Gabbard, Carl,
1948-

ody

Physical Education for Children

Building the Foundation

SECOND EDITION

Carl Gabbard • Betty LeBlanc • Susan Lowy

College of Education
Texas A & M University

 PRENTICE HALL, Englewood Cliffs, New Jersey 07632

Library of Congress Cataloging-in-Publication Data

Gabbard, Carl, (date)
    Physical education for children; building the foundation/Carl Gabbard, Betty LeBlanc, Susan Lowy.—2nd ed.
        p. cm.
    Includes bibliographical references and index.
    ISBN: 0-13-666728-7
    1. Physical education for children. 2. Physical education for children—Study and teaching. 3. Movement education. I. LeBlanc, Betty, (date). Lowy, Susan,
        (date). III. Title.
GV443.G15   1994   93-29648
372.86—dc20   CIP

Editor-in-Chief: **Charlyce Jones Owen**
Project manager: **Benjamin D. Smith**
Production coordinator: **Peter Havens**
Marketing manager: **Bill Hendee**
Copy editor: **Joyce Fried**
Design director: **Anne Bonnano Nieglos**
Cover and interior designer: **Amy Rosen**
Cover photo: **Anne-Marie Weber/The Stock Market**
Formatter: **David Tay**

 © 1994, 1987 by Prentice-Hall, Inc.
A Paramount Communications Company
Englewood Cliffs, New Jersey 07632

Printed in the United States of America

10 9 8 7 6 5 4 3 2 1

ISBN 0-13-666728-7

Prentice-Hall International (UK) Limited, *London*
Prentice-Hall of Australia Pty. Limited, *Sydney*
Prentice-Hall Canada Inc., *Toronto*
Prentice-Hall Hispanoamericana, S.A., *Mexico*
Prentice-Hall of India Private Limited, *New Delhi*
Prentice-Hall of Japan, Inc., *Tokyo*
Simon & Schuster Asia Pte. Ltd., *Singapore*
Editora Prentice-Hall do Brasil, Ltda., *Rio de Janeiro*

Contents

SECTION I
Basis for Foundation

PREFACE   **xi**

1 PHYSICAL EDUCATION FOR CHILDREN   **1**

Developmentally Appropriate Physical Education for Children   1
Other Trends   3
The Values and Purposes of Physical Education   4
References   7
Suggested Readings   7

2 CHILD DEVELOPMENT AND PHYSICAL ACTIVITY   **8**

Total Development   8
Psychomotor Development   13
Cognitive Behavior and Physical Activity   27
Affective Behavior and Physical Activity   28
References   31
Suggested Readings   31

3 THE SCIENTIFIC BASIS FOR MOTOR–SKILL ACQUISITION   **32**

Schema Theory   32
Other Factors Affecting Motor–Skill Acquisition   34
References   36
Suggested Readings   36

4 PHYSICAL FITNESS   **37**

Health Concerns and Children   37
Fitness Concepts   38
Assessment   43
References   58
Suggested Readings   58

SECTION II
Curriculum, Planning, and Teaching

5 CURRICULUM AND PLANNING — 59

Introduction — 59
The Curriculum — 61
Planning Strategies — 64
Theme Development — 70
Unit Planning — 75
Daily Planning — 77
Suggested Readings — 84

6 ORGANIZATION AND INSTRUCTION — 85

Decisions to Be Made — 85
Teaching Strategies — 87
Teaching Styles — 88
Organizational Patterns — 94
Communication Modes — 97
References — 100
Suggested Readings — 100

7 CLASS MANAGEMENT AND DISCIPLINE — 101

Quality — 101
Control Theory and Reality Therapy — 102
Creating a Positive Learning Environment — 105
Behavior Expectations in the Gymnasium — 106
Positive Attitude Development — 107
Communication Skills — 108
Managerial Skills — 109
Guidelines for Developing Discipline Strategies — 117
References — 118
Suggested Readings — 118

8 EVALUATION — 119

Observation — 119
Student Evaluation — 120
Teacher Evaluation — 126
Program Evaluation — 129
References — 130
Suggested Readings — 130

9 CHILDREN WITH SPECIAL NEEDS

Legislation	131
Special Services	132
The Individual Education Program (IEP)	132
Least Restrictive Environment	133
Accommodating Disabled Students in Regular Physical Education	134
Instructional Strategies	134
Specific Disabilities	135
Suggested Readings	136

SECTION III
Program Content

10 LOCOMOTOR SKILL THEMES **137**

Walking	137
Running	139
Jumping and Landing	143
Leaping	156
Hopping	159
Galloping	161
Sliding	163
Skipping	164
Body Rolling	167
Climbing	177
References	283

11 NONLOCOMOTOR SKILL THEMES **184**

Dodging	184
Stretching and Bending	186
Twisting and Turning	188
Swinging and Swaying	190
Pushing and Pulling	194

12 MANIPULATIVE SKILL THEMES **197**

Ball Rolling	197
Throwing	199
Catching	204
Kicking	207
Trapping	212
Bouncing/Dribbling	214
Striking	217
Reference	222

13 MOVEMENT AWARENESS   223

Body Awareness   223
Spatial Awareness   228
Directional Awareness   231
Vestibular Awareness (Balance)   233
Eye-Hand, Eye-Foot Coordination   238
Rhythmic Awareness   244
Visual Awareness   250
Tactile Awareness   253
Auditory Awareness   255
Suggested Readings   258

14 PHYSICAL FITNESS PROGRAM   259

Introduction   259
Basic Instructional Guidelines   259
Exercise Precautions   260
Fitness Values of Selected Activities   263
General Activity Formats   264
Cardiorespiratory Fitness Activities   268
Flexibility Activities   276
Starting Positions for Exercises   277
Muscular Strength/Endurance Activities   285
References   296

SECTION IV

Games, Rhythm/Dance, and Gymnastics Methods and Activities

15 GAMES   297

Introduction   297
Developmental Value   297
Games: Structure and Diversity   297
Game Descriptions   299
Activities for Individuals and Partners (Levels III and IV)   322
Team Sports and Lead-Up Activities (Levels III and IV)   332
Nontraditional Team Sports (Levels III and IV)   398
References   405
Suggested General Readings   405
Suggested Readings and Sources   406

16 RHYTHMS AND DANCE — 408

Progressions — 408
Creative Dance — 409
Structured Dance — 412
Steps in Teaching Structured Dance — 415
Rhythm/Dance Descriptions — 421
Record Sources — 454
Suggested Sources and Readings — 454

17 GYMNASTICS — 455

Safety — 455
Teaching Style — 457
Class Organization — 457
Small Equipment — 460
Large Equipment — 460
Progression — 461
Rhythmic Gymnastics — 461
Teaching Hints — 462
Gymnastic Activities — 462
Suggested Sources — 491
Suggested Readings — 491

18 INTRAMURAL ACTIVITIES AND SPECIAL EVENTS — 492

Basic Considerations — 492
Special Events — 497
Reference — 499
Suggested Readings — 499

APPENDICES

A Physical Fitness Resources — 500
B Rope-Jumping Resources — 502

INDEX — 503

PREFACE

Almost seven years have passed since the first edition of *Physical Education for Children: Building the Foundation*. The second edition has undergone one of the most thorough reviews and revisions of a textbook of its kind. We and Prentice Hall believe strongly that the current edition exemplifies the model contemporary text on children's physical education. Its basic philosophy and content supports quality physical education for children that is *outcome–based* and *developmentally appropriate*. Our position has always been that to develop quality programs for children, the teacher must understand child growth and development and identify specific essential elements and outcomes, based upon that knowledge. In recent years, more and more educators have moved away from the more traditional general "activity-oriented" approach, to programs that reflect professional accountability. This edition of *Physical Education for Children* provides up-to-date knowledge and guidelines for achieving the primary goal of *Building the Foundation* which promotes physical awareness and activity for a lifetime.

Although numerous changes are evident in this edition, two fundamental contemporary elements remain: focus on developmental skill themes in building the movement foundation, and health-related physical fitness. The reader will find that no other text is as complete and practical in regard to the amount of content and integration of these components. The most dramatic revision (expansion) is in the content related to developmental programs for older children. Along with the vast material dedicated to fundamental skill themes (over 30), we have included a comprehensive description of sport skills and other activities that complement refinement of the movement foundation. The class management and discipline chapter has also undergone extensive revision to include the framework of control theory and reality therapy (components of the Quality Schools movement). The focus is on basic needs (teacher and students), self-collaborative evaluation and responsible choices, all necessary components of positive self-esteem. Two chapters are entirely new: Children with Special Needs, and Intramural Activities and Special Events. In essence, given the practical size allowable for a textbook, we pushed and hopefully achieved the limits.

Section I is devoted to an understanding of the "Basis for the Foundation." Chapter 1 introduces the reader to the philosophy and purposes of quality physical education for children, emphasizing current trends and practices. Chapter 2 focuses upon an extensive description of general child development and the contributions of physical activity to growth and "total" development. Chapter 3, The Scientific Basis for Motor–Skill Acquisition, presents scientific information related to how children perform and acquire motor skills. The primary focus of this chapter is on the practical implications of motor learning theory, namely, *schema theory*. Chapter 4 deals with an explanation of physical fitness components and assessment with primary focus on the health related aspects of fitness.

Section II focuses on Curriculum, Planning, and Teaching. Chapter 5 describes the curricular model and integration of fitness activities, developmental movement themes, and game, rhythm, and gymnastic activities into the curriculum. Implementation of the model is presented in the form of yearly, theme, and daily lesson plan formats, along with examples. Chapter 6 deals with organization and instruction. A unique instructional strategy model is provided to present a comprehensive description of the instructional process. Chapter 7 focuses upon the necessary elements for positive class management and discipline. Practical suggestions and techniques creating a needs-satisfying, esteem-building learning environment are provided. Chapter 8, Evaluation, presents a comprehensive discussion of both evaluation and techniques that teachers can use to help them not only understand children better but also their own instructional effectiveness. The information in Chapter 9 addresses issues and provides guidelines relevant to teaching children with disabilities (special needs).

Section III is devoted to Program Content. Chapter 10 through 13 provide a thorough discussion of the fundamental movement themes, each with a subsection for movement description, observation, variability, and enhancement activities. Each theme is accompanied by an enhancement chart identifying a selection of rhythms/dance, game, and gymnastic activities that are developmentally categorized into levels of difficulty. Chapter 14 focuses upon the description and implementation of health-related fitness activities into the curriculum.

Section IV, the first three chapters (15–17), describe methods for teaching a variety of traditional and innovative games, rhythms/dance, and gymnastics. Each chapter also includes charts designating the approximate developmental level of each activity. Chapter 18, Intramural Activities and Special Events, provides a multitude of suggestions and activities that complement the instructional program on exceptional days.

Finally, the Appendices present a useful listing of fitness record selections and rope-jump resources.

Acknowledgments

Since its initial conception, many people have contributed their ideas, professionalism, and support to making the second edition of *Physical Education for Children: Building the Foundation* a reality. We are grateful to the staff at Prentice Hall, especially Charlyce Jones Owen for her support and vision of excellence. To the numerous reviewers over the years, we are most appreciative and are certain that your hard work will make a significant contribution to physically educating America's children.

No work of ours would be complete without acknowledgment of our loving families and those special friends and colleagues whose patience and unconditional support helped us to weather the rough times and celebrate the joys of quality work. Finally, we wish to thank God's children for their continued inspiration for us to do our best as we strive to influence the quality of their lives, which in turn, is the ultimate fruit of our labor.

1

Physical Education for Children

Numerous milestones and innovations have occurred in recent years in physical education programs for children. Along with the nation's dynamic quest for improved health and physical fitness has emerged increasing interest in high-quality physical activity programs for young people. These "happenings" have endowed the profession of teaching physical education to children with the recognition that it is an integral and irreplaceable part of the total school curriculum and child development process. With this responsibility, the professional physical educator is obligated to provide a quality, developmentally appropriate program.

DEVELOPMENTALLY APPROPRIATE PHYSICAL EDUCATION FOR CHILDREN

One of the major features of the contemporary physical education program for children is that it be developmentally appropriate in curricular content and practices. The promotion of these characteristics has been a predominant issue in child education as reflected in several position papers and articles developed by major professional associations including the National Association for the Education of Young Children (BredeKamp, 1987) and the Council on Physical Education for Children (COPEC, 1992). A summary of selected highlights from the COPEC document suggests the following developmentally appropriate practices:

- The curriculum should reflect an obvious scope and sequence based on goals and objectives beneficial for all children. The program should include the components of physical fitness, motor skill development, and plenty of worthwhile practice opportunities to develop stated objectives.
- Testing and assessment should be an ongoing process which is used to establish performance level, individualize instruction, and plan activities.
- Physical education activities should be designed with both the physical and cognitive development of children in mind. Practices which enable children to think critically and apply concepts, as well as gain a multicultural view of the world, should be included.
- Teachers should design activities which provide children the opportunity to work cooperatively and experience the joy and satisfaction derived from regular physical activity.
- Every child should be provided movement activities which maximize participation, learning, and enjoyment.

In essence, *developmentally appropriate physical education* is a high-quality curriculum which is based on knowledge of human development and what is age-appropriate for the group of individuals being served. It takes into consideration the well-established human development premise that there is substantial variation and individual differences among children. Such a program presents activities to children that are sequentially (developmentally) ordered, so that each task takes into account the developmental status of the individual child.

Of the characteristics described in the developmentally appropriate program, the two components that have been the focus for considerable change in recent years are physical fitness and the curricular approach used to develop motor skills.

Physical Fitness

In the last 25 years several advances have occurred in the areas of education, health, and life expectancy; however, it appears that the physical fitness levels of our nation's children may be declining. The results of three national fitness surveys indicate that children and youth (ages six to 17 years) are fatter than their counterparts of the 1960s, exhibit low levels of cardiorespiratory fitness, and score poorly on tests of upper body strength and endurance (National Children and Youth Fitness Study (NCYFS), 1985, 1987; National School Population Fitness Survey, 1985).

Since 1980 the concept of what "physical fitness" means has undergone dramatic change. Traditionally a "fit" child was perceived as an individual who had athletic abilities which were characterized by muscular strength, speed, agility, power, and coordination. Such characteristics, while quite useful in sport participation, have been found to be of minimal benefit to our overall wellness. Today, the meaning of the term physical fitness goes beyond the performance of motor skills. Optimal functioning of all physiological systems of the body, particularly the cardiovascular, pulmonary, and musculoskeletal systems denotes the physically fit person.

According to the American Alliance for Health, Physical Education, Recreation, and Dance (1988) and the American Academy of Pediatrics (1987), physical fitness should focus on the components of health-related fitness to include cardiorespiratory efficiency, muscular strength/endurance, flexibility, and optimal body composition (*i.e.*, proportion of body fat) to lean muscle mass. A news release published by the American Academy of Pediatrics (1987) stressed that

our children's poor fitness report card needs immediate attention. It urges parents and pediatricians to appeal to their local school boards to evaluate their physical education programs. The report strongly recommended that school programs emphasize "lifetime" activities that can be carried into adulthood such as cycling, swimming, jogging, fast walking, aerobics, and tennis. It also stated that schools currently spend too much time on traditional team sports (*e.g.*, football, softball/baseball, basketball) which emphasize "skill" rather than health-related fitness development.

Although a vast amount of evidence indicates that children's health and fitness levels are not adequate, when parents were asked how many days in a typical week they exercised with their child for 20 minutes or more, approximately 60 percent responded that they do not exercise at all with their children (NCYFS, 1987). Along with this lack of lifestyle model and the fact that children are spending more time watching television (approximately 25–30 hours a week), viewing computers, and eating snack foods, the basis for our nation's concern seems evident. The 1985 National Children and Youth Fitness Study reported that only 36 percent of our nation's 10 to 17-year-olds were enrolled in daily physical education programs and approximately 50 percent were participating in appropriate vigorous activity. The NCYFS II (1987), which surveyed children 6–9 years of age, also reported that only one third participate in physical education daily. The fact is that a great proportion of our children get as little as one hour of physical education per week, and much of that activity is game skill oriented. There is no federal law mandating physical education in schools; however, in December of 1987 the United States Senate passed the Physical

Current programs focus upon the development and maintenance of health-related fitness.

Education Resolution. This legislation "encourages" states and localities to provide quality, daily physical education for all children at the elementary and secondary school levels. During discussion on the Senate floor, Senator Ted Stevens noted that:

> "Unlike many of today's educational problems, the remedy is clear and the benefits are almost immediate. This Resolution will be used by parents, educators and administrators alike to ensure that the physical education of our children is not seen as a frill to be cut from school budgets. It will work to reverse the erosion of health and physical education programs, and reaffirm the Greek ideal of a complete education—complete in mind, body and spirit."

As of 1987, eight states had no established time requirements for physical education (American Academy of Pediatrics, 1987). The nation's goals of a more physically fit and healthier young society (and ultimately of the population as a whole) are far from being achieved. A more detailed discussion of fitness and children is provided in Chapter 4.

Curricular Approach to Motor Skill Development

Another essential component in the developmentally appropriate program is the presentation and practice of motor skills. The contemporary program identifies content which is based upon the understanding of psychomotor development. This includes the recognition of individual differences and need for presenting information in sequential (developmental) order. The curricular approach used to accommodate this understanding and need is known as the *developmental skill theme approach*. A developmental theme is the focus of a lesson or series of lessons upon a specific motor skill or movement awareness.

A major aspect of the philosophy supporting this approach is that planning, especially for preschool and primary-grade children (in essence, the foundation), should not focus primarily on game, dance, and gymnastic activities. Rather the focus should be upon the specific "essential elements" (curricular content) corresponding to our knowledge of the developmental behaviors and needs of children.

The primary use of dance, game, and gymnastic activities rather than specific themes still is a popular and widely used approach. This philosophy, called the traditional "activity" approach, is reflected in a decreasing number of texts and curriculum guides in which allotments (or percentages) of time are suggested for activities to be taught during the year. Also connected to this approach is the use of units that focus upon pieces of equipment such as hoops, beanbags, ropes, and balls. Unfortunately, children are frequently taught dance, game strategies, or complex gymnastic stunts before they are able to perform the associative skills needed for efficient performance. Many teachers who focus primarily on activities tend to direct their attention to experiences that are fun, rather than on proficiency of skill performance. This example is of course not meant to attach a characteristic label to all teachers using the activity approach to teaching children, nor does it suggest the total elimination of such practices. Dance, game, and gymnastic activities, even at the preschool-primary level, play an integral role in the development, refinement, and utilization of fundamental skills and movement awareness. The authors of this text suggest only that careful attention be paid to the appropriate application of "activities"; we are not questioning their existence.

OTHER TRENDS

The Teacher

Along with the many changes in philosophy and curriculum concerning children and physical education over recent years have come changes associated with the teacher and teacher preparation. From the early years of supervised recess (and other less desirable conditions) has evolved a sophisticated elementary physical education *specialist*. The specialist is generally an individual who has been educated in the growth, development, and psychology of children as well as in physical education and the psychomotor behaviors of children. Currently, a strong trend in hiring the specialist exists in many parts of the country, mainly because of the exposure and national acceptance that the profession has attained. The acceptance of physical education as an integral part of the "basic" school curriculum in most parts of the nation has brought about the logical response that an unspecialized individual simply is not adequately prepared to direct physical education programs for children. State and local governing agencies are noticeably tightening the preparation requirements for individuals who wish to teach children motor skills and direct physical fitness activities. If a specialist cannot be hired, most state education agencies and universities provide consultative services and resources to school districts. Many universities, realizing that elementary classroom teachers may be responsible for all curriculum areas including physical education, are preparing future teachers with at least a minimum knowledge in physical education for children. Another frequently observable trend is the use of hired teacher "aides" and parent volunteers to supplement the specialist or regular classroom teacher. Unfortunately, some school districts have abused the use of teacher aides by allowing them to be primarily responsible for an entire program; however, their use under the guidance of a specialist can be a definite asset.

Public Law 94-142

Public Law 94-142 (Federal Education for All Handicapped Children Act of 1975) provided public education with a term and concept known as *mainstreaming*. Mainstreaming is the inclusion of children with handicaps into the regular instructional classes and activities with all other children. Among the requirements of the law are:

1. Free and appropriate public education that emphasizes special education and related services for all handicapped children with the "least restrictive environment";
2. The development of an annual individualized education program (IEP) for each handicapped child;
3. A statement explaining the extent to which the child is able to participate in the regular classroom.

The implications of mainstreaming to physical education are strong and far-reaching. Basically it means that handicapped children (now referred to as disabled) may be scheduled in regular physical education classes, if that is the least restrictive environment. Provision for instruction in physical education is clearly defined in the elements of special education. It is noted that each disabled child be afforded the opportunity to participate in the regular physical education program unless the child is enrolled full-time in a separate facility, or needs a specially designed program as prescribed in the IEP. For the physical education teacher, this means possibly individualizing specific portions of instruction to cope with the limitations of each disabled child. Many states and universities now require that future elementary school teachers (regardless of specialization) possess a basic knowledge of the characteristics of exceptional children and that those majoring in physical education take at least one course in adapted physical education (that is, adapting physical activities to accommodate the limitations of specific and general disabling conditions).

Since 1975, tremendous strides have been made in providing educational opportunities, including physical education, to disabled youngsters. Along with the much needed physical education experiences afforded the exceptional child, mainstreaming has provided both disabled and nondisabled children a positive experience of exposure to each other. For more detailed discussion, see Chapter 9.

Title IX

The Educational Amendments Act of 1972 (Title IX) makes it illegal to discriminate between students in matters of education based on gender. The most important implication for elementary physical education is that boys and girls should be taught together except in specific situations. Students may be separat-

The professional educator provides individual guidance to meet the needs of all children.

ed by gender for contact sports (*e.g.*, boxing, wrestling, football) but these types of activities are discouraged in the elementary grades. There may be grouping according to fitness and/or motor skill levels if objective standards are used, but grouping by gender alone is not permitted. In cases where a single evaluation standard would have an adverse effect on one gender (*e.g.*, upper body strength test favoring boys in the intermediate grades), different standards are allowed. Along with providing greater equity between genders, the passage of this act marked a milestone in the advancement of interscholastic and intercollegiate sports participation for females.

THE VALUES AND PURPOSES OF PHYSICAL EDUCATION

Educators generally agree that the primary purpose of education is to help each child develop to his or her fullest potential. With this commitment to individualized and equal education has emerged a revitalized push to educate the "total" child. Educators and parents are being enlightened to an increasing base of information that has strengthened the role of physical education in the elementary curriculum and provided a new dimension to "total" child development. The physical activity programs of today are based upon a vast body of knowledge supported by a number of professional disciplines including medicine, psychology, child development, and education.

The components of total child development are generally accepted as being the three domains of behavior: psychomotor, cognitive, and affective. It is

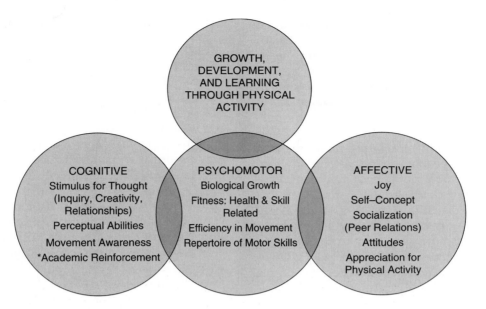

FIGURE 1-1

The contributions of physical activity to child development.

*Refers to reinforcement of academic concepts using specific movement activities

through the development and stimulation of these behaviors that the values and purposes of physical activity programs are given credence. Figure 1-1 illustrates some of the contributions of physical activity to child development as represented by three interrelated circles (that is, behavioral domains). This interrelationship also represents a philosophy that supports the belief that a functioning, happy, "total" individual is one who has attained an acceptable level of behavior in each domain; in many situations, elements from all three must be utilized for the individual to function effectively. Unlike most educational programs, movement, being the child's natural learning medium, is in a unique position to contribute to the development of all three domains and do so effectively!

The following section presents a brief introduction to the contributions (that is, values and basis of purpose) of physical education to the psychomotor, cognitive, and affective development of children. Chapter 2, Child Development and Physical Activity, presents a more detailed treatment of information within the behavioral domains.

Psychomotor Development

Psychomotor behavior includes those responses related to fitness and motor activity, as well as the components of physical growth and development responsible for such functions. It is generally accepted that physical education contributes more to growth and psychomotor development than any other discipline. The merits of physical activity for children in terms of normal growth, development, and health-related

physical fitness are supported by a large body of research. The majority of information suggests that physical activity at an early age is not only necessary for normal growth and development but also enhances the chances of a physically fit adult life.

By using the medium of movement, the physical educator not only has the opportunity to enhance the physical quality of individual lives but to provide for the learning and practice of motor skills essential for a child to attain desirable goals of motor proficiency and recreation.

PHYSICAL ACTIVITY CONTRIBUTES TO THE DEVELOPMENT OF THE FOLLOWING PSYCHOMOTOR BEHAVIORS AND COMPONENTS:

Physical growth and development
Health-related physical fitness
Motor-skill proficiency
Recreational endeavors

Cognitive Development

Primarily composed of the thought processes, such as problem solving, comprehension, evaluation, and creativity, the *cognitive* domain has received the most recognition of all the educational domains. Jean Piaget, one of the most renowned child psychologists, gives a great deal of recognition to the importance of movement and play in the stimulation of cognitive behavior, especially during the child's early years. Exploration, discovery, and problem solving, all used in the physical education setting, have been found most appropriate for the stimulation of cognitive development. A strong interaction exists between movement and cognitive stimulation; children "learn to move," and to the physical educator's credit, "learn through movement." The motor-skill learning mechanism is, in part, a cognitive process. Success is dependent largely upon an understanding (awareness) of the environment, how the actions are to be performed, and reflection of the outcome. Movement and play are stimulating and motivating mediums that offer an exciting dimension to the learning environment. Learning through movement entails thinking and an understanding of *why* as well as *how*.

There are two primary aspects of cognitive development that may be dealt with in movement programs: *perceptual-motor concepts* and the development and reinforcement of *academic concepts*. Evidence suggests that the acquisition of both types of concepts may be enhanced through selected movement experiences. Perhaps one of the most supportive and recognized studies related to this area is the Vanves experiments. Conducted in Vanves, France, after French doctors and educators became concerned with "overloaded" academic programs, the now famous "one third time" program was established (one third to academics, one third to physical education, and one third to art, music, and supervised study). A series of experiments over a 10-year period using control groups indicated that children in the experimental program had better academic performance and were less susceptible to stress, in addition to exhibiting superior levels of fitness, health, discipline, and enthusiasm.

Although a direct relationship between motor activity experience and academic achievement has not been found, strong indirect implications have been presented. Most educators believe that motor activities play an important role in cognitive and perceptual development. With both of these attributes being essential in academic success, the possible link between motor activities and academic achievement may be indirectly drawn. It is perhaps a stronger case for the connection if one assumes that the "total" child possesses a positive attitude not only about himself or herself but also toward learning, which improves the child's chances for classroom achievement. Movement experiences can stimulate motivation and aid in the development of a positive self-concept, both of which are contributing factors in a learning environment.

PHYSICAL ACTIVITY CONTRIBUTES TO THE DEVELOPMENT OF THE FOLLOWING COGNITIVE BEHAVIORS:

Perceptual awareness
Problem solving/strategy
Creativity
Vocabulary
Understanding and communication of concepts and ideas

Affective Development

A desirable goal of educational programs in general should be the development of individuals who can interact effectively with others as well as have self-esteem and self-knowledge. The *affective* domain, responsible for social and emotional behaviors, has received perhaps less attention from educators than the other domains even though the very basis of society and our own personal success depends upon its development. There are many who believe that the moral values of our society (especially among the youth) are decaying and that more moral education should be stressed at the early educational levels. Physical education, through individual and group activities, can foster desirable attitudes about the self, which in turn allow one to understand better the feelings of others. A good physical education setting is a natural learning laboratory in which children interact with individuals, groups, and authority figures. Through properly directed movement experiences, children can confront and develop such positive traits as honesty, courtesy, respect for others, cooperation, fair play, respect for authority and rules, as well as develop healthy assertiveness. A number of research studies support the premise that an adequate level of motor-skill ability is important to the child and the ongoing relationship with peers. Most children place great emphasis and value on motor-skill performance. Educators should not ignore the marked influence that "play" success can have on the social acceptance of children and adolescents. In order to achieve the maximum potential of development and citizenship, emphasis must be placed on values, social interactions, and self-concept during the formative years.

PHYSICAL ACTIVITY CONTRIBUTES TO THE DEVELOPMENT OF THE FOLLOWING GENERAL AFFECTIVE BEHAVIORS:

Pleasure
Self-concept
Socialization
Positive attitudes
Self-discipline

The Physically Educated Child

Ultimately, the outcome of a high-quality program is the *physically educated child*. In 1992, the National Association for Sport and Physical Education (NASPE) as part of its Outcomes of Quality Physical Education Programs document, described the physically educated person as an individual that:

> *Has* learned skills necessary to perform a variety of physical activities
> *Is* physically fit

Does participate regularly in physical activity

Knows the implications of and the benefits from involvement in physical activities

Values physical activity and its contributions to a healthful lifestyle.

These outcomes reflect a major challenge to the contemporary physical educator. As a result of experiences that stress developing the total child, the individual comes to *value*, *know*, and *do*; hence, the desired outcomes of education.

REFERENCES

American Academy of Pediatrics. (1987). Physical fitness and the schools. *Pediatrics, 80*, (3), 449–450.

American Academy of Pediatrics. (1987). News release. September 8, 1987.

American Alliance for Health, Physical Education, Recreation, and Dance. (1988). *AAHPERD health related physical fitness test manual*. Reston, VA: AAHPERD Publications.

BREDEKAMP, S. (Ed.). (1987). *Developmentally appropriate practice in early childhood programs serving children from birth through age 8*. Washington, DC: National Association for the Education of Young Children.

Council on Physical Education For Children. (1992). *Position Statement on developmentally appropriate practices for children*. Reston, VA: AAHPERD Publications.

National Association for Sport and Physical Education (NASPE). (1992). *Outcomes of quality physical education programs*. Reston, VA.: AAHPERD Publications.

National Children and Youth Fitness Study. (1984). Office of Disease Prevention and Health Promotion, U.S. Department of Health and Human Services. Washington, DC: Government Printing Office. Special report in 1985, *Journal of Physical Education, Recreation & Dance, 56* (1), 44–90.

National Children and Youth Fitness Study II. (1987). Special report in *Journal of Physical Education, Recreation & Dance, 58* (9), 50–96.

National School Population Fitness Survey. (1982). The President's Council on Physical Fitness and Sports, Office of the Assistant Secretary for Health.

SUGGESTED READINGS

BARRETT, K. R. (1988). The subject matter of children's physical education. *Journal of Physical Education, Recreation, and Dance, 59* (2), 42–46.

GENTRY, V. (1985). Curricular models of elementary physical education: Traditional and contemporary. *The Physical Educator*, Spring, 59–64.

Healthy children 2000: National Health Promotion and Disease Prevention Objectives (1991). U.S. Dept. of Health and Human Services, Boston: Jones and Bartlett.

Physical activity and well-being. (1986). Reston, VA: AAHPERD Publications.

The value of physical activity. (1986). Reston, VA: AAHPERD Publications.

Whitehead, J. R. (1992). A selected, annotated bibliography for fitness educators. *Journal of Physical Education, Recreation, and Dance, 63* (5), 53–64.

2

Child Development and Physical Activity

Human development can be viewed as a process in which psychomotor, cognitive, and affective factors all interact and contribute to total individual development. Physical activity can have a profound effect on the development of these behavioral domains (thus enhancing total development), for movement is the child's natural learning medium. Physical educators should have a thorough understanding of total child development so the structuring of both physical activities and the learning environment can provide an adequate stimulus for the developmental process.

ers must be able to justify the values of physical activity sessions as more than learning to throw a ball or folk-dance. The sections of this chapter entitled Psychomotor Development, Cognitive Behavior, and Affective Behavior and Physical Activity focus upon the contributions (and implications) of physical activity to those specific behavioral domains.

General Child Development Terminology

Development refers to changes in the individual's level of functioning. Whether in the psychomotor, cogni-

TOTAL DEVELOPMENT

As already mentioned, child development has been conceptualized into three behavioral domains: psychomotor, cognitive, and affective. The psychomotor domain consists of physical and motor abilities based upon biological (growth) and motor (functioning) processes. Cognitive (intellectual) functions include thought processes, language, and memory, all of which contribute to perceptual-motor and academic abilities. The affective domain encompasses those aspects related to feelings, self-concept, and social interaction. These three domains interact in the development of the child and should not be viewed as independent mechanisms.

Children grow, develop, and learn through physical activity. Movement plays a very important role in the "total" developmental process. Movement serves as a vehicle by which children explore, challenge, and conquer the environment around them. To view physical education as relevant only to the psychomotor domain is to place severe limitations on a potentially valuable medium for development. In this age of accountability and individualized education, physical education teach-

tive, or affective domain, the level of functioning is a product of heredity, growth, maturation, and one's experiences (that is, environmental effects).

Heredity, refers to qualities that are fixed at birth and account for many individual traits and characteristics. Heredity is partially or strongly responsible for height, time of tooth eruption, eye and hair color, body build, personality, and intelligence, to name a few. These traits and characteristics may, however, be modified by environmental factors. Consider body build as an example; although build is determined primarily by heredity, it is possible to alter one's body build by using weight training, steroids, and specific diets. The same interaction of environment with heredity may be observed in the intelligence of individuals.

Growth, often used interchangeably with "development" and "maturation," usually refers to an increase in body size such as height or arm circumference. The term may also refer to a change in quantity, such as a growth in one's vocabulary. Although maturation can be a factor in growth (but not necessarily), environmental factors and learning can also contribute.

Maturation is associated with qualitative changes that enable an individual to progress from one level of functioning to a higher level. Primarily innate (that is, genetically determined) and resistant to external influences, maturation interacts strongly with learning and environmental factors to influence development of the child. The fixed order of progression in which humans develop is strongly associated with maturation. Locomotion, for example, develops in a very consistent sequence (sit, stand, walk, run) and at approximate ages. The pace and rate of appearance may vary (usually dependent upon environmental influences), but the sequence generally does not.

Experience, perhaps the most influential factor because it can be easily manipulated (compared with the other factors), refers to those factors within the environment that may prompt changes in various developmental characteristics through the learning process. Learning may be described as a relatively permanent change in behavior attributable to experience or practice, as opposed to natural biological processes.

Although the environment affects development in numerous ways, its principal effect is its influence on learning. Learning, however, is not the only environmental influence that may affect developmental change. Other strong influences are diet, child-rearing practices, and the physical environment (for example, poverty).

Adaptation is the process of altering one's own behaviors to interact effectively with the environment. The term is also used to describe the complex interplay between the child and the environment. The developmental aspects of maturation and the child's experience are interwoven to create behavior.

Developmental Stages

Human development is often classified and studied by stages describing age-related changes in behaviors and growth. Table 2-1 presents the various stages with approximate age range of each corresponding educational level.

Especially during the young years, certain developmental tasks and milestones such as walking, talking, and puberty are attained by all normal children within a general age range. Many educators view the accomplishment of certain developmental tasks as predictive in nature, that is, predictive of later success or failure. Such a viewpoint would also dictate that the child must achieve a specific task by a certain "time." One should be careful, however, when judging age-related behavior, especially during the early years, and in comparison to other behaviors. Individual developmental structures and experiences (or lack thereof) may, and generally do, account for most behavioral differences within specific age groups.

Piaget's Theory of Child Development

Perhaps the most elaborate and fully articulate view on child development theory available is that of Jean Piaget. Piaget theorizes that children pass through a series of behavioral stages from infancy to adolescence. Passage through the stages is the result of

Table 2-1

Developmental Stages

STAGE	APPROXIMATE AGE RANGE	EDUCATIONAL LEVEL
Prenatal	Conception to birth	—
Neonate	Birth to 1 month	—
Infancy	1 month to 2 years	—
Early childhood	2 to 6 years	Preschool to first grade
Middle childhood	6 to 9 years	First to fourth grade
Late childhood	9 to 12 years	Fourth to seventh grade
Adolescence	12 to 18 years	Seventh to secondary completion

adaptation to the environment and organized structures of thought. Piaget (1963) has identified four stages of intellectual development: (1) the sensorimotor period [zero to two years], (2) the preoperational period [two to seven years], (3) concrete operations stage [seven to 11 years], and (4) the period of formal operations [11 and beyond].

As in the situation with most theories using the "age-stage" relationship, the various time periods designated for this model are only approximate. Individual differences may account for the child moving out of a specific stage sooner or remaining longer than is predicted. Because of Piaget's repeated reference to behaviors that involve movement (and motor development) during the sensorimotor period, additional emphasis has been directed there.

Important to the understanding of Piaget's theory of development are the terms *schema, assimilation, accommodation,* and *adaptation.* A schema (not to be confused with Schmidt's Schema theory discussed later, although there are some similarities) refers to the basic unit for an organized pattern of sensorimotor functioning. Examples of schemata include sucking, tossing a ball, and grasping. A schema often functions in conjunction or in sequence with other schema, as when the child combines grasping, throwing, and releasing. When a schema is retained in memory, it may be utilized as programmed or altered to meet the demands of a changing environment. According to Piaget, when children deal with the environment in terms of their current schema (from memory), they exhibit the process of *assimilation.* In this situation, the child utilizes existing schema to perform a task. *Accommodation* refers to the process of modifying basic schema structure to the demands of the environment. For example, the child may use a different type of grip than previously used to handle the shape of a new toy. For Piaget cognitive development is an *adaptation*—the balance between assimilation and accommodation.

SENSORIMOTOR PERIOD (ZERO TO TWO YEARS)

Most of Piaget's writing on this period makes direct reference to movement and psychomotor development. Piaget identifies six stages within this period which cover Simple Reflexes (zero to one month) to the Internalization of Schemes (18 months to two years). Described are the actions of the child as he or she progresses from reflex behaviors to voluntary movement structuring. During the first four months, the child's body is the center of attention and "habits" are formed as well as the reproduction of pleasurable events (*e.g.,* sucking fingers). From approximately four to eight months the child becomes more object-oriented, thus focusing on the surrounding environment. By 12 months, the infant is able to combine previously learned

schemata in a coordinated fashion and perceptual-motor behaviors are more effective. This period (eight to 12 months) also marks the presence of "intentionality" (the separation of means and goals in accomplishing simple tasks). For example, the child may move one doll to reach and play with another one, or manipulate a stick (the means) to bring a toy within reach (the goal).

Piaget refers to the period 12 to 18 months as the beginning for curiosity and interest in novelty. Schemes are developed to explore new possibilities with objects and the period is characterized by trial-and-error learning. From 18 months to two years (Internalization of Schemes) a shift in mental functioning occurs from the sensorimotor plane to the ability to use primitive symbols. A symbol is described here as a sensory image or word that represents an event. This function allows the child to think about concrete events without directly acting or perceiving. One of Piaget's examples refers to a child that opened a door slowly to avoid disturbing a piece of paper lying on the floor. Presumably the child had an image of the paper and what would happen to it if the door were to open rapidly. Also characteristic of this period is the development of "object permanence," that is, the understanding (awareness) that the self is distinct from other objects in space and those objects exist even when no longer in direct perceptual contact. For example, after the rubber duck falls from the playpen and is out of sight, the child searches for it.

PREOPERATIONAL PERIOD (2 TO 7 YEARS)

This period, which extends from preschool to early middle childhood, is subdivided into two stages: the preconceptual stage (two to four years) and intuitive stage (four to seven years). Although still an egocentric, the child, during the preconceptual stage, begins to discover both the environment and self through movement and play. The child must deal with each thing individually for he or she does not possess the ability to group objects. The intuitive stage presents the child as using symbolic language without really understanding the meaning of it. Piaget perceives these limitations as the child's inability to conserve (that is, understand that the basic properties of objects often remain unchanged even after the superficial appearance is altered) and the child's failure to order objects in a series and classify them.

CONCRETE OPERATIONS STAGE (7 TO 11)

During this period the child's thought processes crystallize into more of a system. Children begin to think in a logical manner, and although they cannot yet abstract, they think in terms of the concrete or actual experience. One of the major changes from the preoperational period is the shift from egocentrism to *relativism*. This is the ability to think from various perspectives and to think simultaneously about two or more aspects of a problem. *Reversibility* is also acquired; this is the capacity of relating an event or a thought to a total system of interrelated parts in order to conceive the event from start to finish, or vice versa. A major limitation of concrete thinking is that the child has to be able to perceive an object before thinking in this way. Many times children fail to distinguish between their representation of an event and the actual event itself.

PERIOD OF FORMAL OPERATIONS (11 YEARS AND BEYOND)

In this last stage, as the child enters into adolescence, he or she has achieved the most advanced level of cognition. The child now thinks and reasons beyond the world of actual, concrete experiences. Cognition is logical and systematic problem-solving is used. The child is able to create many hypotheses to account for some event and then test them in a deductive fashion (that is, against empirical data—scientifically).

Table 2-2

Characteristic Behaviors of Children 3 to 4 Years Old (Preschool)

Cognitive Characteristics	Affective Characteristics
Increasing ability to express thoughts and ideas verbally	Egocentric in nature, often quarrelsome, and has difficulty sharing and getting along with others
Unable to sit still for more than a short period of time	Fear of heights, failure, and new situations
Constantly exploring the environment by trial and error	Likes to imitate
Fantastic imagination and fantasy play	Shy and self-conscious
Use of numbers without comprehending concept of quantity	Attitudes formed through family and group play
Can follow directions if not more than two ideas are given	Moral foundation is established
Period of transition from self-satisfying behavior to socialized behavior	Physical aggression decreases; verbal aggression increases
Questions, requests, and commands characterize communication	Likes to play individually or in small groups
	Needs constant encouragement
	Learns appropriate sex role

Table 2-3

Characteristic Behaviors of Children 5 to 6 Years Old (Kindergarten and 1st Grade)

Cognitive Characteristics	Affective Characteristics
Learning to count, read, and write	Seeks individual attention
Short attention span	Dependence and independence fluctuates
Uses such concepts as size, volume, numbers, and weight logically	Possible apprehension toward school
Average first grader reading well by midterm	Tends to be very serious
Interest in what the body can do; often asks "why" about movements	Temper tantrums may occur
Expression of personal ideas and views	Sensitive and individualistic
Teamwork is beginning to be understood	Child wants to help
Highly creative	Expresses affection toward others
Eager to learn and please adults	Competition begins to be enjoyed
Interests include songs, fairy tales, television, movies, rhythmic games, and gymnastic-type activities	Sense of humor
Desires to repeat activities that are known and can perform well	Impatient when waiting for his or her turn
	Enjoys rough-and-tumble activity
	Small-group activities are handled well; poor large-group member
	Responds well to authority, "fair" punishment, and discipline

Table 2-4

Characteristic Behaviors of Children 7 to 8 Years Old (2nd and 3rd Grade)

Cognitive Characteristics	Affective Characteristics
Precise speech production, auditory memory, and discrimination abilities are equal to adults	Shows a need for peer and adult approval as well as being individualistic
Enjoys challenges	Better cooperation in group play
Improvement in use of language and elocution	Likes physical contact
Longer attention span	Wants to excel in skills
Develops ability to plan with and for others	Becoming socially conscious
Capable and willing to accept increased personal responsibilities	Enjoys doing well and being admired for it
	Is a poor loser
	Will admit doing wrong
	Girls and boys begin playing their own games
	Fear of being embarrassed
	Displays jealousy over parent

Table 2-5

Characteristic Behaviors of Children 9 to 12 Years (4th–6th Grade)

Cognitive Characteristics	Affective Characteristics
Capable of abstract thinking and problem solving	Able to control emotions
Attention span lengthens greatly	More self-reliant
Intellectual curiosity increases	Fears being different
Communication continues to be refined, including a vocabulary increase and sentence-structure complexity	Sensitive to criticism
	Increasing independence and identity to peer group
	Boys and girls enjoy team sports; boys concerned with physique and skill; want to display strength
	Personal appearance and activities involving graceful and creative movements are of interest to girls
	Some rejection of adult standards
	Demonstrates less affection
	Constantly worries
	Need for ego to be bolstered
	Peer acceptance is more important than adult acceptance
	Anger is more easily aroused
	Are admired for their sports abilities
	Emotions teeter between love and hate

IMPLICATIONS

Piaget's writings make several references to "action-oriented" activities that involve movement and play; thus his developmental theory has ramifications for every dimension of the play paradigm. Through play (structured and unstructured movement activities), the child is given the opportunity to test novel physical, cognitive, emotional, and social patterns that cannot be accommodated in the real world, thus a buffered form of learning. Once the patterns have been tested through play, they become part of one's memory bank; hence, from a cognitive perspective, play permits the development of intelligence. Play also gives the child the opportunity to practice and expand on existing knowledge.

Characteristic Behaviors of Children

Because the primary thrust of this text is the psychomotor characteristics and needs of children, the above tables, which contain cognitive and affective behavioral characteristics, have been included to provide a more complete understanding of the "total" child. As with other generalizations of behavior related to age and/or educational level, information noted here is approximate, and individual children may deviate considerably, especially in affective behaviors (many of which are based upon one's emotions). (See Tables 2-2 through 2-5.)

PSYCHOMOTOR DEVELOPMENT

This section is devoted to the area known as motor development. *Motor development* refers to those abilities deemed essential in motor skill functioning. It also refers to the study of movement behavior and associative biological change across the "lifespan." In recent years, the term *lifespan motor development* has emerged as a broadening study of lifelong growth, development, and motor behavior (performance). *Motor behavior* is defined as the product of growth and development and describes observable changes in movement. An overview of the phases of lifespan motor behavior with expanded application to the childhood years will be detailed in the latter portion of this section.

The following pages focus upon three subdivisions of psychomotor development: physical growth and development, development of motor skills, and perceptual-motor development. A fourth base of essential information, "physical fitness," will be discussed separately in a later chapter. Preceding the discussion of the three subdivisions is a brief explanation of general growth and development trends and terminology. It should be noted that each of the three areas discussed has an extensive scientific information base and that a thorough discussion of each is beyond the scope of this book. It is the authors' intention to provide the reader with sufficient knowledge with which to understand the mechanisms, capabilities, and abilities of children's motor-skill functioning.

General Trends and Terminology

Cephalocaudal and Proximodistal. These terms refer to the orderly and predictable sequences of physical development. *Cephalocaudal* is physical development that proceeds longitudinally from the head to the feet. This is a gradual progression of increased muscular control moving from the muscles of the head and neck to the trunk, and then to the legs and feet. This phenomenon is characteristic in the developing fetus; the head forms and then the arms and legs. Muscular control is exhibited in the same sequential order. *Proximodistal* development proceeds from the center of the body to its periphery, that is, growth and muscular control occur in the trunk and shoulders before the wrist, hand, and fingers. Both of these trends (that is, of motor control) may be observed in the young child. Preschool children are usually more coordinated in the upper torso of the body before the lower extremities are mastered (cephalocaudal), just as children during early attempts at writing tend to utilize gross shoulder movements before fine-motor cursive forms are achieved.

Mass to Specific (Gross to Fine) Motor Control. Corresponding to cephalocaudal and proximodistal development, *mass to specific motor control* refers to the child's muscular control first over the large muscles before the child is able to differentiate between parts and move them independently. The handwriting example previously described fits this trend as well; during the early attempts, the child uses more parts of the body than are needed.

Bilateral to Unilateral Trend. During the early periods of motor control, movements tend to be *bilateral*; that is, the young child uses either or both hands to manipulate objects. Gradually, preference for and control of a given hand or foot emerge (*unilateral*).

Differentiation and Integration. These two related processes are associated with the increase in motor functioning that stems from neural development. *Differentiation* is associated with the gradual progression from mass (gross) motor control to the more refined specific (fine) movements made by developing individuals. *Integration*, on the other hand, refers to the intricate interweaving of neural mechanisms of various opposing muscle groups into a coordinated interaction with one another.

Phylogenetic and Ontogenetic. *Phylogenetic* skills are movement behaviors that tend to appear somewhat automatically and in a predictable sequence. Such behaviors as reaching, grasping, walking, and running are presumably resistant to external environmental influences. *Ontogenetic* behaviors are those that are influenced by learning and the environment: swimming, bicycling, roller skating, and so forth.

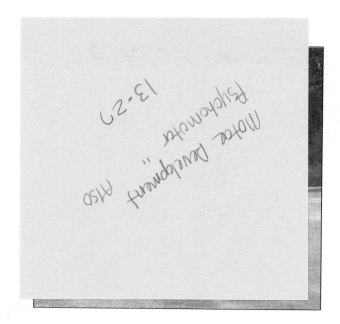

Riding a bicycle is an ontogenetic skill.

Maturation and Experience.　A relevant question in the study of motor development concerns the influence of *maturation* and *experience* (that is, instruction, practice, equipment) in the acquisition of motor skills. Several studies have been conducted to determine whether instruction and practice can significantly affect children's motor skill acquisition or whether maturational factors appear to predominate. The majority of the investigations conducted have used young twins; one twin is given advanced opportunities for practice, whereas the other one receives no instruction or additional practice.

McGraw (1935) concluded in his famous study of twins, Johnny and Jimmy, that, for any task, there appeared to be critical periods when it was most susceptible to change through practice. The author also indicated (as did Gesell, 1928) that phylogenetic skills (that is, those acquired automatically: creeping, walking, running) are more maturationally structured and less subject to modification through practice than are ontogenetic activities. Gallahue (1982) pointed out that, in follow-up studies of their original twin investigations, both Gesell and McGraw found that the trained twin exhibited more confidence in the skills in which he or she had previous special assistance; this suggests a possible benefit from training.

Winnick (1979) concluded from the research literature the following generalizations regarding the effects of early training on skill acquisition:

1. The role of maturation is important, particularly in the early years, in motor development, and skill acquisition. Training rarely transcends maturation, and especially not before neural mechanisms have reached a certain state of readiness. Maturation enables efficient learning to take place.

2. It is important to provide children opportunities to practice those behaviors for which the child is ready.

3. Instruction enhances the development of motor abilities, provided the child's maturational level is high enough to benefit from such experiences.

Individual Differences and Readiness.　Although the sequence of motor-skill development is predictable, the rate of appearance may be quite variable. Each child is unique in that he or she has a timetable for development. It is not uncommon to observe deviations from the "average" by as much as six months in the onset of numerous motor skills. This phenomenon is closely related to the child's "readiness" to learn new skills. Readiness may be defined as a condition of the individual that makes a particular task an appropriate one for him or her to master. Several factors, such as maturation, prior experience, and motivation, promote readiness. Much of our educational methodology is based upon the principles of readiness, that is, preparing individuals for more complex tasks. This same principle should be observed in physical education by developing a foundation of psychological and perceptual-motor readiness, at the same time allowing the child to take full advantage of his or her present maturational level.

Physical Growth and Development

Physical growth and development refers to quantitative and functional changes in the nervous, skeletal, and muscular systems. What follows is a brief review of the physical characteristics of each system.

NERVOUS SYSTEM DEVELOPMENT

The nervous system includes the brain, spinal cord, and the peripheral nerves that innervate (stimulate) the muscles. There are approximately 10 billion neurons (cells) present in the brain at birth; however, numerous structural and functional changes occur as one ages. With differentiation and integration, cells become larger, myelinated, and interconnections are built up among themselves. *Myelination*, or the development of myelin (that is, a white, fatty tissue that forms a sheath around the cell), is primarily responsible for the effectiveness of transmission of nerve impulses. Myelin coats the nerve, serving as an insulation against misdirected nerve impulses, thus allowing for increased speed of muscle action and more precise movement. For the most part, myelination is completed by the 10th or 11th year.

The brain, in terms of total weight, is the organ nearest that of an adult value at birth: 25 percent. This is increased to 90 percent of its final adult weight by five years of age.

The *midbrain* (located in the lower part of the brain) is the portion of the brain most fully developed at birth. Its early developmental importance is in its control of many reflexes exhibited in infants (which disappear with increased development of the cerebral cortex).

The *cerebral cortex* controls voluntary motor responses and is necessary for the acquisition of language, abstract thinking, and virtually all cognitive processes. Development is almost entirely complete by the time the child is four. The motor portion of the cortex that is responsible for control of the upper body (trunk, arms, and hands) is highly developed by six months of age; however, the portion that controls the legs develops later (associated with cephalocaudal development).

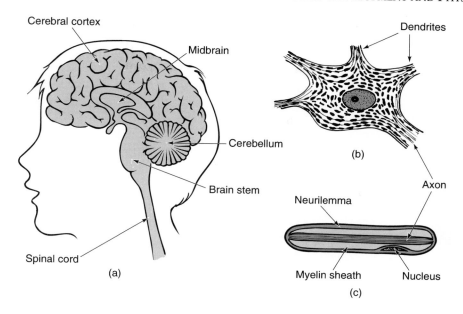

FIGURE 2-1

(a) A representation of major sections of the brain;
(b) a nerve fiber; (c) a cell body.

Also important to the development of motor control and performance are the number of *dendrites* (a branched part of the neuron that conducts impulses toward the cell body), which increase with age. An increase in dendrites and connecting fibers from the associative areas of the cortex (responsible for integrating sensory information and organizing muscular responses) allows for such functions as executing complex motor tasks. Immature development of the cortex severely limits the perceptual and motor abilities of the child.

The last portion of the brain to develop is the *cerebellum*. One of the major functions of the cerebellum lies in its temporal (timing) control or regulation of movement, more specifically voluntary skilled movements. Another functional role is maintaining equilibrium of the body. This is accomplished through interaction with the vestibular apparatus in which information is then transmitted to various muscles responsible for maintaining stability.

SKELETAL DEVELOPMENT (AND BODY WEIGHT)

The skeletal structure of the body originates as soft cartilage tissue before it hardens. Beginning during the prenatal period and extending into late adolescence, this process is known as *ossification*. As with other growth and developmental characteristics, the onset and rate of ossification may differ considerably among individuals. The long bones, such as the radius and femur, have a primary center of growth in the middle of the bone called *diaphysis* and one or more secondary centers at each end identified as *epiphyses*

(Fig. 2-2). Growth occurs both from the center toward the ends and from the ends toward the center. Because the bones of a developing child are not completely ossified, they are relatively soft and flexible. Hence they can absorb more strain without fracturing.

Figures 2-3 to 2-6 present growth patterns of height and weight for individuals two to 18 years of age. Even though children may vary considerably in height and weight, they usually follow a consistent pattern from birth to maturity. The growth patterns for height and weight are generally characterized by alternating phases of faster and slower growth. A very rapid tissue growth occurs during the first two years

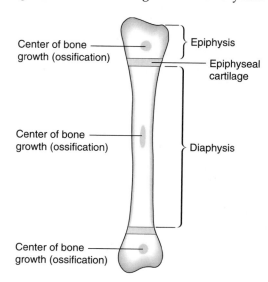

FIGURE 2-2

The growth of long bones.

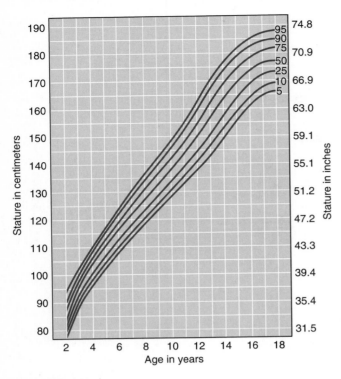

FIGURE 2-3

Boys' stature by age percentiles.

(Source: National Center for Health Statistics, U.S.
Department of Health, Education, and Welfare)

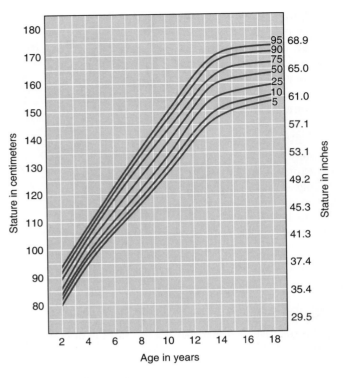

FIGURE 2-4

Girls' stature by age percentiles.

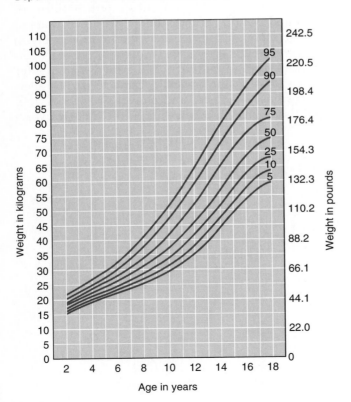

FIGURE 2-5

Boys' weight by age percentiles.

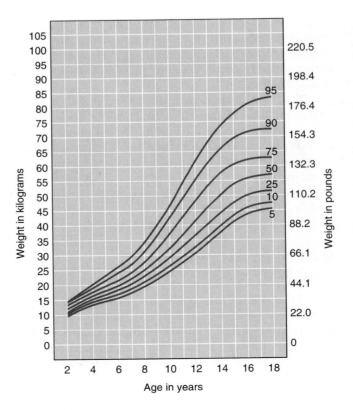

FIGURE 2-6

Girls' weight by age percentiles.

and gradually decreases by age five. A leveling off then takes place until the adolescent growth spurt. Females begin their adolescent growth spurt at approximately nine years of age and reach a peak during the 12th or 13th year. Females are slightly taller than males between the ages of 12 to 14; however, males then become increasingly taller. Males begin approximately two years later (11 years) and reach their peak during the 14th or 15th year. Weight gain follows approximately the same growth pattern as height, with females reaching a peak at about 12 years and boys at 14 years of age. Growth in height is generally completed by age 16 for females and at age 18 for males. Although fluctuating levels may occur in body weight throughout adulthood, growth generally ceases in the early 20's.

MUSCULAR DEVELOPMENT

There are three types of muscle: smooth, cardiac, and skeletal. *Smooth muscle* tissue forms the muscular portion of the internal organs and functions automatically (involuntarily). The muscular portion of the heart consists of *cardiac* muscle, which operates under the involuntary control of the brain. *Skeletal* muscle is unlike either cardiac or smooth muscle in that contractions are voluntarily controlled (that is, brought about by a stimulus from the brain via motor nerves innervating the muscle fiber). Skeletal muscle consists of muscle fibers (that increase in size but not number) that are bound together by a connective tissue that fuses at each end of the muscle to form a fascia (tendon) that is normally attached to a bone. During normal development, muscles grow along with bones, increasing in length and breadth with age. Development generally occurs in a cephalocaudal direction; that is, muscles near the head develop prior to those located in the lower extremities.

An increase in muscle size, whether from normal growth or stimulated by human influence (for example, exercise, drugs), is called *hypertrophy*.

Muscle weight increases approximately 40 times from birth to maturity, which means that the average 12-year-old child has nearly doubled the amount of muscle tissue present at age six.

Generally, as the child increases in age and grows larger, strength increases. Although girls reveal slightly lower strength performance scores at almost all age levels, there is a markedly significant difference between the sexes after the onset of puberty, with the boys being stronger. Researchers explain this difference (which appears in almost all strength tests) by the secretion of testosterone (a hormone), which is accompanied in males by significant (compared to females) increases in muscle weight and size of muscle fibers.

A more detailed coverage of muscular performance and other components of fitness are presented in Chapter 4.

Development of Motor Skills

With the development of certain physical characteristics, as described in the previous section, and with maturity, the child develops the capability of performing motor skills. Although the bulk of our behaviors are learned, one should remember that maturational factors (for example, the readiness of neural mechanisms) set a limit as to what skills and how many can be acquired. As previously noted (and the focus of this review) the acquisition of a motor skill is primarily dependent upon an orderly progression of development.

PHASES OF MOTOR BEHAVIOR

Table 2-6 describes the phases of lifespan motor behavior and the relationship with specific age-related developmental stages (Gabbard, 1992). Subsequent discussion provides an overview of the categories of motor behavior with emphasis on characteristics corresponding to the childhood years.

Table 2-6

Phases of Motor Behavior

Phase	Approximate Age	Developmental Stage
Reflexive	3 mo. fetal to 1 year	Prenatal-Infancy
Rudimentary	Birth to 2 years	Infancy
Fundamental Movement	2 to 7 years	Early Childhood
Sport Skill (Utilization)	8 to 12 years	Middle-Later Childhood
Growth & Refinement	13 to 18 years	Adolescence
Peak Performance	25 to 30 years	Early Adulthood
Regression	30 years +	Middle-Later Adulthood

Reflexive Behavior.   The *reflexive* phase of motor behavior begins with the unborn child and continues into the first year of life. Reflexes are involuntary (that is, uncontrolled) actions triggered by various kinds of external stimuli. They are usually associated with survival or primitive motor responses such as sucking and grasping. Because the full complement of reflexes is well documented in terms of appearance, longevity, and disappearance, they are often used as indicators of an infant's neurological maturity and soundness. Reflexive behavior mirrors the relative immaturity of the nervous system. As the system matures (that is, increased development of the cerebral cortex and associated areas), reflexes are gradually phased out and voluntary control is phased in. Many survival reflexes such as sneezing and coughing stay with us through life.

Rudimentary Phase.   During the rudimentary phase, which begins shortly after birth and terminates at approximately two years of age, voluntary behavior and muscle control gradually develop in a cephalocaudal-proximodistal direction (that is, head, neck, and trunk to feet, and trunk area to periphery). Some characteristic behaviors during this phase are crawling, creeping, walking, voluntary grasping.

Fundamental-Movement Phase.   As the title of this text implies, "Building the Foundation" should be of primary concern to educators. The fundamental-movement-skill areas of locomotion, nonlocomotion (stability), manipulation, and perceptual efficiency (movement awareness) are the foundation upon

which more complex skills are acquired and executed proficiently. For normal children, almost all of the skills and awarenesses associated with their fundamental areas should be acquired with some degree of proficiency by the end of the early childhood period (approximately seven years of age).

The study of children's fundamental motor patterns, especially in the locomotor and manipulative skill areas, has been and continues to be a topic of primary interest among researchers and practitioners. Leaders in this area, such as Wickstrom (1983) have provided information relative to the developmental progression in the acquisition of fundamental-movement abilities. This information has enabled the practitioner to understand better the movements of children. The observation of children's proficiency in movement usually involves a description (and assessment) of a series of movements organized in a particular time-space sequence, known as a *movement pattern*.

A *fundamental* skill (using a fundamental movement pattern) is a common motor activity with a general goal such as running, jumping, throwing, or catching. Each of these skills is identified in the various categories (that is, locomotor, nonlocomotor, and manipulative) of fundamental skills. Descriptions of the various developmental stages of specific skills are typically identified as ranging from *immature* (or *initial*) to *mature*, or *minimal* form to *sport-skill* form. All of these identify the performance traits of children aged two to seven. Fundamental skills are the foundations for more advanced and specialized motor activi-

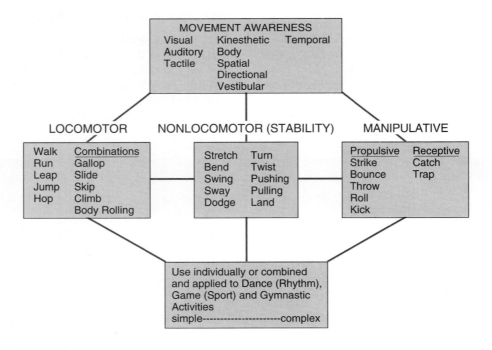

FIGURE 2-7

The foundation of movement awarenesses and fundamental movement skills

ties, known as *sport skills*. Sport skills are mature fundamental motor patterns that have been adapted to the special requirements of a particular advanced movement activity such as pitching a baseball (throwing), jumping hurdles (leaping), or swinging a golf club (striking). All advanced skill movements retain most of the characteristics found in basic patterns, hence the importance of a solid and varied fundamental-movement foundation.

Figure 2-7 presents an illustration of the foundation of fundamental skills and movement awareness and their relationship to more complex movement activities. The skills and awarenesses in each area are not intended to be exhaustive; however, they do represent those commonly identified in the literature.

Generally, by seven years of age, normally developing children have acquired to some degree of proficiency all of the basic postural and locomotor movement skills. Table 2-7 lists the sequence of human locomotion.

Locomotor skills, essential for human transportation, are identified as skills that move the individual through space from one place to another. Most locomotor skills develop as a result of a certain level of maturation; however, practice and experience are essential to reach mature proficiency. The gallop, slide, and skip are more difficult because they are combinations of other fundamental patterns.

Nonlocomotor skills, known also as *stability* skills, are movements executed with minimal or no movement of one's base of support (for example, twisting, bending, swaying). The ability to execute these skills parallels mastery of locomotor skills.

Manipulative skills involve the control of objects primarily with the hands and feet. There are two classifications of manipulative skills: *receptive* and *propulsive*. Receptive skills involve the receiving of objects (for example, catching, trapping), whereas propulsive skills characteristically include imparting force to objects (throwing, striking, kicking).

Table 2-7

Sequence of Human Locomotion

MOVEMENT	PERFORMANCE TRAITS	APPROXIMATE AGE
Rolling	voluntary—stomach to back	3–4 months
	back to stomach	5–6 months
Sitting	voluntary—no support	6–8 months
Crawling		
(body drag)		7 months
Creeping		
(abdomen clear)		8–10 months
Climbing		
stairs (mature pattern)		8–10 months
(descending)		4 years
Standing	pull-up to	8–9 months
	no support	9–12 months
Walking	forward	9–15 months
	backwards	16–19 months
	up steps	18–21 months
Running	attempts	18 months
	true "flight"	2–3 years
	smooth	4–5 years
Leaping		
(extension of running)	one foot take-off/opposite foot landing	3–4 years
Jumping	one foot take-off	1½ – 2 years
	two foot take-off	2–2½ years
	skillful	5 years
Hopping		3 years
(take off and land on same foot)	skillful	6 years
Galloping		4 years
(walk-leap)	skillful	6½ years
Sliding		4 years
(gallop executed sideways)	skillful	6½ years
Skipping		4 years
(step-hop)	skillful	6½ years

Movement awarenesses include those abilities necessary for conceptualization and effective response to sensory information needed to execute a desired motor task (for example, body, spatial, and rhythmic awareness). Chapters 9 through 12 present a thorough discussion of skills and awarenesses that are characteristic of both preschool-age children and older youngsters.

Sport Skill (Utilization) Phase.   The skills and awarenesses that the child acquires during the fundamental-movement phase gradually become more refined in the forms of adaptability and accuracy. By the fourth grade (eight to nine years), social development has stimulated the child's interest in refining those skills used in popular game, dance, and gymnastic activities. During the latter part of this phase, (approximately nine to 12 years; fourth to sixth grade), many of the fundamental competencies are utilized (and continuously refined) in more complex specific dance, game (primarily sport), and gymnastic activities. Fundamental kicking variations, for example, may be refined and adapted to the game of soccer or football (the progression usually begins with lead-up and modified game activities). A number of locomotor and stability skills can be combined to execute more advanced forms of gymnastics and dance.

Growth & Refinement Phase.   While growth occurs during all periods of development, this phase of motor behavior coincides with one of the most significant milestones in human development, the pubertal growth spurt (puberty) that generally begins during the first stages of adolescence. As the levels of hormones rise in the body, changes in muscle and skeletal growth provide a new dimension with which acquired motor skills can be asserted. During the later stages of adolescence, sex differences (mainly favoring males in regard to physical size) become more apparent due primarily to the increased amount of androgen hormones.

Peak Performance.   Most sources place peak physiological function and maximal motor performance between the ages of 25–30 years.

Regression.   While considerable variation among individuals is possible, after 30 years of age, most physiological and neurological factors begin their decline. The earlier developmental processes of cephalocaudal/proximodistal and differentiation/integration begin to reverse, resulting in similar performance characteristics among the very young and older adult. The regression of motor behavior is generally characterized by decreases in cardiovascular capacity, muscle strength and endurance, neural function, flexibility, and increased body fat.

Perceptual-Motor Development

The perceptual-motor process may be described as the monitoring and interpretation of sensory data and the subsequent response to information in terms of some behavior.

Humans have available certain sensory receptors (modalities) that serve to provide information about the environment, their own bodies, and their relationship to each other. These receptors are activated either by external stimuli (light, sound, and so forth) or by the body itself (kinesthetic). Sensations that are derived from such activation are mediated and transmitted through the sensory mechanisms to the central nervous system. Perception, which occurs primarily in the brain, enables the individual to interpret sensory information (stimuli) by associating it with past experiences (memory) and making judgments. These internal judgments are based in large part upon the individual's past experience, which in turn provides the foundation for a motor response (See Figure 2-8.) Perception cannot be viewed as separate or independent from the cognitive or psychomotor domain. Perception should be considered a function that can be learned and modified by varying the

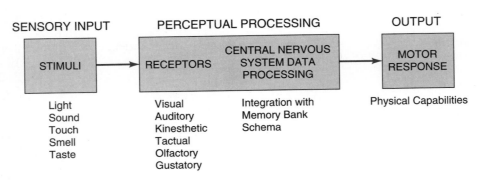

FIGURE 2-8
The perceptual-motor process.

environment. Most learning and development are inherently linked to sensori-perceptual processes, which in effect provide the foundation upon which all related behaviors are built.

The often used term *perceptual-motor development* refers primarily to changes or improvements in the child's capacity to perceive and respond to stimuli as a function of age. As the child develops there is an accompanying increase in sensori-perceptual capacities that allows for greater control of motor behavior. Behaviorally, this means that the child will gradually acquire more complex skills and through practice will perform them proficiently.

Williams and DeOreo (1980) note that as children grow older, three major developmental changes in the sensori-perceptual processes take place: (1) a shift in the hierarchy of the dominant sensory systems, (2) an increase in intersensory communication, and (3) an accompanying improvement in intrasensory discrimination.

The first developmental change is characterized by a shift from the primary use of tactile (touch) and kinesthetic (sense of body position) input to the use of visual information for the regulation of motor behavior. This change in the sensori-perceptual process constitutes development from a crude information-processing capacity (tactile), to the most advanced of all sensory systems in terms of speed and precision: the visual modality. Williams and DeOreo illustrate this shift in behavior with the following jump-rope example. A four-year-old who is attempting to jump a rope being swung by two adults is generally unable to use the visual information from the swinging rope to coordinate bodily movements. The child must first establish an individual pattern of movement and then the rope may be added as those turning the rope aid in the coordination of the task. This behavior suggests that the child is relying on bodily cues (tactile-kinesthetic awareness) to perform the motor task and cannot as yet use available visual information. By the time most children are seven or eight years of age, they have little or no problem in coordinating their bodily movements with the swinging of a rope; thus, as a result of visual input utilization, more rapid and precise judgments can occur resulting in a greater degree of success.

The second developmental change in the sensori-perceptual processes is that of improved *intersensory* communication. This means that as the child grows older he or she is using more of a multisensory functioning, that is, using several sensory modalities for information in regulating motor behavior. For example, the child interrelates auditory with visual information, visual with tactile, and, finally, what is *felt* with both what is observed and heard. In comparison to the seven- or eight-year-old who was superior to the four-year-old in the use of visual information

while jumping rope, the child at this level has developed a capacity for interrelating visual information (swinging rope) to the sounds of the rope as it hits the surface. This level of perceptual-motor development is characterized by a definite trend toward the use of multisensory sources for information and away from isolated functioning of the sensory systems.

The third change in the sensori-perceptual mechanisms is an increase in the discriminatory capabilities of the individual sensory modalities. This change seems to appear simultaneously with improved intersensory communication. At this time the individual sensory modalities become increasingly refined and develop a more detailed capacity for differentiation and discrimination. As a result of this improvement in *intrasensory* functioning, the child is able to make finer discriminations about stimuli, resulting in more efficient motor performance. The child attempting to jump rope at this level possesses greater discriminatory powers than those (children) described previously; thus he or she is able to make better judgments relating to the speed, direction, and movement of the swinging rope.

The developmental changes that have been described form a major portion of the perceptual-motor control upon which effective motor responses are based.

Components of the Perceptual-Motor System: Movement Awarenesses

KINESTHETIC PERCEPTION

Sometimes referred to as the "sixth sense," *kinesthetic perception* is a comprehensive term encompassing the memory and awareness of movement. Unlike the visual, auditory, and tactile sensory modalities that receive information from outside the body, the kinesthetic system is supplied with data from the muscles, tendons, joints, and the vestibular (balance) system. Defined as "awareness of movement and body position," this modality is basic to all movement. Every time an individual moves, sensory information is sent to the cerebral cortex, keeping it informed about the spatial characteristics (positions) of various body parts. This information is used by the brain to decide on programmed movements and to regulate motor behavior.

Kinesthetic perception, like the other sensory modalities, does not operate independently, but integrates with information from other sources to provide the brain with a more complete description of the external and internal environment. It should be stressed that the *visual modality* is a critical source of information to kinesthetic perception. The combination of the two sources dominates the learning and acquisition of motor skills.

Although kinesthetic perception has been described as basic to all movement, the following movement awarenesses have been identified as subdivisions of the modality: body awareness, spatial awareness, directional awareness, and vestibular awareness. It should be stressed that, because each awareness is dependent to a great degree upon each other, they are inseparable in the perceptual-motor process. Some researchers have combined all of the terms into one or two categories, such as body awareness or spatial awareness; however, it is our view that by presenting and understanding the "parts" a better understanding of the "whole" can be gathered, both as a theoretical and, most importantly (and a purpose of this text), as a teaching model.

Body Awareness. Sometimes referred to as "body concept" or "body knowledge," *body awareness* involves the following:

1. Awareness of body parts and their relationship to each other (location and name);
2. Awareness of the capabilities and limitations of body parts;
3. Knowledge of how to execute movements efficiently.

As children increase in age, they become increasingly more cognizant of their body parts in terms of location, name, relationship to one another, capabilities, and limitations. With this knowledge they gradually improve their ability to perform desired movements efficiently. It has been suggested by some child-development experts that only as children begin to define the dimensions of their body (parts and positions) are they able to differentiate among corresponding sectors of the space in which they desire to move. Since the body is a three-dimensional object contained within space, it is conceivable that young children might rely heavily on bodily identifications and dimensions as reference points for initial judgments about dimensions of their desired movement space.

One of the first body awareness characteristics that the child develops is the ability to label body parts. Although essentially an academic function, it is included with kinesthetic perception because of its major thrust and importance to this modality. By the time children are five years of age, they are able to identify approximately one half of their body parts accurately; 100 percent accuracy is usually achieved by 12 years.

Spatial Awareness. Awareness of the position (orientation) of objects in three-dimensional space is termed *spatial awareness*. An extension of body awareness, this perception relies on and can be considered a primary element of the visual modality as well.

However, spatial awareness as defined here refers to the child's perception of spatial relationships, which are based upon visual information and involve egocentric and objective localization of objects in space. *Egocentric localization* can be described as the ability to locate objects in space in relation to oneself. This behavior is characteristic of preschool children who determine the location of an object relative to where their own body is positioned. *Objective localization*, which follows egocentric perception, refers to locating the position of two or more objects in relation to each other. Such behavior is exhibited by older children who can locate an object relative to its nearness to other objects but not in relationship to the location of their own bodies. With the knowledge of space and one's body, the child then has the information upon which to project the body effectively.

Directional Awareness. An extension of body and spatial awareness, *directional awareness* consists of two awareness components: laterality and directionality.

The basis for directional awareness derives from laterality. *Laterality* refers to the conscious internal awareness of the two sides of the body. It may also be described in kinesthetic terms as a "sense of feel" for the various dimensions of the body with regard to their location and direction. Through movement experiences, children become increasingly aware that their bodies have two distinct sides—right and left— and although similar in size and shape, these sides occupy decidedly different positions in space. Children with a good sense of laterality do not need to rely on cues such as a ribbon or watch around their wrist or a ring on their finger to provide information about left and right. Children generally develop laterality at around three to four years, and they then begin to attach the verbal labels of left and right to the sides of the body. However, the ability to label correctly the two sides is usually not fully developed until approximately seven years of age. It is during the time when the two sides of the body are being differentiated that preferences in the use of one of the eyes, hands, or feet over the other appears (that is, lateral dominance). *Handedness* (that is, preference for left or right hand), which appears as early as age four (at this age approximately 84 percent of children are right-handed), may not become permanently established until the age of nine or 10. Before that time, one is likely to observe some unstable periods of preferential hand use. A preference for one foot over the other appears to be established by the age of five years and remains quite stable. Children generally do not exhibit the same degree of lateralization in the use of the eyes as they do for a hand or foot, at any age. Research concerning eye-hand preferences indicates some interesting information for the movement specialist. It appears that five- and six-year-olds exhibit a

Directional awareness allows the child to understand the dimensions of space.

definite mixed preference (that is, the preferred eye is on the side opposite the preferred hand); seven- and eight-year-olds are divided (mixed and pure [same side]); and the majority of children nine to 11 years reveal eye and hand preferences on the same side of the body (Williams & DeOreo, 1980).

Directionality, the second component in directional awareness, refers to the ability to identify dimensions of external space. It is through laterality and directionality that children are able to understand the concepts of space (direction) and to project their bodies left-right, up-down, in-out, front-back, and over-under. These dimensions in external space exist only as they relate to the individual's body position at any given time in space.

Vestibular Awareness. As previously mentioned, kinesthetic perception derives information from within the body itself through the muscles, tendons, joints, and vestibular system. The vestibular apparatus (located in the inner ear) provides the individual with information about the body's relationship to gravity; thus it serves as the basis for *balance* and a "sense of body position." Williams and DeOreo (1980) have summarized the overall functions of the vestibular system as follows:

1. Maintenance of upright posture and equilibrium using the antigravity muscles of the trunk and body for control and postural reflexes;
2. Aid the muscles of the eyes in maintaining visual fixation during bodily movements;
3. Mediation of the body-righting reflexes (balance) using muscles of the head, neck, and shoulders;
4. To merge with receptors from the muscles, joints, and tendons to appraise the central nervous system of the body's spatial orientation;
5. To contribute to the overall perception of bodily movement (kinesthetic sense).

Balance, designated as a skill-related fitness component (as opposed to health-related), refers to the ability to maintain one's equilibrium in relation to the force of gravity. Balance depends primarily upon vestibular awareness; however, basic reflexes and unconscious as well as conscious abilities interrelate to make postural adjustments. Postural balance that occurs as a result of reflexes responding to gravity allows us to maintain upright posture and perform simple tasks such as holding the head erect, sitting,

Table 2-8

Selected Balance Abilities

TYPE OF BALANCE	TASK	APPROXIMATE AGE
STATIC	Balances on one foot 3–4 seconds	3 years
	Balances on one foot 10 seconds	4 years
	Supports body in basic inverted position	6 years
DYNAMIC	Walks on 1-inch straight line	3 years
	Walks on 4-inch-wide beam using alternating steps	3 years
	Walks in 1-inch circular (line) pattern	4 years
	Walks on 2- or 3-inch beam (alternating steps)	4½ years
	Hops (traveling) proficiently	6 years

standing, and walking. Balancing tasks are generally considered as either *static or dynamic*. Static balance refers to the ability to maintain equilibrium while the body is stationary, such as the ability to stand on one foot, tiptoe, or balance on a stabilometer or balance board. *Dynamic* balance is the ability of the body to maintain and control posture during movement. Dynamic balance tasks generally employ walking on balance beams of different heights and widths. Because of its complexity, balance is difficult to isolate and measure; however, some practical methods of assessment such as the ability to walk across a balance beam or stand on one's toes are fair indicators of gross equilibrium. Table 2-8 presents some basic developmental abilities with various balancing tasks.

Although the child's ability to balance begins to stand out after two years of age, it is not until approximately the fifth year that the child possesses the neurological maturity necessary to acquire such skills as roller skating and riding a bicycle.

VISUAL AWARENESS

Many regard vision and kinesthesis (that is, kinesthetic perception) as the two most important senses relating to motor skills. When vision is present, and it is in most motor-skill actions, visual awareness tends to dominate the other senses and may even be used to calibrate information being received from other senses. Approximately 80 percent of all information we perceive comes from the visual modality.

Although all types of visual information are utilized in the execution of motor skills, we will only review a selection of those considered primarily relevant and applicable as aspects of instruction.

Spatial Awareness.   Discussed under kinesthetic awareness, those aspects of spatial awareness concerning relationships or spatial orientation (for instance, making judgments about the positional changes of objects in space) are closely related to the level of visual complexity that the child possesses. The final stages of this complexity are reached by the majority of children by approximately nine years of age.

Depth and Distance Perception.   The perception for spatial relationships involves the ability to distinguish the relationships among distance, depth, and direction. Although the terms are quite similar, *depth perception* refers to the space between two objects in space, whereas *distance perception* refers to the space between the individual and object. A more general definition identifies depth (and distance) perception as the ability to judge relative distances in three-dimensional space. Basically two aspects of vision—binocular and monocular—provide clues for the perception of depth and distance. *Binocular vision*, the forerunner of depth perception, refers to the ability to

focus both eyes accurately on an object to produce a three-dimensional view. *Monocular vision* involves the perception of single-image cues such as those viewed on television or the changing size of objects as we or they move. By the age of six or seven years, children can judge depth as accurately with reduced information, that is, monocular cues, as with binocular cues. With growth, the two types of information become more integrated, thus more efficient.

Figure-Ground Discrimination.   *Figure-ground discrimination* (perception) refers to the ability to distinguish an object from its surrounding background. This perception, as with most meaningful motor-skill performances, necessitates that the child be able to concentrate and to give selective attention to a visual stimulus. Such is the situation when the child attempts to focus upon and catch a white ball that has been hit into the white and blue sky. The child must concentrate and select a limited number of stimuli (ball) from a vast background.

Form Discrimination.   *Form discrimination* involves the ability to recognize differences in shapes and symbols. Very much related to this aspect of visual recognition is *perceptual constancy*; that is, the ability to perceive and recognize an object despite variations in its presentation. These variations may include shape identification from various angles and color recognition (even if partially diminished). Children experiencing problems with this ability are usually unable to match or clearly differentiate similar and dissimilar designs, letters, and objects.

Form discrimination is essential for academic success. Children must learn that two- and three-dimensional forms belong to certain categories (circles, squares, triangles, and so forth) regardless of size, color, texture, or angle of observation. Children three to four years of age tend to rely on form (or shape) rather than color for object identification, whereas by age six or seven, children utilize color and form information in a more integrated manner.

Visual-Motor Coordination.   The ability to coordinate visual abilities with movements of the body is termed *visual-motor coordination*. This aspect of movement combines both visual and kinesthetic perceptions with the ability to make controlled and coordinated bodily movements usually involving eye-hand or eye-foot integration. Development of these actions generally follows the proximodistal (midline to periphery), cephalocaudal (head to toes), and gross to fine motor order. Fine motor tasks, such as lacing shoes or writing, involve the synchronization of small muscles of the hand or foot, which in turn are coordinated with vision. Table 2-9 presents a selection of fine visual-motor behaviors characteristically exhibited by children three to eight years of age.

Table 2-9
Selected Fine-Visual Motor Characteristics of Children 3 to 8 Years Old

AGE (IN YEARS)

3	4	5	6	7	8
Uses hand constructively to direct visual responses	Visual manipulation; does not need support of hands	Understands horizontal and vertical concepts	Copying tasks come easily	Prefers pencil over crayons	Can copy a diamond shape
Skillful manipulations	Discoveries made in depth perception	Copies squares and triangles	Fair ability to print	Ability to make uniform size letters, numbers, etc.	Attempts cursive writing
Draws lines with more control	Laces shoes	Increase in fine finger control		Drawing of person more accurate	Uniformity in alignment of letters
Can copy circles and crosses Stacks 1-inch cubes	Buttons large buttons Orients movements from center of periphery	Colors within the lines Fairly accurate cutting abilities			
Writing utensils handled like adults	Draws a recognizable picture with some detail	Draws a recognizable person			
Strings beads Cuts with scissors					

The successful performance of almost all gross-motor skills requires the integration of visual information with kinesthetic awareness and mechanisms of the motor system. When attempting gross-motor skills such as kicking, throwing, or striking, children must be able to judge accurately the speed and distance of the approaching object, the force to be applied, and the direction of projection. In kicking, for example, visual information is relayed to the brain that gives information about the location of the approaching object. This information integrates with the motor system in the form of a motor program, which enables the child to kick the oncoming ball; this is, of course, a very simplified explanation of a very complex process.

An essential component in the performance of several gross visual-motor tasks is the perception and interception of moving stimuli (catching, striking). Children between the ages of five and 10 vastly improve their ability to track moving stimuli (balls, objects) traveling at a variety of speeds and from various angles. Research indicates that by five or six years of age, children can efficiently track a ball traveling on a horizontal plane. By age seven or eight, children perceive a ball traveling downward or upward more easily, and by age nine they can track an object moving in an arc.

Williams (1967) conducted one of the most recognized developmental studies of perception of a moving object. Children six to 11 years of age had to judge the speed and direction of a projected ball and move as quickly as possible to a location where they thought the ball would land (it landed on a canvas ceiling above the child's head). Results indicated that children six to eight years of age were not capable of integrating their motor behavior with visual information; they reacted quickly, but inaccurately. The nine-year-old children seemed to perceive the complexity of the task; they reacted slower, but were significantly more accurate in their judgments. It was the 11-year-old group, however, that demonstrated a mature interface between the perceptual and motor aspects of the task by responding quickly and accurately. It may be assumed from this and other studies of this nature that complex spatial perceptions involving perceptual anticipation of rapidly moving objects with locomotor movements and manipulative responses are not mature in children until late childhood. Such evidence would make it impractical to expect but a few children six to eight years to catch a well-hit fly ball on a Little League field.

TEMPORAL AWARENESS

Temporal awareness involves the timing mechanism within the body. As previously mentioned, all movements involve spatial temporal characteristics (movement in space within a time structure). The child with a well-developed time dimension generally performs a series of movements in a rhythmical, coordinated manner.

Rhythm, referred to as rhythmic awareness and an instructional theme (along with eye-hand and eye-foot under "temporal awarenesses") in this text, is a basic component of all coordinated movement, and it plays an important role in the everyday lives of children. Rhythm may also be described as the measured release of energy consisting of repeated units of time.

AUDITORY AWARENESS

Auditory perception is dependent upon learning and involves the ability to discriminate, associate, and interpret auditory stimuli. Despite the fact that auditory awareness is one of the most common means by which humans receive information, it has been given little attention in physical education and motor development as compared to other sensory modalities. The importance of an awareness of sound is obvious, however, and awareness of sound may be improved through movement programs. The following are components that appear to be relevant to the instructional program.

Auditory Discrimination.   This refers to the ability to distinguish between different frequencies and amplitudes of sounds.

Auditory Figure-Ground Perception.   Similar to visual figure-ground, this perception involves selecting relevant stimuli from a background of general sounds. This awareness necessitates that the child attend to relevant stimuli in situations where irrelevant sounds are present. A child with underdeveloped auditory figure–ground perception will experience difficulty in hearing the verbal cues from the teacher over the square dance music.

Sound Localization.   This refers to the ability to localize the source or direction of sound in the environment. Without direct visual information, children having problems with this ability would find it difficult to determine the direction of a honking horn or a teacher calling in a playground.

Temporal Auditory Perception.   This aspect of auditory awareness involves the ability to perceive and discriminate variations of sounds presented in time. This perception includes distinction of rate, emphasis, tempo, and order, which are those awarenesses generally needed to perform rhythmic activities using auditory stimuli, like lummi sticks and tinkling.

Jumping rope requires a well-developed time structure.

TACTILE AWARENESS

Tactile awareness (that is, sense of touch) refers to the ability to interpret sensations from the cutaneous (skin) surfaces of the body. Through touch and manipulation of objects, children learn to understand their environment. During early development, children learn to distinguish hot from cold, sharp from dull, wet from dry, and so on. Tactile perception enables the child to cope with and understand his or her world on relatively tangible terms. Previously described as being prevalent during the early stages of perceptual motor development (that is, primary use of tactile-kinesthetic information) and a less sophisticated mode of information input as compared to other modalities, tactile awareness can be quite effective when combined with other modalities.

Along with assisting the child in the development of fine motor skills such as drawing, cutting, and coloring, tactile perception enhances manipulative abilities by providing information relative to contact with objects. Children first learning to walk on a balance beam usually visually guide their movements by looking at their feet and then progress to guidance by "sense of feel." Some movement specialists suggest that we allow children to perform more activities barefoot (and on various surfaces) in support of tactile stimulation as a learning medium.

Two aspects of tactile awareness appear relative to the teaching of young children: tactile discrimination and tactile memory. *Discrimination*, the earliest form of tactile development, involves the ability to distinguish through touch, differentiate between objects, and match objects by tactile information. With tactile discrimination children develop

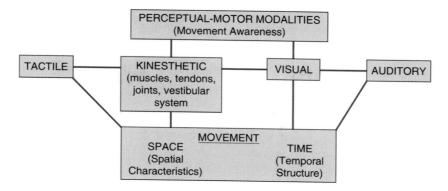

FIGURE 2-9

Intersensory integration and movement.

a corresponding vocabulary such as hard, soft, rough, and smooth. *Tactile memory* refers to the ability to discriminate and apply verbal labels to tactile information.

INTERSENSORY INTEGRATION

The presentation of perceptual modalities as separate components as described in this and other texts should not convey the overall perceptual-motor process as less than very complex. The functioning of any one modality (or component within) is interrelated with and accommodated by the other sensory systems. In the instance of kinesthetic perception, for example, four awarenesses were identified, all of which are interrelated and dependent upon each other for efficient movement. At the same time, visual, auditory, and tactile cues may integrate to enhance information input and facilitate processing. Figure 2-9 illustrates the intersensory integration that results in movement.

COGNITIVE BEHAVIOR AND PHYSICAL ACTIVITY

As previously noted, one of the most recognized theorists in cognitive development in children is Jean Piaget. In his many works, repeated references related to movement (and play) experiences are given. This same belief that motor activity in the form of play contributes to intellectual development has also been mentioned by such noted modern educators as Dewey and Montessori, as well as the ancient Greek philosophers Plato and Socrates. It is with this type of support that educators have recognized the contributions of early movement experiences to the cognitive and perceptual development of children. One could assume that if motor activities play an important role in cognitive and perceptual development, and if both of these attributes are essential in academic success, then an

indirect relationship should exist between motor activities and academic achievement. It should be stressed, however, that the relationship is indirect, for few recognized empirical studies have demonstrated that physical activity directly enhances cognitive abilities. Two of the indirect mediums between movement experiences and academic success are *motivation* and *self-concept*. Through movement experiences both of these behavioral influences may be improved. Many researchers have assumed these behavioral influences enhance the total learning attitude of the child and improve the chances for classroom success.

If educators wish to enhance cognitive skills through movement experiences, the experiences must be "specifically" structured so that they tax the perceptual modality, encourage social interaction, and stimulate cognition.

What follows are some examples of how movement experiences may stimulate and enhance the cognitive skills in children:

1. The use of games and other movement activities should encourage problem-solving rather than replication from demonstration. In these instances, the child is allowed the opportunity to think creatively, logically, and to seek discoveries. Games and other movement-oriented activities may be designed to enhance specific cognitive skills such as attention, memory, and sequencing.

2. Basic to the cognitive development of children is *perception*. Through the various sensory modalities children interact with the environment and challenge information. Movement activities stimulate the perceptual mechanisms of the body as the child develops an awareness for body, space, time, and force. The acquisition of these awarenesses and factors of movement fosters the development of cognitive understanding.

3. Although very little hard research is available at this time, many researchers and teachers believe that *self-concept* is intri-

cately related to academic success and therefore cognitive development. Because participation in movement programs may enhance the child's self-concept, it is suggested that teachers recognize both the physical and the emotional characteristics of their pupils.

4. Another increasingly popular medium between movement activities and academic achievement is *academic reinforcement*. This type of learning medium, generally utilized by elementary classroom teachers, involves the use of specifically structured movement activities to enhance specific academic concepts (usually the basics in language arts, math, science, and social studies). Research comparing the uses of specific movement-oriented programs and traditional classroom methods has indicated superiority for "movement" groups in information gained (Penman, Christopher, & Wood, 1976; Bledsoe, Purser, & Frantz, 1974) and in the retention of material over a period of time (Gabbard & Shea, 1979).

Some of the possible reasons for the success of movement activities in cognitive development (and academic achievement) are listed below:

1. *Motivation.* Very simply, children are interested in movement; they become attentive and eager to participate; therefore the learning process is enjoyable.
2. *Fun.* Not to be overlooked when combined with motivation, together they are prime factors in the learning and retention of information. Children possess a high regard for movement experiences that are fun; therefore any negative thoughts concerning "academics" may be diminished.
3. *Active participation.* Active games and other movement experiences motivate children who have typically short attention spans and get them involved in the discovery-learning process.
4. *Multisensory approach.* This approach refers to the concept that during movement activities the child will utilize more modes of sensory input, namely kinesthetic and tactile awareness, than the child may experience sitting in the classroom. Students generally learn using the visual and auditory modalities. During academic-reinforcement activities, it is quite easy to incorporate visual and auditory stimuli as well as increase kinesthetic and tactile information input (some kinesthetic and tactile awarenesses are involved in most classroom instruction).
5. *Reinforcement.* Academic reinforcement focuses attention to the learning tasks, thus keeping the child involved in the activity.

6. *Retention.* This is perhaps the product of all the factors mentioned; motor-learning specialists have claimed for years that retention of motor-skill learning is higher than "academic" verbal-based learning because of the motivation and processes of neuromuscular feedback.

AFFECTIVE BEHAVIOR AND PHYSICAL ACTIVITY

Another important contribution of physical activity to child development is in the *affective domain*. Affective development as discussed here refers to children's increasing ability to interact with others as well as to understand themselves. Because children's feelings about themselves are markedly affected by the actions and reactions of others, the two cannot be perceived as separate. Few would deny that physical activity contributes to a child's social growth, attitudes, and self-concept, for most of the young child's social contacts are in a play setting. Physical education classes are often referred to as laboratories in which children experience a multitude of social and psychological encounters.

Three major aspects of affective development that are particularly relevant to the physical education setting are: socialization, self-concept, and the development of attitudes.

Socialization

A general definition of *socialization* is that it is a process whereby children learn to interact with others (also known as *peer relations*) and understand what kind of behavior is expected or appropriate in different contexts. A major portion of the socialization process for children involves *play* (a term encompassing all pleasurable physical activity). Play is a primary vehicle by which children learn about themselves and how to interact with their peers. One of the benefits of physical activity is that, in the play environment, children are afforded the opportunity to progress through a ladder of socialization. In general, the following stages of socialization and peer relations may be observed in children.

1. *Egocentric stage* (zero to two years). Also described as the stage of solitary play, this is when the child is the center of the universe, engrossed in his or her own activities with limited contact with others.
2. *Parallel play* (three to four years). During this stage children generally play alongside, but not with, others for extended periods of time. Limited play between two children usually involves the use of the same toys or play apparatus; for example: follow-the-leader-type activities.

3. *Small-group play* (five to six years). Although still enjoying solitary and parallel-play situations, children at this level have the ability and desire to play in small groups of two to four with simple activities of low organization for increasing periods of time. The ability to work with others usually increases at the same time that children learn how to share space, equipment, and ideas, and become less and less egocentric.

4. *Large-group play* (seven to eight years). At this age, most children are eager and capable of participating in large groups (with increasing role complexity) such as found in many dance and team-sport activities. Children at this level are less egocentric and increasingly interested in becoming proficient in motor-skill activities (especially popular team sports) that require more complex behavior and group cooperation.

As with other behavioral characteristics with corresponding age ranges, one should be cognizant of the possible differences between individual children, especially in the psychological realm. Many children (and adults) may never feel "adequate" or "comfortable" when placed in the role of a functioning part of a small-or large-group situation, as commonly found in many game, dance, and sport activities. It is important that teachers attempt to understand both the socio-psychological (psychological behavior in a social setting, which includes emotion and expression) differences among children and their physical and motor-performance variations.

Self-Concept

Self-concept, unquestionably one of the most important components of a child's psychological makeup, refers to one's perceptions and evaluations of the self. Perceptions, or judgments, relative to the self may include personal evaluations about behaviors (for example, academic, motor skills, emotional, physical appearance), or an assumption related to how others perceive those characteristics. Children's successes and their developing tolerance of failures provide a strong influence on self-concept. Many of these events occur in play situations, for movement is one of the primary ways in which children explore and discover themselves and their capabilities. Through movement, children are provided the opportunity to express emotions and identify with a group.

As evidenced by the "hero-type" worship that many young children show for popular athletes, proficiency in motor skills has a great influence on self-concept. Numerous studies have indicated a definite link between high positive peer-group acceptance and motor-skill proficiency, as well as a lower accep-

tance of the less proficient, overweight child (especially among males). There are, however, other influencing factors involved in peer-group acceptance: attitudes toward others (for example, the bully), intelligence to attempt the challenge, and the teacher's acceptance of the individual. The teacher who allows any child to be chosen last, for example, or openly criticizes poor performance may be adding to a child's already negative self-image. Children with a negative self-concept have a tendency to reveal one of two behaviors; they either become more introverted (turn into themselves) or live up to their negative self-image by establishing themselves as failures. These negative feelings about self are often acted out in aggressive behavior.

Gallahue (1989) has described the following factors as components that enhance success in physical activities and allow for the development of a positive self-concept.

DEVELOPMENTALLY APPROPRIATE ACTIVITIES

Activities should be used that meet the needs, interests, and capabilities of children at various developmental stages. Six- and 7-year-olds are not adolescents or adults, and they should not be expected to perform as examples. Forcing children to attempt activities that are beyond their perceptual-motor, physical, and emotional capabilities is not conducive to success; rather, in most cases, failure occurs. Developmentally appropriate activities should be used as a means of enhancing a realistic concept of abilities.

SEQUENCING OF TASKS

Vital to the success of most motor skills, especially more complex ones, is the *sequencing* (that is, difficulty progression) of motor tasks. It seems perfectly logical, for example, to first instruct children on how to perform a tripod or frogstand followed by a headstand, handstand, and cartwheel. Motor learning theory would support the practice of teaching the basics first as well as having children experience success at initial skill learning before attempting more difficult tasks. Children who experience high frequency of failure during early learning stages may give up or not try as hard during future attempts. Competition should not be introduced too early in the learning process and certainly not until the necessary skills can be performed with an acceptable degree of proficiency. Competition necessitates that there be a winner, which is related to success, and in the true sense of competition there must be a loser. Generally speaking, competition for children in kindergarten and first grade should be restricted to self-testing; that is, how many successive bounces before loss of control rather than a relay race involving dribbling a ball. For most young children, failure is a confusing aspect when they attempt to relate the result to self-concept.

ADVENTURE ACTIVITIES

A third way in which physical education programs may have an impact on self-concept is by participation in adventure activities—activities that enhance self-confidence. Such experiences as climbing, swinging on a rope, balancing, crawling, or hanging by the knees challenge the child's courage and imagination while fulfilling the need for mastery that comes from success.

REASONABLE EXPECTATIONS

Teachers can also have an influence on the development of self-concept by helping children establish reasonable expectations of their abilities. Children need to attain goals to feel successful and to establish a positive attitude about their own abilities.

Programmed activities or tasks should not, however, be so low as to not stimulate a challenge and provide discovery. Once reasonable success is secured, new goals should be established in order to maintain a level of challenge. When tasks are too difficult and achievement impossible, frustration and reinforcement of a negative self-concept are likely to follow.

ENCOURAGEMENT

Another area in which movement programs may influence a child's developing self is through direct communication to the child. As previously mentioned in the definition of self-concept, an important aspect involves how children perceive others perceive them. Thus communication of how we feel about the child's accomplishments is very important. Positive remarks and praise, although very effective, should be used appropriately so the child does not perceive your actions as a "game" of constant and sometimes meaningless statements. Children develop self-confidence through accomplishments and from words, attitudes, and judgments of those around them. Many times the way in which the teacher says things makes a difference as well. Instead of negative feedback such as "That was all wrong" or "I do not think you can do this task," teachers should attempt to be more neutral by stating, "You are almost there," and "You are really working hard; perhaps this task is too difficult until we accomplish more basics." If more negative

remarks are necessary (in unusual situations such as display of bad behavior), the child should be communicated to individually and not in the presence of others.

Other techniques and methods that may influence self-concept and be incorporated in the physical education program include the use of individualized movement instruction and teaching strategies that enhance self-reliance, self-discovery, and individual success.

Attitudes

Physical educators have for years acknowledged the development of positive attitudes as a desirable outcome of movement experiences. Attitudes toward physical activity, as in other instances, generally involve feelings of a like or dislike for something. Children form positive attitudes about physical activity if they perceive such experiences as pleasurable or beneficial to the self. The "fun" component is an essential ingredient in the development of positive attitudes, especially with young children. One of the major goals of physical educators should be to establish positive attitudes toward physical fitness. These attitudes will motivate children to be conscious of the benefits of physical activity that are important to them now as well as throughout life. Although not supported by conclusive scientific evidence, positive attitudes toward physical activity carry into adulthood and enhance the quality of one's life, and most physical educators would agree with that statement. It is also assumed that many children who are described as "overweight" or "clumsy" and possess a low self-concept tend to be less "pro" exercise as adults. Teachers of children have a tremendous, if not critical, task before them in establishing positive attitudes that may enhance substantially the quality of mental and physical well-being of individuals. Such practices as using physical activity as punishment (running laps or doing sit-ups), or presenting daily fitness activities in a traditional, boring manner (for example, daily mass calisthenics) are not conducive to establishing positive attitudes. We often hear remarks of former athletes who state that they will never run again because of the memories it brings back related to training. Fortunately, children possess a zest for physical activity; however, they also relate desired movement experiences with events found pleasurable. It is therefore the responsibility of physical educators to build positive attitudes toward physical activity with pleasurable experiences.

Praise is important in the development of a positive self-concept.

REFERENCES

ARNHEIM, D., & SINCLAIR, W. A. (1979). *The clumsy child: A program of motor therapy.* St. Louis: C. V. Mosby.

BLEDSOE, C. J., PURSER, D. J., & FRANTZ, R. N. (1974). Effects of manipulative activities on arithmetic achievement and retention. *Psychological Reports, 35,* 247–252.

GABBARD, C. (1992). *Lifelong motor development.* Dubuque, IA: W. C. Brown.

GABBARD, C., & SHEA, C. (1979). Influence of movement activities on shape recognition and retention. *Perceptual and Motor Skills, 48,* 116–118.

GALLAHUE, D. L. (1989). *Understanding motor development* (2nd ed.). Indianapolis: Benchmark Press.

GALLAHUE, D. L. (1982). *Developmental movement experiences for young children.* New York: Wiley.

GESELL, A. (1928). *Infancy and human growth.* New York: Macmillan.

McGRAW, M. B. (1935). *Growth: A study of Johnny and Jimmy.* New York: Appleton-Century.

National Center for Health Statistics. (1976). U.S. Department of Health, Education and Welfare, 25, June 26, 3.

PENMAN, K. A., CHRISTOPHER, J. R., & WOOD, G. (1976). Using gross motor activity to improve language arts concepts by third-grade students. *Research Quarterly, 48,* 134–137.

PIAGET, J. (1963). *The origins of intelligence in children* (M. Cook, Trans.). New York: W. W. Norton & Co., Inc.

WICKSTROM, R. L. (1983). *Fundamental motor patterns.* Philadelphia: Lea & Febiger.

WILLIAMS, H. G. (1967). *The perception of moving objects by children.* Unpublished study, University of California, Los Angeles, Perceptual-Motor Learning Laboratory.

WILLIAMS, H. G., DEOREO, K. (1980). Perceptual-motor development: A theoretical overview. In C. Corbin (Ed.), *A textbook of motor development,* 2nd ed. Dubuque, IA.: W. C. Brown.

WINNICK, J. P. (1979). *Early movement experiences and development habitation and remediation.* Philadelphia: Saunders.

SUGGESTED READINGS

ECKERT, H. (1987). *Motor development* (3rd ed.). Indianapolis: Benchmark Press.

GABBARD, C. (1992). *Lifelong motor development.* Dubuque, IA: W.C. Brown.

GALLAHUE, D. L. (1989). *Understanding motor development in children* (2nd ed.). Indianapolis: Benchmark Press.

HAYWOOD, K. M. (1993). *Lifespan motor development.* (2nd ed.) Champaign, IL: Human Kinetics.

PAYNE, G. V., & ISAACS, L. D. (1991). *Human motor development* (2nd ed.). Mountain View, CA: Mayfield.

WILLIAM, H. G. (1983). *Perceptual and motor development.* Englewood Cliffs, NJ: Prentice-Hall.

The Scientific Basis For Motor-Skill Acquisition

3

One of the major developments in elementary physical education has been the use of *schema theory* as a basis for teaching and understanding the acquisition of motor skills by children. Few theories of motor-skill learning have had as great an impact or as much support from the scientific community. As with other scientific notions, it has been the role of the practitioner to gather what is believed to be the "best" scientific information available and develop teaching/learning models to facilitate application in a practical setting. This process of "theory into practice," joining the scientific with the practical, is the subject of this section (see Gabbard, 1984).

Understanding the Theory

Schema theory (Schmidt, 1975, 1977) proposes an explanation of how individuals learn and perform a seemingly endless variety of movements. Basically, the theory proposes that humans store in memory past movement experiences. This storage of "movement elements" and their relationship to each other are called *movement schema*. The theory suggests that the motor programs we store in memory are not specific records of the movements to be performed; rather, they are a set of general rules (schemas) to guide performance. An individual calls up his or her schema to program (in a sense, "piece together") movements. Schema theory suggests an explanation (which other theories do not) for two characteristics of human performance. First, individuals rarely repeat a set of movements precisely in the same manner. If a separate program were required for each movement variation performed, our storage capabilities would

be quickly surpassed. Second, individuals are capable of programming movements to fit seemingly novel situations. An example of schema theory in practice is the performance of an individual playing shortstop in baseball or guard in basketball. The shortstop can field a ball from numerous positions—many novel (not practiced)—and return the ball to first base, just as the basketball player can shoot successfully from almost any (unrehearsed) position on the court. Schema theory treats motor programs in much the same manner as concepts are treated in verbal learning. The motor program begins with the cognitive domain and perception of incoming information. The child who has practiced throwing far, hard, soft, or short has a good cognitive sense of what may be in the middle. The same sense of prediction is assumed to be applicable to other movement situations. Abstractions are derived from a large number of similar instances that may represent the relationship among various guidelines needed to identify a particular instance of the concept or produce a particular segment of the movement. The motor schema (concept) for a general skill area (*e.g.*, throwing, jumping) is bounded by dimensions related to space, time, and force. Each dimension represents a continuum that may (depending upon experience) be very limited or quite diverse. The more particular instances generated by the individual, the more abstract the schema becomes. The motor schema enables the individual to select the appropriate level from each dimension to program a task that may be either known or novel. The basketball player calls upon a program consisting of a relationship among distance the ball has to travel, required muscular force, arm speed, and angle of release, all of which may change from one attempt to the other.

"Variability in practice" is the key to a diversified motor-skill foundation.

One of the most fundamental applications and aspects of schema theory is that the learning of a skill can be facilitated by "variability in practice." The theory predicts that practicing a variety of movement outcomes within the same general skill area will provide a widely based set of experiences upon which a schema can be built. Schema theory predicts that individuals with high variability within an area should show superior performance over those with limited experiences. For example, the child who is limited to throwing experiences, using an overhand pattern only, would not be as adept to the performance of a novel throwing task outside that pattern as the child who has had experiences throwing from various positions. Generally, schema research supports what researchers have assumed for a long time: If the task is "closed" (that is, the number of movements is somewhat fixed, as in bowling or swinging a golf club), it is more conducive to practice that one movement pattern than to practice variations. If the task is classified as "open" (that is, the movement responses are somewhat unpredictable, such as playing shortstop in baseball or guard in basketball), it is much better to practice a variety of responses because one never knows what specific movements will be required. It may also be assumed that the more "open" a task is, the more effective will be variable practice.

A strong body of research findings using children (with variable practice conditions) supports the predictions of this theory, namely that variability in practice is a strong variable in determining transfer to a novel motor response of the same class (Shapiro & Schmidt, 1981; Schmidt, 1988).

Implications and Applications

Of course the strongest practical implications of this theory would be in the area of elementary school physical education, because it is at this age when basic motor skills are being established. (Kerr, 1982)

... practice variability is a positive factor in motor learning, especially so for children's motor learning. (Schmidt, 1988)

Schema theory (and variability in practice) strongly suggests developing a solid foundation consisting of a variety of motor-skill experiences early in life. Variability in practice is predictively more effective for children than for adults simply because young individuals have considerably more to learn. Generally, schema theory supports the practice of problem solving during early years rather than the instruction of specific sport skills. With the establishment of a broad motor foundation (schema), children should be in a better position to acquire and apply specific skills, especially in an "open" environment (where conditions vary frequently). Schema theory suggests a progression from a general base to more specific concepts.

Variability In Practice

Schmidt (1977) suggests that in attempting to apply concepts of the schema theory, variability within the same class of movements (for example, throwing) should be structured to maximize the motor program dimensions of space (spatial), time, and force. What follows is an explanation of those concepts when used in the practice situation.

SPATIAL

The *spatial* dimension is best enhanced through movement-pattern variability. Within the schema class of throwing, for example, this dimension may contain variations ("elements") of the overhand, sidearm, and underhand patterns. Each of these can be performed with one of two hands, or both, at dif-

Table 3-1

Throwing

SPATIAL

	Movement Pattern Variations	
Two hands:	One hand (right/left):	
Underhand (from front and either side)	underhand	
	sidearm	
Overhand (overhead, chest pass, from either side)	overhand	Vary base of support (narrow to wide)
	variations	

Directions/Pathways/Levels

Throw up, down, forward, to side, at an angle
Throw while:
  squatting or sitting (low level)
  jumping or leaping (high level)
Throw while moving in various directions:

forward	sideways
backward	diagonally

TIME	**FORCE**
Slow to fast	Throw objects of various sizes and weight
Throwing balls at a stationary target	(*e.g.*, whiffleball, fleeceball, softball,
Throwing balls at a moving target	football, frisbee, playground ball)
Throwing while moving at a target	Throw hard for distance
(stationary/moving)	Throw soft to medium
To a rhythmic beat	Combine distance and accuracy

ferent levels from the ground (squatting, while jumping, and so forth), and with impetus toward various directions.

TIME

The *time* dimension contains information upon which to judge at what speed the spatial (movement) pattern should be activated. Experiences should be provided that develop the continuum that ranges from slow motion to fast.

FORCE

Another dimension along which the motor program might be varied is the amount of *force* that is exerted. Related to time, mass (size), and weight, this dimension can be greatly enhanced with the use of manipulative objects and implements. Experiences that vary the force requirements, such as throwing (using the overhand pattern) to a target from varied distances, and using various size (mass) and weighted balls (weight), should enhance throwing schema and allow increased transfer to a novel task. Table 3-1 presents an outline of practice variation that may be implemented after basic mechanical principles are introduced.

OTHER FACTORS AFFECTING MOTOR-SKILL ACQUISITION

Along with the practical implications of motor-learning theory such as those previously discussed, other factors may enhance or negatively affect the learning of motor skills by children. With a knowledge of these factors, the teacher is in a better position to optimize individual as well as group-learning conditions.

Selective Attention

Critical to the learning of any task is the ability to attend selectively (concentrate) to a specific stimulus while ignoring other simultaneously presented information. The ability to concentrate on one specific feature while performing a task can be difficult for many children. Such may be the situation when a child is attempting to kick or strike a ball, especially if the teacher instructs the child to concentrate not only on specific parts of the movement but also to attend visually to the flight of the object. The experienced performer has less difficulty in attending to multiple sources of information; however, when instructing children it is best to present relative information separately, or within the capabilities of the individual child. Ideally, the teacher must provide an environment that helps the child attend to the most relevant information he or she can process and respond to. For optimal learning, the physical environment should be free of distractions such as irrelevant noises, visual displays, and extra equipment. Instructions should be clearly and concisely transmitted so that they emphasize the most relevant points of the task. Many teachers fail to realize that potential failure by the child may be caused either by an overload of information or the fact that the child is not focusing on the parts of the task, but rather on the result of a demonstration.

Motivation and Interest

Motivation and interest are ever-present factors in the performance and learning of a skill. Motivation is often described as an intrinsic need or desire to perform or learn that prompts one to satisfy that need or desire. Because motivation is intrinsically based, the teacher does not actually motivate the learner, but instead provides conditions that may result in an increased or decreased state of motivation. In reference to motor performance, one of the most frequently utilized motivational constructs is *arousal*. Thus a better description of motivation would be that it is an internal factor that *arouses* and directs a person's behavior. Although motivation and arousal are positive factors in the learning of a skill, research indicates that too much or too little arousal may not be conducive to motor performance and learning. The child has to be aroused to a level of desiring to learn; however, a high degree of arousal, causing anxiety or stress, may not allow the individual to attend to the task optimally. Teachers need to be effective in eliciting arousal, and this may be accomplished through various conditions: providing interesting activities, knowledge of results, realistic goal setting, and degree of success.

As already stated, interest is an ever-present contributing factor to the learning situation. An innovative teacher not only has knowledge of the traditional activities that interest children but is also aware of their current concerns and stimulates new areas of interest. With movement experiences, the stimulation of interest is usually a natural phenomenon and it is the creative and flexible teacher who makes the most of these opportunities. Important to the stimulation of interest is making the activity and learning meaningful to the child, which may best be accomplished by individualizing the learning situation.

Feedback/Knowledge of Results

Feedback refers to all the information that a child receives relative to his or her performance. Feedback may be internal or external, and it might occur during or after the performance of a task. *Internal feedback*, the stimuli coming from within the body, primarily originates with the kinesthetic senses (from receptors in muscles, tendons, joints, and the inner ear). *External feedback* may involve any one or combination of external sources: the five senses or a person such as the teacher. Fitts and Posner (1967) theorize that feedback has three functions (1) to motivate, (2) to change immediate performance, and (3) to reinforce learning. The importance of feedback to the learning process cannot be overemphasized. Teachers should think of feedback as more than knowledge of results, for appropriate information *during* and *after* the task is important for reinforcing correct behavior and possibly modifying incorrect responses.

Although most feedback in physical education is external and produced by the teacher using verbal cues or manual guidance, activities should be presented that encourage internal feedback as well. This may be provided through the introduction of simple skills, which allow for immediate and recognizable results, such as jumping, running, kicking, and throwing. More complex activities, such as learning to dance or performing certain gymnastic stunts, may not be easily analyzed by the child; therefore feedback should be provided during, as well as after, the performance. The teacher should remember that children respond best when they are continuously aware of the performance and results of their efforts. The alert teacher will provide the child with appropriate external feedback and present conditions (activities) that stimulate internal awareness.

Whole and Part Learning

Whole and part learning refers to the presentation and learning of skills in their entirety or in parts, which are then combined to form the complete skill. Important considerations for the teacher will be the complexity of the skill and the abilities of the child. A commonly utilized method (if the task is not too complex) is to begin by teaching the whole and then, if the child is having difficulty, identifying the problem and working on the part(s). Generally it is agreed that complex skills, such as specific dance, track and field, or swimming skills, be taught to students in their logical parts before being presented in their entirety. Because most skills taught to young children are fundamental movements (and not a combination of skills), the whole method is usually appropriate.

Retention and Overlearning

Retention refers to our capacity to remember. It usually entails the ability to repeat an act correctly over a period of time. In terms of motor performance, retention refers specifically to the extent of motor-skill proficiency remaining after a period without practice. Influencing factors on the retention of a skill are *review periods* and *overlearning*. When children are permitted to practice (review) motor skills in spaced intervals, they retain the information longer. Overlearning refers to the continuation of practice on a motor skill after attaining a criterion level of performance, usually determined by the teacher. Overlearning enhances refinement of skill performance and retention by allowing the learning that has

taken place to "set" or "consolidate" (that is, a strengthening of the connection between the sensory and motor apparatus). The teacher should, if possible, allow for adequate practice of skills presented; this needs to be a strong consideration during planning. If the physical education periods are relatively short, (about 15 to 30 minutes) skills from previous periods should be reviewed and, if possible, combined with new skills presented. Children should also be encouraged to practice on their own time, such as during recess or after-school hours.

REFERENCES

FITTS, P. & POSNER, M. (1967). *Human performance*. Belmont, Ca: Brooks/Cole Publisher.

GABBARD, C. (1984). Teaching motor skills to children: Theory into practice. *The Physical Educator, 41*, 69–71.

KERR, R. (1982). *Psychomotor learning*. Philadelphia: Saunders College Publishing.

SCHMIDT, R. A. (1975). A schema theory of discrete motor skill learning. *Psychological Review, 82*, 225–260.

SCHMIDT, R. A. (1988). *Motor control and learning*. 2nd ed. Champaign, IL: Human Kinetics.

SCHMIDT, R. A. (1982). *Motor control and learning*. Champaign, Il: Human Kinetics.

SCHMIDT, R. A. (1977). Schema theory: implications for movement education. *Motor Skills: Theory into Practice, 2*, 36–48.

SHAPIRO, D. C. & SCHMIDT, R. A. (1981). The schema theory: recent evidence and developmental implications. In J. A. S. Kelso & J. E. Clark (Eds.), *The development of movement control and coordination*. New York: Wiley.

SUGGESTED READINGS

MAGILL, R. A. (1993). *Motor learning: Concepts and application* (4th ed.). Dubuque, IA: W. C. Brown.

SHEA, C., SHEBILSKE, W. & WORSCHEL, S. (1993). *Motor learning and control*. Englewood Cliffs, NJ: Prentice-Hall.

SCHMIDT, R. A. (1991). *Motor learning and performance*. Champaign, IL: Human Kinetics.

4

Physical Fitness

Just as parents' beliefs about their children's fitness levels generally do not accurately reflect the child's actual condition, much of our population is also quite naive concerning the implications of unfit children. As previously mentioned, the results of national surveys indicate that American children are fatter than they were 20 years ago, exhibit relatively low levels of cardiorespiratory fitness, possess poor upper body strength/endurance, and the low level of trunk flexibility revealed in boys indicates a good chance of developing back problems in later life.

The two primary areas of medical concern that have prompted the national focus on children's fitness and health are obesity and cardiovascular disease. It has been estimated that nearly one-third of American children are obese and 80 percent of those individuals are destined to become obese adults. Unfortunately, many adults still believe their child's overweight condition is temporary (hence, the baby fat myth) and that they will lose their extra fat tissue as a natural course of development. Obesity is a prevalent disorder among children that is accompanied by significant morbidity. Obese children are at greater risk for several disorders including: hypertension, psychosocial dysfunction, cardiovascular disease, diabetes, and several orthopedic conditions. (Gortmaker, et al. 1987)

Along with time spent viewing television (and playing video games), several researchers point to lack of physical activity in general as a significant cause in producing obesity in children. Current research also points to the school as the primary remediation force for those that are overweight, as well as the best medium for prevention.

Cardiovascular diseases account for almost 50 percent of all deaths in the United States each year. Several lines of research have shown coronary heart disease (CHD) to be a progressive condition with roots in childhood behavior and life-style patterns known to increase an individual's risk of developing CHD in later life (American Journal of Diseases in Children, 1986). Coronary heart disease risk factors such as obesity, hypertension, elevated blood lipids, diabetes, and physical inactivity are not uncommon among young children. Currently there is strong support for early intervention and preventive programs for young children. Increased physical activity and weight control have been suggested as forms of early intervention. There is supporting evidence associated with similar programs for adults that suggests possible benefits. Evidence that diet and physical activity lifestyles are learned early in life is accepted. Programs for children focus primarily on the promotion of healthy attitudes and lifestyles which, if continued into adulthood, will reduce coronary heart disease risk (Parcel *et al.*, 1987).

Common Misconceptions and Facts

The following discussion provides a brief description of popular misconceptions associated with exercise and health-related fitness among children. Refer to Gabbard and Crouse (1988) for a more detailed discussion of the topic and specific references.

Myth: Vigorous aerobic exercise is harmful to children.

Fact: As early as 1879, physicians believed that in children there was a discrepancy in the development of the cardiorespiratory system. It was assumed that the

Myth: Muscles are a sign of being fit.

Fact: Physical fitness involves much more than muscular strength and physical appearance. Other vital components of "being fit" include flexibility, muscular endurance, cardiorespiratory efficiency, and an optimal percentage of body fat/lean muscle tissue.

Myth: Team sports make children fit.

Fact: Some sports, if participation is at a vigorous and continuous level, do promote specific components of health-related fitness (for example, basketball, flickerball, and soccer). Most levels of team sport participation by children, however, are not vigorous and continuous to the point of developing health-related fitness. Many team sports such as football, and baseball/softball, stress motor skills and "skill-related" fitness components (*i.e.*, speed, agility, power, coordination).

The Potential Health Benefits of Physical Activity

Corbin (1987), in an article that presented a comprehensive summary of the well-documented health-related benefits of exercise for adults, asserted that regular physical activity was every bit as effective for children. That fact, and the national concern for our children's low fitness levels and future wellness, has provided what should be a stimulus for change in our educational system and parental care.

FITNESS CONCEPTS

The definition of physical fitness has undergone dramatic change during the last decade. Along with a change in philosophy which now focuses on the health aspects of being fit, a new set of concepts and vocabulary has developed, as well as creative approaches to fitness assessment.

Defining Physical Fitness

The general definition of being fit includes such concepts as the ability to function normally without undue fatigue, and being able to participate in recreational activities without debilitating physical stress. Being physically fit has also been associated with a positive state of wellness which may be influenced by participation in regular physical activity, proper diet, and genetics. In more recent times, the term has been expanded to include not only the components associated with athletic ability and skill-related performance, but also the health-related components of fitness.

large blood vessels developed at a slower rate than the heart, and vessels might not be able to accommodate blood flow created by an exercised heart. Research by Karpovich (1937) and others has helped to dispel misconceptions that large blood vessels developed at a slower rate than the heart, and that these vessels might not be able to accommodate the increased blood flow created by an exercised heart. Current scientific evidence supports the contention not only that children can participate in vigorous aerobic exercise for extended periods but that a healthy child cannot physiologically injure the heart permanently through exercise unless the heart is already weakened.

Myth: Children play hard enough to develop and maintain cardiorespiratory fitness.

Fact: Scientific studies that have monitored children (ages four to 12 years) during school, recess, and the summer report that seldom do these individuals achieve a heart rate during play that would promote cardiorespiratory fitness. Information also indicates that girls are significantly more sedentary than boys, especially during the summer months.

HEALTH-RELATED FITNESS

The central focus of today's philosophy and concern, health-related fitness refers to "those aspects of physiological and psychological functioning which are believed to offer the individual some protection against degenerative type diseases such as coronary heart disease, obesity, and various musculoskeletal disorders" (Falls, 1980). The American Academy of Pediatrics (1987) and the American Alliance for Health, Physical Education, Recreation, and Dance (1988), support this notion by stressing the following four health-related fitness components: **muscular strength/endurance, flexibility, cardiorespiratory endurance, and body composition.**

CARDIORESPIRATORY ENDURANCE

Considered the primary component in health-related fitness, cardiorespiratory endurance is the ability of the heart, lungs, and vascular system to function efficiently for an extended period of time. An efficient system delivers more blood, thus more oxygen to working muscles. The benefits of cardiorespiratory fitness include a lower resting heart rate, and greater resistance to fatigue. Many researchers believe that it protects against coronary heart disease. See Table 4-1 for other health benefits.

BASIC PRINCIPLES

1. The frequency of training should be three to five days per week.
2. Intensity of exercise should be between 60 to 90 percent of maximum heart rate (target heart rate of 145 to 185 beats per minute); techniques for determining heart rate are discussed in Chapter 14.
3. Duration of aerobic activity, when possible, should be 15 to 30 continuous minutes.
4. Activities that develop this component must stimulate large muscle groups and be sustained over a continuous period (*i.e.*, be rhythmical and aerobic in nature, such as running, fast walking, skating, bicycling, rope-jumping, and various endurance games).
5. Anaerobic exercise, characterized by events of short bursts of intensity such as sprinting, pushups, weight lifting, and most games, does not significantly contribute to cardiorespiratory endurance.

Table 4-1
Health Benefits of Regular Physical Activity

Cardiovascular System
- Increased strength of the heart muscle and lowered resting heart rate
- Improved circulation and increased energy stores of the heart muscle
- Increased work efficiency and pumping ability of the heart
- Decreased resting blood pressure in those who are hypertensive
- More favorable blood clotting characteristics

Body Mass
- Greater lean body tissue
- Decreased body fat
- Increased bone density and mineral retention

Muscular Strength and Endurance
- Increased muscle mass and muscular strength
- Improved work efficiency and muscular endurance
- Greater supply of energy fuels in muscle
- Increased circulation in trained muscles

Flexibility
- Increased joint range of motion
- Greater elasticity of muscle and connective tissue
- Lower levels of neuromuscular tension and fewer muscular injuries

General Benefits
- Decreased risk of heart disease and stroke
- Decreased risk of colon and reproductive cancers
- Increased blood high-density lipoprotein (HDL) cholesterol, the "good" cholesterol, and reduced blood triglycerides
- Reduced psychological stress and tension; improved self-perception
- More rapid recovery from physical exertion
- Improved work efficiency and endurance

CONCEPTS COMMUNICATED TO CHILDREN

1. Cardiorespiratory endurance (definition).
2. Improved cardiorespiratory endurance results in: a stronger and more efficient heart, a more effective oxygen- and blood-delivery system, the reduction of coronary heart disease risk.
3. Cardiorespiratory endurance is developed through participation in "aerobic activities."
4. Anaerobic activities have high intensity but are of too short duration to significantly benefit the development of cardiorespiratory endurance.

MUSCULAR STRENGTH/ENDURANCE

This component of health-related fitness may be described on a continuum, ranging from the maximal effort of one attempt to the ability to sustain repetitive muscular contractions over a longer period of time. Strength is generally characterized by a maximum force which in its purest form is one maximal effort. This is exhibited by lifting weights, jumping, throwing, etc. Muscular endurance requires a sustained effort over a period of time such as in performing situps and pushups.

Muscular endurance provides the child with greater resistance to muscular fatigue, thus allowing more work. The relevance of strength to skill-related sport activities is rather obvious; however, there are also health-related benefits. Muscles that are strong, supple, and durable, provide protection to the joints and aid in the prevention of some common postural ailments such as the low-back syndrome found among a vast portion of the adult population.

BASIC PRINCIPLES

1. The recommended frequency is three to five times per week.
2. Use the "overload principle" by progressively increasing the workload (resistance) and or the work duration.
3. The "principle of specificity" dictates that exercise tends to be task specific, that is, if an individual trains for strength, endurance may not be a result as well. Muscular endurance is acquired by performing repetitively (generally 10 to 20 times) with a relatively light weight. Whereas, the strength component can be increased by performing fewer repetitions with an increased load.

   *Single lift maximums (with weights) are not recommended for children. Free weights should only be used under direct and close supervision.
4. Hypertrophy means an increase in muscle tissue. Atrophy denotes a decrease in muscle size.

5. The three types of resistance exercises which develop strength are:

   isometric—a static resistance with no joint movement

   isotonic—a dynamic exercise that involves joint movement variable resistance—a dynamic exercise in which the resistance changes throughout the range of motion

CONCEPTS COMMUNICATED TO CHILDREN

1. Muscular strength/endurance (definition).
2. Muscular strength increases the ability to perform muscular work, reduces the potential of injury, improves the quality of sports performance, reduces stress.
3. Muscular endurance extends the benefits of muscular strength by allowing prolonged periods of physical activity without undue fatigue.
4. Muscular strength/endurance is developed through resistance exercises that overload (greater than normal load) the muscle(s).

FLEXIBILITY

Flexibility, also referred to as joint suppleness, is the degree to which a joint can move through its potential normal range of motion. Flexibility is joint specific and can be improved with movement experiences that promote extending the range of motion. From a health aspect, lack of suppleness often contributes to postural problems and an increased probability of muscular injury. Together with muscle strength/endurance, joint flexibility is a major component in the prevention of back problems, often caused by inactivity which shortens connective tissue in the lower back and thighs, and weakens abdominal muscles. It has been estimated that "low back syndrome" affects approximately 80 percent of adults. While most children appear to exhibit adequate levels of flexibility (especially females), a national fitness survey conducted in 1985 reported low levels of trunk flexibility for a large number of boys (National School Population Fitness Survey).

BASIC PRINCIPLES

1. Flexibility is joint specific. Therefore, select activities that will stretch all major areas of the body.
2. To increase flexibility, overload by stretching muscles farther than their resting length. Stretch to the point just short of where it is painful and hold for 10-30 seconds (repeat). Slow static stretches are more effective than ballistic or bouncing for increasing mobility in the joints and preventing soft tissue injury.
3. If flexibility exercises are to be a part of a comprehensive fitness event including aerobic and muscular strength/endurance

exercises, the flexibility exercises should be performed before *and* after the event.

4. Flexibility and strength training complement each other. When flexibility exercises are incorporated with strength training, the body will not become "muscle bound."

CONCEPTS COMMUNICATED TO CHILDREN

1. Flexibility (definition).
2. Flexibility promotes flowing, efficient movement; reduces the incidence of injury and joint pain; contributes to good posture.
3. Flexibility activities should be used during warm-up and cool-down phases of exercise.
4. Joint suppleness is improved by static stretching exercises.
5. Static exercise involves stretching the muscles to a point just past their normal limit (not to the point of pain) and holding it there (do not bounce!) for 10–30 seconds.
6. Inactivity leads to a rapid loss of joint flexibility.

BODY COMPOSITION

This component of health-related fitness is defined as relative percentages of fat to lean body mass. While a certain amount of body fat is essential for good health, extra adipose tissue is not conducive to being fit. Generally, children who are 10 to 20 percent over recommended weight on "weight-for-height" charts are considered overweight. The obese child would be more than 20 percent over suggested values. A more scientific technique of measurement using skinfold measures (discussed in the latter part of this chapter) has provided more insight into this component of fitness.

An individual's percentage of body fat is determined by several factors, including heredity, diet, and level of activity. For the vast majority of people, the approach to weight control is relatively simple; increase the activity level and/or decrease the caloric intake. While the approach appears simple, the low success rate identifies this problem as most complex. Of all the health-related components, weight control has been the most difficult for children, teachers, and parents to deal with. Weight control in children, to be successful, necessitates a comprehensive fitness program that emphasizes aerobic exercise, proper diet, and strong parental involvement. Fortunately, the physical education setting offers many excellent vehicles to increase one's activity level and forge a basis for a healthy lifestyle of regular exercise (which is a primary factor in the control and prevention of childhood obesity). As previously noted, our nation's children and youth are fatter than they were 20 years ago, and of the 30–40 percent that are overweight, approximately 80 percent will have problems with weight control as adults.

BASIC PRINCIPLES

1. Regular daily physical activity is best for improving body composition.
2. The best type of activity is aerobic exercise that is sustained over increasing periods of time.
3. With children, a variety of activities may be more motivating.
4. A comprehensive program involving exercise, proper diet (at home and school), and parents, is more conducive to success.
5. Before restricting the child's diet dramatically (as many adults do), suggest cutting out high carbohydrate/fat snacks and increase the physical activity level. This approach is much more fun for children because most young people love to play vigorously. Children need a balanced diet to maintain their growth and development. Extreme restriction should be implemented only with the consent and guidance of a physician.
6. Overweight means that an individual weighs more than most children of their sex, height, body frame, and age. Over-fat refers to possessing more fat than the body needs. Obesity describes individuals who are over-fat.

CONCEPTS COMMUNICATED TO CHILDREN

1. Overweight, overfat, obesity, and body composition (definitions).
2. "Percent body fat" refers to the relative percentage of total weight that is composed of fat tissue.
3. Body composition is more important than body weight with respect to health-related fitness.
4. Diet and regular exercise (primarily aerobic-type) are essential to weight control.

SKILL-RELATED FITNESS

Skill-related fitness refers to the qualities that provide the individual with the ability to perform game (sport), dance, and gymnastic activities. Speed, agility, power, balance, and coordination are usually described as athletic abilities, rather than aspects of physical wellness. Reaction time is often placed in this category; however, most experts describe this component as less trainable and more innate than the other items.

While assessment and development of skill-related fitness components have been de-emphasized over the last decade, its inclusion in the school curriculum still merits consideration. While a skill-related fitness program should never be the focus of the overall fitness curriculum at any level, its inclusion may motivate older children to more vigorous participation. Children love to be one of the fastest and strongest. They look up to sports champions as role models, especially during the sports skill phase (approximately eight years and older) of their lives. Realistically speaking, a very small percent of our children will be classified as elite athletes. Our goal is to provide developmentally stimulating instruction for all children. While specific training does enhance the components of skill-related fitness, much of its basic development can be achieved through participation in appropriate performance related activities.

Speed. Speed is the ability to move from one point to another in the shortest possible time. This component is primarily innate; however, it can be improved through practice for technique and body mechanics.

Agility. Agility is the ability to rapidly change direction or body position. Agility is partially innate and reflected by an interrelationship with speed, balance, and coordination. This component is essential to success in several sports and physical education activities.

Power. This component is a combination of strength with explosiveness (speed). Power is the ability to release maximum muscular force at maximum speed. This is a fundamental component required in specific jumping, throwing, and striking tasks. Power can be improved as a result of an increase in strength and practice of technique and body mechanics.

Coordination. Coordination is the ability to integrate motor and perceptual systems into an efficient movement pattern. This function combines the use of two or more body parts (usually eye-hand, eye-foot) and general rhythmical movements to produce a skilled movement. Coordination may also be described as the integration of temporal (timing) and spatial (movement) characteristics to perform motor skills.

Balance. This is defined as the ability to maintain equilibrium and body position. It is influenced by the visual modality and kinesthetic senses (located in the muscles, tendons, and joints). Balance may be divided into three categories: postural, static, and dynamic. Postural balance, the most basic form, is the ability of our kinesthetic sense to provide efficient, upright support and equilibrium. Static balance is associated with deliberate movements that are performed in a relatively fixed position or area, such as balancing on one foot or on a balance board. Dynamic balance is the maintenance of equilibrium while the body is in motion.

POSTURE

It is estimated that 80 percent of the population has some postural deficiency. Posture refers to proper segmental alignment of the body. Most experts agree that prevention, early detection, and correction of deviate postural conditions are important to the quality of one's life and leisure pursuits. Posture is closely interrelated with muscular strength/endurance and flexibility. Poor posture is generally an imbalance in the pull of muscles responsible for maintaining specific postures. A weak musculature is often the problem, for weak muscles have greater difficulty in maintaining good body alignment. In addition to weak muscles due to inactivity, the major causes of poor posture include faulty mechanics caused by poor neuromuscular habits, overdevelopment of one set of muscles at the expense of another, lack of body awareness, illness, injury, and poor diet.

Posture does not exist only in a single position; therefore, its proper use depends upon the type of activity which the body is called upon to perform. The most recognized positions of posture are when the body is standing, walking, and sitting. Postural deviations are usually described in three conditions: lordosis (swayback), kyphosis (roundback), and the most complex—scoliosis (lateral curvature of the spine). These conditions and assessment techniques will be discussed in more detail below under "Assessment."

NUTRITION

The overwhelming consensus of nutrition experts is that optimal health-related fitness cannot be achieved without a proper diet. While much of this nutrition information is covered as part of the school's health curriculum, the physical education teacher should help emphasize the importance and understanding of basic principles. This can be done by working with the health or science teacher during the presentation of that unit, by displaying and reviewing information on the gymnasium bulletin board, and by asking students to do homework assignments related to eating habits and nutritional information. The following terms are considered fundamental to the child's understanding of proper diet, nutrition, and weight control.

Calories and Weight Control. A calorie is a unit of energy supplied by food. All food items contain calories. The more calories a food item has, the more fattening it can be. To lose weight, take in fewer calories, or to gain, increase consumption. Exercise burns up calories. The more vigorous and continuous the exercise, the more calories and stored fat are used up. The best method of losing weight is diet and exercise. By eating less fattening foods and exercising more, the body keeps more lean muscle tissue.

Essential Nutrients. Protein (builds and repairs tissues and provides energy), carbohydrates (supply energy and fiber for digestion), fats (supply energy), minerals (build and repair tissues and regulate essential processes), vitamins (regulate body processes), and water (is an integral component in bodily functions).

Four Basic Food Groups. These are meat, milk, bread/cereal, fruit/vegetable. Table 4-2 presents the calorie equivalent of a child's activities.

Table 4-2									
Calorie Equivalent of Child's Activities (Values denote Kcal per 10 minutes)									

Body Weight in kg

Activity	20	25	30	35	40	45	50	55	60	65
Basketball (game)	34	43	51	60	68	77	85	94	102	110
Calisthenics	13	17	20	23	26	30	33	36	40	43
Cross Country Ski (leisure)	24	30	36	42	48	54	60	66	72	78
Cycling										
10 km/hr	15	17	20	23	26	29	33	36	39	42
15 km/hr	22	27	32	36	41	46	50	55	60	65
Field Hockey	27	34	40	47	54	60	67	74	80	87
Figure Skating	40	50	60	70	80	90	100	110	120	130
Horse-back Riding										
canter	8	11	13	15	17	19	21	23	25	27
trot	22	28	33	39	44	50	55	61	66	72
gallop	28	35	41	48	50	62	69	76	83	90
Ice Hockey (on ice time)	52	65	78	91	104	117	130	143	156	168
Judo	39	49	59	69	78	88	98	108	118	127
Running										
8 km/hr	37	45	52	60	66	72	78	84	90	95
10 km/hr	48	55	64	73	79	85	92	100	107	113
12 km/hr	—	—	76	83	91	99	107	115	123	130
14 km/hr	—	—	—	—	—	113	121	130	140	148
Sitting										
(complete rest)	8	8	9	9	10	10	11	11	12	12
(quiet play)	11	12	14	15	15	16	17	18	19	20
Snow Shoeing	35	42	50	58	66	74	82	90	98	107
Soccer (game)	36	45	54	63	72	81	90	99	108	117
Squash	—	—	64	74	85	95	106	117	127	138
Swimming										
30 m/min										
breast	19	24	29	34	38	43	48	53	58	62
front crawl	25	31	37	43	49	56	62	68	74	80
back	17	21	25	30	34	38	42	47	51	55
Table Tennis	14	17	20	24	28	31	34	37	41	44
Tennis	22	28	33	39	44	50	55	61	66	72
Volleyball (game)	20	25	30	35	40	45	50	55	60	65
Walking										
4 km/hr	17	19	21	23	26	28	30	32	34	36
6 km/hr	24	26	28	30	32	34	37	40	43	48

From Pediatric Sports Medicine (1983), Oded Bar-Or, with permission of Springer-Verlag.

ASSESSMENT

Along with the current change in primary focus from a skill-related to a health-related physical fitness philosophy, has emerged a variety of innovative assessment packages and techniques.

Most fitness tests of the past were designed to assess skill-related items (*e.g.*, speed—50yd. dash, power-broad jump) for children in grades 4–12. Today we find test batteries that emphasize health-related items, or consist of a combination of skill and health-related components. Another very promising trend has been the inclusion of younger children (five to nine years of age) in curriculum materials and assessment batteries. The physical education instructor of today is challenged with several additional and exciting considerations regarding fitness assessment and program integration.

Before reviewing the considerations for fitness assessment, we must ask a few fundamental questions. Why assess the fitness levels of children? If class periods are relatively short (*e.g.*, 20 minutes) and the number of students per class large, should the teacher use valuable time to assess? Why should the teacher conduct a followup assessment at the end of the term? These questions should be considered by the physical education teacher when the yearly plans are being formulated and prior to conducting an assessment program.

Physical education programs across the nation and in specific single communities may be quite simple or complex and diverse. Individual programs may vary significantly in regard to frequency and duration per week, equipment, qualifications of teaching personnel, and availability of aides. There may be a situation when the number of students (or other factors) dictates that fitness assessment would be difficult and impractical to conduct. In such cases, teachers could find themselves conducting a fitness assessment out of habit or tradition, rather than based upon well-thought-out objectives for the overall program. When teachers assess simply from routine, they may find themselves measuring, recording scores, and doing a followup that doesn't really use the information found. The most important ingredient of the fitness curricula is the program of activities that develops and maintains fitness! A good activity program is a must and regardless of class characteristics should be implemented at an acceptable level. If at all practical, fitness assessment should be conducted at the beginning of the school year to screen for individuals who will require special assistance. Assessment data also provides information from which fitness program objectives can be developed. The follow-up assessment, usually conducted seven to eight months later, provides information about the progress of both students and the program. Such information can be used to track the progress of students from year to year, or to provide information if the individual transfers. Many teachers use the followup data to evaluate school or district results and set objectives for the coming year. Fitness results may also be viewed as one form of teacher accountability.

Considerations for Fitness Assessment

While the integration of a health-related activity program into the curriculum is the primary consideration, successful fitness assessment also requires much deliberation regarding:

Assessment Instruments
Time of Year (initial/follow-up)
Conditioning/Practice
Recording/Reporting of Results
Remedial Intervention
Assessing The Exceptional Child

ASSESSMENT INSTRUMENTS

The assessment of physical fitness entails the potential measurement of several fitness-related items including body weight/height, posture, health-related components, and items that evaluate skill-related performance.

BODY WEIGHT/HEIGHT

The measurements of weight and height in children are generally considered fundamental growth estimates that may have a wide margin of error due to individual differences. Body composition (a health-related component) is more important than body weight with respect to health, hence height/weight charts can be misleading regarding this component. Two testing programs (that will be described later in this section) use a "body mass index" as an option in assessing body composition; the index represents a ratio of weight to height. General weight/height charts are of some value in estimating the typical growth characteristics of individuals. The use of such charts as a screening technique may have merit in determining extreme deviations in weight or height. Such conditions can be unhealthy and require further testing and a physician's opinion. See Chapter 2 for weight and height values for children and youth.

POSTURE

Most experts agree that early detection, correction, and preventive programs for posture are important to the quality of one's everyday life and recreational pursuits. While "correct" posture is usually defined as proper alignment of body segments (focusing on the spinal column), a universal description is somewhat difficult since proper posture is needed while an individual is standing, sitting, moving (*e.g.*, walking, running), and lifting. Since a general assessment can be derived from the standing position, and the focus is on the spinal column, this position will be featured here.

Some schools administer postural assessment as part of a general health screening or as a State requirement to determine the presence of scoliosis, one of the most debilitating postural deviations. Every school program should provide some type of assessment if at all feasible. Posture awareness on the part of children is important for two reasons. First is the health-related fitness aspect; a body in proper alignment is a body balanced with muscular strength and flexibility. Second, posture training is "lifetime" training in that the child will carry the information and hopefully the conditioning into the adult years. While there are several different techniques that can be utilized in postural assessment, subjective evaluation is the most frequent method, primarily because it

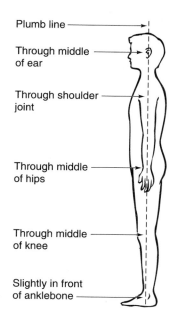

FIGURE 4-1

Figure side view.

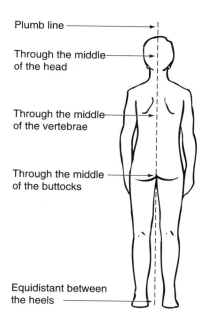

FIGURE 4-2

Figure rear view.

is less expensive and less time-consuming than other methods. The school nurse usually coordinates the assessment with the help of other teachers (often the physical educators). One of the most popular and convenient techniques is the use of a plumb line or string with a weight on one end that is hung in a doorway or archway. Males wear shorts and females wear shorts and halters or tight-fitting swimsuits. When screening females, an adult female should always be present. Figures 4-1 and 4-2 depict good standing posture as judged by the use of a plumb line.

COMMON POSTURAL DEVIATIONS

Lordosis (swayback). Lordosis is characterized by an exaggerated forward curvature of the lumbar spine and prominence of the sacrum and buttocks (Fig. 4-3). Many young children, especially females three to five years of age, exhibit slight characteristics of this condition that are due to immaturity, but these are usually resolved between the ages of seven and nine. Weak abdominals, gluteals, and hamstrings along with tight psoas and lumbar extensors are most often the cause for lordosis; however, the problem could be a fixed structural deformity.

Kyphosis (round upper back). Kyphosis is an exaggerated thoracic curve (Fig. 4-4). The upper back shows a sharp angulation which in its pronounced state results in the condition commonly known as hunchback or humpback. Kyphosis is not a common condition among normal children in the public school setting, but is seen more frequently in the adult years—often being associated with the degenerative process.

Rounded shoulders (forward shoulders). Rounded shoulders is a forward deviation of the shoulder girdle in which the shoulders are pulled forward by strong chest muscles (pectoralis minor and serratus anterior) due to the weakened condition of the upper back muscles (trapezius and rhomboids) attached to the scapulae. Rounded shoulders is a common postural deficiency that many children experience and should not be confused with Kyphosis (round back), a distinctly different postural deviation. Rounded shoulders exhibits shoulder tips that are positioned in front of the normal gravitational line, and arms with increased inward rotation which can cause many other compensatory changes in alignment of body parts. Some of these are:

> *Forward head* exhibited by the head and neck being displaced forward;
> *Hollow chest* exhibited by a lowered chest position causing a lowered diaphragm resulting in more shallow breathing;
> *Lordosis* to compensate for the increase in the thoracic curve;
> *Hyperextended knees* to compensate for the increase in the lumbar curve.

Scoliosis (lateral curvature of the spine). Scoliosis is a lateral curvature of the spine that can take either of two forms: a C- or S-shaped curve (Fig. 4-5). Scoliosis is a very debilitating condition if undetected and untreated, and signs of scoliosis should be reported to parents and medical personnel immediately. The key indicators for scoliosis are uneven shoulder, scapulae, and hip heights. The higher shoulder may also be carried more forward. One leg may also be

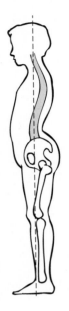

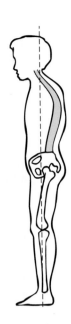

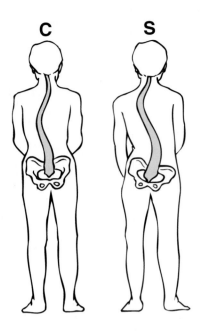

FIGURE 4-3
Lordosis (swayback).

FIGURE 4-4
Kyphosis (round upper back).

FIGURE 4-5
Scoliosis (C and S curves).

longer than the other, thereby exhibiting uneven knee creases at the back of the knees.

The Adams position is a useful technique to help determine if the lateral curvature is functional (still flexible) or structural (permanent).

To assume the Adam's position the child stands with feet parallel and comfortably apart and while gently holding palms together, bends forward from the hips. The knees are kept straight, head and neck are relaxed (Raggedy Ann style). While in this position the back should appear smooth and symmetrical on both sides of the spine. If, however, there is a rise along one side of the thoracic or lumbar spine then a structural scoliosis is suspect, and parents must be notified immediately.

The following type of posture assessment chart is recommended because of its specific screening characteristics and easily understood reporting feedback (Fig. 4-6).

Recommended exercises and activities conducive to the development of good posture can be found in Chapter 14.

Health- and Skill-Related Tests

Physical fitness assessment batteries of today present the teacher with a diversity of choices in measuring and assessing fitness components. Some tests focus entirely on skill-related performance items, while others provide a combined approach, or emphasize the assessment of health-related items. Modern commercial programs now offer the teacher comprehensive

packages which may include instructional materials, an award system, and computer aids for reporting and storing results.

CRITERION- AND NORM-REFERENCED TESTS.

Most physical fitness tests have been developed using norm-referenced measurement theory. Norm-referenced tests are designed to detect individual differences. Generally, the purpose of such tests are to compare an individual's performances to those of others, as well as detect superior and substandard achievement. Frequently test results are stated in terms of "the top five percent," or "your flexibility score was in the lower 25 percent." Norm-referenced tests are essential when selectivity (among the group) is a testing objective. Many teachers like to group children by norm results for remedial activities, and some children find stated norms motivate them to achieve higher levels.

Criterion-referenced tests are a rather new and promising trend. Instead of comparing an individual's score to a norm scale representing a 1–99 percentile range, criterion-referenced tests compare the achievement to a "standard" score. This standard score (based on norm data) represents mastery or an acceptable level of fitness. These standards are judged sufficient to establish and maintain a healthy lifestyle. There is no emphasis on comparing an individual's performance to that of others. This approach to measurement goes along with the often-asked and debat-

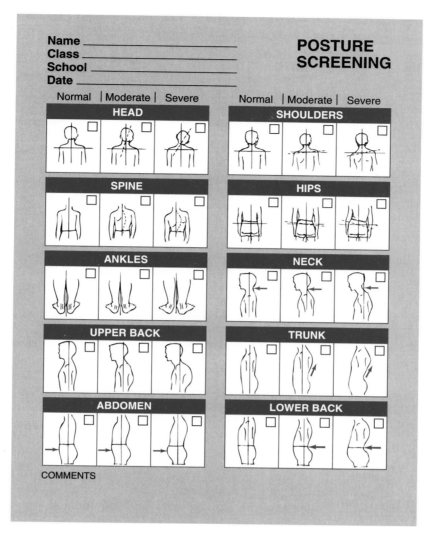

FIGURE 4-6

Posture assessment chart.

ed questions—what constitutes being fit and how fit do we need to be. If the 50th percentile in cardiorespiratory endurance is acceptable, does it mean that a child scoring at the 48th percentile is unfit? Test batteries that utilize this approach designate a single standard (or minimum) score for grade level and, if appropriate, sex of the individual.

Modern physical fitness test batteries focus on the components of health-related fitness (cardiorespiratory efficiency, muscular strength/endurance, flexibility, body composition) or a combination of health- and skill-related items (speed, agility, power, coordination). Table 4-3 presents a list and brief description of recommended test batteries (all provide comprehensive fitness packages) suitable for children. The following are brief descriptions of some of the recommended test items used in the assessment of health- and skill-related fitness. For more (and possibly updated) information on complete packages, details,

and the complete set of updated norms (or criterion standards), the reader should contact the appropriate source provided in Table 4-3.

Cardiorespiratory Assessment.   The most utilized tests for assessing cardiorespiratory (aerobic) fitness are the one-mile or nine-minute run/walk (for ages five to 12 years), or the 1.5 mile or 12-minute versions for individuals 13 years of age and older. Two alternatives to this standard protocol have been recommended. The expert panel which designed the National Children and Youth Fitness Study II (1987), recommended that children under age eight only run a half mile, due to the younger child's relative short attention span and fact that most children have not been trained to run farther. It was also the panel's contention that a half mile would serve as a good educational medium to introduce the child to pacing and long-distance running. The panel did point out that there is no physiological reason why a young child cannot run a mile.

Table 4-3

Fitness Testing Batteries

Name	Level	Norms (N) Criterion Std. (C)	Component/ Test Item	Source
AAHPERD Physical Best	Ages 5–18	(C)	**Cardio.** (1 mi. walk/run; opt. one-half mi. for 6–9 yrs.) **Body Comp.** (skinfolds; body mass index) **Strength/Endur.** (1 min. modified sit-ups; pull-ups) **Flexibility** (sit & reach)	AAHPERD Publ. 1900 Association Reston, VA 22091 (703)476-3400
Fitnessgram	Grades K–12	(C)	**Cardio.** (1 mi. walk/run) **Strength/Endur.** (modified situps; pull-up/flexed arm-hang) **Flexibility** (sit & reach) **Body Comp.** (skinfold; body mass index) **Agility** (shuttle run opt. for K-3)	Fitnessgram Institute for Aerobics Research 12330 Preston Rd. Dallas, TX 75230 (214)701-6885 Ext. 6886
Fit Youth Today (FYT)	Grades K–12		**Cardio.** (20 min. steady state jog for 4–6; 12 min. K-1, 15 min. grades 2–3) **Strength/Endur.** (2 min. bent-knee-curl-ups) **Flexibility** (sit & reach) **Body Comp.** (skinfolds; body mass index)	American Health Fitness Found. 6225 U.S. HWY 290E Suite #114 Austin, TX 78223 (512)465-1080
The President's Challenge	Ages 6–17	(N)	**Cardio.** (1 mi. walk/run) **Flexibility** (V-sit reach/ sit & reach) **Strength/Endur.** (curl-ups; pull-ups) **Agility** (shuttle run)	Department of Health & Human Services The President's Council on Physical Fitness and Sports Washington, DC 20001

While the training of the child and motivation should be strong considerations, most exercise physiologists would contend that distances of less than a mile would have questionable validity for the assessment of cardiorespiratory fitness. The Fit Youth Today (FYT) program recommends the use of a 20-minute steady jog for grades 4–6. The objective of the test is to determine a student's ability to cover a prescribed distance during a 20-minute period. The developers describe the task as a sub-maximal aerobic evaluation and emphasize the accepted standards to develop and maintain cardiorespiratory fitness (*i.e.*, 20 continuous minutes for at least three days per week). Standards for children in grades K-3 are reduced: 12 minutes of continuous aerobic activity for K-1, and 15 minutes for grades 2–3.

Flexibility. All four of the assessment batteries listed in Table 4-3 utilize the sit-and-reach for the assessment of flexibility. The sit-and-reach is a test of truck flexion that is related to low back, hip and hamstring suppleness. Figure 4-7 depicts a child in the reaching position.

Muscular Strength/Endurance. The standard protocol for assessing abdominal strength/endurance is with the bent-knee curl-up (sit-up). The only major difference found among fitness batteries is task duration; a one-minute or two-minute period. The Fit Youth Today program recommends the two-minute period and comparison to a criterion standard, stressing proper curl-up form rather than speed. Figure 4-8 illustrates the curl-up (top position).

FIGURE 4-7
Sit-and-Reach position

While the assessment of upper body strength/endurance is categorized under health-related fitness, there has been much debate as to its health value. Those individuals that support its inclusion in this category contend that it is an element of overall physical working capacity that complements cardiorespiratory fitness and abdominal strength/endurance. Opponents view this component as more performance-related by asking the question "how strong do individuals need to be to be healthy?" Their point is that strong individuals are not necessarily healthy and the level of muscular strength required in our everyday lives is minimal. While this debate is sure to continue, the merits of developing upper body strength/endurance (with the emphasis on endurance) surely justifies its inclusion in the activity program and, depending upon philosophy, should be considered as an assessment item.

The most common tests of upper body strength/endurance have been the pull-up/chin-up (with palms away from the body) for boys, and flexed-arm-hang for girls. The 1985 National Children and Youth Fitness Study I (ages 10–18) used the chin-up test (palms toward the body) with boys and girls. An inherent problem among these tests has been the "zero score" dilemma. Results of the 1985 NCYFS found that 30 percent of the boys and 60 percent of the girls scored zero on the test. Test items such as pull-ups and the flexed-arm-hang provide very poor measurement sensitivity at the low end of the range (Pate *et al.*, 1987). Since a large number of students score zero on these tasks, their motivation and acceptance of the test items is usually low, thus defeating one of the primary objectives of the fitness program. Due to the zero-score problem, the developers of the NCYFS II (1987) pilot-tested a "modified pull-up" with the six to nine-year-old population. The test was declared an improvement over the pull-up and flexed-arm-hang tests since only five percent of the sample were unable to perform one modified pull-up. The test is appropriate for boys and girls, and at this time there are no norms available for children over nine years old (refer to the AAHPERD Physical Best Test for more information). Traditional pull-ups and the flexed-arm-hang are considered appropriate with children nine years and older.

Body Composition.   There are several methods that may be used to detect the amount of body fat in children. While the underwater weighing procedure is perhaps the most accurate means of estimating the proportion of lean body weight and body fat, it requires laboratory facilities and is therefore impractical as a field test. The use of skinfold calipers to estimate body fat has proven to be quite acceptable and the most recommended procedure. Nationwide norms and criterion standards are available for children six to 13 years of age for estimating body fat from medial calf, triceps, and subscapular skinfolds. It

FIGURE 4-8
Curl-up (top position)

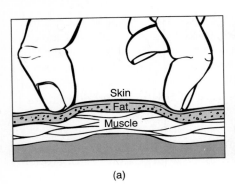
(a)

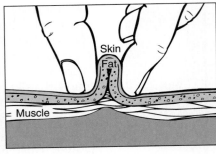
(b)

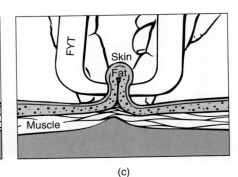
(c)

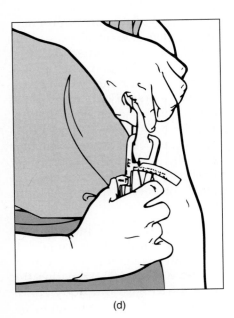
(d)

FIGURE 4-9

Proper grasp of skinfold

is recommended that for purposes of evaluation, the sum of two sites be used. However, if only one site is measured, the triceps or medial calf is suggested.

Vital to the accurate assessment of skinfolds is an acceptable skinfold caliper and a reliable tester. A properly calibrated instrument should register zero when closed and exert a constant pressure of 10 grams/mm^2 throughout the range of skinfold thickness. Lange, Lafayette, Harpenden, or similarly constructed calipers are recommended. The Fit Youth Today program has field-tested and also recommends a quality plastic caliper if the other brands are unavailable. Tester reliability should also be a concern. Teachers should be thoroughly familiar with the testing protocol and practice to enhance accuracy before the testing session begins. Instructors are also encouraged to attend assessment workshops and view audiovisual tapes. The American Alliance for Health, Physical Education, Recreation, and Dance and Human Kinetics Publishers (reference provided) have developed a training tape to aid skinfold assessment.

Figure 4-9 (a,b,c,d) illustrates the proper grasp of the skinfold between the thumb and forefinger. The muscle will not be grasped since it is firm; grasp firmly but do not induce pain. With younger children the tester may wish to allow the child an opportunity to feel the pinch of the caliper in a playful manner to assure them that it is not a "shot." The contact surfaces of the caliper should be placed one centimeter (one half-inch) below the finger pinch. Do not place the calipers at the base of the skinfold. The reading is to the nearest millimeter. Three measurements are taken at each site and the middle value recorded.

The triceps is measured with the right arm in a relaxed position at the side of the body. The measured site is taken over the triceps with the skinfold parallel to the axis of the upper arm (Fig. 4-11d).

The medial calf skinfold is taken at the inside of the right calf in the area of maximal girth (Fig. 4-10). The right foot is placed on a bench (flat chair, or crate) with the knee flexed at approximately 90 degrees.

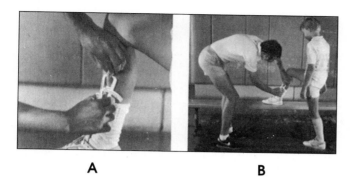

A   B

FIGURE 4-10

Medial calf skinfold

FIGURE 4-11

Subscapular (and triceps) skinfold sites

The **subscapular** site (right side of the body) is one centimeter below the inferior angle of the scapula in line with the natural contour lines of the skin (Fig. 4-11). Girls should wear halter-tops or tight fitting swim suits and an adult female should always be present.

Most national testing programs provide an alternative to skinfold testing in the form of a Body Mass Index. The index uses the individual's body weight and height values to calculate a ratio of body weight to height (weight in kilograms divided by height in meters, squared). In situations when skinfold measurement is not feasible, this alternative should be considered.

Skill-Related Items. Of the skill-related fitness components described in this text, only speed, agility, and power have been recommended and frequently utilized in assessment batteries. The assessment of balance presents several measurement problems and reliable norms have not been available. The softball throw was used to assess coordination and power in fitness batteries in the past, but has been omitted in recent years. In 1985 the National School Population Fitness Survey (The President's Council On Physical Fitness and Sports) established national norms for children six to 17 years of age on measures of speed, agility, and power.

Running speed is most frequently measured with the 40– and 50-yard dash.

Agility. The ability to change directions rapidly is usually measured by having the child run as rapidly as possible through an obstacle or shuttle course. The object of the shuttle run is to run as quickly as possible, back and forth, between two parallel lines marked on the floor 30 feet apart.

Power. This component of fitness is generally assessed by measuring the explosive power of

the lower limbs. The most recommended tests are the standing long jump and vertical jump, however very little norm data has been available for the vertical jump. Some fitness batteries have included tests of upper body power in children (*e.g.*, basketball throw while kneeling, softball throw), but its acceptance on a national scale has not developed.

TIME OF YEAR

Generally, due to the need to condition the children before testing, it is recommended that assessment begin no earlier than three to four weeks after the beginning of the school year. The follow-up assessment, if conducted, should be no earlier than the last week of April and no later than the first week of May (based on a September 1 to June 1 school year)—thus allowing for makeups, recording, and reporting of results.

CONDITIONING/PRACTICE

One of the primary objectives of all fitness programs should be to develop a positive attitude toward regular vigorous exercise. This task is not an easy one, yet it may be much more difficult if unprepared and extremely unfit students are required to take fitness tests. The first three to four weeks of school should be devoted to basic health-related conditioning and quality practice, if the item is skill-related. This conditioning period allows the child to safely progress into higher levels of activity without the "shock" of unexpected discomfort which can be experienced in running and muscular endurance activities (*e.g.*, sit-ups, pull-ups). This preparation period also allows the child an opportunity to practice skill-related technique and pacing for running events. If the items are skill-related (such as the shuttle run or long jump), a good teacher demonstration and

Table 4-4

Cumulative Fitness Record

NAME _____

Grade	K		1		2		3		4		5		6	
Date	Fall	Spr	Fall	Spr	Fall	Spr	Fall	Spr	Fall	Spr	Fall	Spr	Fall	Spr
Age														
Height (in/cm)														
Weight (lb/kg)														
Posture Rating														
Component	SC	%	SC	%	SC	%	SC	%	SC	%	SC	%	SC	%
Distance Run														
Skinfolds														
Sit-ups														
Sit-and-reach														
Flexed-arm hang														
Standing long jump														
Shuttle run														
40-yard dash														
50-yard dash														
Softball throw														
Pull-ups														

repetitive practice may be essential to the child's accomplishing his/her best performance. Teachers should always be concerned with the child's safety. An adequate preparation period minimizes the chance of physical and mental harm. Another precaution includes making sure that each child has had a recent medical checkup and that the child is fit for vigorous physical activity. This may be accomplished by checking with the school nurse, reviewing the records yourself, or asking parents in a written-permission form.

RECORDING/REPORTING OF RESULTS

Recording, data dissemination, and record-keeping can be done in various ways. Most of the recommended assessment batteries provide recording and record-keeping forms, and include computer software. School districts and individual teachers may wish to create their own materials due to individual or administrative preference or available funds. Regardless of what form the record may take, it should be transmitted to the parents in a way that is interpretable and provides recommendations for improvement if needed. A more permanent cumulative record (year-to-year) of results is essential to keeping track of performance; these results are usually stored on heavy-weight file cards.

The use of computers with available software packages has become quite helpful in fitness assessment. Individual results can be entered into the computer and personalized reports printed on a form that is "parent ready." Other advantages include time saved in processing large populations, versatility in analysis and printed results, developing norms, and making comparisons. A list of computer software sources can be found in the Appendices. In Table 4-4 an example of a cumulative record is presented and Figure 4-12 is an example of a computer generated fitness report card.

REMEDIAL INTERVENTION

Remedial intervention is the result of the identification of individuals with low fitness levels and the subsequent inclusion of remedial activities into their physical education program. One of the primary objectives of fitness assessment is to identify individuals that fall below the "acceptable" level of fitness for their age and, if appropriate, gender. If using norm-referenced data, the point of identification for recommending remedial intervention is usually around the 30th percentile (and below). It also seems reasonable to assume that the individuals whose scores fall between the 30th and 50th percentiles may also require special attention. However, their fitness levels are more likely to improve through the regular health-related program. The students whose

FITNESSGRAM®

Commited to Health Related Fitness

NAME **Joe Jogger**
SCHOOL **Fitnessgram School**
DISTRICT **Fitnessgram Test District**

GRADE **05**   PERIOD **05**
INSTRUCTOR **Brown**

	SCORE	HEALTH STANDARD

One Mile   ACCEPTABLE RANGE

min:sec	
7:07	11:00

11:00

DATE	HEIGHT	WEIGHT
MO – YR	FT – IN	LBS
9–87	4–04	63

Situps

number	
33	30

30

Congratulations Joe! Your scores on four of five test items were equal to or above the health standard. Keep up the good work!!

Pullups

number	
1	1

1

These activities are recommended:

Sit and Reach

inches	
9.0	10.0

10.0

To improve the flexibility of the lower back and posterior hip and thighs: sitting toe touches, knee tucks and the sit and reach stretch.

Body Composition

% body fat	
14.2	25.0

25.0

The FITNESSGRAM is a valuable tool in assessing each student's fitness level and for monitoring height/weight development. The test items provide information on the following:

- aerobics capacity –– measured by the one mile walk-run
- abdominal strength and endurance –– measured by the modified sit-up
- upper body strength and endurance –– measured by either the pull-up or the flexed-arm hang
- low–back and posterior thigh flexibility –– measured by the sit-and-reach
- body composition –– indicated by one of the following assessments:
    a) calculation of percent body fat from skinfold measurements of the triceps (back of upper arm) and calf(inside of lower leg)
    b) Body Mass Index which is a ratio of weight to height
       (weight in kilograms divided by height in meters squared)
- speed with change of direction –– measured by the shuttle run (optional item in grades K-3)

The shaded area of each bar indicates the range of performance for students of the same age and sex. The minimum acceptable score for each test is slated in the column "Health Standard". The minimum acceptable scores have been set by a panel of experts and were determined to be the level of fitness recommended for good health. Activities for improving fitness are recommended as determined by each student's performance on the FITNESSGRAM test.

Developed by
Institute for Aerobics Research
Dallas, Terxas

Sponsored by
Campbell Soup Company

FIGURE 4-12
Computerized fitness printout

scores fall in the lower 30 percent may not be able to complete a single sit-up, pull-up, or run without pain. These children will require special remedial activities before fitting into the regular program. Some school programs may be fortunate enough to have aides that can work with these students during the class period or at a time outside of the regular session. One method of individualizing within the regular fitness program is through the use of fitness stations. For example, 10 stations for strength/endurance may be arranged in order of difficulty, thus allowing the child needing remedial attention to accomplish tasks at the first two or three stations, as well as challenging the stronger individuals at other stations. More ideas and activities are described in Chapter 14.

ASSESSING THE EXCEPTIONAL CHILD

Since Public Law 94-142 (the Education of All Handicapped Children's Act) approximately 80 percent of all handicapped children have been "mainstreamed" into regular classrooms. Many of these exceptional children, especially those with mental disabilities, are in regular physical education classes and it is their right and the physical educator's obligation to assess their fitness. While participation of the exceptional child in the regular fitness assessment should be considered on an individual basis, the teacher should be cognizant of possible inequities. Some exceptional children cannot be measured on specific fitness items due to their handicaps. For example, the child that is visually impaired will be at a disadvantage in the shuttle run, or the child with only one arm would be at a disadvantage in perform-

ing pull-ups. Even the mildly mentally disabled child, which physical educators will have most often in the regular classroom, may be at a disadvantage due to his or her inability to comprehend and respond accurately with the proper muscular movements. Rarick and Francis (1960) found that when fitness tests commonly administered to normal children were given to mentally disabled children, their scores were lower and demonstrated a positive relationship to IQ scores. This does not mean that all mentally disabled students should be administered special tests. The decision should be on an individual basis and may require only a slight modification of the fitness test being utilized.

A meaningful measure for each individual can be devised by charting progress rather than comparing to an established set of norms. All unfit children are exceptional; disabled students frequently have lower fitness levels because of the tendency to be less active. Winnick (1988) and other experts in physical education for exceptional children present a convincing case for classifying according to general ability, thus measuring abilities rather than disabilities. Since exceptional children can possess a variety of physical or mental impairments, the issue of fairness with regard to using a standard fitness battery is questionable. This is an issue, however, that is still developing and currently has not been resolved. Table 4-5 presents a list of recommended physical fitness tests for exceptional children. It is suggested that the physical educator evaluate the capabilities of each exceptional child and decide upon the appropriate modification, test battery, or test items. When possible, the primary criteria for test selection should be based upon its health-related value, rather than skill performance characteristics.

Table 4-5

Physical Fitness Tests for Exceptional Children

Name	Source
Special Physical Fitness AAHPERD (1986) (Mentally Retarded)	AAHPERD Publications Association Dr. Reston, VA 22091 (703)476-3400
Motor Fitness Test for the Moderately Mentally Retarded (1976)	AAHPERD Publications
Buell Adaptation of the AAHPERD Health and Youth Fitness Test (1982)	AAHPERD Publications
Testing for Impaired, Disabled & Handicapped Individuals (N.D.)	AAHPERD Publications
Physical Fitness Testing for the Disabled (1985)	Human Kinetics Box 5076 Champaign, IL 61820

PROGRAM MODELS

The 1985 and 1987 National Children and Youth Fitness studies reported that approximately 97 percent of all elementary school children participate in physical education; about one third do so daily and the average frequency is three days per week. While this is certainly not ideal (our nation's goal is for 100 percent participation in daily physical education), it could (through teacher dedication) be an acceptable duration for developing physical fitness. It is now a commonly known fact that 20 minutes (or more) of regularly scheduled aerobic exercise at least three times a week can develop an acceptable level of cardiorespiratory fitness. While this formula was initially developed for adults, exercise physiologists also recommend this amount and more for children 14 years and younger (Haskell, Montoye, & Orenstein, 1985).

The basis for the relatively disappointing fitness levels of children appears to be related to the type and amount of activity. The American Academy of Pediatrics (1987) highlighted this problem by stating "Schools should decrease time spent teaching the skills used in team sports . . .," and went on to suggest that school programs promote a lifelong habit of aerobic-type exercise. The traditional focus of the elementary curriculum has been games, rhythms/dance, and gymnastics for the primary grades, and team sports at the intermediate levels. A strong trend that has developed since 1980 has been an emphasis on "skill themes," *i.e.*, a primary focus on developing motor skill proficiency, rather than the learning of traditional games and dances. This effort appears to have added immensely to strengthening the quality of elementary instruction; however its role in significantly improving fitness levels is questionable.

The major controversial issue in physical education for children today is curricular content emphasis. Curriculum supervisors and teachers must decide if the priority of program goals is to develop specific health-related fitness, master fundamental and sport motor skills, or a combination of the two. Unfortunately, as evidenced by the recent fitness survey findings, the priority of our goals has not been to develop "healthily" fit children and youth. Many teachers have been mislead by the assumption that participation in a general game, dance, and gymnastic ("activities") curriculum is sufficient to develop and maintain physical fitness. This misconception is perhaps partially due to the notion that skill-related performance is synonymous with being physically fit. Also contributing to the problem is a lack of understanding of the significance of health-related fitness.

TRADITIONAL CURRICULAR MODELS

The vast majority of traditional curricular models focus on the attainment of fundamental skills and sport skill mastery. While most curriculum guides and elementary textbooks emphasize the importance of health-related physical fitness, few sources provide specific suggestions for integration of content into the "activity" curriculum. Models of this type usually treat the development of physical fitness based on two general approaches: **general activity approach** and use of a **warm-up/introductory phase** in the lesson.

General Activity Approach. This method contends that the components of physical fitness (both health- and skill-related) are developed sufficiently as a result (or byproduct) of the general activity curriculum. The development of fitness is not separate from the skill development program and the motor skill content is the primary focus of the curriculum.

Warm-up or Introductory Phase. This curricular approach also focuses on motor skill mastery and the assumption that physical fitness can be developed as a result of the general activity program. There is, however, a phase of the lesson (usually the first five to 10 minutes), that focuses on "general" fitness activities (*e.g.*, calisthenics). The intent of this activity is to warm the body up for the next phase of the lesson and provide a level of general conditioning.

The assumption that physical fitness, especially health-related components, can be developed to an acceptable level as a byproduct of the general activity program is questionable and has not been supported by the scientific community. It is accepted that specific game, dance, and gymnastic activities can stimulate specific fitness development. However, to assume that a general program makes this contribution is questionable.

MODELS EMPHASIZING SPECIFIC FITNESS DEVELOPMENT

The following three general fitness models focus on the development and maintenance of specific health-related fitness components. The models are general in nature due to the diversity of class frequency and duration, finances, and instructional assistance found among school programs. All three of the models support the philosophy that the specific components of fitness (health-related) should be systematically treated to provide for greater accountability toward achieving fitness objectives. The three approaches described are the (1) Specific Fitness Phase, (2) Separate Fitness and Motor Skill Days, and (3) the Comprehensive Approach. It is also quite feasible that programs may be developed by integrating selected characteristics of the various models.

Specific Fitness Phase.   The basis for using this approach focuses on the contention that the specific components of fitness should be systematically addressed on a daily basis and in addition to the motor skill curriculum. In an integrated curriculum (*i.e.*, objectives are to achieve health-related fitness and motor skill mastery), the authors recommend that the initial phase of the daily lesson be the Fitness Phase and its duration be approximately one third to one half of the total class period. The remaining time would be devoted to motor skill instruction. This approach is more conducive to fitness development if the class period is 45 minutes to one hour, allowing at least 15 to 20 minutes to be devoted to attaining specific fitness objectives. Class periods that are 30 minutes or less may find this approach more difficult. The basis for this format was derived from the recommended training principle that aerobic exercise (cardiorespiratory endurance) should be emphasized at least three times a week for a duration of at least 15–20 minutes. The type of activities need not be entirely specific to developing the individual component(s). However, the "primary" objective should be component-specific. An example of a "multicomponent" activity is aerobic dance, which stresses aerobic fitness and develops flexibility and muscular strength/endurance. In a class period of 45 to 60 minutes, it is quite practical to achieve fitness objectives and provide motor skill instruction. Many teachers that have 30-minute class periods have used this general approach and found that 10–12 minutes was an acceptable duration of vigorous activity with younger children (K-3).

While a daily (five-day) physical education program is ideal and one of our profession's goals, the average frequency per week is three days of instruction.

If, for example, the class days are Monday, Wednesday, and Friday, the development of fitness could still be feasible by stressing all three health-related components during the initial phase of the lesson. There are numerous multicomponent activities (*e.g.*, aerobic dance, fitness stations) that could fulfill this need. If the class duration is relatively short, a separate-day approach should be considered. In Table 4-6 a systematic approach to fitness component development for a five-day and three-day per week program is presented.

Separate Fitness and Motor-Skill Days.   The primary justification for using this approach is usually time limitations. Many teachers contend they cannot do an adequate job of developing fitness and motor skills in a class period of less than 30 or 40 minutes. An "adequate" time is dependent upon individual teaching styles, classroom management, etc. With this in mind, Table 4-7 depicts a separate-day approach for a five-day week. The basis for this plan is the belief that developing physical fitness should receive top priority and should be stressed at least three days per week, with the remaining two days devoted to motor skill instruction. This approach also requires that the format for each of the three days stresses "multicomponent" activities.

Separate-day programs of less than five days per week (for example, a three-day-per-week format) presents the teacher with several additional considerations and a less than desirable situation. In this case the teacher has two basic options. One option would be to strive for high involvement each day in both fitness and motor skills. It may be that the teacher stresses fitness activities for the first seven to 10 minutes (of a 20-minute period) and, when practical, selects motor

Table 4-6

5-day and 3-day formats

MONDAY	TUESDAY	WEDNESDAY	THURSDAY	FRIDAY
AEROBIC	FLEX MUSCULAR STRENGTH/ENDUR	AEROBIC	FLEX MUSCULAR STRENGTH/ENDUR	AEROBIC

MONDAY	WEDNESDAY	FRIDAY
	AEROBIC FLEXIBILITY MUSCULAR STRENGTH/ENDURANCE	

Table 4-7

Separate day approach (5-day week)

MONDAY	TUESDAY	WEDNESDAY	THURSDAY	FRIDAY
FITNESS	MOTOR SKILLS	FITNESS (MULTI-COMPONENT)	MOTOR SKILLS	FITNESS

skill activities that have a high fitness value for the remaining period of time. (See Chapter 14 for fitness values of common motor skill activities). Another option that has been successful is the use of a "fitness-oriented recess," hence a **fitness break** to complement the regular physical education program. With this option, motor skill development would be stressed on each of the three-day program sessions and fitness activities would be the focus during "fitness breaks."

Fitness breaks are applicable to any of the models described in this chapter. They are an innovative activity that complements any fitness program or, in some situations, can be the primary method for developing physical fitness. Similar only in time format to the traditional recess, a fitness break emphasizes vigorous physical activity for a duration of 15 to 20 minutes. This may be on a daily basis, or conducted on select days of the week. Since most schools allow time for a recess in the morning and afternoon, the fitness break would substitute for either of the periods, thus maintaining one "free" recess period. Classroom teachers can supervise this period after receiving instructional information from the physical education teacher or through inservice workshops. It is not uncommon to observe classroom teachers and administrators participating in the sessions and, in fact, this practice can serve as a positive motivator for student behavior. Frequently used activities are: rope-jumping, jogging, fast walking, aerobic dance, calisthenics, and roller skating (bring your own). The primary objective is continuous activity, which can be monitored with a whistle, bell, air horn, and watch (or preferably a large clock). In locations where very cold winters are commonplace, warm shelters generally present a space problem for large numbers of children participating in aerobic activities (the gymnasium is being used for regular physical education classes). Solutions to this problem vary considerably, due to the physical characteristics of the school.

Comprehensive Approach. This innovative approach provides a glimpse at what some school programs are currently doing and others should be striving toward. The comprehensive approach is based on the sound reasoning that the responsibility for developing health-related fitness should not lie entirely with the physical educator. This format is a cooperative effort that entails strong goal-setting and the involvement of the physical educator, health educator, food service personnel, auxiliary staff (aides, parent volunteers), and periodic consultation with a physician. Program goals are health-related and focus on preventive medicine as well as remedial objectives.

A 1987 article by Parcel and colleagues, developers of project Go-For-Health, reported that elementary school children consume too much fat and sodium from a typical school lunch, and do not participate in physical activity of significant intensity or duration to develop cardiorespiratory fitness. While this information sup-

ports other findings that have been discussed in this text, the opinion of the medical profession and developers of such programs as Go-For-Health, Heart Smart, The Heart Treasure Chest, and the Sunflower Project, contend that a successful remedy to the "diet-exercise" problem requires a comprehensive and cooperative approach.

The general format of a comprehensive program includes specific objectives for each of three basic components: **physical education, classroom instruction** (knowledge), and **food service**. A typical comprehensive program provides:

Health-related fitness assessment
Screening for heart disease risk factors
Health-related physical activity (in the regular physical education class and during "fitness breaks"), the focus being 15–20 minutes of continuous aerobic exercise at least three times per week
School breakfast/lunch diet that is low in fat, sugar, and sodium
Remedial intervention with high-risk students; morning and afternoon activity sessions and counseling of parents
Classroom instruction to develop a knowledge base related to healthy lifestyle behaviors

This approach is truly a comprehensive and cooperative effort to address the health of our children today and the quality of their lives as productive adults. Specific information related to classroom instruction content and other program details (most materials begin with kindergarten) can be requested from sources provided in Table 4-8.

Chapter 14 provides recommendations and guidelines for program implementation, and activities that can be used to enhance specific fitness components.

Table 4-8

Comprehensive Program Sources

Project Go-For-Health
    Dr. Guy Parcel, Associate Director
    Center for Health Promotion Research and Development
    School of Public Health
    The University of Texas Health Science Center
    Houston, TX 70036
Sun Flower Project
    Shawnee Mission
    Instructional Program Center
    6649 Lamar
    Shawnee Mission, KS 66202
The Heart Smart Program
    National Research and Demonstration Center
    L.S.U. Medical Center
    1542 Tulane Avenue
    New Orleans, LA 70112-2822
The Heart Treasure Chest
    American Heart Association, National Center
    7320 Greenville Avenue
    Dallas, TX 75231 (or local AHA affiliate)

REFERENCES

American Academy of Pediatrics. (1987). Physical fitness and the schools, *Pediatrics, 80,* (3), 449–450.

American Academy of Pediatrics. (September, 1987). News release. Appeal to schools: increase p.e. programs.

American Alliance for Health, Physical Education, Recreation, and Dance. (1988). AAHPERD Physical best. Reston, VA: AAHPERD Publications.

American Journal of Diseases in Children. (1986). Editorial: Can (should) the pediatrician wage preventive medicine war against coronary heart disease? *140,* 985–986.

CORBIN, C. (1987). Physical fitness in the K-12 curriculum. *Journal of Physical Education, Recreation, & Dance, 58,* (7), 49–54.

FALLS, H. B. (1980). Modern concepts of physical fitness. *Journal of Health, Physical Education and Recreation, 51,* 25–27.

GABBARD, C. P., & CROUSE, S. (1988). Children and exercise: Myths and fact. *The Physical Educator, 45* (1), 39–43.

GORTMAKER, S. L., DIETZ, W. H., SOBOL, A. N., & WEHLER, C. A. (1987). Increasing pediatric obesity in the U.S. *American Journal of Diseases of Children, 141,* 535–540.

HASKELL, E., MONTOYE, H., & ORENSTEIN, D. (1985). Physical activity and exercise to achieve health related physical fitness components. *Public Health Report, 199* (2), 202–211.

Human Kinetics Publishers, Inc., Dept. 966, Box 5076, Champaign, IL.

National Children and Youth Fitness Study II. (1987). Special report in *Journal of Physical Education, Recreation, and Dance, 58* (9), 50–96.

National Children and Youth Fitness Study I. (1985). Special report in *Journal of Physical Education, Recreation, and Dance, 56* (1), 2–48.

National School Population Fitness Survey. (1985). The President's Council on Physical Fitness and Sports, HHS—Office of Assistant Secretary for Health, Research Project 282-84-0086.

PARCEL, G. S., SIMONS-MORTON, B. G., O'HARA, N., BARANOWSKI, T., KOLBE, L., & BEE, D. (1987). School promotion of healthful diet and exercise behavior. *Journal of School Health, 57,* (4) 150–156.

PATE, R., ROSS, J., BAUMGARTNER, T., & SPARKS, R. (1987). The modified pull-up test. *Journal of Physical Education, Recreation, and Dance, 58* (9), 71–73.

RARICK, L., & FRANCIS, R. (1960). Motor characteristics of the mentally retarded. *Competitive Research Monograph, 1,* DE-35005, U.S. Office of Education.

SHERRILL, C. (1986). *Adapted Physical Education and Recreation.* Dubuque, IA: Wm. C. Brown.

WINNICK, J. (1988). Classifying individuals with handicapping conditions for testing. *Journal of Physical Education, Recreation, and Dance, 59* (1), 34–37.

ARNHEIM, D., AUXTER, D., & CROWE, W. (1973). *Principles and methods of Adapted Physical Education.* St. Louis, MO: C.V. Mosby.

SUGGESTED READINGS

AAHPERD. (1986). Physical activity and well-being. AAHPERD Publications. Reston, VA: AAHPERD.

AAHPERD. (1986). The value of physical activity. AAHPERD Publications. Reston, VA: AAHPERD.

ROWLAND, T. W. (1990). *Exercise and children's health.* Champaign, IL: Human Kinetics.

SALLIS, J. F., & MCKENZIE, T. L. (1991). Physical education's role in public health. *Research Quarterly for Exercise and Sport, 62* (2), 74–77.

WHITEHEAD, J. R. (1992). A selected, annotated bibliography for fitness educators. *Journal of Physical Education, Recreation, & Dance, 63* (5), 53–64.

5

Curriculum and Planning

This book divides the physical education curriculum into two categories:

1. Building the Foundation (Levels I–II). Development of fundamental skills and movement awarenesses necessary for the execution of efficient motor performance.
2. Utilization of the Foundation (Levels III–IV). Refinement of fundamental movement behaviors and development of specific game, dance, and gymnastic skills generally associated with children in grades 3–6.

These two curricular categories were adopted because they parallel closely the developmental phases of motor behavior outlined in Chapter 2. While traditionally teachers have used grade levels and ages to place children into one curriculum or the other, rarely do children develop skills in such an orderly fashion. Skills develop at widely varying rates among children within any one grade level; therefore, the use of grade designations in planning may be inappropriate for addressing individual differences. With this in mind the authors propose the use of four skill proficiency levels (Levels I–IV) rather than grade designations for designing and selecting skill development and enhancement activities. These levels of movement skill proficiency exist independently for every skill contained in the curriculum.

A brief description of the generic levels of skill proficiency follows:

LEVEL I

Inconsistency is most characteristic of this level. The child is not able to consciously control or repeat movements. Manipulated objects are usually being chased rather than caught, bounced, or trapped. Movements seem awkward, random, and frequently have unnecessary actions included.

LEVEL II

The child begins to consciously control movements and can repeat familiar patterns frequently. Combinations of movements are difficult and complete concentration is required for success.

LEVEL III

Movements become more automatic and are easily repeated. The child is able to adjust movements to suit variable situations and combine several skills into a successful performance. We might say this child has a well-developed fundamental skill schema and is ready to learn more complex game/sport, dance, and gymnastic skills.

LEVEL IV

Movements at this level are automatic so that the child may easily adjust to unpredictable and novel situations. Skills are performed in a smooth and effortless manner in a variety of situations. This child is able to "utilize the foundation."

There are skill proficiency indicators for each of these levels which will help the teacher recognize the level at which children are performing in a given skill area. These indicators also enable the teacher to deter-

Table 5-1

Generic Levels of Skill Proficiency and Curricular Categories

BUILDING THE FOUNDATION
(fundamental movement phase)
LEVELS I–II   Pre-K–2nd
                 ages pre-7
(TRANSITION)
LEVELS II–III   3rd
                 ages 8–9
(UTILIZATION)
(specific-advanced phase)
LEVELS III–IV   4th–6th
                 ages 9->

mine how stable the child is within a given level. When stability is established at one level, then the teacher must challenge the child with initial activities from the next higher level. Specific skill proficiency indicators are provided at the beginning of each skill chapter (Chapters 10, 11, and 12).

Table 5-1 illustrates the authors' conceptualization of the relationships among the curricular categories, the child's chronological age, and skill proficiency level.

The reader is cautioned that while Levels I and II may be associated with pre-school to second grade and Levels III and IV with third through sixth grade, as many as three skill levels may be found at any one grade level. For example, a child in the first grade may be performing at Level III in catching and at Level I in striking. On the other hand a 10-year-old may be performing at Level I on all skills. The level of skill proficiency of each child is determined by experience and level of developmental maturity.

The challenge for the physical educator, as for all teachers working with grade level groups, is to effectively individualize material by skill level so each child can be challenged by the activity and will progress at a reasonable pace so as to experience success. It is hoped that the addition of skill proficiency levels to the generally accepted grade level designations will enable the teacher to have more realistic expectations for children with very diverse backgrounds and abilities. However, in view of the fact that schools are divided by grade levels, the curriculum planning presented here will also be organized according to grade level. This does not in any way hinder the use of skill proficiency levels as a tool for individualizing planning at the theme, unit, and daily levels.

As with any area of scholarly inquiry in which a new textbook emerges, much of the information and concepts contained here were developed from and/or inspired by existing materials and knowledgeable individuals. In holding to the promising trends noted in the 1980s, the authors firmly believe that the use primarily of dance, game, sport, and gymnastic activities is not the best approach for building acceptable levels of fitness and motor-skill proficiency in children. The philosophy or assumption that fitness and motor-skill proficiency develop merely as a result of participation in fun-filled activities has not been acceptable to the authors for many years, and that belief is even stronger today. The primary mission of this text is to support the developmental-theme approach and to emphasize the health-related fitness concept. A curricular model is presented that is as scientific as practicality permits and at the same time blends the more traditional with contemporary instructional approaches. Figure 5-1

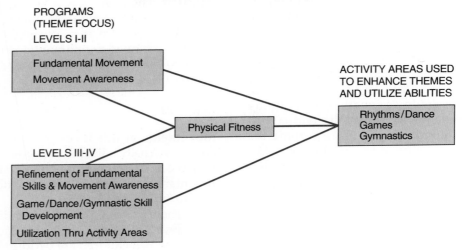

THE GENERAL CURRICULAR MODEL

PROGRAMS
(THEME FOCUS)
LEVELS I-II

Fundamental Movement
Movement Awareness

ACTIVITY AREAS USED
TO ENHANCE THEMES
AND UTILIZE ABILITIES

Physical Fitness

Rhythms/Dance
Games
Gymnastics

LEVELS III-IV

Refinement of Fundamental
Skills & Movement Awareness

Game/Dance/Gymnastic Skill
Development

Utilization Thru Activity Areas

FIGURE 5-1

Outline of the curricular model

illustrates the general concept of integration and relationship between the contemporary approach and use of traditional activity areas.

THE CURRICULUM

Levels I–II Building the Foundation

"Building the Foundation" (Levels I–II) refers to program emphasis that focuses upon the development of:

1. Health-Related Physical Fitness
2. Movement Awareness
3. Fundamental Movement Skills

The basis for this program model was derived from knowledge related to the developmental psychomotor abilities of children as described in the previous chapters. It is with this information, plus years of experimentation and practical implementation, that the following model is presented.

In addition to a predetermined, structured plan for implementing the physical fitness component of the program (discussed in Chapters 4 and 14), the use of developmental themes is the framework by which the movement foundation is constructed, refined, and utilized with proficiency. A developmental theme focuses on a specific fundamental movement skill or movement awareness whereas the traditional unit focuses on several skills specific to a given sport, dance area, or gymnastic activity.

Table 5-2 presents the fundamental movement skills and movement awarenesses used to plan and implement the theme concept.

The following is a brief review and explanation of each category.

MOVEMENT AWARENESS

Body Spatial	Directional Temporal	Vestibular Visual	Auditory Tactile

Movement awareness refers to a specific component of the perceptual-motor system that is basic and essential to movement efficiency and motor-skill performance. The execution of all motor tasks requires the utilization of sensory information and perceptual mechanisms. The components of movement awareness are, in essence, the substructure of the movement foundation. Following this line of reasoning, one may assume that anything other than a primary emphasis upon these components would not fit the developmental theme concept. Basic components such as eye-hand and eye-foot coordination, for example, can be viewed as the foundation for proficiency with fundamental manipulative skills (*e.g.*, throwing, catching, kicking, trapping). Activities within an eye-hand and eye-foot theme would be much more diverse and generalized than fundamental throwing or catching themes and therefore merit separate and specific emphasis. An eye-foot theme, for example, may include kicking and trapping activities as well as jumping, leaping, hopping, and walking with eye focus on lines or between ladder rungs. Eye-hand activities would also be quite generalized and include several gross motor skill (*e.g.*, rolling, bouncing, throwing, catching, striking) activities and fine-motor tasks. Vestibular awareness (stability) is another example of a basic component that influences the execution of virtually all fundamental skills.

Table 5-2

Fundamental Movement Skills and Movement Awareness

MOVEMENT AWARENESSES	FUNDAMENTAL LOCOMOTOR SKILLS	FUNDAMENTAL NONLOCOMOTOR SKILLS	FUNDAMENTAL MANIPULATIVE SKILLS
Body	Walking	Dodging	*Propulsive*
Spatial	Running	Stretching/bending	Rolling
Directional	Leaping	Turning/twisting	Throwing
Temporal	Jumping (and landing)	Pushing/pulling	Bouncing/Dribbling
Rhythm	Hopping	Swinging/swaying	Striking
Eye-hand	Galloping		Kicking
Eye-foot	Sliding		
Vestibular	Skipping		*Receptive*
Visual	Body Rolling		Catching
Auditory	Climbing		Trapping
Tactile			

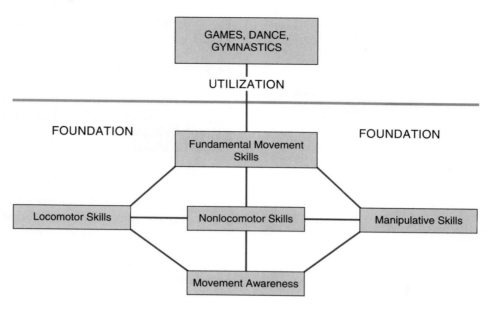

FIGURE 5-2

The "foundation" and "utilization"

Without question all developmental-theme models as well as traditional approaches characteristically require a great deal of overlapping of movement abilities. This overlapping should be perceived as beneficial and a natural characteristic of human psychomotor behavior. The important point is that the specific psychomotor abilities of children are stimulated through a predetermined and varied program of activities.

We hope through this discussion to demonstrate the "foundational" importance of awareness themes which allow and encourage exploration in movement of preparatory abilities that facilitate effective and efficient performance of all gross and fine motor skills.

Figure 5-2 illustrates the integration of movement awarenesses with fundamental skills establishing the "foundation" for development of more specific movement skills used in sports, dance, and gymnastics.

FUNDAMENTAL MOVEMENT SKILLS

| Locomotor | Nonlocomotor | Manipulative |

Along with an efficient movement awareness base, the acquisition of fundamental movement skills form the foundation for development and performance of more complex motor tasks (game, dance, gymnastic skills). Most research findings have shown that instruction may be a significant factor in the level of proficiency achieved. This information, in addition to the propositions of "schema theory" and "movement variability," strongly suggests the importance of identification and enhancement of individual perceptual-motor elements (awareness and movements) of the

desired "motor program." Most complex motor tasks and many individual fundamental movement skills consist of a combination of two or more skill characteristics. Mastery of individual components of the task would appear to provide a better chance for success, as well as greater proficiency with individual fundamental skills. For a more detailed discussion of the role and description of the fundamental skill categories, see Chapters 10–13. The following is a brief review of category descriptions.

The three categories of fundamental movement are:

LOCOMOTOR SKILLS	Propel the individual through space from one location to another.
NONLOCOMOTOR SKILLS	Characterized by stability executed with minimal or no movement of the base of support.
MANIPULATIVE SKILLS	Controlling of objects, primarily with use of hands and feet.

See Table 5-2 for a complete listing of fundamental movement skills.

Levels III–IV Utilization of the Foundation

"Utilization of the Foundation" (Level III–IV) refers to program emphasis for children who have acquired proficiency at the "foundation" level (Levels I–II). This curriculum refines those movement awarenesses and fundamental skills acquired during the previously discussed foundation phase and utilizes them in more

Table 5-3

Utilization of the Foundation

PROGRAM EMPHASES LEVELS III–IV

Fitness (Health and Skill-Related Components)
Refinement of Movement Awarenesses and Fundamental-Movement Skills
Introduction to (and utilization of "foundation" abilities) activities involving greater motor-task
    complexity:
        Game (individual, dual, team)
        Dance (creative, folk, square, aerobic)
        Gymnastic (stunts/tumbling, small & large equipment, rhythmic)
Introduction of knowledge concepts, (for example, rules and strategies) and principles related to
    skill areas and fitness.

dynamic challenges in individual/team sports, games, dance, and gymnastics. During this period, children refine specific motor abilities and combine various patterns of movements (locomotor, nonlocomotor, manipulative) in an attempt to execute more complex dance, game/sport, and gymnastic tasks. It can be assumed that it is the composition (that is, degree of movement dimension variability and proficiency) of the foundation that determines motivation and chances of early success in many of the complex motor tasks. See Table 5-3 for suggested program emphases and Table 5-4 for suggested program content.

The primary emphasis is on specific tasks. Whereas during the foundation phase, catching and throwing were generalized with movement variability, the skills are now utilized in more specific motor-task situations such as fielding and throwing in the game of softball. Within these motor-skill areas, sev-

Table 5-4

Suggested Content for Levels III–IV

GAMES

Low Organization	Individual/Partner		Team*	
Relays	Bowling Activities	Frisbee	Basketball	Soccer
Tag	Croquet	Horseshoes	Hockey (Field/Floor)	Softball
Simple Group Games	Deck Tennis	Shuffleboard	Football	Volleyball
	Hackey sack			Track & Field
	Paddleball	Handball	Hocker	Korfball
	Paddle Tennis	Sidewalk Tennis	Speedball	Netball
	Pickleball	Volley Tennis	Team Handball	Pillo Polo
	Badminton			Flickerball
			Toppleball	

*Creative/Cooperative Games***

RHYTHMS/DANCE

Rhythms
Creative
Folk
Square
Aerobic***

GYMNASTIC ACTIVITIES

Stunts
Tumbling
Small Equipment (rope jumping, juggling, others)
Large Equipment
Rhythmic Gymnastics

* Team activities emphasize a variety of lead-up games
** May be incorporated with other games or presented as a separate
content area.
*** Aerobic dance is not truly dance in the same sense as folk, cre-
ative, and square, however, it is listed under dance because of its
importance as a fitness activity.

eral variations and combinations of fundamental skills can be used. A more detailed discussion of the integration of the theme and unit approach will be addressed later in the chapter.

PLANNING STRATEGIES

Planning is essential for effective teaching, and effective teachers plan with a goal in mind. This is true for all educational endeavors, and physical education is no exception. The end result of effective planning is a smooth lesson that achieves stated objectives by maximizing the use of time. Instruction that does not produce minimal change of behaviors over a reasonable period is "wasted" time and the tax-paying public is not keen on paying for experiences that do not positively affect students' behaviors. Physical education must be presented as more than supervised recess, and effective planning is one of the major tools in accomplishing this mission.

Physical educators are accountable for their students' accomplishment of fitness and skill objectives just as mathematics teachers are responsible for attainment of stated math-skill objectives by their students. The physical education class of today is an important segment of the child's educational day in which their wonderful energy is focused on healthful exercise and on learning how to move better—experiencing more fully the joy of graceful and effective movement.

Crucial to effective planning for physical education is a thorough understanding of the overall goals of the profession. The goal of physical education is to promote the development of the total child through the psychomotor, cognitive, and affective domains. The authors believe that the physical education environment presents the child and teacher with unique opportunities for development of organic fitness, motor skills, and cognitive and affective abilities. The world of play is the child's natural environment for expression and learning. Wise teachers will take advantage of a child's natural instincts to be active and, through appropriate and creative planning, present an environment where learning can be realized by both process and product. Systematic planning is a tool utilized by the teacher to ensure that stated objectives are accomplished. Plans are made at three different levels. First is the *yearly plan*, then *theme* (Levels I–II) and *unit* (Levels III–IV) plans, and finally the *daily lesson* plan is made.

Yearly Planning

The yearly plan is a flexible outline of the general content areas and amount of time to be devoted to each area. You might look upon the completed yearly plan as the blueprint for the year's building efforts, and as the end result of a significant amount of preplanning. This scope (what will be presented) and sequence (order of presentation) will be different for each grade level because of maturational and skill-level changes of the students from year to year. The yearly plan in general serves three purposes:

1. Provides a written plan for accomplishment of stated program goals. Most school districts insist on this evidence of professionalism.
2. Provides written evidence of accountability to the appropriate governing agencies and the public.
3. Helps the teacher make certain all of the content areas are given a realistic proportion of the allotted time.

PRIMARY CONSIDERATIONS WHEN PLANNING FOR THE YEAR

Prior to beginning initial plans there is a certain amount of background information the teacher should gather. These data are rather general but as necessary as the more specific information required later. Prior to initiating the yearly plan the teacher needs to survey the following:

1. Nature of the community as reflected by the known customs and mores;
2. Philosophy of the school district as reflected by the goals and objectives of the school board;
3. Needs and interests of the children as reflected by their behavior (successful teachers are constant "people-watchers");
4. Available facilities and equipment as reflected by the current inventory;
5. Campus time/frequency structure for physical education as reflected by the school schedule (this may be negotiable with the school administrator);
6. Competencies of the teacher as reflected by past performance and continual updating of professional knowledge.

While all of these factors may affect the planning process, information relative to facilities/equipment, class sizes, and time/frequency structure can vary within the same school district. A yearly plan developed for a school that schedules physical education three times a week (30 to 45 minutes per class) will be quite different from a plan developed for a daily program.

Specifically, the number of days available for physical education during the year will determine the amount of emphasis that can be placed on the various content areas. A program which meets for only three days a week would have fewer days devoted to the theme of body awareness, for example, than would a program which meets five days a week.

It would be convenient if the teacher could assess the motor, fitness, cognitive, and affective abilities of the students prior to writing the plans; however, this is generally not practical. A reasonable yearly plan can be developed by the teacher based on knowledge about the student population. This information can come from many sources (such as past experience, current written resources, talking with veteran teachers, and perusal of school records). This topic will be discussed later in the chapter titled Evaluation.

A more accurate analysis of each grade level can be accomplished at the beginning of the year through informal (but critical) observations of such key items as the following:

1. Movement awareness (body, spatial, vestibular, etc.)
2. Selected fundamental and advanced motor skills
3. Health-related fitness levels to include:
Cardiorespiratory endurance
Abdominal and upper body
strength/endurance
Flexibility

The results of these observations will enable the teacher to revise, if necessary, the amount of time to be devoted to various content areas of the yearly plans for each grade level. Planning the yearly curriculum for each grade level is not easy, for it is not based on arbitrary choices. The curriculum is based on the developmental readiness and movement-skill needs of children at that developmental level—which may not be consistent with age or grade and may vary widely.

CONTENT PLACEMENT

After identifying general content, the next step in yearly planning involves sequence, that is, general placement/order of activities on the school calendar. While this may vary also, certain activities are accepted as being presented at specific times of the year (*e.g.*, soccer in the fall, basketball in the winter, softball in the spring). Placement of activities on the calendar necessitates another important general consideration: method of placement. There are two recommended methods for content placement: modified and solid (block).

MODIFIED METHOD

This method suggests that a segment of time be shared between two or more activity areas or skills. For example, at Levels I–II during a five-day week (a

week is the most frequent unit of planning) a locomotor skill can be presented two or three days and a manipulative skill two days with a movement awareness theme on the remaining day. At Levels III–IV soccer skills may be presented three or four days and another activity area the remaining days. This method provides both continuity and variety. Continuity over a period of days promotes effective instruction and planning. This method also considers children who may not enjoy participating in the same skill area every day of the week.

At Levels I–II the modified method is most often recommended because the skills and awarenesses are best presented in one-, two- or three-day blocks—depending on the complexity of skills and maturity level of the students. At Levels III–IV one day may be set aside as a "break" or "mod" day. The activities presented on the "mod" day should provide a change of pace and be simple enough to be completed in a single class period. Some "mod" day content suggestions include: rhythms, simple dances, simple stunts, small equipment gymnastic activities, individual and partner games, and cooperative and creative game activities.

The modified method is the method most preferred by the authors because it offers continuity, flexibility, and variety for teacher and student.

SOLID METHOD

A solid or block method represents an extended period of instruction (that is, five days a week) devoted exclusively to one content area. This method is recommended primarily for Levels III and IV. Its primary asset is that there is no disruption during the presentation of skill development content. This type of plan requires a highly interested group of children and, while variety is not provided from another content area, an assortment of skill-development activities can provide motivating challenges.

Both methods of content placement provide the teacher with a great degree of planning flexibility. After a feel for general planning and instruction has been achieved, many teachers find it desirable to combine both methods of content placement.

PLANNING PROCEDURES

Until now, the planning discussion has focused on skill proficiency levels. At this point, in order to simplify the yearly planning process, we will revert to traditional grade level designations. Most school systems organize their placement of students in physical education classes by grade level; so the yearly curriculum outline will be most useful if it also is done by grade level.

The "Building the Foundation" curriculum will be used for grades K or Pre-K, 1, and 2 where the learners are likely to be at proficiency Levels I and II. "Utilization of the Foundation" is for grades 4 through 6 where the learners are likely to be at proficiency Levels III and IV. Grade 3 is considered a transition period because at the beginning of the year students often are still developing basic skills, primarily at Level II. It is likely that later in the year they will be ready to use those skills in more complex game/sport, dance, and gymnastic activities. Therefore it may be desirable for grade 3 to spend the first half of the year with the "Building the Foundation" curriculum and the second half with "Utilization of the Foundation." It will depend on the specific group of children for which the plan is being developed.

In order to begin, the teacher needs the school calendar (holidays, inservice days, etc.) and the curriculum content outlines (see Table 5-2 and Table 5-4). You will note that health-related fitness is not treated as a separate content area in either curriculum because fitness development is within the scope of each daily lesson. Each class period should be paced so that the activity demand is vigorous enough to promote health-related physical fitness development. However, the teacher may want to have "special fitness days" for motivational purposes or in order to have a stronger health-related fitness basis (as noted in Chapter 4). These fitness days would need to be scheduled on the calendar.

Each yearly curriculum outline (one for each grade) will reflect the philosophical beliefs of the teacher, school, and community as well as facilities, equipment availability, and weather considerations. The following curriculum outlines reflect the authors' general suggestions and should be viewed as flexible guidelines rather than the last word (see Tables 5-6, 5-7, and 5-8).

"BUILDING THE FOUNDATION" (GRADES K-2, 3)

As you look at the yearly curriculum outline begin the following procedure:

1. As you mark the names of the months, keep in mind the seasons and weather conditions.
2. Place an X on the inservice days; if you don't have exact dates but know that your students will only be in class 175 days of the 180, simply place five X's arbitrarily on the outline.
3. During the first few weeks, lessons will include movement themes as well as time spent acquainting students with the area and class management routines.
4. Beginning with the third week, fundamental movement themes are presented in two-day segments in rotational order of locomotor, nonlocomotor, manipulative, with one day a week devoted to movement-awareness themes. The single-day lessons (usually movement-awareness themes) can be presented on Monday, Wednesday, or Friday. The two-day lessons should be taught on consecutive days.
5. Fitness assessment days should not begin before an appropriate conditioning period has been completed—usually in four to six weeks. The last six weeks should also include time for fitness testing and a culminating activity—such as a Field Day.

The modified method of content placement is recommended. Table 5-5 is an example of a general format for grades K-2.

As you plot in the locomotor, nonlocomotor, manipulative, and movement awareness days, you need to balance time allowed for each theme. This balance can be accomplished by using the columns in Table 5-2 to insert the skills in the designated movement category (i.e., locomotor, nonlocomotor, manipulative, movement awareness). Tables 5-6, 5-7, and 5-8 are examples of partially completed (that is, three six-week blocks) yearly plans. The rest is generally repetitive, that is, a continuance of the system.

6. The preschool-kindergarten curriculum outline (Table 5-6) should include all themes somewhat equally (approximately four lessons per theme) except for the auditory, visual, and tactile themes. They are approximately two lessons each. Note that certain nonlocomotor themes (stretch/bend, turn/twist) are presented on a consecutive two-day period. The plan also reflects an adjustment due to inservice days.
7. The first grade curriculum (Table 5-7) will display less time spent on body, spatial, directional, and walking themes. In this example, the movement-awareness day has been set on Wednesdays. After the initial walking theme is presented, the focus is dropped and, in this plan, more rhythm is added. Keep in mind that if more rhythm is desired, it may be presented through the enhancement selection of appropriate locomotor, nonlocomotor, and other movement-awareness themes.
8. The second grade curriculum (Table 5-8) limits its focus on body, spatial, and directional-awareness (after a review), as well as on visual, auditory, and tactile themes; additional time is allocated to rhythm and manipulative themes. Note that throwing/catching and kicking/trapping themes are now placed together and that, in this example, two rhythm days are on consecutive Wednesdays. (This is optional. There could be more rhythm days in a row, or the rotation could continue allowing only one day for each theme.)

Table 5-5

Yearly Curriculum Outline: "General Format"

General Format for Grades K-2

1st

#	M	T	W	T	F
1	Introduction		Spat Aware	Body Aware	Direct Aware
2					
3	Loco		Move Aware	Nonloco	
4	Manipu		Move Aware	Fitness Testing	
5					
6					

2nd

#	M	T	W	T	F
1					
2					X
3					
4					
5					
6					

3rd

#	M	T	W	T	F
1					
2					
3					
4	X				
5					
6					

4th

#	M	T	W	T	F
1					
2					X
3					
4					
5					
6					

5th

#	M	T	W	T	F
1					
2					
3					
4					
5					
6	X				

6th

#	M	T	W	T	F
1					
2					
3	Fitness Testing				
4					
5					
6					

— Field/Play Days —

X = inservice/work days

Table 5-6

Yearly Curriculum Outline: Preschool/Kindergarten

1st (6 weeks)

	M	T	W	T	F
1	Introduction		SA	SA	BA
2	BA	DA	DA	Loco Walk	
3	MA Rhythm		Nonloco Dodge	Manip Ball Roll	
4	MA Eye/H		Loco Run	Fitness Testing	
5	MA Eye/Ft		Nonloco Stretch/Bend	Manip Throw	
6	MA Vestib		Loco Leap	Nonloco Turn/Twist	

2nd

	M	T	W	T	F
1	MA Vis	Manip Catch		Loco Jump	
2	MA Aud	Nonloco Push/Pull		Manip Bounce	
3	MA Tact	Loco Hop		Swing/Sway	X
4	MA BA	Manip Strike		Loco Gallop	
5	MA SA	Nonloco Dodge		Manip Kick	
6	MA DA	Loco Slide		Nonloco Stretch/Bend	

3rd

	M	T	W	T	F
1	MA Rhythm	Manip Trap		Loco Skip	
2	MA Eye/H	Nonloco Turn/Twist		Manip Ball Roll	
3	MA Eye/Ft	Loco Body Roll		Nonloco Push/Pull	
4	MA Vestib	Manip Throw		Loco Climb	
5	X	Nonloco Swing/Sway		Manip Catch	
6	MA Vis	Loco Walk		Nonloco Dodge	

SA, Spatial Awareness; BA, Body Awareness; DA, Directional Awareness; MA, Movement Awareness Theme.

Table 5-7

Yearly Curriculum Outline: 1st Grade

1st

	M	T	W	T	F
1	Introduction		SA	BA	DA
2	Loco Walk		MA Rhythm	Nonloco Dodge	
3	Manip Ball Roll		MA Eye/H	Loco Run	
4	Nonloco Stretch/Bend		MA Eye/Ft	Fitness Testing	
5	Manip Throw		MA Vestib	Loco Leap	
6	Nonloco Turn/Twist		MA Vis	Manip Catch	

2nd

	M	T	W	T	F
1	Loco Jump		MA Aud	Nonloco Push/Pull	
2	Manip Bounce		MA Tact	Loco Hop	
3	Nonloco Swing/Sway		MA SA	Manip Strike	
4	Loco Gallop		MA BA	Nonloco Dodge	
5	X	MA Rhythm	MA DA	Manip Kick	
6	Loco Slide		MA Rhythm	Nonloco Stretch/Bend	

3rd

	M	T	W	T	F
1	Manip Trap		MA Eye/H	MA Rhythm	X
2	Loco Skip		MA Eye/FT	Nonloco Turn/Twist	
3	Manip Ball Roll		MA Vestib	Loco Body Roll	
4	Nonloco Push/Pull		MA Vis	Manip Throw	
5	Loco Climb		MA Aud	Nonloco Swing/Sway	
6	Manip Catch		MA Tact	Loco Run	

Table 5-8

Yearly Curriculum Outline: 2nd Grade

1st

	M	T	W	T	F
1	Introduction		SA	BA	DA
2	Loco Walk Run		MA Rhythm	Nonloco Dodge	
3	Manip Ball Roll		MA Eye/H	Loco Leap	
4	Nonloco Stretch/Bend		MA Eye/Ft	Fitness Testing	
5	Manip Throw/Catch		MA Vestib	Loco Jump	
6	Nonloco Turn/Twist		MA Rhythm	Manip Bounce	

2nd

	M	T	W	T	F
1	Loco Hop		MA Rhythm	Nonloco Push/Pull	
2	Manip Strike		MA Eye/H	Loco Gallop	
3	Nonloco Swing/Sway		MA Eye/Ft	Manip Kick/Trap	
4	Loco Slide		MA Vestib	Nonloco Dodge	
5	X	MA Rhythm	MA Ryhthm	Manip Ball Roll	
6	Loco Skip		MA Rhythm	Nonloco Stretch/Bend	

3rd

	M	T	W	T	F
1	Manip Throw/Catch		MA Eye/H	Loco Body Roll	
2	Nonloco Turn/Twist		MA Eye/Ft	Manip Bounce	
3	Loco Climb		MA Vestib	Nonloco Push/Pull	
4	Manip Strike		MA Rhythm	Loco Run	
5	Nonloco Swing/Sway		MA Rhythm	Manip Kick/Trap	
6	Loco Leap		MA Eye/H	Nonloco Dodge	

Table 5-9

Yearly Curriculum Outline: 3rd Grade

1st

	M	T	W	T	F
1	Introduction Cooperative Games		Rhythms		Run/Leap
2	Dodge		Rhythms		Throw/Catch
3	Jump/Hop		Rhythms		Stretch/Bend Turn/Twist
4	Kick/Trap		Rhythms		Fitness Testing
5	Soccer		Rhythms		Soccer
6	Gallop/Slide/Skip		Rhythms		Push/Pull Swing/Sway

2nd

	M	T	W	T	F
1	Football Activities		Eye/Hand/Foot		Football Activities
2	Run/Jump		Eye/Hand/Foot		Dodge (X)
3	Ball Rolling Bowling		Eye/Hand/Foot		Stunts Tumbling
4	Stunts/Tumbling		Eye/Hand/Foot		Climbing
5	Dribble		Eye/Hand/Foot		Basketball
6	Basketball		Eye/Hand/Foot		Basketball

3rd

	M	T	W	T	F
1	Folk		Cooperatives		Dance
2	Folk		Cooperatives		Dance
3	Strike		Cooperatives		Volleyball
4	Jump (X)		Cooperatives		Volleyball
5	Stunts		Cooperatives		Tumbling
6	Creative		Cooperatives		Dance

4th

	M	T	W	T	F
1	Catch/Throw		Rhythms		Small Equip. Gymn.
2	Frisbee		Rhythms		Strike (X)
3	Floor		Rhythms		Hockey
4	Small Equip.		Rhythms		Gymnastics
5	Folk		Rhythms		Dance
6	Run/leap		Rhythms		Stretch/Bend

5th

	M	T	W	T	F
1	Ball Roll		Eye/Hand/Foot		Jump/Hop
2	Turn/Twist		Eye/Hand/Foot		Kick/Trap
3	Gallop/Slide		Eye/Hand/Foot		Push/Pull
4	Strike		Eye/Hand/Foot		Climb/Skip
5	Softball		Eye/Hand/Foot		Softball
6	Swing/Sway		Eye/Hand/Foot		Dribble

6th

	M	T	W	T	F
1	X		Large Equip. Gymnastics		
2			Indiv./Partner Games		
3	Fitness Testing		Track & Field		
4			Track & Field Dance		
5			Gymnastics Cooperative Games		
6			—Field/Play Days—		

X = inservice/work days

9. When a theme is dropped from the yearly curriculum outline, this means that particular content area is no longer emphasized as a theme topic. However, there is always considerable overlapping of the movement awareness and fundamental skills so those skills that no longer receive emphasis are still being utilized by children as they participate in themes that focus on other skills.

10. The third grade curriculum (Table 5-9) will be a blending of the Building the Foundation curriculum and the Utilization of the Foundation curriculum. The general planning method still focuses on the rotation of themes, however combinations are stressed and complementary activity units are introduced.

"UTILIZATION OF THE FOUNDATION" (GRADES 4–6)

The initial task of yearly planning for grades 4–6 (Levels III–IV) is similar to the procedure followed for grades K–3. The calendar is set up in regard to months, inservice days, introductory days, fitness assessment, and a culminating activity.

1. The next procedure is to indicate priorities by establishing percentages for the areas of games, dance, and gymnastics. Though the following percentages are suggested, each teacher will understandably make modifications to suit specific school circumstances.

	GRADE 4	GRADE 5	GRADE 6
Games/Sports	40%	40%–50%	40–60%
Dance	30%	25%–30%	20–30%
Gymnastics	30%	25%–30%	20–30%

See Table 5-4 for suggested content for each of the areas of games/sport, dance, and gymnastics.

2. Determine number of days allotted for each area based on percentages. For example: after placing the inservice, testing, introductory, and culminating activity days, approximately 162–165 days will be available for content allotment.

GRADE 4			
	%	days	
Games	40	66	(165 × .40)
Dance	30	49.5	(165 × .30)
Gymnastics	30	49.5	(165 × .30)
	100%	165.0	

3. Determine number of days for each unit within each area. For example:

	GRADE 5		GRADE 6	
Dance	(25%)	(41 days)	(20%)	(33 days)
Folk	20		13	
Square	15		13	
Creative	6		7	
	41		33	

4. Determine placement of units on the yearly calendar; see Tables 5-10 and 5-11 for examples.

After completing the yearly plan for each grade level, the teacher is ready to begin planning themes (Levels I–II) and units (Levels III–IV).

THEME DEVELOPMENT

Theme development represents the second level of planning. A developmental theme is a resource packet which focuses on one movement awareness or fundamental skill. Each of these awarenesses and fundamental skills serves as a very important component of the psychomotor "foundation." The theme packet contains information needed by the teacher who wants to develop within each lesson the variability in practice that is the core of the developmental-theme approach. The wide range of movement-variability experiences facilitate the child's developing schema, which enables the individual to become a more versatile and successful mover. Remember, the more complete the theme packet, the more valuable it becomes for daily lesson planning. Visualize having a file of resource packets on all 32 themes!

The teacher is faced with two choices when beginning the composition of a developmental skill or movement-awareness theme. A theme can be developed to include all information necessary for any of the skill levels likely to be observed in grades K-6 (Levels I–IV), or the teacher may choose to develop a theme containing the necessary information for lessons to be taught only at certain grade levels. Because most elementary physical education specialists will teach grades K/1–6, the authors believe the more complete packet to be the most practical. Remember, the theme is an organizational tool for the teacher to use in facilitating planning of daily lessons. During the development of each theme, the teacher keeps in mind that this step in planning is one of the most stable of the three planning levels (yearly, theme, daily), and will not have

Table 5-10

Example of Modified Plan: Yearly Outline 5th Grade

(Each weekly block below is laid out across the days M | T | W | T | F, with many activities spanning Monday–Tuesday and Thursday–Friday.)

Table 1

Week	M / T	W	T / F
1	Introduction	Games	Low Organization
2	Rhythms/Dance	Cooperative	Games
3	Football/Flickerball	Gymnast Stunts	Football/Flickerball
4	Football	Gymnast Stunts	Football
5	FB Test Fit.	Gymnast Stunts	Testing Fitness
6	Individual Games	Gymnast Stunts	Individual Games

Table 2

Week	M / T	W	T / F
1	Partner Games	Rhythm Dance	Partner Games
2	Soccer	Rhythm Dance	Soccer
3	Soccer	Gymnastics Stunts	Soccer
4	Dance*	Gymnastics Stunts	Dance / ⊠
5	Dance	Gymnastics Stunts	Dance
6	Partner Games	Gymnastics Stunts	Partner Games

Table 3

Week	M / T	W	T / F
1	Basketball	Rhythms/Dance	Basketball
2	Basketball	Rhythms/Dance	Basketball
3	Gymnastics	Rhythms/Dance	Gymnastics
4	Tumbling & Stunts	Rhythms/Dance	Tumbling & Stunts
5	Volleyball	Rhythms/Dance	Volleyball
6	Volleyball	Rhythms/Dance	Volleyball

Table 4

Week	M / T	W	T / F
1	Gymnastics Tumbling	Games Cooperative Indiv./Partner	& Stunts
2	Dance	Games Cooperative Indiv./Partner	Dance / ⊠
3	Choice**	Games Cooperative Indiv./Partner	of
4	Team	Games Cooperative Indiv./Partner	Game(s)
5	Floor/Field Hockey	Games Cooperative Indiv./Partner	Floor/Field Hockey
6	Floor/Field Hockey	Games Cooperative Indiv./Partner	Floor Field Hockey

Table 5

Week	M / T	W	T / F
1	Individual Games	Gymnastics Small Equipment	Partner Games
2	Partner Games	Gymnastics Small Equipment	Partner Games
3	Dance	Gymnastics Small Equipment	Dance
4	Dance	Gymnastics Small Equipment	Dance / ⊠
5	Softball	Gymnastics Small Equipment	Softball
6	Softball	Gymnastics Small Equipment	Softball

Table 6

Week	M / T	W	T	F
1	Gymnastics	Dance	Gym	⊠
2	Large	Dance	Apparatus	
3	Track	Dance	Fitness Testing	
4	Fitness Test	Track & Field		
5	Track		Field	
6		—Field Days—		

	Days	Percent
Games	100	61
Dance	30	19
Gymnastics	32	20
180 − 18* =	162 days	100 %

* Dance (rhythms, creative, folk, square, aerobic).

** Additional Team Games (e.g., team handball, korfball, speedball).

* 18 "non-theme" days (introduction, testing, inservice days, field days).

Table 5-11

Example of Solid/Modified Plan: Yearly Outline 6th Grade

1

	M	T	W	T	F
1	Introduction		Games Low Organization		Dance
2	Gymnastics		Football/Flickerball		
3			Football/Flickerball		
4					✕
5	Testing		Fitness	Gym.	
6	Gymnastics				Dance

2

	M	T	W	T	F
1		Individual/Partner Games			
2			Soccer		
3			Soccer		
4			Gymnastics		✕
5			Gymnastics		
6			Dance		Gym

3

	M	T	W	T	F
1		Basketball			Gymnastics
2		Basketball			Gymnastics
3		Dance			Gymnastics
4	✕	Dance			Gymnastics
5		Volleyball			Gymnastics
6		Volleyball			Gymnastics

4

	M	T	W	T	F
1			Gymnastics		✕
2			Dance		
3			Dance		
4			Field/Floor		Dance
5			Hockey		Dance
6			Gymnastics		

5

	M	T	W	T	F
1		Individual/Partner Games			
2			Dance		
3			Gymnastics		
4			Dance		✕
5			Softball		
6			Softball		

6

	M	T	W	T	F
1		Gymnastics			Dance
2		Individual/Partner Games			
3		Dance		Fitness Testing	
4	Gymnastics			Track/Field	
5			Track/Field		
6		—Field Days—			

	Days	Percent
Games	81	50
Dance	41	25
Gymnastics	40	25
180 – 18* =	162 days	100%

*18 "non-theme" days (introduction, testing, inservice days, field days).

to be repeated each year. Of course, the conscientious teacher will want to update the skill-development and enhancement-activity sections if she/he discovers specific items in these two areas inappropriate for her/his students. This type of updating should be ongoing and will not entail recreating the entire theme packet; other elements of the theme are fairly constant. Each theme should reflect all that is needed to enhance the development of that particular skill. The contents of a skill-theme packet are as follows:

CONTENT OF THEMES:

1. Instructional objectives
2. Organizational procedures
3. Safety reminders
4. Equipment (items and quantity)
5. Special contingency plans
6. Evaluation procedures
7. Skill development/movement variability activities
8. Enhancement activities
9. Culminating activity
10. References

Instructional objectives are statements that describe the expected performance of students after they have *completed a unit of instruction*. These objectives, although they describe student behavior, are not as specific as the behavioral objectives of daily

lesson plans. Objectives are written to describe expected performance in the psychomotor, affective, and cognitive areas as they relate to the theme topic. A more detailed section on writing objectives is presented later in the chapter.

Organizational procedures are most thoroughly dealt with in the daily lesson plan. However, the following organizational decisions are part of theme development and should be included in the theme packet:

1. Possible teaching style selections;
2. Possible organizational pattern selections;
3. Visual, written, and auditory task stimuli. (Mini-posters on 8 ½ × 11 paper make excellent references for larger posters, which can be developed later when needed for daily lessons.)

Safety reminders are both specific to the theme being taught and to general safety rules pertinent to the class at all times. Safety awareness is just as relevant to the child as it is to the teacher. Design posters for the class that reflect safety.

Equipment needed for the entire theme should be listed, as well as quantities needed for each item based on number of students in the class and available equipment. Posters and other visual aids can also be included in this list.

Special contingency plans are always needed when the children are scheduled to play outside, especially when there is a possibility of bad weather. These alternative plans should include activities that will continue to enhance stated objectives relevant to that theme. With a kicking theme, for example, many eye-foot activities such as jumping rope, hopscotch, and hackey sack would be appropriate in more limited space areas. In addition, during teaching of themes normally taught in the gym, the class might experience interruptions in which the gymnasium is needed for other activities (such as setting up voting booths for elections). This possibility should also be considered during the planning of each theme, and plans should be formulated so that as little disruption as possible will be experienced by students. For example, during a rhythms theme in which children are learning to use their bodies and small equipment (balls, streamers) in rhythm to music, an appropriate alternative activity (for use in a small area like a hallway or classroom) might be tapping balloons or lummi sticks in rhythm to chants or music.

Further plans might also include procedures appropriate for larger-than-usual classes in the gym. When the teacher(s) finds it necessary to combine two classes in a space usually reserved for one, it may or may not be possible to continue with instruction that will enhance the objectives of the present theme. During such times, the use of stations are more desirable than mass games for larger groups.

Evaluation procedures for assessing student performance and progress should be described in detail and examples of all task sheets and/or skill tests contained in each theme (see Chapter 8, Evaluation, for suggestions).

Skill development/movement variability activities focus on "variability in practice" as interpreted from Schmidt and others (see Chapter 3). Activities to be included in this part of the theme are created by varying the skill around the four dimensions presented in Table 5-12.

Although somewhat similar to the movement concepts (that is, movement analysis model) proposed by Laban and modified by others, this model represents a practical interpretation of schema theory with the addition of the authors' preference for the "relationships" concept found in other curricular models.

In Chapters 10–13 a large number of movement possibilities (movement variability) are listed which were derived from the above dimensions. In the theme plan these variations must be translated into activities and listed in order of complexity. Translating the movement variability into movement challenges (or problems) is the best generally accepted method for accomplishing this transition. For example, in a throwing theme at Level II an appropriate challenge might be to have the child see how many different directions a ball can be thrown using an overhand pattern. In a running theme, Level I children can be challenged to see how many different ways they can hold their arms when they run. The number of movement-variability tasks for a given theme is limitless. The challenge for the teacher lies in developing interesting movement problems that will motivate children to explore ever more varied movements—thereby strengthening their movement schema.

Enhancement activities are chosen from the areas of games, dance, or gymnastics. Every effort must be made by the teacher to choose enhancement activities that will best help the students test out and enjoy the skills they are acquiring in a dynamic environment. Enhancement activities are listed at the end of each skill chapter. Each theme should have a variety of enhancement activities listed (with references) for each skill level. Each lesson drawn from the theme utilizes one or more of these enhancement activities.

The culminating activity is planned as the last movement experience for each theme taught. This is not the same as an enhancement or final activity of a daily lesson. The culminating activity is much more involved and may take as long as three to four days (field day or tournament), an hour (PTA program) or entire class period (class contest or creative dance routine). Only one culminating activity need be planned for each theme. In most cases, the entire class performs as a unit. This activity is normally a creative experience for the younger children (entire class performing a movement rendition of a fairy tale) or it may be a low-key contest for older stu-

---

Table 5-12

Theme Development Movement-Variability Phase (Schema Enhancement)

DIMENSIONS

SPATIAL (variation in movement pattern)

Basic Patterns
Direction (path of movement)
   up/down   forward/backward
   left/right   zigzag   curved
Levels (height at which movement
   is performed)
   low/medium/high

FORCE (amount of muscular exertion)

light to heavy
related to: distance/height projected
             size/weight of objects
             manipulated

TIME (speed at which movement is performed)

   slow motion to fast
   sudden/sustained
   smooth/jerky (also known as "flow"
   of movement)

RELATIONSHIPS (movement with objects and/or
                people)

Objects   small equipment/large equipment
            (attached and apart)
People   solo/partner/group/mass

dents (entire class involved in an obstacle course relay or a mini-track meet). Seasonal and PTA programs that involve one or all grade levels of the school offer fine opportunities for a single culminating activity of skills learned over a period of time. Keep in mind that this single event is an option available to the teacher, who will make the decision to use or not use it on an individual class basis. Another point to keep in mind is that one culminating activity containing multiple challenges (like a mini-track meet) could serve all four levels.

References should include specific music from specific albums, texts, tapes, and other sources.

It should be quite evident that the development of movement-awareness and fundamental-skill themes is a creative task for the teacher. After completing several of these themes, however, the teacher will be accustomed to the format, and the time required to plan such a theme will decrease. The teacher who has a file of well-developed themes possesses an indepth and task-specific resource library from which effective daily lessons can be planned. Well-developed themes normally can be used year after year with minimal updating required.

Other aspects of theme planning to consider are:

1. Most teachers will find it more efficient and appropriate to pair certain fundamental skills (*e.g.*, jumping and landing, swinging and swaying, pushing and pulling, twisting and turning, stretching and bending).

2. Even though such themes as throwing and catching and kicking and trapping are usually performed together, because of their complexity they are focused upon individually during early learning periods (Levels I and II).

3. Themes should also be developed around the health-related physical fitness components: cardiorespiratory endurance, muscular strength, endurance, and flexibility (see Chapter 14).

UNIT PLANNING

The unit plan is the most frequently used second level tool (yearly plans are the first level) for organizing instructional materials for Levels III and IV. A unit is a resource packet focusing on a specific game, such as frisbee golf; concept such as physical fitness or sportsmanship; sport such as volleyball; dance such as square or folk; or gymnastics. It is important to note, however, that themes can and should still be used when warranted with teaching units. In this case, movement variability can play a significant role in the development of sport-skill proficiency as used in the ever-changing conditions of dynamic games. For example, within a lesson where the skill of base running is going to be the sport skill theme, the variability of practice includes change of speeds, levels, and directions. The contents of a unit are almost identical to that found in a skill-theme packet (refer to the previous section for a more detailed discussion on items 1, 2, 4, 6, 11).

CONTENT OF UNITS:

1. Instructional objectives
2. Organizational procedures
3. Safety reminders
4. Equipment (items and quantity)
5. Special contingency plans
6. Evaluation procedures
7. Skill development—scope and sequence
8. Enhancement activities
9. Culminating activity
10. Block plan
11. References

Safety reminders are specific to the unit being taught. For example, gymnastics, softball, and gym hockey have specific safety concerns that are inherent to those activities. General safety reminders that are pertinent to the physical education class at all times should also be stated. Children at grades 4, 5, and 6 should be expected to demonstrate a relatively mature concern for safety at all times. Posters designed to emphasize safety should be utilized.

Special contingency plans are always needed when the weather impinges on the play area. Regardless of where the unit will be taught, special contingency plans should be indicated. One never knows when a particular teaching station will be unavailable. These plans, which are alternatives, should include activities that will continue to enhance the stated objectives of the unit with some being appropriate for small areas, classroom, and double-sized classes.

Let's consider a basketball unit for sixth graders. Examples of appropriate activities that would continue to enhance those skills specifically needed for basketball might include:

Juggling—for eye-hand coordination;

Jumping rope—for leg strength and endurance, cardiorespiratory endurance, eye-foot coordination, rhythm, agility, dynamic balance;

Speed passing (nerf balls)—for eye-hand coordination, reaction-time, deception.

Skill development for the unit should be listed as scope (the breadth of skills to be learned) and sequence (the progressive order of presentation). The authors suggest listing all the skills in order, from simple to complex. For example, the spike and overarm serve in a volleyball unit would be listed in the scope but not necessarily taught to a Level III student. Modifications for each skill level can be easily implemented.

Enhancement activities will include lead-up games, cooperative games, creative games/dance, structured dance, gymnastics routines, and sometimes the regulation sport.

The culminating activity is planned as a cooperative, creative, or competitive event to close the unit. The following culminating activity possibilities can be considered:

Sports Units—tournament, playday, field day, student-faculty competitive game, intramurals

Dance Units—PTA program, open house, school assembly, community demonstration, small group competition, marathon dance, after school, ethnic programs

Gymnastic Units—competitive routine, PTA program, open house, basketball/volleyball halftimes (at the junior or senior high school), intramurals

The block plan is a schematic representation of the unit on a day to day basis. Each grade level will have a separate block plan. Only the "what" to be taught is written for each day, the "how" is a function of the daily lesson plan.

Obviously, developing a teaching unit is no easy task. However, like the theme packet, once developed the teacher has a valuable resource from which will spring many lessons for several grades and ability levels. Minimal updating will be required for well developed sports, dance, and gymnastic units.

Writing Objectives

Writing objectives are often viewed by beginning teachers and some seasoned teachers as a futile exercise. The authors value objectives, however, for several reasons:

1. Objectives help to organize the learning material.
2. Developmentally appropriate objectives that identify specific behavioral outcomes provide the teachers with realistic assessment criteria.

3. Specific objectives demonstrate that the teacher believes in teacher accountability.
4. When children are aware of the objectives they are better able to understand the "education" of physical education.
5. Written objectives help to keep the "educational team" (principal, teachers, students) on track.
6. Objectives enable teachers to be more prescriptive to specific situations and more sensitive to interpersonal relations between the teacher and student and among the students themselves.

EACH OBJECTIVE STATES:

1. **Who** (the student) will do
2. **What** (the observable skill or behavior—*e.g.*, jump) under what
3. **Conditions** (rope on the ground) and to what
4. **Degree** of competency (eight consecutive) to indicate a minimum (average) level of success.

The following are examples of (1) general (nonmeasurable) objectives and (2) specific (measurable) objectives:

1. The students should know how to jump rope.
2. At the end of the year, while using a rope stretched out on the ground, kindergarten students will repeatedly jump back and forth over the rope for eight consecutive successful jumps.

Notice that the measurable objective states what the students will do, rather than what they should be able to do. By writing this objective the teacher is saying that all of the kindergarten children are expected to develop the skill to enable them to jump back and forth over a rope resting on the ground. Furthermore, each student is expected to be able to jump for eight consecutive jumps without mistakes. The following are examples of affective, cognitive, and fitness objectives (non-measurable and measurable).

AFFECTIVE

1. The students should be good sports (nonmeasurable).
2. The third-grade students will demonstrate good sportsmanship by taking turns while performing jump-rope skills and turning the rope (measurable).

COGNITIVE

1. The students will chant while jumping rope (nonmeasurable).
2. The fourth-grade students will chant (without cues) three of the four jump-rope chants previously taught (measurable).

FITNESS

1. The students will become more physically fit (nonmeasurable).
2. The fifth-grade students will demonstrate an improvement in their level of cardiorespiratory endurance by jumping continuously (with or without a rope) for one minute longer than performed at the beginning of the semester pretest (measurable).

Specific objectives obviously require more thoughtful preparation than general objectives. However, if the accomplishment of an objective is to be an indicator of success, then the objective must be measurable. In order to be measurable, it must be specific. Both teacher and student can measure success or failure when both know the performance expectations. When an objective is conquered, the next higher objective in the progression is attempted.

All of the above are examples of instructional objectives (expected performance outcome of students who have completed a *unit* of instruction).

Behavioral objectives follow the same format of Who, What, Conditions, and Degree; however, they indicate the desired performance outcome at the end of a class period. The following examples are offered as possible behavioral objectives for a gymnastic unit. You will note that in some content areas the performance objectives even offer a built-in safety mechanism. For example, if students know that prior to attempting a fully extended headstand they must satisfy the behavioral objective of " . . . complete 10 tripod lift-ups (knees lifted from elbows) without hesitation . . . ," the teacher has eliminated the famous "crick in my neck" and "fell flat on my back" hazards that suddenly appear. During the tripod lift-ups, the neck, back, and arms are being strengthened and the sense of balance enhanced. At the completion of that behavioral objective the students can safely go on to the next, more difficult objective (*e.g.*, the fully extended headstand). Another advantage of writing these specific performance objectives is that the teacher is forced to focus on the critical criteria for successful performance, and then teach the skills in a safe progression that stimulates healthy practice sessions leading to more rapid success for the individual student. One more comment about objectives: it is beneficial to let students know the objectives of the lesson. This serves several purposes. Objectives:

1. Help keep students and teacher focused on the goals of the lesson.
2. Promote the "education" in physical education.
3. Help students realize that their physical education teacher values the lessons they plan and the children they teach.
4. Encourage the development of goal awareness and self-assessment in the children.

5. Provide a yardstick with which to measure daily progress of the class. A short critique focusing on which objectives were and were not accomplished offers excellent content for the "huddle phase" of the lesson, and a starting place for ensuing lessons.

The following list of verbs will assist the teacher in writing behavioral objectives for physical education classes.

BEHAVIORAL VERBS FOR PHYSICAL EDUCATION (EXAMPLES)

PSYCHOMOTOR DOMAIN

bat	hold	stretch
bend	hop	strike
bounce	jump	sway
catch	kick	swim
chase	leap	swing
clap	pull	throw
climb	punch	toss
crawl	push	trap
dodge	roll	turn
gallop	run	twist
grab	skip	walk
grip	slide	
hit	stamp	

COGNITIVE DOMAIN

assess		
check	describe	measure
circle	evaluate	name
copy	identify	question
count	list	show
define	match	state
demonstrate	ask	tell

AFFECTIVE DOMAIN

ask	complete	participate
attempt	cooperate	praise
challenge	defend	share
choose	evaluate	suggest
	offer	tolerate

DAILY PLANNING

At the third level of planning the daily lesson is developed. The daily lesson plan is a flexible yet highly specific and detailed outline of one day's lesson for each grade level. This plan, like the yearly plan, is developed on a grade level basis because that is the

Table 5-13

Physical Education Daily Lesson Plan

THEME _____ LESSON _____ GRADE _____ # _____

EQUIPMENT _____

SAFETY PRECAUTIONS _____

OBJECTIVES _____

_____

_____

_____

_____

_____

_____

REFERENCES _____

_____

_____

Time (min.)   Area Layout

_____   (⅛) FITNESS:

_____   (⅜) SKILL DEVELOPMENT/MOVEMENT VARIABILITY:

_____   ENHANCEMENT:
                              (As skill proficiency is acquired more time should be
                              allowed for this phase)

_____   HUDDLE:

EVALUATION: _____

way children are grouped for physical education. However, it is important to remember that within one class as many as three distinct skill proficiency levels can exist. Therefore, it is at this level of planning (individualized daily planning) that the teacher really meets the needs of all the children.

The information on the daily lesson plan will be drawn directly from the theme and unit resource packets, and arranged in a way the teacher determines will most appropriately meet instructional objectives for a particular class. There will be a degree of similarity among classes at each grade level, so the teacher may devise one plan for the first grade as long as desired variations for individual classes within that grade level are noted on the plan. There are four phases common to all lesson plans:

> Health-Related Fitness
> Skill-Development
> Enhancement
> Huddle

The generally accepted time allotments for a typical physical education lesson are one third health-related fitness, two thirds skill development and enhancement combined, with at least one minute reserved for a "huddle" or summary. The amount of time devoted to each phase, however, is flexible and highly dependent upon the established instructional objectives for each day—as well as the amount of time allotted for physical education by a specific school district. For example, given a 30-minute lesson in which the primary objective is to elevate the heart rate for a sufficient time to achieve a training effect, it would be necessary to devote at least 20 minutes toward this objective, thereby leaving only 10 minutes for the remaining parts of the lesson. Another very typical example is the degree of flexibility among skill-development and enhancement phases needed—especially at Levels III and IV where more complex skills and enhancements are being developed. Following a fitness phase, it is not uncommon to have a lesson completely devoted to skill development (frequently gymnastics lessons) or completely devoted to enhancements (frequently sports and folk dance lessons). Moreover, some daily lesson plans (especially those involving stations) will have sufficient content material to warrant their use for two days.

Daily Lesson Plan Content

Table 5-13 presents a suggested daily lesson plan form. Many teachers prefer to devise their own forms. However, the authors believe that certain specific information is necessary for the smooth execution of a daily lesson, and that information should be common to all lesson plans.

Theme or unit title will come from the areas of movement awareness, fundamental skills, games, individual and team sports, dance, gymnastics, or fitness. Theme titles may include: body awareness, running, or throwing. Unit titles may include: soccer, folk dance, or large apparatus. Fitness titles may include: cardiorespiratory endurance, agility, or flexibility.

Lesson title will reflect the focus of one day's lesson. A theme focus for running might be pathways or pattern variations. A unit focus for soccer might be dribbling or position play.

Grade level and *Class Number* are listed on the lesson plan along with class period (for example, third period, second grade, 32 students).

Equipment needed indicates not only what equipment is needed for that lesson but also quantity of each item. Audio-visual teaching aids should be included.

Safety precautions that are specific to that lesson are listed. General class rules for safety should be posted where they can be seen daily.

Objectives covering all three domains (psychomotor, affective, and cognitive) are stated in *behavioral terms* (remember, theme/unit objectives were stated as instructional objectives). Clear and concisely stated behavioral objectives become tools for assessment at various times during the lessons. An efficient method for stating behavioral objectives on lesson plans is to make the initial statement of "The student will" followed by the desired performance, conditions, and criteria for successful completion of each behavioral objective (for example, while standing five feet away, catch five out of eight beanbags tossed by a partner). Classes with children who have special needs may require additional and/or modified behavioral objectives (and equipment).

References will include all resources used to complete the lesson plan. Good lesson plans can be used year after year with only minimum modifications. Accurate references are valuable timesavers.

Area layout indicates the spatial organization for the class and the teacher. The diagram should include where the children will be as well as equipment, traffic patterns, positions of stations, and so forth. The teacher's position should be fluid most of the time. Beginning teachers will want to note the most advantageous locations for effectiveness of instruction, safety, and other supervisory needs.

The Four Phases of the Daily Lesson

The following section will focus on each phase of the daily lesson plan and relate to the skill proficiency levels (I–IV). Keep in mind that the primary tool for the execution of the theme and unit is the daily lesson plan. It is at this level that ideas from the curricular model are put into practice.

HEALTH-RELATED FITNESS PHASE

As stressed throughout the text, the development of health-related physical fitness is a primary goal of the overall elementary program.

In this phase of the lesson, activities are presented that are based on specific fitness objectives that have been formulated to develop a physically fit child. In Chapter 4 the concepts and rationale that are used to formulate objectives, and several systematic plans (general models) for integration into the overall curriculum, were presented. Ideally, a five-day plan is used when there is adequate time (45–60 min) to accomplish motor skill and fitness objectives. Approximately one third to one half of the session should focus on specific fitness components. Mondays, Wednesdays, and Fridays the aerobic component could be emphasized, and on Tuesdays and Thursdays flexibility and muscular strength/endurance stressed. Specific component emphasis for this plan does not imply that other components should not be incorporated into the activity; it implies primary emphasis. If the three-day or separate-day format were used, specific component emphasis would not be as concentrated. With these formats, the goal of each lesson is to provide activities that stimulate all three health-related components. Due to the importance of this portion of the curriculum, Chapters 4 and 14 address the specific needs of this phase of the lesson. Included in Chapter 14 are basic instructional procedures, exercise precautions, activity formats, suggestions for selecting activities (based upon fitness value), and descriptions of activities used to develop health– and skill-related fitness components. Refer to Chapters 4 and 14 for detailed discussions specific to this phase of the daily lesson plan.

The following reminders are offered:

1. Select a systematic plan for implementing fitness objectives.
2. Instructions should be brief but clear.
3. Maximum participation is essential; there should be little or no waiting in line or other delays.
4. The use of music can enhance motivation and smoothness of movement.
5. If games or obstacle courses are used, they should already be known or require minimal instruction.
6. Use a variety of fun activities to maintain interest.
7. Begin with moderately vigorous movement, quickly moving to more vigorous demands for the children. Opportunities for individual pacing should be provided if needed.
8. Strive toward 15–20 minutes of continuous aerobic activity three times a week.
9. The entire class period should be paced so that the activity demand will appropriately stimulate the development of health-related fitness.

TEACHER'S ROLE DURING THE FITNESS PHASE OF THE LESSON

1. Be an enthusiastic motivator.
2. Have the area ready when students arrive.
3. Begin quickly (brief but clear directions). Save game and dance teaching for skill development.
4. Use music at every opportunity.
5. Encourage pacing when needed by individual students.
6. Praise good effort as evidenced by accelerated breathing, rosy cheeks, accelerated heart rate, and perspiration.
7. Teach the children how to locate their "heart beat" (chest, neck, wrist).

SKILL-DEVELOPMENT PHASE

Movement variability (Levels I–II) is the nucleus of the daily lesson in the "Building the Foundation" curriculum. It is during the movement-variability phase that students are provided with a variety of opportunities to explore, experiment, and test out the many ways a particular fundamental skill can be performed. During this phase there exists a laboratory-type of attitude with the teacher and students in partnership as they use specific skills in a variety of predictable and unpredictable situations. In this way each child updates his or her functional-movement vocabulary.

Through the variables of space, force, time, and relationships with objects and other people, the students continue to develop their personal schema of concepts and movement patterns that will enable them to respond more efficiently and effectively to both novel and familiar movement challenges. The students receive the challenges or problems verbally or through the use of task sheets (or posters). The predominant teaching styles are guided discovery and problem solving. It is important that the teacher overplan this phase of the lesson, for it is better to have too many challenges than to run out of ideas!

The movement-variability challenges and problems are extremely important and should be written with care. The teacher should begin by first recalling all of the performance characteristics that exemplify the mature, proficient movement pattern of that specific skill. The beginning teacher may even want to write down these characteristics. Take running, for example. The characteristics described in the skill chapter include:

1. Slight forward lean of the trunk;
2. Arms swing vertically in opposition to the legs;
3. The support foot hits the ground rather flat and close to the center of gravity;
4. The knee of the support leg bends slightly after contact;
5. The driving leg extends at the hip, knee, and ankle;
6. The recovery knee quickly comes forward as, simultaneously, the lower portion of the same leg draws the foot toward the buttocks.

With a clear understanding of what the mature form is supposed to look like, the teacher is ready to begin listing the variability opportunities. At this point it is necessary for the teacher to consider all the uses of that skill and how those movement requirements can be reproduced in the physical education class. Then the teacher will consider varying the use of that specific skill (running) through the applications of the variables—time, space, force, and relationships. The list of challenges/problems will represent a rather complete sample of challenges and movement problems appropriate for the various skill levels represented by children. Teachers should consider the children moving along a continuum from simple to complex skill proficiency. In a single class there will be children performing at various stages along that continuum. Each child's progress can be facilitated or hindered by the movement demands made during the movement-variability phase. Therefore the listing of challenges/problems should be from simple to complex and stated in general terms, so each child can become a versatile successful problem-solver while operating at his/her individual level.

The challenges presented to the children should stimulate them to apply what they know about the skill, and use that skill in ways they may not have thought of before (*e.g.*, "Can you run faster when your body leans forward or backward?" "What happens to your speed if you hold your arms down at your sides while running?"). Each skill chapter in this text provides many cues to the teacher as stimuli for development of imaginative and realistic movement-variability challenges.

The following are examples of throwing challenges (and the variability focus) appropriate for Levels I through II (See Table 5-12).

Level I—How many different ways can you throw the beanbag? Can you throw the beanbag over your head (space)? Can you throw the beanbag behind you (direction)?

Level II—Can you throw the ball to the wall fast three times (time)? How far can you throw the ball (force)? How many times can you and your

partner throw the ball to one another without mistakes (relationships)? Can you throw the ball to your partner's knees (level)?

For Levels III–IV, skill development is the portion of the lesson in the "Utilization of the Foundation" curriculum in which new skills are introduced, and both new and old skills are practiced. Though similar to Levels I and II in that the student must be given a wide variety of challenges, there is also a major change in focus within each skill. The focus now moves from refinement of fundamental skills into developing specific skills required for success in a given game/sport, dance, or gymnastic activity. Let's carry the throwing example through Levels III and IV.

Level III—Can you hit a target while running towards it (space, direction, rhythm)? While stationary and being guarded, can you throw the ball to your moving partner (space, direction, time, relationships)?

Level IV—While trying to avoid an opponent can you successfully pass to a partner, causing your partner to reach (high, to either side, low) for the ball (space, time, force, relationships)?

Traditionally this has been a time of extensive use of enhancement activities since the children are able to use their fundamental skills well enough to play the game. However, growing discrepancies between skill performance levels limit excessive use of game and sports enhancement activities. Due to the nature of skill demands in dance and gymnastics, this is less often a problem. In order to dance the "Cotton-Eyed Joe," you must be able to perform the steps in sequential order and in rhythm to the music. Similarly, in gymnastics you need to know several specific gymnastics skills such as the forward roll, cartwheel, and front scale prior to being able to construct a routine.

The challenge to the teacher is to plan creative ways to keep the children interested in skills practice so proficiency of each of the fundamental skills is justifiably improved. Each child should demonstrate improvement in each fundamental skill each year, and teachers should be held accountable for this learning. This improvement should lead to more effective performance in the enhancement areas of games/sports, dance, and gymnastics. The skills can be presented using a variety of teaching styles, depending on the complexity of the movements required. Using more complex movement-variability challenges with a problem-solving or guided-discovery style will serve to strengthen the child's schema—especially at Level III. However, many complex skills will require a more direct approach. That is, a demonstration highlighting specific skill points followed by a directed skill practice or drill.

This portion of the lesson must be well organized so that specific skill objectives may be realized.

THE FOLLOWING REMINDERS ARE OFFERED:

1. Move quickly from the fitness phase to the skill-development phase. Equipment must be ready and instructions should be brief. Difficult transitions should be noted on the lesson plan to ensure the teacher has thought through the procedure for moving from one phase to the next.
2. When demonstrating, give at least two full views employing both slow speed and operational speed.
3. Observe critically for possible formation of inefficient skill habits (for example, arms and legs not in opposition when throwing a beanbag), and be ready to employ guided-discovery techniques to facilitate movement toward more efficient skill.
4. Be imaginative when posing variability challenges through the use of space, time, force, and relationships.
5. Liberal use of various equipment facilitates more intensive practice.
6. Refrain from stating the challenges in the same way or using the same drills day after day.
7. Respond to the children's movement with appropriate feedback techniques. Remember, there can be secondary learning by children on the periphery if feedback is given so that several children can hear.
8. Create drills for Level IV students that incorporate some of the requirements of the actual game/sport.
9. Incorporate key skill points into feedback remarks.

THE TEACHER'S ROLE DURING THE SKILL-DEVELOPMENT PHASE OF THE LESSON

1. Clarify the challenges to those who indicate this need.
2. Motivate all students to full participation.
3. Encourage unique (rather than only the familiar) movement solutions for Levels I and II.
4. Guide the students towards proper body mechanics for the efficient execution of the more specific skills required for utilization of the foundation.
5. Observe constantly and give accurate feedback on skill attempts and affective behavior.
6. Use every teachable movement in a positive manner.

ENHANCEMENT PHASE

Although not every lesson will necessarily end with an enhancement activity, (*i.e.*, the skill-development phase may continue for the duration of the class period), the enhancement phase is considered by the authors to be a very complementary part of the lesson that can add significantly to the development of each skill. When approximately 80 percent of the children are able to perform the skills being practiced with some semblance of accuracy (see Chapter 8), a carefully chosen enhancement activity can further this development in an enjoyable way. Skills are reinforced as they are used in dynamic games, dance activities, or gymnastics skills.

Enhancement activities for Levels I–II are focused on the theme being developed. In one example, the children have been participating in a balance theme and have become relatively proficient in balancing on low beams while in various static and dynamic positions, and can also combine locomotor movements and balance activities. These skills could then be enhanced as the students are taught how to use the mini-trampoline. Indeed, they would use many of the same movements while balancing on the trampoline and in the air. Likewise, a game such as "Stop and Go" would provide opportunities for enhancing the development of balance skills. Performing the dance "Seven Jumps" would offer additional opportunities to demonstrate balance skills. Through participation in this organized activity the students are able to use the skill(s) they have been developing in a dynamic way, thereby moving that development to a higher level. Again, it is important for the teacher to overplan this segment of the lesson. If one enhancement activity proves to be inappropriate for that particular group of students, another can be introduced immediately. Although teachers often prefer those activities with which they are most familiar, every effort should be made to plan a variety of activities that will draw from all three content areas of games, gymnastics, and dance.

Level III–IV enhancement activities are chosen to utilize the skills being developed in the game/sport, dance, or gymnastics unit. Care should be taken to ensure there is an appropriate relationship of drill to enhancement. This transition is most important for early success to occur—especially in dynamic game situations. For example, a lesson utilizing a static passing drill followed by a game with opponents requiring more dynamic movements would not promote early success. On the other hand, use of a transition game without opponents requiring dynamic movement would be a more natural progression. The following reminders are offered:

1. Enhancement is a means to an end (namely, skill development) not an end in itself.

2. Evidence of adequate skill development should be demonstrated by at least 80 percent of the class prior to moving from the skill development to the enhancement phase.

3. Variety of enhancement activities from games, dance, and gymnastics for Levels I–II is very important.

4. A progressive relationship of drill to enhancement activity must exist at Levels III–IV.

5. In order to promote the use of games and dances during away-from-school time, children must know the games and dances well.

6. Allow for a demonstration or a trial run of relays, tag games, and other similar activities so that all students have a functional understanding of what will be required of them. Older students may only need a demonstration, while younger students usually require a practice prior to the real event. Remember, if you allow one of the teams to demonstrate a relay or other competitive event, that specific team will have an advantage over the other teams. A trial run for all teams is usually the fairest and often the safest choice for the teacher to make. Children with inadequate skill development should not be expected to participate in competitive events. The teacher's choice is either to schedule competitive and cooperative events simultaneously and let the students choose, or to avoid the competitive events until all the children have the appropriate skill development.

7. Children can choose appropriate enhancement activities if they are encouraged and educated to do so.

THE TEACHER'S ROLE DURING THE ENHANCEMENT PHASE OF THE LESSON

1. Have all needed equipment ready and the area marked off appropriately (use of ropes, bases, or cones is most efficient).

2. Divide the class (if necessary) quickly and fairly.

3. Explain the event and safety procedures clearly and quickly (use of visuals can speed up this process).

4. Ask specific questions to evaluate students' understanding of the events. To ask "Are there any questions?" is not nearly as effective as "Raise your hand if you can explain how you will know how someone is 'it.'"

5. Encourage students to show their support for the winning team by clapping for the winners, and teach the winners to congratulate their opponents for their good effort, fair play, and team spirit.

6. Encourage cooperative play among team members by praising this behavior when it is demonstrated by the students.

7. Initiate variations in the event when needed to provide opportunities for maximum participation.

8. Be constantly aware of possible safety hazards.

9. Cease the activity on time, allowing for a one-minute "huddle" before dismissal.

10. Officiate quickly and decisively when necessary.

11. Make changes or simply cease an enhancement activity that is not providing opportunities for skill development.

HUDDLE PHASE (REVIEW AND FEEDBACK)

The last few minutes of each class period can bring a very special closure to the daily lesson. The teacher calls the children to "huddle" and discusses what went on during that day's lesson. This phase provides an opportunity for teacher and students to relate to one another on a more personal level. Remarks may focus on a number of items, including skill and affective behaviors. It is best to stress the positive events that occurred. However, it is also correct to talk about inappropriate behaviors and discuss the advantages of appropriate behaviors versus possible consequences if the inappropriate behavior continues (relating this to the standing class rules for such behaviors). The teacher might also want to mention the events planned for the next day's lesson.

THE FOLLOWING REMINDERS ARE OFFERED:

1. This is a time for enhancing affective and cognitive skills.

2. All equipment should be placed aside prior to coming to the huddle. When outdoors this may mean some of the children in the last class of the day will bring the cones and balls with them to the huddle where they will be placed to one side.

THE TEACHER'S ROLE DURING THE HUDDLE PHASE OF THE LESSON:

1. Provide an accepting atmosphere where the children will feel free to express themselves.

2. Ensure that the lesson ends on a high note even if that psychological high is simply a promise by all to try their best tomorrow! (Remember The Little Train That Could?)

3. State all expectations clearly so the children understand what is expected of them.

4. Insist that the transition from enhancement phase to huddle phase is executed quickly.

5. Allow the children to verbalize their enjoyment of the lesson *and* what they learned. This can be accomplished by referring back to the objectives for the lesson. Ask the children, "How many were able to catch the ball five times?"

EVALUATION

At the end of each class period (or, more realistically, for elementary teachers this will be done at the end of the day) the teacher should evaluate the progress of each class in meeting the objectives of the lesson. This evaluation is important not only for making adjustments to the next lesson but also for next year's plan. There is no need to keep making the same mistakes year after year regarding progressions, methodology, or activity selections.

GENERAL SUGGESTIONS FOR THE TEACHER

1. View planning as one of several keys to being an effective teacher. To quote one sage, "Work will win where wishing won't."

2. Most of the educational settings are on a rigid time schedule; therefore, appropriate planning is crucial.

3. Flexibility is a necessity for teacher and students alike. Yearly and daily plans are meant to serve as guidelines—*flexible* guidelines.

4. By Thursday of each week the plans for the coming week should be completed.

5. A short period of time each day should be spent reviewing what will be taught the following day and checking on the necessary supplies and equipment. Some teachers prefer the time prior to leaving their campus each day, while others prefer early morning planning.

6. Preplanning provides the teacher with a more trouble-free teaching experience than if plans are left till the last minute when it may be too late to secure needed equipment, facilities, etc.

7. Students should be given the opportunity to provide feedback to the teacher regarding their likes and dislikes. However, the teacher is responsible for the year's goals and objectives being met through a curriculum that allows skills to be taught and learned.

8. Teachers who realize the value to the total educational experience will become enthusiastic about planning the yearly curriculum, movement-awareness and fundamental-skill themes, and daily lesson plans that have a purpose and that result in academic, motor, fitness, and affective achievements for students.

9. Skeletal outlines are appropriate for initial planning purposes, but these should not be considered sufficient for daily plans that need considerable detail.

10. Teachers who expect a lot from students should also be willing to write creative lesson plans prepared in a way that facilitates student's enthusiam about participating in a lesson that is different, challenging, exciting, and—at times—unpredictable. Teachers should not be afraid to take risks when planning lessons.

11. Provide for early success experiences.

12. Plan for student leadership opportunities.

13. Be enthusiastic, positive, and accountable.

14. Observe the children's performance carefully and respond verbally to what you see.

15. Reinforce desired behavior.

SUGGESTED READINGS

DAUER, V. P., & PANGRAZI, R. P. (1992). *Dynamic physical education for elementary school children*, 10th ed. Minneapolis: Burgess.

DAVIS, R. G., & ISAACS, L. D. (1992). *Elementary physical education: Growing through movement*, 3rd ed. Winston-Salem, N.C.: Hunter.

GALLAHUE, D. L. (1993). Developmental physical education for today's elementary school children (2nd ed.). Madison: Brown & Benchmark.

GRAHAM, G., HOLT-HALE, S. A., & PARKER, M. (1993). *Children moving: A reflective approach to teaching physical education*, 3rd ed. Palo Alto, CA: Mayfield.

KIRCHNER, G. (1992). *Physical education for elementary school children*, 8th ed. Dubuque: William C. Brown.

NICHOLS, B. (1990). *Moving and learning*, 2nd ed. *The elementary school physical education experience.* St. Louis: Mosby.

6

Organization and Instruction

Along with the knowledge of what to teach, the teacher must have the ability to organize the class and select an effective style of subject matter presentation. The fact is, however, there are numerous styles of presentation and organization. Which is best? The topic deserves much consideration before a thorough understanding can be assured, and then a direct answer to the preceding question usually reflects personal preference. A number of teaching strategies (combination of style, organization, and communication mode) can be used effectively to present the same subject matter; each has advantages and disadvantages, depending upon the specific class situation, content, and desired learning process (Gabbard, 1983). The important criterion in the selection of a strategy is knowledge of the "process," its inherent characteristics, and implications for the development of the child. Although research indicates that most teachers do not vary their style of teaching, a considerable body of evidence suggests that the most effective teachers are those who do vary the teaching and learning environment.

Muska Mosston (1981, 1986), whose work in physical education has had considerable impact upon the teaching profession, describes teaching as a constant chain of decision-making events. Teachers in all subject areas are engaged in decisions about objectives, organization of the class, subject matter, evaluation, and specifics related to the environment, to name a few. Every successful lesson is developed from a number of decisions that can be grouped into three categories: preparation (precontact with students), contact, and postcontact (reflection of the lesson). Table 6-1 reveals some of the major decision-making events that occur prior to, during, and after each lesson.

Even if accomplished in the subject area, the teacher who does not consider such components as number of students, amount of time, and resources available may allow a great deal of undesirable events to occur. The selection of a teaching strategy(s) is dependent upon the detailed understanding of numerous precontact factors. If eye-hand coordination (using balls) is the chosen theme, for example, one's selection of a teaching strategy may be severely limited or dependent upon equipment, facilities, and number of students. Are there enough balls so that each child receives one, or are there 12 balls for 35 children? How many vaulting boxes are available for jumping? Are there two for 30 children, or six for the same amount of students? Conditions could vary considerably and, in many instances, class size may vary significantly within the same school setting.

An important point to consider when planning is to be prepared for the unexpected. For example: Your selected location is outside and it rains! Or the ground is wet and the principal (or you) forgot that the fifth graders are scheduled to practice for the school play in the gym. Few if any teachers do not experience such unexpected occurrences. So, have an alternative set of plans in your lesson-plan book, or at least in your mind. Can you use another large area, classroom(s), or the hallways? Are you going to modify the scheduled lesson (if the situation continues), or use an unrelated activity?

A successful lesson is based upon planned decision-making that takes into account all phases of the learning and instructional process.

Table 6-1

Chain of Decision-Making Events

Decision Categories	Components And Decisions

Precontact
(preparation)
	1. General subject area/objectives
	   a. Fitness Activity
	   b. Skill Development
	   c. Enhancement Activity
	   d. Review
	2. Learning/ability level(s)
	3. Number of students
	4. Equipment/material
	5. Facilities/location
	6. Time
	7. General class attitude and anticipated learning climate (how much responsibility is the class ready for?)
	8. Selection of a teaching strategy
	   a. Style
	   b. Organization pattern
	   c. Communication mode (verbal, written, visual, auditory)
	   d. Teacher's role
	   e. Student's role
	   f. Communication
	9. Specific subject matter
	   a. Quantity (desired amount to be accomplished)
	   b. Quality (performance level)
	10. Evaluation of performance (assessment procedures, other)

Contact	1. Adjustment to precontact decisions (weather, mishap, other) 2. Observation of behavior 3. Adjustment to observed behavior 4. Assessment (against criteria) 5. Feedback (type: gesture, touch, verbal)
Postcontact *(reflection)*	1. Assessment of teaching strategy 2. Assessment of student performance 3. Assessment of teacher performance

TEACHING STRATEGIES

The term *teaching strategy* refers to a process of manipulation of the learning environment. Each strategy is a composite of several possible variables (Fig. 6-1). The essential ingredient in a strategy is the *style* of presentation of subject matter. Along with the style, the instructor may select from a number of *organizational patterns* and *communication modes* (Gabbard, 1983).

One commonly used method of comparing styles is to place them on a continuum denoting general characteristic qualities (Fig. 6-2). As one observes the continuum, it is important to keep in mind that no style is superior in every situation. The continuum is not necessarily a "style versus style" representation, but rather something that highlights the relationships. Each style has advantages that are unique to the style itself and that must be effectively matched with the uniqueness of each class (that is, students, equipment

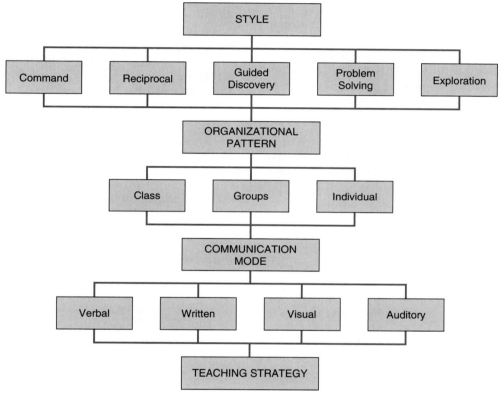

FIGURE 6-1
The teaching strategy model.

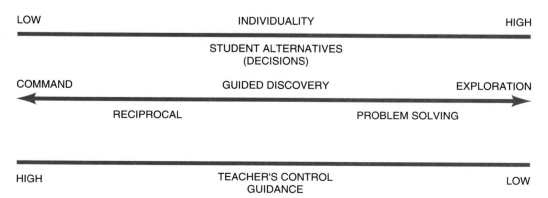

FIGURE 6-2
Teaching style continuum.

available, and other variables), subject matter, and learning outcomes perceived by the teacher. The master teacher is one who has the knowledge and experience in matching various conditions and content with an array of teaching styles and organizational patterns to produce the best results.

The best teachers are those who possess a wide repertoire of teaching strategies. They are not afraid to mix and combine styles. After experimenting with each style and becoming well versed with its characteristics, learn to modify it to suit your individual needs and desired outcomes. There is nothing as monotonous as a teacher who uses the same style over and over. This procedure stifles both student and teacher.

One last thought—a teaching strategy is only as good as the practitioner. It is hard work to understand the mechanisms involved in the teaching/learning process, but careful preparation and attention to detail are critical for a successful outcome.

TEACHING STYLES

COMMAND

The *command* style is considered by many as the most limiting because of the few opportunities for decision-making offered the student. The uniqueness and individuality of the student is not acknowledged in a pure command approach. Frequently utilized for mass instruction, where all students are required to perform the same task at the same pace (relays, mass calisthenics), this style is usually characterized by teacher demonstration (and/or explanation) and student replication. The teacher allows little if any deviation from the presentation. During some lessons involving gymnastics and dance, this tight control is desirable. Here, it is important that the teacher using this style not appear rigid and mistrusting, but rather be perceived enthusiastically, as desiring that the students learn the skills in an efficient and safe manner.

It is the control characteristic that perhaps influences many new teachers to use this style and seasoned teachers to apply it at the beginning of the school year. When tasks are presented using this style, the teacher usually provides a demonstration and verbal explanation of the task(s), or conveys the material using written direct task instructions (task sheets). Examples of direct command statements are:

1. Bounce the ball with your right hand five times; then switch to your left and bounce it five times.
2. Jump up with both feet and land on one. Jump up with both feet and land on both at the same time.

3. Kick the ball with your right foot to the wall, and after it rebounds trap it with the same foot. Switch to the left foot and do the same.

An essential element in this style is the demonstration and/or explanation of the task. If the teacher is going to demand strict adherence to the task criteria, then it is necessary that these criteria be clearly understood by the student. Demonstration is perhaps the most efficient means to make criteria clear. The teacher must be very careful, however. An incorrect or poorly executed demonstration can confuse the child or lead to inadequate performance of the skill. It should also be noted that the command style of teaching is not as practical for the development of motor schema as other styles because of its emphasis on specific movement outcomes—which excludes the variability needed for schema development. There are, however, several advantages to the command style of subject matter presentation:

1. Clear objectives and specific skill acquisition (the student learns what you have specifically stated). There are skills that can most effectively be presented with the direct style (dance steps, some gymnastic and sport-skill movements, specific exercise movements).
2. Efficiency in terms of time and organization (especially with large classes). Research findings in support of the command style suggest that if the objective is to teach a specific skill within a relatively short period of time, this mode of presentation is superior to problem-solving methods (Toole & Arink, 1982).
3. Some children respond better to the security of knowing what to do, how to do it, and where to go.
4. Class control and safety (such as when teaching gymnastics or swimming).
5. Requires less knowledge of subject matter and dealing with unpredictable questions (as in problem solving). This is perhaps an advantage for the new teacher in a new situation; however, this may also be considered a major shortcoming.

The command style of teaching does have a place in the teaching/learning environment. Situations arise when this style is desirable; however, it should not be used extensively because of the limits it sets on individual creativity, self-discipline, and movement variability—items deemed essential to the total development of young children.

RECIPROCAL

This method of presentation is characterized by a grouping of two or more individuals and is frequently referred to as a partnership. Although the reciprocal style inherently necessitates that students are grouped (that is, a form of organizational pattern), its unique reciprocal qualities justify its placement as a style in this model.

The reciprocal style is structurally similar to the command style except that interaction and feedback about performance are provided immediately by a peer(s) rather than by the teacher. This style is accomplished by grouping the students into partnerships of at least two (most frequently two or three), with one being the observer that provides feedback (to the performer) based on criteria established by the teacher. After this process, the cycle continues with students switching roles. Although this method can be used with younger children (Levels I–II), a sufficient level of maturity is required for maximum effectiveness. Students must be able to understand and carry out the teacher's criteria; thus they are responsible for a major portion of the instructional process. Second, the observer should be able to communicate effectively with the student performing the task. This type of behavior is generally observed with students in the intermediate-grade levels.

Of utmost importance is the teacher's clarity and effectiveness in conveying the established criteria to the partnership. With a clear demonstration and explanation of the task(s), teachers have also found it helpful to provide written task sheets (discussed later) outlining the criteria and, if possible, presenting a visual model of the task. While the teacher should be observant of the environment at all times, direct communication with the partnership (that is, interacting with the feedback process) should take place only through the observer (not the performer) unless safety is a factor.

The advantages of this style, aside from the grouping arrangement, provide for a unique learning opportunity. Characteristically, this method provides for a one-to-one teacher/student interaction with immediate feedback of performance, thus enhancing the potential for skill development. Provided the teacher presents a clear explanation of task criteria (and follows up with supportive materials), additional benefits of this style would be mental practice and the potential for overlearning (that is, repetition). Also unique and supportive of this style is the potential for enhancement of self-concept. The image of being an instructor and assisting in the learning process can be a rewarding experience for the student.

Although this style provides many advantages, it can also present problems in the learning process. A certain level of mental maturity is essential. The potential problem arising when a child is teamed with a partner who is overly critical can be serious. The opposite may also occur, when very little reciprocal communication takes place. The quality of communication and feedback is the essential component in this teaching style. The teacher's explanation of the task criteria and the grouping of students are central to the effectiveness of the reciprocal process.

Further information related to the reciprocal style may be found in the Organizational Patterns section of this chapter.

An extension of the reciprocal style which recently has gained popularity among educators is the use of cooperative learning. *Cooperative learning* requires that children be grouped and activities structured so that a feeling of positive interdependence among group members be established. The outcomes of this approach to learning are that students can increase academic performance, gain a sense of locus of control, improve social relationships, and enhance language skills, as well as develop physical skills.

Teachers can incorporate this approach into the reciprocal teaching style by following a few specific recommendations. First, structure activities so that group members are dependent upon each other for portions of learning. To foster this interdependence, the teacher should give only one informational copy of, for example, a rules worksheet, or skill concepts list, to the group. Then each group member should be responsible for teaching a part of the information to the rest of the group. Once the information has been shared or learned, the students proceed to an activity designed to use the information. During this activity each student should perform one of the specific roles from the following list:

Performer, student who performs the skill set by the teacher or group members;
Recorder, student who writes the number of trials or key points of the group discussion or even a report;
Observer, student who watches the performer, evaluates, and gives feedback;
Presenter, student who reports the groups' progress to the class or teacher;
Timer, student who keeps track of the practice time or discussion time;
Leader, student who keeps the group on task and makes assignments assuring that the group follows through with the task;
Collector, student who retrieves the equipment from the teacher and puts it away when finished.

These are most of the roles that are possible, but not all of them will necessarily be used in each cooperative learning experience. For example, the first time this approach is used the teacher may want to keep it simple by using pairs of students rather than larger groups. In this situation, only the roles of performer and observer are used. Also, with small groups, one student may assume more than one role. Whatever roles are used the teacher needs to be sure that the roles are rotated or reversed so that students can experience each facet of the process.

The success of cooperative learning experiences is dependent on each student fully understanding what is required so he or she can fulfill the role. Whether the teacher gives the information verbally, and uses a demonstration, or gives a handout with the information, it is critical that the teacher monitor the process very closely to ensure that all are clear about expectations.

One final word of advice—all parties involved in this process must assume responsibility for creating a physically and emotionally safe environment for learning. To be successful, the students must demonstrate a willingness to work with all students, to make mistakes, to take risks, and to share responsibilities. The teacher must model these behaviors as well.

Guided Discovery, Problem Solving, and Exploration

The following styles present a dramatic cognitive shift from the command process. The change is from demonstration/replication (stimulus/response) to a gradual increase in intellectual freedom and opportunity for *creativity* and the development of *critical thinking skills*.

With the command approach the student followed a set of guidelines with few if any allowable alternatives. Now the student is presented with the opportunity to think, inquire, and discover; *the process becomes as important as the product*! A demonstration of the "right way," of giving the answer, occurs very seldom, if ever, when utilizing these styles. At this point, the teacher needs to consider the following: Are *the students* ready for the organizational and intellectual freedom? Can I better serve the needs of the child with one of these processes? Is the presentation of this theme best conveyed using one of these styles? *Am I ready to present the material effectively using one of these styles?*

Communication

Essential to the success of any style is the line of communication between teacher and learner. The teacher presents a stimulus to which the student reacts. The teacher must be a careful and continuous observer in order to respond effectively to the student's performance with appropriate ongoing challenges and feedback. In other words, the student and teacher are communicating through the verbal and motor avenues. In the guided discovery, problem solving, and exploration styles the process becomes as important as the product. A common element that all the styles exhibit is the presentation of tasks or movement stimuli in problem–solving form. Although the majority of the communication is presented verbally, there is a growing popularity of nonverbal problem-solving communication (for example, task sheets, cards). The characteristic differences between guided discovery,

problem solving, and exploration are in the amount of guidance and openness conveyed through statements; exploration offers the least guidance and greatest openness, whereas guided discovery conveys the most teacher guidance of the three styles.

The success by which a teacher can get a student to learn depends on the manner in which the student comprehends the information presented. Teachers should phrase tasks or inquiries in an indirect manner through questions and/or challenges without giving away the direct answer, or giving the student a feeling of being commanded.

Teachers should be diverse (as well as challenging) in their presentations. Too often teachers rely on the phrases "Can you . . . ?" "How many ways . . . ?" and "In how many ways can you . . . ?" The following are examples of phrases that can be used to diversify task statements and inquiries:

> "Can you dodge this ball with your upper body?"
> "Show me. . . ."
> "Who can . . . ?"
> "How can you . . . ?"
> "Try. . . ."
> "Could you . . . ?"
> "Find a way. . . ."
> "What other ways . . . ?"
> "How many ways can you . . . ?"
> "What different ways are there to . . . ?"
> "If you. . . ."
> "How else can you . . . ?"
> "Is there another way . . . ?"
> "Is there a better way . . . ?"

After presenting the problem(s) or stimuli to the class, the teacher's role is far from completed. Communication now extends to reinforcement and providing students with knowledge of their performance (feedback). Feedback can be offered in a variety of ways; however, negative statements very seldom if ever are appropriate. In matters of safety, the teacher may have to be negative if an immediate response is necessary. Praise may be given to a student without verbal statements, and in large classes nonverbal communication may be used frequently. This type of recognition may be in the form of a nod, a smile, or a body gesture. The teacher should, however, try to interact verbally with as many students as possible, giving priority to those who may be "stuck" or who require extra psychological support.

Regardless of teaching style (including *command*), it is essential that the teacher have the attention of all students, especially for initial guidance and delivery of learning information. Voice is both an essential teaching tool and valuable asset. For it is not only what is said but *how* it is delivered that provides understanding and motivation. A teacher's enthusiasm is contagious! Two teachers presenting the same material and using the same script may get far different responses from the same class. It is a common occurrence observed in teacher-education classes that an enthusiastic personality and voice can completely turn around an unassured class of children. Many teachers comment that their afternoon classes (especially the last) do not seem to respond as well as their classes before lunch. The problem, in part, is probably the teacher's delivery. Learn to pace yourself, unless you have an extremely enthusiastic personality and possess a strong voice. Know when to be loud and soft. Be careful not to convey fear by being too loud and direct when a soft, caring voice may be needed.

In order to present an effective delivery, the teacher needs to get the attention of the class. A signal should be established that signifies "stop, look, and listen!" Depending upon the size and personality of the class, this may be done with the voice, a beat on a drum, a clap of the hands, or a whistle. The class needs to understand the importance of this signal, for it is used not only for task delivery but also in an emergency and as an indicator that class time is over.

For delivery, the teacher should be positioned so everyone can see and hear. A scattered or semicircle formation, with students and teacher facing each other, is quite effective. In specific situations it may be best to have the students sit down. This technique controls excessive movement when attention is desired; however, children should not be expected to sit still or be too attentive except for short periods of time. Keep verbal statements short, concise, motivating; your job is to get them moving!

GUIDED DISCOVERY

The *guided discovery* style has been described by Mosston (1981) as the first process that cracks the cognitive barrier and embodies the discovery concept. Guided discovery uses the process of inquiry to guide students to the discovery of an end–product predetermined by the teacher. Basically, the teacher sets the scene through a series of questions, which brings the students to where a common starting point can be assumed. After establishing a foundation, the teacher then guides the students through a carefully planned sequence of steps consisting of questions or clues. Because it is not known how the students will respond, each step is based on the response given by the students in the previous step. If the students are too far off track, the teacher must guide them back to the target—remembering not to reveal the answer, however. Ideally, each succeeding question narrows in on the target (predetermined objective) until self-discovery is realized by the student. Figure 6-3 illustrates the ladder effect of this style.

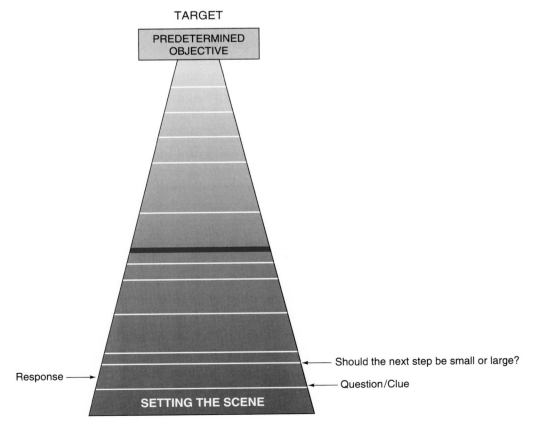

FIGURE 6-3
The ladder effect of Guided Discovery.

Essential to the success of this style is the teacher's awareness of the following factors as described by Mosston (1981):

The objective (target)
The direction of the sequence of steps
The size of each step
The interrelationship of the steps (general progression)
The speed of the sequence.

The following suggestions may help to facilitate a smooth development of the guided-discovery process:

1. After stating the challenge, always wait for the student's response; be patient, it takes time to think.
2. Reword the challenge if you must, or state it more simply. If after a reasonable amount of time no response is given, you probably took too big a step. Ask questions to clarify, motivate, or extend.
3. Always reinforce student responses with positive statements (unless safety is in jeopardy); negative ones tend to inhibit student responses.
4. Remember, observe then respond by stating what you have seen; follow this by a question to clarify, motivate, or extend; *observe-reflect-question* (praise when appropriate).

Example:
Predetermined objective—Vertical jump for height

1. proper landing (balls of feet with knees bent)
2. crouch (and toes leaving the floor last)
3. use of arms

QUESTIONS TO SET THE SCENE

Today we are going to discover jumping for height. Challenge: pretend that you are jumping up and reaching for an apple that is hanging high above your head. How would you jump to grab it? Try jumping a few times.

Questions: On what part of your feet did you land? How many places on your feet could you land? After trying all three (flatfooted, ball, heel), which is the most comfortable? Did you land with your legs straight or were your knees bent? Select a partner and allow him or her to observe while you jump. Can anyone think of some reasons for landing on the balls of one's feet? Let's talk about the takeoff. Have you discovered any factors that you could share with us that could help us go higher? Good; we have identified the arms and legs as major factors in the takeoff. Let's all practice jumping with our arms in various positions.

Try to identify one that lifts you the highest. Share your discoveries with others around you. Would someone like to share some discoveries with us? John says to swing your arms down and then up as your body moves up. Try it! Do you feel a difference? As your body moves up, how do you propel yourself up with your legs? Some of you are crouched deeply and others are just barely squatting down. Does this make a difference? Try different depths. Which depth allows you to go the highest? What part of your foot leaves the floor last? Sally says that she can feel her toes push hard against the floor. What do you feel? Would it help if you extend your hand and fingers to grab the apple? How much higher can you reach if you do? Now let's review the discoveries that we have made. Can we put some of our discoveries together well enough to explain to our friends and parents how to jump the highest and grab something?

Ideal for primary-grade children, this style of presentation allows the teacher to provide intellectual inquiry and at the same time accomplish a designated (specific) objective(s). The concept of variability in practice and an understanding of the discovery process by the student are greatly enhanced with this style, especially when compared to the command presentation.

Guided discovery does present possible problems, however. The style has been described as the most difficult for the teacher to master because of the amount of verbalizing and high degree of task competence and knowledge of task sequence required. It may be viewed as time-consuming because of the question-response process. With large groups or groups that possess an extreme range of abilities, this style may present other problems.

PROBLEM SOLVING

With *problem solving* emerges individuality, creativity, critical thinking, and variability within a general movement area. Where guided discovery is closed-ended (that is, the teacher guides the student to a specific discovery), problem solving is an open-ended process. Each new and different problem leads students to a variety of solutions that, while challenging, are within the student's own unique ability. The teacher still chooses the general subject matter area; however, the student may discover what he or she wishes within that framework. There is room for making new discoveries. Mosston (1981) describes problem solving as a self-perpetuating process. The act of discovery itself becomes a reinforcing, motivating agent that drives the child to continue to seek additional solutions and alternatives.

Problem Design.   All problems presented to students must be relevant to subject matter, student readiness, and experience of both the group and the individual. What can be discovered using this style?

Skills/Movement Variability. This refers to skills that may or may not be designed for specific situations, but ones that enhance the movement schema of a general skill area. Example: In discovering how to roll the body, a number of rolling skills may be acquired. The rolling schema may be greatly enhanced as the child strengthens the dimensions (spatial, time, force) of that skill area, which may help prepare him or her for novel and ever-changing tasks and conditions.

Relationships. Through problem solving, relationships among parts of the body, equipment, and other bodies are discovered. "Most or perhaps all movements are performed in some relationship to their antecedents and their consequences" (Mosston, 1981).

Concepts. As a result of the problem-solving process, students discover an understanding of the concepts upon which movement performance is based. An understanding of time, space, force, and relationships, and the functions and use of strength, endurance, flexibility, and the cardiorespiratory system (to name a few), may be discovered through problem solving.

Preferences. As a result of performing a variety of movements, understanding how the body moves, and judging relationships, the child can make personal judgments as to which movement is the most or the least effective and efficient for specific conditions.

Quantity/Limits. By performing a set of movements in various situations, the child develops an idea of quantitative performance and limitations. How far can I kick the ball using the inside of my foot? How fast can I run backwards? Can I jump higher [vertical jump] by swinging my arms upward? How far can I bend my trunk forward?

STEPS IN THE PROBLEM-SOLVING PROCESS

1. Identify the skill theme (ball dribbling, jumping, others). Have a clear understanding of the sequence of progression of the skill.
2. Focus upon a specific area (dribbling and moving, jumping for distance, and so forth).
3. Identify a dimension(s) of the skill to focus upon (that is, an element of space, time, force).
4. Design the problems, keeping in mind the desired discovery of skills/variability, relationships, concepts, preference, and quantity/limits.
5. Presentation of problems. Keep in mind that demonstration or disclosing solutions is rarely done! Being an open-ended process, problem-solving questions should be structured in the same manner: allowing solutions, yet stimulating the student to continue inquiring (as opposed to guided discovery of the solution). It will be noted later in this section that the questions can be presented to the class as a whole, in groups, or individually (using problem-solving task sheets).
6. Problem solving. Remember to allow time for students to explore. Refrain from offering additional questions unless children need them for clarification or motivation.
7. Discussion and demonstration of solutions. If possible (class size allowing), all students should have the opportunity to reveal their solutions. Although theoretically there is no "wrong" answer as long as it is appropriate for the problem (yet some answers are recognized as "better"), guidance may provide the student with more meaningful discoveries that result in a broader information base, which may serve further to enhance the schema.
8. Reinforcement. Verbal reinforcement and individual assistance are essential to keeping the process flowing and being motivational for the student. If the student becomes "stuck" (can't think of a solution) on a specific problem, which may occur frequently with younger children, the problem-solving process can be perceived as frustrating, therefore unsuccessful. If such conditions arise it is best to shift over to guided discovery and guide the student away from the frustration and to some solution. Not all children will do well with problem solving.

Problem-solving provides numerous opportunities to enhance the movement schema.

Example

General subject matter area: Ball Dribbling (Level 1)

Specific Theme: Dribbling while moving in various directions

Primary Focus: Body position and ball control; dimensions of space, time, and force.

Background: Children have explored with ball bouncing/dribbling; using two hands and one-hand variations while in their personal space

QUESTIONS (GENERAL STIMULUS)

Let's start out by dribbling with two hands, then one hand (if you can), while staying in your personal space. Can you change hands? Try to change the level of bounce: at your knees, waist, chest. Now, using your preferred hand, move in different directions. Try forward and backward. What other directions can you move to? Is it easier to control the ball while bouncing it high or low? Are we remembering to not slap at it? Change speeds; moving first slowly then faster. Are you still keeping control of the ball? If you feel ready, try changing hands while moving in various directions.

Problem solving is not designed to develop a specific skill, nor is it the most efficient style in terms of time or teaching large groups of children. This style is, however, an excellent means for allowing the children the opportunity to understand how their bodies move and to develop schema.

EXPLORATION

The *exploration* style can be utilized quite effectively with elementary-level children. This process takes advantage of the child's intrinsic interests in exploration and experimentation. Compared to guided discovery and problem solving, exploration is more open-ended and offers the least amount of teacher guidance. The teacher designs problems and allows students to explore as they wish, with additional guidance provided only for safety purposes or adjustment owing to lack of communication (for instance, the student did not understand the statement). Generally, exploration is associated with that which is novel. This style is very effective when introducing a new piece of equipment or presenting old equipment or movement skills in a new atmosphere of creativity.

This style is also appropriate at the beginning of a lesson when introducing a new theme before a more guided style is applied. The uniqueness of the exploration style lies in its flexibility and accommodation to various ages and problem-solving abilities. Exploration instructions from the teacher are generally limited to a few wide-open statements such as:

1. Explore handling and bouncing the ball with your hands.
2. Select a ball (various sizes) of your choice and explore ways of balancing it on various parts of your body.
3. What can you and your partner do with a hula hoop?
4. Can you create a new jump-rope routine and chant?

The role of the teacher during exploration is to be aware of safety hazards and to stimulate thought in youngsters who appear "stuck." If needed, it is helpful to inspire children to observe others. This practice, often performed naturally, stimulates thought for movement and creativity. With some children, the teacher may need to compensate somewhat by inspiring with pertinent questions that do not guide too much, but ask the child to respond to thoughts about his or her movement abilities that are related to the area of exploration.

ORGANIZATIONAL PATTERNS

As noted in Fig. 6-1, teaching styles and organizational patterns are independent, yet a teaching strategy must combine elements of both. An *organizational pattern* is utilized to group students so the desired teaching style may be presented. The basic organizational patterns are: class, groups (two or more), and individual instruction. A number of combinations (styles and patterns) are possible. Some may be more advantageous under ideal conditions (small class size and lots of equipment); however, many teachers find themselves in less than ideal settings.

For example, problem solving and guided discovery are very effective if the class size is small and an abundance of equipment is available. Instruction is therefore usually directed to the entire class, and the teacher moves around to interact. But what if there are 60 students in the class and equipment is limited? Can the teacher still provide problem solving? Yes! The alternative is grouping at stations and using written problem-solving techniques (task sheets, cards, other devices). The master teacher is one who can combine style with organization to challenge both the conditions and the student.

Class Instruction. In this pattern, the students are presented information as a whole. Using the desired style, the teacher communicates the same message (command or problem) to the entire class at the same time. Students work as one unit, usually in a scattered formation, responding to the instructions presented.

Group and Individual Instruction. If the teacher wishes to organize the children so that more than one activity can be presented at the same time, dividing the class into units (groups or individual) is excellent.

EYE-FOOT COORDINATION

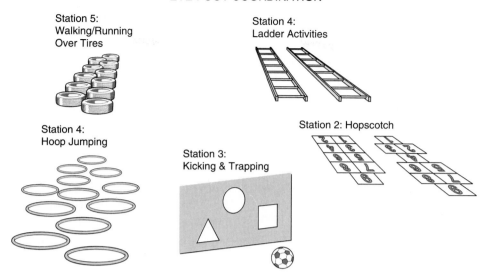

FIGURE 6-4

Station work with a theme.

The use of stations, also known as *learning centers*, has become a very popular and useful technique designed to accommodate group and individual instruction (individual stations). With stations, students are assigned, or allowed the freedom, to perform a task or set of tasks at a number of activity areas that are usually related to a specific theme (Fig. 6-4).

This pattern, one of the most utilized in physical education, is praised by many for its effectiveness in providing sufficient practice of a skill.

A unique quality of stations is that stations may be combined with various styles quite effectively. Among the options are:

1. Dispersing into units (groups) that perform tasks demonstrated or directed by written, auditory, and/or visual materials (task cards, sheets, posters, tape recorders) at each station;
2. Dividing the class into units that perform problem-solving activities as stimulated by written, auditory, and/or visual information.

Basic Station Arrangements

1. Single Task. In this arrangement, each unit (group or individual) is presented a single task at each station. The task could be the same; if so, no rotation (movement to the other stations) is necessary. This arrangement is effective for separating students so maximum utilization of space is obtained. Another option provides a single, yet different task at each station. With this arrangement the units rotate from station to station, thus providing maximum efficiency of equipment use when not enough is available for all to engage in the same activity.

2. Multiple Tasks. Same as the single-task arrangement, except that at each station more than one task is presented.

With both basic arrangements, the teacher has a number of options in terms of rotation, starting, stopping, and duration between stations.

Among the options are:

1. Setting a specific amount of time for the completion of the task(s) at each station, then giving a signal (whistling, clapping hands, using the voice) for each group to rotate in a designated order (that is, clockwise, station 1 to 2 to 3 . . .).
2. Students (individual) have the choice of pace and location. This is a self-operating design that requires the individual to be in control of his or her own performance and behavior. Students may be given complete freedom or they may be told to complete "at least three of the six stations." A word of caution here: (1) standards must be established by the teacher in regard to number of students allowed at a station at one time, and (2) students need to work up to this freedom with limited decisions.

There are many advantages associated with dividing a class and using stations. One is that stations provide maximum utilization of space and equipment; skills can be practiced without waiting in long lines. Another advantage is that a large number of activities can be conveyed (to large classes) without the direct verbal guidance of the teacher. Stations, in addition to individualizing instruction, can be used to group children by ability (if the task requires this) and promote social interaction.

Using Formations to Organize Activity

There are a variety of formations that may be used by the teacher to convey instruction and organize movement activity. Although it is quite common for an entire class (one unit) to be arranged in a single formation, one of the positive characteristics of formations is that they can be used to divide classes into smaller units. When used correctly, formations provide time efficiency and ease in organizing both small and large numbers of children. While some arrangements emphasize uniformity and may be characteristic with teacher-centered (*e.g.,* command) teaching styles, others emphasize more freedom with movement space, which is generally more appropriate with child-centered styles (guided discovery, problem solving, and exploration). Table 6-2 presents some of the most commonly used instructional activity formations with children.

Hoffman, Young, and Klesius (1981) have suggested the following additional considerations for organizing students:

1. If in an outside area, face the students away from, or at an angle to, the sun so they are not looking into the sun.
2. Face the students into or at an angle to the wind so the teacher's voice, when standing in front of the students, is carried toward them by the wind.
3. Keep equipment to be used later in the lesson out of sight, either in a bag, equipment cart, or another area, in order to avoid distracting the students.
4. Choose an activity area that minimizes distractions.
5. Observable boundary markers for movement space are easier for students to respond to than abstract instructions. An area marked off by plastic containers, flags, cones, or painted lines is easier for students to adhere to than instructions such as, "Don't go too far away" or "Stay in line with that tree."
6. The teacher should circulate among the students to provide individual teaching points, ask and respond to questions, give reinforcement, or intervene in a potentially hazardous situation.
7. When speaking to the whole class, the teacher should be in a position to view all the children, regardless of the formation used, and to observe the actions of each student.

Offering additional options in the selection of a teaching strategy is *communication mode,* that is, the mode with which the teacher wishes to convey material. The general options (often combined) are verbal, written, visual, and auditory. The *verbal mode* consists of spoken communication through personal contact, usually between the teacher and student (the most utilized form). An *auditory mode* may be presented using records or tapes that convey the style of presentation selected.

The remainder of this section is devoted to the *written* and *visual* modes of communication; both have been found to be effective and motivating alternatives in the learning process.

THE USE OF WRITTEN AND VISUAL INFORMATION

Task cards, task sheets, and posters can be used most effectively with group and individual organizational patterns. Providing written and/or visual information, these techniques promote individualization and convey the instructional style desired by the teacher. Through these media, tasks may be presented directly (command), or be designed to stimulate the problem-solving abilities of children.

Along with promoting general individuality, task materials offer some very functional benefits:

1. Inform about what and how; especially if a demonstration or explanation was not provided.
2. Help the child remember what was presented in demonstration or explanation.
3. Provide a record (task sheet) for the teacher, student, and parent (optional) of what was expected and to what degree it was accomplished.
4. Provide the flexibility of meeting individual abilities with multiple tasks of varying degrees of difficulty.
5. Release the teacher from the role of direct communicator to the entire class, thus allowing the teacher to interact with individuals.
6. For young children, preschool to first grade, who may not be at a level to comprehend written statements or words adequately, posters with visual information (figures, pictures, other media) provide a means of problem solving without direct teacher communication.

Examples

Poster conveying a direct style of presentation.
Poster information conveyed with figures.

Table 6-2

Instruction and Activity Formations

Formation		General Description And Suggestions	Examples Of Use
File	X X X X X X X X X X X X X X X X X X X X X X X X X X X X X X X X T	Position one child for each line desired, equidistant apart, then signal the class to line up behind these children, forming single files. Children may also stand side by side (line formation). For relay activities, be sure that teams are even and limited to 6 to 8 per line.	Relays, simple games, marching, simple stunts
Circle	(circle of x's)	Children form a circle by following the teacher around in a circle. Other methods include all joining hands and forming a circle, or having the class take positions on a circle printed on the floor or play area. The teacher should stand at the edge of the circle when talking, not in the middle. For maximum participation, limit number of children to 8 or 10.	Circle games and dances, parachute activities, marching
Semicircle	(semicircle of x's with T)	Arrange children in a line facing their leader, then have them join hands and form a half-circle.	Most practical for giving instructions and demonstrations, and skill practice
Scattered	(scattered ⊗ symbols)	Children find a spot in the play area. Unless partners or small groups are together, each child should be at least an arm's distance apart. Set geographical boundaries. Be sure to move around the area and interact.	Great for problem-solving and exploratory activities, tag games, stunts, creative dance

Table 6-3

Eye-Foot Coordination

STATION #1—LADDER ACTIVITIES

1. Walk forward, stepping on each rung.
2. Walk forward, stepping between the rungs.
3. Walk backward, stepping on each rung.
4. Walk backward, stepping between the rungs.
5. Walk sideways, stepping on each rung.
6. Walk sideways, stepping between each rung.
7. Hop forward between the rungs.
8. Hop sideways between the rungs.

Task card (could be sheet or poster) with problem-solving information.

EYE-FOOT COORDINATION
STATION 1–LADDER ACTIVITIES

FIGURE 6-5
Poster conveying visual stimuli.

Table 6-4

Task Card: Eye-Foot Coordination

STATION #1—LADDER ACTIVITIES

Watch where you want your feet to move!

1. Can you walk in different ways from one end to the other without touching the floor?
2. Try walking across by stepping on the rungs only and facing in different directions.
3. Are there other ways to walk across the ladder?
4. Is there a way to cross without stepping on the rungs or spaces between?
5. Have you discovered a direction other than forward in which to cross?
6. If you were a rabbit, how would you move to the other side? Be careful. Be sure to watch where your feet are going to move next.

Table 6-5

Eye-Foot Coordination

LEARNING CENTER TASK SHEET

NAME _____   PERIOD _____

Completed				TASKS
				Ladder
				I can:
				1. Walk forward by stepping on the rungs only
				2. Walk backward by stepping on the rungs only
				3. Walk sideways on the rungs
				4. Hop between the rungs to the end
				Tires
				I can:
				1. Walk across the tires
				2. Run across the tires
				3. Run, stepping in the middle of each tire
				4. Walk across, placing one foot in each tire
				5. Run across in the same way
				6. Hop in the middle of each tire to the end
				Hoops
				I can:
				1. Leap from hoop to hoop
				2. Hop from hoop to hoop
				3. Run across placing one foot in each hoop
				I can:
5	10	15	20	1. Hit the target from 5, 10, 15, and 20 feet away (3 trials)
5	10	15	20	2. Hit the target by kicking with my opposite foot
				3. Trap the ball with my right foot
				4. Trap the ball with my left foot
				Hopscotch
				I can:
				1. Play a successful game of American Hopscotch
				2. French Hopscotch
				3. Italian Hopscotch

Task sheet with checklist; may be completed by student, with partner or teacher.

REFERENCES

BROOKFIELD, S. D. (1987). *Developing Critical Thinking*. San Francisco: Josey-Bass Publishers.

DUNN, S., & WILSON, R. (1991). Cooperative learning in the physical education classroom. *Journal of Physical Education, Recreation and Dance*. August, 1991, 22–28.

GABBARD, C. (1983, Fall). A teaching strategy model: The integration of style, organization and communication mode. *Journal of Teaching in Physical Education*, 16–21.

MOSSTON, M., & ASHWORTH, S. (1986). *Teaching physical education* (3rd ed.). Columbus, OH: Charles E. Merrill.

MOSSTON, M. (1981). *Teaching physical education* (2nd ed.). Columbus, OH: Charles E. Merrill.

TOOLE, T., & ARINK, E. A. (1982). Movement education: Its effect on motor skill performance. *Research Quarterly for Exercise Sport, 53*, 156–162.

SUGGESTED READINGS

BEYER, B. (1987). *Practical strategies for the teaching of thinking*. Boston: Allyn and Bacon.

BROOKFIELD, S. D. (1987). *Developing critical thinking*. San Francisco: Jossey-Bass Publishers.

DUNN, S., & WILSON, R. (1991). Cooperative learning in the physical education classroom. *Journal of Physical Education, Recreation and Dance*. August, 1991, 22–28.

GABBARD, C., & McBRIDE, R. (1990). Critical thinking in the psychomotor domain. *Journal of the International Council for Health, Physical Education, and Recreation. 26*(2), 24–27.

HELLISON, D. R., & TEMPLIN, T. J. (1990). *A reflective approach to teaching physical education*. Champaign, IL: Human Kinetics.

HURWITZ, D. (1985). A model for structure of instructional strategies. *Journal of Teaching in Physical Education, 4*, 190–201.

SIEDENTOP, D. (1991). *Developing teaching skills in physical education* (3rd ed.). Palo Alto, CA: Mayfield.

7

Physical Education for Children

Concerned and progressive educators who realize many of the old ways aren't working any longer want methods to improve the learning environment in schools. Not only in the educational setting, but throughout our world there is a sense of ordered chaos—in marriages, families, classrooms, businesses. Wherever people are relating to one another and trying to accomplish something—there often is confusion, misunderstanding, disrespect, alienation and lack of quality performance. The demands on each person are multifaceted, and children especially experience the stress. However there also seems to be developing a new level of human consciousness of what is needed for us to be able to relate successfully in our contemporary world with all of its demands. One can observe common strands of this awakening consciousness to reality whether the setting be families, schools, businesses, churches. There is a sincere response from people who want things to work as they were meant to work, and an earnest desire to find the "best way" for humans to behave in ways that satisfy their needs (needs-satisfying) without interfering with the rights of others. There is also an expressed need for a strengthening of self-discipline attitudes and behaviors. How can we as adults create and maintain learning environments that set the parameters for (a) the satisfaction of individual needs and (b) encourage learning, self-evaluation, self-discipline, and restitution?

Class management and discipline is presented here as the product of three viewpoints, all focusing on enhancing quality in the elementary school physical education setting. First, we consider the philosophies, attitudes and techniques of reality therapy and its underlying basis of control theory. Second, we add the 62 years of collective teaching experience of the authors. Third is the experience of managing students, teachers, equipment and space in school environments.

The reader is encouraged to take the following thoughts and ideas, test them and choose those which will best assist in creating a physical education learning environment that is needs-fulfilling, non-coercive, respectful and encourages self-evaluation.

Class management is defined in this text as "definite procedures used to create a positive learning environment permitting needs-satisfaction of students and teacher, promoting learning of lifetime values and skills, and preventing serious disruptions of the learning process." Discipline comes from the Latin word *disciplina* which means learning. This learning refers specifically to the discipline of self. Discipline regarded in this way is regulated by what we *value* rather than by some discomfort to be avoided. Discipline is not defined in this text as something the teacher does to the students to get them to conform to the teacher's standards.

The subtitles of this chapter focus on quality, control theory, reality therapy, positive learning environments, behavior expectations, positive attitude development, communication skills, managerial effectiveness, discipline strategies, punishment and restitution.

QUALITY

In recent years there has been a growing interest in the Quality Schools Movement as described by Glasser (1986, 1990), and the institute of Reality Therapy. The ultimate goal in education is quality of knowledge and life skills. Quality is hard to define but is almost always recognized when seen. We define quality as that which is distinctively good and continually getting better. Quality performance is the best we can do at the time. Professional teachers know change is needed in our schools and they are extremely frustrated by the increasing absence of self-discipline among the student population, the magnitude of lack of quality, and the lack of support for themselves.

In a Quality School teachers teach, and students learn, how to evaluate their own work in a life skills curriculum being taught in ways that satisfy their needs (needs-satisfaction). When students experience satisfaction in the school setting, there is no need for manipulation or coercion. In the physical education setting we have a very fertile environment for teaching quality of life skills and values. We are working in the child's favorite world—the world of play, activity and creativity. The teacher's biggest challenge is the managing of such a unique learning environment. It is not how much variety, how much equipment, how many points, or how much space, except as these things play a role in needs-satisfaction. In a well-managed physical education class there are many opportunities for satisfying all basic psychological needs for both the students and teachers.

Students prefer a safe environment with known boundaries, one in which they experience respect and can learn meaningful content and how to relate to others without constant disruption. They become frustrated when they are unable to experience needs-satisfaction, and teachers become frustrated when the children are not achieving in quality ways. Parents expect their children to learn both course content and proper behavior when involved with others in cooperative and competitive endeavors. Everyone wants teachers and students to move towards quality—the best they can do at the time. Teachers and administrators know that the effectiveness of class-management strategies greatly influence the quality of teaching and learning that occurs in classes.

The strength of the desire for quality of learning prompts teachers to search for effective class-management strategies which will facilitate movement towards quality performance in both students and teachers. Quality performance, is a satisfying experience as the basic needs of belonging, power, freedom and fun are met. Quality feels good! When teachers and students are working together effectively, all experience satisfaction and quality performance is generated.

The public fears that students who are allowed to demonstrate hostility, disrespect, and lack of self-control within the structured environment of the schools will eventually manifest this unacceptable behavior to a greater extent in society at large. Growing up has never been easy, and the school environment is difficult for everyone. It's hard managing workers who don't want to be there. Perhaps we all need to remind ourselves that getting to know self as a needs-satisfying organism is basic to all quality living, and that learning to live qualitatively requires patience, bumps and bruises, self-discipline, mutual respect and trust. The old methods haven't worked for a long time. It's time for a change. It's time for all those involved with educating children to treat each other as they personally want to be treated—with respect, and non-manipulative, growth-enhancing attitudes.

The authors recognize that the manner in which teachers handle class management and discipline is closely related to their philosophical beliefs. Most of the current management and discipline practices in the schools is based on stimulus-response theory which depends on consequences, rewards, and punishment to *coerce* students into conforming to the standards of the teacher. This approach doesn't facilitate the life skills of self-discipline, respect, responsible, needs-satisfying choices that generate quality living. In this chapter you will be asked to consider another set of behavioral beliefs as explained through control theory.

CONTROL THEORY AND REALITY THERAPY

Control theory (Glasser 1990, 1986) is a biological theory which explains the physiological and psychological behavior of all living organisms. When applied to human behavior, it is the theory of how humans control what happens to them in their attempts to satisfy one or more of the five basic needs divided into two categories of physical needs and psychological needs.

physical needs
1. *survival and reproduction* (water, food, warmth, air, sex), and,

psychological needs
2. *love and belonging* (acceptance, affection, fellowship),
3. *power* (self-evaluation, self-esteem, recognition, achievement, influence),
4. *freedom* (independence, making choices, self-direction), and
5. *fun* (play amusement, recreation, pleasure relaxation, joy).

The following is a common playground example:

Example: Some of the students choose to stay in line, waiting their turn as their perception of the best behavior to satisfy their need for belonging (for which they look to the teacher.) This picture of obedience is in their brain as an effective way to receive attention and respect from an adult. They first learned the effectiveness of this behavior as children relating to a parent. On the other hand, some of the children whose needs are not being satisfied may choose not to obey the command of the teacher. One student, to satisfy power and freedom needs, may choose to steal the ball from a peer and throw it at the target.

Another may choose to clown around to satisfy a need for peer acceptance. Another child may behave in very defiant or aggressive ways out of his/her need for power. The child's inner picture in this case might be that of aggression and violence to dominate another person—his/her experience of home life.

In other words, it's not much fun waiting in a long line for a turn. Those that refuse the required behavior will do so either because they do not have the picture of obedience as an effective behavior for needs-satisfaction, or other needs are stronger at that moment.

The following beliefs are unique to control theory:

1. All behavior is purposeful and directed toward needs-satisfaction.
   Example: Student bullies other students to satisfy power need; student always compromises to satisfy love and belonging needs.

2. Though we share a common reality our perception of reality is individual.
   Example: The physical education setting is a common reality, however, one's attraction or avoidance to this setting is influenced by the individual's perception of the strength of the setting for needs-satisfaction.

3. Motivation is internal, not external. This is not to say that what happens in external reality is not important. Although the outside event can have a lot to do with the behavior chosen, it cannot cause behavior. The outside event provides information and one's perception of the outer reality is just that—the perception of one individual. Both information and the way it is delivered is important. How one chooses to act on the perception of this information is up to each individual. The degree of importance of the required behavior is also decided by each individual. According to the degree of its importance, the individual will cooperate or not.
   Example: A students will engage in quality practice of gymnastic skills only to the degree that she/he is motivated by an internal need (*i.e.,* belonging, power, freedom, fun).

4. We can't control others; we can only control ourselves. Students want to learn appropriate ways of satisfying needs. Except through coercion, the teacher cannot "make" students behave. Though a person may seem to follow the control of someone more forceful, the choice to comply will happen only if the person thinks the requested behavior is the best thing to do at that particular moment. Compliance does not mean the person has necessarily changed a belief, or that behavior will transfer to times other than the present.

   Example: The student, even though bored with the same worn-out skill drills, may behave without questioning in a highly restrictive physical education class. The choice to participate without question is made not in freedom, but under coercion. To ask for something that would satisfy a fun, freedom or power need might bring on punitive or embarrassing consequences. The student chooses to not risk but does not change his/her thinking ("this is boring!"). In this kind of environment, quality of performance will not be present and individuals may not meet their needs for freedom and power.

5. When basic needs are not being met, there is the experience of some level of pain. The experience of basic needs being satisfied brings forth some level of pleasure. In both cases the pain or pleasure is not something that is done to the person but rather an experience of ownership through the freedom of choice.
   Example: The pain of not being chosen for the intramural volleyball team (frustration of love and belonging, power, fun needs) and the pleasure of completing both free throws (satisfying a power need) are common examples of ownership.

Reality therapy (Institute of Reality Therapy) is an action-oriented approach that teaches individuals how to effectively control their behaviors to meet their needs. This is not just a counseling tool, but an attitude towards life that teaches self-evaluation and self-discipline. Students can learn to identify their needs, self-evaluate, and choose behaviors that are responsible, effective and caring. When ineffective behaviors exist, there is still the choice to correct the behavior. With help, most students are capable of restitution. This process will be discussed later in the discipline section.

Behavior, rather than being just "thinking," or "feeling," or "doing," is understood as *total behavior* made up of four components: doing, thinking, feeling, and the physiological response of the body. "Control" in control theory and reality therapy is not the control of dominance, but the control of *choice of behaviors* based on internal needs that are innate. Glasser uses the image of a car (Figure 7-1) to describe total behavior. The engine represents our needs and the steering wheel represents our decision-making, our wants (note, only one driver!). The front wheels can be steered, the rear wheels follow. The front wheels represent our choices of doing and thinking. The rear wheels represent the feeling and physiological components. When our needs are not being satisfied it is best to use the thinking and/or doing components rather than focus our attention on how we feel emo-

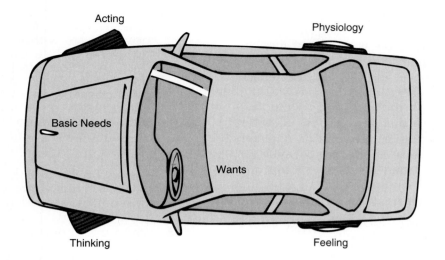

FIGURE 7-1

Total Behavior

tionally or physiologically. Usually as we change our actions and our thinking the feelings will begin to change as will the physiology. In the following example you will note that the behavior ranges from aggression to passive-aggression to withdrawal.

Example: A child is being shunned on the playground. Her need for love and belonging is frustrated; she feels powerless and certainly isn't having any fun. There are several choices before her: she can choose to locate and join another group or pair up with another child (thinking and doing); she can disrupt the play of the group that shunned her by grabbing their jump rope and running off with it, or she can tell the teacher. If her pictures (mental images of past quality experiences) for satisfying her need for love and belonging are limited to that one small group that has shunned her, she will most likely either choose to tell the teacher, to withdraw and refuse to play, to disrupt the game, or get sick. If she has a less restrictive set of pictures for satisfying her love and belonging needs, then she will likely choose to find another playing group. If the learning environment is highly regimented and she must remain with the learning group to which she was assigned, and fears the consequences of disrupting the group, she will probably choose to tell the teacher, or withdraw and depress, or stay with the group and not do her best (passive-aggressive). Whatever behavior she chooses, it will be the behavior that she thinks is her best choice for her needs-satisfaction in this situation.

Very large classes require efficient class-management procedures.

CREATING A POSITIVE LEARNING ENVIRONMENT

Like the classroom, the gymnasium is meant to be a place of learning. However, it can become the scene of a never-ending battle in which teacher and students struggle to satisfy individual needs. When this happens, the casualties are usually heavy and most often detrimental to desirable learning.

In an educational environment that links needs-satisfaction and learning, students more easily place a positive value on learning. The physical education class offers multiple opportunities for satisfaction of all the basic needs. Quality experience in this learning environment can do much to facilitate the child's attitude about school in general. When the child values learning and school, behaviors will be chosen that enhance learning rather than behaviors that fight against it. Both students and teachers have these basic internal needs that influence behavioral choices. The teacher's job is to be aware of the needs and do all she/he can to create a class environment that allows the basic physical and psychological needs to be acknowledged and satisfied.

Control theory states that all human behavior is purposeful and chosen as a person's current best attempt to satisfy one or more basic needs. Keeping in mind that we have the ability to fulfill our needs and can do this for ourselves, it follows that a healthy learning environment will offer students and teacher the opportunity to satisfy their needs while learning new skills and refining known skills. This learning environment will be a place of nourishment, challenge and growth for students and teacher

alike, rather than a place of punishment, guilt, and shame. As manager of the learning environment, the teacher sets the tone for a positive or negative learning environment. The quality teacher leads the students in focusing on needs-satisfaction, respect, self-evaluation and responsible quality performance.

In a physical education class being taught by such a teacher, the following conditions will be observable:

1. The setting is perceived by the students to be psychologically safe, where threats are noticeably absent, expectations are realistic, ineffective behaviors (i.e., mistakes) are allowed, restitution is encouraged, early success is common, and feedback is appropriate.
2. The students are treated as worthwhile individuals capable of learning and meeting their needs in responsible and appropriate ways.
3. Progressive acquisition of motor, cognitive and affective skills are diligently planned with positive expectancy of their attainment.

The physical education setting can be a very needs-fulfilling environment for all students and teachers as well. The main characteristic that needs to be lessened is that of coercion. Let's look at some communications examples (Table 7-1) of how this might be accomplished.

The reader might want to think of teacher comments that would be considered coercive. Most of us have experienced and provided a lot of coercion thinking it was the best way to motivate. Has it worked to facilitate change of attitudes and/or behaviors?

Table 7-1

Less-coercive Teacher Messages

SITUATION	NON-COERCIVE COMMENTS
Students won't participate.	What are you trying to tell me? What do you want?
Student is frequently off task during skills practice	What are you supposed to be doing? Can you do that? What do you need?
Student is disrespectful.	Is this the way you want to behave? What do you need? How can you make this right?
Student lies.	Is this the way you want to behave? What do you most need right now?
Student breaks a class rule.	What's the rule? Can you do that? What do you need so you can follow the class rule?

There are many teacher tasks that facilitate the development of a positive learning environment. One very important task is learning the children's names—no easy task when you may see 500–600 students per week. Children experience satisfaction of their needs for power and belonging when the teacher calls them by name. The teacher's frequent use of the student's names will model needs-satisfaction behavior that the students can use to help one another.

Systems that permit the rapid learning of names are valuable tools for the teacher. We suggest the following:

1. Study the class rolls prior to the first class day. Surnames of former students and siblings may be recognized. The wise teacher will refrain from referring to former students as this may be perceived as the initial step of a long line of comparisons.
2. Arrange the class in alphabetical squads (an even number of squads if possible) prior to the first class meeting. Squads should contain no more than six students.
3. On the first day of class, call the roll and make notations beside names that will help recall faces. The entire class can become actively involved in this process by repeating each student's name after the teacher calls it.
4. Play at least one name game on the first day (e.g., "Back-to-Back Tag" with partners introducing one another to the entire group).
5. Each evening during the first week review squad lists and recall faces (now you know the importance of the notations suggested in item 3).
6. Each day have on an index card a small number of names and diligently set a goal to learn them before the end of the class period.

Students who misbehave find a certain security in anonymity. Children hearing their name become more responsible for their behavior.

Other teacher tasks that facilitate the development of a positive learning physical education environment are the prompt beginning for each class, and a specific beginning and stopping signal for an activity. A special signal for immediate attention (e.g., two sharp blasts of whistle) and cessation of activity is important for several reasons, the two most important being safety and efficiency. The stop signal should be well-known and the accompanying expected behavior should be practiced by the students. Any number of games (e.g., Freeze Tag variation) can help the students learn to listen while moving, and to "stop-freeze" on the appropriate stop signal.

BEHAVIOR EXPECTATIONS IN THE GYMNASIUM

Each child has a deep need to experience the satisfaction of her/his basic psychological needs of love and belonging, power, freedom to make choices, and having fun. Each teacher has the same basic needs to satisfy and, in the class setting, the greatest need for most teachers is for the children to listen, relate with respect, and cooperatively engage in learning tasks. The professional teacher will help students learn behaviors that allow student needs to be satisfied while teachers also experience needs-satisfaction. How does the teacher do this? How do the teacher and students best relate to one another in this non-coercive, self-evaluating, fun environment and learn the appropriate skills and values?

We know that coercion will not generate needs-satisfying experiences or facilitate change. This approach has been used in the educational setting for a long time with minimal positive results.

The reality therapy process is offered as a method for teachers and students to effectively work together in needs-satisfying ways. Remember, reality therapy is the process that everyone can use to put control theory to work in their lives. This process also provides a very clear and simple way for the teacher to model desirable behaviors appropriate for the school setting and for life in general. The focus of reality therapy is always on cooperative (*i.e.*, teacher and student) problem-solving for the "better way" rather than on the power struggle (*i.e.*, teacher *vs* student) of "my way is best."

Some of the students' need for power is satisfied when they know what is expected of them, and are encouraged to self-evaluate on an ongoing basis. The teacher can enable this self-evaluation by observation and open-ended questions (*e.g.*, "How are things going?" "Can you do what is expected?" "Is that easy/difficult for you?"). The caring teacher will allow practice time for expected behaviors that may be new or difficult so that all students are given opportunity to understand the expectations and can feel good about their quality performance—the best they can do at the time. The expectations must be fair, with the probability that everyone will be able to meet them at some level. Granted, not all children will progress at the same rate; however, individualization was never meant to give license to behaviors less than those each student is capable of performing.

Perhaps one of the most difficult decisions a teacher must make is the prioritizing of student behaviors. It is neither practical nor desirable to react to each and every student behavior whether it is positive or negative. Naturally, there are those undesirable behaviors that require an immediate corrective response on the part of the teacher (see discipline strategies)—especially when the inappropriate behavior creates a safety hazard (physical or psychological).

All rules and consequences need to be posted; they should be few in number, simply stated, and agreed to by all concerned. Rules will vary according to school system expectations, teacher philosophies, and maturity of the students. Rules for appropriate behaviors in the elementary school physical education class need to include:

1. Be safe at all times.
2. Listen and follow directions.
3. Cooperate.
4. Freeze on signal.
5. Respect others and equipment.
6. No chewing gum.

Behavior expectations for the students should focus on needs-satisfaction and quality performance. The first rule of thumb is to consider all the children as worthy human beings capable of learning (although not always at the same pace), and meeting their own needs. Teachers should help children to understand the many similarities all humans have in common rather than to emphasize differences. The authors encourage the beginning teacher to realize that children bring to school more than their bodies and lunch pails. Differences in lifestyles and cultural background cannot and should not be ignored. Neither should they be emphasized nor used as an excuse by teachers or students to explain away different expectations of children coming from different cultural backgrounds. Teachers need to make an effort to understand how the children's backgrounds relate to the children's needs and to use that knowledge to guide youngsters to quality performance and greater needs-satisfaction. Teachers most clearly demonstrate respect for all people when they facilitate the learning of all students; this responsible teacher behavior helps each student to progress toward becoming fully the person he or she was created to be.

POSITIVE ATTITUDE DEVELOPMENT

Very young children usually come to school thinking everything is going to be great in school. This attitude will especially be prevalent if the child comes from a needs-satisfying home environment. Sometimes, the teacher may not be in the children's quality world, but the caring adults in their lives have told them to obey. Wanting to please these significant adults, they obey. However, if the teacher persists in asking them to do things that are not needs-fulfilling, or the teacher is coercive, he/she may never gain acceptance into the children's quality world. The way for the teacher to gain admittance into their children's quality world is to understand the different ways through which the children are able to experience needs-satisfaction. For example:

1. Doing funny things and laughing are fun.
2. Being listened to feels important (power)
3. Making choices gives me a sense of freedom and power.
4. Being allowed to figure out ways to correct mistakes allows me to feel confident and worthwhile.

Teachers have excellent opportunities to facilitate the development of positive attitudes within students. Often adults take a child's good behavior for granted and find themselves responding to negative behaviors while ignoring appropriate behaviors. Positive attitudinal development can be reinforced on a daily basis through ongoing self-evaluation by the students and the teacher's creative and prudent use of positive feedback. For children, the effort towards quality is of great importance and the quality teacher will not let it go unnoticed. A student-teacher chose to remind students of quality behaviors by listing "exceptional" behaviors on a poster (Figure 7-2). The attitude of respect for one another (use of self-space principle can be very effective in this regard) and for equipment

EXCEPTIONALS
Individual performance effort
Over-all performance class effort
Sustained cooperative effort
Obeying the rules effort
Safety effort
Listening effort

FIGURE 7-2
Non-coercive Behavior Expectations

must be taught, reinforced, and frequently retaught. For example, when two or four children carry a tumbling mat, the mat should not get a "floor burn" from being dragged. Teachers who model respect for others and for property will help students to be more open in their dealings with authority figures. Students who struggle with unmet needs for power and freedom, and who do not have a way of effectively meeting their power and freedom needs, will usually have difficulty working with obvious authority figures. An attitude of respect and cooperation with authority is sometimes more naturally fostered when the teacher is liked and respected by the students and the students experience love and belonging. Attitudes of cooperative play and honorable competition can be fostered through well-chosen games and good officiating. The responsible attitude of safety can be fostered as the children realize they too are responsible for the safety of their play environment.

Positive attitude development is also influenced by opportunities to learn behaviors that are appropriate for satisfying individual needs. It is very important that the teacher always keep in mind the child's struggle with the desire for instant needs-satisfaction. The more needs-satisfaction the child experiences at home the easier it will be for her/him to agree to do the "work of today" even though the "pay-off" might not be until later. This "later" dilemma is often experienced in the school setting, and frustrates the student's needs of feeling important (power), making choices (freedom), working in groups (belonging), and pleasure (fun). Let's face it, learning is work, and the more academic the subject, the harder it is to keep the environment needs-fulfilling. All the more reason for the teacher to pay particular attention to the many small opportunities in a class period for the child to lead (power), choose activities (freedom), work in groups (belonging), and laugh (fun). The teacher who demonstrates such respect and compassion for the students will greatly facilitate the ability to delay some needs-gratification. This is the heart of self-discipline.

Unfortunately some children come to school from a background of constant needs-gratification regardless of appropriateness of behavior. These "overly-indulged" children frequently disrupt the give- and-take interactions necessary in all class settings, where each child is striving for satisfaction of many individual needs. The other extreme is the child who comes to school with such a backlog of needs-satisfaction deprivation that much of her/his behavior is inappropriate, because in fending for himself/herself, needs may be met but behaviors quite likely are not appropriate, respectful, safe for the individual or others. Lawrence (1987) in *People types and tiger stripes* reminds us that the adult world has the responsibility to help children learn that satisfaction can be expected, and appropriate behaviors learned.

Each time children experience the freedom and limits of trusting their perception of what is expected and trusting their judgment of what is appropriate, their positive attitudinal development as well as self-confidence and respect for self, others and the environment are enhanced. Not only will students learn behaviors more appropriate for the school setting, they will also carry these skills into the adult world and enjoy higher levels of autonomy, freedom, love, and happiness.

COMMUNICATION SKILLS

Both class management and discipline procedures require considerable reflection and planning by the teacher and discussion with the students. The complex verbal and nonverbal interactions between and among students, and between students and teacher require ongoing interpretation by both teacher and students.

Effective teachers must be able to communicate to the learner the essential information needed. A common mistake of beginning teachers is to present more information than is needed for the initial learning to begin. Successful teachers have found the following reminders effective when presenting a lesson.

1. Teacher enthusiasm helps generate student interest in lesson content.
2. Body language and facial expressions should be congruent with what the teacher is expressing verbally.
3. Detailed, but flexible lesson plans facilitate a more orderly presentation of the lesson. Beginning teachers especially will want to include on the lesson plan the key points for each skill being taught.
4. Class atmosphere should be friendly, with the teacher modeling a sincerity about the expected accomplishment of the lesson.
5. Questions, challenges and specific feedback ashould be used to obtain and maintain student attention and to help them stay focused on the objectives of the lesson.
6. Objectives of the lesson are shared with the students at the beginning of the lesson. Let's say the objective is to dribble the basketball 20 feet without looking at the ball. The objective can be shared either verbally ("Kevin, what goal will you set for yourself so you will know when you have done your best?"), or written (chalkboard or poster stating incremental goals).
7. Students are encouraged to state personal objectives for each class period.
8. Demonstrations are presented in both side and front views.
9. Demonstrations are performed, when possible, as key points are spoken. Students need to see skills demonstrated both in slow speed and operational speed.

10. Eye contact and frequent use of names help the students stay focused.

11. Asking the questions, "How will you know when you are doing well? What are the benchmarks you want to set for yourself?", may help keep the student's interest high, be needs-satisfying for power and freedom, and facilitate self-evaluation.

12. Visualization (mental images) helps to clarify (e.g., "Can you finish your forward roll in good form, stretched tall as if you were an Olympian?").

13. Questioning techniques help the teacher evaluate how students are receiving the instruction (e.g., "Michael, in what direction are you to rotate when you hear the signal?").

14. Current events and historical records are used to call attention to current high achievers (ranging from disabled through professional, children through adult, local through international). This data can be announced (verbally, or bulletin board) by teacher and/or students.

There will be many opportunities for the teacher, through good communication techniques, to model respect and friendliness to the students. So often we say things to children without realizing the effect on the child. The quality school teacher will want to send messages to the student that are non-coercive, encourage self-evaluation, and enhance self-esteem. This sets the environment for students and teacher to have greater regard for self and the other person. Students who experience this kind of respect will then begin using it among themselves.

Table 7-2 offers examples of messages that block communication and diminish self esteem compared to messages that facilitate communication and self-esteem. Note in the drawings where self-esteem is so impacted that the figures have no eyes, and no ears because when addressed in these abrasive ways the student becomes hostile, closes down, can't see or hear and eventually gives up (no hands) trying to do anything. The seeing, hearing, doing, happy figures depict a student maintaining dignity and a sense of well-being. This student grows in self-esteem and is able to perform with quality.

MANAGERIAL SKILLS

The effective teacher must be a skilled manager of time, space, people, and things. Research tells us that the smoothness of transitions between phases of the lesson and between activities is of utmost importance to the level of success of the lesson. The momentum or flow of the lesson is closely related to the transitions because when these factors are efficiently managed, the students are provided a maximum amount of quality learning (practice) time. There are many factors to consider such as management of equipment, grouping of students, use of space, and so forth.

Many school districts have a behavior management policy. This facilitates promoting good behavior throughout the school. It is up to the physical educator to develop the specifics about the unique teaching environment of physical education.

The following managerial techniques have been used by teachers who are considered to be effective managers.

1. Use "My Job—Your Job" technique to establish the responsibilities of teacher/students. In this process, both teacher and student become responsible for the success of the class. Questions are asked not to control, or to coerce, but to enable the development of a learning team, all working for quality levels of needs-satisfaction and performance. In this clear-cut way the teacher shares with the students his/her view of teacher as leader of a learning environment. Some of the questions that need to be cooperatively explored are: Whose job is it to teach? Whose job is it to learn? Whose job is it to motivate? Whose job is it to listen, problem-solve? Whose job is it to discipline? Whose job is it to model appropriate behaviors? Whose job is it to create a safe learning environment? These questions are not to just be answered "ours" or "yours," but through discussion to facilitate awareness and exploration of the big picture as well as some of the specifics of the learning environment. Obviously, some of these questions will not be asked of very young children, but all should be seriously considered in the teacher's personal reflection.

2. Develop lesson plans that include such information as predicted time for each phase of the lesson, kind and amount of equipment and clearly stated objectives, and alternative ways of achieving the objectives.

3. Use an established routine to begin class.

4. Provide task cards (individual or at stations) to give instructions to the students.

5. Post (usually in a central area) as much class information (team assignments, rotation, procedures, class rules) as is appropriate for the maturity level of the students. Encourage students always to check their "message center". Issue positive reinforcement to those who look for information upon entering the gym ("Kathy, I noticed you reading the new poster. Can you tell the class what it says?").

6. Encourage the development of self-management skills in the students by frequently reinforcing "hustling," cooperation, self-evaluation, initiative, and other positive self-management behaviors.

7. Set up the necessary equipment before class begins. When appropriate, encourage leadership by letting students assist in storing equipment.

Table 7-2

Messages That Block—Messages That Facilitate

Messages that Block Communication and Impact Self-esteem.	Messages that Facilitate Communication and Self-esteem.
What are you doing?	Would you find a more effective way of handling this? Thank you.
You *always* have a problem!	Would you want to problem-solve this situation?
You *never* seem to know what to do!	What are you supposed to be doing?
Don't talk back to me!	Say more about what you need.
Stop that behavior!	What are you trying to tell me from your behavior?
	What do you want me to know?

"Students can more easily and more naturally translate reality therapy and control theory messages into positive regard for themselves and their teachers.

Angele Marino, ACSW, LMSW-ACP: LMFT
Reality Therapy Certified
Expressive Therapies Center, Houston TX

Secured equipment is less of a distraction during instruction.

8. Teach time-saving routines for equipment issue and retrieval, for reporting scores, and for taking skills tests.

9. Teach several methods for students to use in securing equipment. When additional instruction is being given, younger children may have to be told (or given no more than two choices) a method to use, while older students may choose (from several possibilities) to place the equipment between their feet, or hold equipment overhead, to prevent the distraction of bouncing balls during instruction.

10. Use frequent positive and corrective feedback interactions that have both informative and value content (*e.g.*, "Nice work, class, it only took 20 seconds to put the jump ropes back on the hook (information)—now we have time to play with the parachute (value). Bill, you're certainly staying with this task; I have counted at least 10 tries (value/information). Do you think stepping out on the foot opposite your throwing arm will help your accuracy?" (information).

11. Emphasize the importance of time by challenging classes to complete management-type tasks quickly (organizing groups, handling equipment, and so forth). Low-keyed competition can also be effective. Classes can compete against each other, or against their previous scores. Let the students help set the desired standard for quality.

12. Maintain low percentages of management time in such circumstances as transitions between activities, waiting in line, taking attendance.

13. Demonstrate energy, enthusiasm, and "hustle" behavior as you teach the class. This will encourage the students to become more involved with both the content and the process of the lesson, and remain on task for longer periods of time.

14. Invite the students to enter into the learning for the day. I know everyone is excited about today's activity on the fitness equipment; listen well, so everyone will know the rotation procedure.

15. Teach a variety of ways to quickly organize into teams of all sizes.

16. Move about the periphery of the class rather than maintaining a static position in the center. Try to keep your back to a wall rather than to a group of students.

17. Scan the entire class frequently.

18. Use a release signal to let students know when to begin an activity.

Ineffective Teacher Behaviors

Some teacher behaviors can contribute to disruption and confusion within the learning environment. Kounin (1970) indicated that smooth transitions and appropriate momentum are the most important management skills for promotion of work involvement and class control. What follows is a summary of the key points of Kounin's research regarding the effect of teaching behaviors on the flow and momentum of a lesson.

"Jerky" transitions are caused by teacher "thrusts," which occur when a teacher suddenly interrupts an activity in progress without regard to the effect on flow of the lesson. This interrupts the concentration of the students. For example, a group of students playing a game are told abruptly to stop the activity and join another group involved in another activity. It would be more effective to tell the students they had one minute to finish the game. Another cause of jerky transitions can be caused by teacher behavior that Kounin calls "dangles" interrupting an activity in progress to initiate a second activity. Later, the teacher may return with a "flip-flop" to the first activity (*e.g.*, a class working with lummi sticks is stopped while the teacher takes a lunch count [dangle], then lummi activity is resumed [flip-flop]). The lunch count must be handled before or after the activity. Obviously, jerky transitions are not desirable teacher behaviors because of the accompanying confusion and interruption of momentum that encourages student misbehaviors.

Teachers can also interrupt the flow of a lesson if they take too long between activities. The teaching behaviors of "overdwelling" or "fragmentation" are frequent teacher disrupters. Teachers who talk too long experience difficulty in holding the attention of the children. Too much information is boring to children and often a waste of time. A better approach is to give the bare essentials of directions and proceed with the activity. The teacher can give additional information as it is needed by the students. Overdwelling on misbehavior is perceived by children as nagging, and is detrimental to the overall learning environment. Fragmentation occurs when group tasks are broken into too many small steps ("Line up and, one by one, put your rope on the hook, then return to your squad line." When everyone has completed that task—"Now go get a playground ball, one at a time and come back to your squad line, and sit down"—"hold the balls, hold the balls," and so on). A more efficient procedure is to say, "On the signal, take your jump rope to one of the hooks and hang it evenly, then get a playground ball, and see how many times you can toss it to yourself and catch it while walking back to your self-space—for every time the ball touches the floor take away one catch." Of course the developmental level will determine the quantity of instruction that can be given at any one time.

Though the flow of a lesson can be negatively influenced by both student and teacher behaviors, awareness is the first step toward eliminating disrupters in the learning process. Videotapes and tape recordings will help teachers determine the frequency of disruptive behaviors.

Positive Teacher Behaviors

Students report their desire for teachers who care about them and make the learning of relevant life skills and knowledge fun. Throughout this chapter the impor-

tance of needs-fulfillment and quality performance have been stressed and we have looked at communication skills. There are many ways for a teacher to be a positive influence for quality (Table 7-3). The single most important teacher behavior identified by Kounin is "with-itness" (as in "eyes in the back of the head"). Students perceive such a teacher as an alert teacher who takes teaching and learning seriously and is capable of accurately reading each situation. For example, when a discipline problem arises, the teacher sees it early, and is able to stop the incident before it grows into a larger problem. Likewise, this teacher notices student success, and celebrates that with the student. Now we will look at some specific teacher behaviors and strategies that can enhance learning in a needs-satisfying environment.

Discipline Strategies

Is it lack of discipline or lack of understanding that has such a grip on students, teachers and all who play a role in the education of our youth? Are the real culprits lack of self-discipline, lack of quality performance, lack of respect? Students, parents, teachers, administrators, the general public—all have a stake in the way students are taught, managed and encouraged to do their best. "Us against them" won't work. The teacher is the adult professional and must find the way that will instill attention, respect, self-discipline and quality performance. What is the best way to help students who sometimes make mistakes, sometimes are unhappy, unproductive and uncooperative in school?

From birth, we have made behavior choices that seemed the best way at the time to do what we think would most satisfy one or more of our basic needs. Often what we need is not clear to us and this is especially true for children. The door to better understanding which need is unsatisfied is to be able to name our feelings. Children want to feel *good* and they know the difference between feeling good and not feeling good. The perceptive teacher and parent will look for ways to help the child transfer this recognition of how they feel to what they need. The child will ask for food or something to drink without an understanding that their survival need is calling for attention. They ask for food because of an inner knowing that says they need food to feel good at that particular moment. The same can be said for wanting the laughter (fun), fellowship (belonging), achievement (power), and choices (freedom) of play.

It is not the intent of this chapter to explore all available disciplinary philosophies. Many seasoned teachers pick the best techniques from a number of disciplinary systems. The following specific strategies are suggested to assist the teacher in teaching life-skills that enhance self-esteem, teamwork, self-evaluation and quality performance; and, can be used to enhance discipline techniques already in place.

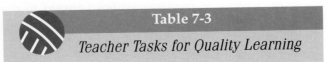

Table 7-3

Teacher Tasks for Quality Learning

Learn student's names promptly and use frequently
Invite the students into the learning process
Teach life skills and self-evaluation
Begin and end class on time
Provide a safe and respectful non-coercive environment

RESTITUTION

There are times when a teacher needs a quick control system that is not too coercive and helps students take control of their actions. They also need a system to help students restore themselves when their behavior has been inappropriate and they don't feel good about it.

Restitution (Gossen, 1993) is a reality-based strategy for resolving conflict using a needs-satisfying procedure. Depending on the circumstance, it can be very quick, or it can require considerable reflection and planning. All the control theory and reality therapy concepts apply to this process of restitution, which can be explained simply as finding a way to make a situation better: and allowing the one acting inappropriately to restore her/himself and allowing justice for the one(s) offended. The focus of restitution is on helping the students to strengthen themselves; it is based on the premise that children want to be happy, and can change themselves and their behavior. Restitution is not something outside ourselves to be learned, rather it is something we tap into that is innate.

Ineffective behavior is an inevitable variable of the human condition. In the process of becoming aware of their needs, children explore many different ways to get what they want. Operating in a dynamic of gross behaviors in need of fine-tuning, some choices are less effective than others and are often labeled as mistakes—meaning wrong. Being "wrong" usually makes a child feel fearful and shuts down self-esteem and creative problem-solving. However, if we accept that all behavior is purposeful, then most of these "mistakes" are actually behaviors that are "not as effective" as one would desire for the well-being of the student, teacher and class. The behavior, being purposeful, is still that child's best attempt at that time to get what he/she wants and experience needs-satisfaction.

Students who work and play in an environment where ineffective behavior is treated as an opportunity for learning do not experience fear of making mistakes. This frees the student to learn simple and creative ways to engage in restitution. One thing that makes a behavior ineffective is if it violates the rights of another—even though the ineffective behavior is thought by the student to be his/her best behavior choice, persisting in such behavior will actually not result in needs-satisfaction for the offender.

Non-judgmental questions offered by the teacher facilitate the problem-solving process as the child searches for creative ways to restitute self and restore a balance in the relationship. A true restitution can not be mandatory and serves first to restore the self-esteem of the offender, although the one whose rights have been violated also benefits.

There are two kinds of circumstances that could call for restitution. In one circumstance there is a wrong done to another person, and the offender is not feeling good about it. (This would include accidents.)

The teacher's role in this situation is first to reassure the student that he/she still "belongs" and then to help the student gain some perspective on what is happening and to make plans for change. In this circumstance the student will usually have more choices in the planning stage ("What do you want to do?"). The question, "What's happening?" asked in a patient, non-judging, matter-of-fact manner will hopefully allow the child to be in touch with still being accepted and of experiencing the freedom to state truthfully what has happened. The questions, "Is this the way you want to be?", "Are you getting what you need?" are to help the child get to the value judgment. It's important to help the child to be able to express what he/she values (e.g., "I want to be in a cooperative relationship." "I want to be having fun." "I want to be captain once in awhile." "I want to be choosing my own partner.") Once the student can verbalize what she/he wants (values), the plan to get what is needed (e.g., to be captain) can be explored, committed to, and implemented.

The other kind of circumstance is when an established rule, process, or program is being violated. This is a circumstance where the student does not have many options and, in fact, it may boil down to the choice of either obeying the rule or suffering the consequences. In this case the question,"What are you supposed to be doing?" helps the teacher enter into the circumstance without immediately judging the child (providing the tone of voice isn't accusing), and also checks out if the child actually knows what the rule or process is that has been assigned. The question helps the child to focus on her/his understanding of what task is to be completed, and also allows the opportunity for her/him to answer—"I'm not sure." or "I don't know." The second question "What are you doing?" helps both teacher and student focus on the behavior and the question, "Is it helping you?" begins the self-evaluation process necessary to get underneath the behavior to the value judgment. At this point, the teacher will be getting a pretty clear picture of what need the student is trying to satisfy.

The questions found in Table 7-4 will help the teacher facilitate self-evaluation behaviors and appropriate behavioral change in the students.

CONSEQUENCES

Whereas restitution focuses more on being and inner strengthening for self-discipline, consequences focuses more on doing as the rules require. In other words, the students learns to conform to an external rule. Most often teachers look at consequences as removal of a privilege, additional assignments, detention. Most consequences are really punishments designed to bring misery more so than change. Sometimes, either because of immaturity of the student, or the strength of the rebellion, a student will not be able to cooperate. At such times the student is choosing the consequences rather than to work out a restitution.

Table 7-4	
Reality Therapy Evaluative Questions to Get to the Value Judgments	
When things aren't working right	**Working with established rule, process or program**
Many options available	Few options available
What do you want? What do you need?	What are you supposed to be doing?
What are you doing? What's happening?	What are you doing?
Is it working? Are you getting what you need?	Can you follow the rules?
What do you want to do? Do you need some help?	Restitution or consequences?

For a consequence to have a positive outcome, it must provide opportunity to shape a positive behavior—one that will lead to change. When looked at this way each misbehavior can truly be seen as an opportunity to learn new needs-satisfying behaviors.

TIME-OUT

The time-out disciplinary technique is used for those times when the student's ineffective behaviors are interrupting the learning process for self or others. "Time-out" provides the opportunity for a disruptive student to get in touch with feelings. What is needed is a more effective way that allows for the needs of the student, teacher and class to be satisfied. This temporary removal from the activity of the class permits a time of "respite" for creative planning and regrouping. Not viewed as a punishment (even a teacher can announce, "I need to take time-out."), the process allows the student an opportunity to learn a life skill for dealing with stress. To initiate the process the teacher (without anger) removes the child by saying,

> John, since you have said you do not want to plan a restitution, then the consequence you are faced with is time out. This would not be what I would want for you, but the choice is yours. Would you like to reconsider restitution? "No?" Okay, then you have repeatedly used the equipment in a dangerous way; and now you are choosing time-out. So now what is the rule? What are you supposed to do? That's right. Go to the time-out area and think about the class safety rules, especially the rules for the horizontal ladder. When you want to obey the rules, and you can tell me how you are going to act I will let you back into the activity.

The location of the time-out area (chair, bench, floor) should be on the periphery of the class and in full view of the teacher. The teacher may tell the child to face away from the class. If a child is sent to the time-out area a second time during the same class period, he or she must remain there the rest of the period. Every effort must be made by the teacher for this to be a time of reorganizing (creative problem solving) for the child. Most young children have not developed an aversion to play activity; however, if it becomes apparent that a child is trying to avoid the activity, then an alternative technique, (*e.g.,* teacher-student conference) needs to be used.

TEACHER-STUDENT CONFERENCES

The relationship between teacher and students is most critical to the overall success of the learning environment. It is important that students view teachers as caring, fair, competent and consistent. Children, out of their need for love and belonging and power, normally want to please adults. This desire to please will usually be prompted either when they are afraid of angering the adult, or when they seek approval. Of course, teachers would prefer that children obey because they are happy, feel safe, and enjoy what they are learning. When a child does not follow the rules or procedures of the class, the teacher should first look inward for the reason. Teachers should ask themselves, "What am I doing, or not doing, that may be encouraging this child to act this way?" A violation of any of the good teacher practices listed previously under managerial skills (such as unclear rules, not paying attention to all of the students, and high percentage of management time) can adversely affect the behaviors of individual students or even an entire class.

Once the above question has been answered, then it is appropriate for the teacher to consider possible handicaps of the student (*e.g.,* poor hearing or sight, poor nutrition, perceptual motor problems, emotional problems). These questions can only be answered by the teacher making the effort to know the student. This can be accomplished by obtaining data from several sources: the child, parents, permanent records, school counselor, nurse, other teachers.

Sometimes all it takes for the student to be more cooperative is for her/him to realize that the teacher's goal is to help the student get their needs met, improve fitness and motor skills and thereby enjoy physical activity. Besides modeling this in the class setting the teacher-student conference offers another opportunity for this to be communicated.

When a teacher confers with a child privately, several things must occur. First of all, the child must not feel threatened by the thought of a "talk with the teacher." Simply say to the child, in a friendly non-threatening manner, "Meagan, I'd like to talk to you today after your lunch. I was thinking about asking Miss Jones if you could come to the physical education office when you have finished eating. Would that be okay with you?"

Second the problem must be stated as it is perceived by both teacher and student. The teacher should be honest, gentle and direct, (*e.g.*,"Meagan, you don't seem to be having much fun when you are in your physical education class. Do you suppose we could talk about this?") This invitation needs to convey genuine interest and not be accusatory. Use the reality therapy questions to help the student get in touch with needs that are not being met when in the physical education class. This is not the appropriate time to lecture on class rules, behavior, and so forth. However it is the time for the teacher to state her/his need for rules to be followed and for Meagan to learn more appropriate behaviors. Meagan will benefit by the teacher's modeling of honoring the needs of all—teacher, Meagan and class.

Third, help the student self-evaluate, and then together come up with a plan that will help him or her to experience and evaluate needs-satisfaction and enjoy the time in physical education. Last, schedule another meeting to evaluate his/her progress. This evaluation is a cooperative effort and can be very needs-fulfilling for both the student and teacher.

The following questions (adapted from Glasser) may help the student enter more fully into the self-evaluation process.

1. What are your strongest points?
2. What works best for you? Why?
3. What help could you use to do a better job?
4. How do you see yourself helping others in the class?
5. What one thing do you want most to improve?
6. Do you need any help in making this change?

TEACHER-PARENT CONFERENCES

Most parents want to help their children be successful in school, and certainly all parents have the right to know of their child's successes and failures. Just as academic reports of progress are given to parents, so too should behavior reports be issued. At the kindergarten and first-grade level most children respond very well to teacher intervention of their misbehaviors. By the second grade, however, some students have begun to test authority figures and therefore require more sophisticated disciplinary strategies. Children who chronically choose to behave inappropriately are asking for something they need and are not receiving. Often the child cannot even label what it is that is needed.

The authors believe that parents should be apprised when inappropriate behavior becomes frequent. The first step is for the teacher and the student to try to work things out by using some or all of the strategies mentioned earlier. Without a doubt, the least effective method for dealing with inappropriate behavior is to send the student to the principal. When teacher and student reach an impasse, then the parents should be called and a parent-teacher conference arranged. During this conference the teacher's job is to communicate concern for the child's apparent unhappiness and lack of quality work. It is important that the teacher conveys to the parent the desire to come to a better understanding of the child's needs. The goal of the conference is to find ways to help the child get more of his/her needs met in the school setting through more effective behaviors. This requires some serious problem-solving on the part of the teacher, parent and child. Matter-of-fact reporting of the specific incidents where the child has demonstrated inappropriately aggressive behaviors toward self or others will be helpful. The teacher should carefully avoid being drawn into an argument about the validity of the facts reported. The best way to communicate with a defensive parent is to gently and specifically keep the focus on the goal of finding the best way to help the child meet his/her needs so the student can do his/her best at school and home.

The reality therapy questions presented earlier in the chapter will help maintain the focus for the conference. Trying to explain control theory and reality therapy to the parent might be experienced as threatening. Just stay with the concepts by using the questions. The following is offered as a possible sequence to follow when meeting with a parent of a child not experiencing success in the classroom:

1. State what you want for the child. See if parent wants the same.
2. Explain what you have been doing to help the child become more self-disciplined and produce quality work.
3. Describe how it is not working.
4. Express your desire to find a way(s) that will work.
5. Ask for parental input.

6. Develop a plan with the parent. Let each state their level of commitment.
7. Discuss how each of you will work with the child
8. Set a date for the evaluation of the plan

Sometimes, rather than aggressive behaviors, the child will habitually withdraw from the activity or from the other children. Still other children may choose to say they will do something, and then do nothing (passive-aggressive). All three of these behavior choices are unhealthy and must be addressed.

Once the parent believes in the teacher's sincerity, then real progress can be made provided both teacher and parents choose to cooperatively seek a better understanding of the child's needs and come to some agreement about their individual roles in helping the child. Rather than demanding specific behaviors, it is better to help the child learn how to choose appropriate need-fulfilling behaviors. The school counselor can also be a valuable resource for parents, teachers and child. Before culminating the conference, it is important that the parent understand what the teacher is willing to do to help the child and *vica versa*. It is also important that parents and teacher continue to communicate with one another about the progress that the student demonstrates. The child, knowing that both home and school are working together, may experience some satisfaction of his/her needs for belonging and power. Hopefully, opportunity for choices and fun will be built into the plan. With this experience of needs-satisfaction, the child can become more engaged in experiencing the new expectations and respond positively by learning more appropriate behaviors. This is not to say that correcting inappropriate behavior is easy and that change will be rapid and painless. However, a cooperative team approach (when it is realistic, accepting, non-coercive and fair) is more likely to bring about desired results, allowing the student, parent and teacher to experience needs-satisfaction.

Just a word about the presence or absence of the child at the time of the conference. If the teacher decides that it is in the child's best interest for the parent and teacher to meet alone, the teacher can still set the stage for the child to be more comfortable about the upcoming conference. It is important that the child not feel "it's them against me." Asking the student what he/she thinks would be important for the parent and teacher to discuss (*e.g.*, "Is there something you would like for me to say?...to ask?") can actually be part of the self-evaluation process. Each case will be different, and what the teacher wants to avoid is setting up a power struggle. This might happen if the child is present in the confer-

ence. The entire process should help the child to engage in self-evaluation and tap into the inner desire to be a cooperative and successful contributor to the overall learning process, rather than placing the child in a coercive setting that brings about change out of fear.

SOME THOUGHTS ON PUNISHMENT

The need for punishment becomes apparent in situations of severe, chronic misbehavior. Though punishment does have a role to play, most children will respond positively to some of the disciplinary strategies that we have discussed. However, when the child does not choose restitution, or the consequences aren't working, and punishment seems to be inevitable, the authors strongly encourage the following guidelines.

1. Treat each child with respect and dignity.
2. Refrain from using physical exercise (*e.g.*, calisthenics and running) as punishment.
3. Administer necessary punishment objectively, quickly, and fairly.
4. Once the punishment is completed, the slate is clean.
5. Group punishment is most often ineffective.
6. Refrain from using peer group pressure (even if it seems positive). Some who can be manipulated by peer pressure are susceptible to being manipulated regarding alcohol, drugs, sex, smoking, reckless driving and other inappropriate student behaviors.

BEHAVIOR GAMES

As the name implies, behavior games—a disciplinary strategy described by Siedentop (1983)—uses a game format in which the specific goal is the learning of a specific class behavior. The game is played intermittently during the regular lesson for the day. Behavior games are introduced only when the behavior of a class is especially deviant (for example, many of the students are not paying attention to the stop signal, which is supposed to elicit very specific behavior.

Specific standards for the class are established, and everyone in the class can earn the rewards. The teacher's goal is for everyone to progress to the point at which the desired behavior is demonstrated regularly, therefore signaling that the game is no longer needed. Though this technique is used to change undesired behavior, it should not be viewed by teacher or students as punishment, but rather as quality practice and a fun way to gain total class improvement. The following is an example of a behavior game suitable for Levels II-IV.

Current Undesirable Behavior When signal sounds, most of the children continue to play, to use the equipment, and to talk to one another.

Desired Behavior When the signal sounds, the children should stop, not talk, put equipment down, and listen to the teacher.

Game Structure

1. Entire class plays; all can win.
2. Class is divided into four to six squads; children choose squad names and mascot (optional).
3. Game will be played until 90 percent of students in the class are demonstrating desired behaviors.
4. Reward will be choice of fitness activities on Friday.
5. Game can be played during any lesson being taught; the game is ongoing.

Game Procedure This is an illustration of how a behavioral game can be played.

1. A timer (out of sight of the children) will go off at a time set by the teacher.
2. When the timer sounds, all must stop, place equipment on the floor, quickly move to the designated area for their squads, face the teacher, place hands on hips, and not talk. This must be done within 10 seconds.
3. The teacher will determine quickly which squads are successful and record this on a worksheet.
4. The teacher signals continuation of the lesson and resets the timer.
5. Initially, a timer buzzer should sound four or five times during a 30 minute period. Each behavioral game incident should take no more than one minute (maximum) from the lesson.
6. At the end of the period, the teacher totals the yards for each squad (10-yards for each win) and moves the squad marker accordingly on the poster of a football field (an example to record progress in the game).
7. The objective is to score a touchdown.
8. A touchdown qualifies for 10 minutes of "choice of activity" on Friday.
9. The teacher should state that the normal stopping signal (voice, whistle, other) can also signal the beginning of the behavioral game.
10. If one or two students persist in preventing their squad from winning, the teacher should encourage that squad to help squad members react more quickly. When a mainstreamed child is involved, the teacher must determine what level of conformity can be expected from the child.
11. The game should reward appropriate behaviors, and not punish inappropriate behaviors (unless it becomes absolutely necessary, at which time yards can be deducted).

GUIDELINES FOR DEVELOPING DISCIPLINE STRATEGIES

Central to what is contained in the following guidelines—regardless of the problem a child might have—he/she has the right to be treated with respect at all times. No student should be allowed to engage in behavior that can cause injury to self, or that violates the rights of peers or the teacher. The less coercive environment will have fewer disciplinary problems.

Guidelines for developing discipline strategies include:

1. List areas of misbehavior you may encounter (*e.g.*, inattentiveness, poor self-control, lack of persistence, off task, disrespect for others, inappropriate use of equipment).
2. Know what behaviors (by degrees) you will tolerate, and what behaviors you will stop. Have predetermined methods for discouraging inappropriate behaviors.
3. Keep class rules short and simple (four to six should suffice).
4. Post rules, rewards, and consequences.
5. Explain rules, rewards and consequences to students, parents and administrators.
6. Teach, during the first week of school, a process for restitution.
7. Explain teacher's rights and student's rights. Go through "My Job–Your Job" process.
8. Use the reality therapy questions to redirect behaviors before they become ineffective.
9. Explain that ineffective behaviors (mistakes) can be fertile ground for learning. Without fear of mistakes, a person can

Eye contact is critical when disciplining a student.

actively reorganize her/his perception and discover creative solutions.

10. Call the student by name when asking the student to change behavior.

11. Discuss with students that mistakes (ineffective behaviors) are bound to happen, and that the focus will be on finding more effective behaviors.

12. Explain that it's the child's choice to choose the appropriate behavior, restitution, or consequences.

13. Be a role model for your students; act and speak in the same manner as you expect of them.

14. Focus remarks on the child's behavior rather than on the child ("Tom, what are you supposed to be doing at this station?" rather than, "Tom, why are you not following instructions?").

15. Be very aware of what is going on in your class areas and let the students know how aware you are by timely responses to both appropriate and inappropriate behaviors.

16. Strive to interact with the child fairly when he/she refuses to self-evaluate and do what is required.

17. Avoid coercion and help guide the child toward self-management (see Table 7-2 on less coercive messages).

18. Interact with students on a personal level, and personalize those rules that are applicable to one or a few members of a class.

19. Refrain from imposing excessive rules on the entire class when only a few need additional constraints.

20. Help with individual difficulties in a manner that does not cause undue attention, or embarrassment.

21. Stress choosing good behavior rather than avoiding bad behavior.

22. Help students (with prompts, cues) learn to choose good behavior.

23. Work with individuals to correct behaviors. Group punishment, unless the entire group is at fault, is not a fair disciplinary technique.

24. Apply the "ripple effect." Appropriate interactions directed at one individual, but heard by several on the periphery, will often prevent others from choosing the same inappropriate behavior.

25. Consistently follow through with feedback when appropriate.

26. Strive to maintain a reasonable momentum, encouraging students to remain on task.

27. Choose methods for reinforcement, corrective feedback, and restitution that are developmentally appropriate.

28. Post expected behaviors and call to students' attention, when appropriate.

29. Initiate cooperative behaviors. Teachers, parents, and administrators who work together have higher ratios of success in changing inappropriate behaviors. The teacher is the logical lead person within this triad.

30. Be firm, consistent, fair and friendly. Remember the goals of positive attitudinal development, self-discipline, self-confidence, and respect for self, others and the environments.

REFERENCES

GLASSER, W. (1984). *Control theory: a new explanation of how we control our lives.* New York, NY: Harper Collins.

GLASSER, W. (1986). *Control theory in the classroom.* New York, NY: Harper and Row.

GLASSER, W. (1969). *Reality therapy* New York, NY: Harper Collins.

GLASSER, W. (1990). *The quality school: managing students without coercion.* New York, NY: Harper Collins.

GOSSEN, D. C. (1993). *Restitution: restructuring school discipline.* Chapel Hill, NC: New View Publications.

KOUNIN, J. (1970). *Discipline and group management in classrooms.* New York, NY: Holt, Rinehart and Winston.

LAWRENCE, G. (1987). *People types and tiger stripes: a practical guide to learning styles.* Gainesville, FL: CAPT, Inc.

SIEDENTOP, D. (1983). *Developing teaching skills in physical education.* Palo Alto, CA: Mayfield.

The Institute for Reality Therapy, 7301 Medical Center Drive, Suite 407, Canoga Park, CA 91307, (818) 888-0688

SUGGESTED READINGS

CHARLES, C. M. (1981). *Building classroom discipline.* New York, NY: Longman.

CRUICKSHANK, D. R. (1980). *Teaching is tough.* Englewood Cliffs, NJ: Prentice-Hall.

DOBSON, J. (1977). *Dare to discipline.* Wheaton, IL: Tyndale House Publishers.

ERNST, K. (1972). *Games students play.* Millbrae, CA: Celestial Arts.

GLASSER, W. (1969). *Schools without failure* New York, NY: Harper and Row.

GLASSER, W. (1993). *The quality school teacher.* New York, NY: Harper Collins.

GOOD, E.P. (1992). *Helping kids help themselves* Chapel Hill, NC: New View Publications.

HELLISON, D. (1978). *Beyond balls and bats.* Washington, DC: American Alliance for Health and Physical Education, Recreation and Dance.

LONG, J.D., and V. H. FRYE (1985). *Making it till Friday.* Princeton, NJ: Princeton Book Co.

POWERS, W. T. (1973). Behavior: *The control of perception.* Chicago, IL: Aldine Publications.

8 *Evaluation*

By definition, the process of education implies that a change, a modification, or an adjustment of behavior will occur as a result of experience. Changes occur in both student and teacher behaviors. These changes may be minor adjustments in a daily lesson for the teacher, or advancements in skill learning for the student as a result of experiences in the learning environment. Change is a constant in education, and evaluation of changes no matter how small must also be constant. Learning to observe and assess children in activity will enable the teacher (and the student) to locate strengths and weaknesses and make the necessary adjustments toward attaining the established goals of physical education.

This chapter is designed to provide teachers with techniques for evaluating both students and themselves. The first part is devoted to student evaluation, and the second to teacher evaluation. Both are equally important to the success of any program.

OBSERVATION

Observation of change is the first step in the evaluation process. The teacher and student gain important information about progress toward stated goals through skillful observation.

There are several different types of observation that may occur in the physical education environment—from a general observation of health habits (grooming, posture, and so forth) or social interactions, to more specific observations of skill performance. From the moment a class arrives, the teacher can begin evaluating the students' health, fitness level, motor skills, attitudes, social, emotional, and cognitive development, all based on observation.

Students also gain important information about their performance by observing demonstrations or other students in action. Sometimes both teacher and student will be looking for the same change in behavior. Regardless of who or what is being assessed, the keen observer must know specifically what to expect and only then can it be determined whether or not the

Teachers who make notes about student progress are more accurate.

movement, social interaction, or knowledge was achieved. For example, if the focus of the lesson is on running, observation of (and focus on) specific movement behaviors, such as the action of the arms, legs, torso, speed, and distance covered, can be used in the assessment process. In order to be accurate in evaluating the child's running form, the teacher should choose only one or two factors to note at each observation until a total picture is drawn. Likewise, the students should be taught to focus on only one or two factors at a time when observing a demonstration.

The key to good observation is pinpointing ahead of time specifically what is to be noticed about the child's movement or behavior. When students are observing each other, the teacher should use a reciprocal or cooperative teaching style (see Chapter 6). One child is then assigned the role of observer and is responsible for noticing the key skill points such as arm action, body position or foot placement in running.

STUDENT EVALUATION

Frequently, the physical education teacher is expected to evaluate the student's physical, motor, social, emotional, and cognitive growth, and to keep records and report on student development. This is a monumental task requiring a great deal of discipline and organization on the part of the teacher. The following section on student evaluation outlines techniques for evaluating and assessing student progress in the above areas.

HEALTH

General health appraisal is a daily responsibility. The teacher looks for signs of illness, neglect, abuse, or emotional strain by scanning the class at the beginning of the period. *Scanning*, as an observation technique, should be done by looking from left to right at the class, noting unusual skin color or markings (such as bruises), unkempt appearance, body odors, unusually fatigued or extremely fidgety children. These children may have problems that will greatly affect their performance and growth.

Should the teacher notice anything unusual about a child's appearance that would indicate possible child abuse or neglect, the proper school authority (usually the principal) should be notified immediately.

Assessment of the child's physical growth and functioning is generally a combined effort with the school nurse. A yearly assessment of height, weight, vision, hearing, and posture should be made. A record of growth is kept either in the nurse's office or frequently with the fitness record, which is the physical education teacher's responsibility (see Chapter 4, Physical Fitness).

PERCEPTUAL MOTOR SKILLS

Several good tests exist that may be used to assess the child's perceptual development. Table 8-1 lists selected assessment tools.

When choosing a standardized test, the teacher must consider the time available for testing and the ease with which the test can be administered. The teacher may want to screen the students first for potential problems then administer the test only to those children who exhibit obvious weaknesses. The teacher can select a simple activity for each of the perceptual-motor areas and scan the class, noting children who are having obvious difficulty with the task. For example, to assess balance, students may be asked to stand on one foot for five seconds; the teacher notes in the scan which students are hopping around unable to maintain a balanced position. To assess directional awareness, students may be asked to place beanbags in different positions in relation to themselves and others. Difficulty in placing to the front, back, side, over, under, or between can be noted as a weakness. A copy of the Dayton Sensory Motor Awareness Survey for Four- and Five-Year-Olds is provided as a simple and easy-to-administer screening device (see Table 8-2). Children with obvious problems should be singled out for further testing and remedial work.

In order to evaluate by means of scanning technique, the teacher must know the students' names. For some, this is a monumental task, and teachers often neglect to make an effort. The following technique, which has been used successfully, serves the dual purpose of providing a record of observations and a vehicle for learning children's names.

First, organize the class into squads, rows, circles, or any formation that can be organized quickly. Each child must be assigned a spot within that formation which they take each time the teacher calls for the formation. This may be done alphabetically, by size, or any way the teacher wishes. The teacher then makes a checklist containing each child's name in the spot occupied. While scanning, the teacher glances at this sheet and circles the name of the child who is either having difficulty or who has completed the task assigned. This type of checklist is excellent for screening fundamental-skill performance, especially among large groups.

FUNDAMENTAL MOTOR SKILLS/SPORT SKILLS

The assessment of fundamental and advanced (sport) motor skills should be both objective and subjective. The teacher is concerned with performance outcomes such as the ability to toss and catch a ball consecutively (product-oriented), as well as the form with which the skill is executed (process-oriented); therefore, two different types of evaluation are appropriate.

Table 8-1

Summary of Selected Assessment Tools

Title	Age Range (Yrs.)	Items	Comments
Denver Developmental Screening Test DDM P.O. Box 20037, Denver, CO 80220	Birth to 6	fine motor, gross motor, personal-social, and language skills (105 items; short form available)	charts depict at what age level 25, 50, 75, and 90 percent of "normal" children can accomplish specific tasks.
Bruininks-Oseretsky Test of Motor Proficiency American Guidance Service Circle Pines, MN 55014	4 ½ to 14 ½	gross motor, gross and fine motor and fine motor skills (eight sub-tests; short form available)	a valid test of motor proficiency as measured by the performance of a child on a given day
Basic Motor Ability Test-Revised In D. Arnheim & A. Sinclair, *The Clumsy Child*, St. Louis: C. V. Mosby	4 to 12	eleven tests designed to evaluate small-and large-muscle control, static and dynamic balance, eye-hand coordination, flexibility	while validity has not been reported, test-retest reliability was found to be .93. The norming sample was 1,563 children; expressed in percentiles
The Fundamental Movement Pattern Assessment Instrument In B. McClenaghen & D. Gallahue, *Fundamental Movement: A developmental and remedial approach.* Philadelphia: W. B. Saunders.	across ages	five fundamental skills; throwing, catching, kicking, running and jumping	used to classify skill level performance into initial, elementary or mature stage of development changes over time
Test of Gross Motor Development (Dale Ulrich) Austin, Tx: Pro-Ed.	3 to 10	twelve locomotor and object control skills	test was standardized on a sample of 908 children in eight states. Instructions well written and easy to understand

Objective Evaluation. The *objective* evaluation of a skill is generally thought of as a skill test. Because there are no standardized tests for fundamental skills, they must often be devised by the teacher. When devising a skill test the following guidelines should be observed:

1. The test should be designed to measure only one skill.
2. The test should be inexpensive and easy to administer, with time and space factors always considered.
3. The test should accurately reflect the skill it intends to measure. A running test, for example, should reflect the factors of speed and distance.
4. The test should discriminate between high and low levels of skill development. If all children score within two points of each other, for example, it would indicate that

the test was either too hard or too easy and the teacher should adjust accordingly.
5. Scores obtained can be standardized and added to other test battery scores to obtain a total score. A total score can be used to form individual and class profiles, which will in turn enable norms to be established for school or district populations. For example, it may be desirable to group tests in locomotor skills into one test battery—similarly nonlocomotor and manipulative skills for comparison purposes.

The use of objective skill testing is more appropriate for Level III students (and above) whose fundamental skills are ready for refinement. Objective tests may be necessary to point out those students who have not attained a basic level of skill development. Johnson and Nelson (1986) suggest the following uses of sport skill tests (Levels III–IV):

Table 8-2

Dayton Sensory Motor Awareness Survey for 4- and 5-Year-Olds

DATE OF TEST _____

NAME _____ SEX _____ BIRTH _____ CENTER _____

_____

Body Image. One half point for each correct part; nine points possible.

_____ 1. Ask the child to touch the following body parts:

Head _____	Ankles _____	Ears _____	Stomach _____	Elbows _____
Toes _____	Nose _____	Legs _____	Chin _____	Back _____
Eyes _____	Feet _____	Mouth _____	Waist _____	
Wrists _____	Chest _____	Fingers _____	Shoulders _____	

Space and Directions. One half point for each correct direction; five points possible.

_____ 2. Ask the child to point to the following directions:

Front _____ Back Up _____ Down _____ Beside you _____

Place two blocks on a table about 1 inch apart. Ask the child to point:

Under _____ Over _____ To the top _____ To the bottom _____ Between _____

Balance. Score two points if accomplished.

_____ 3. Have the child stand on tiptoes, on both feet, with eyes open for 8 seconds.

Balance and Laterality. Score two points for each foot; four points possible.

_____ 4. Have the child stand on one foot, eyes closed, for 5 seconds. Alternate feet.

Laterality. Score two points if the child keeps his feet together and does not lead off with one foot.

_____ 5. Have the child jump forward on two feet.

Rhythm and Neuromuscular Control. Score two points for each foot if accomplished six times; four points possible.

_____ 6. Have the child hop on one foot. Hop in place.

Rhythm and Neuromuscular Control. Score two points

_____ 7. Have the child skip forward. Child must be able to sustain this motion around the room for approximately 30 feet.

Integration of Right and Left Sides of the Body. Score two points if cross-patterning is evident for each.

_____ 8. Have the child creep forward.

_____ 9. Have the child creep backwards.

Eye-Foot Coordination. Score two points if done the length of tape or mark.

_____10. Use an 8-foot tape or chalk mark on the floor. The child walks in a crossover step the length of the tape or mark.

Fine Muscle Control. Score two points if paper is completely crumpled. Score one point if paper is partially crumpled. Score zero points if child needs assistance or changes hands.

_____11. Using a half sheet of newspaper, the child picks up the paper with one hand and puts the other hand behind his back. He then attempts to crumple the paper in his hand. He may not use his other hand, the table, or his body for assistance.

Form Perception. Score one point for each correct match.

_____12. Using a piece of paper with 2 inch circles, squares, and triangles, ask the child to point to two objects that are the same.

Form Perception. Score one point if circle is identified correctly. Score two points if the triangle and square are identified correctly.

_____13. Ask the child to identify by saying, "Point to the circle." "Point to the square." "Point to the triangle."

Hearing Discrimination. Score one point if the child taps correctly each time.

_____14. Ask the child to turn his back to you. Tap the table with a stick three times. Ask the child to turn around and tap the sticks the same way. Ask the child to turn his back to you. Tap the table again with the sticks (two quick taps, pause, then two more quick taps). Have the child turn back to you and tap out the rhythm.

Eye-Hand Coordination. Score one point for each successful completion.

_____15. A board is used with three holes in it. The holes are ¾, ⅝, and ½ inch in diameter. The child is asked to put his finger through the holes without touching the sides.

By permission of the Dayton, Ohio, Public Schools, W. T. Braley, consultant.

Table 8-3

Fundamental Skill Task Sheet

Name _____
Date _____ Age _____
Class _____

Skill: Dodging

	Task	Date Completed
1.	Weave through 6 cones spaced 5 ft. apart without touching any cones.	
2.	Change direction on a whistle signal 7 out of 10 times without falling.	
3.	Avoid a partner's tag for 15 seconds.	
4.	Avoid a ball thrown below the waist from 20 ft. 7 out of 10 times.	
5.	Weave through 6 cones spaced 5 ft. apart while carrying a ball without touching any cones.	
6.	Avoid a partner's tag for 30 seconds.	
7.	Hand dribble *or* foot dribble a ball while weaving through the cones without touching them or loosing the ball.	
8.	Weave through the 6 cones for 20 seconds and pass at least 20 cones.	
9.	Hand dribble or foot dribble past an opponent 30 ft. 3 out of 5 times.	

1. To measure achievement in specific sport activity for purposes of evaluating the instructional program and, along with other information, for grading purposes.
2. Skills tests enable teachers and students to objectively plot individual progress throughout the course and, conceivably, from year to year.
3. For diagnostic purposes, by pointing out needs for special emphasis at each particular grade level in which a sport is taught.
4. In some cases, skills tests can be used for competition in intramural programs and for rainy day activities.
5. Skills tests can be used as a means of interpreting the program and its accountability to administration, parents, and the public.
6. Skills tests serve as excellent motivational devices.
7. As a teaching aid to supplement instruction and to be used for practice.

The results of objective tests can be recorded on a master sheet, or students may be allowed to self-test and record the results on task sheets. Task sheets are often more valuable because they can be used to report to parents, and the children are more intimately involved with their own progress when they are responsible for recording their own performances. Task sheets enhance any program and grading system by individualizing learning in an atmosphere of minimum competition. Task sheets are fun to create and can be very diverse (see Tables 8-3 and 8-4). The following guidelines will aid you in formulating a task sheet system:

FUNDAMENTAL SKILL AND MOVEMENT AWARENESS TASK SHEETS SHOULD:

1. Include specific tasks based on skill proficiency indicators for each level of skill proficiency (Levels I–IV), to be developed from theme objectives.
2. Game, dance and gymnastic task sheets can be devised for one skill at two levels (Levels III–IV) or for several skills at a single level.
3. Task sheets must be organized in a progressive manner so that children who complete tasks at one level of proficiency have the opportunity to advance to the next level.
4. Each task must be specific and have a criterion for completion similar to those established in lesson objectives. It is important that children be able to fill out their own task sheets.
5. Sufficient time to complete the task sheets should be allotted. Children can complete the forms as they are able to perform the tasks, or a specific task sheet period may be set aside.
6. The teacher should hold the task sheets until they are complete before sending them home with the children or in the report card.
7. Periodic review of the task sheets will provide the teacher with valuable feedback about individual progress.

Table 8-4
Objective Sport Skill Task Sheet

TASK SHEET
UNIVERSITY LAB SCHOOL
GRADES 4–6

NAME _____
DATE _____ AGE _____

SKILL: BASKETBALL SHOOTING
             Tasks to be completed at your own speed
SKILLS AT TEN FEET

	COMPLETED (CHECK)
1. TWO HANDED SET SHOT (3 OF 5 SHOTS) SUCCESSFULLY	
2. ONE HANDED SET SHOT (3 OF 5 SHOTS)	
3. GRANEE SHOOTING SKILL (3 OF 5 SHOOTING TRIALS)	
4. HOOK SHOT (RIGHT OR LEFT) ANY DISTANCE (2 OF 5 SHOTS)	
5. LAY UP SHOT-RIGHT SIDE—ANY DISTANCE (3 OF 5)	
6. LAY UP SHOT-LEFT SIDE—ANY DISTANCE (3 OF 5)	
7. LAY UP SHOT-FRONTAL APPROACH (3 OF 5)	
8. SHOTS COMPLETED AT THE FOLLOWING DISTANCES AND DIRECTIONS ANY STYLE	
A. Side Approach 15 Feet (2 of 5) B. Front Approach 15 Feet (2 of 5)	

9. JUMP SHOT
    A. 5 Feet (3 of 6)
    B. 10 Feet (2 of 5)	

Subjective Evaluation. Periodic evaluation of a child's movement patterns will provide the teacher with important information about the child's skill development, which should be used in planning future lessons. To be effective, the teacher must aid the child in progressing from one stage of motor-skill development to another more advanced stage. To do this the teacher must first determine what stage the child has already achieved. Table 8-1 contains selected assessment instruments for this purpose.

Another choice is a skill-development check sheet. A good skill check sheet is a valuable tool. The teacher should list the positive skill points to be observed and then check them off as they are achieved (Table 8-5). To list the skill points, refer to the individual skill chapters (checklist examples provided with many skills) and study the skill descriptions. The check sheet can also be used by students when engaged in cooperative learning (Chapter 6). The observer watches the performer and then gives the information to the recorder, who notes the information on the check sheet.

SOCIAL DEVELOPMENT

The child's social development is many-faceted. The teacher needs to evaluate and foster positive attitudes about physical activity, sportsmanship, and authority.

Social development also involves group dynamics such as leadership, sharing, and cooperation. The evaluation of the child's social development is primarily a subjective appraisal. Unfortunately, many teachers wait until report card time to evaluate seriously this area of development, and then they assign a satisfactory or unsatisfactory grade to this complex area of development. The teacher must decide what social skills can be realistically expected of the children and should not try to evaluate behavior that has not been specifically taught.

A checklist can be used to systematically observe and record these behaviors. Table 8-6 is an example of a social development checklist. The (+) indicates a positive occurrance of the behavior and a (-) indicates a negative occurrence. If the teacher notices a listed behavior on a given day then a + or - is recorded. In this way a social development profile is arrived at. The teacher can then use this information when reporting to the parents, or to encourage children to behave more appropriately.

COGNITIVE DEVELOPMENT

The child's cognitive development in the primary grades (and intermediate grades) involves the ability to solve problems, understand physical education

Table 8-5

Skill Development Check Sheet

SKILL THEME: DODGING

Name	Lowers center of gravity in preparation to dodge	Changes direction quickly	Regains balance at the completion of dodging maneuver	Uses feinting-type movements

Table 8-6

Social Development Checklist

Name	Follows Directions	Stays on Task	Stops on the Whistle	Works Cooperatively with Others	Helps with Equipment	Enters & Leaves Gym in Orderly Way

concepts, laws of motion, and the vocabulary associated with movement. The teacher can best observe these factors by evaluating the child's ability to listen and move appropriately. Written instruments can be devised by the teacher to facilitate communication of the assessment to the child. These must be kept simple; often pictures are very helpful to the child's understanding. The teacher can use task sheets very effectively to evaluate the child's understanding of movement concepts and vocabulary. Table 8-7 is an example of a cognitive concept task sheet that could be used to determine the child's understanding of directional vocabulary. To use this the teacher can read the directions to children who cannot read.

REPORTING PROGRESS

Student progress reports are generally required by most school systems in the form of grades. In the primary grades a satisfactory/unsatisfactory system is usually employed, and intermediate grades usually require a percentile or A-B-C-type grade. Both of these grading systems are very difficult for the physical educator for a number of reasons:

1. Diversity of skill levels
2. Number of students
3. Actual contact time.

The need for a more descriptive type of evaluation is apparent.

Table 8-7

Directional Awareness Task Sheet

Name _____

Grade _____

	Complete
1. Draw an X next to the circle ○	
2. Draw a box □ inside the circle ○	
3. Draw a line ___ over the circle ○	
4. Draw a triangle △ between the two circles ○ ○	
5. Draw a line ___ under the circle ○	
6. Draw a box □ around the circle ○	

It is suggested that a task-evaluation-sheet system (see discussion of task sheets in this chapter) be utilized for reporting student progress to parents because task sheets can describe achievement in terms of skill performance and depict what was actually achieved. A further benefit of task sheets for reporting purposes is that they can serve as guidelines for parents who wish to help their children improve. Task-evaluation sheets point out specific areas of performance and skill levels that enable the parents to understand the specific skills and activities performed in the physical education classroom. This type of system also reduces grade competition among children and enhances individualized learning.

Public information and parents' understanding are basic to an effective and involved elementary program, and task sheets provide a vehicle for providing information about our programs to the public in understandable terms.

If the teacher is bound by the school system to assign a letter or numerical grade, the most important concern is to establish guidelines or criteria ahead of time and communicate to the children, and if possible their parents, what is necessary to achieve each grade.

TEACHER EVALUATION

Teacher evaluations are often informal and performed by the school administrator. They are generally viewed by the teacher as a negative experience. The informal assessment based on a five-minute visit provides the teacher with little valuable information about teaching effectiveness. In order to increase effectiveness with children, the teacher must receive relevant feedback about teaching performance. The teacher may employ self-evaluative, student-assisted, or peer-assisted techniques to obtain concrete information about the effectiveness of instructions, interactions with students, management skills, practice opportunities, and teacher movement through the learning environment.

INSTRUCTIONS

Giving clear and concise instructions to a group of students from varying backgrounds is challenging for even the most experienced teacher. Teachers usually receive immediate feedback about the effectiveness of their instructions as they observe children begin the activity. Confusion about where to go and what to do will generally look like disruptive behavior as the youngsters try to respond to unclear directions. The teacher can obtain immediate feedback about the quality of instructions by asking questions of the children relating to the instructions that have been given. For example, the teacher might ask Betsy, once Betsy has been given instructions, "What will you do after you get your ball?" Betsy's answer will provide the teacher with the information about the quality of instructions before the students even begin the activity.

Tape-Record. One of the easiest and most informative techniques for evaluating the ability to give instructions clearly is to tape-record verbal instructions as they are given. The teacher can easily wear a portable recorder, which the students will soon become familiar with, so that all verbal exchanges may be recorded during a lesson. The teacher should tape different classes and at the end of each class make comments about whether or not the class seemed to run smoothly. When analyzing the tape to improve performance, the teacher should ask these questions:

1. Did I repeat myself frequently?
2. Did the students have a lot of questions before they began the activity?
3. Did I have to shout to be heard?
4. Did my verbal directions take longer than necessary?
5. What evidence did I have that the students understood my directions?

Student Questionnaire. Children can provide valuable information about the effectiveness of instructions and other teaching skills by answering a questionnaire such as the one offered in Table 8-8. The results of such a questionnaire must be interpreted in conjunction with other techniques because this type of instrument will only provide the teacher with information about the children's reactions to teaching.

The written instrument must be simple and the required answers concrete. Using faces on the answer sheet and having the teacher read the questions will increase the effectiveness of the instrument for the primary-grade child.

Interactions. The amount and the quality of interactions a teacher has with students greatly influence teaching effectiveness. The teacher should try to interact either verbally or nonverbally with each child in a class during a lesson. Information about the teacher's interaction patterns with the students can be obtained from the tape-recording technique or the student questionnaire. When using the tape-recording technique, the teacher should calculate (1) the percentage of positive, negative, and neutral comments made during a class; and (2) the percentage of children involved in interaction.

Interaction Checklist. An interaction checklist (Table 8-9) can be used to determine interaction patterns between teacher and students during a lesson.

Table 8-8

Student Questionnaire: Reaction to Teacher/Student Interaction

DIRECTIONS: Circle the Face That Best Describes Your Teacher

My teacher gives me good directions.

My teacher will repeat directions if I don't understand them.

My teacher gives me a second chance to learn what I need if I don't the first time.

My teacher calls me by name.

My teacher talks to me politely.

My teacher keeps me working the whole class period.

Table 8-9

Interaction Checklist

Child's Name	Talked to	Smiled at	Touched	Total
Joan	///	/		4
John	/	//		3
Charles	/			1
Carol	//	/		3
Janice		/		1
Bill	#### #### ///	///	////	20
Totals	20	8	4	32

An analysis of the checklist data can provide information about:

1. The sex and race of the children who get the most attention in the class;
2. Whether the skilled or unskilled get more attention;
3. Whether an individual or group of children is being ignored.

A colleague who knows the names of all the children in the class can make a tally in the columns of the checklist. This record can also be derived from a videotape, or even a tape recorder for verbal interactions only. The authors recognize the difficulty of this task; however, the effective teacher will utilize whatever means are available to obtain the information necessary for the development of an optimum learning environment. The tally results can be placed on a graph, which will provide a pictorial representation of the data that have been collected.

Feedback Checklist.   A feedback checklist can give the teacher valuable information about the type and quality of the reinforcement provided to the students (see Table 8-10). The teacher should provide feedback about both movement behavior and social behavior.

This type of checklist will be best kept by a colleague enlisted to help the teacher evaluate teaching skills. The colleague chooses several children to observe and codes feedback statements made by the teacher. Using the checklist, positive and negative statements are tallied. The teacher should strive for a 2:1 ratio of positive to corrective feedback.

MANAGEMENT SKILLS

An analysis of management skill utilizes time as a measure of student behavior and involvement. The following techniques involve a time-sampling of behaviors (both teacher and student behaviors) that occur during a lesson, and these techniques will provide the teacher with a better picture of one facet of teaching effectiveness. These instruments can be administered by a colleague, or the teacher can use the tape recorder to gather information during the lesson.

Placheck (Siedentop, 1983).   A planned activity check can be conducted to determine the percentage of students involved in meaningful activity during a lesson. The teacher or evaluator scans the class for 10 seconds at five-minute intervals using the left-to-right technique and counts the number of students involved in either productive or nonproductive activity (which is based on the behavioral objectives for the lesson). It is easier to count the number of students in the behavior category in which the fewest are involved, and then calculate the percentage involved in meaningful movement.

$$\frac{\text{number of students exhibiting productive behavior}}{\text{number of students in class}} \times 100 = \text{percentage of productive behavior}$$

The goal of the teacher should be for 90 percent of the students to be involved in meaningful activity. Five or more plachecks during a lesson of 30 minutes will provide the teacher with a good profile of teaching effectiveness.

Table 8-10

Feedback Checklist

TEACHER _____   DATE _____
OBSERVER _____
THEME _____

Teacher Feedback

Child's Name	Movement Behavior		Social Behavior	
	Positive	Corrective	Positive	Corrective
George	////		/	
Todd	/	////		##### //
Susan	##### #####	/	///	
Ben	#####	/		///
Kristin		////	/	
Total	20	10	5	10

Directions: Mark a slash each time the teacher gives feedback about movement behavior (i.e., "Great catch, John. You really watched the ball all the way"), or social behavior (i.e., "Susan, you put your equipment away very quickly today") occurs. Include both positive and corrective feedback.

Table 8-11

Practice Opportunities Checklist

TEACHER _____   DATE _____

OBSERVER _____

LESSON TIME _____

Practice Opportunities

Child's Name	Throwing Overhand	Throwing Underhand	Throwing Sidearm				

PRACTICE OPPORTUNITIES

The more children practice a skill, the more likely they are to acquire proficiency in that skill. Therefore, an analysis of teacher effectiveness should include a calculation of practice opportunities provided by the teacher in the lesson. Recording on a practice opportunities checklist (Table 8-11) can be done by a colleague. Several children are singled out for observation and a tally kept of the number of times each child practices a given skill. The teacher then adds up practice opportunities for each child and utilizes the information to improve the lesson.

SUPPORT GROUP

A systematic evaluation of teacher performance can aid the teacher in pinpointing some problems and highlighting some strengths. However, not all teaching skills can be systematically analyzed. Therefore, the teacher needs to develop a support group of trusted colleagues with whom questions, problems, and triumphs can be discussed. Often teachers in the same school district can arrange to meet once a month for discussion and sharing as part of a teacher inservice program.

The support group should be used to improve teacher performance by fostering positive feelings and building the self-confidence of its members. Gripe sessions about students, administrators, parents, and other teachers are inappropriate and will be self-defeating to the goal of improved teaching.

PROGRAM EVALUATION

The final area of evaluation to be considered by the teacher is that of the overall program. Specific questions need to be answered about how well the actual execution of the program meets the established objectives. The first step is to review the goals that were established at the beginning of the year.

To determine how effectively these goals have been met, the teacher has several sources available:

1. lesson plan comments;
2. student skill- and fitness-assessment records;
3. anecdotal notes;
4. parental and administrative comments.

A formative review (three or four per year) of these sources will provide the most realistic overview as opposed to a summative review (at the end of the year).

REFERENCES

JOHNSON, B., & NELSON, J. (1986). *Practical measurements for evaluation in physical education* (4th ed.). Minn: Burgess Publishing.

SIEDENTOP, D. (1983). *Developing teaching skills in physical education* (2nd ed.). Palo Alto, CA: Mayfield.

SUGGESTED READINGS

BARRETT, K. R. (1977). Studying teaching: A means for becoming a more effective teacher. In Logsdon, B. J., Barrett, K. R., Broer, M. R., *et al. Physical education for children: A focus on the teaching process.* Philadelphia: Lea & Febiger.

CLARKE, H., & CLARKE, D. (1987). *Application of measurement to physical education (6th ed).* Englewood Cliffs, NJ: Prentice-Hall.

GALLAHUE, D. L. (1982). *Understanding motor development in children.* New York: Wiley.

HENSLEY, L. D., MORROW, J. R., & EAST, W. B. (1990). Practical Measurement to Solve Practical Problems. *Journal of Physical Education Recreation and Dance.*

GRAHAM, G., METZLER, M., & WEBSTER, G. (1991). Specialist and classroom teacher effectiveness in children's physical education. *Journal of Teaching Physical Education,* 10(4).

McGEE, R. (1977). Evaluation of processes and products. In Logsdon, B. J., Barrett, K. R., Broer, M. R., *et al. Physical education for children: A focus on the teaching process.* Philadelphia: Lea & Febiger.

WICKSTROM, R. L. (1983). *Fundamental motor patterns* (3rd. ed.) Philadelphia: Lea & Febiger.

SAFRIT, M. J. (1990). *Introduction to measurement in physical education and exercise science.* St. Louis: Mosby

9

Children with Special Needs

FIGURE 9-1

Disabled Students with a peer partner participate in physical education

The number of children in the public schools with disabilities receiving special education services has reached 4.2 million, which represents about 11% of the school age population (Department of Education, 1989). These figures draw attention to the need for special education in the public schools. However, they do not clearly represent the magnitude of need of persons who can benefit from special physical activity designed to accommodate individual needs. Furthermore, the number of individuals with multiple disabilities is also increasing due to a

higher rate of survival among infants born prematurely, and advanced medical technology helping keep children with one or more disabilities alive. Because of this situation and recent legislation concerning individuals with disabilities, the challenges for public school teachers to meet the needs of such children are of particular concern. This chapter briefly describes the legal boundaries, and instructional and program considerations concerning placement and integration of children with disabilities into the regular physical education program. For additional information, refer to the Suggested Readings list. The importance and abundance of this extensive body of information has generated several textbooks and separate educational courses.

LEGISLATION

The Individuals with Disabilities Education Act (IDEA) of 1990 (P.L. 101-476), along with previous legislation governing disabled (the Education of the Handicapped Act of 1975 [P.L. 94-142], 1983 [P.L. 98-199] and 1986 [P.L. 99-457]) has mandated and provided funding for more extensive services to individuals with a broader range of disabilities, and covering a longer age span, than ever before. Children are included from birth under present legislation because it is believed that intervention with appropriate services early in the lives of the disabled will enhance their quality of living. A *disabled* school-aged person is anyone of school age who has a physical or mental impairment that substantially limits one or more major life activities like: caring for one's self, performing manual tasks, walking, seeing, hearing, speaking, breathing, learning, or working.

Furthermore, individuals who have drug or alcohol dependency, attention deficit disorder, diabetes, severe allergies, arthritis, epilepsy, communicable diseases like human immunodeficiency virus, learning disabilities, or are socially maladjusted and, as a result of such impairments have limits in the above-mentioned major life functions, are included in this legislation. Physical Education is clearly defined and included as a component of this legislation. According to P.L. 94-142, physical education activities should involve the development of physical and motor fitness, fundamental motor skills and patterns, and skills in aquatics, dance and individual and group games and sports (including intramurals and lifetime sports). Also included are the terms: special physical education, adapted physical education, movement education and motor development. The two most essential features of physical education for children with disabilities are the teaching of the regular physical education curricula and the inclusion of individualized programming for the child.

The outcomes of this legislation for physical education teachers have been to demonstrate the need for teachers to:

1. Outline behavioral objectives in detail and be accountable for evaluations.
2. Keep parents fully informed.
3. Ensure that education takes place in the most integrated setting with children who are non-disabled, if possible.

Working with disabled children in the public school setting requires a range of services designed to meet the needs of each child.

FIGURE 9-2

In challenger baseball programs, disabled children participate in organized sports

SPECIAL SERVICES

Direct Services

Direct services in the public school are supplied by several key individuals, and are designed to teach the curricula sanctioned by the School Board. These services include: adapted physical education, which modifies traditional physical activities to enable the child with disabilities to participate safely, successfully and with satisfaction; corrective physical education, which is designed to remediate deficiencies in posture or mechanical alignment of the body; remedial physical education, designed to rehabilitate or develop functional movement as a motor prerequisite for functional motor skills; and regular physical education, designed to develop functional motor skills and physical fitness. These services are provided either by an "adapted physical educator" or the regular physical education teacher. Unfortunately, the area of "adapted physical education" has been sorely neglected and inadequately programmed in the public school, so that placement of children into regular physical education classes occurs even when that may not be the most appropriate and least restrictive environment for a particular individual in a specific activity. The most important considerations for determining what services will be needed for the child are developed in the Individual Education Program (IEP) discussed later in this chapter.

Related Services

Related services are used in the public school to help children gain benefits from the intended outcomes of the direct services. Related services include physical, recreational and occupational therapy. The role of related services is to assist in the development of a physical prerequisite to a skill. For example, when a child does not have enough strength or flexibility to perform a skill to be used in the regular physical education program the physical educator can request the services of a physical therapist for the child.

The choice of services, program, method, or intervention for the individual child must have accountability so that significant positive changes in one or more behaviors is clearly demonstrated. Therefore, written records are required to document progress towards specific goals. These documentations of progress and programming of direct and related services are developed in the IEP.

THE INDIVIDUAL EDUCATION PROGRAM (IEP)

The *IEP*, initially required by P.L. 94-142, is developed by a committee which includes a local Education Association representative who is qualified to provide and supervise the administration of special education, the child's parents, the teachers who have direct responsibility for implementing the IEP and—when appropriate—the child. The IEP is developed to advance the child in incremental steps, beginning at the child's current level of ability. Each IEP must include the following information:

1. An assessment of the child's current level of educational performance.
2. Program plans, to include a statement of long-term goals, and short-term objectives.
3. A recommendation indicating the least restrictive environment for the child, including related services needed.
4. A time line for the start of services, periodic reviews and projected ending date.
5. Specific evaluation criteria to be used to determine if the long- and short-term goals are being met.

Physical education is involved in this process because of the close connection between the development of physical skills and fitness and social living skills that facilitate independent living. Physical education contributes to the overall well-being of the disabled child by meeting his or her needs in the following ways:

1. Developing recreational motor skills for independent functioning in the community.
2. Developing physical fitness for health maintenance.
3. Developing ambulatory skills to master mobility at home and in the community.
4. Developing physical and motor prerequisites to self-help skills for independent living.
5. Developing physical and motor prerequisites to vocational skills for independent living.

6. Developing motor skills needed for participation in self-fulfilling social activity.

These long term goals should be incorporated into the IEP. Once this IEP is developed, the needs of the child will dictate the type of program that will be most beneficial. Implementation sometimes requires modification of the learning environment, and usually requires changes in the teaching strategies employed. Placement of the child into the least restrictive environment is the ultimate goal.

LEAST RESTRICTIVE ENVIRONMENT

The least restrictive environment is the one that offers the learner the greatest opportunity to progress with the fewest barriers to overcome. As much as is possible, the disabled should be educated with those who are not. However, when a child is not ready either physically, socially, or emotionally, to participate with nondisabled classmates, the outcomes of forcing the child to be *mainstreamed* (mainstreaming occurs when a disabled child is included in the regular physical education or other class) can be disastrous. Furthermore, the transition of disabled children from a segregated setting, with a full-time special physical educator, to a regular physical education program should be a gradual process—planned for with great care. Table 9-1 shows a gradual progression of options for the disabled learner which moves him or her towards full integration—from the most restrictive to the least restrictive environment. It must be noted here that this progression is designed to be used with care. Each situation the child will encounter in a regular physical education environment must be evaluated, and the necessary support systems employed to ensure suc-

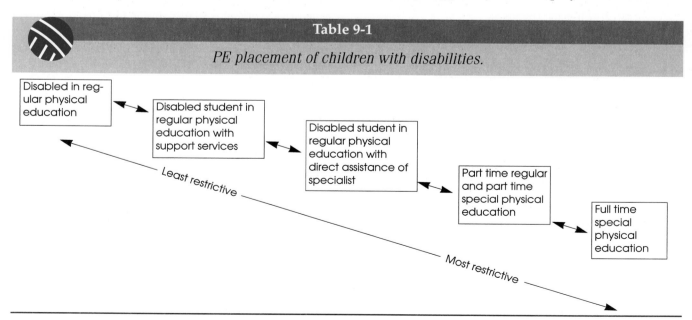

Table 9-1

PE placement of children with disabilities.

Disabled in regular physical education

Disabled student in regular physical education with support services

Disabled student in regular physical education with direct assistance of specialist

Part time regular and part time special physical education

Full time special physical education

Least restrictive

Most restrictive

cess. For example, students who possess adequate or above motor and fitness abilities, but have a cognitive disability, must first learn rules and strategies in a special environment before they can effectively participate in traditional games and sports in a regular physical education environment. Likewise, students who have physical disabilities often need support services to participate in regular physical education.

When determining the appropriateness of placement of the disabled child, several factors must be considered. First, the attitude and ability of the regular physical educator must be considered. The regular physical educator must be able to accommodate for individual differences, and possess an attitude of acceptance of all children. Second, the nature of the activity to be performed and, finally, the available support systems must also be considered. These three factors must be assessed each time the activity changes in class.

Integration of the disabled child into a regular environment is prepared for before it occurs. The transition from special to regular physical education is facilitated by the special physical educator, who serves as liaison between the regular physical educator and the special and related services dictated by the child's IEP.

The special physical educator must first prepare the disabled child by discussing with him or her what to expect in the new environment. Then the regular physical educator must be prepared. The special physical educator can facilitate this by:

1. Offering informal training in mainstreaming strategies.
2. Providing background information on the disabled child's needs and describing major components of the disability.
3. Analyzing modifications needed to properly program for the disabled child.
4. Inviting the regular physical educator to attend the IEP meeting.
5. Helping the regular physical educator develop more individualized teaching strategies.

Finally, classmates must be prepared before the arrival of the disabled child by creating an accepting environment and a heightened awareness and concern for disabled peers. Also, the classmates of the disabled child need to be able to cooperate and work as a group, developing fair systems for game-playing that take into consideration individual strengths and weaknesses. Occasionally, nondisabled classmates can assume a handicap with a blindfolded, or confined to a scooter, during participation to help develop sensitivity towards the disabled child. Most importantly, nondisabled classmates can be helping partners for the disabled child—an honor many will want to experience.

Full integration can occur only when the disabled child has been fully accepted by the other students.

ACCOMMODATING DISABLED STUDENTS IN REGULAR PHYSICAL EDUCATION

Today's physical educator will often be including disabled children in the regular program when that is determined to be the least restrictive environment for them. In order to do this effectively, the teacher needs to make use of teaching strategies which individualize instruction as much as possible. The use of pre-arranged written objectives developed in the child's IEP will facilitate this process, as will the use of a system which allows and enables learners to direct and evaluate their own learning.

INSTRUCTIONAL STRATEGIES

Group and Individual Organization

Using group or individual organization with a variety of learning centers can facilitate inclusion of the disabled child quite effectively. The teacher organizes the class so that each student is working at his or her own pace at each station using task cards to stay on track with what needs to be done (see Chapter 6 for detailed information on this type of organization). The children's tasks are developed according to their own capabilities and needs as established in the IEP. The nondisabled students also use task cards to facilitate their activity. In some cases, disabled and nondisabled may be doing the same activities and in others they may not. It is also possible to provide partners for the disabled child in this type of organization. However, the partnering should be mutually beneficial, with the disabled child also having responsibility for helping his/her partner when appropriate. This type of organization really allows for and facilitates a developmentally appropriate physical education program for all children. Organizing into stations is most useful when working on individual skills. When participation in group activities is required, then a different strategy must be employed.

Modifying tasks

When the disabled child is to participate with classmates in a group game or dance activity, then some modification of the game, dance, or task may be necessary. For example, a child in a wheelchair may not be able to play in a group game with an equal chance at success with nonwheelchaired peers. If the classmates were required to participate on scooters, the disadvantage would be somewhat equalized. Likewise, a visually impaired child would have a great advantage if classmates were blindfolded for participation in a game. The most important guideline to follow when modifying activities is that the modifications enable participation by all children and discourage spectatorship.

Partnering

Another option for inclusion of the disabled in group activities is to use a buddy system whereby a nondisabled child is the partner and assistant to the disabled child. Again, in using the buddy system, participation should be facilitated. It should be an honor to be chosen as the "buddy" for the day, and this honor should be bestowed very carefully on children who have shown empathy for, and acceptance of the disabled child.

Problem Solving

Finally, the use of the problem-solving teaching style, with open ended questions that have a variety of acceptable solutions, will enable each child in the class to progress at his/her own rate. A further advantage of this style for the disabled is that it allows the child to find solutions that may be uniquely adapted to that child's individual characteristics and needs (Chapter 6 includes a complete discussion of this teaching style).

Communication Mode

It is particularly important to remember to vary the communication mode employed when dealing with diverse groups of children. A child with a visual impairment will need to have word pictures drawn and may need to have kinesthetic information provided through physical manipulation. On the other hand, a hearing-impaired child will need more visual information. The teacher must be cognizant of all the options available and use a variety of communication modes as much as possible.

SPECIFIC DISABILITIES

The teacher of physical education may encounter many children with special needs. These can generally be placed into four broad categories which frequently overlap. The following is a brief description of some of the specific conditions which can be encountered in the public schools.

Physical Disabilities

Physical impairments affect about 3 percent of the school age population, and are characterized by either a sensory deficiency or musculoskeletal restriction.

Sensory impairments most frequently fall into two categories; visual and auditory. A visual impairment is present when performance is negatively affected even when corrective lenses are worn. Children with visual impairments are assisted by the inclusion of more tactile kinesthetic, and auditory information in the environment. An auditory impairment is present when there is difficulty in the child's processing verbal information without amplification. Children with hearing aids generally have few limitations when participating in physical education activities. However, when the teacher is positioned behind them, they may not be able to hear, so they are helped when positioned close to the teacher and the teacher maintains eye contact with them. It must be noted that perspiration may cause the hearing aid to malfunction and the child will not be able to hear the teacher. Also when the hearing aid must be removed for an activity such as swimming, then a buddy will facilitate the smooth inclusion of the child into the program.

Cardiovascular problems can be a result of congenital heart disease, rheumatic heart disease, coronary heart disease, or hypertensive heart disease. Restriction in the amount or duration of an activity for these children can range from mild to severe. It is imperative that the teacher work closely with the child's physician and monitor the child for signs of severe stress.

Neurological disorders which result from damage to the brain or spinal cord are often characterized by paralysis(partial), weakness, tremors or uncoordinated movement. Cerebral palsy and epilepsy are the two most common neurological disorders seen in children. Social integration and peer acceptance are particularly important to these children; both goals can be facilitated by a good physical education program. Motor-skill tasks may have to be modified for the child, and the teacher should work in close conjunction with the child's physician.

Musculoskeletal conditions include arthritis, postural deviations, and generally any condition that limits the child's ability to move efficiently. Activities for children with such disabilities should be individually determined with the advice of the child's physician. Specific information on postural deviations is contained in Chapter 4.

Mental Retardation

Children with below normal levels of intellectual functioning have a disability called mental retardation. The primary cause of mental retardation is brain damage which occurs to the central nervous system before birth. Often mentally retarded children exhibit low motor coordination as well as low intellectual ability. This may be due, however, more to the fact that this group of disabled has suffered from neglect of motor-skills training. A life of inactivity can result in poor motor coordination. Also their participation is somewhat limited by their ability to comprehend how to move. When working with mentally retarded children, the teacher should demonstrate rather than tell how to do something, and provide manual assistance when possible. Simplify instructions and gradually develop the child's movement vocabulary by labeling movements as they are learned, and using repetition.

Emotional Disabilities

Some of the emotional disabilities that can interfere with children's ability to learn include: inappropriate behaviors, trouble maintaining interpersonal relationships, and developing physical symptoms in response to personal or school problems. This group of disabled school-age children has been estimated to contain variously between two and 20 percent of the population. Teachers should be alerted to the prevalence of this disability and the need to be aware of the concerns of children who exhibit its symptoms. Consistency is the key to dealing with an emotionally disabled child. The teacher must provide a stable and orderly environment with clearly defined limits that enable the child to feel secure.

Learning Disabilities

The learning disabled child is one who has difficulty in one or more of the following: the ability to read, write, think, speak, spell, or do mathematical functions. Excluded from this category are children whose problems stem from a physical disability or mental retardation, and children whose problems stem from cultural, economic or environmental conditions.

Often these children appear developmentally normal except that, for an unknown reason, they fail to perform up to expected grade levels in school. Success is extremely important for this child who struggles academically in school. The teacher needs to use small increments in progressions so the child experiences success most of the way to learning a task. Focus particularly on body awareness, spatial awareness and directional awareness activities (see Chapter 13 for activity ideas).

Success in teaching children with disabilities for a nonspecialist depends on several factors. First the teacher must accept the disabled child and be able to motivate him/her towards improvement. The teacher must have a genuine desire to integrate the child into the regular program, and the ability to individualize and personalize instruction. The environment must be conducive to learning, where all children feel free to experiment and explore. These are not very different from the qualities and skills required of teachers of nondisabled.

SUGGESTED READINGS

AUXTER, D., HUETTIG, C., & PYFER, J. (1993). *Adapted Physical Education and Recreation*. Boston, MA: Mosby.

BORDNER, G. A. & BERKLEY, M. T. (1992). Educational play: meeting everyone's needs in mainstreamed classrooms. *Journal of the Association for Childhood Education International, 69*, 38–40.

DUCHANE, K. & FRENCH, R. (1991). Preparing students and teachers for Effective Mainstreaming in Physical Education. *The Physical Educator*. 95–99.

KARPER, W. B., & MARTINEK, T. J. (1982). Mainstreaming handicapped students into physical education: Initial considerations and needs. *The Physical Educator, 39*, 13–15.

MAELAND, A. F., (1992). Identification of children with motor coordination problems. *Adapted Physical Activity Quarterly. 9*, 330–342.

NIETUPSKI, S. H., MCDONALD, J., & NIETUPSKI, J. (1992). Integrating elementary students with multiple disabilities into supported regular classes. *Teaching Exceptional Children. 24*, 6–9.

10

Locomotor Skill Themes

Movement Description

Walking is the shifting of weight from one foot to the other, with at least one foot contacting the surface at all times. During the movement, each leg alternates between a supporting phase and swinging phase. The heel strikes the surface first as the back leg pushes off, shifting the weight to the leg in front. The body leans forward slightly after the lead foot contacts the surface. The weight is then transferred from the heel to the outside of the foot, the ball of the foot, and the toes. The base of support (with feet parallel to each other, toes straight) should be approximately shoulder-width apart. The arms swing rhythmically in opposition to the legs; the right arm swings forward with the left leg and the left arm moves forward with the right leg (Fig. 10-1).

Movement Observation

The first walking movements can be observed in children aged nine to 15 months, with most acquiring the skill by 12 months. Walking sideways and backwards occurs approximately four to five months after walking forward is achieved. Around the age of 4 years, the child has achieved an adult style of walking that is

FIGURE 10-1

Mature walking pattern.

FIGURE 10-2

Foot placement deviations.

137

characterized by an easy, rhythmic stride with a smooth transfer of weight.

Figure 10-2 illustrates base of support variations that are related to many problems in walking gait. As previously described, the feet should be close together (shoulder width), with toes pointed straight ahead. Toeing out slightly may be all right; however, an exaggeration may cause the child to walk on the inside of the foot rather than shifting weight from the heel to the outside of the foot. Walking pigeon-toed (toeing in) may result in a flat-footed step and a knock-kneed condition.

COMMON PROBLEMS

1. Swinging the same side arm and leg forward simultaneously (the arms should swing freely in opposition to the legs);
2. Failure to flex the ankle, knee (stiff), or hip joints, which may cause bouncing or jarring of the body;
3. Incorrect posture as characterized by a forward tilt of the head and body, rounded shoulders, and a tilted pelvis (the head and body should be erect);
4. Dragging the heel (push upward and forward from the toe).

Movement Variability

Walking is the most utilized and basic skill that an individual possesses. Used alone or in combination with other movements to form complex skills, walking is the foundation of locomotion.

SPATIAL

MOVEMENT-PATTERN VARIATIONS

Trunk bent forward or sideward.
Vary base of support (wide to narrow).
Vary length of steps (short to long).
On heels; on toes.
Knees stiff.
Vary arm position (straight out, at side, overhead; arms thrusting forward together or alternately; swing arms together from side to side).
Hands on knees; clasped behind back or neck.
Place one foot directly in front or in back of the other.
Sideward (and cross one foot over the other).
Walk on all fours.
Legs kicking up high in front, back, sideward.

DIRECTIONS/PATHWAYS/LEVELS

In place	Change directions	Over
Forward	Low level (knees bent)	Under
Backward	High level (tiptoe)	Zigzag
Circle	Around	Lower and raise the body

TIME

Slow to Fast	Jerky
	To musical accompaniment or rhythmic beat
	Smooth

FORCE

| Hard | Uphill | Lightly |
| Soft | Downhill | Knees lifted high |

ADDITIONAL MOVEMENT VARIATIONS

Walking in creative ways.
Walk like animals (ostrich, penguin, duck, road-runner).
Walk (on all fours) like a bear and crab.
Walk "happy" and "sad."
Walk "carrying a heavy load."
Walk on apparatus (benches, balance beams, boards, ropes).
Walk with a partner (side by side, same and opposite direction; back to back, front to front; one behind the other, both facing forward; *all of the variations with variable hand placement*).
Walk as if in a parade.
Walk as if on ice; in mud; on eggs.
Turn, twist, stretch, and bend while walking.
Walk through an obstacle course; forward and backward.
Walk like a tightrope walker in the circus.
Walk like an astronaut in space.
Clap hands under thighs while walking.
Walk like a robot.
Walk with a military goose-step.
Throw and catch an object while walking.

Combine walking with other locomotor skills (walk, run, skip, walk).

Use walking in a gymnastics routine.

Use walking as a movement in dance (see Table 10-1, Movement Enhancement).

Teaching Hints

Provide a visual model of good walking posture.

Provide activities that stress keeping the trunk erect.

Emphasize pushing off from the toes.

Stress walking with the head up and arms swinging freely.

Skill Concepts Communicated to Children

Keep your head up and your trunk straight.

Point toes straight ahead.

Walking is similar to running except one foot is always in contact with the ground.

Your heel is the first part of your foot to contact the ground, and your toes are the last to leave as you walk.

Arms swing opposite the action of your legs in a relaxed, rhythmical manner.

Swing leg from hip.

Swing arms and hands forward easily.

RUNNING

Movement Description

Running is an extension of walking and is primarily characterized by a phase in which the body is propelled with no base of support (flight phase) from either leg. Because of the nonsupport phase, the movement is less stable than walking and demands more bodily control. Jogging, a popular form of running, generally presents a slower pace, more bouncing, and a shorter stride length. As the child propels at greater speeds, more flight time occurs, and there is longer stride length and less bounce. By the age of

Movement Enhancement

Table 10-1

Walking Enhancement Chart

GAMES	LEVEL	GYMNASTICS	LEVEL		LEVEL

Follow the Leader
Command Cards
	I–III	Camel Walk
		Ankle Walk
		Walking Chair
		Bear Walk
		Lame Puppy Walk
		Duck Walk
		Elephant Walk
		Gorilla Walk
		Inch Worm
		Directional Walk
			I&II	Loobie Loo
				Mulberry Bush
				Farmer in the Deli
				The Snail
				Sally Go Around
				   the Moon
				Did You Ever see
				   a Lassie
				Ten Little Indians
				Oats, Peas, Beans,
				   and Barley
				London Bridge
					I&II

Animal Walk Relay Walking Robot Cars Fetch and Carry Relay Freight Train Relay Boiler Bust Kneeling Tag Marching Ponies Caged Lion Squirrels in the Tree Corners Slow Poke Hook-on Red Light Santa's Reindeer Charlie Over the Water Play Footsie	I&II	Crab Walk Knee Walk	II	Jolly is the Miller Come Let Us Be Joyful Ach Ja Shoo Fly The Wheat Glow Worm, Bingo, Greensleeves Gustaf's Skoal	II II&III
		Dance/Rhythm/Rhymes			
Mousetrap Old Man/Old Lady Rescue Relay Fire Engine Bronco Tag Circle Jump Relay Old Plug Chariot Race	II&III	Sing A Song of Six- Pence Baa, Baa, Black Sheep Blue Bird	I&II		

FIGURE 10-3

Elementary running pattern.

five, children generally present good running form. They have progressed from the ability to run in a straight line fast to changing direction and dodging.

The majority of children 4 to 8 years of age exhibit running patterns that can be classified as either elementary or mature. McClenaghan and Gallahue (1978) characterize the two stages as follows:

ELEMENTARY STAGE

In the elementary stage, there is an observable but limited flight phase. Although the arms appear to be achieving adequate vertical distance, there is limited horizontal movement. The support leg extends somewhat at takeoff; however, at the height of recovery to the rear, the recovery foot swings across the midline before it is swung forward to the contact position.

MATURE STAGE

In the mature stage, the arms are bent at the elbows in approximate right angles and are swung vertically in a large arc in opposition to the legs. The recovery knee is raised high and is swung forward quickly while the support leg bends slightly at contact and then extends completely and quickly through the hip, knee, and ankle. Length of stride and duration of flight time are at their maximum. There is very little rotary movement of either the recovery knee or foot as length of the stride increases.

Another description of the mature running pattern as summarized by Wickstrom (1983) suggests that:

1. The trunk maintains a slight forward lean throughout the stride pattern;
2. Both arms swing through a large arc in a vertical plane and in synchronized opposition to the leg action;
3. The support foot contacts the ground approximately flat and nearly under the center of gravity;
4. The knee of the support leg bends slightly after the foot has made contact with the ground;
5. Extension of the support leg at the hip, knee, and ankle propels the body forward and upward into the nonsupport phase;
6. The recovery knee swings forward quickly to a high knee raise and simultaneously there is flexion of the lower leg, bringing the heel close to the buttock.

Movement Observation

Most young children acquire an acceptable level of running without formal instruction. This naturally acquired level of proficiency is attributable in part to the amount of experience (time and movement variability) gathered through structured activities and free play. Nevertheless, observation and analysis can both enhance specific phases of the mature runner's form and identify the inexperienced individual.

FIGURE 10-4

Mature running pattern.

Elementary

Mature

FIGURE 10-5
Running check-sequence.

COMMON PROBLEMS

1. Running in an erect position (slight forward lean should be maintained);
2. Running with the heel touching the surface first (for sprints) or on the toes during long-distance runs (should run on balls of feet during fast, short runs; in long-distance running the heel touches first);
3. Running with feet turned (exaggerated) in or out (feet should be straight);
4. Swinging arms from side to side or allowing to flop at sides (bend elbows at right angles and swing hands and arms forward); motion should resemble putting hands in and out of front pockets);
5. Rearing head far back (head should be positioned straight in direction of run).

When assessing the running pattern, this check-sequence illustration may prove helpful to the instructor and child (Fig. 10-5).

Movement Variability

For pure running efficiency it is important that basic fundamental principles be utilized; however, many movement and game-type activities call upon the child to move in a running fashion using a variety of unorthodox patterns (some being novel to the child). Practice variability allows the child an opportunity to utilize and refine basic patterns as well as experience a variety of situations that call for bodily adjustment to novel running situations.

SPATIAL

MOVEMENT PATTERN VARIATIONS

Vary base of support (wide to narrow)

Use short, medium, and long strides

On balls of feet (sprint)

On heels-to-toe (jog)

Vary arm position;

Straight out to side; in front; over head; swinging from side to side; folded

Hands on head, waist, shoulders

Knees up high

Crossover step right; left

DIRECTIONS/PATHWAYS/LEVELS

In place

Forward; backward

Sideways (left and right)

Upgrade and downgrade

Over, under, and around objects

Low (squatting down partially)

High (spring into the air)

Changing directions

In circles (clockwise and counterclockwise); zigzag

TIME

Slow to fast

Jog

Change speeds while moving

To music accompaniment or rhythmic beat

Running to clapping of hands

Uneven

Even

Jerky motion

Running through an obstacle course offers the opportunity to enhance agility.

FORCE

Hard	Heavy
Soft	Quiet
Weak	Loud
Light	Shift weight with emphasis

ADDITIONAL MOVEMENT VARIATIONS

Run like various animals.

Run like a character you know.

Pretend you are running in the sand or mud.

Run the pattern of a letter, number, or shape.

Run with a partner (side-by-side holding hands).

Run obstacle-course variations.

Run and stop on a signal.

Run and dodge stationary objects or people.

Combine running with other forms of locomotion (jump, leap, walk, skip, gallop).

Run relays.

Run, playing follow the leader.

Run while throwing and catching objects.

Run while shuffling your feet.

Run and touch the ground.

Run while looking over your shoulder.

Run like a rag doll or tin soldier.

Run up and down hills or stairs.

Pretend you are running against a strong wind.

Use running as a movement in dance (see Table 10-1, 10-2, Movement Enhancement).

Movement Enhancement

Table 10-2		
Running Enhancement Chart		

GAMES	Level		Level	DANCE/RHYTHMS	Level
		Box Ball			
		Fire Engine			
Corners	I&II	Boiler Bust	I&II	Hickory, Dickory, Dock	I&II
Kneeling Tag		Beater Goes Round		Sally Go Round the	
Jet Pilot		Indian Running		Moon	
Marching Ponies		Bronco Tag			
Command Cards		Frog in the Pond		Pease Porridge Hot	II
Forest Lookout		Old Plug		Jump Jim Joe	
Cars		Run for Your Supper		Danish Dance of	
Squirrels in the Tree		Flytrap		Greeting	
Hook-on		Thread the Needle		This Old Man	
Red Light		All Up Relay			
Birds and Cats		Cat and Rat			
Santas Reindeer		Count-3-Tag			
Charlie Over the Water		Mousetrap			
Catch the Witch		Rescue Relay			
Man from Mars		Race Around the Bases			
Caged Lion		Old Man/Old Lady			
		Fire on the Mountain			
Wild Horse Round-up	II&III				

Skill Concepts Communicated to Children

Run on the balls of the feet (for sprinting).
Head up, eyes forward.
Bend your knees.
Relax your upper body.
Breathe naturally.
Lean slightly into your run.
Lift your knees.
Bend your elbows and swing the arms freely.
Contact the ground with your heels first
    (for jogging).

JUMPING AND LANDING

Movement Description

Jumping consists of movements that project and suspend the body momentarily in midair with the following basic characteristics: (1) a one- or two-foot takeoff with two-foot landing; (2) two-foot takeoff and one-foot landing. Although classified as a jumping variation, the leap and hop are treated separately in this text because of their extensive use. Wickstrom (1983) describes the following jumping tasks in terms of progressive difficulty:

Jump down from one foot to the other (leap).
Jump down from two feet to two feet.
Jump up from two feet to two feet.
Run and jump from one foot to the other (leap).
Jump forward from two feet to two feet.
Jump down from one foot to two feet.
Run and jump forward from one foot to two feet.
Jump over objects from two feet to two feet.
Jump from one foot to same foot rhythmically
    (hop).

FUNDAMENTAL JUMPING VARIATIONS AND APPROXIMATE TIME OF ACCOMPLISHMENT

One-foot takeoff–Opposite-foot landing (jump down; simple leap)	1 ½ years
One-foot takeoff–Two-feet landing	2–2 ½ years
Two-feet takeoff–One-foot landing	2 ½ years
Two-feet takeoff–Landing (broad jump)	4 ½–5 years
One-foot takeoff–Same-foot landing (hop)	4–6 years

Jumping, regardless of movement variation, is usually attempted with one of two purposes in mind: for height or distance. For either purpose, the hips, knees, and ankles must be bent in order for force to be produced through extension; therefore, takeoff should be from a half-crouched position.

Jumping for Height

If the primary purpose of the jump is to achieve height, the knees should be bent (crouched position) and the arms lowered with the elbows slightly flexed. As the knees straighten, the arms swing upward. The body stretches and extends as far as possible into the air. The landing should be on the balls of the feet, with the knees flexed to absorb force of impact.

DEVELOPMENTAL PROGRESSIONS OF THE VERTICAL JUMP AND REACH*

Stage 1. Note the crouching position (illustrated in Fig. 10-6) in which the legs are bent to initiate force. Upward motion is initiated with the arms while the child's head is focused in the direction of the target. After takeoff, the body is fully extended; however, in the upper series, the nonreaching arm is not in an effective position, whereas (in the lower series) the arm is swung downward as the reaching arm stretches upward.

Stage 2 (mature). The preparatory phase is characterized by flexion at the hips, knees, and ankles. A vigorous forward and upward lift by the arms begins the jump; drive is continued by forceful extension at the hips, knees, and ankles. Upon landing, the ankles, knees, and hips flex to absorb the shock (Fig. 10-7).

Jumping for Distance

To achieve the greatest distance, as in the standing or running long jump, there should be a forward lean, which is counterbalanced by swinging the arms backward and then forcefully forward. The angle of takeoff should be about 45°. The landing should be on the heels first, after which the body's center of gravity shifts forward to maintain balance.

DEVELOPMENTAL PROGRESSIONS OF THE STANDING LONG JUMP*

Stage 1. The jumping action of the standing long jump is not initiated effectively by the arms, because of their limited swing. Arms move in a sideward-downward or rearward-upward direction to maintain balance during flight. At takeoff, the trunk is propelled in a vertical direction with little emphasis upon the length of the jump. The preparatory crouch is limited and inconsistent with regard to the degree of leg flexion. The extension of the hips, legs, and ankles is incomplete at the takeoff of the jump. Because the child is experiencing difficulty in using both feet simultaneously, one leg may precede the other at takeoff and upon landing (Fig. 10-8).

*Material in the section adapted from McClenaghan and Gallahue (1978), and Wickstrom (1983).

FIGURE 10-6
Vertical jump: Stage 1.

FIGURE 10-7
Vertical jump: Mature pattern.

FIGURE 10-8
Standing long jump: Stage 1.

FIGURE 10-9

Standing long jump: Stage 2.

FIGURE 10-10

Standing long jump: Mature pattern.

Stage 2. In this stage, the arms are utilized more effectively to initiate the jumping action. They initiate the pattern at takeoff and then move to the side to maintain balance during the jump. There is only a slight change (from Stage 1) in the position of the trunk at takeoff; namely, limited forward lean. The preparatory crouch is deeper and more consistent. At takeoff, the legs, hips, and ankles extend more; however, they remain somewhat bent. During the flight, the thighs are held in a flexed rather than the more effective extended position (Fig. 10-9).

Stage 3 (mature). In the preparatory phase the crouch is deep and the arms swing backward and upward. At takeoff, the arms swing forward and upward with the thrust being initiated in a horizontal direction (angle of takeoff approximately 45° to 50°). As the body moves forward, the hips, legs, and ankles extend in succession. During flight, the hips flex, bringing the thighs to a position nearly horizontal to the surface. The lower legs extend prior to landing. The knees bend upon impact and body weight continues forward and downward. The arms reach forward to keep the center of gravity moving in the direction of flight (Fig. 10-10).

Movement Observation

Young children begin jumping naturally as soon as they develop the abilities necessary to project their bodies through space with extended flight. As strength, balance, and coordination levels increase,

movement pattern proficiency improves as well as desired height and distance.

In screening for possible weaknesses and determining fundamental jumping ability, the following movement-pattern tasks should be observed:

1. Jumping down from a height of 12 inches using a one-foot takeoff and two-feet landing; two-feet takeoff and two-feet landing.
2. Jump forward using a one-foot takeoff and two-feet landing.
3. Jump forward using a two-feet takeoff and landing.
4. Jump over, onto, and out of a circle with a diameter of 2 feet.
5. Jump onto a box (12 inches high) using a two-feet takeoff and landing.
6. Jump backward using two feet to two feet and one foot to two feet.
7. Run and jump from a one-foot takeoff and two-feet landing.

COMMON PROBLEMS

JUMPING

1. Failure to flex the hip, knee, and ankle joints on takeoff (takeoff should be from a crouched position);
2. Failure to swing arms forward or upward in time with takeoff (if jumping for height, the arms should swing upward as the knees are straightened and the body stretched;

when jumping for distance, the arms swing forward and upward explosively);

3. Failure to extend the legs on takeoff;
4. Upper part of body leaning forward in the jump for height (should stretch and reach vertically);
5. Standing too erect when distance is desired (there should be a forward lean and the angle of takeoff approximately 45°).

LANDING

1. Landing flat-footed (should land on balls of feet if jumping for height and on heels if projecting for distance);
2. Landing with feet too close together (width should be same as hips);
3. Knees rigid (knees and ankles should give on landing);
4. Head down (should keep chest and head high, with eyes fixed on direction of movement);
5. Bending forward at the waist (rebound with a small jump into a standing position).

When assessing the standing long jump (two-feet takeoff/two-feet landing), the following check-sequence chart may prove helpful to the instructor and child (Fig. 10-11).

If one is assessing the vertical jump, it is important to provide an overhead target to elicit an effective performance. The target may be an object (bag, ball, balloon) tied to the end of a light rope, horizontal rod, or the tester's hand. For advanced jumpers, chalked fingers, or chalk held in the hand and used to mark the achieved height on a wall, work effectively.

Movement Variability

Jumping and landing are perhaps the most utilized fundamental skills aside from the basic running pattern. A strong schema is necessary if children are to challenge the many and varied jumping and landing tasks that will confront them in almost all movement activities. Aside from the fundamental jumping and landing schema used in performing simple dance, game, and gymnastic activities, jumping variations are an integral part of many advanced movements. Fundamental jumping forms the foundation for such activities as the running long jump, high jump (with variations), and triple jump. Few individual and team-sport activities are performed without some form of jumping. In basketball, for example, players frequently perform a lay-up, jump shot, jump ball, rebound, and jump into the air to retrieve high passes.

Stage 1

Stage 2

Stage 3

FIGURE 10-11

Standing long jump: Check sequence.

SPATIAL

In any sport or movement activity in which an object is thrown or hit and must be caught, a jump is frequently utilized (volleyball, baseball, football, lacrosse, racquetball).

Proficiency in dance and gymnastics activities is often based upon one's ability to project through space and land accurately.

MOVEMENT-PATTERN VARIATIONS

Jumping

One-foot takeoff-two-feet landing

Two-feet takeoff-one-foot landing (right/left)

Two-feet takeoff-two-feet landing

Jump in a tuck position

Jump in a pike position

Jump in a straddle position

Jump and reach out or up

High jump variations (hurdle, scissors, roll)

Gymnastic vaulting variations

Upright (standing erect)

Arms in various positions (at sides; swinging forward and backward, or side to side; making circles; folded or extended)

Vary base of support (narrow to wide)

Hands in various positions (on knees, hips, behind head, on head)

Landing

Right foot

Left foot

Both feet

With right foot forward

With left foot forward

With arms in various positions

On heels

With knees bent

On toes

With feet apart

With feet together

Straddle position

Squat position

With feet crossed

Right foot and right hand

Right foot and left hand

Left foot and left hand

Left foot and right hand

(All of the following are performed on a soft mat or trampoline:)
On seat
On knees
On stomach
On back

DIRECTIONS/PATHWAYS/LEVELS

In place

Upward

Forward, backward, sideward

Change directions while jumping

Off objects (bench, box)

Onto objects

Over objects

Low (knees bent)

TIME

Slow to Fast

Change speeds while jumping

To a rhythmic beat

To musical accompaniment

FORCE

JUMP

For distance	For height	For height/distance
Hard	Heavy	
Soft	Smoothly	
Lightly	Loudly	

LAND

Lightly   Hard

ADDITIONAL MOVEMENT VARIATIONS

Jump like a bouncing ball.

Jump into and out of hoops on floor.

Jump with objects on head.

Jump with a partner (side by side, face to face, back to back, face to back; using a variety of hand placements).

Jump like various animals (rabbit, kangaroo).

Land on designated spots (squares, colors, numbers).

Land on different surfaces (mats, sponge, sand).

Combine jumping with nonlocomotor movements (jump and turn, twist).

Jump while bouncing a ball, while throwing or catching objects.

Combine jumping with other locomotor movements.

Jump onto, on and off a mini-trampoline or springboard.

Play hopscotch games.

Try jumping rope and vaulting (discussed in the next two sections of this chapter).

Hopscotch is an excellent and popular enhancement.

Jumping Rope

Movement Description

Traditionally labeled as an activity for young females, *jumping rope* has gained popularity in recent years due in part to its publicity as a fitness tool. Sometimes referred to as *rope skipping*, jumping rope can be achieved using a variety of movements such as skipping, leaping, hopping, and jumping, all of which require that the performer clear a rope(s) in motion (jump) and land (rebound).

EQUIPMENT AND BASIC BODY POSITION

Equipment.   There are several kinds of ropes available, ranging from sash cord to the more expensive Olympic-style plastic links with turning handles. Homemade ropes can be constructed of inexpensive clothesline and adhesive tape (tape the cut ends to avoid fraying). An excellent idea is to color-code the ropes to indicate length.

The length of the rope can definitely affect the child's performance. To determine the proper rope length, have the child stand in the center of the rope; the ends should be approximately armpit level (Fig. 10-12). Generally, an assortment of ropes in 6-, 7-, and 8-foot lengths are appropriate for elementary-school children (preschool children most often utilize a 6-foot rope). Adults will find that a 9-foot rope works well. Long jump ropes should be from 15 feet to 20 feet long. Thickness of the rope may also vary: the authors recommend ⅜-inch to ½-inch thicknesses.

Basic Body Position.   The ends of the rope should be held loosely in the fingers with the thumbs positioned on top of the rope and pointing to the sides. The elbows are positioned close to the sides, with hands and forearms pointing slightly forward and away from the body. The rope is started by swinging the arms and shoulders in a circular motion. The wrists and fingers should supply the force necessary to initiate further turning action. The jump is executed with the body erect, a slight push off the toes, and a straightening of the knees, which provides for the lift (approximately one inch). The landing should be made on the balls of the feet with the knees bent slightly to cushion the shock. Specific jumping steps will demand variations in takeoff and landing position; however, the basic principles of posture should apply.

BASIC MOVEMENT PATTERNS

It is suggested that rope-jumping patterns and activities be presented in the following order of teaching progression: (1) jumping movements using stationary ropes (or basic jumping, no ropes), (2) long-rope jumping, and (3) jumping using individual ropes.

Because basic jumping and jumping using stationary ropes are discussed in the first section of this chapter, only patterns utilized with long and individual rope jumping will be discussed here.

JUMPING WITH LONG ROPES

After the child has been exposed to basic jumping and stationary-rope activities, a confidence in the ability to time one's jumping movements to rhythm is at a level that is appropriate for introduction of the next rope-jumping category—long-rope jumping. This form of rope jumping is usually performed with one or more children jumping over a rope being turned by at least

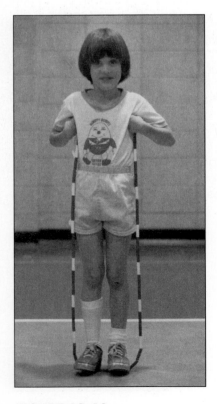

FIGURE 10-12
Determining proper rope length.

FIGURE 10-13
Long-rope jumping.

two others (Fig. 10-13). There are two ways that the rope can be turned, which allows the jumper a choice of entries: front door and back door.

Front door means that the child enters from the side where the rope is coming down. The jumper waits until the rope is moving away before entering.

Back door entry is from the side where the rope is coming up. The jumper does not enter until the rope has passed its highest point and is moving downward.

To enhance the rhythmic process, rhymes and chants are very helpful. Children enjoy making up jumping verses, and such a practice is an excellent activity to stimulate creativity (refer to Movement Enhancement section for jumping–rope chants and rhymes).

Using the front door (easiest) and then back door entry, the following progression should prove effective in teaching children to jump using long ropes.

1. Run under the rope.
2. Enter, jump once, and exit.
3. Enter, jump several times, and exit.
4. Enter, hop once, and exit (repeat with opposite foot).
5. Enter, hop several times on one foot, and exit (repeat with opposite foot).
6. Enter, hop on alternate feet, and exit.
   The child should now be ready for more variations to develop schema (refer to Movement Variability section).

JUMPING WITH INDIVIDUAL ROPES

The challenge of turning one's own rope and performing various jumping movements makes this category of rope jumping more difficult than fundamental long-rope jumping (the authors acknowledge that there are some very difficult movements and routines using long ropes).

As with previous rope-jumping activities, music and rhymes/chants can be very helpful in the timing process and stimulation of creativity.

All jumping movements can be varied in speed: slow time, fast time, and double time. An explanation for each of these components is given in the Time

FIGURE 10-14
Jumping with individual ropes.

dimension, contained within Movement Variability. Also related to timing is the *rebound*; this is a hop in

FIGURE 10-15
Two-foot step.

place as the rope passes overhead. A rebound is used only in slow time with the purpose of carrying the rhythm between steps.

BASIC ROPE-JUMPING STEPS

The rope-jumping steps that follow are presented in approximate order of difficulty.

FIGURE 10-16
Alternate-foot step.

Two-Foot Step. The two-foot step consists of a two-feet takeoff and two-feet rebound (or landing). The rebound phase is executed while the rope is approximately overhead (Fig. 10-15).

Alternate-Foot Step. The alternate-foot step is characterized by a takeoff and rebound on the same foot (hop), then a switch to the opposite side to continue the same procedure. The rebound step is executed while the rope is passing overhead (Fig. 10-16).

Swing Step. The swing step is nearly identical to the alternate step, except the *free leg* swings forward, backward, or to the side during the rebound phase (Fig. 10-17).

FIGURE 10-17
Swing step.

One-Foot Hop. The one-foot hop is similar to the alternate-foot step, except the performer continues hopping on one foot for several rotations of the rope before switching to the opposite foot (Fig. 10-18). This series of movements requires a higher level of balance and general body coordination than does the alternate–foot step.

FIGURE 10-18
One-foot hop.

Rocker Step. In the rocker step, one leg is always forward and the weight is shifting from the back foot to the forward foot. As the rope passes under the lead (front) foot, the weight is shifted in a forward motion, allowing the back foot to lift and for the rope to pass under. The performer should then rock back, shifting the weight to the back foot (Fig. 10-19).

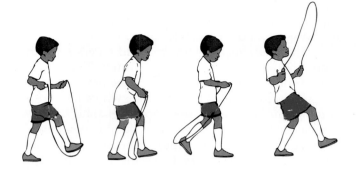

FIGURE 10-19
Rocker step.

Stride Step. The stride step starts with the legs in a stride position (one foot forward) with the weight equally distributed on both feet. As the rope passes under the feet, the performer changes foot position and continues (Fig. 10-20).

(a)   (b)   (c)

FIGURE 10-20
Stride step.

Cross-Leg Step. The cross-leg step begins with one leg crossed in front of the other. As the rope passes under the feet, the legs are crossed in the opposite direction and the pattern continued (Fig. 10-21).

FIGURE 10-21
Cross-leg step.

FIGURE 10-22
Side-shuffle step.

Side-Shuffle Step.   As the rope passes under the feet, the performer pushes off with the right (or left) foot and sidesteps to the left, landing with the weight on the left foot (Fig. 10-22). The pattern is then continued in the opposite direction.

Crossing Arms.   When combined with any selected jumping step, crossing arms while turning the rope provides an interesting challenge for the more advanced jumpers. Once the rope has passed overhead and begins a downward movement, the left (or right) arm crosses over the right and the right hand is brought up and placed under the left armpit (Fig. 10-23). The next jump is executed in this position; the performer now has the option of continuing in the crossed-arm position or alternating positions.

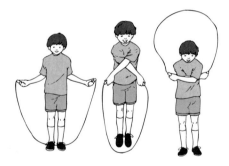

FIGURE 10-23
Crossing arms.

Movement Observation

Depending upon experience and ability, children will enter programs with a wide variety of rope-jumping proficiency. Generally there will be little difference in skill levels between boys and girls at the primary stage; however, girls seem to extend their interest for the activity over a longer period of time. Recent publicity on rope-jumping routines for fitness has helped influence the idea that this activity is not exclusively feminine.

Assessment is essential in determining the entry point of the individual. Corresponding to teaching progression, the following items should also be guidelines for assessment: (1) allow the child an opportunity to jump rhythmically without a rope(s) in motion (jumping in time to a rhythmic beat); (2) allow the child to jump using long ropes turned by others (5 to 10 jumps are considered successful); and (3) allow the child to jump using individual ropes in motion.

Assessment of individual rope-jumping skills can be grouped according to movement pattern and number of turns completed; for example.

NUMBER OF TURNS

Basic two-foot (fast)	_____
Basic two-foot (slow)	_____
Alternate-foot (fast)	_____
Alternate-foot (slow)	_____

The teacher sets a certain criterion to be challenged to meet the requirement for a specific level (that is, Level I, 5 turns; Level II, 10 turns; and so forth).

COMMON PROBLEMS

1. Landing flat-footed (the child should bend slightly at the knees and ankles and land on the balls of the feet);
2. Landing on the rope (in most instances due to incorrect timing; instruct the child to concentrate on movement of rope; offer feedback as to "too soon" or "too late"; slow down rope speed);
3. Not jumping high enough (again, this may be because of incorrect timing or placement of the rope); the rope should hit the surface in front (with individual rope) of the child, thus creating auditory feedback, a cue in the timing process.

Movement Variability

SPATIAL

MOVEMENT-PATTERN VARIATIONS

I. *Long Ropes*
   A. *Basic Steps*
      one-foot, two-foot variations; leap, hop
   B. *Variations*
      Combine basic steps
      Place hands in various positions (on head, waist, arms crossed)
      Jump with feet in various positions (in, out, close, wide)
      Rope variations
      • Double Dutch—two ropes turned alternately, inward (two turners)
      • Double Irish—two ropes turned alternately, outward (two turners)
      • Egg Beater—two ropes turned at right angles by four turners (more ropes may be added)

II. *Individual Ropes*

  A. *Basic Steps*

    two-foot, alternate foot, swing, one-hop, rocker step, stride, cross-leg, side shuffle, crossing arms

  B. *Variations*

    Combine basic steps

- Toe touch—swing right (or left) foot forward or sideward and land; touch heel with toe of free foot;
- Heel-toe—jump with weight landing on right (or left) foot, touch left heel forward; on the next jump, land on same foot, but touch opposite toe to heel; alternate landing foot;
- Heel click—while performing the swing-step sideward (right foot lead), instead of executing a hop (on rebound) when the rope is overhead, raise the left foot to click the heel of the right foot; alternate lead foot;
- Step and tap—this is executed by pushing off with the right (or left) foot and landing on the left. While the rope is overhead, brush the sole of the right foot forward and then backward; alternate push-off foot;
- Create jumping routines from dance steps (Schottische, Bleking);
- Jump with feet in various positions (close, wide, pointed out).

DIRECTIONS/LEVELS/PATHWAYS

I. *Long Ropes*

  Forward body motion on turn of rope
  Backward body motion on turn of rope
  Sideward (shuffle)
  Combinations (change directions while in motion)
  Facing turner; side to turner
  Low level (knees bent)

II. *Individual Ropes*

  Forward body motion on turn of rope
  Backward body motion on turn of rope
  Sideward
  Diagonal
  Combinations
  Low level (knees bent)
  Change direction of rope motion (nonstop jumping); forward to backward (as rope starts downward, swing both arms to the left (or right) and make a halfturn facing in the opposite direction. Next, spread the arms and start turning.
  Jump with rope turned laterally (rope swung around the body sideways).

TIME

  Slow Time—slow rope with slow feet movement and a rebound. Rope passes under the feet on every other beat.

  Fast Time—fast rope with fast feet movement. Rope turns in time with beat; twice the speed of slow time. Rope speed is approximately 120 to 180 turns per minute.

  Double Time—slow rope with fast feet movement. Rope moves in slow time while the performer executes two steps; passing of rope at feet and overhead.

  Pepper Time—fast rope with slow feet movement. Two or more turns of the rope while the performer's feet are off the ground.

To a rhythmic beat or musical accompaniment;

Use of rhymes and chants. (see Movement Enhancement).

FORCE

  Rebound soft; hard
  Turn the rope hard; soft
  Jump to achieve various heights.

ADDITIONAL MOVEMENT VARIATIONS

Long Ropes. Jumping with partners (start together, or additional jumpers move in while the rope is in motion)

  face to face; back to back; face to back
  alternate role of jumping and turning, with rope in constant motion
  partners attach themselves at various sites and jump (hands on waist, shoulder)
  bounce a ball to a partner or self
  throw a ball to a partner
  jump with more than two

squat down and touch the surface (one, then two hands)

create a routine to music.

Individual Ropes. Jumping with partners (start together, or the extra jumper moves in while the rope is in motion)

  face to face; back to back; face to back
  the extra jumper changes directions
  change role of turning rope
  one jumper holds on to the other at various sites (hands on waist, shoulder, and so forth)
  stand side by side, clasp hands (or arms around waist, shoulders), and turn rope with outside hands
  side by side, raise inside knees or touch knees
  the "extra" jumper bounces a ball
  turning the rope, facing each other, one partner moves in (jumps), then out; partners alternate; another variation is to have one partner move in, followed by the other

jump with three partners (one in front, one behind the turner)

jump with an individual and long rope (long rope being turned by others in usual fashion)

Create a routine using music

Jump rope (running) through an obstacle course.

VAULTING

Vaulting, classified as a gymnastic activity, involves a coordination of movements that enable one to bound over an obstacle(s). The obstacles most often used in physical education classes are boxes, benches, and beams. Mini-trampolines, springboards, and beatboards are frequently utilized to aid in the takeoff phase of the vault. Whatever the type of apparatus used in the activity, it is highly desirable that the apparatus be adjustable to accommodate the size and skill level of the participants. There are a number of acceptable models on the commercial market.

Because the use of a springboard or similar apparatus aids in the takeoff phase of some vaulting activities, it is recommended that children be introduced to such apparatus and be allowed adequate practice (with variability) before attempting to vault over obstacles. The control of the body while in flight is an essential prerequisite to this activity. Therefore some forms of vaulting, especially the more complex movements, should be regarded as advanced forms of jumping.

Beginning Vaulting Progression (Nonrunning Approach). Apparatus can be a bench beam, horse, or box; surface approximately knee high to start. (Note: Material in this section is adapted from O'Quinn, 1990.)

PUSH OFF

FIGURE 10-24

Place one foot on the top and push off to the other side.

BOUNCE OFF

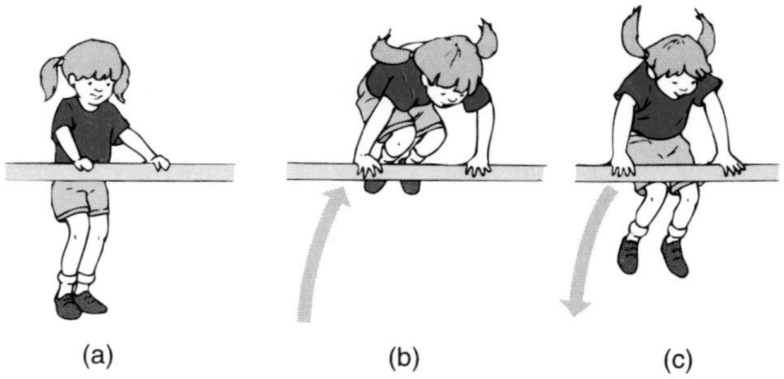

FIGURE 10-25

With hands on the top, jump up and bend the knees (don't land on the top).

(a)　　　(b)　　　(c)

KANGAROO HOP

(1)　　　(2)　　　(3)　　　(4)

FIGURE 10-26

Jump up and over.

HIGH PUSH OFF (START AT WAIST LEVEL)

FIGURE 10-27

HIGH BOUNCE UP

FIGURE 10-28

HIGH KANGAROO HOP

FIGURE 10-29

TOE TOUCH

FIGURE 10-30
Jump up and touch the top with your toes.

ONE FOOT ON

FIGURE 10-31
Jump up and land on one foot.

TWO FEET ON

FIGURE 10-32

VAULTING WITH MOVING APPROACH

The basic *moving approach* in vaulting consists of a series of running steps and a two-feet takeoff from the floor or bounce apparatus (springboard, beatboard, mini-trampoline). Figure 10-33 illustrates the basic approach and two-feet takeoff. Beginning several yards away from the takeoff point, the child runs into a one–foot liftoff, then brings the legs together for the two-feet takeoff position (which is also the landing on the bounce apparatus or surface). The landing should be on the balls of the feet with the knees slightly bent. The takeoff is performed with a slight forward body lean and hands in place to clear the obstacle.

FIGURE 10-33
Basic approach and two-feet takeoff.

Basic Vaults (Running-Step Approach). Basic jumping skills and bounce apparatus proficiency are a prerequisite when beginning the running-step approach.

The practice-variability method is certainly applicable. However, caution should be taken and spotters utilized as with any potentially hazardous activity. The beginning vaulting movements—bounce off (low and high), kangaroo hop (low and high), toe touch, one foot on, and two feet on—should be the first basic vaults attempted using the running-step approach. *All of the following vaults are performed using a two-foot takeoff:*

FLANK VAULT

With both hands on the top of the apparatus and legs extended toward the right side, the child's right hand is released and motion continued forward until a bent-knee landing is achieved (Fig. 10-34). This vault may be executed from a right or left side takeoff.

SQUAT VAULT

As the child bounds over the obstacle, the hands touch the top as the knees are tucked up close to the chest. The knees should be slightly bent upon landing (Fig. 10-35). The usual landing is on two feet; however, after that is accomplished the child may vary the phase, such as turn, twist (just before landing), or perform a forward roll after landing.

STRADDLE VAULT

The jumping technique is similar to that of a leapfrog. The child reaches forward with extended arms and extends the legs to the side. Maximum height is essential to ensure clearance. The legs are brought together and knees bent slightly upon landing (Fig. 10-36).

HEAD VAULT

The head vault is to be performed only by the highly skilled child. A spotter should be on

FIGURE 10-34
Flank vault.

FIGURE 10-35
Squat vault.

FIGURE 10-36
Straddle vault.

FIGURE 10-37
Head vault.

each side of the apparatus. As the child moves upward, both hands and then the head are placed on the top of the box. When the child becomes overbalanced, the fingertips are used to push off and direct the landing (Fig. 10-37). Caution should be taken by reminding the child not to push off too early and thus fail to clear the apparatus.

Teaching Hints (General Jumping)

Avoid having children jump in socks or in gym shoes that have poor traction.

Emphasize coordinated use of the arms and legs.

Reinforce jumping by measuring individual jumps with a yardstick.

Place a mat on the floor for landing.

Stress proper landing techniques.

Emphasize to the child the need to maintain control while the child is in the air.

Skill Concepts Communicated to Children

Swing your arms forward, bend your knees, and push off with your toes.

Push off equally with both feet.

Your toes leave the ground last.

Lean forward slightly.

Keep your legs shoulder width apart for landing preparation.

LEAPING

Movement Description

A *leap* is similar to a run (it may be described as an extension of the run); however, a leap presents more flight, as well as greater height and distance. A leap is also characterized by a one-foot takeoff and opposite-foot landing (Fig. 10-38).

On the takeoff, the toe of the lead foot leaves last, while the ball of the landing foot contacts the floor first. The movement is usually preceded by several running steps, which add to the momentum needed to produce height and distance. A forward upward motion of the arms also gives added momentum to help carry the body.

Movement Observation

Without a running start, it is difficult to project the body to the necessary height and distance to execute a successful leap. The combination of a run and leap is

FIGURE 10-38
Leaping.

Movement Enhancement

Table 10-3
Jumping and Landing Enhancement Chart

GAMES	LEVEL	GYMNASTICS	LEVEL	DANCE/RHYTHMS/RHYMES	LEVEL
Hopscotch Games	I–III	Rope Stunts	I&II	Ten Little Indians	II
		Lazy Rope		Bleking	
Play Footsie		Snake Rope		Seven Jumps	
Train Station	I&II	Circle Rope		Hansel and Gretel	
Hoop Hop		Straight Rope		Jump Jim Joe	
Toss, Jump, and Pick		V-Rope		The Popcorn Man	
		Rope Rings			
Eyeglasses	II&III	Frog Jump		Rope-Jump Rhymes	II&III
Weathervane		Jack in the Box		Apple, Apple	
Sticky Popcorn		Missile Man		All in Together	
Jump the Clubs Race				Ask Mother	
Stool Hurdle Relay		Knee Slapper	II	Be Nimble, Be Quick	
Jump the Shot		Heel Slap		Birthday	
Over the Brook		Heel Click		Blind Man	
Sack Relay		Human Spring		Bobby, Bobby	
Frozen Beanbag		Jumping Tubes		Bubble Gum	
Here to There		Bouncing Ball		Bulldog	
Slow Poke		Top		Call the Doctor	
Frog in the Pond		Up-String		Cinderella	
Deep Freeze		Toe Touch		Charlie McCarthy	
Islands		Tuck Jump		Chickety Chop	
Chinese Hurdle		Rabbit Jump		Down in the Meadow	
In the Creek		Jumping Swan		Down in the Valley	
Kangaroo Relay		Pogo Stick		Hippity Hop	
Circle Jump Relay		Kangaroo Jump		Hokey Pokey	
Deck The Halls		Leap Frog		I Love Coffee	
High Water		Knee Jump		Ice Cream Soda	
		Split Jump	II&III	Lady, Lady	
		Jacknife		Mabel, Mabel	
		Flank Vault		Mama, Mama	
		Squat Vault		One Two, Buckle My Shoe	
		Straddle Vault		Teddy Bear, Teddy Bear	
				Tick-Tock	
				Vote, Vote	

difficult for many preschool children, although the basic pattern can be achieved. Movement-pattern variations should be held to height and distance during the early learning stages.

COMMON PROBLEMS

1. Not pushing off with enough force to suspend the body in air (push up, stretch, and extend);
2. Failing to swing the arms forward and upward;
3. Landing on heels or flat-footed (land on ball of foot);
4. Landing on both feet (land on opposite foot from takeoff leg);
5. Taking off and landing with stiff knees (knees should be ready to push, lift, extend, and give with the landing).

Movement Variability

While running, children often leap spontaneously when challenged to step over obstacles or space. A leap enables them to hurdle the area (or object) and continue the running pattern; such is the situation in many sport activities. A leap is preferable to a jump while catching an object (basketball, football, baseball) because the running pattern can be continued easily. Leaping can also be observed in such activities as gymnastics, the martial arts, and track (triple jump and hurdling).

Except when combined with other movements, the leap is not very easy to use in dancing with others, but it can be frequently observed in solo rhythmic routines.

SPATIAL

MOVEMENT-PATTERN VARIATIONS

Vary takeoff foot.
Vary arm position (at sides, on head).
Leap with same leg and arm forward; alternate sides.

DIRECTIONS/PATHWAYS/LEVELS

Forward	Various path patterns
Upward	At a low level; high level
To the side (left, right)	Over objects

TIME

Slow to fast	To musical accompaniment or rhythmic beat

FORCE

For height	Land soft; hard
For distance	

ADDITIONAL MOVEMENT VARIATIONS

Leap from a stationary position.
Leap like a deer.
Leap over objects (rope(s), bean bags, blocks, hurdles).
Leap over a stick or rope in high-jump fashion (gradually increased).
Leap a distance across two lines (gradually widened).
Clap your hands as you leap.
While leaping, catch a ball.
Leap across ropes on the floor at evenly (and unevenly) spaced intervals.
Vary the running pattern before the leap.

"Leap the Brook" is a traditional and challenging activity.

Leap, landing on the X's on the floor.
Leap, forming different patterns.
Leap with a partner (side by side holding hands or without attachment).
Change directions.
Combine leaping with other locomotor movements (run, leap, jump).
Use the leap as a movement in dance (see Movement Enhancement).

Teaching Hints

Combine leaping with two or three running steps.
Provide definite objects or barriers to leap over.
Encourage leaping with either foot.
Suggest imagery-leaping for young children (over mud puddles, or running rivers).
Use devices that "give" if the child comes in contact with an object being leaped over.

Movement Enhancement

Table 10-4

Leaping Enhancement Chart

GAMES	LEVEL	GAMES	LEVEL	DANCE/RHYTHMS	LEVEL
Hopscotch Games	I–III	High Water	I&III	La Raspa	II
Follow the Leader		Here to There		Fool's Jig	
Over the Brook		Eyeglasses			
Command Cards		Jump the Clubs Race			
Leapfrog Relay		Deep Freeze			
Hoop Hop	I&II	Stool Hurdle Relay			
		Slow Poke			
Hurdle Relay	II&III	Frog in the Pond			
		Spoke Relay			
		In the Creek			
		Chinese Hurdle			
		Islands			

Skill Concepts Communicated To Children

Push upward and forward with your rear foot.
Stretch and reach with your forward foot.
Keep your head up.
Lean forward slightly at the trunk as you leap.
Alternate your arm action with your leg action.
Push up, stretch, and reach.
Swing arms up and forward.
Run, run, leap.

HOPPING

Movement Description

Hopping is characterized by a takeoff from the surface on one foot and landing on the same foot (Fig. 10-39).

Execution is very similar to a jump, but it presents more difficulty in two instances: (1) balance must be maintained across the base of one foot only, and (2) one leg must provide the force necessary to propel the body into space. In hopping, the child should take off and land on the ball of the foot while flexing the hip, knee, and ankle joints to absorb the landing. The free leg, while it may be moved, is bent under the body so that it makes no contact with the floor.

Movement Observation

Before a child can properly execute a hop, he or she must be able to balance on one foot and have enough strength to propel the entire body using the force of only one leg. A child of 3 ½ years can usually perform one to three hops, but it is not until approximately 6 years of age that children have mastered the task proficiently. Identification of problems in hopping may be detected easily by directing each child to hop along a straight line (using right and left foot) and over a small object (block, beanbag). Many of the problems associated with hopping are related to lack of balance, leg strength, and experience, which in most instances can be improved upon with proper guidance.

FIGURE 10-39
Hopping.

COMMON PROBLEMS

1. Landing flat-footed, instead of on the ball of the foot;
2. Inability to propel very far up into space because of being too earthbound (should lift arms up);
3. Taking off on one foot and landing on the other foot or both feet (should take off and land on the same foot);
4. Taking off and landing with stiff knees and ankles (hips, knees, and ankle joints should be flexed slightly to absorb shock of landing);
5. Taking off with the trunk bent too far forward, backward, or sideward (body should lean slightly in the direction of the takeoff leg, with the angle of takeoff close to vertical).

Movement Variability

Hopping is an integral component in many dance, game, and gymnastic activities. It is used in hopscotch, jump rope, skipping, dance steps (step-hop, schottische, polka, mazurka, tinikling), as well as a component in endless movement combinations.

SPATIAL

MOVEMENT-PATTERN VARIATIONS

Hop on right foot; left foot.
Hop with trunk tilted forward, backward, or sideward.
Short, medium, and long hops.
Free leg placed in various positions (extended forward, sideward, backward, or bent up high in front or at side).
Hop with hands in various positions (on head, behind head, on hips, around knee of free leg).
Hop with arms in various positions (at sides, straight out in front, straight out at sides).
Click heel of hopping foot to free leg heel.

DIRECTIONS/PATHWAYS/LEVELS

Upward	Hop in place
Forward; backward; sideward	Hop over
Low (knees bent)	Change directions/levels
High	

TIME

Slow to fast	To the rhythm of music, or a rhythmic beat

FORCE

For height	Soft, lightly
For distance	Heavily

ADDITIONAL MOVEMENT VARIATIONS

Hop and turn.

Hop, forming a pattern (number, letter, shape).

Hop over objects (ropes, beanbags).

Hop with a partner (side by side, face to face, back to back, front to back; hand placement variable).

Hop like a wooden soldier (short hops with a stiff body).

Hop through an obstacle course; over, around, in and out (tires, ropes, ladders, hoops, cones, tape).

Hop on a trampoline or bouncing board.

Hop while holding the nonhopping leg (foot).

Hop holding the nonhopping leg in various positions.

Hop with eyes closed.

Hop and clap your hands.

Hop using a jump rope.

Hop while dribbling a ball.

Pop a balloon with foot while hopping.

With a partner, try to "mirror" each other.

Combine hopping with other movements (run, jump, skip, step, walk, leap, gallop).

Hop while catching, throwing, or juggling (with a partner).

Hop and kick.

The Hop in Dance.   Hopping is usually combined with other movements for use in partner dancing. The hopping movement is found in the following traditional dance steps:

Skipping—discussed separately in this chapter.

Step-hop—a combination of a walk and hop. The walk is strongly accented and the hop executed in place. The step-hop is performed to the two beats of an accompaniment in ¾ meter time.

Schottische—a combination of three short running steps and a hop. The accent is on the first run and the hop is executed on the foot that takes the third run. The movements are performed in ¾ meter time.

Polka—a combination of a hop and three springy walking steps performed on the balls of the feet. These movements are usually performed in a sideward direction. Preliminary lift for the first walking step is initiated by the hop. The walking step is taken sideward with the outside edge of the lead foot. The feet are brought together into a closed position by the second walk. The third walking step is taken in the same direction as the first, completing the combination in an open position, held for part of the fourth count. The movements are performed to one equally divided and one unequally divided pulse interval in ¾ meter time.

Mazurka—a combination of two springy walking steps and a hop. The two walking steps are taken forward and the hop is performed after the second walking step on the same foot. The movements are performed in ¾ meter time.

Teaching Hints

Avoid letting children perform hopping activities when wearing only socks or gym shoes that have poor traction.

Use marks on the floor to hop to and over.

Emphasize coordinated use of the arms and legs.

Skill Concepts Communicated to Children

Hop up in the air on one foot and down on the same foot.

Stay on the balls of feet while hopping.

Arms should be used for balance.

Reach for the sky.

Crouch halfway down for takeoff.

Hopping is used in many traditional dance steps.

Movement Enhancement

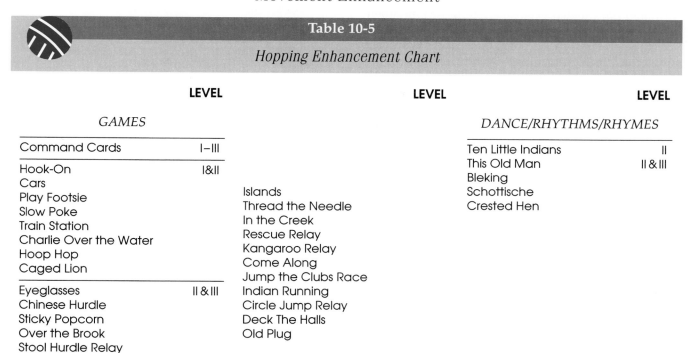

	LEVEL			LEVEL			LEVEL
GAMES						*DANCE/RHYTHMS/RHYMES*	
Command Cards	I–III					Ten Little Indians	II
Hook-On	I&II					This Old Man	II & III
Cars						Bleking	
Play Footsie			Islands			Schottische	
Slow Poke			Thread the Needle			Crested Hen	
Train Station			In the Creek				
Charlie Over the Water			Rescue Relay				
Hoop Hop			Kangaroo Relay				
Caged Lion			Come Along				
			Jump the Clubs Race				
Eyeglasses	II & III		Indian Running				
Chinese Hurdle			Circle Jump Relay				
Sticky Popcorn			Deck The Halls				
Over the Brook			Old Plug				
Stool Hurdle Relay							
Here to There			*GYMNASTICS*	I–II			
Deep Freeze							
Frozen Beanbag			Rope Stunts				

Table 10-5

Hopping Enhancement Chart

GALLOPING

Movement Description

Galloping is an advanced extension of walking combined with a leap. It is similar to a slide except the directional progress is forward or backward. Just as the slide, the rhythm is uneven (Fig. 10-40).

The lead leg thrusts forward, supporting the weight, while the rear foot quickly closes behind the lead foot and takes the weight. In a series of gallops, the same foot takes the lead. The takeoff is from the ball of the rear foot and landing is on the ball of the forward foot.

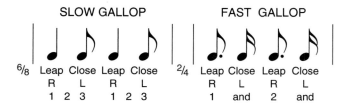

FIGURE 10-40

Galloping.

Movement Observation

Galloping (and skipping) are two of the most difficult locomotor skills for young children to master. This may be partly due both to lack of experience with the movement and complexity of the skill, which is a combination of locomotor movements. Galloping rarely appears before 4 years of age, and children usually do not achieve the mature stage until 6 ½ years.

COMMON PROBLEMS

1. The rear foot is not brought up quickly to support weight;
2. Lack of a "sliding" movement;
3. Lack of flexibility in lead leg (lead leg should be lifted and bent);
4. Tempo too slow;
5. Weight not taken on heel of lead foot (increase stride of leg in front);
6. Failure to stay on toes of foot in rear (take shorter steps on rear leg);
7. Stride of leap too short (should be long-short uneven rhythm);
8. Body too erect (body's center of gravity should be shifted forward);
9. Trailing leg passes in front of lead leg.

Movement Variability

Although not utilized extensively in most fundamental and advanced movement programs, galloping is known as one of the traditional dance steps with variations that range from the simple to complex when combined with other locomotor movements.

SPATIAL

MOVEMENT-PATTERN VARIATIONS

Alternate lead foot	Alternate stride length
Change arm position (at sides, overhead, in front)	Legs stiff; very loose
	Base of legs set wide; set close together

DIRECTIONS/PATHWAYS/LEVELS

In place	Low Level	Around
Forward	Change Directions; Levels	Between
Backward		Curve
Circle (clockwise, counter-clockwise)	Zigzag (through cones)	
High Level	Turning gallop (lead foot acts as a pivoting center)	

TIME

Slow to fast	To a rhythmic beat or musical accompaniment

FORCE

Heavy	For distance (strong leaps)
Lightly	

ADDITIONAL MOVEMENT VARIATIONS

Gallop with a partner (one behind, both facing forward or side by side; hands joined optional).

Combine galloping with other locomotor movements (slide, gallop, run, leap, step, skip).

Gallop through an obstacle course (cones, beanbags, ropes).

Gallop while throwing and/or catching.

Gallop like various animals (race horse, mule).

Gallop like a bouncing ball.

Use a wand and ride a horse.

Be a horse on a merry-go-round.

Be a horse carrying a heavy load.

Gallop over two ropes ("jump the river").

Gallop in different patterns (C, Z, S, 7, 9).

Use the gallop as a movement in dance (see Movement Enhancement).

Teaching Hints

Begin with exploratory experiences then progress to skill drills.

Stress not crossing the feet.

Stress bending of the knees, trunk leaning forward, and staying on the balls of the feet.

Rhythmical accompaniment aids in galloping.

Skills Concepts Communicated to Children

Keep one foot in front of the other.

Use arms as needed for balance.

Move on the balls of the feet.

Lean forward slightly at the waist.

Movement Enhancement

Table 10-6
Galloping Enhancement Chart

GAMES	LEVEL		LEVEL	DANCE/RHYTHMS/RHYMES	LEVEL
Command Cards	I-III	Boiler Bust		Sally Go Around the Moon	I&II
		Man from Mars		Loobie Loo	
		Gardner and Scamp		Paw Paw Patch	II
Run For Your Supper	I&II	Caged Lion			
Marching Ponies				Pease Porridge Hot	
Cars		Come Along	II&III	Hobby Horse	
Charlie Over the Water		Beater Goes Round			
Flowers Blowing in the Wind		Thread the Needle			
Broomstick Relay		Cat and Rat			
Hook-On		Catch the Witch			
Santa's Reindeer		Indian Running			
Buffalo Bill		Rescue Relay			
Wild Horse Round-Up		All Up Relay			
Corners		Bronco Tag			
		Old Plug			

SLIDING

Movement Description

Sliding consists of a long-short uneven movement pattern that is executed in a sideward direction (Fig. 10-41).

When sliding to the right, the right foot moves sideward, taking the weight, and the left foot follows quickly. The same foot always leads. The first step is a slow gliding movement and the second a quick closing step. The movement should be performed on the balls of the feet, with the weight shifted from lead to follow-up foot. After the follow-up foot catches the lead foot, a slight hop (with little height) occurs; balance is easily maintained, and the body is ready for a quick change of direction or continuation on the same pathway. The slide is the easiest way to move continuously in a sideward direction.

Movement Observation

By 5 years of age, most children are ready to learn sliding, provided they have had some success with hopping movement. The uneven rhythm that is characteristic of sliding, galloping, and skipping presents a more complex challenge to the child (as compared to running, jumping, and hopping). If a child is having difficulty, the skill should be broken down and practiced at a slow tempo. Children find it easier to slide with one side leading, but both need to be practiced.

COMMON PROBLEMS

1. Sliding on the heels rather than on the balls of the feet;
2. Failure to shift weight from the lead to follow-up foot;
3. Hopping too high and not gaining distance (hop should be slight and provide momentum for next movement);
4. Legs too stiff (both knees should be bent).

Movement Variability

Variations from the basic movement can be seen in many sport and dance activities. Sliding movements are frequently utilized in skating, basketball, badminton, tennis, volleyball, and baseball (also softball). Sliding is also a basic step found in many dances.

SPATIAL

MOVEMENT-PATTERN VARIATIONS

Change lead foot	Change feet position
Slide with arms in various positions	(heel to heel, heel to side)
Change slide lengths	

DIRECTIONS/PATHWAYS/LEVELS

Sideward to the right; to the left	Low level (knees bent); high level (on toes)
Change directions	Around objects

TIME

Slow to fast	To musical accompaniment or rhythmic beat

FORCE

For distance (short to long)	Heavily
With a high lift (hop); slight lift	Lightly

ADDITIONAL MOVEMENT VARIATIONS

Sliding with a partner (facing, holding both or one hand; facing, without holding hands; one or two hands on partner's hips, facing or one behind the other; hand(s) on shoulders, facing or one behind; side by side, holding one hand(s) or without holding hands; side by side, skater's style; back to back, holding one hand, both hands, or none).

Slide in a circle with others (hands joined, facing toward or away from center).

While sliding, form various patterns (shape, letter, number).

Slide through an obstacle course.

FIGURE 10-41
Sliding.

Catch and throw objects while sliding.

Slide so a hand(s) can touch the floor.

Combine sliding with nonlocomotor movements (slide, turn, slide, bend).

Combine sliding with other locomotor movements (slide, skip, slide, gallop, run).

Use the slide as a movement in dance (see Movement Enhancement).

Teaching Hints

Rhythmical accompaniment can aid in sliding.

Stress keeping the knees slightly bent, trunk forward, and staying on the balls of the feet.

Skill Concepts Communicated to Children

Step to the side.

Draw foot up toward the other and do a slight hop.

Do not bounce.

Slide the feet.

SKIPPING

Movement Description

Skipping is a rhythmic combination of a walking step and hop. It consists of stepping forward on one foot, quickly hopping on the same foot, then duplicating the process on the opposite foot (Fig. 10-42).

To maintain balance and provide the body with upward momentum, the arms should be swung forward and upward in opposition to the legs while hopping. The weight should be on the balls of the feet throughout the movement.

Movement Observation

Skipping may be the most difficult locomotor skill for young children to acquire. Successful performance requires the combination of two fundamental movements—a walking step and hop—that must be executed in an uneven but rhythmic pattern. Skipping is usually the last locomotor skill to be acquired. Research indicates that skipping appears at approximately 5 years of age; however, it is usually not perfected until about age 6 ½.

Aside from lack of experience, especially among males, young children experiencing difficulty in skipping usually have problems with the hop or coordination of movements. Initial remediation should focus upon the child's ability to hop and then the step-hop combination.

COMMON PROBLEMS

1. Inability to hop (work on the hop, then the combination; step-hop);
2. Landing flat-footed (should land on toes);
3. Stepping on one foot and hopping on the other foot (should step and hop on same foot);
4. Failing to swing the arms in opposition to leg movements (arms should swing forward and up in opposition to legs while hopping);
5. Body lean is too far forward or backward (slight lean toward movement direction, with vertical takeoff on hop).

Movement Variability

Although not used in many sport and game-type activities, skipping is a traditional dance step used in many folk dances.

Movement Enhancement

Table 10-7						
Sliding Enhancement Chart						
	LEVEL		**LEVEL**			**LEVEL**
GAMES		Hook-On		Come Along		
		Cars		Charlie Over the Water		
Command Cards	I–III	Flowers Blowing in the		Indian Running		
Slow Poke	I&II	Wind		Rescue Relay		
Gardener and Scamp		Man From Mars		Beater Goes Round		
Catch the Witch		Santa's Reindeer		Thread the Needle		
Corners				All Up Relay		
Caged Lion		Cat and Rat	II&III	Kinder Polka		
Old Man/Old Lady		Chimes of Dunkirk		Jump Jim Joe		
		A Hunting We Will Go		Ach Ja		
DANCE/RHYTHMS/RHYMES				Little Brown Jug		
		Pease Porridge Hot	II	Carousel		
Loobie Loo	I&II	Paw Paw Patch				
Sally Go Round the Moon						
Baa, Baa, Black Sheep						

FIGURE 10-42

Skipping.

SPATIAL

MOVEMENT PATTERN VARIATIONS

Vary base of support
(feet wide; narrow)

Skip with arms in various
positions (folded,
straight out, at sides)

Change lead foot (right, left)

Skip with hands in various
positions (on head, on
hips, behind head)

Skip on tiptoes

Free knee
swings out to
side, or bent up
high in front

DIRECTIONS/PATHWAYS/LEVELS

In place	Low (body crouched)	
Forward	Around	In and out
Backward	Over	
Sideward	Various patterns	
High (on toes)	(circle, square, zigzag)	

TIME

Slow to fast

Slow motion

To musical accompaniment or
rhythmic beat

FORCE

Lightly   High on the hop

Heavily   Low on the hop

ADDITIONAL MOVEMENT VARIATIONS

Skip with your eyes closed.

While skipping, catch and throw a ball or beanbag.

Skip and clap your hands.

Skip low, touching the ground with the hands.

Skip through an obstacle course.

Skip rope.

Skip with a partner (side by side; face to face;
right or left sides together; arm and hand
placement variable).

Movement Enhancement

Table 10-8
Skipping Enhancement Chart

GAMES	LEVEL	DANCE/RHYTHMS/RHYMES	LEVEL		LEVEL
Command Cards	I–III	A Hunting We Will Go	I&II	Fool's Jig	
Santa's Reindeer	I&II	Loobie Loo		Maypole Dance	
Old Man/Old Lady		The Muffin Man		Jolly Is the Miller	
Slow Poke		Did You Ever See A		Grand March	II&III
Corners		Lassie?		Gustaf's Skoal	
Run for Your Supper		Oats, Peas, Beans,		Skip to My Lou	
Hook-on		and Barley		Little Brown Jug	
Cars		Baa, Baa, Black Sheep			
Catch the Witch		Paw Paw Patch	II		
Gardener and Scamp		Hansel and Gretel			
Flowers Blowing in the Wind		Round and Round the			
Man From Mars		Village			
Caged Lion		This Old Man			
Charlie Over the Water		Shoo Fly			
Boiler Bust		Pease Porridge Hot			
Mousetrap	II&III	The Wheat			
Come Along		The Popcorn Man			
All Up Relay		Seven Jumps			
Rescue Relay					
Thread the Needle					
Beater Goes Round					
Indian Running					

Skip and add other locomotor movements (skip, jump, slide).

Skip and add nonlocomotor movements (skip, and turn).

Use skipping as a movement in dance; best performed to music in ⅝ meter time (see Movement Enhancement).

Teaching Hints

Child should be able to gallop with either leg leading before learning skipping.

Child should be able to hop on either leg before learning skipping.

Provide a slow-motion demonstration if necessary.

If child has difficulty with the pattern, take his or her hand and skip with the child.

Skill Concepts Communicated to Children

Step forward and hop up.
Swing arms up.
Skip on the balls of the feet.
Keep eyes forward.
Bend the knees.
Relax the upper body.

BODY ROLLING

Movement Description

Body Rolling is one of the earliest locomotor abilities acquired. Before infants crawl or creep they can be observed rolling from stomach to side, stomach to back, back to side, and later back to stomach.

FIGURE 10-43
Log roll.

Rolling may be described as: (1) moving along a surface by turning over and over, and (2) forming into a mass revolving over and over. Rocking, which is to move or sway to and fro or from side to side, is often used in the preliminary stages of rolling development, especially as a component in rolling backwards or sideways.

The rolling schema, consisting of a multitude of directional and axis roll patterns, can be developed extensively utilizing a system of progression with practice variability.

BASIC LOG ROLL

The easiest roll to execute is performed with the child lying across one end of a gymnastics mat with arms stretched overhead (Fig. 10-43). The child tries to roll across the mat evenly, keeping the body in a straight line. Initial attempts may be performed without demanding that the child roll across the mat evenly.

FORWARD ROLLING PROGRESSION

(Note: Material in this section adapted from O'Quinn, 1979.)

FIGURE 10-44
Bunny Hop.
Jump out and land with hands first.

FIGURE 10-45
Look Behind.
Peek between legs and balance.

FIGURE 10-46

Tip Over.   Duck down slowly and tip over.

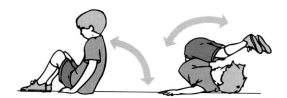

FIGURE 10-47

Back Rocker.

FIGURE 10-48

Seat Lifter.   Do the back rocker, rock forward, then reach out and lift seat off the floor.

(a)   (b)   (c)   (d)   (e)   (f)

FIGURE 10-49

Forward roll.

Forward Roll.   The forward roll is characterized by the child starting in a standing position, then squatting down with the arms extended forward and the fingers pointing straight ahead. There is a push-off from the toes, a rising of the seat, and the chin is tucked to the chest. The arms and hands receive the body weight as the force is transferred to the base of the neck and the top of the shoulders as the roll continues. The arms assist the forward motion by moving forward until first a crouch, then a standing position, is attained (Fig. 10-49).

FIGURE 10-50

Step-Jump Roll.

FIGURE 10-51

Reach-Over Roll.

FIGURE 10-52

Dive Roll.

FIGURE 10-53

Side roll.

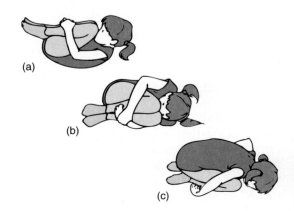

Side Roll. Starting in a back-lying position, with the elbows, knees, and nose tucked in, the performer rolls like a human ball in a sideward direction (Fig. 10-53).

BACKWARD ROLLING PROGRESSION

FIGURE 10-54
Back Rocker.

FIGURE 10-55

Back Balance.   Do the back rocker and hold balance.

FIGURE 10-56

Shoulder Balance.   With palms of the hands pointing backward, rock back and balance.

FIGURE 10-57

Reach and Look.   While performing a "back rocker," look sideways at an extended hand. (Fig. 10-57).

FIGURE 10-58

Toe Touch.   While performing the "reach and look," one foot is extended over the head to touch the floor.

FIGURE 10-59

Back Shoulder Roll.   Combine a "rock back," "toe toucher," and rollover.

FIGURE 10-60

Sit Back.   Sit, rock back, balance on shoulder, and return.

FIGURE 10-61

Sit Back to Shoulder Roll (diagonal roll).

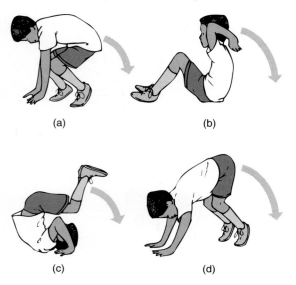

(a)   (b)

(c)   (d)

FIGURE 10-62

Backward roll.

Backward Roll.   The backward roll is the most diffi-cult basic roll to execute because weight has to be taken on the arms as the body rolls in the backward motion. With the back facing the mat, the child rocks forward slightly, pushing off with the hands, and rolls backward while keeping the knees close to the

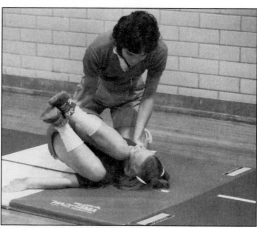

FIGURE 10-64

Spotting a backward diagonal roll.

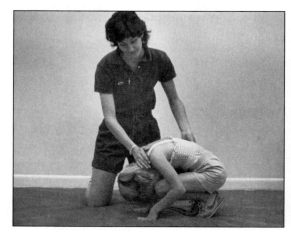

FIGURE 10-63

Spotting a forward roll.

chest and chin down. The backward motion continues until the weight is well over the shoulders; at that time the hands push off the floor, exerting enough force to lift shoulders off mat and allow head through and then bring the body to a landing position on the knees and toes (Fig. 10-62).

Movement Observation

Aside from focusing on skill performance, the instructor should constantly be aware of possible hazards, especially when children are attempting unfamiliar rolls. *Spotting* demands that the instructor understand what the child is going to do next and be ready to assist by giving momentary support (psy-chological and physical). Figures 10-63 to 10-65 illus-trate proper spotting techniques for the forward and backward rolls.

Forward Roll.   The spotter, positioned on the left side of the child in a kneeling position, places the right hand on the back of the child's left thigh and left hand on the back of the child's head. As the child rolls forward, the right hand pushes up against the thigh while the left hand tucks the head. (Fig. 10-63).

FIGURE 10-65
Spotting a backward roll.

Backward Diagonal Roll. Facing in the direction of the backward roll, the spotter takes a kneeling position on the child's left side. The right hand is placed under the child's left shoulder and the left hand on the lower back ready to assist (Fig. 10-64).

Backward Roll. Positioned in a standing posture on the right side of the child, the spotter places the hands on the child's hips. As the child rolls backward, the spotter gently lifts upward and then backward (Fig. 10-65).

COMMON PROBLEMS

FORWARD ROLL

1. Body collapses to one side; little use of the arms and hands (arms and hands should take the body weight and push evenly);
2. Too much weight taken onto the head (head should slide through the roll, not be a primary support);
3. The performer does not achieve an ending on the feet (body should be curled with knees tucked in until erect position; arms not coming off the mat as the shoulders touch may also cause lack of momentum).

BACKWARD ROLL

Child cannot roll over backwards:

1. Roundness of back not held during roll (knees should be positioned close to chest);
2. Hands not positioned properly to exert force necessary to accomplish rollover (refer to placement of hands in Fig. 10-62).

Movement Variability

Rolling, a movement youngsters find naturally fascinating, has an extended utility far beyond the basic rolling foundation. Variations of the founda-

tion can be observed in such activities as gymnastics, dance, football, soccer, volleyball, trampolining, wrestling, and judo.

SPATIAL

MOVEMENT-PATTERN VARIATIONS

ROCKING (forward and backward with hand and leg position variations)	FORWARD AND/OR BACKWARD ROLL
LOG ROLL	Walking takeoff
Vary arm positions (at sides, crossed, over-head)	One-foot takeoff
Vary leg positions (crossed, wide, close)	Running takeoff
SIDE ROLL	Diving takeoff
Vary arm/hand position (on ankles, shins, knees, chest, behind head)	Kneeling takeoff
	One-knee takeoff
See Figures 10-89 and 10-90 (Human Ball and Egg Roll)	Squatting takeoff
	Standing takeoff
Vary leg position(crossed)	Legs crossed (takeoff and/or landing)
	More than two parts (takeoff and/or landing)
	Vary arm/hand position (close, wide, grasping feet, ankles, knees, chest)
	Vary leg position (crossed, wide, close, one in front of the other)

DIRECTIONS/PATHWAYS/LEVELS

Backward	Down	Low and High level (vary bend of knees)
Sideways	Change directions	Roll in a circle
Forward	Under	
Up	Over	

TIME

Slow to Fast	Changing speeds
	To a rhythmic beat
	To musical accompaniment

FORCE

Smoothly	Roll, diving over objects (mats or markers)
Soft	
Hard	

ADDITIONAL MOVEMENT VARIATIONS

Forward Rolling Progression Using a Spring Board*

FIGURE 10-66

Land and Squat.

FIGURE 10-67

Land and Bunny Hop.

FIGURE 10-68

Land, Bunny Hop, and Tip Over.

FIGURE 10-69

Knee Slapper and Tip Over.

*Note: Material in this section adapted from O'Quinn, 1979.

FIGURE 10-70
Seat Kicker and Tip Over.

FIGURE 10-71
Seat Kicker and Forward Roll.

FIGURE 10-72
Jack Knife and Forward Roll.

FIGURE 10-73
Straddle Bounce and Forward Roll.

FIGURE 10-74

Full Twist and Forward Roll.

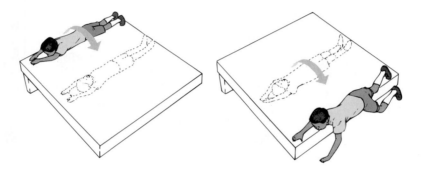

FIGURE 10-75

Rolling Using a Tumbling Table*

Log Roll.   Start on the stomach and then the back.

(Note: Place well-cushioned mats around the table.)

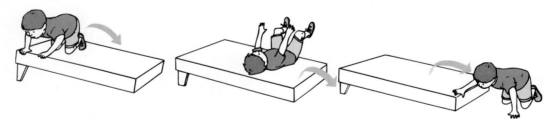

FIGURE 10-76

Dog Roll.

FIGURE 10-77

FORWARD MOTION ROLLING

Tip Over.

*The tumbling table can be purchased from Physical Fun Products, Inc., Box 4548, Austin, Texas 78765.

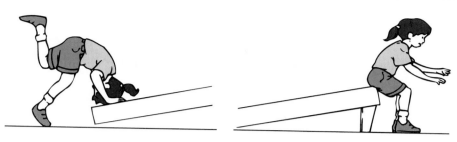

FIGURE 10-78
Kick Roll Up.

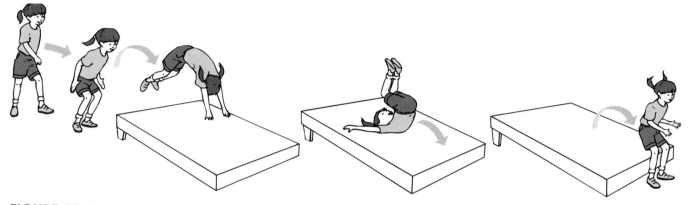

FIGURE 10-79
Step Jump Roll.

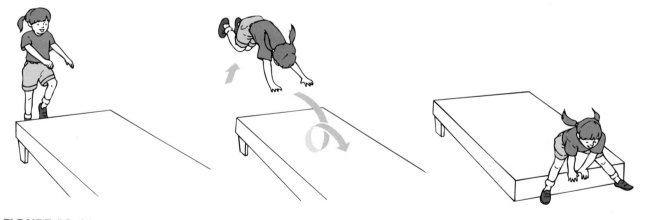

FIGURE 10-80
Step Jump, Roll, and Straddle.

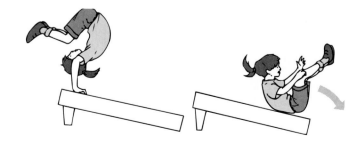

FIGURE 10-81
Tuck Roll Down.

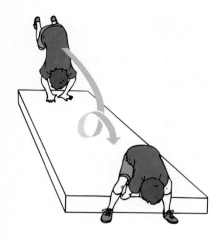

FIGURE 10-83
Pike Roll Down. Keep legs straight. Backward motion.

FIGURE 10-82
Straddle Roll Down.

BACKWARD MOTION ROLLING

FIGURE 10-84
Tip Over.

FIGURE 10-85
Roll Back to Feet.

FIGURE 10-86
Roll Back and Straddle.

FIGURE 10-87
Roll Back and Leap.

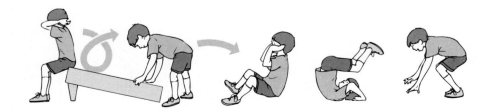

FIGURE 10-88
Straddle Roll Back and Tuck Roll Back

FIGURE 10-89
Human ball.

ADDITIONAL MOVEMENT VARIATIONS

Sideward Rolling Variations

Human Ball. Beginning in a sitting position with feet flat on the mat, knees bent, and held close to the chest, the hands are locked together around the lower legs. The child rolls first to one side, then the other, on the shoulder (Fig. 10-89).

Egg Roll. From a sitting position, the arms are stretched down the inside of the knees and the hands are wrapped around the lower legs to overlap the ankles. The child rolls as in the Human Ball movement (Fig. 10-90). How many other arm and leg variations can you create?

MISCELLANEOUS VARIATIONS

Dive and roll (over and under objects).
Roll with something in hand(s).
Combine rolling with other locomotor movements (jump and roll).
Combine rolling with nonlocomotor movements (balance and roll).

FIGURE 10-90
Egg roll.

Roll onto, along, and off apparatus (balance beam, bench, plank).
Roll after catching an object.
Roll and stop on signal.
Roll up in a blanket and unroll.
Roll down an incline (hill, ramp).
Roll in a cardboard box.
Play "Follow the Leader"; use various rolls.
Roll with a partner.
Roll with a hoop.
Toss a ball against a wall, then roll and catch.
Allow children to create "rolling routines" (with and without musical accompaniment).

Teaching Hints

See Chapter 17, Gymnastics.

Skill Concepts Communicated to Children

Stay tucked in a small ball throughout the forward roll on back.
The head should touch the floor as little as possible, so push off on the hands to compensate.
Keep the chin against the chest.
Push evenly with both hands.
Focus the eyes on an object in front to help roll in a straight line (forward roll).

Table 10-9		
Rolling Enhancement Chart		
LEVEL		
GAMES		
Round Stones		I–III
Command Cards		
Wagon Wheels		II&III

CLIMBING

Movement Description

Climbing is moving upward or downward (ascending and descending) by using hands and feet, with the upper limbs usually initiating primary control. Climbing, an outgrowth of creeping, is often performed before walking, especially if the opportunity to practice is made available. Shortly after the child learns to move in an upright position, the child then attempts to ascend and descend obstacles (usually stairs and steps). This form of climbing is performed without the use of the upper limbs, and although it is prevalent among older children, it will not be discussed in this chapter.

FIGURE 10-91

(a) Start of marking-time pattern; (b) completion.

FIGURE 10-92

(a) Start of cross-lateral pattern; (b) completion.

Depending upon the climbing condition (stairs, ladders, frames, nets, ropes), a number of movement patterns may be utilized by the child.

During the initial stages of stair and ladder climbing, the child moves in a "marking-time" pattern, that is, stepping up or down on the level with the same foot each time followed by the trailing foot to the same level. This type of behavior is frequently observed in children two years of age. (See Fig. 10-91(a), (b).)

It is after this stage that the child demonstrates the alternate-foot ascent and descent characterized by a cross-lateral pattern, that is, alternating sides, right-left, or vice versa, with only one foot on each level. (See Fig. 10-92 (a), (b).)

Children are usually capable of descending ladders by five years, and at six years of age they are proficient climbers in general. Espenschade and Eckert (1980) summarize the studies in stair-climbing ability as follows:

1. Ascending is achieved prior to descending at the same level of achievement.

2. An activity is accomplished with help before it is performed alone.

3. The child will negotiate a shorter flight of stairs before a longer flight.

4. Stairs with lower risers are mastered prior to those of adult size.

FIGURE 10-93

Lying to sitting.

ROPE CLIMBING

Movement-pattern variations performed on vertical climbing ropes vary with the "hands only" technique usually not observed among primary-grade children because of upper body strength and endurance limitations.

ROPE-CLIMBING PROGRESSIONS

Lying to Sitting.   In the lying position, the child pulls up the upper body into a sitting position. This is executed by placing one hand over the other, moving up the rope. To return to the lying position, the child places one hand under the other, moving the hand on top first (Fig. 10-93).

Lying to Standing Position.   While keeping the knees straight as possible, the child pulls, using the hand-over-hand technique until in the standing position. Again, the child moves hand under hand to lower the body down to the lying position (Fig. 10-94).

Hanging.   While standing close to the rope, the child grasps it as high as possible with both hands and pulls, bringing the feet up off the floor. This position is held for progressively longer periods of time (Fig. 10-95).

Climbing.   Positioned close to the rope, the child grasps it firmly as high as possible with elbows straight and hands close together. The knees should be bent and feet crossed over the rope. As the child attempts to move up the rope, the knees are straightened and elbows bent. To initiate the pull, the hands move up as high as possible (one hand at a time; hand over hand during initial stages), followed by an upward pull of the knees (Fig. 10-96).

To descend, the foot grip is released as the hands move, using the "hand-under-hand" technique. The body should always be positioned close to the rope. The child should be instructed not to slide down the rope because of possible body burns, loss of control, and orthopedic injuries.

FIGURE 10-94

Lying to standing position.

FIGURE 10-95

Hanging.

FIGURE 10-96

Climbing.

Swinging. The child grasps the rope firmly and backs up before running forward. While moving forward, the child slides the hands up and jumps onto the rope. The feet are crossed around the rope and squeezed firmly (Fig. 10-97).

Climbing, aside from being a primary mode of early-stage locomotion, is an excellent means of developing young bodies. Research indicates that children who participate in regular programs utilizing climbing apparatus (overhead ladders) should reveal significantly increased upper body muscular strength/endurance levels as a result of the experience. This is compared to children who have limited opportunities on climbing-type apparatus during the day. Unfortunately, many of our pre- and elementary-level schools today do not provide adequate outdoor play environments, and as a result children there may be deprived of a very essential benefit to their motor development. The overall contributions of general play activities on muscular strength and endurance—common weaknesses in children—should not be underestimated.

Climbing apparatus offer children a wide variety of opportunities to enhance a great number of developmental components.

Movement Observation

A point of observation that the instructor should always be concerned with is safety, especially among those children who are learning control of their bodies in early developmental stages. The instructor should consider such factors as apparatus height, depth, distance between rungs and surface, as well as the child's strength and endurance limitations and perceptual-motor capabilities. When observing the climber, points of periodic focus should be on foot placement, hand grip, eye focus, and general body coordination. Remembering that children are children, and sometimes their confidence borders on the reckless, one should always be alert for possible trouble.

FIGURE 10-97

Swinging.

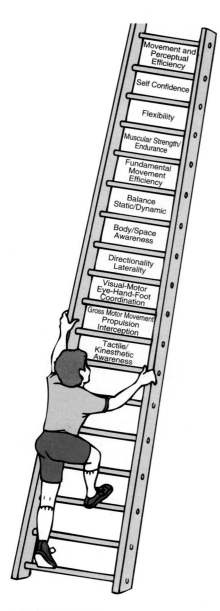

FIGURE 10-98

Contributions of climbing apparatus to child development.

COMMON PROBLEMS

1. Inability to use alternating hand and/or foot placement.
2. Failure to grip the grasping object efficiently.

Movement Variability

Considering the wide variety of climbing challenges that children may encounter, opportunity and variability of practice should be regarded as prime factors to enhance proficiency. Climbing behavior among children depends to a large degree on whether or not they have been exposed to specific challenges. As previously mentioned, climbing apparatus vary widely in dimension and type. Equipment variability, an asset to the development of movement schema, certainly can be experienced in the climbing program.

SPATIAL

MOVEMENT-PATTERN VARIATIONS

Step-Type Apparatus (alternate lead side)

Unilateral—Same side leg and then arm movement; opposite leg and then arm follow to same level (marking time).

Simultaneous Unilateral—Movement from same side leg and arm simultaneously followed by opposite-side movements to same level.

Cross-pattern—One side leg moves then opposite side arm, alternating sides.

Simultaneous Cross-pattern—One side leg and opposite arm move simultaneously, alternating sides:

Dragging legs

Replacing feet position with knees

Without using hands

Using one hand (alternate)

With knees together/wide

Arms together/wide

Using various grips (thumbs under bar, thumbs over bar)

Changing forearm positions (pronated, supinated)

With the back facing the obstacle.

Rope- and Pole-Climbing Patterns

Refer to Rope-Climbing Progressions in earlier section.

DIRECTIONS/PATHWAYS/LEVELS

Ascending (upward)	Sideways (moving across; ascending or descending)
Descending (downward)	Varying levels (degree of incline/decline Backwards (head first or reverse)

TIME

Slow to fast	To musical accompaniment
	To a rhythmic beat

FORCE

Force requirements related to: (1) degree of incline and decline, and (2) amount of weight carried during movement.

ADDITIONAL MOVEMENT VARIATIONS

Climbing

Mountains or hills on hands and feet.

While carrying a pack on the back.

With a partner (holding hands or attached by a rope).

Climbing Apparatus

FIGURE 10-99
Stairs

FIGURE 10-100
Boxes

FIGURE 10-101
Cargo Nets

FIGURE 10-102
Frames

FIGURE 10-103
Ladders

FIGURE 10-104
Ropes

FIGURE 10-105
Poles

Teaching Hints

Always insure that a spotter is present and in correct position.

Instruct children to wrap thumbs around the object (rope, pole) when climbing with the use of the hands.

Place a mat under the climbing apparatus.

Stress alternating hand-and-foot action.

Skill Concepts Communicated to Children

Place thumbs around the bar.

Use the arms to pull and the legs to push.

Move one hand and the opposite leg at the same time.

Use a follow step and/or a follow grasp.

Movement Enhancement

Table 10-10 Climbing Enhancement Chart	
	LEVEL
GAMES	
Bridges	I–III
DANCE/RHYTHMS/RHYMES	
Jack the Giant Killer Let's Pretend	I&II

REFERENCES

ESPENSCHADE, A. S. & ECKERT, H. D. (1980). *Motor development* (2nd ed.). Columbus: Charles E. Merrill.

McCLENAGHAN, B. A. & GALLAHUE, D. L. (1978). *Fundamental movement: A developmental and remedial approach.* Philadelphia: W. B. Saunders.

O'QUINN, Jr., G. (1990). *Teaching developmental gymnastics.* Austin: University of Texas Press.

WICKSTROM, R. L. (1983). *Fundamental motor patterns* (3rd ed.). Philadelphia: Lea & Febiger.

11

Nonlocomotor Skill Themes

Movement Description

Dodging is any sharp change of direction away from an original line of movement. Dodging skills are required to avoid physical contact with one or more objects or individuals that may be either stationary or moving.

Dodging may only require the movement of a portion of the body away from the object or person to be avoided. For example, only the upper portion of the body need be moved to elude a tagger with outstretched arms, whereas the lower portion of the body must be moved to avoid a stationary object or a tagger attempting a tag on the leg.

The dodge is executed by lowering the center of gravity by bending the knees and then shifting all or part of the weight away from the object or pursuer, and then regaining balance by taking a step in the direction of the shift or in the original line of motion. Effective dodging movements include a variety of locomotor and nonlocomotor skills such as jumping, running at different speeds, twisting, bending, falling, and rolling.

Movement Observation

Young children develop rudimentary dodging skills at an early age. As they learn to walk they must also learn to avoid stationary objects in their path. However, the more dynamic situations encountered in games and crowded conditions require a very efficient and mature dodging pattern that must be developed through practice in a variety of situations.

COMMON PROBLEMS

1. Failure to lower the center of gravity (bend the knees and sometimes bend at the waist in preparation to dodge);
2. Failure to stop forward momentum to shift the weight effectively away from pursuer or object (stop forward movement first, then shift the weight or lean away);
3. Maintaining one position too long (push off quickly in new direction);
4. Failure to use deceptive movements (practice feinting to each side and using different body parts).

Movement Variability

The ability to dodge people or objects effectively in game-like situations is dependent on one's experiences in avoiding moving objects and people. The various conditions that demand dodging movements are rarely the same, so it is very important to practice dodging in as many different and novel situations as possible to enhance the refinement of this skill.

Dodging, probably best known for its use in dodgeball, is also extensively utilized in such sports as football, basketball, hockey, and soccer.

SPATIAL

MOVEMENT-PATTERN VARIATIONS

Vary base of support (narrow to wide)	Arms held high
Knees bent	Arms held low
Legs straight	Legs in stride position
Flat-footed	Legs in parallel position
On toes	Upper body stiff

184

Dodging is a skill used in more advanced games like soccer.

Movement of:
head
shoulders
abdominal muscles
hips
knees
legs
feet
combinations of body parts

Upper body relaxed
Base stationary
Base moving
Body shapes:
twist away
curl away
stretch away

DIRECTIONS/PATHWAYS/LEVELS

Forward; backward; sideways (left and right).
Move to a low level (knees bent, squat), high, middle level.

Change directions on a signal while moving.
Avoid stationary objects in space by changing direction as one encounters them.
Run and dodge in a zigzag or circular path.

TIME

Slow to fast
Combinations

Accelerate forward movement
Decelerate forward movement
Even movement
Jerky movement
Dodge on a drum beat
Change direction quickly without stopping movement.

FORCE

Hard
Soft

Weak
Shift weight quickly
Dodge stationary objects by jumping over them.

ADDITIONAL MOVEMENT VARIATIONS

Dodge balls thrown from different distances.
Dodge various size playground balls (size 5, 6, 7, 8, 10).
Dodge yarnballs.
Dodge a rolling hula hoop.
Use feinting movements before dodging.
Combine different locomotor skills while dodging stationary objects or people.
Dodge objects thrown at varying speeds.
Dodge thrown objects by jumping over them or by ducking from them.
Change running speed while moving forward to avoid a tagger.

Movement Enhancement

Table 11-1

Dodging Enhancement Chart

GAMES	LEVEL		LEVEL		LEVEL
Buffalo Bill	I & II	Fire Engine	II & III	Mousetrap	III
Gardener and Scamp		Wild Horse Round-up		Exchange Dodgeball	
Cut the Pie		Hop Tag		Roll Dodgeball	
Partner Tag		In and Out		Balance Dodgeball	
Birds and Cats		Crossover Dodgeball		Goal Tag	
Scarecrows and Crows		Poison Circle		Snake Catcher	
Seven Dwarfs		Come Along		Snowball	
		Back to Back		Blue and Gold	
		Guard the Toys		Freeze Ball	
		Octopus		Stealing Sticks	
		Square Dodgeball		Chain Tag	
		Triangle Dodgeball		Chase the Bulldog	
				Man from Mars	
				Flies Up Dodgeball	

Dodge while dribbling a ball (around cones, chairs, people).

Run and dodge through an obstacle course.

Dodge objects or people with a partner (hands joined).

Teacher Hints

Use activities that first demand changing direction on a verbal command, then add stationary objects, finally add moving objects that must be avoided.

Emphasize bending the knees.

Practice dodging in all directions and use different levels to avoid becoming one-sided.

Practice deceptive-type movements utilizing head, shoulders, eyes, and trunk.

Stay away from dodgeball activities until the child reaches a mature stage of development.

Skill Concepts Communicated to Children

Stop one's movement before dodging one way or the other.

Bend the knees and stay low.

Use different body parts to fake movements; use head, shoulders, and hips.

Change one's speed to fake opponent before dodging.

STRETCHING AND BENDING

Movement Description

Stretching is extending or hyperextending any of the joints of the body to make the body parts as long or as straight as possible. Stretching movements are generally done either to increase flexibility or the range of motion of the joints; therefore, they should be done in a controlled manner. Good balance should be required before a maximum stretch is attempted. Children need to understand that stretching involves some minor discomfort and that gradual and static stretching should precede maximum efforts.

Bending, or curling, the body is accomplished by flexing any or all parts of the body at the joints. The structure of the individual joints will determine the range of motion each joint is capable of producing. Bending motions are used both as preparatory actions, as in bending knees before jumping, and ending actions, as in catching a ball by bending the elbows.

Bending is often a preparatory movement for stretching, and both bending and stretching aid in the achievement of maximum force, speed, and distance in combined movements.

The flexibility of the joints can be increased by gradually exerting more force as joints are flexed or extended. If increased flexibility is to be obtained,

A wide stretch.

Bending different body parts at a low level.

then bouncing or bobbing movements should be avoided when bending and stretching. Children should be encouraged to feel the change in movement kinesthetically as the action shifts from towards the body center to away from the body center.

Movement Observation

A stable base of support is necessary for all bending and stretching movements; consequently, the analysis of a child's pattern should start at the base. Observation should focus on the physical appearance of the child. A heavy or very tall child, for example, may have trouble fully bending the trunk.

COMMON PROBLEMS

1. Stretching and bending movements that are jerky (stress smooth continuous movement, use flowing type music);

2. Being unable to stretch or bend through the full range of motion (gradually increase flexibility through slow, smooth stretching and bending movements);

3. Loss of balance while bending or stretching (strengthen supporting muscle groups).

Movement Variability

Complete bending and stretching movements greatly enhance the aesthetic beauty of dance and gymnastic activities and increase the child's ability to succeed in the performance of more refined dance and gymnastic skills. A very tight tuck (bent) position, for example, is essential to successful performance of a forward roll. Likewise, a good stretched position is important to the performance of pirouette turns (turning on one foot in dance).

Bending and stretching movements are effective dodging maneuvers for tag and dodgeball games; therefore practice for these skills needs to be dynamic.

SPATIAL

MOVEMENT-PATTERN VARIATIONS

Bend and stretch with different supports

legs together	on heels	on side
legs apart	on one leg	on back
legs crossed	on seat	on arms
on toes	on stomach	on head and arms

Bend and stretch different body parts

neck	waist
shoulders	hips
elbows	knees
wrists	ankles
fingers	toes

Bend and stretch different combinations of parts with different supports.

DIRECTIONS/PATHWAYS/LEVELS

Bend and stretch
at high, medium, and low levels;
forward, backward, and side to side;
to trace pathways in the air with different body parts—curved, straight, and zigzag;
Bend one body part in one direction and stretch another the opposite direction.

TIME

Bend or stretch

slowly	on a drum beat
continuously	evenly
quickly	unevenly
to music	

FORCE

Bend or stretch

farther than before	close to the ground
hard	smoothly
soft	roughly
in the air	

ADDITIONAL MOVEMENT VARIATIONS

Hang from a chinning bar—bend and straighten the knees, hips, elbows, neck.

Imitate animals or plants that bend or stretch.

Bend and stretch different body parts while balanced on a box, balance beam, or balance board; use different supports.

With a partner, stretch by gently pushing the partner to stretch farther; bend around the partner in different ways.

Grasping a wand with two hands, bend and stretch to reach the toes from different positions: standing, lying down on back, on front, others.

Stretch and bend while holding different sized and weighted objects in the hands or feet.

Move across the floor by bending, then stretching, the entire body.

Form the letters of one's name by alternately bending and stretching different body parts; use a partner or a group.

Curl or bend around or inside a ball, cone, hoop, rope, or wand, then extend or stretch out over these objects.

Bend to grasp objects on the floor, then stretch to reach objects placed out of reach.

Teaching Hints

Stress smooth continuous movement; use flowing-type music.

Increase flexibility gradually by using slow, smooth stretching and bending movements.

Strengthen supporting muscle groups to aid in balance.

Practice bending and stretching in many positions and utilizing many body parts.

Skill Concepts Communicated to Children

Stretch far enough that it hurts a little.

Stretch slowly and smoothly—do not jerk and bounce.

Alternate stretching and bending to obtain maximum effort.

Try to stretch or bend a little farther each time.

FIGURE 11-1
Twisting.

FIGURE 11-2
Turning.

Movement Enhancement

GAMES	LEVEL	GYMNASTICS	LEVEL	RHYTHMS AND DANCE	LEVEL
Table 11-2					
Stretching and Bending Enhancement Chart					
Command Cards	I–III	Giraffe Walk	I & II	Hokey Pokey	I & II
Follow the Leader		Row Your Boat		Limbo	II
Skin the Snake		Long Stretch			
Octopus		Lame Dog Walk			
		Blow Up The Balloon			
Partner Tag	I & II	Over the Head			
		Sky Scraper			
Popcorn	II	Pick the Grass			
		Bear Walk			
Hop Tag	II & III	Inch Worm			
Parachute Play		Egg Roll			
Crossover Dodgeball		Log Roll			
In and Out					
Guard the Toys		Egg Sit	II		
Back to Back		Ankle Walk			
Big Snake		Double Roll			
		Bridge			
Balance Dodgeball	III	Straddle Seat			
Snake Catcher		Rocking Horse			
Fly Trap		Corkscrew			
Exchange Dodgeball		Thread the Needle			
Chain Tag		V-Sit			
Goal Tag		Rhythmic Ball Gymnastics			
Roll Dodgeball		Rhythmic Wand Gymnastics			
Chariot Race		Rhythmic Hoop Gymnastics			
		Rhythmic Ribbon Gymnastics			

TWISTING AND TURNING

Movement Description

Twisting is the rotation of the body or any of its parts around an axis with a stationary base. Children often call these movements *turning*. For example, one can turn or twist one's head and those movements would look the same.

Turning is a circular movement of the entire body through space, releasing the base of support. Movement of individual body parts without the whole body moving is referred to as *twisting*, not turning.

In twisting and turning movements the base of support should be broadened, and the center of gravity should be lowered to provide a stable position for the next movement and to maintain balance. To twist effectively, the body parts on which the movement is based should be fixed or stable. A slight twist in the opposite direction will add momentum to a turn. The turn from a standing position can be executed by jumping, hopping, or shuffling with the feet and should be made in multiples of quarter turns.

In both twisting and turning, the body should remain relaxed through the range of movements. The speed of these movements can be increased by shortening the length of the moving parts, as a basketball player does when pivoting; he or she draws the ball in close to the body.

Movement Observation

Maintaining balance is a key factor in twisting and turning movements. An analysis of a child's form should be focused on the base of support both at the beginning of the movement and at the conclusion.

COMMON PROBLEMS

1. Losing balance in either twist or turn (widen base of support and lower the center of gravity at start and finish of movement in the turn; maintain body alignment throughout movement; don't bend over);

2. Being able to turn one way and not the other (initiate turn by moving one part in the desired direction first—usually the head works best—then combine body forces as skill increases);

3. Landing from a turn stiff-legged (bend the knees when landing and relax);
4. Moving too fast to control the body (perform slow movements until control is achieved);
5. Losing balance or sliding while twisting (hold supporting limbs or parts firm).

Movement Variability

Twisting and turning movements are most commonly used in gymnastic and dance activities. A varied schema is crucial in order to transform these simple movements into the more complicated movement patterns required in such activities as tumbling and apparatus work. An advanced concept of twisting is essential, for example, to execute a round-off on the floor. Turning and twisting movements are present in most dance forms, and their uses in creative movement are numerous. Twisting and turning maneuvers are also a part of dynamic game skills where dodging or quick changes of direction are required. Twisting skill is especially important in manipulating rackets and long-handled implements for striking objects.

SPATIAL

MOVEMENT-PATTERN VARIATIONS

Twist or turn
vary base of support (narrow to wide)	with arms in close
on toes	on one foot
on heels	knees
stiff-legged	seat
knees bent	hips
arms high	shoulders
low	head turning only (advanced)

with arms extended in front
    in back
    to the side

Twist arms	shoulders
legs	hips
head	upper body
	lower body

Twist using different supports and upper body parts
    arms around legs
        around head
        around waist
        around tummy
        around hips
        around knees

DIRECTIONS/PATHWAYS/LEVELS

Twist or turn	Turn while moving in
right or left	straight,
up or down	curved,
high level	zigzag paths
low level	

Twist body parts in opposite direction.

TIME

Twist or turn
to music	evenly
on a drum beat	unevenly
continuously	
slow to fast	

FORCE

Hard
Soft
Turn while high in the air or close to the ground
Smoothly
Roughly

ADDITIONAL MOVEMENT VARIATIONS

Throw a ball into the air and turn or twist to catch it at different levels.

Twist and turn on balance beam, boxes, ladders, benches.

Twist body around hanging rope or double ropes; on rings.

Twist and turn at the same time.

Twist with or around a partner.

Turn a partner as many different ways as possible.

Mirror a partner's twist-and-turn movements.

Twist in different ways while passing an object back and forth to a partner.

Twist one body part around another.

Using a rope on the floor, turn in different ways while crossing it.

Make shapes with a jump rope and the body.

Twist as if swinging a wand, racket, bat, or other implement around the body.

Twist or turn while carrying various-sized and weighted balls.

Turn and twist while moving under and through obstacles.

Teaching Hints

Stress a wide base of support and lower center of gravity at the start and finish of the movement.

When children are turning, stress maintaining body alignment throughout the movement.

To initiate a turn, first move one body part in the desired direction—usually the head works best—then combine forces as skill progresses.

Practice turns and twists to both sides.

Stress bending the knees and relaxing when landing from a turn.

Have the children slow their movement until control is achieved.

When children are twisting, stress holding the supporting limbs firm as they twist.

Children should start with quarter turns and progress to half turns and then full turns as mastery is achieved.

Table 11-3
Twisting and Turning Enhancement Chart

GAMES	LEVEL	GYMNASTICS	LEVEL	RHYTHMS & DANCE	LEVEL
Command Cards Follow the Leader	I–III	Human Ball	I & II	Turn the Glasses Over	I & II
Partner Tag	I & II	Top Wring the Washrag Twist Away	II	Pease Porridge Hot Hansel and Gretel Klapptanz	II
Shoe Twister Human Tangles Crossover Dodgeball Poison Circle Hop Tag Back to Back In and Out Guard the Toys Leap the Brook Skin the Snake	II & III	Floor Touch Thread the Needle Back Scratcher Twist Under Stick Twist Crazy Walk Corkscrew Churn the Butter Crane Twist Greet the Toe Forward Turnover			
Exchange Dodgeball Roll Dodgeball Balance Dodgeball Goal Tag Snake Catcher	III	Rhythmic Wand Gymnastics Rhythmic Ball Gymnastics Rhythmic Hoop Gymnastics Rhythmic Ribbon Gymnastics			

Skill Concepts Communicated to Children

> Twisting means keeping one or several body parts on the ground while moving other parts around them.
>
> Turning means to lift one's whole body off the ground and move it around.
>
> Land from a turn with knees bent and body relaxed.
>
> Twist slightly in opposite direction first before turning.
>
> When twisting, place one or more body parts firmly on the ground.

SWINGING AND SWAYING

Movement Description

Swinging movements are pendular or circular movements of the arms, legs, trunk, head, or whole body that occur when the moving part is below the axis. The axis can be another body part, usually a joint (shoulder, hip, knee, elbow), or a fixed object like a bar, which a child can grasp and swing underneath.

Swaying is the same circular type of movement except that the moving part is above the axis. A complete circle of the arms, for example, would involve both swinging and swaying movements.

The pendular motion used in swinging is greatly aided by the force of gravity, whereas swaying movements demand more muscular force to overcome the gravitational pull. For example, for the arms to complete a full circular motion starting above the head, little force need be applied as the arms swing downward below the shoulders, but the arms will stop as speed decreases in the upward portion of the swing unless force is applied to continue the motion back over the head.

Child swinging a leg.

Child swaying arms.

In both swinging and swaying motions, when the body is in contact with a supporting surface, momentum of the swinging or swaying part (arm, leg, head) can be transferred to the rest of the body, thus causing movement in the same direction. Also, the speed of the moving part can be increased if the elbow, knee, or entire body is kept straight or extended.

Movement Observation

Swinging and swaying both involve controlling the force of gravity to effect a continuous and graceful movement pattern. Particular attention needs to be focused on the use of gravity in the downward portion of swinging movements, and the exertion of force in the upward portion of swaying movements for the smoothest and most rhythmic action.

COMMON PROBLEMS

1. Loss of body control when swinging or swaying too hard (reduce or eliminate force on downward portion of swing, and allow the weight of the body part swinging to be the force);
2. Movements stiff and jerky (relax body parts, use music to suggest more graceful and continuous movement);
3. Being unable to swing or sway through the full range of movement (increase flexibility of the joints and muscles);
4. Being afraid to swing on high objects like bars and rings (teach proper landing techniques; that is, drop off or dismount at the back of the swing when momentum is briefly slowed).

Movement Variability

Swinging and swaying movements are most commonly associated with dance and gymnastic activities;

however, these fundamental movements are also the basis for the manipulative game skills of throwing, striking, and kicking. Therefore, a great variety of experiences in swinging and swaying movements will greatly enhance a child's movement proficiency as he or she progresses through the elementary grades.

SPATIAL

MOVEMENT-PATTERN VARIATIONS

Supports

Swing or sway arms and upper body with a wide base of support with a narrow base of support
on toes, on heels
legs stiff
knees bent
on one foot
knees
seat
Swing or sway legs and/or lower body standing on one foot
on knees
on seat
on stomach
on back
on shoulders
Using different supports, vary the extension of swinging or swaying
body parts
elbows or knees bent or extended
ankles or wrists bent or extended
Swing or sway different parts to the front, back, or side of the supporting body.

DIRECTIONS/PATHWAYS/LEVELS

Swing or sway
at high, medium, and low levels
right or left
up or down
two body parts in opposite directions
trace straight, curved or zigzag paths with arms, legs, head.

TIME

Swing or sway different body parts

slowly	to different musical rhythms
quickly	to a drum beat
evenly	
unevenly	
continuously	

FORCE

Hard
Soft
Evenly
Unevenly
Swing using only force of gravity
Use individual parts then add whole-body movements.

ADDITIONAL MOVEMENT VARIATIONS

Swing or sway several body parts at the same time.

With a partner, mimic swinging or swaying motions, then do the opposite: one swings the other sways.

Using ribbons or streamers, swing and sway at different levels, speeds, directions, alone and with partners.

Join with a partner and swing or sway together as one.

Swing or sway hoops or wands alone or with a partner.

Swing and sway poi-pois with one hand, then two at the same time; add a body sway to the routine.

Swing and sway holding onto different sized and weighted balls; use one hand or two.

Swing a jump rope doubled up, then extended; continue around to a sway.

Swing various implements around the body using one hand or two; use wands, rackets, ropes, or bats.

Create images for swinging and swaying movements: sway like a stalk of corn, a willow tree, or a flag in a brisk wind.

Swing or sway holding onto a bar.

1. With the body underneath:
   a. Swing one foot up and touch the bar (Fig. 11-3).
   b. Pull one knee up between elbows, then two.
   c. Lift one foot and hook the toe around the bar, then hook one toe, pull the other leg through, and turn over backward (Skin the Cat; Fig. 11-4).
   d. Pull through and balance with legs straight (Basket; Fig. 11-5).
   e. Swing with the body in different positions: straight, curled, or twisted.
   f. Swing slow, then fast.
   g. Grasp the bar with knees or hands.
   h. Drop off at different points in a slow swing.

2. With the body on top of the bar:
   a. Place one knee over the bar and grasp with hands—swing back (Fig. 11-6).
   b. Place both knees over the bar, swing back, and catch on knees or drop back to a basket (Fig. 11-7).

3. In a front support, arms straight, bar at hips (Fig. 11-8):
   a. Swing legs forward and back underneath bar.
   b. Sway head, shoulders, and upper body.
   c. Bend arms and support weight at hips.
   d. Lean forward and roll over.

4. Pulling to a support:
   a. Perform flexed arm hang with chin above bar, then pull knees up into a ball (Fig. 11-9).
   b. Curl knees above the bar (Fig. 11-10).
   c. With someone helping, child swings legs over the bar while pulling toward it (Fig. 11-11).
   d. Unassisted—pull with arms while kicking over the bar (Fig. 11-12).

FIGURE 11-3
Swinging one foot up to touch the bar.

FIGURE 11-4
Skin the cat.

FIGURE 11-5
Basket.

FIGURE 11-6

Child hooks one knee over bar and swings back under the bar.

FIGURE 11-7

Child sits on top of bar, both legs over, and drops back to a basket.

FIGURE 11-8

Front support position.

FIGURE 11-9

Flexed-hang knees in tuck.

FIGURE 11-10

Flexed-hang knees over the bar.

FIGURE 11-11

Pullover assisted.

FIGURE 11-12
Pullover unassisted.

Teaching Hints

Use music to relax children and encourage graceful and creative movements.

Stress dismounting apparatus at the back of the swinging movement, and the need to bend knees upon landing.

Stress swinging through the full range of motions.

Skill Concepts Communicated to Children

Allow the weight of one's body parts to pull into a swinging motion.

Relax the muscles when swinging different body parts.

Hold muscles firm when swaying.

When swinging on bars or rings, let go at the back of the swing and land with knees bent.

By adding more force by pumping, one will swing faster and may go all the way around.

PUSHING AND PULLING

Movement Description

Pushing is exerting force against an object or person either to move the object or person away from the body or to move the body away from the object or person. For example, pushing a small box will cause it to move away from the body, whereas pushing on a wall will cause the body to be moved and not the wall!

Movement Enhancement

Table 11-4

Swinging and Swaying Enhancement Chart

GAMES	LEVEL	GYMNASTICS	LEVEL	RHYTHMS & DANCE	LEVEL
Command Cards Follow the Leader	I–III	Elephant Walk	I & II	Hickory Dickory Dock	I & II

Crossover Dodgeball
Poison Circle
Guard the Toys
Octopus
	II & III	Skin the Cat
		One-Knee Swing-up
		Underswing
		Pull Over
		Rhythmic Gymnastics:
		  Ball
		  Hoop
		  Ribbon
		  Wand
			II	Shoo Fly
				Skip to My Lou
					II

Exchange Dodgeball Roll Dodgeball Balance Dodgeball Snake Catcher	III				

Pulling is the application of force that causes objects or people to move toward the body. If the body moves, then pulling will cause the object to follow, as in pulling a wagon; however, if the body remains stationary because of the weight of the object, then pulling will trigger an isometric contraction of one or more muscle groups.

For both pushing and pulling, the body's center of gravity must be lowered and the base of support broadened in the direction of the pull or push. All body forces used in pushing or pulling must be directed either toward (in pushing) or away (in pulling) from the center of the weight of the object to be moved. Both pushing and pulling movements should be smooth and controlled, especially when used to move heavy objects. Further, when maximum force is to be exerted, care should be taken to keep the back in a straight position to avoid using the weaker back muscles to impart force.

Movement Observation

Poorly executed pushing and pulling movements can and frequently do cause injuries to the back. Therefore it is imperative that careful observation and analysis of pushing and pulling skills be conducted in order to identify potentially inefficient movement patterns and also to enhance the development of mature patterns.

COMMON PROBLEMS

1. Inability to maintain balance for the duration of the action (widen base of support);
2. Inability to impart maximum force (lower the body and get in line with the direction of the force);
3. Using jerky and inflexible movements (gather body forces and push or pull steadily and evenly);
4. Using an improper body position to lift or pull objects (bend at the knees and keep the back in reasonable alignment).

Movement Variability

Pushing and pulling actions are required in a large variety of game, dance, and gymnastic activities as well as in daily activities not normally associated with physical education. Therefore a variety of practice situations are important to enable the child to adjust to the changing requirements of pushing and pulling movements.

Pushing and pulling movements are most commonly associated with combative games like wrestling and tug-of-war, but they are also used in the games of football and shuffleboard.

Child pushing.

Child pulling.

SPATIAL

MOVEMENT-PATTERN VARIATIONS

Vary base of support (narrow to wide)
On toes
On heels
Flat-footed
Stiff-legged
Knees bent
Using different body parts
feet, legs, hips
shoulders, back, arms, hands, wrists
legs in stride position
legs in parallel position
standing on one foot
upper body stiff
upper body relaxed
arms high, low, in front, in back
stationary base
base moving

DIRECTIONS/PATHWAYS/LEVELS

Forward   Near
Back   Far

Right, left side
Upward
Downward
In
Out
High
Low

Over
Around
Under
In between
Different angles
Circular motion
Figure-8 motion

TIME

Slow to fast
Continuously
Even or uneven
Accelerating, decelerating

To drum beat
To beat of music
To clap of hands

FORCE

Hard
Soft
Lightly
Smoothly
Roughly

Evenly
Steadily

ADDITIONAL MOVEMENT VARIATIONS

In pairs, push:
  finger to finger
  shoulders together
  side by side
  feet to feet
  back to back
  seat to seat
  knee to knee

PULL

reaching between legs
locking wrists
hand to hand from standing, sitting and prone
  positions.

Use tug-o-ropes alone to pull on different body
  parts, and in pairs to pull a partner in different
  positions and with different body parts.
Use rhythm wands to push and pull against alone
  and in pairs.
Push or pull a partner on a scooter in open
  space or through obstacles.
Use objects of various sizes and weights to push
  or pull through space (balls, beanbags, boxes,
  cones, hoops, others).
Use a giant tug-of-war rope in a group to pull.
Pull in a group in circle formation holding hands.
Push or pull objects with implements (wands to
  push beanbags or ropes to pull cones).

Teaching Hints

Use lightweight objects at first and gradually
  increase the weights.
Stress controlled movements; no jerking or tug-
  ging.
Stress good body alignment and relate to every
  day activities (keep back erect).
Stress widening the base of support and lowering
  the center of gravity.
Stress using all body forces and not just arms and
  back.

Skill Concepts Communicated to Children

Keep the back straight.
Bend the knees.
Spread legs apart forward and back.
Push or pull steadily and evenly.
Use one's whole body.

Movement Enhancement

Table 11-5
Pushing and Pulling Enhancement Chart

GAMES	LEVEL	GYMNASTICS	LEVEL		LEVEL
Commands Cards	I–III	Pull the Wand	I & II	Push the Donkey	II
Parachute Play		Push the Wand Together		Pull the Donkey	
Follow the Leader		Push and Clap		Push-ups	
		Rocking Horse		Jack-in-the-Box	
Tug-of-War	II & III	Crocodile Crawl		Shoulder Wrestling	
		Stand-up		Leg Wrestling	
		Sawing Logs		Rooster Fight	
Pull the Tail	III			Seal Slap	
Circle of Friends		Elevator	II	Push War	
Volleyball (Scooter)		Elbow Wrestling		Foot Push	
		Stand-up		Toe Push	
		Going Down		Crab Fight	
		Climbing Ropes		Pull-over	
		Partner Pull-up			
		Push 'em into Balance			

12

Manipulative Skill Themes

Movement Description

Rolling consists of imparting force to an object that maintains contact with the surface. It is a fundamental manipulative skill that enables a child to learn how to control the speed and direction of the object. The body can be positioned in a sitting or standing posture. If standing, the ankles, knees, and hips will be flexed, head up, and the trunk inclined forward so the hands and the ball will be in close proximity to the ground during the swing.

ELEMENTARY STAGE

In the elementary stage (Fig. 12-1) the child usually sits in straddle position and pushes or bats the ball with one or both hands. If both hands are used they seldom push evenly, thus causing problems with direction. If the skill is attempted from a standing position, the legs are straight or slightly flexed at the knees and the ball is pushed from between the feet with little or no attention paid to focus or follow-through.

MATURE STAGE

By the age of six years most children will demonstrate the mature stage (Fig. 12-2) as they roll a ball from a semicrouched position with the nondominant foot slightly in front of the other. The ball may be grasped with one or both hands held to the dominant side of the body. The arms are slightly flexed at the elbow as the child moves the ball toward the floor. The child focuses on the target. As the ball reaches the floor, both hands are placed at the back of the ball and move in a coordinated manner to propel the ball in the desired direction. Follow-through is in the direction the ball is going. Weight transfer is from back to front. At this stage the child is able to focus on the target area and be rather successful.

Movement Observation

Ball rolling is one of the first game skills a child masters. The first steps of understanding direction and force can be developed through activities and games that utilize ball rolling. Because a rolling ball only uti-

FIGURE 12-1
Elementary ball rolling.

FIGURE 12-2

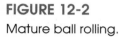

Mature ball rolling.

lizes two dimensions of space (forward-backward and sideward) it is more easily controlled and caught than a thrown ball, which utilizes a third dimension of space (up and down).

COMMON PROBLEMS

1. Poor placement of hands (hands should be behind the ball; fingers pointing down);
2. Failure to transfer the weight backward and then forward (offer word pictures like shoveling dirt or mopping the floor);
3. Failure to release the ball at the proper time (slip the ball gently onto the floor);
4. Failure to step forward with the appropriate foot (foot opposite the ball side);

5. Lack of follow-through and/or focus on the target (reach for the target).

When assessing the ball-rolling pattern, the following check-sequence illustration (Fig. 12-3) may prove helpful to the teacher and child.

Movement Variability

Many elementary games require the skill of rolling a ball. The child needs to learn how to control the direction, force, and speed of the object being manipulated. Children should be encouraged to progress to the one-hand roll (from either side) as quickly as possible. Practice-variability should also include rolling the ball from a moving posture. A well-developed rolling

FIGURE 12-3

Check-sequence, ball rolling.

schema can later be used in more complex situations found in bowling, bocci, shuffleboard, curling, and team handball. The rolling-movement pattern also offers a foundation for the skill needed for horseshoes, and softball pitching.

SPATIAL

MOVEMENT-PATTERN VARIATIONS

Using two hands; one hand (left and right)
Straddle-sitting
Straddle-standing (feet parallel)
Stride-standing (alternate lead foot and rolling hand)
Crouched
Kneeling (both knees and one knee stride standing, feet parallel)
Arms positioned in front of body; at either side
While moving
Vary base of support (narrow to wide).

DIRECTIONS/PATHWAYS/LEVELS

Roll ball:
Straight ahead, diagonally left, right, backward (side and between legs), in a curved pathway;
While traveling (walking, running) forward, backward, and sideways;
While lying on floor, kneeling, standing, jumping (levels).

TIME

Slow to fast   To a rhythmic beat

FORCE

Hard   Roll for distance
Soft   Roll for accuracy
Objects of various sizes and weights

ADDITIONAL MOVEMENT VARIATIONS

Roll a ball with a partner.
Roll to a moving target.
Combine other fundamental skills with rolling a ball.
Roll a ball down a balance beam, up a plank, around a large foam doughnut.
Have a bowling tournament.

SUGGESTED GENERAL PROGRESSION

1. Roll a ball from straddle position, ball held with both hands between the legs.
2. Roll ball from either side of the body while standing in stride position (two hands, then one).
3. Roll a ball diagonally from either side of the body.
4. While moving, roll a ball to a stationary and a moving target.

Movement Enhancement

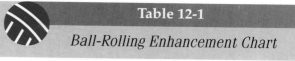

Table 12-1
Ball-Rolling Enhancement Chart

	LEVEL		LEVEL
GAMES		Hit the Pins	II & III
		Roll Dodgeball	
Rat poison	I & II	Bowling Relay	
Box Ball		Straddle Bowling	
Call a Guard		1, 2, 3 You're Set Free	
Charlie Over the Water			

Teaching Hints

Use balls of different sizes and weights; however, do not use heavy objects such as a bowling ball during initial experiences.
Emphasize eyes on the target.
Work first on distance and moderate speed, then accuracy.
Provide quality variability of practice around suggested progressions and ability level.

Skill Concepts Communicated to Children

Allow one foot to lead.
Coordinate shift of weight to back foot with backswing of arm.
Arm giving force is fully extended at completion of backswing.
Release the ball as it passes the forward foot.
Follow-through is in direction of desired pathway of the ball.
Eyes shift from target to ball.

THROWING

Movement Description

Throwing is a complex manipulative skill in which one or both arms are used to thrust an object away from the body and into space. Depending on many factors (size of child, size of object, and so forth), the throw may be underhand, overhead, overarm, or sidearm. There is also a two-handed overhead throw that is used for projecting large balls. The mature throwing pattern is a complex skill requiring the coordination of many body parts. Of the three most common styles—overarm sidearm, and underhand—the unilateral overarm style is the form most commonly used and most thoroughly studied.

During the developmental stages, children demonstrate many different throwing patterns; however, Wickstrom (1983) reports an absence of any definite or precise order for the onset of the variations.

FIGURE 12-4
Two-hand underhand throw.

FIGURE 12-5
Two-hand overarm throw.

In normal-developing children 4 to 8 years of age, two distinct stages of throwing can be identified: elementary and mature.

ELEMENTARY STAGE

First attempts at throwing are usually represented by the two-hand underhand (Fig. 12-4) and two-hand overarm (Fig. 12-5) throws. As the child's hands mature, a smaller ball will encourage the development of the basic one-hand overhand throw, and one-hand underhand throw.

By four or five years of age most children demonstrate a throwing pattern in which the body more or less faces the target as the arm swings side-ward, upward, and backward to a flexed elbow position with the hand held behind the head. There is some trunk rotation when the arm is swung backward as well as when the ball is thrust into space. The forward motion of the throwing arm is accompanied by a forward flexion of the trunk, resulting in a shift of body weight as a forward step is made with the leg on the throwing side of the body (Fig. 12-6). Follow-through is forward and downward.

MATURE STAGE (OVERARM)

The mature stage of overarm throwing (Fig. 12-7) is a coordinated sequence of moves in which the body is used to impart force and speed in an efficient and effective manner. Balance is assisted through the use of transfer of weight and the horizontal movement of the nonthrowing arm. The child assumes an open stance with the throwing shoulder pointed diagonally to the rear and slightly dropped. There is a marked increase in trunk rotation as the weight shifts to the rear foot, the arm swings backward, upper arm assumes a right angle to the body, and the elbow is flexed at a 90° angle. As the forward motion begins, the trunk rotates through the hips, spine, and shoulders, bringing the upper arm to a position straight out from the shoulder with the elbow leading the forearm (thumb pointing diagonally to the rear). At this point the forearm quickly extends fol-

FIGURE 12-6
Elementary stage overarm throw.

FIGURE 12-7

Mature stage overarm throw.

lowed by a snap of the wrist as the ball is released. The transfer of weight from the rear foot is completed by a step forward (and slightly lateral) of the opposite foot. The follow-through is forward and diagonally downward across the midline of the body. The following summary characterizes the general movements associated with the mature overhand throwing pattern:

Feet are slightly apart with forward foot opposite throwing arm.

Trunk rotates to throwing side and weight shifts onto rear foot.

There is a definite rotation through hips, legs, spine, and shoulders.

Weight shifts and there is a step with the opposite foot just before the ball is released.

Elbow extension occurs just before release as body continues follow-through.

MATURE STAGE (UNDERHAND)

While most of the throwing performed in games and sports is overarm rather than underhand, the underhand pattern is exhibited in several activities including softball pitching, horseshoes, bowling, and other tossing-action oriented games.

When extreme windups are eliminated, skilled underhand throwers demonstrate the following pattern (Figure 12-8):

FIGURE 12-8

Mature Stage underhand throw.*

1. A forward step with the opposite foot, slight forward trunk flexion, and a backward swing by the throwing arm. The pelvis and upper spine rotate backward in the process.
2. Forward rotation of the pelvis, followed in close sequence by upper spine rotation and arm flexion.
3. Ball release when the hand of the throwing arm is at a point just forward of a vertical line through the shoulder.

Movement Observation

Research has provided considerable evidence describing improvement in throwing performance from late infancy through childhood. Although some children progress to the elementary stage of throwing without formal instruction and an abundance of practice, many do not attain mature pattern characteristics without some proper experiences (that is, practice and instruction). Although the skill of throwing requires the coordination of many body movements, throwing proficiency can be realized by the age of five or six by children engaged in play experiences (with meaningful feedback) that stimulate proper throwing behaviors.

Early analysis and correction of ineffective throwing behaviors will help children achieve this important game skill.

COMMON PROBLEMS

1. Beginning stance is "square" when facing the target (place contralateral foot more forward than foot on the throwing side of the body);
2. Failure to shift weight to rear leg (engage child in forward-backward, rocking-type movements—with and without ball play);
3. Failure to rotate the trunk (practice twisting and turning movements with head and feet in a stationary position; encourage a preparatory reaching back of the throwing arm to open up the stance);
4. Positioning the ball too close to head or behind head (90° elbow joint);
5. Positioning the upper arm close to the body (90° shoulder joint, elbow out);
6. "Palming" the ball (hold ball away from palm—grip with fingers);
7. Failure of elbow to lead the forward arm swing (elbow out in front);
8. Releasing the ball too soon or too late (snap of the wrist and release of the ball occur simultaneously as forearm extends);
9. Failure to extend forearm quickly (fling the forearm, wrist, hand, ball);
10. Failure to follow through (reach for the target, back foot follows through, and weight is transferred to it; distance throws encourage this movement);
11. Inability to hit "target" (refrain from requiring children to throw for accuracy until they have acquired the mature throwing pattern);
12. When throwing underhand, failing to release the ball at proper time (reach directly for the target).

Elementary Stage

Mature Stage

FIGURE 12-9

Check-sequence, overarm throwing.

Trunk rotation is considered to be key in the development of overhand throwing proficiency. The gradual evolution from the trunk acting as a "block" with little or no rotation to the pelvic-initiated rotation will be encouraged by experiences that stimulate overhand throwing for long distances.

When assessing the throwing pattern, the following check-sequence illustration (Fig. 12-9) may prove helpful to both the instructor and child.

Movement Variability

Games at all levels offer opportunities for children to use either the underhand, sidearm, or overarm throw. The use of quality variability to provide a healthy throwing schema is very important if the child is to develop throwing patterns that allow success in dynamic game situations. The mature overarm throw movement is commonly used in lead-up games and in the following sports: softball, baseball, football, volleyball (serve), and the racquet games for smash and serve (tennis).

SPATIAL

MOVEMENT-PATTERN VARIATIONS

Two hands:	One hand (right/left):	Vary base of support
Underhand (from front and either side)	underhand	(narrow to wide)
Overarm (overhead, chest pass, from either side)	sidearm overarm variations	

DIRECTIONS/PATHWAYS/LEVELS

Throw up, down, forward, to side, at an angle
Throw while:
    squatting or sitting
    jumping or leaping
Throw while moving in various directions
    forward, sideways
    backward, diagonally

TIME

Slow to fast   To a rhythmic beat

FORCE

Throw objects of various sizes and weights (whiffleball, fleeceball, softball, football, frisbee, playground ball).
Throw hard for distance.
Throw soft to medium.
Combine distance and accuracy.

ADDITIONAL MOVEMENT VARIATIONS

Throwing against a wall or other rebound material;
Throwing while maintaining a stiff posture (Tin Man);
Throwing while exhibiting an exaggerated relaxed posture (Raggedy Ann);
Throwing while performing locomotor skills (running, skipping, galloping);
Throwing to a partner;
Throwing balls at a stationary target;
Throwing balls at a moving target;
Throwing while moving to target (stationary/moving);
Throwing while being guarded.

SUGGESTED GENERAL PROGRESSION

1. Use the two-handed underhand and two-handed overarm patterns, feet parallel then contralateral (feet and arms in opposition), throw:
   short, then long distances;
   to a large target on the wall;
   to a stationary partner;
   to a moving partner;
   while moving (forward, backward, left, right) to a stationary target;
   to a moving target while moving.
2. Use the one-hand overarm pattern (following the same progression).
3. Use the one-hand underhand pattern (along with the progression outlined for the previous patterns; use right and left hands). The one-hand underhand and one-hand overarm patterns can be introduced within the same time frame.

Teaching Hints

Provide a quality variability of practice.
Encourage distance throws with balls easily gripped in one hand.
Provide "soft" balls (yarn, sponge) at the beginning and progress to more firm (whiffleball, "soft" softball).
Think of creative ways to help the children learn the necessary trunk rotation (rotating forward and out from under the ball).
Stress freedom of elbow from the body.
Stress speed of movement, hip rotation, and follow-through.
Emphasize the need for "leading the receiver" when throwing to a moving partner.
Work on distance and then accuracy.

Skill Concepts Communicated to Children

Keep eyes on target.
The leg opposite the throwing arm is out in front.
Turn shoulder toward target.

The shoulder of the nonthrowing arm should point toward the target.

Elbow is held away from the body.

Ball is held with fingers and thumb positioned near the ear.

Body weight moves from back foot to forward foot as ball is thrown.

The elbow leads the way, followed by wrist.

Swing rear foot forward and follow through.

Movement Enhancement

Table 12-2
Throwing Enhancement Chart

GAMES	LEVEL
Beanbag Ring Throw	I
I Don't Want It Ring the Tire Triangle Dodgeball	I & II
Ball Toss Gap Ball Individual Dodgeball One Step Poison Circle Sock-It-to-Me-Ball 25 Throws	II
Can Can Canoes and Rapids Club Guard Square Dodgeball Skeet Ball Old Plug	II & III
Catch Up Hand Grenade Snowball Call a Guard Crown The King Flies Up Dodgeball	III

CATCHING

Movement Description

Catching is a fundamental manipulative skill that involves stopping the momentum of an object and gaining control of it by use of the hands. During the early stages of catching, moving objects are first trapped (stopped and held) with one or more body parts. The acquisition of eye-hand coordination enables the child to attempt the manipulative skill of catching in which an aerial object is grasped and controlled through the use of the hands and sometimes the arms. Basically, the mature stage of catching is characterized by placing the hands in a position for effective reception of the aerial object, which is grasped with the hands in such a manner that control is demonstrated. A functional understanding of time-space relationships and the coordination to make the necessary bodily adjustments must be achieved before the child will be able to demonstrate a proficiency in catching a moving object.

By the age of four years, most children can successfully catch an aerial ball from the frontal horizontal plane. This is, however, primarily a cradling movement of the arms (trapping a large ball against the chest) and generally does not involve just the hands. Depending upon experience, children generally acquire mature pattern characteristics between five and six and a half years of age.

ELEMENTARY STAGE

By five years of age, most children have usually progressed to the elementary stage of catching (Fig. 12-10). Standing in a stationary position, the child tracks the incoming aerial ball, and the eyes close only as contact with the ball is felt or sometimes immediately preceding contact. The arms are held slightly bent in front of the body and the child attempts to make initial contact with the hands prior to ball-arm contact. The timing of the grasp with the flight of the ball and the immature coordination of the two hands working together often necessitate the continued use of the upper body to help secure the ball (Fig. 12-11). Ball size becomes increasingly important during this stage. During the transition stage from arms predominant to hands predominant, the use of smaller balls will encourage grasping with the hands rather than scooping attempts of the arms. It is not uncommon for a child who can catch a large ball with the hands to regress to the trapping movements against the body with the initial change to smaller balls.

FIGURE 12-10
Elementary stage, catching.

FIGURE 12-11
Trapping the ball against the chest.

MATURE STAGE

By the age of six and a half, most children demonstrate the mature stage of catching proficiency (Fig. 12-12) with large balls. From a stationary position, the child tracks the incoming aerial ball to final contact with the hands. The elbows are slightly bent as the arms are held relaxed at the sides or in front of the body. The hands move forward to meet the approaching ball, which is caught solely with the cupped hands, as the force of the object is absorbed by hands and arms. At this stage, arm and body adjustments to variations in the flight of the ball are also attempted. The following characteristics summarize the movements associated with the mature catching pattern (ball traveling on the frontal horizontal plane):

Body is in alignment with incoming object.
Arms are held relaxed at sides and elbows flexed.
Hands and fingers are relaxed and slightly cupped and point toward the object.
Eyes follow the flight of the object.
Arms give upon contact to absorb the force, and fingers close around object.
Weight is transferred from front to back.

FIGURE 12-12
Mature stage, catching.

Both the elementary and mature stages of catching have all been characterized with the child in a stationary catching position. It should be noted that not until about 10 or 11 years of age are most children capable of perceptually judging flight projection from a nonpredetermined distance and angle. Such may be the case during many game and sport activities when the child attempts to catch a fly ball.

Movement Observation

Just as with throwing, many individuals fail to achieve the mature stage of catching because of lack of experience and/or lack of proper instruction. Along with varied practice conditions, children should be provided with feedback and reinforcement related to their performance. Several factors may affect catching performance: ball size, speed, and angle of approach. Although it is easier for children to catch a larger ball, their response tends to result in a more elementary form of catching, namely "trapping." The use of too small a ball may also produce undesirable responses. As a general rule, the ball should be large enough so that the child can cup it effectively, yet is not too small that a high degree of visual-motor control is required. Such factors should be kept in mind as the teacher observes catching performance. It is very easy to present tasks that are too difficult for the child to complete; thus appropriate tasks, keen observation, and feedback are vital to the attainment of optimal performance.

COMMON PROBLEMS

1. Failing to watch object until contact with hands ("watch the ball into your hands");
2. Failing to "give" with ball (as ball contacts hands, elbows should flex to "give" with impact);
3. Putting heels of hands together; thus object bounces out (hands should be held in opposition to each other, slightly apart to accommodate ball size, with thumbs held upward);
4. Keeping fingers straight and rigid; object bounces off and injury may occur (hands and fingers should be relaxed and slightly cupped);
5. Inability to vary the catching pattern for objects of different weights and sizes, and inability to adapt to objects approaching from various angles to the body (provide variability in practice);
6. Improper stance (feet should be slightly apart in forward stride position allowing weight to be transferred from front to back);
7. Reaching out to the side to catch; therefore not being in line with the incoming object (line body up with the object).

FIGURE 12-13
Check-sequence, catching.

When assessing the throwing pattern, the following check-sequence illustration (Fig. 12-13) may prove helpful to the teacher.

Movement Variability

The importance of proficiency in catching to success in a variety of game and sport situations is obvious. Ample practice opportunities that are diverse and meaningful to the child are essential to the attainment of a mature schema and successful performance. The skill of catching can be utilized in numerous elementary game activities and in such refined sport areas as basketball, softball, baseball, soccer, team handball, and volleyball. Lacrosse requires an *absorbing* skill similar to that found in catching.

SPATIAL

MOVEMENT-PATTERN VARIATIONS
Catch with both hands; right hand; left hand.
Vary base of support (narrow to wide).
Overhand; underhand.
Catch object with hands at varied positions (examples):

Overhead (overhand)	Below waist (underhand)
Chest level (overhand)	At knees (underhand)
Body fully extended	To either side of the body

Body stationary
Body moving
Standing on one foot

DIRECTIONS/PATHWAYS/LEVELS
Moving
    forward to catch an object
    backward to catch an object
    sideways to catch an object
    diagonally forward to catch an object
    diagonally backward to catch an object
    dodging (zigzag) prior to catching an object.
Low (sitting; full squat, back straight; lying-down positions)
High (jumping up)
Middle (partial squat)
Catching an object:
    incoming from front; side
    from various angles
    sdown from above.

TIME

Reaction time/rhythm
    Draw object to center of body quickly
    Draw object to center of body slowly
    Move slowly to catch an object
    Move quickly to catch an object
    Catch a slow-to-fast-moving object
    Catch a bounced ball
    Juggling two or three objects.

FORCE

Vary weight and size of object caught: (beachball, tennis ball, ping-pong ball, playground ball, beanbag, volleyball, fleeceball, frisbee, football).

ADDITIONAL MOVEMENT VARIATIONS

Clap hands a number of times before catching objects.
Perform locomotor or nonlocomotor movement(s) before catching a released ball.
Throw and catch with a partner(s).
Catch a ball rebounding from the wall.
Catch and throw a ball to a rhythmic beat or music.
Catch a ball while rebounding from a mini-tramp.
Catch a deck tennis ring.
Catch a hula hoop rolling toward (away from, along side of) the participant.
Catch a bouncing ball; a rolling ball.
Catch with one eye closed.
Catch and toss lummi sticks with a partner (to rhythm).
Catch a small ball while playing jacks.
Catch with a scoop, glove, or carton.

SUGGESTED GENERAL PROGRESSION

1. Traps a rolling ball.
2. Catches a rolling ball with both hands while kneeling and standing.

Sight-impaired children can play many games with verbal cues and appropriate equipment.

3. Catches a bouncing ball.
4. Catches an aerial ball with a scoop.
5. Catches an aerial ball with either hand.
6. Catches an aerial ball while moving in different directions.
7. While moving catches ball over the shoulder.
8. Catches a fast-moving and bouncing "grounder."

Teaching Hints

Use soft objects (beanbags, foam balls, yarn balls) with initial instructional periods.
Use objects that are highly colored.
Start with large objects and progress to smaller ones.
Let the students occasionally choose size of objects.

During initial learning experiences, provide the child with a background (from where the object is approaching) that does not provide complex figure-ground problems or distractions (auditory and visual).
Play games that emphasize catching and throwing.

Skill Concepts Communicated to Children

Get in the path of the ball.
Stand with feet in forward stride position.
Curve fingers.
Keep one's eyes on the ball.
Reach for the ball.
Pull ball in toward body.
"Give" with the impact.

KICKING

Movement Description

Kicking is a manipulative skill pattern in which the foot is used to strike an object. The *placekick* (stationary ball) is the foundation for other kicking skills such as kicking a moving ball and punting. Good dynamic balance is critical to the development of successful kicking skills. Foot *Dribbling* will also be discussed, because it represents a variable of the basic kicking pattern. The reader is reminded, however, that a consistently mature kicking pattern should be developed prior to attempting to dribble.

Movement Enhancement

Table 12-3
Catching Enhancement Chart

	LEVEL		LEVEL		LEVEL
GAMES					
Ball Toss	II	Cross Over	II & III	Long Ball	III
25 Throws		Call Ball		Hot Ball	
Freeze Ball		Ring Toss		End-Zone Ball	
		Beach Ball		Overtake Ball	
		Bat Ball		Beanbags	
		Circle Ball		Hoop Activities	
		Beat Ball		Crown The King	
		Circle Stride Ball		Flies Up Dodgeball	
		Pass and Duck			
		Up the Field			
		One Step			

FIGURE 12-14
Elementary stage, kicking.

ELEMENTARY STAGE

The elementary stage of kicking is characterized by the absence of a pronounced backswing as the kicking foot sort of jerks forward to push or punch at the ball. The arms are held sideways for balance and there is little follow-through (Fig. 12-14).

MATURE STAGE

In the mature stage (Fig. 12-15), the support foot is placed beside the object to be kicked and the kicking leg with knee bent swings freely from the hip through an arc toward the object to be kicked. The knee is quickly extended as the foot contacts the object and the body leans back for balance. The kicking leg continues its movement forward in the direction of the flight of the object. The eyes should be on the object at all times, and the arms should be relaxed and move in opposition with the legs.

Movement Observation

Kicking is a unique game skill that requires dynamic balance from a small base of support. A general prerequisite ability to kicking is the ability to assume a balanced position on one leg (this occurs at approximately two years of age). As early as possible in the development of this skill, young children should be encouraged to kick for distance because this requirement encourages the child to move the kicking leg through a larger arc. The mature kicking pattern requires the kicker to use full range of hip and knee joints.

Children enjoy kicking, and when they are exposed to sufficient practice opportunities the skill can be acquired relatively early. However, the child often experiences difficulty when trying to kick in childhood games. When kicking a stationary ball, children are hampered by ineffective placement of the support foot. When punting, they experience difficulty controlling the drop of the ball, and when dribbling they experience difficulty controlling the path of the ball. The two main kicking skills—placekick and punt—require accurate foot placement of both support foot and kicking foot. In addition, the punt requires accurate timing of the kicking foot as it meets the descending ball. The dribble requires complex balance adjustments as well as a kinesthetic knowledge of the application of force placed on the ball. By the time children reach the age of five or six years, with appropriate experiences they should demonstrate the characteristics of a mature movement pattern. As the mature pattern becomes established and the ability to produce force increases (with age) the child begins to make more precise adjustments in accuracy with complex tasks such as punting and kicking a rolling, bouncing, and/or aerial ball.

COMMON PROBLEMS

PLACEKICK

1. Inadequate backswing (pushing action) from the hip of the kicking leg (encourage one or two steps prior to kicking);
2. Inaccurate placement of support foot (foot should be a "shadow" to the ball, that is, to the side and slightly behind);
3. Lack of force (punching action) when striking the ball (leg should "whip" through the ball and arms should move in opposition);
4. Ball "pops up" (contact should be slightly below center; follow-through should be forward and toward the midline of the body);
5. Foot misses the ball completely (keep focus on the ball throughout the kick, and check position of body behind ball);
6. Ball rises dangerously soon after kicked (avoid placing toe under the ball; encourage soccer type side-of-the-foot kick).

FIGURE 12-15
Mature stage, kicking

Full follow-through when punting.

When assessing the placekick pattern, the above check-sequence illustration (Fig. 12-16) may prove helpful to the teacher and child.

PUNT

1. Ball "pops" with little force (hold ball forward with outstretched arms and drop it straight down; contact is made on top of foot while leg is extended);

2. Insufficient force (take one or two preliminary steps, whip the kicking leg through the ball, look for the extended leg on follow-through);

3. Lack of balance while kicking and after kicking (hold ball in front of body, arms outstretched, move arms in opposition to legs during follow-through, lean trunk forward during follow-through, widen the base slightly);

4. Poor timing with the drop of the ball (arms are outstretched, ball is dropped—not pitched).

Dribbling (short taps keep the ball in control).

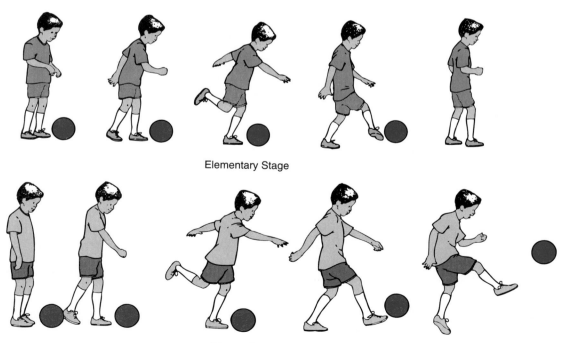

Elementary Stage

Mature Stage

FIGURE 12-16
Check-sequence, placekick.

FIGURE 12-17

Check-sequence, punting.

The following check-sequence illustration (Fig. 12-17) of the punt may prove helpful to teacher and child.

DRIBBLE

1. Excessive force applied to the ball (take small steps and tap the ball using alternate feet);
2. Inability to control body balance (hold arms out for balance, take small steps, flex knees slightly);
3. Loss of control of ball (lightly tap the ball, use side of foot nearest ball, avoid contact with toe of foot, nudge the ball in the direction of choice).

Movement Variability

Children enjoy kicking objects and they should be encouraged to explore the various ways of kicking as soon as they have the balance required for running. A variety of objects of different sizes and weights should be supplied during practice variability, and kicking for distance should be encouraged initially as this promotes a full leg swing. Fundamental kicking skills are utilized in numerous low-organized and lead-up games as well as soccer and football. The kicking movement can also be found in dance and gymnastics.

SPATIAL

MOVEMENT-PATTERN VARIATIONS

(*Note:* Initial exploration should encourage the use of both feet for kicking.)

PLACEKICK

Use inside, outside toe, heel, and instep of foot.
Kick from a prone position; supine position, crab position; squat position.
Kick standing; feet parallel (vary the distance apart).
Kick with stiff legs.
Step into the kick (that is, run, walk).
Vary arm position (at sides, hands on hips, straight out in front, above head, across chest).

PUNT

Stride stand; kicking leg back; arms straight forward; ball held waist high with hands on either side exerting equal pressure, near end of football turned slightly to the kicking side.
Vary distance of feet apart.
Single step into the kick.
Multiple steps into the kick.

DRIBBLE

Use either side of foot.

DIRECTIONS/PATHWAYS/LEVELS

forward
either side
diagonally right, left
under an object, through a hoop, over an object
zigzag pathway while dribbling
curved pathway.

TIME

Execute kicking pattern slow to fast.
Kick to rhythm of music or drum.

Consecutive kicks (dribble).
Kick a ball repeatedly against a wall.

FORCE

Kick a light to heavy object lightly.
Kick a light to heavy object hard.

Kick for distance.

Kick for accuracy.
Kick for height.

ADDITIONAL MOVEMENT VARIATIONS

Kick a ball to barely avoid an obstacle.
Kick a ball to hit an obstacle.
Kick while running, leaping, galloping, sliding, or skipping.
Kick a ball back and forth with a partner.
Kick a ball to a person moving at various angles away and toward the ball.
Dribble a ball while maneuvering around objects and people.
Use imaginary movement stories that encourage kicking moves.
Use the kicking movement while dancing (see Movement Enhancement).

A kicking movement in dance.

SUGGESTED GENERAL PROGRESSION

All tasks are for distance unless otherwise noted.

1. Stationary child kicks a stationary ball forward.
2. Moving child kicks a stationary ball forward.
3. Stationary child kicks a ball that has been rolled straight to the child.
4. Moving child kicks a moving ball forward.
5. Stationary child punts a self-bounced ball.
6. While taking one step with nonkicking foot, child punts a dropped ball (emphasize distance, then accuracy, then distance/ accuracy).
7. Child takes two steps (R, L) and punts (R) for distance, accuracy, distance/accuracy)
8. Stationary child kicks and punts ball to a partner.
9. Child dribbles in general space; no set pathways.
10. Child dribbles along a set straight pathway.
11. Child dribbles along a set curved pathway.
12. Child dribbles and passes laterally to a teammate repeatedly.
13. Child dribbles against an opponent.

Teaching Hints

Provide settings for distance kicking; mature kicking pattern should be established prior to focusing on accuracy.

Practice using both right and left foot.

Practice kicking in all directions.

Provide different sized, weighted, and shaped balls (round and elliptical; foam balls of all shapes are recommended).

Space children far enough apart so distance kicking will be encouraged and safety hazards will be prevented.

When punting and placekicking, stress full follow-through.

When dribbling, stress short, soft, taps.

Frequently use the term "ball control" during dribbling practice.

Refrain from placing children in games until they have developed the control and balance necessary for safe and successful participation.

Encourage use of the kicking-movement pattern in combination with other fundamental skills (rhythmic locomotor/nonlocomotor work).

Relate kicking patterns used in dance to those used in maneuvering balls.

Provide additional balance work for those who need it.

Skill Concepts Communicated to Children

Keep eyes on the ball at all times.

Foot should contact ground ball just below mid-line of ball.

Drop (not toss) the ball to be punted.

Arms and legs work in opposition.

Kick "through" the ball for follow-through.

Inside of foot kick is best for controlling the height of the ball.

Movement Enhancement

Table 12-4

Kicking Enhancement Chart

	LEVEL
GAMES	
Circle Kick Ball Hot Ball Kick the Pin Moon Soccer	I–III
Boundary Ball Place Kickball	II & III
Crab Soccer Battle Ball Circle Soccer Soccer Dodgeball	III

The following dances can be used if the low kick (often combined with a hop) is used as a movement variation.

	LEVEL
DANCES	
Looby Loo Hokey-Pokey Did you Ever See a Lassie?	I & II
Hansel and Gretel Seven Jumps	II
Hora	III

FIGURE 12-18
Good focus on the approach.

> Center of gravity changes during a strong kicking movement, arms are important in maintaining balance.

_____

TRAPPING

Movement Description

Trapping is a receptive skill in which a ball is received and controlled by the body without the use of the hands. The trunk, legs, and feet are the body parts most frequently used to block the ball's flight and cause it to drop vertically to the ground and be con-

trolled by the child. In the case of ground balls, the ball may be stopped or merely slowed down.

ELEMENTARY STAGE

In the elementary stage the child meets the ball with an unyielding body. Only minimal attention is given to the direction of force of the object. The child's goal is simply to obstruct the ball's progress without using the arms or hands. Actual control is seldom accomplished during this stage.

MATURE STAGE

The mature stage of trapping is much like catching. The body is aligned with the oncoming ball and focus is maintained on the ball as the ball approaches the body (Fig. 12-18). Upon impact, the trunk, leg, or foot gives with the ball as the force is absorbed and the ball is controlled. As the ball falls to the ground the leg and/or foot is used to control the ball prior to it being propelled again. The arms are held relaxed and out from the body for balance.

Movement Observation

Trapping is a skill that is utilized in various games of low organization as well as the team sport of soccer. There are numerous ways to trap a ball. Initially, students should trap balls that come from directly in front of them. The sole-of-the-foot trap (Fig. 12-19a) and lower-leg trap (Fig. 12-19b) will offer the most control during this stage. Later progressions will include trapping a ball that is traveling along a diagonal path. The inside-of-the-foot trap will be more effective for balls traveling diagonally. As the child progresses to trapping moving balls while the body is also moving, con-

FIGURE 12-19
(a) Sole-of-the-foot trap; (b) lower-leg trap.

FIGURE 12-20
Body absorption of force.

siderable care must be taken to make sure the child maintains balance when making the necessary adjustments to receive the force of the ball effectively. When the ball is trapped with the sole of the foot, the child must understand the concept of retarding the force of the ball by allowing the foot to meet the ball softly, the object being to control the path of the ball and then to redirect the ball along a new path. An effective verbal cue such as "heel down, toe up" can serve as a skill-technique reminder. Whether using the sole of the foot or the inside of the foot, the child must be encouraged to absorb the force and then redirect the ball (that is, dribble or pass) as quickly as possible. When the ball is trapped with the leg or body, the concept of force absorption will help the child control the ball whose momentum is absorbed by the child's body and allowed to drop at the child's feet (Fig. 12-20).

COMMON PROBLEMS

1. Failure to align the body with the path of the ball (keep eyes on the ball);
2. Inadequate visual tracking (eyes follow the ball until the ball contacts the body);
3. Failure to absorb the force of the ball, causing the ball to rebound off the foot (give as the ball contacts the body);
4. Transferring body weight to the ball, thus causing a fall (keep body weight on support foot and keep heel lower than the toe or sole-of-foot trap);

5. Failure to bend the knees when trapping with the legs (keep knees bent until ball is trapped between shins and ground).

Movement Variability

The similarities between catching and trapping should be emphasized as the child develops his or her trapping schema. With the growing interest in soccer in the United States, many elementary-grade children are very interested in their development of efficient eye-foot coordination skills. In soccer-type games the feet, legs, and body will be used to stop the momentum of the ball in a controlled manner.

SPATIAL

MOVEMENT-PATTERN VARIATIONS

Trap with chest, upper legs, lower legs, feet (right, and left)   Body stationary
Body moving
Vary arm positions (up, horizontal, down)
Vary the base of support (narrow to wide)

DIRECTIONS/PATHWAYS/LEVELS

While body is moving:
forward,
diagonally,
sideways,
back to trap.
Body stationary and ball moving:
toward,
to left and right side,
from behind,
at angle toward.
Levels: crouching the body to meet the ball
high (springing into the air)
middle (standing)
low (partial squat, sitting, lying down).

TIME

Trap while traveling from slow motion to a fast rate.
Trap a moving ball slowly to quickly.

FORCE

Trap a light to heavy object (fleeceball, nerfball, soccer ball).
"Give" lightly with the ball, or forcefully trap it.

ADDITIONAL MOVEMENT VARIATIONS

Clap hands prior to the ball making contact with body.
Trap a ball and immediately send the ball sideways, diagonally, forward, backward.
Trap objects other than balls (beanbags, foam shapes).

SUGGESTED GENERAL PROGRESSION

1. While standing, trap a rolling ball coming from directly in front, using the sole-of-the-foot trap.
2. While standing, trap a rolling ball coming from directly in front using the lower-leg trap.
3. While standing, trap a rolling ball coming diagonally from the left or right, using the side-of-the-foot trap.
4. While standing, trap a bouncing ball coming from directly in front, from the left, from the right using the side-of-the-foot trap, thigh trap, or body trap.
5. While moving, repeat the traps described in items 1 through 4.

Teaching Hints

Provide a variety of different sized balls traveling at various speeds.

Use soft balls (yarn balls, nerf soccer balls, and partially deflated playground balls) in the early progressions.

Use soccer balls only after students are able consistently to trap lighter, softer balls.

Partially deflated balls are more easily controlled.

Use large beanbags at beginning of aerial ball traps progression.

Keep children at lower progressions until contact with the ball is consistent (that is, consistently trap rolling ball, then bouncing ball, then aerial ball).

Emphasize the give of the body part(s) as contact is made with the ball.

Stress consistent eye contact with the ball.

Emphasize "heel down, toe up" for sole-of-the-foot trap.

Emphasize control of the ball after it is trapped.

Larger foot surface enables greater control.

Stress moving the ball immediately after the trap.

When first learning to body trap, girls can protect chest by crossing arms in front of chests.

Movement Enhancement

Table 12-5

Trapping Enhancement Chart

GAMES	LEVEL
Circle Kick Ball Hot Ball	I–III
Boundary Ball	II & III
Crab Soccer Soccer Dodgeball Battle Ball Circle Soccer	III

Skill Concepts Communicated to Children

Keep the eyes on the ball.

Line up the body with the path of the oncoming ball.

As the ball reaches the body part(s), "give" with the force of the ball; this may necessitate a slight jump backward.

Angle the body part(s) so ball will be deflected toward the ground.

BOUNCING/DRIBBLING

Movement Description

Bouncing and dribbling, manipulative skills requiring considerable eye-hand coordination, are means of propelling a ball in a downward direction. The development of bouncing originates as the child drops a ball, causing it to bounce, and attempts to strike the object repeatedly. As the child's ability progresses, control of the ball increases and the term *dribbling* is applied. It is at the dribbling stage that the child has learned to place the hand in relation to the center of the ball and meets the ball as is rebounds, maintaining contact with it as long as possible. Although few research studies have focused on this topic, the developmental sequence for ball bouncing/dribbling appears as follows:

1. Bouncing and catching;
2. Bouncing and "slapping" on the rebound;
3. Dribbling with the ball in control;
4. Dribbling with the child in control;
5. Advanced dribbling abilities such as utilized in basketball.

Along with the described developmental sequence, the child will generally exhibit the following proficiency characteristics:

1. Bounce with both hands and catch;
2. Bounce with dominant hand and catch;
3. Bounce with both hands repeatedly;
4. Bounce with dominant hand repeatedly;
5. Bounce with nondominant hand repeatedly;
6. Alternate hand while bouncing continuously;
7. Dribble (continuously and with control) with either hand and alternating;
8. Dribble while traveling.

While some two-year-olds may exhibit a degree of proficiency in two-hand bouncing, it is not until approximately five or six years of age that the mature pattern is mastered.

FIGURE 12-21
Elementary stage, dribbling.

FIGURE 12-22
Mature stage, dribbling.

ELEMENTARY STAGE

At the elementary stage of development (Fig. 12-21) the child, while performing at a somewhat successful level, generally exhibits the following characteristics:

1. While striking the ball, the fingers are together and stiff.
2. The striking action is from the shoulder or wrist only, resulting in slapping.
3. The hand is repelled from the ball at time of contact.
4. Control of bouncing is not continuous.
5. Ball rebounds to a level other than at the waist.

MATURE STAGE

The following characteristics are found in the mature pattern stage (Fig. 12-22) of one-hand ball dribbling:

1. Feet placed in a narrow stride position and the body flexed at knees, hips, and waist, with a slight forward trunk lean.
2. The ball is contacted with fingers spread and propelled (pushed) to the floor by elbow extension and follow-through.
3. Height of bounce is maintained at waist level.
4. Focus is occasionally on the ball, but student is also able to focus away from the ball.

Two aspects of ball bouncing and dribbling—bouncing to another individual and foot dribbling—are discussed in separate sections (Throwing and Kicking).

Movement Observation

While some two-year-olds may exhibit some degree of ball-bouncing proficiency, it is generally not until approximately five or six years of age that the ability to repeatedly bounce a ball is acquired. At this stage eye focus is constantly on the ball and there is little locomotor movement. Both experience and visual-motor control in the form of eye-hand coordination are essential to the acquisition of ball-handling skills. A lack of coordination (that is, timing) between visual information and motor response may account for many of the problems associated with poor performance.

COMMON PROBLEMS

1. Using the palm of the hand to slap the ball (use fingers to push the ball and ride back with the rebounding ball);
2. Bouncing the ball too high or too low (consistent force should be applied to maintain ball at waist level);
3. Inability to maintain a stationary position while dribbling (if this is the desired task);
4. Poor concentration on the ball;
5. Insufficient follow-through, causing the ball not to return to waist level (the hand should meet the ball as it rebounds, maintaining contact as long as possible while the arm pushes with follow-through of arm, wrist, and fingers).

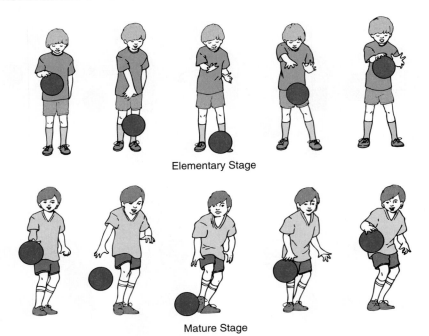

Elementary Stage

Mature Stage

FIGURE 12-23

Check-sequence, dribbling.

When assessing the bounce/dribble pattern, the following check-sequence illustration (Fig. 12-23) may prove helpful to both the teacher and child.

Movement Variability

While bouncing/dribbling are basically task-oriented game and sport skills, they do provide the child with opportunities for increasing the general schema, which is important to overall conceptualization and motor control of objects. Along with utilization in numerous elementary game activities, dribbling is also applied to the sport activities of basketball, speedball, and team handball.

SPATIAL

MOVEMENT-PATTERN VARIATIONS

Using two hands | While stationary
Using one hand (dominant/nondominant) | While moving
Changing hands | Vary base of support (wide to narrow)

DIRECTION/PATHWAYS/LEVELS

While moving body:
  forward;
  backward
  sideward
  (left and
  right)
  diagonally
  changing
    directions

While moving body:
  over, under and
    around objects
  in circles
  zigzag
  curved line
  changing
    pathways

Low level
  (on knees,
  squatting,
  sitting)
Medium level
  (standing)
High level
  (on toes,
  while
  jumping)

Moving the ball at various points from the body (in front, to side, under legs, around legs).

TIME

While moving (traveling)   To music accompani-
  slow to fast   ment or rhythmic beat
Moving ball slow to fast

FORCE

Vary size and weight of ball   Push soft to hard
  (junior size basketball,   (ball at low to
  volleyball, playground   high level;
  balls 7 to 10 inches,   below knees, waist).
  rhythm balls).

ADDITIONAL MOVEMENT VARIATIONS

Outline letters, names, words.
Join with a partner(s); to the same beat; alternating balls.
Go through an obstacle course (chairs, hoops, cones, under and over ropes).
Perform while blindfolded.
Perform while following lines on the floor (straight, curved, zigzag, circles).
Play one-on-one with a partner.
Perform other movements between bounces (twist, spin, turn, squat, jump).
Use different locomotor skills while bouncing/dribbling (walk, jog, run, leap, skip, gallop, hop, slide).
Jump over and/or move under the ball as it rebounds.
Create a dribbling routine (music enhances this activity).
Dribble while moving up and down stairs.
On different surfaces (concrete, wood, carpet, tile, dirt).

SUGGESTED GENERAL PROGRESSION

1. Stationary child bounces seven-to nine-inch ball in front of body using both hands.
2. Kneeling, child bounces ball in front of body using both hands.
3. While standing/kneeling, child bounces ball to various heights on either side of and in front of the body.
4. While moving, child bounces ball using both hands.
5. Stationary child dribbles ball with dominant/non-dominant hand in front and to either side of body.
6. While moving, child dribbles ball using either hand and switches hands.
7. While moving, child dribbles along a set pathway (straight, curved, zig-zag) with minimal eye-contact on the ball.
8. While moving, child dribbles and passes laterally to a teammate repeatedly.
9. Child dribbles and shoots for goal.
10. Child dribbles against an opponent.

Teaching Hints

Provide the child with a medium sized and weighted ball (8- to 9-inch playground ball) before force (weight and size)-variability activities are presented.

Keep in mind the stages of ball-bouncing progression and provide variability around these stages.

Do not use enhancement activities (games) that require a high level of ball control before such abilities are reasonably acquired.

After the child has achieved a degree of proficiency with the dominant hand, provide practice with the nondominant side.

Stress eye focus on the ball during initial learning periods and work toward kinesthetic (that is, a sense of feel for where the ball is) awareness with the advanced child.

Skill Concepts Communicated to Children

Keep one's eyes on the ball.
Control the bounce with the fingers and wrist.
Push the ball slightly forward and downward.
Follow through.
Keep the level of the ball below the waist.

STRIKING

Movement Description

Striking is an action in which the hand(s) or an implement is used to give impetus to an object. As a skill, striking does not present well-defined

Movement Enhancement

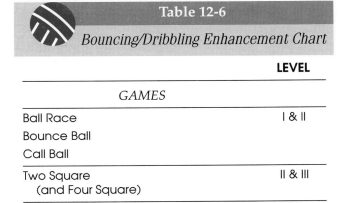

Table 12-6

Bouncing/Dribbling Enhancement Chart

	LEVEL
GAMES	
Ball Race	I & II
Bounce Ball	
Call Ball	
Two Square (and Four Square)	II & III
Bucket Ball	III
Wall Ball	

sequences. The child may be confronted with numerous striking situations that require the use of the hand(s), head, or various implements to hit stationary or moving objects (usually balls). Striking patterns may be influenced greatly by the size, weight, and length of the implement, as will the nature of the object struck. Kicking, also considered a striking task, is treated separately because of its importance as a fundamental skill.

Striking develops in much the same sequential order as throwing in terms of general age-level performance. This is dependent, however, upon movement opportunities and availability of developmentally appropriate equipment (that is, weight and size). This skill appears to start from the overarm motion, as in throwing, with the child facing the object and primarily utilizing the arms and hands. This method of striking an object is replaced with the underarm and most commonly used sidearm pattern (across a horizontal plane); however, the initial selection of pattern is highly dependent on the position of the object in space. By 3 years of age, the child can be observed using the sidearm striking motion, with one arm being the primary initiator of the movement. The more common employment of both arms, such as in batting, is generally not exhibited even at a minimal proficiency level until the child is 4 to 5 years of age.

Children who are given special assistance with equipment of appropriate weight and size tend to progress faster from striking in a vertical plane (that is, facing the object squarely, extending the forearms, striking downward) to the more effective motion predominating in a horizontal plane.

FIGURE 12-24

Elementary stage, one-arm striking.

ELEMENTARY ONE-ARM STRIKING PATTERN

This pattern is generally performed with the use of the preferred hand or implement. The child exhibiting an immature pattern will (if attempting to strike an object directly in front) utilize an overarm motion (Fig. 12-24).

The legs are usually stationary, or a forward step is presented with a unilateral (that is, same arm-leg) pattern. The trunk is bent forward slightly, and little if any trunk rotation is present.

MATURE ONE-ARM STRIKING PATTERN

Before contact is desired, weight is shifted to the back foot, while the trunk rotates approximately 45° to 90° to a cocked position. With the hand drawn back, force is delivered quickly as the weight shifts (forward), body rotates, and the arm moves horizontally to contact the object. Force is maximized as the child exhibits follow-through in the predetermined direction (Fig. 12-25).

TWO-ARMS (BATTING)

As with the immature one-arm pattern, initial attempts using both hands reveal a downward vertical swing (Fig. 12-26). The child faces the object squarely, bends forward at the trunk, and extends the forearms. Much of the force is delivered as the wrists are uncocked. As the skill develops, the child attempts to strike the object using a sidearm pattern. In the early attempts, the arms initiate most of the movement, for there is limited weight shift, hip and trunk rotation, and follow-through. The pelvis and trunk rotate as a unit, appearing to be a result of the forward arm motion rather than force initiated.

MATURE BATTING PATTERN

The child reveals characteristics of a mature pattern (Fig. 12-27) by initiating movement with a forward weight shift, rotation of the hips and trunk, followed by a smooth arm swing. The wrists are uncocked just before contact with the object.

In greater detail, the preparatory and executory phases of mature two-arm striking (horizontal) can be described (and used for assessment) as follows (Wickstrom, 1983):

1. Feet positioned approximately shoulder-width apart. Body position is perpendicular to the line of flight of the oncoming ball.
2. Trunk is rotated to the right (for right-handed batters); weight is shifted onto the right foot.
3. The lead elbow is held up and out from the body with the bat held off the shoulder. Striking arm moves back parallel to path of oncoming ball.
4. Eyes follow the flight of the ball until just before contact is made (visual tracking).

FIGURE 12-25

Mature stage, one-arm striking.

FIGURE 12-26
Elementary stage, batting.

FIGURE 12-27
Mature stage, batting.

5. Body weight shifted forward (onto opposite foot) in the direction of intended hit.
6. Hips and trunk rotated in direction of intended hit with the hips leading.
7. Arms move forward into contact and follow-through action.

Wickstrom (1983) indicates that although each striking skill (one-arm, two-arm variations) has its own unique characteristics, all contain a basic sequence of three movements: step–turn–swing. Those movements are described as follows:

1. Body weight is shifted in the direction of the intended hit while shoulders and arms are coiled in the opposite direction.
2. Hips and spine are rotated in rapid succession in the same direction as the weight shift.

3. Arm(s) swings around and forward in close succession with the other rotatory movements.

Although not described in this section, other striking variations utilized by children such as in volleyball-type activities also contain elements of the basic sequence described.

Movement Observation

Although young children may exhibit a proficient striking form, another developmental factor, *coincident timing*, especially of a moving object, may present difficulties in the performance outcome. Each striking task presents the child with a unique timing situation. Developmentally appropriate activities

	Successful	Needs Extra Practice	Comments
STATIONARY/PITCHED BALL (ONE-ARM)			
Side-stride foot position			
Rotation through hips and torso			
Arms moves horizontally			
Ball contacted opposite forward foot			
Path of swing elongated with follow-through			

Table 12-7

Checklist For Striking

are essential for outcome success. It is highly unlikely that a child under the age of seven could successfully strike (with bat) a ball thrown fast by another child of the same age. This acknowledgment by youth-sport administrators may be observed in the form of a sport modification called *T-Ball* (that is, the ball rests on a stand). Children can, however, acquire with some degree of movement and outcome proficiency most striking skills (especially with slow or stationary objects) if given the advantage of developmentally appropriate equipment and practice.

Evaluation checklists may be developed from basic sequence items described, and descriptive components from one- and two-arm patterns; see Table 12-7 for an example.

COMMON PROBLEMS

1. Failure to contact object (if speed of the object is within the perceptual capability of the child, failure to focus visually on the object is a probable cause). Another is lack of practice with timing. Have the child practice watching the object and timing the act; first from a stationary position (T-stand or ball on top of cone) and then suspended on a string;

2. Striking an object while standing with too narrow or too wide a base of support (approximately shoulder-width apart);

3. Rotating body too little; failure to rotate the body backward (twist the body away from the direction one plans to hit);

4. Keeping the elbow in too close to the body when arm action is involved (hold arms away from body, "wings up");

5. Striking a hard object with relaxed fingers and arm (if using hand only, think of the hand as a solid club head);

6. Failure to use sufficient backswing (the body should rotate approximately 90°, and the implement move through an arc of 180° before contact; bat should be held back during stance so less time is spent on backswing);

7. Failure to grip implement tightly (tighten-release-tighten grip for awareness);

8. Striking an object too far above (topping) or below, lifting its center of gravity (meet the ball squarely);

9. If striking a moving object, failure to get in line with it before contact (body weight should shift in the direction of the intended hit while shoulders and arms are coiled in the opposite direction; focus on ball and position the body appropriately prior to contact);

10. Failing to follow-through after the object has been contacted (move implement through the ball);

11. Lack of power (probable causes: facing incorrectly, poor weight shift, incomplete extension of forearms and wrists, weak grip, and improper contact with object).

Movement Variability

The diverse nature of striking requires the child to be familiar with several implements (varying in size and weight) in varying circumstances of object position and timing; therefore, variability in practice is essential for general striking competency. Such practice would allow the child opportunities to perform under a multitude of spatial, force, and timing conditions. Various forms of striking are fundamental to many primary movement activities, and they are used extensively in such advanced sports as volleyball, tennis, golf, racquetball, handball, baseball, and hockey.

SPATIAL

MOVEMENT-PATTERN VARIATIONS

Using one- and   vary foot placement:
  two-arm variations:
  overarm   shoulder width
  sidearm   narrow to wide
  underarm
  oblique (golf-type swing)
  backhand
Ball: strike while in:
  stationary   personal space
  swinging   moving
  vertical bounce
  moving toward

DIRECTIONS/PATHWAYS/LEVELS

Vary level: (ground to reach height) and position
  of object in space
Vary level of body while striking:
  lying
  sitting
  kneeling
  squatting
Strike from above, below, side, and straight forward.
Lean forward, backward, and sideward while
  striking.
Strike object to fly in different directions.

TIME

Striking: stationary object; swinging slow to fast
  an object moving toward slow to fast
  an object from various distances of origin

FORCE

Striking with: soft to hard impact
  light to heavy implements
  implements of varying sizes

ADDITIONAL MOVEMENT VARIATIONS

Strike: objects against wall
  objects over barriers (nets, ropes)
  objects to contact a target
Use of:
  either hand   beanbags
  large paddles (plastic preferred) balloons
  ping-pong paddles   foam balls
  racquetball rackets   whiffleballs
  tennis rackets   tennis balls
  badminton rackets   yarn balls
  plastic bats   racquetball balls
  plastic clubs (golf type)   ping-pong balls
  plastic hockey-type sticks   shuttlecocks

SUGGESTED GENERAL PROGRESSION

1. Strike a stationary ball placed on floor with hand (alternate hands).
2. Strike a ball being rolled back and forth between hands.
3. Strike a ground ball with hand(s) to a partner.
4. Strike a ball off batting tee (or cone) with hand(s).
5. Strike a suspended ball with hand.
6. Strike a balloon with hand(s) and lightweight implements.
7. Strike a suspended ball with implements (moving from short handle to long handle).
8. Strike a balloon back and forth with others.
9. Strike an object held in hand.
10. Strike a bounced ball first with the hand, then with lightweight racket.
11. Strike a stationary ball off tee with lightweight bat.
12. Strike a ball swinging suspended from a rope with hand, then with implement.
13. Strike an object on floor with club (hockey stick or pillo polo club).
14. Strike a thrown ball after it bounces once.
15. Strike a ball rebounding from a wall.
16. Strike a moving object on floor with hockey-type stick.
17. Using an implement, strike an underhand thrown ball with implement (for instance, a scoop).
18. Using an implement, strike an overarm thrown ball with implement.
19. Strike a self-tossed ball with an implement (fungo hitting).
20. Strike a moving object with implement while moving.

Teaching Hints

Before learning striking skills, the child must demonstrate the ability to track an object approaching from various angles.

Prior to actual striking (with an implement), the child should be given opportunities to hold a short implement and make pathways in the air at various levels and in various directions from the body. Free-swinging movements should be emphasized.

Extensive work with short streamers will help the child acquire the relaxed swing necessary for effective striking.

Imagery such as "the arm acting like a swinging gate" is encouraged.

Objects to be hit should range from large to small, light to heavy.

Light objects such as balloons, nerf balls, and beach balls will help allay fear of the ball.

Check frequently for proper grip.

Stress proper stance; use markers on ground or floor as reminders.

Encourage "floating elbows" away from the body.

Stress follow-through in initial instruction.

Skill Concepts Communicated to Children

The top hand should touch the bottom hand when using both arms to strike.

Keep the eyes on the ball right up to contact.

Shift the body weight from back to forward when beginning the swing.

The bat should only have to be moved forward when the decision is made to strike.

Arms and wrists are extended on impact with the object.

Allow the arms to continue swinging after impact (follow-through).

Follow-through is in the direction one wants the object to go.

The swing should be level—like a swinging gate.

Feet remain in contact with the ground when contacting the ball.

The bottom hand is the last hand to let go as the bat is dropped by the side.

REFERENCE

WICKSTROM, R. L. (1983). *Fundamental motor patterns* (3rd ed.). Philadelphia: Lea & Febiger.

Movement Enhancement

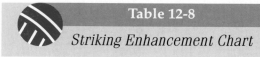

Table 12-8
Striking Enhancement Chart

GAMES	LEVEL
Beach Ball Nerfs Hot Rolls	I & II
Ball and Stick Relay Two Square Four Square Toppleball Call Ball Balloon/Feather Relay	II & III
Bat Ball Fistball Tetherball Flies Up Dodgeball	III

13

Movement-Awareness Themes

Movement Description

Body awareness is the impression the child has of one's own body parts and their capabilities for movement. Body awareness, sometimes called body image or body schema, is essential to efficient movement and is the foundation of total movement awareness. Development of a child's body schema involves (1) identifying and locating one's body parts, (2) understanding their relationship to each other, (3) knowing how to use the body parts, and (4) understanding their capabilities.

An important part of the young child's vocabulary should be the names of body parts. The child's movement experiences should enhance body-part recognition and allow body-part relationships to develop the body schema progressively.

The young child first learns to identify body parts by name and then is capable of understanding their relationship to each other, how they are used, and the variety of movement capabilities for each.

Although most five-year-olds can identify and locate the majority of their body parts, they should be evaluated on their ability to do so by means of a checklist before other body-awareness activities are attempted.

Movement Observation

A child's body-awareness capabilities can be evaluated by observing a game of "Simon Says" where the leader verbally asks the group to touch different body parts. Children should be able to locate the following body parts:

ears	mouth	nostrils	buttocks	fingers
eyebrows	chin	shoulders	arms	hands
eyelashes	cheeks	chest	elbows	wrists
hair	nose	back	thigh	waist
hips	stomach	forehead	knees	feet
toes	soles	heels	fingernails	scalp
ankles	trunk	spine	neck	earholes
lips	tongue	side	forearm	thumb
palm	knuckles	calves	legs	

Children can also be asked to use various parts of the body to do something, as in the following examples:

Stamp your feet	Twist your neck
Clap your hands	Nod your head
Wiggle your nose	Snap your fingers
Open your mouth	Shrug your shoulders
Bend your knees	Close your eyes
Bend your elbows	Wiggle your toes

The teacher can very effectively use a checklist to help identify children who have problems with the above activities.

COMMON PROBLEMS

1. Errors or slowness in response to touching and using the correct body parts (physically move the correct body part as a cue for the child);
2. Hesitancy in movements (give positive feedback immediately when beginning correct responses);
3. Inability to extend or contract different body parts fully (physically manipulate the body part for the child until the child gets the feel of the full range of motion);

Body awareness involves a knowledge of how the various body parts can move.

4. Inability to coordinate the movement of two body parts at the same time.

Movement Variability

Development of a solid body schema is essential to all motor-skill development. Body-awareness activities will serve to enhance the following:

1. A vocabulary and awareness of names and location of essential movement parts of the body;
2. The relationship of one body part to another;
3. The ability to move and be aware of the role and capabilities of body parts (understanding what and how we move);
4. The ability to contract and relax specific muscle groups, and feel differing amounts of force.

These are all essential components of meaningful movement and, as such, comprise the fundamental basis of all game, dance, and gymnastic activities.

COMBINING BODY AWARENESS WITH A MOTOR PROGRAM

SPATIAL

MOVEMENT-PATTERN VARIATIONS

Move as many different body parts as possible while:
    sitting
    standing
    lying on back, stomach
    lying on side
    kneeling

balancing on one, two, three, four, or five body parts.

Move one part at a time all around as many different places as it will reach, then move several different parts the same way.

Move different body parts while moving across the floor using different locomotors (walking, running, skipping, hopping; try some novel patterns too).

DIRECTIONS/PATHWAYS/LEVELS

Move individual body parts:
    forward
    backward
    sideways
    at a high or low level
    tracing different pathways in the air;
        try straight, curved, zigzag.
Move two different body parts at the same time:
    both in the same direction
    in opposite directions
    at the same level
    at different levels
    with the same pathway
    tracing different pathways
Move different body parts at one time in the same direction; in different directions.

TIME

Move individual body parts:
    fast
    slow
    accelerating their speed
    decelerating their speed

Children place body parts in relationship to hoops.

in time to musical accompaniment
to a drum beat.
Move two different body parts at:
the same speed
different speeds
Contract and extend different limbs quickly, then very slowly.

FORCE

Move individual body parts:
smoothly
roughly or jerkily
hard
soft
while airborne
with a stable base.
Move two or more body parts with the same force or different force.
Extend a body part farther then before.
Hold a body position longer and longer each time.

ADDITIONAL MOVEMENT VARIATIONS

1. Use flash cards to:
   a. Show figures with missing body parts; children move missing part.
   b. Show individual body parts; children identify and move shown body part or try to hide the diagrammed part. Children can try to touch shown body parts with a partner's same body part.
   c. show body in relation to walls or objects; children imitate the position shown on the card: O is a hoop, X is the child.
   d. Show the direction different body parts face in relation to objects and walls: O is a hoop, represents the direction the body part should point.
2. Using verbal commands, have children show body part relations to different walls. Use wall identifications like:
   a. pictures
   b. outstanding physical features
   c. outside objects

   d. geographic locations; north, south, east, and west.
   Examples:
   a. Sit with elbows pointing toward the number wall.
   b. Lie down with head toward the animal wall.
3. Move body parts in relation to other body parts; for example, move with elbows behind feet; move with feet higher than head.
4. Move an object in relation to body parts. Move beanbag around knee.
5. Move body in relation to an object. Move under the rope, feet first. Balance with hands inside and feet outside the hoop.
6. Move body in relation to an object and a wall. Balance with one foot inside the hoop pointing toward the north wall, and one hand inside the hoop pointing toward the east wall.
7. Play "one behind." Instructor touches body parts and children stay one behind by beginning to touch the same body part after the instructor has touched the second body part. Use verbal cues also.
8. Laterality (left-right recognition) may be enhanced by asking the children to move right- and left-side parts ("Lift your right leg," "Close your left eye"). Example: With children lying on their backs, ask them to move various parts, such as:
   Lift your legs
   Lift your arms
   Touch your elbow to your chest
   Lift your right arm
   Touch your ankles together
   Touch your knees
   How many parts can you lift off the floor at one time?
9. Paste one part of a body such as the eyes or nose (cut out from magazines) on paper and have the child draw the rest of the person. Draw incomplete faces or stick-people on paper to be mimeographed and distributed for completion.
10. State and ask the children to complete the following:

I comb my	(hair)	I snap my	(fingers)
I shrug with my	(shoulders)	I smell with my	(nose)
I squat with my	(hips, knees)	I throw with my	(hand, arm)
I kneel on my	(knees)	Food goes to my	(stomach)
I write with my	(fingers)	I hear with my	(ears)
I taste with my	(mouth, tongue)	I wave with my	(hand)
I clasp with my	(hands)	I walk with my	(feet)
I bend at the	(waist, elbow, knee)	I lick with my	(tongue)
I brush my	(hair, teeth)	I catch with my	(hands)
I sleep on my	(back, side)	I jump with my	(feet)
I kick with my	(feet)	I see with my	(eyes)
I chew with my	(teeth)	I wear earrings on my	(ears)
I wear a belt around my	(waist)		

11. Identify the following joints by name and ask the children to move them in as many positions as possible; then ask the following: How many ways can you move your neck? What movements can you make with your toes? Will your fingers move side to side? Up and down? Can you move your hips around in a circle shape? Which body part can be moved the least, your shoulders or waist? Show me how your knees move when you run, walk, skip, jump.

12. Cut pictures of people from magazines and then cut into smaller pieces and have the children reassemble. Paper dolls may be cut and reassembled also.

13. Have the children outline each other on large sheets of paper. Instruct them to color a designated part of the outlined body in a specific color.

14. Have the children make people using vegetables (carrots, corn, peppers), marshmallows, gum drops. Attach paper parts for the body with glue, or use toothpicks if preferred.

15. *Space*
    Make shadow designs using an opaque projector or other light source. The child stands with back to the light and casts a shadow on the screen or wall. Ask questions, or direct activities such as:
    a. "Move only your fingers, now your toes, your head, your elbows. Keep watching your shadow as you move them in many ways."
    b. "How many different ways can you make your arms bend? What part of your arm bends? (elbow) Can you make your arms bend at the elbow and then stretch them out again? Watch your shadow as you move." Same sequence, but with legs (bend at the knee), head (bend at the neck), feet (bend at the ankle), hands (bend at the wrist), body (bend at the hips).

    c. "Can you make a design with your shadow? What else can you make your shadow do? Can it jump up? Can it hop? Can it walk? Can it run in place? Can it leap? Can it skip?"
    d. "See what else your shadow can do."

16. *Human Sticks*
    Six children work together to make the shape (with their bodies) of a human stick figure lying on the floor. At first, parts may be assigned: "John, you be the head." "Sara, you be the right arm."
    Once the body is made, the parts may move. "Sara, you are the right arm. Can you make it stretch? How else can you make the arm move?" Do the same with other children. You may ask the children to respond to commands such as: "Bend the right leg. Raise the right arm. Bend the left arm."

17. *Body-Part Jumping*
    Draw a large stick figure of a person (use tape or chalk) on the floor for each child. The children are asked to hop or jump from one body part to another.
    a. "Can you stand on the head and jump to the neck?"
    b. "Can you jump from the neck to the right hand?"
    c. "Jump from the right hand and see if you can land on the waist."
    d. "Can you jump from the waist to the left hand?"
    e. "Now try jumping from the left hand to the left foot."
    f. "See if you can jump from the left foot to the right foot."
    g. "Stand on the right foot. Can you walk up the right leg, jump to the head, and then walk backwards to the left foot?"
    h. "Stand on the right hand. Can you hop on one foot to the left hand?" Many other variations are possible and should be used.
    i. "Stand in front of your stick figure. I will call out the name of a body part, and you run and stand on it as fast as you can. When I blow the whistle come back and stand in front of your stick figure ready for the next call. Head! Pause long enough to be sure that every child has responded correctly, then blow the whistle. "Leg!" And so forth.

18. *Build a Floor Body*
    Using beanbags, boxes, cans, hoops, balls, wands, ropes, build a body on the floor.
    a. "Can you build a human body using the boxes, hoops, cans, beanbags, and other materials you see here?"
    b. When the children have finished, ask them to study for several minutes the body they created. Afterward, take the different parts, stack them in a pile, and see how quickly they can put the body back together again. For added interest let the children give their body a name (Fred, Sam, Hazel, Lucy). "Let us take

'Sam' apart and stack him in a pile. When the whistle blows, see how fast you can put 'Sam' back together again."

19. *Space Walk*

Use a gym floor, sidewalk, or other open area on which patterns may be painted or taped. Directions may be painted beside each floor pattern, such as: hop right, hop left, and so forth. Children start at the beginning and follow the painted space walk. The space walk may include anything the teacher deems necessary. If directions are placed on movable cones instead of being painted on the sidewalk they can be changed periodically. Children unable to read may be talked-through the space walk by the teacher.

20. Discovering body awareness is a partnership. Divide the children into pairs. Explain that together they have 4 hands, 4 feet, 2 heads, 4 elbows, and so forth. Moving across and attached in any manner, the children must solve a series of movement problems. Examples:

a. "Can you (both) move across the mat with only three feet touching the mat?"

b. "With six parts of your body touching?"

c. "Can you move to the other side without touching the mat with your feet?"

d. "Show me a movement with one elbow touching the other's ankle."

e. "Move across knee to knee and try to be different from the others."

Mirror games enhance body awareness.

21. *Relationships with Mirror Activities*

Have a child stand in front of a full-length mirror. The other children give directions to locate body parts. The child can only look at his or her reflection in the mirror when touching the designated part with one hand. When he or she makes a mistake, the child giving the last instruction takes the mirror position.

Movement Enhancement

Table 13-1
Body Awareness Enhancement Chart

GAMES	LEVEL	GYMNASTICS	LEVEL	DANCE/RHYTHMS/RHYMES	LEVEL
Command Cards	I–III	Blow Up the Balloon	I & II	Tall and Small	I & II
Beanbags		Jack in the Box		Reach to the Skies	
Follow the Leader		Pogo Stick		Two Little	
				My hands	
Hoop Hop	I & II	Stand Up	II	This Is the Circle	
Charlie Over the Water		Turk Stand		that Is My Head	
Birds Have Feathers		Knee Walk		Make a Fist	
		Balance Stand		Rest Rhyme	
Hot Ball	II & III	Tripod		Hokey-Pokey	
Chinese Hurdle		Wring and Washrag		Looby Loo	
Skin the Snake		Tummy Balance		Did You Ever See	
Frozen Beanbag		Rocking Horse		a Lassie?	
Deep Freeze		Egg Sit		Heads, Shoulders,	
In the Creek		Balance Board Activities		Knees, and Toes	
		Human Bridge		Where Is Thumbkin?	
		Side Balance			
		People Pyramids		Seven Jumps	II
		Thread the Needle			

a. Repeat the above activity, but have the child use both hands to touch the body.

b. Repeat the above activities but indicate the right or left parts of the body in the mirror reflection.

Teaching Hints

Use physical manipulation and touching of different body parts to help children identify their parts.

Have children draw pictures of the movement of different body parts.

Use flash cards to cue children on body parts and positions.

The use of rhymes and songs help children remember their body parts.

Use a jointed doll to demonstrate where the body bends.

Skill Concepts Communicated to Children

All body parts have specific names.
One body part can lead a movement.
Muscles can contract and relax.
A contraction makes muscles shorter.

SPATIAL AWARENESS

Movement Description

The ability to orient oneself to the position of other people and objects in space and the knowledge of how much space the body occupies is fundamental to all movement. *Spatial awareness*, an extension of body awareness, relies on and may be considered a primary element of the visual modality. Children possessing this awareness are more likely to become adept at maneuvering themselves in a constantly changing environment without collisions. An extension of spatial awareness, namely *directional awareness*, which enables the child to perceive the dimension of objects in space and their position in relation to themselves, is considered to be an important readiness skill for both reading and writing as well as fundamental movement. Directional awareness and its components—*laterality* and *directionality*—are discussed in a separate section of this chapter because the development of this awareness is vitally important to both academic and movement success.

Movement Observation

The child's spatial awareness is developed to a degree upon entrance into kindergarten; however, a heightened awareness is essential to success in the school environment. Children should exhibit a knowledge of how much space their bodies occupy, an internal awareness of left and right, the ability to move their bodies into general space without collisions, and the ability to locate objects in space in relation to themselves and other objects. The key to spatial awareness is developing a keen visual perception of the position of objects in space in relation to oneself and other objects.

The development of spatial awareness occurs in two phases; thus evaluation of this awareness should also be divided into two parts. The child is first able to locate objects in relation to his or her own body position in space (*egocentric localization*). This ability can be observed by positioning the child in relation to an object in space. A school desk, a chair, or a bench is a good object to use as these provide a full range of relationship possibilities. The child should demonstrate the following body-position relationships:

over	near to
under	far from
beside	around
in front of	across and between
behind	(two desks or objects)

The second phase, *objective localization*, is the ability to locate two or more objects in relation to each other and independent of oneself. The child demonstrates the development of this awareness by positioning two different objects in space and observing the following relationships of the objects to each other:

behind	under
next to	between
close to	in front of
far from	inside of
over	outside of

Two balls of different sizes may be used or any two different objects of choice. The use of a hoop or box as one object provides for the inside-outside projection to be demonstrated. Again, when observing these two phases of development the teacher would do well to maintain a checklist (see Chapter 8, Evaluation) of each relationship to keep track of when the child achieves the desired response.

Generally, children exhibiting poor spatial orientation have difficulty judging position in space, estimating distance, knowing the dimensions (coordinates) of space, and perceiving relationships between objects.

COMMON PROBLEMS

1. Errors or slowness in positioning oneself or an object (physically position the child or object so that the child may better visualize the relationship required);

2. Difficulty in judging distance from a target (person or object) from self;

3. Clumsiness in movement or collisions with others and objects in space (check visual acuity and reinforce movement without collisions);

4. Lack of understanding of the relationship possibilities (demonstrate the various terms).

Movement Variability

A good understanding of spatial relationships is fundamental to all meaningful movement and is important in the acquisition of academic skills. Spatial awareness activities will reinforce the following:

1. The ability to move in general space without collisions.
2. An understanding of how much space one's body occupies.
3. The ability to locate objects in space in relationship to oneself and other objects.

Without the development of this awareness, children's movements will appear clumsy and awkward as they attempt to move through space.

COMBINING SPATIAL AWARENESS WITH A MOTOR PROGRAM

SPATIAL

Explain the difference between *personal* and *general space*. A hoop can be used to demonstrate this when stationary; the area inside the rim and one or two steps outside is one's personal space; if the hoop is rolled over the floor, then it is in general space.

In general space:
Stand with front toward, back, side, and other side of teacher.
Lie on back, stomach, side, and other side.
Make the body:
tall—small
wide—narrow
curved—stretched
twisted—straight

Move into general space using various locomotor patterns; move:

forwards	diagonally
backwards	following a curved, straight, or
sideways	zigzagged path

Move to something near; far.
Move to something larger or smaller.
Walk the outline of various geometric shapes: circle, square, triangle, and so forth.
Roll across a mat and observe how much space the body occupies.
Try this with body narrow, then wide, and observe the difference.
Place foot in one spot and stretch the body as far as it will go—forward, backward, sideward, and upward.

TIME

Move slowly and quickly through space, staying as far and close from everyone as possible.
Vary the speed (by accelerating then decelerating) through space without collisions; make quick changes in direction on signal, then try changing in slow motion.

Developing an understanding of symmetry.

FORCE

Cross the room taking first large steps, then small. Estimate the least number of steps necessary to cross the room.

Step very lightly or forcefully.

ADDITIONAL MOVEMENT VARIATIONS

1. In the classroom or gym, walk carefully among desks, chairs, or cones without touching the objects. Use different locomotors. Move fast, then slow, and change directions, levels, and pathways periodically.

2. Set out various-sized objects to step *over* (boxes, chairs, balls, hoops, cones, milk cartons, others).

3. Set out objects at various heights to go *under*.

4. Design obstacle courses using tunnels, chairs, cones, ladders, boxes, and other objects that challenge the child to adjust to a variety of objects in space. Allow children to design their own obstacle courses.

5. Set out balls or blocks of various sizes at various points in the play space. Direct children to:

   walk to the farthest small ball,
   walk to the closest large ball,
   run to the nearest medium-sized ball, and so forth.
   Vary the locomotor pattern used.

6. Line up the entire class in a straight line, shoulder to shoulder, then have children spread out to arm's length apart. Do this also in a square or circle figure.

7. With a ladder flat on the floor:
   Move forward between the rungs; backward.
   Creep on hands and knees between the rungs.
   Jump, hop, or run between the rungs. Go over two at a time.
   Bounce a ball between the rungs.
   Toss a beanbag back and forth between stepping between the rungs.
   Walk on the rungs or sides of the ladder. Go forward, backwards, and sideways.
   Place the ladder on its side. Creep in and out of the space going forward and backward.

8. Using a hoop flat on the floor:
   Move in and out of it going forward, backward, and sideways. Find as many different ways of doing this as possible.
   Have a partner hold the hoop on edge or flat off the ground and explore different ways of going in and out of the middle.
   Roll the hoop and go over it or through it before it stops rolling.

9. With a partner:
   Stand: side by side,
   facing each other,
   back to back.
   Move about the room, maintaining this relationship with the partner.
   Move away from the partner; now toward the partner.
   Move far from and close to the partner.
   Walk around the partner.
   Have the partner lie on the floor and then step over and into the spaces formed by the body parts.

Movement Enhancement

Table 13-2
Spatial Awareness Enhancement Chart

	LEVEL		LEVEL		LEVEL
GAMES		Jump the Shot	II & III	Chimes of Dunkirk	
		Over the Brook		The Muffin Man	
Follow the Leader	I–III	Frog in the Pond		Turn the Glasses Over	
Hopscotch Games		In the Creek			
		Islands		Children's Polka	II
Brownies and Fairies	I & II	Rattlesnake		(Kinder polka)	
Hoop Hop		Man From Mars		Round and Round	
Rescue Relay		Cut the Pie		the Village	
Cat and Rat				Seven Jumps	
Charlie Over the Water		*DANCE/RHYTHMS/RHYMES*		Crested Hen	
Gardener and Scamp				Greensleeves	
Seven Dwarfs		Bluebird	I & II	Lummi Sticks	
Squirrels and Trees		Loobie Loo		Grand March	
Jet Pilot		Did You Ever See		Skip to My Lou	
		a Lassie?			
Eyeglasses	II & III	Farmer in the Dell			
		Hokey-Pokey			

Have the partner make a shape and go under it. Explore different ways of doing this.

10. Jump rope in place, then move across the floor (see Chapter 9 for ideas on jump-rope techniques).

11. Gymnastic (and jumping) activities (see Vestibular Awareness section in this chapter for more ideas).

12. Place a rope on the floor in different directions and then go over it in various ways.

Teaching Hints

Use a variety of objects of different shapes and sizes when schema is being developed.

Use flash cards to show the various relationship variations.

Obstacle courses should provide variety in spacing of objects as well as size and shape of objects to maneuver in and out of.

Have children trace their body shape and then observe or measure how much space they occupy.

Skill Concepts Communicated to Children

The body can be maneuvered through space by altering its size, shape, direction of travel, and level.

The body has certain relationships with other people and objects according to its location in space.

An understanding of the following terms:

near	around	below
far	center	between
close	in front	in
over	behind	out
under	above	

DIRECTIONAL AWARENESS

Movement Description

Closely associated with body and spatial perception is the awareness of the body with regard to location and direction. *Directional awareness* consists of two awareness components: laterality and directionality.

Laterality is defined as an internal awareness that the body has a left and right side. In the hierarchy of awareness development, body awareness is thought to emerge first, followed by the emergence of laterality. Laterality is also thought to be a basic prerequisite for the subsequent emergence of directionality.

Directionality is the external projection of laterality. This component of the awareness gives dimension to space. A child possessing good directionality is capable of conceptualizing left-right, up-down, front-back, and various combinations.

Catching over the shoulder is an advanced directional-awareness task.

Movement Observation

Children with a good sense of laterality do not need to rely on cues such as a ribbon or watch around their wrist or a ring on their finger to provide information about left and right. Without a fully established awareness, children may, in addition to movement difficulties, encounter laterality problems in discriminating between various letters of the alphabet (for example, b, d, p, q).

Although it is not unusual for the 4- and 5-year-old to experience confusion in direction, teachers should be concerned for the older child who consistently exhibits such difficulties.

The following signs are easily recognizable by the teacher and may indicate a deficiency in a child's directional awareness:

1. General difficulty with responding to instructions emphasizing direction (conceptualizing and producing a motor program);

2. Inability to shift weight to maintain balance when jumping, hopping, or leaping;

3. Difficulty in using feet alternately;

4. Difficulty in maintaining rhythm while performing locomotor skills.

Movement Variability

It is through movement experiences that the child has the opportunity to conceptualize and respond to directional information. Both laterality and directionality give dimension to space and facilitate the child's determination of where he or she is in relation to other phenomena in the environment. A variety of movement experiences is essential to enable the child to develop a strong schema that reflects a diverse conceptual foundation.

COMBINING DIRECTIONAL AWARENESS WITH A MOTOR PROGRAM

SPATIAL

A variety of locomotor, nonlocomotor, and manipulative-skill movement activities should be performed that emphasize the following aspects of directional awareness:

left-right	over-under-around
up-down	clockwise-counterclockwise
front-back	curved
forward-backward	zigzag
sideward-diagonally	

TIME AND FORCE

Movement experiences incorporating diversity in the spatial dimensions just mentioned may also be enhanced through movements that vary from slow to fast (that is, object and person), through musical accompaniment, and through varying levels of force production (weak to strong).

EXAMPLES OF GENERAL MOVEMENT EXPERIENCES

Using a finger, point as directed; to the right, left; in front, in back, behind, to the side, to the top and bottom (of objects), over your shoulder, between your legs. With the eyes closed, point to objects in the gym, the door, the stage, the clock.

Move below, over, under, and between objects in the gym (chairs, beams).

Move body parts in a specific direction. Put your arms in back of you; put your hands in front of you; put your arms in back of the same side; point both of your hands to one side; put your arms between your legs; put your fingers under your feet; put your elbow below your hips; put your feet over your head.

Using a designated locomotor skill, move to specific points in the area: the nearest large ball, the nearest small ball, the farthest small ball, the farthest large ball.

Relationships (people): Step over (*Johnny*); stand near (*Sally*); stand between (*Joe*) and (*Pat*); touch another child's right hand; touch another child's left ear; touch another child's right shoulder; touch another child's left knee; touch another child's right foot.

While using hoops, beanbags, or carpet squares, stop in the direction instructed.

Move through an obstacle course that has written and/or visual directional instructions.

As the teacher presents a flash card indicating directional term or arrow, respond with a series of movements in that direction.

Using hoops, move around, inside, over, through, and in and out.

Place a number of parts inside the hoop (two or three).

Move on scooter boards through an obstacle course (consisting of cans, cartons, chairs, other objects).

Follow lines or maps drawn on the gym floor.

Using a ladder lying flat, follow directional cues such as, walk *between* or *on* the rungs; walk *forward*, *backward*; step *over*; walk *beside*; lead with the foot, and so forth.

Walk in different directions with coffee-can stilts.

European rhythmic activities:

Run in circular formation. On signal, change places with the student opposite.

When the tamborine sounds, run away from the circle and scatter in all directions; on the second signal, return to the circle.

On signal, run in clockwise, circular formation while circling the right hand above the head (repeat activity counterclockwise with left hand circling).

On signal, run backward in circular formation; on signal, run toward the center in four steps, turn around in place four steps, run away from the circle in four steps, and continue to run in clockwise, circular formation. Repeat sequence each time new signal is given.

Angels in the Snow (lying on backs):

Slide both arms along the floor and touch hands together overhead.

Slide both legs apart as far as possible.

Slide arms and legs along the floor at the same time.

Move the left arm overhead.

Move the right leg to the side.

Move the left arm overhead and the right leg to the side at the same time.

Relationships (partner):

Move around your partner to the right; to the left.

Move over your partner.

Elementary directionality task.

Move under your partner.

Move under some of your partner's body parts.

Touch the top of your partner; the bottom.

Stand behind your partner; beside; in front of.

Touch the body parts of your partner that the teacher names (left wrist, right hip).

Beanbag activities:

Hold the beanbag in the right hand; the left hand.

Place the bag on the left shoulder; the right shoulder.

Place it on the lowest part of the body; the highest part.

Try to place the beanbag on the floor in front; in the back.

Move around the beanbag at a low level.

Move over the beanbag at a high level.

Activities with balls:

Bounce with the right hand; the left; with both hands.

Bounce the ball twice with the right hand; twice with both hands, and twice with the left hand and continue.

Change directions while bouncing the ball.

While bouncing the ball, change hands.

Chalkboard activities:

Draw vertical and horizontal lines as directed; up, down, right, left.

Twist board activities:

Twist, moving arms in the direction given; for example, both to one side; one forward, one back; one up, the other back making clockwise and counterclockwise movements.

Teaching Hints

Ask children to repeat directional terms practiced (Level I).

Use a variety of equipment to reinforce directional concepts (scooters, cones, hoops, tape, cans, cartons, chairs, balls).

Emphasize directional terms with locomotor movements (especially during skill development, games, and dance activities).

Skill Concepts Communicated to Children

The body can move through space in several directions.

An understanding of the following terms:

up/down	clockwise/counterclockwise
forward/backward	diagonal
right/left (sideways)	straight/curved/zigzag

VESTIBULAR AWARENESS (BALANCE)

Movement Description

The ability of the child to maintain body position while counteracting the force of gravity is *balance*. Proficiency in balance requires the child to maintain control of the body both in *stillness*, as in maintaining held positions, (standing on one foot or performing a head stand), and in *motion*, as in locomotor, nonlocomotor, and manipulative skills. Both static balance and dynamic balance are essential to all meaningful movement.

Movement Enhancement

Table 13-3

Directional Awareness Enhancement Chart

GAMES	LEVEL		LEVEL	DANCE/RHYTHMS/RHYMES	LEVEL
		Mousetrap	II & III		
		Cat and Rat			
Command Cards	I–III	Beater Goes Round		Jack in the Box	I & II
Follow the Leader		Ship Wreck		Turn the Glasses Over	
		Indian Running		Chimes of Dunkirk	
Back to Back	I & II	Go Tag		The Muffin Man	
Partner Tag		Islands		Loobie Loo	
Scarecrows and Cranes		Here to There		Hokey-Pokey	
Squirrels in the Trees		Guard the Toys		Jack in the Box	
Catch the Witch		Hop Tag		Right Hand, Left Hand	
Cat and Rat		In and Out			
Hot Ball				Orchestra Leader	II
Birds and Cats		Mousetrap	III	Round and Round	
Cars		Exchange Dodgeball		the Village	
		Roll Dodgeball		Greensleeves	
Race Around the Bases	II & III	Balance Dodgeball		Skip to My Lou	

FIGURE 13-1
Static balance.

Static balance is generally accomplished before *dynamic balance*. A young child learns to stand unassisted before attempting to take his or her first steps. Consequently, children need to experiment with a variety of held positions (Fig. 13-1) before they can be expected to try different body positions in motion (Fig. 13-2). For example, a child who cannot balance on two hands and one foot could not be expected to experience success with the lame-dog walk.

A child's stability is greatly influenced by muscular control, fitness of the inner ear, ability to concentrate, and by past experience with balancing activities. It is necessary for the child to sense a change in the relationships of the body parts and then to compensate rapidly and precisely for those changes in order to maintain balance.

Movements that indicate an ability to compensate for changes in body-weight distributions include:

1. Raising of both arms to catch balance;
2. Bending of knees or lowering of whole body to maintain balance;
3. Using stepping patterns where the weight is transferred from one foot to another without hesitancy along a straight line or balance board.

Movement Observation

Keen observation of both static and dynamic balance will ensure maximum motor development of these two perceptual motor abilities. Research indicates that evaluation of dynamic balance can best be accomplished by observing children moving on a balance beam or a line on the floor that is approximately 6 cm wide x 2.5 m long (10 cm high if off the ground). Static balance can be evaluated by timing and observing children standing on a balance stick 1≤ x 1≤ x 12≤ with the foot placed lengthwise on the long axis.

FIGURE 13-2
Dynamic balance.

COMMON PROBLEMS

STATIC BALANCE

1. Failure to use arms to catch balance (extend arms out to the side to aid in balancing);
2. Consistent use of only one arm or one side to regulate body weight (stress the use of both sides by practicing bending to one side then the other).

DYNAMIC BALANCE

1. Failure to use arms and consistent use of only one arm or one side (see above for static balance);
2. Need to walk or run very fast to maintain balance (slow down walk and focus eyes at the end of the beam);
3. Being unable to use a step-like pattern and constantly leading with the same foot when moving forward (stress stepping pattern on a line on the floor first);
4. Looking down at the feet (eyes should focus up or at the end of a balance beam);
5. Hesitancy and looking backward to maintain balance (stress good straight posture and body weight over the center of gravity while moving slowly at first).

Movement Variability

The fundamental stability skills of infants are for the most part maturationally determined. Control of the head, neck, and trunk, as well as sitting and standing, is usually accomplished when the child develops sufficient strength. However, development of the basic stability necessary to accomplish locomotor, nonlocomotor, and manipulative skills requires a variety of experiences and opportunities to explore both static and dynamic balancing activities on and off equipment.

Training should take place through several kinds of balance tasks including those in which some kind of visual stress is imposed (for instance, an eyes-closed balance task), in tasks where the child is asked to move and maintain equilibrium (beam walking), as well as in activities in which the child's center of mass remains relatively fixed (static balances of various sorts).

Balancing may be made increasingly difficult for a child by imposing stresses of several kinds.

1. The area on which the child is balancing may be made smaller (decrease the width of the balance beam).
2. Some kinds of visual stress may be imposed, ranging from the easiest (watch a stable point), through increasingly difficult (specific instructions about what should be done with the eyes) to requiring the child watch a moving point that moves from left to right across the line or beam which the child is attempting to walk.
3. The platform on which the child is asked to balance may be made increasingly unstable. An example would be to ask the child to balance on a small board with some kind of runner or knob underneath it.
4. In static balances, the child's base of support may be decreased or the center or mass may be raised, that is, "Stand on one foot ... lift your arms (or knee) higher."

SPATIAL

MOVEMENT-PATTERN VARIATIONS

Balance on:
   one body part; foot, knee, seat, shoulders, stomach;
   two body parts; feet, hand and foot, knees, knee and hand, seat and foot;
   three body parts; 2 feet-1 hand, 2 hands-1 foot, 1 knee-2 elbows, and so forth;
   four body parts;
   five body parts;
   six body parts.
Change base of support from wide to narrow.
Move on the above combinations of body parts.
Change the body shape while balanced on different parts; use curled, stretched, and twisted shapes.

DIRECTIONS/PATHWAYS/LEVELS

While balanced on different body parts, move another:
   forward
   backward
   left to right (sideways)
   in a circular, zigzag, or straight pathway in the air.
Balance on different parts at high, medium, or low level.
While moving on different body parts and combinations, go:

   forward
   backward
   sideways
   in a zigzag, straight, or curved path.

TIME

Change balance shapes or move with different body parts on the floor:
   quickly
   slowly
   accelerating
   decelerating
   evenly
   jerkily
   on a drum beat
   hold one position long, one short, and one medium.

FORCE

Take a body shape that is strong- or weak-looking.
Feel the force of the muscles when holding positions for longer and longer periods of time.
Move into different balances very slowly then quickly.

ADDITIONAL MOVEMENT VARIATIONS

Stability can be greatly enhanced by balancing and moving on various equipment. This section will include a progression of problems for each piece of stability equipment.

BALANCE BEAM

(About 4 inches wide; a tape line on the floor may be used.)

1. Walk forward, sideways, and backward.
2. Balance on different body parts and move from one balance to another without falling off.
3. Try turning around at different levels.

4. Use different locomotors—run, jump, hop, leap, and skip along beam.
5. Carry different objects as you move: beanbags, hoops, wands, balls.
6. Balance beanbags on different body parts.
7. Pick up objects placed on beam as you move along it.
8. Step over different objects on the beam: hoops, beanbags, blocks. Vary the height and distance between objects.
9. Go under obstacles placed over the beam.
10. Manipulate objects as you move along the beam; toss and catch a ball, bounce it on the floor, move it around your body and so forth.
11. Play follow the leader.
12. Find different ways to get on and off the beam.

TIRES

(Old truck and car tires work well. Place them flat on the ground.)

1. How many ways can you move around the tire?
2. Go over the tire; use the center as you go over; first put one foot in.
3. Now try both feet.
4. Bounce on the tire.
5. Bounce off and on in different directions.
6. Place tires in a sequence flat on the ground and move across without touching the ground, without touching the tires, or by stepping only in the middle of each tire. Use different locomotor patterns.

BALANCE BOARD—ROCKER BOARD

1. Balance on your feet; use a wide base, then a narrow base.
2. Balance on different body parts and different combinations, maintaining your balance as you change positions.
3. Balance with a partner; try to change levels and still stay on.
4. Manipulate different objects; toss and catch a beanbag to yourself, then to someone else; bounce a ball around you, use a hula hoop.
5. Pick up objects on your board while balancing.

TRAMPOLINE

Creative use of the trampoline* can result in the development of endurance, coordination, balance, and self-confidence. Rebound stunts like the knee drop, seat drop, and front drop should be reserved for the older child. Trampoline activities should be organized for small groups so that there is maximum opportunity for turns, and a few safety rules need to be established. To ensure safe use of the trampoline, children should (1) jump alone and (2) crawl onto and off of the trampoline bed.

The following problem variations are designed to enhance the development of the child's overall balance.

1. Crawl around the bed of the trampoline.
2. Walk on the bed forwards, sideways, and backwards.
3. Roll on the bed; log-roll then try forward rolls, backward rolls, egg rolls.
4. Bounce with two feet in the middle of the bed, feet close then apart.
5. Teacher holds a 4-foot pole or stick across and close to the bed. The child first steps over the stick then jumps over it. The stick can be raised or lowered as the child desires.
6. Jump making quarter turns, half turns.
7. Hop on alternating feet.
8. Find different ways to hold the arms while jumping; try moving them.
9. Find different ways to hold and move the head and jump.
10. Touch different body parts while jumping.
11. Try doing some jumping jacks.
12. Grasp different objects while jumping: beanbags, hoops, balls. Try to toss and catch these while jumping.
13. Try jumping rope or other rope maneuvers while jumping.
14. Count out loud the number of times one can jump.
15. Try jumping to different jump-rope songs and chants.
16. Jump and face different positions on a compass or a clock.
17. Play Simon Says and have children face different directions on command.
18. Jump with light weights on hands or ankles.

LADDER

(Horizontal on the floor or at a slight incline.)

1. Cross on hands and feet or knees front first, then back first.
2. Cross using just the feet forward, backwards, and sideways.
3. Step, jump, or leap between the rungs only.
4. Use only the side rails to cross; vary directions.
5. Carry different objects while traveling across.
6. Manipulate different objects when crossing.
7. Try to pass a partner without losing balance.

---

*Note: Close supervision by the teacher is important when using the trampoline.

HOOPS, WANDS, OR ROPES

(These can be laid on the floor.)

1. Walk along your equipment forward, backward, and sideways.
2. Change the shape of the rope and travel on it.
3. Use different body parts as you travel on your obstacle.
4. Make interesting bridges over your obstacle by using different body parts.
5. Combine with a partner to bridge both your obstacles.

BEANBAGS

1. How long can you balance on a beanbag? Try eyes closed, on one foot.
2. Make bridges over a beanbag.
3. Balance your beanbag on different body parts as you find different balance positions.
4. Balance your beanbag on different parts as you move through space with different locomotor patterns. Create your own locomotors.

PARTNERS

(Use a mat underneath.)

1. How many ways can you balance on a partner when the partner's base is:
   a. hands and knees* (Fig. 13-3)
   b. back-lying (Fig. 13-4)
   c. upright—knees bent and feet spread wide (Fig. 13-5)?

OBSTACLE COURSE

How many ways can you move over the equipment without losing your balance? (See Fig. 13-6.)

Teaching Hints

Have children experiment with different arm positions as they attempt to balance.

Practice balance activities on a line on the floor before going on a balance beam.

Hold up numbers for the child to identify as he or she moves forward and/or backward to encourage proper focus.

Start activities at a lower level and progress to high levels as skill improves.

You may offer a hand to assist in balance each time, thus encouraging the child to grasp less tightly.

Stress squeezing muscles to maintain held positions for longer periods of time.

*Note: Weight should be placed only over the hips or shoulders, never on the small of the back.

FIGURE 13-3
Hands and knees base.

FIGURE 13-4
Back-lying base.

FIGURE 13-5
Upright base.

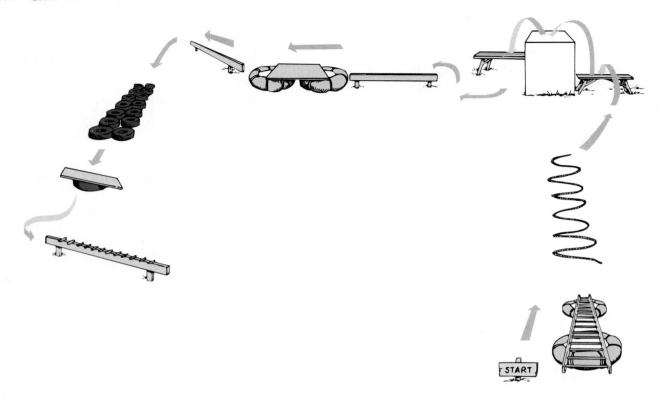

FIGURE 13-6

Skill Concepts Communicated to Children

Look at something out in front of you as you balance.

Extending the arms out to the sides will help maintain balance.

When walking on a beam, alternate the feet as you go.

If you lower your body or widen your base you will balance better.

Balancing the body in different positions is like balancing a scale: the body parts must be equal on both sides of the center.

EYE-HAND, EYE-FOOT COORDINATION

Movement Description

As a group, rhythmic awareness, eye-hand coordination, and eye-foot coordination represent the teaching themes related to the development of temporal awareness. As the child's spatial world is developing, so is the time structure that is responsible for the coordinated interaction of various muscular and sensory components.

Visual-motor coordination, the ability to coordinate effectively the hand and/or feet with that which is perceived visually, begins very early in a child's life.

Through appropriate movement opportunities this ability develops into the gross– and fine-motor control of eye-hand and eye-foot movements that are the end products of synchrony, rhythm, and sequence. The development of eye-hand and eye–foot efficiency demonstrates the presence of an established time structure within the body of the child. This perceptual process of seeing a stimulus and effectively responding with the hands and/or feet encompasses more than the fundamental manipulative skills of throwing, catching, volleying, striking, bouncing, and kicking that are covered in separate skill chapters. This ability is the basis upon which the fundamental skills mentioned are effectively performed; therefore its inclusion into the curriculum for children is vital.

Eye-hand coordination as described in this chapter is the perceptual motor awareness that enables the child effectively to touch, grasp, release, flick, and tap objects with the hands. Effective *eye-foot coordination* enables the child to step in specific patterns and maneuver objects with the feet and toes.

Movement Observation

The child's eye-hand and eye-foot coordination, like other controlled movements, develops from the midline of the body to the periphery. Therefore gross movements involving mostly the shoulder become more refined as the elbow, wrist, and hand develop strength and coordination. By seven years of age the

Movement Enhancement

Table 13-4
Balance Enhancement Chart

LEVEL		LEVEL		LEVEL	
GAMES		Hand Wrestling		Spanker	
Command Cards	I–III	Stand-Up		Stiff Knee Pick-up	
Follow the Leader		Rocker		Mule Kick	
Whistle Stop		Rooster Fight		Bent Knee Hop	
		Wheel Barrow		Jump Foot	
Hoop Hop	I & II	Row Boat		Frog Dance	
Kneeling Tag		People Pyramids		Frog Stand	
		Mule Kick		Head Stand	
Balance Dodgeball	II & III	Rabbit Jump		Hand Stand	
Over the Brook		Seal Crawl		Forearm Balance	
Deep Freeze		Forward Roll		Thigh Balance	
Frozen Bag Relay		Ankle Walk		Angel Balance	
Islands		Step Over the Wand		Sitting Balance	
Spoon and Ball Relay		Bear Walk		Three-Man Mount	
Hopscotch Games		Balance Stand		Backward Roll	
Freeze Ball		Inch Worm		Backward Extension Roll	
In the Creek		Dog Run		Eskimo Roll	
Kangaroo Relay		Duck Walk		Cartwheel	
Animal Walk Relay		Egg Roll			
GYMNASTICS		Egg Sit		**RHYTHMS AND DANCE**	
Lame-Dog Walk	I & II	Heel Slap		Hokey-Pokey	I & II
Frog Jump		Kangaroo Jump		Mulberry Bush	
Animal Walk Obstacle Course		Thread the Needle		Loobie Loo	
Leap Frog		Turk Stand			
Human Ball		Tripod		Round & Round the Village	II
Log Roll		Double Knee Balance		Jump Jim Joe	
Measuring Worm		Stoop and Stretch		Limbo	
Wring the Washrag		Crane Dive		Seven Jumps	
Crab Walk	II	Cork Screw		Hora	
Frog Squat		Coffee Grinder		Zip Code 001	
Bouncing Ball		Twister		Cat's Meow	
Churn the Butter		Blind Touch			
Double Walk		Tummy Balance			
		Tightrope Walking			
		Push-ups			
		Single Squat			
		Sit-Up			

child (with a varied activity background) can be observed manipulating with moderate levels of success objects such as jacks, marbles, and puzzles.

Children performing at the elementary stage (Fig. 13-7) of eye-hand coordination may be observed making very deliberate movements with their hands toward objects they wish to touch or grasp. When they release an object there is a tendency to release too early or too late. Attempts at tapping or flicking objects result in more of a punching movement due to their lack of synchrony of the body parts involved. At the less-than-mature stages of eye-foot control, children attempting to step in specific patterns (for example, stepping on the rungs of a ladder resting flat on the floor) will exhibit great concentration and deliberate movement with their feet. As a child's eye-hand and eye-foot coordination matures, the movements will become more reflexive.

Children with poor eye-hand and eye-foot coordination are going to exhibit performance problems with those activities in which they must visually track and manipulate either an object or themselves in response. While the gross-motor manipulative skills (striking, kicking, throwing, catching, bouncing) and fine-motor movements (sorting, rhythm sticks, tracing, tapping) are most frequently associated with these abilities, other common movement skills such as jumping, walking, running, and climbing depend

FIGURE 13-7
Children's movement at the elementary stage requires considerable concentration.

upon an adequate visual-motor efficiency. A lack of coordination between visual information and motor response may account for many of the problems associated with poor performance. The difficulties encountered by the child frequently stem from a general integration, which may be the basis for immature performance across a number of fundamental skills, such as those previously mentioned.

COMMON PROBLEMS

Examples of general visual-motor (that is, eye-hand and eye-foot coordination) integration problems are:

1. Difficulty in keeping eyes on the ball as it crosses midline of the body;
2. Moves head instead of eyes;
3. Inability to touch or hit ball as it moves;
4. Difficulty in receiving objects;
5. Reaching out for ball and moving head back; closing eyes as ball approaches;
6. Hesitancy in deciding which foot to use to step; always trying to see where to step;
7. While walking across ladders or objects on floor, the child has problems adjusting length of step to varying distances.

Movement Variability

Visual-motor efficiency, being the essential component in the majority of gross– and fine-motor-skill proficiency, demands a diversified movement experience foundation. Because of its importance to performance, programming should begin early in the child's education before gross-motor manipulative skill movement-pattern concentration. Eye-hand and eye-foot coordination experiences should include (but certainly not be limited to) the commonly accepted gross-visual-

motor skills of throwing, catching, kicking, and striking. Climbing horizontal and vertical ladders, walking on rungs of a ladder placed flat on the ground, tagging peers in games, tapping musical instruments, stepping in and out of hoops, and playing hop-scotch—all enable the child to experience variability of practice that will result in an enhanced general eye-hand and eye-foot coordination. With a strong schema the child can concentrate on movement-pattern proficiency and be more likely to acquire the skills needed for advanced activities such as juggling, combatives, select folk dances (for example, tinikling), and frisbee. With a background of varied experiences, the child is also equipped to respond effectively to the constantly changing sport-skills environment.

The authors would like to emphasize that the experiences suggested for schema enhancement stress the visual-motor component of performance. This entails the use of a focal point; for example, throwing at a target, hopping from square to square, and stepping (walking) between the rungs of a ladder.

SPATIAL

Movement-pattern variability with movement variations in different directions and at low to high levels from the ground should include:

GROSS-MOTOR MANIPULATIVE SKILLS

Rolling balls to a designated target (bottles, bowling pins);
Throwing/tossing objects to a designated target (picture, bucket, hoop);
Catching (with hands, scoops) objects of various sizes (balls, beanbags, rings);
Striking objects of various sizes (balloons, drums, balls) with the hand(s) and implements (rackets, paddles, bats, sticks);
Ball bouncing using various ball sizes;
Grasping (climbing ladders, poles, ropes);
Clapping.

Combining Eye-Hand Coordination With a Motor Program

JUGGLING

The following progressions are suggested in the teaching of juggling:

1. Practice tossing and catching one object—using the dominant hand, then the nondominant hand—until consistency of toss height is achieved. Children should quietly chant "toss, catch" during this stage.

2. Using an object in each hand, practice tossing and catching. Children quietly chant "toss, catch"—(dominant hand); "toss, catch"—(nondominant hand). Repeat this unilateral exercise until toss height and rhythm have been established.

3. Using two objects, toss and catch bilaterally. Children quietly chant "toss" (dominant), "toss" (nondominant), "catch" (nondominant), "catch" (dominant). The second object is tossed as the first object starts to fall.

4. Using two objects, toss and catch using only one hand. One object is held in the fingers and the second one is secured by the thumb in the back of the hand. As object held by fingers is released, the second object rolls toward fingers to be tossed as first object starts to fall. Students quietly chant "toss, toss," "catch, catch." Repeat with nondominant hand.

5. Three-object juggling begins with two objects being held in the dominant hand (as in item 4 above) and one object held in the nondominant hand. Begin by tossing object A from the dominant hand, followed by object B from the nondominant hand. Practice in cycles of three tosses, three catches, then begin again. When three tosses can be successfully caught, move to four, then five, and so on. Concentration becomes very important, and it is best to have a set number in each cycle until the movements become more reflexive.

TEACHING HINTS

1. Small, firm beanbags or commercial "juggling cubes" should be used (weighted paper balls wrapped with tape are also effective).

2. Height of toss should be no higher than where child can comfortably reach overhead.

3. Catching should be between waist and shoulders (closer to waist).

4. Facing and about two and a half to three ft. from a wall will help to stabilize the toss (Fig. 13-8).

5. Insist that students master the two-object bilateral juggle with consistency in toss height as well as rhythm before progression to three-object juggling.

6. Appropriate music (¾ or ⁴⁄₄ time) can help to establish the rhythm of juggling.

7. Set the number of tosses and catches low at first so students can experience success without losing control of the objects. This will help to eliminate repeated struggling with inconsistent tosses.

8. Refrain from rushing the students into a new phase before they have mastered the present phase.

9. Establish 25 "toss-catches" without dropping an object as the goal for each phase prior to moving onto the next progression.

10. Focus should be on the apex of the tosses (Fig. 13-9).

11. Early success is very important if students are to be intrinsically motivated to continue practicing.

12. Teachers should juggle frequently to give the students a role model.

FIGURE 13-8
Facing a wall to help stabilize the toss.

FIGURE 13-9
Focus is on the apex of the toss.

TIME AND FORCE

The experiences described thus far may be enhanced through movements that also vary from slow to fast (that is, object and person) with musical accompaniment, and through varying levels of force production (soft to hard).

EXAMPLES OF GENERAL MOVEMENT EXPERIENCES

Roll a ball underhand using two hands (then one) to knock down tennis ball cans.
Throw a beanbag underhand to a bucket or within a hoop.
Throw a fleeceball at a target on the wall.
Catch a large playground ball on the right side, left side, overhead and below the knees.
Catch a beanbag with both hands; the right hand, left hand.
After blowing soap bubbles, catch and pop them.
Bounce a playground ball with two hands, then one hand.
Bounce a ball between the rungs of a ladder.
Shoot a small playground ball through a lowered basketball goal.
Hit a balloon with the hand to try to keep it in the air.
Hit a balloon back and forth with a partner.
Roll a hula hoop and keep it going by hitting it with the hand.
Using a plastic bat or racket, hit a whiffleball suspended from a string.
Hit a foam ball with the hand back and forth on the floor with a partner.
Beat designated points (X's) on a drum with a stick to a rhythm.
Climb play apparatus that includes various types of ladders.
Climb cargo nets and playground fire poles.
Clap hands with a partner using rhymes (pat-a-cake).

FINE-MOTOR MANIPULATING SKILLS

Stacking objects
Dropping small objects on targets   Pegboard
Marbles
Jacks   String activities
Finger symbols

COMBINING EYE-FOOT COORDINATION WITH A MOTOR PROGRAM

SPATIAL

Movement-pattern variability with movement variations in different directions and at low to high levels from the ground should include:

GROSS-MOTOR MANIPULATIVE SKILLS

Kicking objects of various sizes
Hacky Sack activities (kicking)
Trapping (with feet) objects of different sizes

LOCOMOTOR SKILLS

Walking and running across, through, and on pieces of equipment (ladders, ropes, hoops, cones, obstacle course);
Leaping, jumping, and hopping over, onto, and between various points (equipment, lines, squares, marks on surface).

TIME AND FORCE

The experiences mentioned may be enhanced through movements that also vary from slow to fast, with musical accompaniment, and through varying levels of force production.

EXAMPLES OF GENERAL MOVEMENT EXPERIENCES

Kick a large playground ball around the room.
Dribble a soccer ball between a course of cones.
Punt a lightweight ball into the air.
Hit a suspended ball with the foot.
Push a beanbag around the room with one foot while sitting,
Keep a balloon in the air by using the feet.
Trap a large playground ball with both feet while standing and sitting.
Walk on lines drawn on the floor.
Walk on a balance beam.
Walk between and on the rungs of a ladder.
Run in and out of a course of hoops without touching one.
Leap over a low hurdle.
Leap from hoop to hoop.
Play hopscotch
On a letter grid, jump on the letters representing your name.
Air-write with feet.
Pick up marbles with feet.

Teaching Hints

Select fundamental skills that best accommodate the developmental level of the child: rolling a ball underhand using two hands before one-hand throwing, and simple jumping before hopping, and so forth.

Movement Enhancement

Table 13-5

Eye-Foot Coordination Enhancement Chart

	LEVEL		LEVEL		LEVEL
GAMES		Long and Short Combo	II & III	*DANCE*	
		Soccer Steal			
Boundary Ball	I & II	Formation Jumping		Marching	I – III
Hoop Hop		Crab Soccer	III		
Hot Ball				Bluebird	I & II
Train Station		*GYMNASTICS*		Oats, Peas, Beans,	
Traffic Cop				and Barley Grow	
		Rope Stunts	I – III		
Kick the Beast Relay	II	Lazy Rope		Bleking	III
Potato Race		Snake Rope		Zip Code 001	
		Circle Rope			
Hopscotch	II & III	Straight Rope			
Jump the Shot		V-Rope			
		Rope Rings			

Movement Enhancement

Table 13-6

Eye-Hand Coordination Enhancement Chart

	LEVEL		LEVEL		LEVEL
GAMES		Crown The King		Three Little Monkeys	I & II
		Ball and Stick Relay		This Little Clown	
Carry and Fetch Relay	I & II	Marbles		Over the Hills	
Circle Stride Ball				Row, Row, Row	
Hot Potato		Hand Soccer	III	Dig a Little Hole	
Beanbag in a Can Relay		Jacks		Ten Fingers	
Throw and Go		Lamb Over the Wall		Little Fish	
Clothespin Drop		Eggs in the Basket		Bunny	
Buffalo Bill		Around the World		If I Were a Bird	
		Cherries in a Bucket		Two Little	
Cat and Rat	II	Lazy Susan		Left and Right	
		Pigs in a Pen			
B-B Ball	II & III	Fast Charlie		Names in Rhythm	II
Agents and Spies		My Ball		Rhythm Echo	
Magic Wand		Par Three		Dance of Greeting	
Blue and Gold		Scoot to the Hoop		Morse Code	
Brownies and Fairies		Sweep-up Relay		Lummi Sticks	
Kneeling Tag		Volleyball (Scooter)			
Seven Dwarfs					
Finger Toss		*DANCE/RHYTHMS/RHYMES*			
Over and Over					
Top Hat Tag		Pease Porridge Hot	I & II		
Pebble Flip		Itsy Bitsy Spider			
Call and Guard		Here Is the Beehive			
		I'm a Little Teapot			

- Provide large focal points (targets, balls, other objects).
- Encourage use of both right and left hands and feet.
- Stress concentration on the focal point (keeping eyes open.).
- Use eye-hand activities when confined in classroom, (that is, bad weather).

Skill Concepts Communicated to Children

Keep the eyes on the object (focal point).

RHYTHMIC AWARENESS

Movement Description

All meaningful movement takes place in a time structure, which, when organized, is rhythmical. *Rhythmic awareness*, therefore, refers to the child's ability to move (utilizing fundamental movement skills) or to make sounds that are repetitive, patterned, and result in balance and harmony of movement or sound.

Children develop rhythmic awareness through experiences that stress (1) moving to or singing with already established rhythms (for example, recorded music, drum beat, singing, chanting, or clapping) and (2) creating movements or sounds in their own time structure. The beauty of rhythmic activity is that it is inherently pleasurable for the child. One has only to observe children at play to notice their frequent use of chants (nonsensical and meaningful) and repetitive movements, which give them great enjoyment. Rhythmic activities using songs and chants (for instance, alphabet song, "Ten Little Indians") enhance the learning of many fundamental academic skills and contribute greatly to the development of fundamental motor abilities. Musical accompaniment may be a valuable teaching technique for the teacher instructing children to coordinate their movements in such activities as skipping, galloping, or bouncing a ball.

To develop rhythmic awareness in children is to develop an internal time structure that is consistent and meaningful to the child. The basic elements of rhythm are pulse beats, accents, measures, patterns, and qualities that are internalized and reinforced through selected movement activities.

Pulse beats are the division of time into equal intervals. The intervals between pulse beats may vary depending on the speed of the piece (music or other accompaniment), but the amount of time that each interval between pulse beats occupies must be exactly the same. A child who can time the climax of a movement with the exact moment of the beat is said to be moving in response to pulse beats. This is no simple feat even for many adults.

The first step in helping children understand this difficult element is to offer many opportunities to move to a musical accompaniment without requiring an accurate response. Not only is the frequent use of music with movement motivating but it provides the necessary experience of moving within a time structure, which will later enable the child to adapt to an established rhythm. The kindergartener and even the first-grade child should not have his or her attention drawn to an inaccurate response to pulse beats, but rather should be encouraged to develop movements that are regular and repetitive in the child's own time framework. Children at this age develop the awareness of pulse beats by repeating similar movements over and over with an accompaniment much like chanting a nursery rhyme repetitively. Simply using locomotor movements for expressive purposes will accomplish this goal. Once children can repeat movements like clapping, tapping, or walking in place at regular intervals, then they are ready to attempt to order their movements around established beats.

All movements can be timed to coincide with established pulse beats. In locomotor skills, the moment of contact of the foot or other body parts with the floor is timed to coincide with the beat. In rhythmic running, for example, the foot should touch the floor at the same time as the pulse beat occurs. With nonlocomotor skills and other creative movements, the beginning of the movement should coincide with the beat. Manipulative movements should be timed so that contact of the object either to the floor or to the body coincides with the beat. For example, bouncing a ball to a pulse beat would require that the ball contact the floor or the child's hand at the moment of the beat.

Accents are the extra impetus placed on certain beats that divide pulse beats into a series of equal groups, called *measures*. There is an innate tendency to accent alternate beats to create a strong-weak sequence, which simulates the body's heart beat or respiration. In all movement there is a point at the beginning, middle, or end at which added force is applied or released. For example, an accent naturally occurs at the beginning of pushing or pulling movements and most locomotors. However, the accent of a stretching movement is at the end of the complete stretch rather than at the beginning. In more continuous movements there is an accent in the middle of the movement. Swinging and swaying are examples of this, with the accent at the bottom or middle of the swing as opposed to either end of the movement. In most common dance steps, as well as locomotor movements, the primary accent occurs at the beginning of the movement. Children respond to accents first by learning to clap on the accented pulse beats and then by making some other forceful movement or step instead of clapping. Large, forceful movements and, of course, stamping and clapping are the simplest response to accents. Changes in direction, level, and size of movement can also delineate an accented pulse beat.

Measures are equal groupings of pulse beats that are marked by accents. The major accent generally occurs on the first beat of each measure and a lesser accent may occur on the third beat of a four-beat measure. The number of beats in each measure defines the *meter*. A measure that has two beats is a *duple meter*, and one that has three beats is a *triple meter*. The meter established by music or other accompaniment will dictate the types of movements possible. The most common meters used in children's dance and locomotor skills are the *quadruple meter* (four beats; used for walk, run, jump, hop, leap, and other even-movement patterns) and 6/8 meter (six beats in two groups of three; used for skips, slides, gallops, and other uneven-movement patterns).

Counting out the amount of time and duration of music and movements is an important skill in developing an awareness of the element of measures. For example, in quadruple meter the beats are counted 1-2-3-4, 2-2-3-4, 3-2-3-4 and so on for the number of measures required. In this way the child and teacher can keep track precisely of the amount of time a particular movement sequence occupies. This is especially important when children are trying to coordinate group–movement sequences, repeat movement patterns exactly, or the teacher is designing a sequence for a program. The key concept here is that children learn to count out measures and keep accurate track of the duration of a particular sequence. Naturally, this skill is somewhat advanced and should not be required of the kindergartener or even the first-grade child. By second grade the children may begin counting measures and ordering movement sequences to those measures. It is suggested that the quadruple and 6/8 meters be worked with first, as these are the simplest and most common in children's dance.

Children can make a strong movement on an accented beat to show their understanding of this element.

Patterns are achieved when movements or sounds are put together so that they are not equal to each other in time. One part of the movement will take longer than another. When skipping, the step part takes two pulse beats and the hop portion takes one, totaling three beats and two movements. Any time a movement is uneven, a rhythmic pattern occurs, as with the gallop, slide, two-step, and polka. Another possibility is to have a pulse-beat interval that is divided equally (for instance, two or three equal parts) followed by an undivided interval that spans the same amount of time. The resulting pattern follows a two-to-one ratio with the first movements being half as long as the second. Two runs followed by a walk, or two walks followed by a slow walk are examples of an even-movement pattern. Very simply, unless one movement is continued in exactly the same way for a long time, a movement pattern usually results. The movement pattern, then, is a combination of movements that occupy varying amounts of time.

Qualities are attributes that distinguish rhythmic movements from each other. Two children can perform the same movements in the same time structure and yet the performances can appear totally different. One has only to vary the size and/or speed of movement to change the quality of the performance. A child who is swinging his or her arms in a wide arc will appear very different from another who is swinging the arms in a small arc, and yet both may be performing the same skill in the same time period. This difference in "quality" of rhythmic movement is the result of variations in the intensity (that is, size and force) and tempo (speed) of the movements. These variations that distinguish one child's movements from another represent the beginning of creative expression.

The terms used to describe the elements of rhythm are presented for the teacher's clarification only and will not necessarily be used with the children. Words easily understood by the children should be substituted for the terms presented here.

For example, the concept of accents can be conveyed by using words like loud and soft beats or strong and weak movements. Tempo can be communicated as fast or slow movements. The idea of meter can be described as skipping (uneven) beat or walking (even) beat. In this way children can develop an understanding of the elements of rhythm through movement experiences that are commensurate with their ability to understand terminology, thereby developing a functional movement vocabulary. It is not necessary for them to memorize definitions for the technical terms or even to know those terms; what is most important is that their schema is reinforced in such a way that they can respond accurately to and create movement sequences to a variety of rhythmic accompaniments. If this is accomplished, then the later learning of specific folk and square dance steps (as well as other more complicated skills that demand rhythm and timing) will be much easier for them.

Children use movement to express emotion.

CREATIVITY

Fostering creativity in the child is a very important task that is often overlooked by teachers who are anxious to "teach." Creativity is not something that can be taught as such, but rather must be stimulated and then given room to grow. It is sometimes very difficult for a conscientious teacher to step back and allow the children to move as they feel, and yet this very freedom is crucial for the development of creative expression. The following are some practical suggestions to help the teacher foster blossoming creativity in children.

Begin with *imitative activities*. Children are very adept at pretending to be familiar animals, people, fairy caricatures, objects, and events. It is important to choose a stimulus for imitation that is familiar to all and suggests movement possibilities. The following list of categories offers some ideas:

Living creatures
    (animals and people; real and imaginary)
Natural events
    (weather, climate, and nature activities)
Objects
    (transportation, machines, toys)
Familiar events
    (movies, sports, circus)
Poem, fairytale, simile, and double simile
    (move as a pelican, move as a pelican just after lunch).

Remember that the children themselves may be your greatest source of ideas. They have been playing "let's pretend" since they were two, and certainly haven't forgotten how.

Allow children to move first without accompaniment and then add a rhythmic structure (drum beat, piano, record, other sources).

Progress to *interpretative activities*. These stimuli should encourage children to express moods, feelings, and actions. There should be a lot of variations in movement as each child expresses his or her own ideas about surprise, for example.

Have children interpret art through movement. Variations in texture, shape, size, and color provide stimulus for creative-movement activities.

Use props like ribbons, scarves, wands, and hoops that enable children to shed their self-consciousness about movement by focusing their attention on the prop.

Encourage movement patterns that demonstrate a wide variety of space, time, force, and relationship variations.

Movement Observation

The ability to "keep time" and move rhythmically demands three basic skills. Children must be able to *attend* to the accompaniment, *identify* the pulse beats, and then *order* movements around them.

Five- and six-year-old children may find it hard to synchronize their movements with an accompaniment, especially when the pulse beats deviate from their own natural rhythm. Consequently, these children should be exposed to an accompaniment in a way that is relaxed so that their movements can occur with the accompaniment and without tension. It is particularly important to avoid continual drilling on this matter and to allow the child to develop his or her own "timekeeping ability" through free-movement activities.

The seven- and eight-year-old (second and third grader) can be expected to order their movements more accurately to pulse beats. The child will find a walk in place easier to control than a walk forward, skips and gallops easier than a run, and small jumps easier than hops to an accompaniment. At this point it may be necessary to motivate the child to try to identify and order movements around pulse beats, because the child may be more interested in moving only for movement's sake. Children's development will be greatly enhanced by the use of gamelike activities that challenge them to be accurate. Working with lummi sticks and tinikling poles are particularly useful in motivating children toward accuracy.

Once the child has mastered an accurate response with simple movements of arms and legs to a series of beats, the teacher can then expect to see accents and rhythmic patterns, movements with equipment, partners, and in different directions, levels, and so forth.

Movement Variability

Discovering the inherent rhythm in movement and being able to move rhythmically greatly enhance the child's motor-skill development. The discovery of the child's internal rhythm should result in more fluid and coordinated movement patterns. A child who has not developed a basic level of rhythmic awareness may exhibit movement patterns that appear awkward and clumsy, characterized by a stumbling, uneven walking pattern as opposed to a smooth and even transfer of weight.

In the skill chapters, rhythm is a part of the time variable used to provide the child with a repetitive signal for movement. Depending on the child's age and experience, success in ordering movements to the accompaniment will vary. Regardless of the success exhibited, the teacher should continue frequently to use an accompaniment with fundamental movement skills.

When developing rhythmic awareness through movement, activities should be provided that follow a progression.

1. First allow the child to explore movement patterns (both creative and established, locomotor, nonlocomotor, and manipulative) in the child's own time structure. That is, the child determines his or her own pulse beats and accents, and moves accordingly.
2. The child should be encouraged to establish sequences of movements and repeat them.
3. The child may then work with a partner and use small equipment.
4. Group activity should be organized by the teacher until the child is able to demonstrate proficiency.
5. Once the child is comfortable creating movement patterns without accompaniment, then rudimentary clapping, slapping, and stomping should be encouraged to an established rhythm (music, poem), followed by locomotor and nonlocomotor movements.
6. Keeping time can then be expanded to using small manipulative equipment, instruments, and then working with a partner.
7. Finally, a sequence of movements to established rhythms can be expected.

AUDITORY RHYTHMIC ACTIVITIES

Rhythmic awareness is also developed through the use of singing rhythms, finger plays, and rhymes. These activities offer opportunities for combining movement and socialization to rhythmic patterns. Use of these rhythmic activities demands movement responses that serve to reinforce the child's internal awareness of pulse beats, accents, patterns, and tempo in an enjoyable manner. A further benefit of auditory rhythmic activities is that they heighten children's ability to attend to an accompaniment as they listen for the action directions and sing along.

Singing rhythms are those songs that appeal to youngsters and suggest action possibilities by telling a story. Children will sing along as they create movements to go along with the songs in this category. As they sing the song over and over, they internalize the rhythm of the song through enjoyable repetition.

Finger plays are fun.

Finger plays incorporate singing or chanting short and simple rhymes with specific hand and finger actions. These rhymes are easy to learn and help to develop the accompanying finger dexterity in children.

Rhymes and poems present further stimulus for developing rhythmic auditory awareness. Most kindergarten youngsters are familiar with a variety of nursery rhymes and learn new ones easily as they perform actions to them. These differ from finger plays in that they may involve whole-body movements as the children act out the words to the rhyme or poem.

The enhancement section of this chapter contains a list of appropriate singing rhythms, finger plays, and rhymes.

COMBINING RHYTHMIC AWARENESS WITH A MOTOR PROGRAM

The following activities stress moving in response to a pulse beat and, by necessity, require an accurate motor response. There is, however, another aspect of dance that stresses interpreting and expressing feelings and ideas through movement without attending to an external time structure. This is called *creative dance*. Creative dance experiences are usually the first exposure a child has to the world of dance. As the child explores the fundamental-skill and movement-awareness themes, he or she should be encouraged to key-in on the quality of the movements that communicate different feelings and emotions.

For example, a strong, forceful stretch as opposed to a slow, smooth stretch will communicate a totally different feeling. Children need to experience the full range of their creative-movement capabilities by being encouraged to try new and different actions that they have not yet explored. Communication experiences should be followed by sequencing and phrasing or patterning activities where the child must combine various movements to make a statement.

Finally, the child will be able to create a total dance by putting together several sequences that express an idea, feeling, activity, or movement awareness.

It is difficult and probably unwise to isolate rhythmic experiences from creative experiences because of the many possibilities for movement which exist. Therefore, this section on rhythmic practice should be utilized in such a way as to encourage individual creative expression following the above progression. The use of a variety of stimuli will greatly enhance the child's creative capabilities. We suggest:

A variety of music and sounds;
Instruments created by children;
Reading poems and stories to interpret;
Viewing art work to interpret;
Creating movements around props.

SPATIAL

Perform at the moment of beat:

Clap hands or floor.
Slap different body parts.
Tap feet.
Make small hand gestures.
Make large arm gestures.
Bend and extend different body parts: knees, elbows, fingers, wrists, neck, waist, hips; shrug shoulders.
Push and pull, swing and sway, twist and turn on the beat.
Walk in place.
Perform the various locomotors moving forward.
Change directions every fourth beat or accented beat.
Change movement patterns (skip, gallop, slide) on accents.
Move only on accented beats, pause on other beats, freeze (shape) on accented beats.
Combine locomotor and nonlocomotor movements into a pattern and perform over again.
Experiment with all movement possibilities and body parts in this dimension.

TIME

Move slowly so that one movement occupies more than one beat (half as fast).
Let one movement last an entire measure.
Move quickly so that more than one movement occupies one beat (twice as fast).
Combine different speed movements into a pattern (that is, two steps and a slow walk = four beats); try different combinations.
Make movements that accelerate from half as fast to on beat to twice as fast.
Make movements that decelerate from twice as fast to half as fast.
Make movements that are sustained (last two or more beats).
Make sudden movements that last only part of a beat.
Move body in sustained (slow) maneuver; let a body part(s) (head, arms) move on accents.

FORCE

Vary the quality of movements by contrasting actions that are:

strong, then weak
hard, then soft
heavy, then light
firm, then fine or loose.

ADDITIONAL MOVEMENT VARIATIONS

Try the following partner relationship possibilities for rhythmic-movement sequences:

advancing-retreating	together-apart
meeting-parting	above-below
mirroring-matching	behind-in front of
following-copying	over-under
questioning-answering	on-alongside

In a large group move in succession or unison.

Create rhythmic movement sequences that utilize the following:

hoops	scarves
wands	flags
streamers	rings
balls	other props of the children's creation

Create rhythmic sequences in relationship to large apparatus.

use:
 ladders
 mats
 beams
 bars
 other
go:
 over-under
 through, inside, outside
make shapes:
 around
 under
 over
 between

Create tapping sequences in 4/4, 3/4, 2/4, and 6/8 time, using lummi sticks. Work alone, in pairs, then in a group.

Remember to vary the direction, level, and speed of the sequence.

Use rhythm instruments in a movement sequence:

bells
triangles
sand blocks
tambourines.

Teaching Hints

1. Use simple, uncluttered sounds to establish rhythms; consider using:
   a. your voice (singing or chanting)
   b. a rhythm drum
   c. a tambourine
   d. a xylophone
   e. lummi sticks
   f. finger cymbals
   g. records with an unchanging beat (country and western, marches, and simple rock–and–roll music works well.)
   h. homemade instruments
2. Avoid too much loud drumming; use other percussion instruments for variation.
3. Always require a movement response when exploring rhythms.
4. Hand waving, tapping on and off the body, shaking the head are all good responses to begin with.
5. The ability to create a movement pattern demands time and encouragement. Allow sufficient time for the children to explore; stand back, and don't interfere except to support the work in progress.
6. Allow children time to perform their creations.
7. You need not be a dancer to teach creative rhythms, so don't be afraid to try.
8. Use props and imagery like scarves, hoops, picture, sounds, and feelings to stimulate creative movement.
9. Avoid telling the children how something moves, but rather allow them to decide on their own movements.
10. When children seem inhibited, try outlandish similes ("How would you move if you were a piece of bacon on a really hot sidewalk, a stork walking in peanut butter, a grasshopper on top of a moving bowl of jello?").

Skill Concepts Communicated to Children

All movements occur in a time structure.

When movements are ordered and repetitive, then they are rhythmical.

Pulse beats and accents can be identified in movements and sounds.

Movement Enhancement

Table 13-7

Rhythmic Awareness Activity Chart

RHYTHMIC GAMES	LEVEL	SINGING RHYTHMS	LEVEL		LEVEL
Marching	I & II	A Hunting We Will Go	I & II	Ten Little Indians	II
The Crazy Clock		You Can		How Do You Do,	
Levels		Little Miss Muffet		My Partner	
Orchestra Leader		Look! See!		Clap Your Hands	
Lummi Sticks		Yankee Doodle		Bingo	
		Keep It Moving			
Rhythm Echo	II	Hinges		FINGER PLAYS	
Threes and Sevens		Butterfly			
Names in Rhythm		Up, Down, Turn Around		Here Is the Beehive	I & II
Reverse Ranks		Teddy Bear		The Little Clown	
Line or Circle Clap		Toot the Flute		I'm a Little Teapot	
		Jack in the Box		Over the Hills	
RHYTHMIC GYMNASTICS		The Little Green Frogs		Row, Row, Row	
		Top of the Morning		Dig a Little Hole	
Balls	II	Spinning Tops		Ten Fingers	
Hoops		Mulberry Bush		Little Fish	
Wands		Ten Little Jingle Bells		Bunny	
Ribbons		Loobie Loo		If I Were a Bird	
		Farmer in the Dell		Two Little	
		Did You Ever See		Left and Right	
		a Lassie?		Itsy Bitsy Spider	
				Three Little Monkeys	

NURSERY RHYMES (I)

The following familiar nursery rhymes are listed in order of difficulty. Start with the first line and devise a movement sequence that is true to the rhythmic pattern. Use locomotor, nonlocomotor, and various body movements that may suggest the words, but not necessarily. Add succeeding lines one at a time. Choose rhymes familiar to the children because the rhythmic sequences for those will be well established.

Twinkle, Twinkle Little Star
Hot Cross Buns
Sing a Song of Sixpence
Baa, Baa, Black Sheep
Pussy Cat
Ding Dong Bell
Pease Porridge Hot
Fee Fi Fo Fum
One, Two, Buckle My Shoe
Diddle Diddle Dumpling
One, Two, Three O'Leary
Tom, Tom, the Piper's Son
Hickory Dickory Dock
Humpty Dumpty Sat on a Wall
Little Miss Muffet
Ride a Cock Horse

RHYMES AND SAYINGS (I & II)

The following sayings can provide stimulus for short movement compositions. Children should be encouraged to create their own movement patterns to the lines.

"April showers bring May flowers."
"Birds of a feather flock together."
"A bird in the hand is worth two in the bush."
"All is not gold that glitters."
"The early bird catches the worm."
"An apple a day keeps the doctor away."
"Rain, rain go away, Little Johnny wants to play."
"A stitch in time saves nine."
"Early to bed, early to rise, makes a person healthy, wealthy, and wise."

CHANTS (I & II)

Chants provide a rhythmic pattern that is continuous and enables children to create movement sequences or just move various body parts rhythmically to their accompaniment. Chants may be created by the children out of nonsense syllables or familiar words.

Who Put the Cookies in the Cookie Jar?
Ice Cream
I Went to the Store
Valentines
Tim Tam Toes Tap

VISUAL AWARENESS

Movement Description

A child's ability to perceive and react to visual stimuli is crucial to his or her future academic achievement. Unfortunately, many children entering school are deficient in at least one of the three types of perception necessary to good visual awareness.

Movement Enhancement

Table 13-8

Rhythmic Awareness Activity Chart (continued)

	LEVEL		LEVEL		LEVEL
DANCES		Danish Dance of Greeting		Oh, Susanna	
London Bridge	I & II	Seven Jumps		Bleking	
Chimes of Dunkirk		Hansel and Gretel		Badger Gavotte	
Hokey-Pokey		This Old Man		Glowworm	
Jack the Giant Killer		The Popcorn Man		Skip to My Lou	
Oats, Peas, Beans, and Barley		Paw Paw Patch		Klapptanz	
I See You		Kinderpolka		Danish Schottische	
Birds in the Nest		Ach Ja		Crested Hen	
		Hobby Horse		Hora	
Round and Round the Village	II	Fool's Jig		Grand March	
Sally Go Round the Moon		Shoo Fly		Gustaf's Skoal	
Jolly is the Miller		Limbo		Little Brown Jug	
Jump Jim Joe		Bow Belinda			
		The Wheat			
		Maypole Dance			

A sound visual awareness is necessary to maneuver through obstacles of varying sizes and shapes.

Good visual awareness involves effective functioning of depth, form, and figure-ground perceptions.

These three perceptive abilities account for approximately 80 percent of the information received as stimuli. Therefore, a sound visual awareness is fundamental to success in most fundamental movement skills.

DEPTH PERCEPTION

This is the ability to judge distances in three-dimensional space. Development of depth perception increases the child's ability to utilize external cues in determining depth, distance, and size.

FORM PERCEPTION

This is the ability to recognize forms, shapes, and symbols. Related to form perception is perceptual constancy: the ability to recognize categories of shapes regardless of size, color, texture, or angle of observation. The young child may have difficulty perceiving that the huge airplane on the field is the same size and shape as the one several thousand feet above in the sky. Research indicates that children four to seven years of age may rely on different perceptual information to identify objects. Four-year-olds generally rely on form or shape, rather than color, whereas five-year-olds tend to use color for identification. By the time children are in the second grade (seven years), color and form are utilized more equally to identify objects. Progression in development proceeds from ill-defined globulous masses to the differentiation of elements within objects.

Children with inadequate form perception may have difficulties in such activities as differentiating letters, numbers, sorting objects, and engaging in movement activities that involve moving objects or boundary lines.

FIGURE-GROUND PERCEPTION

This refers to the ability to perceive and distinguish a figure separate from its ground: being able to select specific stimuli from a mass. The child who attempts to catch a thrown ball must be able to screen out obstructive stimuli (sky, clouds, children, buildings, trees) while sighting and concentrating on the ball.

Movement Observation

A child with poor visual awareness may appear clumsy and may have problems with academic subjects. Movement is an excellent medium for enhancing the development of visual awareness. A good visual schema will form the basis for all future learning.

The following signs are easily recognizable by the teacher and may indicate a deficiency in visual awareness:

1. clumsiness in daily activities
2. difficulty in coloring large symbols
3. difficulty in matching symbols and shapes
4. inability to recognize and interpret symbols correctly
5. difficulty in form and depth perception
6. inability to reproduce letters, numbers, and symbols correctly

If remedial work is indicated, the teacher may select from a number of specially designed programs to aid in the correction of deficiencies.

Movement Variability

A sound visual awareness is essential to the learning of all motor skills. Consequently, visual awareness training should begin when the child is preschool age to ensure maximum development. In public education the kindergarten child should receive visual training at the beginning of the school year and

Figure-ground perception.

should be evaluated periodically throughout the year to determine possible weaknesses. Visual training should continue through the primary grades to ensure a readiness for learning.

Parents should be encouraged to participate at home with the child in some of these activities.

COMBINING VISUAL AWARENESS WITH A MOTOR PROGRAM

SPATIAL

Move through space, staying as far from everyone else as possible.

Move as close to everyone as possible (without touching); vary the size of the space.

Vary the direction of travel.

Place one body part close to someone and another part far away.

Try different body parts and combinations of parts.

Trace the path of different shapes on the floor:

circles	ovals
squares	straight, curved, and zigzag lines
rectangles	alphabet letters
triangles	numbers

Move at different levels while traveling through space.

Move one body part at three different levels: high, medium, and low.

Make the body into the above shapes both flat on the floor and while standing up.

Trace the above shapes in the air with different body parts; try fingers, hands, feet, head, elbows, knees.

Go toward a wall that has animal pictures on it, pick out one animal, and try to imitate it with your movement.

Find someone in the class wearing the same color tennis shoes as you and go to that person.

TIME

Move through space as quickly or as slowly as possible *without collisions*.

Match movements to a drum beat while traveling through space.

Move the body into different shapes first quickly then as slowly as possible; try this first while standing then while lying down.

Change shapes and levels on a drum beat.

FORCE

Move about the room with very smooth/jerky motions without collisions.

Move about, sometimes exploding into the air then staying very close to the ground, without touching anyone.

Move quietly and loudly.

ADDITIONAL MOVEMENT VARIATIONS

1. Have children sort different objects into like piles; use buttons, toothpicks broken into different lengths, geometric shapes, colored objects, etc.

2. Have the child catch a balloon thrown by the teacher then progress to large balls and beanbags, then small balls and other objects.

3. Try to juggle first two beanbags, then two balls, then three objects.

4. See if the child can bounce a ball with different body parts: elbow, knee, head, wrist.

5. Keep a balloon aloft by batting it with different body parts.

6. Leap across different objects placed on the ground without touching them. Leap over a hula hoop, a jump rope or two placed parallel, a wand, a traffic cone, etc.

7. Move in and out, and over and under different obstacles that are off the ground without touching them.

8. Push a small object while creeping across the floor.

9. Show a picture to the child, then hide it, and have the child recall as many things as he or she remembers.

10. Have the child duplicate a pattern you have just drawn after you hide it from view.

11. Find as many different ways as you can to sort a group of objects like buttons; groceries, beads, clothes, kitchen items, and so forth.

Teaching Hints

Plan many and varied spatial dimensional cues and reference points for judging distance (depth perception).

Stress recognizing similarities and differences among shapes.

Have students reproduce a variety of shapes with their bodies.

When teaching figure-ground perception, first limit the number of stimuli in the background and use white or light solid colors.

Gradually add stimuli to the environment.

Skill Concepts Communicated to Children

The body can recognize a variety of shapes that one can see.

One can move through space without collisions.

One can locate specific objects in space.

Movement Enhancement

Table 13-9							
Visual Awareness Enhancement Chart							
	LEVEL			**LEVEL**			**LEVEL**
GAMES		*GYMNASTICS*			*DANCE*		
What's Missing? Peripheral Vision Finding Different Objects	I–III	Animal Walk Obstacle Course		I & II	A Hunting We Will Go Did You Ever See a Lassie?		I & II
Nuts and Bolts Letter Race Change It	I & II	Partner Stunts		II	Round and Round the Village Jolly Is the Miller Shoo Fly Paw Paw Patch		II
Clothespin Drop Ping-Pong Bounce	II & III						
I Pass These Scissors to You	III						

TACTILE AWARENESS

Movement Description

Tactile awareness involves the ability to discriminate among objects through touch and the ability to remember the feel of various objects in order to categorize them. Tactile perception is a very basic component of all manipulative skills and plays an important role in all exploratory learning. Through feeling and manipulating objects, the child experiences a variety of sensations that not only have a survival value but also contribute to a better understanding of the environment. The sense of touch enables children to distinguish objects with different feels and further enables them to manipulate a variety of objects more effectively.

Fundamental tactile awareness begins in infancy when a baby first grasps objects at about three months of age. The child very quickly learns to differentiate among soft and hard objects, hot and cold, and rough and smooth objects. The total sum of these preschool experiences will determine the child's tactile awareness when he or she enters kindergarten. A child who has been offered a variety of different textured and shaped objects to manipulate through the preschool years will be better equipped to relate to novel objects in grade school than one who has been deprived of these experiences.

By the time children enter school they should be able to describe and identify familiar objects without the aid of a visual cue.

Movement Observation

Children with tactile awareness problems can be easily identified through simple observation in tactual discrimination activities. The teacher should look for the following behaviors:

1. Inability to discriminate tactually (without visual cues) among different-sized coins, or fabrics with different textures. Other objects may be used here.
2. Complains of clothes irritating the skin; may avoid wearing a coat;
3. Craves to be touched or held;
4. Avoids touch and reacts negatively to physical contact;
5. When the child's eyes are closed, child is unable to identify fingers as they are touched.

Identification of objects without visual cues develops a keen tactile awareness.

Movement Variability

Developing tactile awareness is necessary to learning both fundamental manipulative and primary educational skills. Tactual awareness can be practiced very effectively through a variety of movement activities.

COMBINING TACTILE AWARENESS WITH A MOTOR PROGRAM

SPATIAL

Move on different surfaces while barefooted:
  hard floors
  lawns
  beaches, sandy and rocky
  balance beams
  mats.

Use different locomotors and move at different levels and directions.

Blindfold children and have them:
  follow tape marks (while barefooted) that form different paths: straight, curved, and zigzag; identify the pathway;
  feel a cardboard shape, then walk that shape and name it;
  feel different textures, then move like that texture, and label the texture.

Perform isometric exercises using different amounts of pressure.

Trace different shapes on the child's back and have the child move in those shapes.

TIME

Move at varying speeds on different surfaces.
Accelerate and decelerate on different surfaces.
Move on a drum beat on different surfaces.
On signal, make sudden changes in direction on different surfaces.

FORCE

Move like different heavy objects/light objects.
Move up high in the air or close to the ground on different surfaces.
Make jerky or smooth movements on various surfaces.

ADDITIONAL MOVEMENT VARIATIONS

1. Touch the various parts of the body of a child with various objects. Ask the child to name or move the parts touched and to identify the characteristics of the objects used for touching.

2. Have children perform isotonic and isometric exercises with various objects: balls, hoops, wands, and beanbags can be used.

3. Have children climb ropes, cargo nets, ladders, and other playground equipment that have different textures.

4. Have children move through, over, or under a variety of obstacles, including tires, trampoline beds, mats, playground equipment, boxes, benches, beams, etc.

5. Have blindfolded children feel the position of another child while he or she is in movement, then ask them to name the skill or reproduce it.

6. Have blindfolded children identify, discriminate among, and categorize different objects.

7. Have children work in pairs and push each other across the room slowly, with one child providing just enough resistance for the pushing child to move the other child slowly. Try this:
   a. with palms touching.
   b. standing back to back.
   c. standing shoulder to shoulder.
   d. using any other pair of body parts.

8. Have the children stand about 10 inches from the wall, facing it. They lean toward it and pretend to push it back with their hands.

9. Have the children press against the floor or other rigid surface with the whole body in both face-up and face-down positions, first with eyes closed, then with eyes opened.

10. Have children kneel with hands on floor below shoulders and slightly turned inward, thighs at right angles to the floor, back straight. Ask the children to press "holes" in the floor with the hands. Hold while the teacher counts to three, then relax.

11. Have children stand with back about four to six inches from a wall. Tell them to lean backward and press against the wall with the back as hard as possible. Still pressing, tell them to slide down to a position as if sitting on a chair, with knees bent and back flat against the wall. Slide up to the original position.

12. Use different body parts to manipulate different objects. Use hands, feet, elbows, wrists, knees, heels, etc.

Teaching Hints

Utilize familiar objects for tactual discrimination tasks.

Encourage children to label objects by the feel of them.

Use objects with homogeneous shapes, textures, size, or weight for sorting.

Skill Concepts Communicated to Children

Objects can be hard, soft, rough, smooth, sticky, slimy, and so forth.

The feel of an object can be determined by body parts other than the hands.

The shape of an object can be determined just by feeling it.

Table 13-10				
Tactile Awareness Enhancement Chart				

	LEVEL		LEVEL	LEVEL
GAMES		*GYMNASTICS*		Egg-Sit
				Forward Roll
The Feely Bag	I–III	Bear Walk	I & II	Backward Roll
		Inch Worm		Trampoline
Partner Tag	I & II	Egg Roll		Shoulder Wrestling
		Log Roll		Leg Wrestling
Back To Back	II & III			Push War
Put in Order		Eskimo roll	II	Foot Push
Memory Ball		Bridge		Toe Push
Sandpaper Numbers		Rocking Chair		Rhythmic Ball Gymnastics
and Letters		Corkscrew		
		Thread the Needle		

AUDITORY AWARENESS

Movement Description

Auditory awareness refers to the ability to discriminate, associate, and interpret auditory stimuli in order that such information may become meaningful to the individual. More specifically, the following is involved:

1. The ability to locate and identify sounds;
2. The ability to retain and respond to auditory commands;
3. The ability to respond to a rhythmic accompaniment;
4. The ability to distinguish among sounds that are both similar and dissimilar;
5. The ability to comprehend verbal communication.

    Four components of auditory awareness appear to be relevant to enhancement by movement activities. These are discussed below.

AUDITORY FIGURE-GROUND

This component is the ability to distinguish and concentrate on relevant auditory stimuli while ignoring irrelevant stimuli within an environment containing general auditory information. Children with inadequate functioning of the *auditory figure-ground* component have difficulty concentrating on verbal instructions and responding to directions.

AUDITORY DISCRIMINATION

This refers to the ability to distinguish between different frequencies and amplitudes of sounds. Included in the *auditory discrimination* component is *auditory constancy*, namely the ability to recognize auditory information as the same under varying circumstances.

Children with poor discrimination abilities usually exhibit problems in rhythmic activities, games, and dances, all of which are dependent on such skills.

SOUND LOCALIZATION

Sound localization involves the ability to determine the source or direction of sound. Being able to locate individuals, animals, or objects (for example, cars horns) with limited or no immediate visual information is something that must be experienced in order for the child to be effective and safe in his or her environment.

TEMPORAL AUDITORY PERCEPTION

This component refers to the recognition and discrimination of variations of auditory stimuli presented in time. Especially relevant during the presentation of rhythmic and dance activities, inadequacy in *temporal auditory perception* may hinder the child's movement as she or he attempts to interpret tempo, rate, emphasis, and order of auditory stimuli.

    The existing variations of abilities in auditory perception may be attributable to differences in ability or differences in early parental training (awareness depends upon learning). Therefore, unless training occurs many children will have difficulty in hearing and following the teacher's instructions in school. Further problems in listening and reading comprehension may occur because the child cannot distinguish between, and attend to, auditory cues.

Movement Observation

A child who is deficient in auditory awareness will appear to be inattentive and at times disobedient. Some behaviors that suggest poor listening skills include:

Auditory awareness is a key component of rhythmic awareness.

1. An inability to identify common sounds without visual cues;
2. An inability to follow simple directions that are clearly stated;
3. Poor performance in dance activities;
4. An inability to understand verbal commands.

Although all children benefit greatly from auditory training, the child who is deficient needs to be placed in a remedial program to ensure future ability to learn in the classroom.

Movement Variability

Movement provides an excellent medium for practicing listening skills. When learning to follow directions it is more motivating for the child to actually show understanding through movement than to demonstrate understanding verbally.

Teachers must stress that noise be kept to a minimum so that their voices can be heard by all children when giving directions. Following directions should be made a challenge for the children.

COMBINING AUDITORY AWARENESS WITH A MOTOR PROGRAM SPATIAL

On command, have the children:
touch or move different body parts;
form different shapes with their bodies;
move across the floor with different locomotors;
move at different levels: high, medium, and low;
trace curved, straight, and zigzag pathways as they move through space;
change directions as they move;
touch the floor with different body parts.

TIME

On command, the children should be able to:
stop and start movement;
accelerate and decelerate movement;
go at different speeds;
move different body parts in time to a rhythmic accompaniment (try a drum beat, tambourine, lummi sticks, or recorded music that has a simple beat);
imitate different clapping patterns and sequences.

FORCE

On command, the children should be able to:
move with jerky movements;
move with smooth movements;
move with heavy or light movements;
move close to the ground or high in the air;
make hard and soft gestures with the arm or other body parts.

ADDITIONAL MOVEMENT VARIATIONS

1. Have children identify with their eyes closed the following common sounds:
   a. sharpening a pencil
   b. closing a window
   c. turning on the water fountain
   d. turning on a light
   e. knocking on a door.
2. Have children identify (with their eyes closed) an object when it is dropped, or the number of times a ball bounces when dropped.
3. Have children point with eyes closed in a direction where they believe a designated sound (ringing bell, ticking clock, etc.) is coming from.
4. Have children identify with eyes closed various rhythm instruments.

Identifying common sounds and directions without visual cues.

5. Have children move in conjunction with changes in volume of music. Loud music would suggest large movement, and soft music would suggest small movement, for example.
6. Repeat different rhythmic patterns and sequences using lummi sticks, ribbons, or poi pois.
7. Have blindfolded children try to identify the voices of other children in the class.
8. Have children follow simple directions, for example:
   a. march loudly for five steps
   b. bounce the ball eight times
   c. clap hands twice.
   Make this into a game and challenge the children to be accurate in their responses.
9. Jump rope to music.
10. Give commands as children perform on apparatus.
   (The following activities are to be performed blindfolded or in a dark room:)
11. Ask children to move toward or away from a voice or other auditory signal.
12. Provide children with paper cups or other objects. Have them throw the objects a particular distance and then find them as quickly as possible.
13. While in a restricted space, have children move about without touching each other. They may make their own sounds while moving. Make the activity more difficult by further restricting the space.
14. Ask children to roll balls to each other on the grass.
15. Ask children to throw objects at a sound. For example, children may shoot baskets by aiming toward an audible beeper.

16. Arrange an obstacle course in which the order of direction is dependent upon sound. For example, sounds emitted from tape recorders, electronic beepers, or record players may be used. In addition, children may be stationed at various obstacles to lead youngsters in the correct order by calling, clapping, or creating sounds with objects.
17. Associate a movement such as hopping, jumping, rolling, or skipping with a particular sound. For example, a clap may mean a hop; a bell may mean a jump; a horn may mean a skip; a strike of a triangle may mean a squat. Make sounds in a particular order and ask children to respond with appropriate movement in the same order.

Teaching Hints

Keep noise to a minimum so that all children may hear the directions.
Use a variety of vocal notations; sometimes loud, sometimes soft.
Use different sounds to signal different types of movement.
Challenge the children through games that demand good listening skills.
Use music during activity.

Skill Concepts Communicated to Children

Sounds may come from a variety of places.
One can replicate auditory commands in movement.
One can tune into one sound among other sounds and respond to just one cue.

Table 13-11

Auditory Awareness Enhancement Chart

	LEVEL		LEVEL		LEVEL
GAMES		Little Red Fox		Chimes of Dunkirk	
		O'Leary		Farmer in the Dell	
Prui	I–III	Attention Relays		Hokey-Pokey	
Go Touch It		Knock-Knock		Looby Loo	
Kitty, Kitty		Colors		Did You Ever See a Lassie?	
Giants, Dwarfs, and People	I & II	Math Merriment	III		
Birds Have Feathers				Ten Little Indians	II
Just Now		*DANCE AND RHYTHMS*		Klapptanz	
Cat and Rat				Bingo	
Boiler Bust		I'm a Little Teapot	I & II		
		Row, Row, Row			
Indian Chief	II & III	If I Were a Bird			

SUGGESTED READINGS

ANDREWS, G. (1976). *Creative rhythmic movement for children*. Englewood Cliffs, NJ: Prentice-Hall.

BARLIN, A. (1979). *Teaching your wings to fly*. Santa Monica, CA: Goodyear.

BRUCE, V. R. (1970). *Movement in silence and sounds*. London: G. Bell & Sons.

DIMONDSTEIN, G. (1971). *Children dance in the classroom*. New York: Macmillan.

HARRIS, J., PITTMAN, A., WALLER, M., (1987). *Dance a while* (2nd ed.). Minneapolis: Burgess.

JOYCE, M. (1993). *First steps in teaching creative dance to children*. Palo Alto, CA: Mayfield.

JOYCE, M. (1984). *Dance technique for children*. Palo Alto, CA: Mayfield.

KIRCHNER, G. (1985). *Physical education for elementary school children* (6th ed.). Dubuque, IA: Wm. C. Brown.

LOGSDON, B. J., BARRETT, K. R., BROER, M. R., *et al.* (1984). *Physical education for children*. (2nd ed). Philadelphia: Lea & Febiger.

MURRAY, R. L. (1975). *Dance in elementary education*. (3rd ed.). New York: Harper & Row.

WEIKERT, P. S. (1989). *Teaching Movement and Dance*. 3rd ed. Michigan: High Scope Press.

14

The Physical Fitness Program

Physical fitness is a cornerstone of this text. As noted in Chapters 4 and 5, the fitness program should receive the highest priority and not be left to chance or viewed as a byproduct of the motor skill curriculum. The elementary physical education program provides the opportunity to develop the foundation in which positive attitudes and adult lifestyle behaviors are formed. For a program to be successsful, carefully thought out goals must be set and specific objectives developed.

The intent of this chapter is to extend the information provided in Chapters 4 and 5. In those sections, discussions relative to concepts, assessment, and general curriculum planning were presented. This chapter focuses on program implementation. The following material will provide practical information on basic instructional procedures, exercise precautions (including potentially harmful exercises), selection of activities based on fitness value, and activity formats. This chapter also includes a selection of exercises and activities

that can be used to develop lessons to enhance the components of health-related fitness. The authors believe that the skill-related components of fitness (agility, speed, power, coordination, reaction time, and balance) will be enhanced in this age range as children participate in the general program; therefore specific enhancement activities have been excluded.

BASIC INSTRUCTIONAL GUIDELINES

1. Select activities that are specific to developing designated fitness component objectives. Primary focus should be on the development of cardiorespiratory efficiency, flexibility, and muscular strength/endurance.
2. Plan carefully to exercise all major muscle groups (that is, legs, trunk, arms, and shoulder girdle).
3. Introduce fitness activities by using the principle of progression, that is, progress slowly with the level of difficulty, duration, and intensity.
4. Set reasonable goals and plan for student success so optimal progress and enthusiasum is created and maintained.
5. When feasible, individualize the presentation of activities to accommodate the less-fit student and challenge those individuals that exhibit greater abilities.
6. While it is not always possible at the elementary school level, ask that students wear appropriate shoes and attire when participating. This issue will be discussed in more detail in Cardiorespiratory Fitness Activities.
7. Every effort should be made to make the fitness activity fun-filled and motivating. An enthusiastic teacher is the key element toward accomplishing this goal.

8. Select activities that provide maximum participation.

9. Omit elimination-type activities from the program or, when appropriate, modify to maximize activity. This practice could also be extended to the skill development phase of the lesson. For example, rather than have a child sit out after being tagged or hit with a ball (dodgeball), the child may complete 25 jumps with a rope and re-enter. Another example suggests that the teacher "aerobicize" an activity that characteristically has children waiting in lines and standing for extended periods. During a softball or kickball game for example, children in the field or waiting in line must jog in place (or in circles) between the time that a ball is hit and the runner is safe.

10. If the activity requires partners, assign individuals of comparable size.

11. Opportunities for student leadership should be considered for children above the second grade.

12. When introducing a new exercise (or reviewing), demonstrate clearly the proper form and provide cognitive information regarding value, names of muscles used, and exercise concepts. Cognitive information should be presented on the child's level of understanding.

13. Select an efficient organizational arrangement to begin class. Teachers that have large groups may wish to assign students to numbered floor spots, numbered lines, or behind lines that are designated by specific names or words. Designated lines are popular because of the ease in forming groups for fitness activities. Regardless of the arrangement, sufficient spacing between individuals is needed, especially if the initial activity calls for exercising in this formation.

14. When possible, plan motor skill activities (during the skill development phase of the lesson) that continue stimulating the components of health-related fitness.

EXERCISE PRECAUTIONS

Inherent in almost any physical activity is the potential for injury or adverse reactions. Teachers should constantly be aware of this possibility for the child's sake and the reputation of the program.

Before children are allowed to participate in the physical education program (especially the fitness assessment and development portions), the teacher should seek information to determine if there is a medical or psychological reason for limited participation or exclusion. This information can be found in the student's medical files and through a conference with the school nurse. Teachers should also send home an information request and permission form to the parents. This information helps in verifying that the child can participate in vigorous physical activity and that he or she has been examined by a physician within the past year.

Common ailments that are reported to the nurse and physical education teacher are: bronchial asthma, anemia, epilepsy, diabetes, heart problems, and respiratory concerns. While none of these conditions should automatically exclude the child from physical activity, the range of severity dictates that each case be considered individually with the advice of the child's physician and parents. The fitness levels of individuals exhibiting these diseases can range from low-fitness (with extreme limitations) to future athletic champions. It has been suggested by some authorities that many children with these conditions are perhaps overprotected and are not as fit as they could be due to habitually low activity levels.

One of the standard practices of teacher observation is to check students for unusual physical or psychological characteristics or behavior. Climatic conditions are another safety consideration that may warrant the teacher's attention. Children's bodies are less efficient than adults' at regulating extreme hot and cold temperatures during exercise. While children usually have physical education in the gymnasium or apply extra clothing during winter months, in warm and hot weather the teacher should be aware of the possibilities of dehydration and heat-related illnesses such as heat cramps, heat exhaustion, and heat stroke. All of these are preventable! During warm weather, the teacher should limit intensive exercise and allow students to drink plenty of water and rest sufficiently; lightweight clothing and a hat are also recommended. The teacher should also be scanning the class frequently for signs and symptoms of heat-related illnesses and overexertion. The general signs that precede heat-related illnesses are: unexplained headache, a throbbing head, chills, nausea, disorientation, dry skin, and loss of motor coordination. If the teacher suspects a student of being ill, the student should be moved to a cool place and the school nurse, a paramedic, or physician called. According to the American College of Sports Medicine (1983), extra caution should be taken if the temperature is above 82 degrees and the humidity is high. Other signs that may indicate overexertion and require medical assistance are: excessive breathlessness or shakiness long after the activity is completed, blue lips or nail beds, cold clammy skin, profound fatigue and a poor recovery rate, and muscle soreness lasting more than 24 hours.

Potentially Harmful Exercises

Always present a clear demonstration of exercises. While students are performing the activities, the teacher should be scanning for improper form or potentially dangerous movements. Children often forget what was presented during the demonstration or try to be creative and extra physical. Teachers often find themselves reminding students about basic exercise principles (*e.g.*, when stretching, apply pressure smoothly and do not bounce). The following section presents 13 exercise movements that the present authors and others (Timmermans & Martin, 1987; Corbin & Lindsey, 1983) have identified as not recommended or potentially harmful.

1. Straight leg sit-up (stressful on lower back).

FIGURE 14-1

Alternatives: Bent Knee Sit-Up, Reverse Sit-up, Crunchy.

2. Sit-up with hands behind neck (places undue pressure on the cervical spine).

FIGURE 14-2

Alternative: fold arms across chest; hands on opposite shoulder.

FIGURE 14-3

3. Double leg lift (stresses lower back and can overstretch abdominal muscles).

FIGURE 14-4

Alternative: reverse sit-up, knee to chest.

FIGURE 14-5   **FIGURE 14-6**

4. The Plough (promotes forward head; can injure neck and back if balance is lost).

FIGURE 14-7

Alternative: one-leg stretcher.

FIGURE 14-8

5. Inverted bicycle (similar to the Plough).

FIGURE 14-9

6. Back bend (arching) (stresses lower back and overstretches abdominal muscles).

FIGURE 14-10

7. Wrestler's Bridge (similar to back bend with severe stress on neck).

FIGURE 14-11

8. Hurdler's stretch (abnormal stress placed on bent knee; can also strain groin).

FIGURE 14-12

Alternative: lateral straddle stretch (with or without towel).

FIGURE 14-13

9. Quadriceps stretch (if the knee is bent 120° or more, can damage cartilage and ligaments).

FIGURE 14-14

Alternative: use opposite hand and foot

FIGURE 14-15

10. Ballistic ballet bar stretches (some experts believe that when the extended leg is raised 90° or more and the trunk is bent over the knee, sciatic nerve inflammation can occur).

FIGURE 14-16

Alternative: bent leg (low level) stretches.

FIGURE 14-17

11. Standing toe touch (can overstress muscles and ligaments of the lumbar).

FIGURE 14-18

Alternative: sitting stretches.

FIGURE 14-19

12. Deep knee bends (duck walk) (can damage knee joints when knees are bent more than 90°).

FIGURE 14-20

Alternative: half-squats (less than 90°).

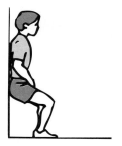

FIGURE 14-21
Wall Seat

13. Neck hyperextension (moving the head forward or backward during exercise. Neck circling can pinch arteries and nerves at the base of the skull).

Alternative: use this activity moderately (no circling movements) and while supporting the neck with a hand, also refer to Figure 14-61. (Yes, No).

FITNESS VALUES OF SELECTED ACTIVITIES

One of the primary tasks of the teacher is to select activities that are appropriate for the performance level of the children and provide objective-oriented fitness value. The President's Council on Physical Education and Sports (1986) conducted an expert panel survey to determine the health-related and general well-being benefits of popular physical pursuits. At the bottom of the ratings were golf, softball, and bowling. These activities also happen to be among the most active recreational pursuits in our society. At the top of the list were jogging, bicycling, swimming, and skating. The physical education teacher can make a significant impact on the types of activities that children participate in during their leisure time. The concept of recreational pursuits and fitness-oriented activities should be differentiated from one another with the understanding that most recreational activities are skill-oriented rather than health-related. Teachers should introduce children to fitness and skill-related recreational activities that have lifelong potential and provide the highest fitness value possible. Recreational activities such as bowling, golf, archery, and fishing, should not be viewed as substitutes for fitness development, but as separate leisure time pursuits.

Activity selection for the school program warrants considerable deliberation. As with the majority of schools today, time is short and program goals are to accomplish both health-related and motor-skill objectives. Many teachers will find that just as with fitness activity selection, they need to choose motor-skill and sport activities with consideration to their health-related benefits. It is not uncommon in the traditional elementary curriculum to find four to six weeks being allocated to a softball or bowling unit. If time is a limitation, this practice certainly is questionable. A more reasonable plan would limit the instructional time for low-fitness sports and other activities to five to ten days, and focus on skill attainment rather than extended practice and tournament play. In almost all communities, children can find youth sport activities for additional recreational endeavors. Few schools provide the resources and time structure that enable physical education teachers to develop optimal physical fitness and mastery in all the popular sports. The physical educator's primary responsibility should be to develop healthy children (and lifestyle behavior) and, as conditions permit, introduce them to basic and advanced sport skills for their recreational pursuits.

Table 14-1 presents the health-related benefits of selected physical activities. The activities are of a general nature, rather than specific game, dance/rhythms, and gymnastic events. As previously noted and generally understood, many simple games and rhythm dance activities offer minimal health-related benefits. The activities presented are rated high (H), medium (M), or low (L) in regard to the five health-related factors and an overall value. Teachers may select an activity for the specific fitness component benefits or for its value as a general multicomponent contributor. If the teacher needs a general activity to accomplish several component objectives, careful review of its contribution to each component should be considered. Good general activities such as jogging and rope jumping, for example, contribute little to the development of flexibility, thus additional exercises would be required.

While it should not be emphasized as a primary goal of the program, the inclusion of sports and other advanced skill-related activities does merit consideration in the intermediate grade curricululm. Children in the sports-skill phase of motor development (approximately eight years and older) find these activities a motivating force in their voluntary participation. Much of this is due to our nation's obsession with skill-related events and the focus on athletic heroes. Teachers traditionally include specific sports and other skill-related activities in the curriculum based on popularity or the desire for the child to learn a "fun" activity, rather than for the unique skill-related benefits. While this process may have some realistic merit and is not likely to be revised dramatically, there may be times when the teacher may wish to be selective. Just as with the health-related selection process, skill-related activities may also be chosen for the specific component contribution. If one of the program goals is to provide children with opportunities to develop defined skill-related fitness abilities, then specific component assessment must be administered and, if improvement is needed, specific activities prescribed. Table 14-2 provides the skill-related fitness values of selected general physical activities.

Table 14-1

Health-Related Benefits of Selected Physical Activities

Activity	Cardiovascular Fitness	Strength	Muscular Endurance	Flexibility	Weight Control	Overall Rating
Backpacking	M	M	H	M	M	M
Badminton	M	L	M	M	M	M
Baseball	L	L	L	L	L	L
Basketball	M	L	M	L	M	M
Basketball-Vigorous	H	L	M	L	H	M
Bicycling	H	M	M	L	H	M
Bowling	L	L	L	L	L	L
Calisthenics	L	M	M	M	L	M
Canoeing	M	L	M	L	M	M
Circuit Training	M	M	H	M	M	M
Dance, Ballet	M	M	M	H	M	M
Dance, Aerobic	H	M	M	M	H	M-H
Dance, Folk	M	L	M	L	M	M
Football	M	M	M	L	M	M
Gymnastics	M	H	H	H	M	M-H
Hiking	M	M	H	M	M	M
Jogging	H	L	M	L	H	M
Judo	L	M	M	M	L	M
Racquetball/ Paddleball	M-H	L	M	L	M-H	M
Rope Jumping	M	L	M	L	M	M
Skating, Ice	M	L	M	L	M	M
Skating, Roller	M	L	M	L	M	M
Skiing, X-Country	H	M	M	L	H	M
Skiing, Downhill	L	M	M	L	L	L-M
Soccer	M-H	M	M	M	H	M
Softball (slow)	L	L	L	L	L	L
Swimming	M-H	M	M	M	H	M-H
Table Tennis	L	L	L	L	L	L
Tennis	M	L	M	L	M	M
Volleyball	M	M	L	L	M	M
Walking (brisk)	M	L	M	L	M	M
Waterskiing	M	M	M	L	M	M
Weight Training	L	H	M	L	M	M

GENERAL ACTIVITY FORMATS

As the teacher selects activities to achieve fitness objectives, he or she may choose a specific exercise to develop a specific component (*e.g.,* jogging/cardiorespiratory, sit-ups/strength/endurance). Or the teacher can select a single format that allows for the development of several fitness characteristics. While the opportunity to concentrate on specific components with precise exercise(s) is ideal, this practice may not be feasible with some school programs due to time limitations or curricula model. Conditions in many schools require that each fitness phase of the lesson incorporate the multicomponent approach; for example, the three-day-per-week fitness

model. The remainder of this chapter will describe the following general activity formats: fitness stations (circuit training), challenge (obstacle) courses, calisthenics (and calisthenics to music), and aerobic dance. Specific exercises and activities that may be used with fitness stations and calisthenic routines can be found in the component sections in the latter part of this chapter.

Fitness Stations (Circuits)

This arrangement is one of the most popular and versatile of the general activity formats. Fitness stations are a circuit of exercises that allow students to move from one task to another. One version requires that the students attempt to complete as many stations as

Table 14-2

Skill-Related Benefits of Selected Physical Activities

Activity	Balance	Coordination	Agility	Power	Speed
Archery	M	H	L	L	L
Backpacking	M	M	M	M	L
Badminton	M	H	M	M	M
Baseball	M	H	M	H	M
Basketball	M	H	H	H	M
Bicycling	H	M	L	L	M
Bowling	M	H	M	M	M
Canoeing	M	M	L	M	L
Dance, Aerobic	M	M	M	L	L
Dance, Ballet	H	H	H	M	L
Football	M	M	H	H	H
Gymnastics	H	H	H	H	M
Hiking	M	M	M	M	L
Jogging	M	M	L	L	L
Judo	M	H	H	H	H
Racquetball/ Paddleball	M	H	H	M	M
Rope Jumping	M	M	M	M	L
Skating, Ice	H	M	M	M	M
Skating, Roller	H	M	M	M	M
Skiing, X-Country	M	H	M	H	M
Skiing, Downhill	H	H	H	M	L
Soccer	M	H	H	M	M
Softball (slow)	M	H	M	M	M
Swimming	M	M	M	M	L
Table Tennis	M	M	M	M	M
Tennis	M	H	M	M	M
Volleyball	M	H	M	M	M
Walking	M	M	L	L	L
Waterskiing	M	M	M	M	L
Weight Training	M	M	L	M	L

possible in the allocated time. The individualized version allows the student to exercise at stations designated by the teacher or desired by the student. The merits of the individualized format is that it can address the needs of the less-fit child (requiring remedial exercise) and challenge the student that possesses greater abilities. The circuit of stations can focus on a single fitness component (*e.g.,* muscular strength/endurance or flexibility) and provide different tasks requiring various levels of difficulty. Or it can emphasize a multicomponent presentation in which all or several fitness components are addressed at the various stations. With students needing remedial exercise (*e.g.,* they cannot do a single sit-up or pull-up), this format allows the teacher to provide exercises appropriate for their fitness level, while at the same time addresses the needs of the average and more-fit students. The following guidelines and instructional procedures should be considered.

1. Generally, each circuit should consist of six to nine stations safely spaced in a relatively large area.
2. Select an exercise on the basis of its specific fitness benefits that corresponds with class objectives.
3. Individualize the circuit as much as feasible.
4. Students should be able to perform the tasks independently.
5. Demonstrate proper exercise form and provide clear instructions. Posters are an excellent medium for providing task instructions and visual displays of proper exercise form. Teachers should not count on all students remembering specific instructions. A visual display (illustration) of the exercise may aid in minimizing potential injuries, as well as keeping students on task. Posters can be taped to walls, hung on poles, or tacked to stands for outdoor use. The displays should contain concise instructions

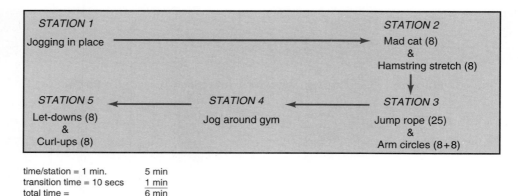

STATION 1		STATION 2
Jogging in place	→	Mad cat (8)
		&
		Hamstring stretch (8)
		↓
STATION 5	STATION 4	STATION 3
Let-downs (8)	← Jog around gym ←	Jump rope (25)
&		&
Curl-ups (8)		Arm circles (8+8)

time/station = 1 min.	5 min
transition time = 10 secs	1 min
total time =	6 min

FIGURE 14-22

Fitness circuit layout

that are readable from at least six feet away. Black and blue colors on a light background provide the best visibility. Red is not a preferred color unless placed on a white background. While large displays and colorful lettering and illustrations can add fun and enthusiasm to the activity, teachers need not be artists to create acceptable posters. A copy machine that enlarges can aid the teacher in producing displays. It is not unusual to find teachers that have made dozens of posters with a variety of themes for use with this format.

6. With the non-individualized plan (*i.e.*, students complete all stations), distribute students equally among stations to maximize equipment use and minimize waiting. Divide the total time allocated (after instructions) by the number of stations, thus setting a designated time limit per station. Allow eight to 10 seconds to change stations. A whistle is a popular device used with large classes to signal a station change; one blow means 30-second warning, two blows mean change. Music tapes can also be used to manage the station rotation. Record music to play the required time (one to two min.) at a station, then record eight to ten seconds of silence for rotation to the next station. Continue this procedure to cover the required amount of time. Some exercise stations may require more time to complete than others. To help minimize such a situation, one solution would be to increase the number of sets required or present multiple exercises at the easier stations.

Challenge (Obstacle) Courses (Appropriate for Levels II-IV). This is similar to the fitness circuit format except students must individually (or in pairs) negotiate each task on the course against a personal or standard time challenge. Since the basic concept is for each student to complete every task, individualizing is minimal, unless flexible (or no) time standards are established. The fitness focus of challenge courses are usually on skill-related components; namely, speed, agility, coordination, power, and balance. Tasks requiring a degree of muscular strength/endurance are also popular. When designing challenge courses, the teacher must not make any single task insurmountable. The individual challenge should be on the time that it takes to complete the course, rather than on the completion of a specific task. Ostacles such as a climbing rope or high climbing box may need modification before being allowed as an appropriate task for all students.

If a time standard is used, multiple levels of achievement are recommended. After setting up the course, the teacher should personally run through it for a safety check, then estimate a completion time from which three or four standards may be established. The teacher may wish to solicit students to aid in establishing standards. With multiple standards, students can be motivated to achieve the next level on a personal rather than collective basis. Figure 14-23 illustrates a sample challenge course. Popular challenge tasks include:

walking/running (around cones, chairs; through tires, hoops; short sprints)
stunts (Crab, Bear, and seal walks, log rolls) gymnastic skills (vaulting, forward rolls)
climbing (boxes, ropes, poles)
jumping/hopping (over hoops, ropes, cane poles)
hurdling
high jump
crawling (over and under objects; low poles, mats, boxes)
rope jumping (set number of turns)
push-ups, sit-ups, pull-ups, jumping jacks

Calisthenics

Calisthenics are traditionally a set of individual exercises that are performed in unison while students are positioned en masse. This often-highly-structured format requires that students follow the exercises, rhythm, and progression according to the standard

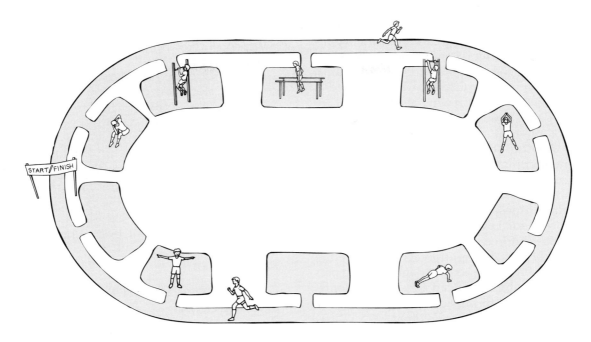

FIGURE 14-23
CHALLENGE COURSE

chosen by the activity leader. This activity format provides minimal opportunities for individualizing and, with younger children, such highly structured routines are inappropriate. In its traditional format, this system often frustrates the less-fit student who is unable to meet the designated standards, and is of minimal challenge to students that possess greater abilities. The value of the calisthenic format as a daily physical fitness routine is quite questionable.

Calisthenics usually consist of exercises that develop flexibility, strength and muscular endurance. Synonomous with the term calisthenics is the class arrangement that the activity usually requires. That is, students are positioned (en masse) in squad lines or on designated numbered spots. Teachers with large classes sometimes find this arrangement appropriate and a good starting place for the initial phase of the fitness lesson. A common exercise selection is stretching and other light flexibility work performed prior to a more strenuous phase of the lesson. Specific and intensive exercise can be developed within this format. However, when feasible, students should be allowed to complete the designated exercise at their own intensity level (*i.e.*, work load, repetitions).

CALISTHENICS TO MUSIC

Long before aerobic dancing was introduced people were exercising to music, which is a time-tested motivational aid for most exercise programs. Calisthenics to music is a unique fitness program due to its simplicity and adaptability. With 4/4

music playing in the background, children can exercise vigorously (for aerobic benefit) or easily (for general warm-up and flexibility work), moving to a memorized regime of calisthenics taught by the teacher, or an impromptu routine led by teacher or students. As long as the exercises are performed correctly and in time to the music, students can enjoy the physical and emotional benefits of this activity. Transitions and phrasing (critical in aerobic dance routines) are of little importance provided the students are able to move from one exercise to another without much interruption of rhythm. This format for exercise is often a follow-the-leader type of activity, though sometimes it is a structured routine. Depending on space constraints, objectives, and creative abilities of the leader, this format may or may not include locomotor skills, and may or may not enhance cardiorespiratory endurance. Generally, it is designed to enhance muscular strength and endurance, flexibility, and coordination, and is appropriate for all levels (I–IV).

The advantage of calisthenics to music over regular calisthenics is the additional motivation created by the music, and the less structured format. The teacher may choose calisthenics to music over aerobic dance in situations where simplicity of routine is needed because of time constraints, multiability levels, or lower ability levels of the students.

Aerobic Dance

Aerobic dance is an enjoyable and motivating medium for developing health-related physical fitness. As a general activity, aerobic dance is rated as one of the best contributors to developing cardiorespiratory fitness, flexibility, and muscular endurance. Its versatility lies not only in the possible exercise variations, but also in the type of music that can be used—including rock, jazz, country, swing and classical.

Aerobic dance is unique in its format of choreographed steps phrased specifically for the accompanying piece of music. The steps, which include locomotor and nonlocomotor movements, are put together so that movement and music complement one another. Another bonus of this activity is its popularity as a lifetime fitness endeavor. Aerobic dance is most appropriate for Levels III–IV (the intermediate grades), because children at these levels can learn the routines quickly and dance at levels that raise the heart rate effectively. Some aerobic dances can be performed effectively by advanced Level II students. However, calisthenics to music is generally a more appropriate activity for younger children.

The following basic instructional procedures should be considered for both aerobic dance and calisthenics to music:

1. When exercising to music with children in grades K-3, the exercises should be very basic and the speed of the music relatively slow. The developmental motor-skill abilities of younger children generally do not enable them to follow a quick-paced exercise or dance routine.
2. For most routines, the tempo of the music should be 120 to 140 beats per minute.
3. Movement increments should be organized by units of four, eight or 16 counts. If phrases are repeated, it is desirable to repeat the previous movements as well.
4. Introduce exercise movements with greater complexity progressively and gradually.
5. Allow extra time for transitions (aerobic dance) to be thoroughly learned.
6. Alternate high-intensity movements with less strenuous ones.
7. Encourage capable upper grade children to create their own routines. Offer guidance on appropriate music selection.
8. Use cue words to assist the children in anticipating the changes in movements and staying with the beat of the music. Example, Jog, Bounce, Reach.
9. An enthusiastic teacher and leader are the key to an enjoyable and motivating fitness experience.

The following list is a partial compilation of popular movements that can be used in aerobic dance and calisthenics to music. There are numerous possible combinations and routines that can be created. Table 14-3 displays a sample routine appropriate for intermediate grade children.

STEPS

Walking/marching/jogging (in place, directional)
Hop/step-hop
Bleking/schottische/polka/waltz
Rocking step/slide/grapevine
Bounce/skip/lunge
Jumping jacks/turn

ARM MOVEMENTS

Circles/flexing and extending/clapping/finger snaps
Swings/punching motion/slapping (legs)

LEG MOVEMENTS

Leg kicks (to side, front, back, chorus line)
Knee lifts (front, side)
Toe touches

FLOOR EXERCISES (FOR CALISTHENICS TO MUSIC ONLY)

Sit-ups (curl-ups)/push-ups/V-sit
Side leg raises (with straight leg while on side)
Crab kicks

ROPE JUMPING
STRETCHING

overhead, sideways (side bends), stand or sit

CARDIORESPIRATORY FITNESS ACTIVITIES

Cardiorespiratory (aerobic) efficiency is the single most important element in physical fitness. The ability of the heart, blood vessels and lungs to respond effectively to the demands of muscular activity are critical to the child's physical wellness and success in vigorous motor performance activities. There is a consensus among the medical profession that physical education programs that focus on vigorous aerobic-type activities may provide preventive characteristics in regard to obesity and cardiovascular disease. The basic assertion is that programs of this type should begin with the young child if appropriate lifestyle behaviors are to be realized with adults. Properly presented, cardiorespiratory activities can be one of the most enjoyable and motivating experiences in the school program.

Review of Basic Concepts and Principles

1. Frequency of cardiorespiratory exercise should be three to five days per week.
2. Intensity should be between 60 to 90 percent of maximum heart rate, approximately 145 to 185 beats per minute (see Table 14-4).

Table 14-3

Sample Aerobic Dance Routine (Intermediate)

Music: any lively 4/4 music* for example When The Saints Go Marching In or a Sousa March
Begin each pattern to the right (step, lunge, turn, etc.)

	Counts		Repetitions
Part I	8	1. Marching (knees high)	8
	8	2. Side lunges	4
	16	REPEAT 1 AND 2	
Part II	8	3. Jumping Jacks to the four winds-right (make 1/4 turn to the right with each j.j.)	4
	8	4. Repeat to the left	4
		5. Jog to the front (vigorous arms & legs)	8
	8	6. Jog backwards (hands on hips, legs straight, kicking forward)	8
Part III	8	7. Skip in place (knees high, vigorous arms)	8
	4	8. Jump and clap (make 1/4 turn to the right)	2
	4	9. Jog forward (class will be moving to the right)	4
	48	Repeat 7, 8, 9 three more times until class again faces front	
Part IV	12	10. Jog to form a circle (when in position continue jogging counter-clockwise in circle)	12
	4	11. Jump & clap (fast)	4
Part V	6	12. Skip to center	6
	2	13. Jump and clap (fast) (1/2 turn to face out)	2
	6	14. Skip out to circle	6
	2	15. Jump and clap (fast) (1/4 turn left to face counter-clockwise)	2

Note: 12, 13, 14, 15 can be repeated if the music selection is longer

Cue Card

I   March — 8 2
      Lunge — 4 2

II   Jumping Jacks to the four winds — R
      Jumping Jacks to the four winds — L
      Jog forward — 8
      Jog backward — 8

III   Skip — 8
      Jump and clap — 2
      Jog — 4

IV   Jog to circle — 12
      Jump and clap-center — 4

V   Skip-center — 6
      Jump/clap/turn — 2
      Skip-out — 6
      Jump/clap/turn — 2

*See the Appendices for a list of commercially developed aerobic dance music sources.

3. Duration, when possible, should be 15 to 20 continuous minutes.

4. Aerobic-type activities (requiring large amounts of oxygen and performed for long periods) are the key to development and maintenance.

5. Non-aerobic activities (short bursts of intense activity:sprints, weight lifting) do not significantly contribute to the development of this component.

6. Be sure that students have had a medical examination within the last year and their parents have approved their participation in an aerobic fitness program.

7. Teacher enthusiasm and physical vitality are key determinants in a successful cardiorespiratory endurance program.

8. Determining target heart rate—when the situation and understanding of the children permits, the teacher will want to introduce the concept of heart rate and its significance in exercise. Aerobic activities such as jogging, jumping rope, and aerobic dance provide excellent opportunities for developing this understanding and allowing students to monitor themselves. Children at all ages can develop some level of understanding regarding heart (pulse) rate, however with younger children (below third grade) the traditional techniques of measuring heart rate may be somewhat time consuming and awkward. While the monitoring of heart rate can aid in the understanding of one's performance level, it should not be considered an absolute must, especially with younger children. The primary objective of the cardiorespiratory program is for children to exercise aerobically for a duration of 15–30 minutes (with a target time of 20 continuous minutes).

Healthy children are capable of vigorous aerobic activity, and working heart rates of 200 beats per minute are not unusual. Target heart rates can be estimated by using the values in Table 14-4. These values are based on the accepted formula: 220 (predicted maximum heart rate) minus the child's age, multiplied by the selected intensity level.

The individual program should focus on progressively increasing the intensity level and duration of the activity with the emphasis on time. A recommended strategy for children is to progress from five to 20 minutes of continuous activity (hence, the focus on duration). The emphasis can then change to targeting the intensity level. A reasonable increase in duration is three to five minutes per week. The practice of continuous activity for 20 to 30 minutes is the primary objective. After the concept and procedures of determining individual heart rate are understood (and it may take a while), then duration with progressive increases in intensity can be incorporated. With children, an approximate target heart rate range of 60 to 80 percent intensity should be encouraged during the activity. This would mean that a nine-year-old should attempt to exercise at a heart rate of between 126 and 169 beats/minute and try to maintain around 150 beats/minute.

The preferred sites for measuring heart (pulse) rate are at the wrist (radial artery) and neck (carotid artery). Some experts caution the use of the neck for repeated measures over a short period, due to the possible decrease in blood flow to the brain. Pressure should never be placed on both carotids simultaneously. Figure 14-24 illustrates a child taking a pulse rate at the two sites. After the pulse location is found, it is taken for 15 seconds (using a cue from the teacher or a wall clock with second hand) and the number multiplied by four to determine the beats per minute (bpm). With both techniques, the index and second fingers are pressed easily until the pulse is found. With younger children (below the third grade level), these techniques may be somewhat cumbersome and distract from the primary objective of continuous aer-

Table 14-4

Target Heart Rates

Age	Predicted Maximum HR	Intensity Level				
		60%	65%	70%	75%	80%
5	215	129	140	150	161	172
6	214	128	139	150	161	171
7	213	127	138	149	160	170
8	212	127	138	148	159	170
9	211	126	137	148	158	169
10	210	126	136	147	158	168
11	209	125	136	146	157	167
12	208	124	135	146	156	166

FIGURE 14-24

Taking pulse rate: (a) left at cartoid artery; (b) right, at radial artery

obic activity. Younger children can grasp the basic understanding after an explanation of the heart's function during exercise and by placing a hand over their rapidly beating chest. The basic understanding should be that when we exercise, our heart beats faster and the more vigorous the exercise, the faster it beats. As a result of this activity, the heart becomes more efficient in pumping blood (oxygen) to the working muscles. This concept can be easily demonstrated by using one of the two techniques (wrist or neck) in the following experiment. Conduct this activity with individual monitoring and in pairs—with the students measuring each other's heart rates. Allow students to record values on paper and encourage their practicing this procedure at home and on the playground.

RECOMMENDED ACTIVITIES (ALL PERFORMED AEROBICALLY FOR OPTIMAL BENEFITS):

Brisk Walking	Cycling
Jogging	Swimming
Aerobic Dance	Skating
Jumping Rope	Cross Country Skiing
Aerobic Jumping	
Vigorous Games	
Vigorous Folk Dances	
Dual Activities	Team Sports
	Basketball
	Soccer
Paddleball	Flickerball
Handball	Hockey (floor/field)
	Speedball

Selected Activity Descriptions

WALKING

In recent years, a national trend toward brisk walking as a health-related fitness activity has provided an excellent medium for increasing the physical activity levels of adults and children of all ages. Research does support the use of brisk walking as a healthy activity and suggests that the benefits are similar to jogging, cycling, and aerobic dance, with less potential for injury and exercise burnout. With the less-fit child (*e.g.*, overweight), a walking program may be much more appropriate than jogging and running. The primary asset of brisk walking is that it increases one's

---

Table 14-5

Heart Rate (Exercise and Recovery)

Activity	Heart Rate (bpm)
Take Resting Rate	(15 sec.) × 4 =
Run In Place (or small group circles) for 2 minutes	(15 sec.) × 4 =
Recovery Rate after 2 minutes	(15 sec.) × 4 =
Recovery Rate after 4 minutes	(15 sec.) × 4 =

aerobic activity level and, therefore, aids in the prevention and remediation of obesity and other risk factors associated with heart disease and poor health. Walking is also an excellent outside-of-school exercise that can be done with the whole family while having a conversation!

Noted walker Robert Sweetgall has written an excellent book, *Walking for Little Children*, and developed an innovative Walking Wellness program that is highly recommended. Much of the following was inspired by his work.

Characteristics and Teaching Hints

1. Proper walking technique requires that the child walk heel-toe with weight directly over the feet and the arms swinging freely to and fro at the sides. An energetic arm swing is vital to an efficient brisk movement pattern. While walking hand-in-hand with another child may be appropriate in some situations, only about half of the exercise benefits (and calorie expenditure) are attained. Common errors include: sloughing (walk tall), toes pointed out or in (feet should point in straight line of travel), and lack of arm swing. See Chapter 10 for specific characteristics of the walking movement pattern.

2. As with jogging, for optimal benefit, the walker should elevate the heart rate to an appropriate level (120 to 170 bpm) and continue the activity for 20–30 minutes. Since brisk walking is not as stressful as jogging or running, the duration of walking can extend to 45 minutes or one hour with practice. Unlike jogging for children in general, emphasis should be on intensity (briskness) and duration.

3. Walking can be done every day. While 20–30 minutes is encouraged, even five- and ten-minute brisk walks have value toward total physical activity per week—a method that some physicians are recommending.

4. While brisk walking is more beneficial to cardiorespiratory development, Sweetgall and Neeves (1987) recommend that fast, short workouts be alternated with slow, long walks to allow for muscle recovery. It has been noted by the authors that slow, long walks are also beneficial because of the calorie burning function. The "hard-easy" principle of training is recommended.

5. A warm-up and cool-down phase should be done by gradually starting and ending with slow walks.

6. Generically there are three walking gears: slow, medium, and fast. For training purposes with children, "easy" (normal) and "brisk" appear to be the most practical paces. Paces that are too slow or too fast usually cause an awkward movement pattern, resulting in mechanical inefficiency. A brisk walk constitutes a medium/fast pace for children, which would be approximately 14–19 minutes per mile (3–4 mph). An easy walk would take approximately 22–25 minutes to cover a one-mile distance. Since stride length varies considerably among children four to 13 years of age, the concept of "easy" and "brisk" is quite individual, therefore values may vary considerably.

7. Use hills to increase intensity.

8. It takes the average child 2,200 footsteps to walk one mile.

Activities

1. Create field trips that the children can walk to and from. Depending on conditioning and grade level, one- to three-mile trips at the beginning of the year, and two- to five-mile walks later in year should be attainable goals.

2. Provide a "walk break" during one of the regularly scheduled recesses. Teachers are encouraged to participate.

3. Use motivational incentives such as mileage charts to record distances completed during the school day. Plain block charts, animal (*e.g.*, segmented snake or caterpillar) charts, and map charts (walk across the state, county, or nation) are popular. If funds are available, certificates, ribbons, or T-shirts may be given after a significant mileage goal is achieved.

4. Indy 500. Make a large oval walking track in the gym or outdoors (use cones). The teacher or leader will need three light signals; green (walk fast), yellow (slow), and red (stop after completing the round). The signals can be made out of cardboard and painted or cut out of heavy construction paper. Paint-mixing sticks make excellent handles. Distribute paper plates for "steering wheels". The leader stands at the start/finish line and begins the race (in groups up to 15–20) with the green signal. After two or three minutes (heart rates are up), a yellow signal can be used to slow down the walking pace. No jogging is allowed. If a child wishes to stop, a "pit-stop" may be taken in a designated pit-stop area. However unless in discomfort, the child should be encouraged to walk slowly and not stop completely. Recorded automobile sounds or racing music can provide additional stimulus for enthusiasm.

5. Walk The Ball. In pairs, students walk side by side while bouncing a small rubber ball. The objective is to keep bouncing the ball back and forth while maintaining the desired walking pace. Variations are numerous: vary pace, catch after two bounces, walk backwards, and catch with other hand.

6. Straw Walk. Establish a small (up to 200 yards around) indoor or outdoor (or both) walking track. Set a time limit of five to 10 minutes to complete the walk. As each child passes the starting line, a straw is given. Cones divided equally around the track are used to calculate distances of less than a full lap. With the final time limit signal (whistle), children move to the nearest cone and freeze. The objective is to collect as many straws as possible within the time limit. This activity provides an individual challenge to collect more straws each session and is an excellent technique for increasing heart rates. Depending on the distance of the course, teachers may wish to set standards of walking performance. Example: eight straws Level III, five straws Level II, two straws Level I.

JOGGING

Jogging is one of the highest rated and most enjoyable ways to develop cardiorespiratory fitness and muscular endurance in the legs. The majority of children love to run and participate in activities that test their speed and endurance. Jogging takes no special equipment (other than good running shoes) and can be done almost anywhere. While there are numerous benefits to a good walking program, especially for the less-fit individual, there will be several children that will prefer and immensely enjoy the feeling of moving with greater speeds. Jogging/running programs have become very popular at the elementary school primary and intermediate grade levels. It is not uncommon to find a high level of participation in school-based (voluntary) running clubs. These kinds of activities are an excellent medium for developing lifetime fitness behaviors and a healthy attitude toward vigorous physical activity.

Characteristics and Teaching Hints

1. While running with speed is not totally discouraged, the emphasis in the aerobic program should be on jogging and being able to cover long distances. Jogging is defined as an easy running pace that the individual is able to maintain for long distances. As the individual's cardiorespiratory fitness develops, it is not unusual for the jogging pace to increase as well. See Chapter 10 for illustrations depicting the mature jogging/running movement pattern. Key points unique to jogging include:
   a. Land on the heel of foot (not on the front as in sprinting), rock forward and push off with the ball of the foot.
   b. Elbows and hands should be held at a relaxed position (approximately waist level), with the elbows flexed no more than 90 to 100 degrees. Swing arms directly forward and backward.
   c. The stride should be smooth and even (do not overstride), with the back positioned as straight as possible and head up.
   d. Breathe normally (and perhaps deeply) through the nose and mouth.
   e. Avoid excess bouncing.
2. Equipment and attire—appropriate shoes and clothes are essential for preventing jogging-related injuries. During warm days, loose, comfortable clothes should be worn. In cold weather, sufficient covering of the body (sweatshirts, windbreakers) and exposed areas (gloves, ear muffs, cap) is important. A shoe designed for jogging should be encouraged; shoes designed for basketball, tennis, and the street (hard sole) are not recommended for long-distance running. Children should not be allowed to jog with bare feet.
3. Caution should be taken with jogging in warm temperatures. Allow plenty of water to be drunk and scan class frequently for heat-related illnesses.
4. Establish an indoor and outdoor jogging area with markers or number of laps required to complete a set distance. If possible, provide a jogging surface that is not hard. A track, grassy area, or dirt road is preferable to concrete and asphalt surfaces.
5. Warm-up and cool-down phases are important parts of any jogging/aerobic activity. Children should stretch and engage in a gradual increase in speed (fast walk to light jog) before the main jogging activity, and cool down afterwards by gradually reversing the process (light jog, fast walk and stretch). When practical, warm-up and cool-down phases should last for approximately three to five minutes each. Recommended flexibility exercises follow (descriptions can be found in Flexibility Activities section):

One Leg Stretcher	Lateral Straddle Stretch
Sitting Stretches	Quadriceps Stretch (use
Thigh Stretch	opposite hand/foot)
Bent Leg Stretches	Double Knee Hug
Shoulder and	Butterfly
Chest Stretch	Psoas Stretch

6. The concept of proper pacing should be taught and practiced. Children have a natural tendency to want to race, especially when running with others. As previously noted, the goal is for children to be able to jog continuously for at least 20 minutes. This objective requires that the children be conditioned gradually and with proper pacing strategy. Emphasis should be on jogging duration (time), rather than speed (intensity).
7. There are three general types of jogging/running programs (jog-walk-jog, continued jog,

Fartlek). From these methods, several combinations are possible. It is the teacher's job to assess the students and individualize the program as much as possible. Some children may be limited to and prefer a vigorous walking program, while others will develop or possess the abilities and desire to run (rather than jog) a set distance.

(a) The jog-walk-jog method is generally used to condition students for increasing the time it takes to cover a set distance. Over a designated distance, such as a half mile, the student is allowed to jog and walk as needed. Another variation of this method requires that the student jog and walk specified increments. Example: jog 220 yards, walk 110 yards. Jogging increments can be gradually increased and the walk portion decreased until a set goal is attained.

(b) With the continued jog method the student jogs the entire designated distance. Goals to achieve greater distances (two to two and a half miles; approximately 20 minutes) are the priority. For students with the ability to run at an even pace for an extended period, the continued run strategy may be a more appropriate activity.

(c) Fartlek training, also referred to as speed play, is a stimulating method that focuses on a frequent change of pace. With a class divided into small running lines (of eight to ten), a leader changes the pace of activity by walking, jogging, running, and sprinting for a designated distance (usually to a landmark), or short period of time, and over different surfaces (grass, track, hills) when feasible. The leader must be aware of the limitations of the group and not over-exert or leave behind a group member. Rest (walk or slow jog) phases between intensive bouts are vital to optimal student motivation and task completion. Teachers may wish to group students by ability. A more formalized and systematic version consists of the teacher gradually increasing the duration and intensity of specific phases of the activity.

Sample

brisk walk	2 minutes
jog	2 minutes
run	30 seconds
sprint	15 seconds
(repeat jog, run, sprint)	
brisk walk	30 seconds

Activities

1. Jogging Clubs. Similar to the walking clubs previously described, jogging clubs provide motivational opportunities for children to extend their running desires while developing cardiorespiratory fitness and a healthy lifestyle behavior. With the emphasis now on health-related fitness, more and more schools are organizing Roadrunner and Healthy Jogger clubs with wall displays depicting individual student mileage records. While the teacher will want each able student to do at least some walking/jogging as part of the general program, jogging clubs (with the aim of extending mileage) should be voluntary. Teachers should also be careful about allowing students to make up missed days with double or triple distances. The aim is for the child to develop an attitude for regularly scheduled activity. Missed days should be completed at other times scheduled by the teacher (e.g., before school, after school).

2. Indy 500. (see description in walking section)

3. Indian Running. Students jog in a line (following a leader) or in a large circle. On a signal (whistle, drum beat, or "go"), the last person in line sprints or runs to the front and becomes the new leader. While the last person is running to the front, the other children should maintain a steady jogging pace. The last person should run on the outside of the circle (use cones to designate) or to the right of a line formation.

4. European Rhythmic Running. This activity consists of an easy-paced jog that is done to the accompaniment of a drum or tom-tom. The primary purpose is to develop a rhythmical jogging/running pace that can be sustained for prolonged distances. The activity begins in a circle formation with the children clapping their hands to the beat of the drum. After a rhythmic beat is established, the children jog in place while standing one behind the other, ready to move as instructed. Variations include:

using a parachute (clockwise/counter-clockwise)
varying the path of movement (random or specific pathway) by a line leader
varying the speed (tempo) slow jog to sprint
leaping high on accent (hard) beat or whistle
jogging and leaping with a partner
changing places with another while moving in wide formation
freezing on the signal (double beat or whistle)
lifting knees high and regular
making a full turn in four jog steps
clapping hands while jogging (every beat/specific beats)
jogging randomly, then return to circle formation on a signal
on command "center", jogging toward center four steps, turn and return to circle
tossing and catching a bean bag on a specific beat or step (every fourth)

JUMPING ROPE

Jumping rope, also called rope skipping, is an excellent cardiorespiratory and general coordination activity. Much of the current popularity associated with jumping rope (rope skipping) is due to the The American Heart Association's Jump Rope for Heart program. This program has triggered a national phenomenon that has introduced millions of children to this excellent lifetime aerobic activity. No longer considered an activity primarily for young girls, jumping rope has developed into a favorite form of exercise and leisure activity for both sexes and all ages. Many schools and communities take great pride in their programs, as evidenced by making it the focus of presentations to parents, organizing clubs, and other groups, and forming highly skilled teams with spirited names such as the "Skip-Its", "Heart Beats", and "Palpitations."

Teaching Hints and Activities

1. See Chapter 10, Jumping Rope, for information related to equipment, basic body position and rope-jumping steps. The rope-jumping steps are presented in the approximate order of difficulty beginning with the Two-Foot Step.

2. There will be some primary grade level children, especially preschool to second grade, that will not be able to jump an individual rope effectively enough to produce an aerobic effect. As a fitness activity, aerobic jumping (with and without stationary ropes) may be more appropriate. With some practice, most children in the third grade and older will be able to effectively perform the basic rope-jumping patterns.

3. It may be helpful to begin each new step without a rope.

4. Partner jumping (individual ropes). Several steps are possible when one child turns the individual rope and another child joins in. If this activity is conducted for fitness purposes, the exercise should include sustained actions for both individuals with as little waiting as possible. The teacher should note that for beginners the action of running into a jumping pattern can be difficult, therefore it may be more appropriate to begin with the child already in position, then progress to the run-in.
   Examples:
   (a) One child turns and the other stands in front in preparation to run in.
      Run in and jump together face to face; could place hands on turner's waist or shoulders
      Run in and jump with back to turner
      Match selected jumping steps
      Change turn direction; forward or backward

   (b) Partners stand side by side with inside hands joined while turning rope with outside hands.
      Face in the same direction
      Face in opposite directions; join right, then left hands
      Lock inside elbows
      Lift inside knees
      Match selected jumping steps
   (c) Partners stand back to back while holding a single rope in right hand, then left hand.
      Change direction of rope turn
   (d) One child turns the rope while the other stands in back ready to run in. The runner moves in and grasps the partner's shoulders or waist as they jump together.
   (e) Three children jump; one turns the rope (forward or backward), one runs in from the front, and the other runs in from behind.
   (f) Two children turning individual ropes face each other; one turns forward and the other backward with both jumping over each rope.

5. Jumping with long ropes (two rope turners and one or more in the middle) is not as conducive to aerobic fitness as individual rope jumping.

6. Store ropes by hanging on hooks, pegs, or over boxes and stands; this prevents troublesome tangles.

7. Develop the initial stages of a jumping step before adding music, especially with beginners. Children should first try the new step without a rope. At this stage, musical accompaniment may provide additional motivation and help the child maintain a steady and continuous rhythm. Music with a 4/4 rhythm works well.

8. Several popular folk dances, especially those with a 4/4 rhythm such as polkas and schottisches, provide excellent jump-rope routine music. Among the favorites are:

Shoo Fly	Bleking	Hora
Pop Goes The Weasel	Schottische	
The Popcorn Man	Polka	
Loobie Loo	Little Brown Jug	

9. The teacher and intermediate grade students can have great fun creating routines to popular rock-and-roll, jazz, country-and-western, and rhythm-and-blues tunes.

10. There are several excellent commercial jump-rope records available. (See the Appendices for a list of selected records and sources.)

11. Mileage charts similar to the ones used with walking and jogging are good motivational aides. Children can "Skip Across America" on maps that depict mileage between major cities; for example, each minute of continuous jumping equals five miles.

12. Jump Rope for Heart provides an exemplary set of curriculum materials and activity suggestions. Contact the nearest American Heart Association office or the American Alliance for Health, Physical Education, Recreation, and Dance: Director Special Events. (AAHPERD, 1900 Association Drive, Reston, VA 22091, (703) 476-3488)

AEROBIC JUMPING

Similar to aerobic dance, aerobic jumping routines are rhythmical, continuous activities that involve a diversity of arm and leg positions. Aerobic jumping routines offer children good cardiorespiratory exercise and are superb lead-ups to rope jumping and exercise(aerobic) dance. Using lines on the floor or stationary ropes, younger or less—skilled children can use basic and creative one—and two—foot movement patterns to develop cardiorespiratory fitness by jumping for prolonged periods of time. For children that have mastered the basic and advanced rope–jumping steps, aerobic jumping can provide a new challenge that is similar to aerobic dance.

Teaching Hints and Activities

1. With and without musical accompaniment, use a variety of basic jumps: leap, one-foot takeoff/two-foot landing, two-foot takeoff, and hop.
2. As a lead-up activity to jumping with a rope or as an additional challenge for the proficient rope jumper, use the basic and advanced individual rope-jumping steps described in the previous section.
3. Vary arm positions: hands on hips, overhead, jogging position, clasped behind head, straight out to sides or in front, clapping, etc.
4. When using music, begin with 4/4 musical selections (see rope jumping). Progress to eight and 16 repetition patterns and calisthenics and aerobic dance routines include jumping. (See the Appendices for a list of aerobic selections.)
5. Allow older children to lead informal routines or create their own on paper as a project and present them to the class.
6. Use cue words to present step changes. Examples: "hop right-4," "leap forward," "kick left-4."
7. Emphasize efficient jumping patterns that allow for sustained (aerobic) activity, rather than short bursts of exercise followed by rest. Hopping or jumping relays that are brief non-aerobic bouts of exercise are more beneficial to leg endurance and power than cardiorespiratory fitness.
8. Alternate less-forceful steps (alternate step, heel-toe, leap, rocker step, swing step) with heavy movements (repeated hops and hard two-foot landings).
9. Jumping floor patterns (using marked lines or ropes) are excellent instructional aids. Popular patterns include: straight line, circle, rings of inner circles, snake (lazy rope), V, parallel lines, 4-square, and hopscotch patterns. See Rope Stunts under Gymnastics for descriptions of floor patterns.

Vigorous Games & Dances

There are several traditional games and dances available that can potentially provide an aerobic experience. While some are basically aerobic in nature if prolonged, others can be easily modified (that is, aerobicized) to provide the stimulation needed for cardiorespiratory development. For example, games and dances that use slower locomotor movements (such as walking) may be modified, when practical, by substituting a faster form of locomotion (skip, slide, run). If the activity is too brief to provide an aerobic effect, it can be repeated several times or phases prolonged. Team sport activities such as basketball, soccer, field/floor hockey, speedball, and flickerball include stimulating activities such as related relays, drills, and modified games. Aerobic benefits may also be derived through prolonged participation in individual and partner activities such as paddleball, badminton, and frisbee. Table 14-7 presents samples of commonly used games and dances that are potentially aerobic. Descriptions of activities can be found in Chapters 15 and 16.

FLEXIBILITY ACTIVITIES

Flexibility is the measure of the range of movement possible at each joint. The importance of overall flexibility has been clearly established (Chapter 4) as an essential component in one's health-related fitness. The experiences presented in this section are suggested as appropriate to improve both static and dynamic levels of flexibility as well as joint strength. Another fitness concern—posture—is also directly influenced by the child's flexibility.

REVIEW OF BASIC PRINCIPLES & TEACHING HINTS

1. The muscle must be stretched beyond its normal length.
2. If possible, stretch all muscle groups daily, otherwise at least three days a week.
3. Hold each stretch for 10 to 30 seconds, repeat for five to six repetitions and three to five sets (cycles).
4. Slow static stretches are best, do not bounce.

Table 14-7

Sample of Vigorous Games & Dances

Games		Dances	
Levels I & II	Jet Pilot	Levels I & II	A Hunting We Will Go
	Charlie Over the Water		Muffin Man
	Scarecrow and Cranes		Sally Go Around The Moon
	Whistle Stop		Bow Belinda
	Wild Horse Roundup		Dance of Greeting
	In the Creek		Hansel and Gretel
	Hop Tag		Jump Jim Joe
	Partner Tag		Maypole Dance
	Chain Tag		Little Brown Jug
	Galloping Lizzie		
	Shadow	Levels III & IV	Paw-Paw Patch
	Circle Chase		Pease Porridge Hot
	Line Touch		The Old Man
			Hopp Mor Annika
Relays (I–IV)	Locomotor Relay		The Popcorn Man
	Circle Post Relay		Carousel
	Rescue Relay		Created Hen
	Zig Zag Relay		Oh Susanna
	Shuttle Relay		Patty Cake Polka
	Two-Legged Relay		Black Nag
			Tinikling
Levels III & IV	Capture the Flag		
	Pirate's Gold		
	Trees		
	Steal The Treasure		
	Grabbing Sticks		

5. Flexibility is joint specific.
6. Flexibility exercises should be used to warm up and cool down.
7. Flexibility enhances efficient movement and may reduce the incidence of injured muscles.
8. Adequate strength and flexibility contribute to good posture.
9. Use flexibility exercises as a pacing technique inserted between strength and muscular endurance activities.

RECOMMENDED GENERAL ACTIVITIES

Movement stories
Static stretching exercises
Calisthenic exercises
Fitness stations (circuit)
Aerobic dance
Selected
Games
Rhythms/Dances
Gymnastic Activities

STARTING POSITIONS FOR EXERCISES

Various starting positions are used for the activities presented in this section. The following illustrations are offered for clarification.

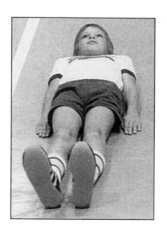

FIGURE 14-25
1. Supine

FIGURE 14-26
2. Prone

FIGURE 14-27

3. Hook Lying

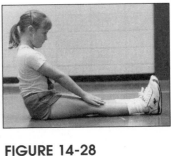

FIGURE 14-28

4. Long Sit

FIGURE 14-29

5. Straddle Sit

FIGURE 14-30

6. Hook Sit

FIGURE 14-31

7. Cross-Leg Sit

FIGURE 14-32

8. Sitting on Heels

FIGURE 14-33

9. Standing

FIGURE 14-34

10. Straddle Stand

FIGURE 14-35

11. Front Leaning Rest

Selected Activity Descriptions

Movement Stories.   Through the medium of movement stories, children can be stimulated to execute many moves that will serve to test out and improve the range of motion of their joints. As the teacher verbalizes a fairy tale or short story, the students act out the roles of various people or animals in the story. Through the use of variability of time, force, space, and relationships, the children can be required to perform stretching, agile moves that will both stretch and strengthen the various joints of the body. The joints most often used in such imaginative activities are the spinal vertebrae, hips, knees, ankles, shoulders, elbows, wrist, and fingers (especially if climbing apparatus is available).

Wands also offer excellent challenges for flexibility as the body attempts to move over and under individually held wands. (See Fig. 14-39.)

FIGURE 14-36

12. **Side Leaning Rest**

FIGURE 14-37

13. **Hands and Knees**

FIGURE 14-38

14. **Crab**

FIGURE 14-39

STATIC AND DYNAMIC STRETCHING EXERCISES

LEGS

FIGURE 14-40

1. **Hamstring Stretch.**
   Starting position: lying on back.
   Procedure: Extend one straight leg up toward the ceiling; later grasp toes and try to keep knees straight.

FIGURE 14-42

3. **Lateral Straddle Stretch.**
   Starting Position: straddle sit.
   Procedure: Bend one leg so sole of foot touches inside thigh of other leg. Bend forward over the outstretched leg, reaching both hands towards the foot. The head is pulled over the straight knee. Hold 6–10 seconds.

FIGURE 14-41

2. **Butterfly.**
   Starting Position: hook sit.
   Procedure: Place soles of feet together, hands grasp legs above the ankles and pull feet close to the body. Gently press knees towards the floor and hold the position for 10 seconds. Back and neck are held straight.

FIGURE 14-43

4. **Quadricep Stretch.**
   Starting Position: prone position.
   Procedure: Alternate pulling each lower leg toward the buttocks; both legs can also be pulled simultaneously.

FIGURE 14-44

5. **Foot to Head.**
   Starting Position: crossed-leg sit.
   Procedure: Alternate pulling each foot to head.

6. **Calf and Arch Stretch.**

Starting Position: standing—arms held out in front.

Procedure: Slowly squat while keeping heels flat on the floor; place hands on floor in front of feet and continue to stretch calf and feet muscles; rock slowly back and forth, allowing heels to rise only if necessary; emphasize keeping heels in contact with the floor as much as possible.

FIGURE 14-45

7. **Leg, Foot, Back Stretch.**

Starting Position: hands and knees, tops of feet resting on floor.

Procedure: Alternate sitting back on heels while extending the arms forward; emphasize keeping entire surface of lower legs and tops of feet in contact with the floor.

FIGURE 14-46

8. **Calf Stretch.**

Starting Position: front lean against wall, standing 1 ½ to 2 feet from the wall.

Procedure: Lean forward to bring chest as close to wall as possible (head may be turned to one side) while keeping back and knees straight and heels flat on floor. Increase standing distance from wall as flexibility permits.

FIGURE 14-47

9. **Heel Walk.**

Starting Position: standing.

Procedure: Walk on heels with legs straight and toes pointing toward the ceiling; first attempt should be two sets of 10 yards each.

FIGURE 14-48

TRUNK

1. Low Back Stretch.

Starting Position: straddle sitting.

Procedure: Alternate pulling torso toward each leg; torso can also be pulled straight forward through legs. In long sit position, pull torso over both knees. Do not lock knees. Hold each position a minimum of 10 seconds.

FIGURE 14-49

2. Low Back Stretch (pelvic tilt).

Starting Position: hook lying, arms at sides.

Procedure: Inhale deeply, allowing the abdomen to rise (diaphragmatic breathing); exhale while pressing back to the floor (Use abdominal muscles to push your backbone into the floor); continue pressing until all air is exhaled; repeat the procedure four to six times.

FIGURE 14-50

3. Mad Cat.

Starting Position: hands and knees, head up, focus straight ahead, back relaxed.

Procedure: Arch back up by pulling in the abdomen, tightening the buttocks, lowering the head, and exhaling; hold until exhalation is completed, then relax, letting the back and abdomen sag while inhaling, head returns to starting position, repeat cycle rhythmically for six repetitions.

FIGURE 14-51

4. Psoas Stretch.

Starting Position: long lying.

Procedure: Alternate hugging each knee to the chest while keeping outstretched leg flat to the floor; emphasize keeping low back in contact with floor.

FIGURE 14-52

5. Trees.

Starting Position: moderate straddle stand, arms by sides or held straight overhead.

Procedure: Slowly allow the upper body to bend right, left, forward, and backward; when arms are held above the head more weight resistance will be experienced.

FIGURE 14-53

6. Washing Machine Twist.

Starting Position: straddle standing.

Procedure: Slowly twist the body rhythmically from right to left; arms may be held in various positions, and head should turn in direction of twist.

FIGURE 14-54

7. Supine Tuck.

Starting Position: Hook lying.

Procedure: Hug both legs to chest, knees separated and pulled to shoulders, hips pulled off of floor. Head and shoulders maintain contact with the floor. Hold a tight tuck for 10–20 seconds.

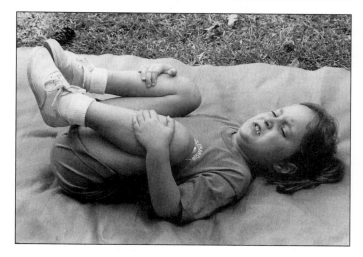

FIGURE 14-55

ARM AND SHOULDER GIRDLE

1. Shoulder Stretch No. 1.

Starting Position: standing, arms at sides.

Procedure: Alternate pulling shoulder blades together while rotating arms outward and back (thumbs point to rear) and pulling shoulders forward while rotating shoulders and arms forward and inward.

FIGURE 14-56

2. **Shoulder Stretch No. 2.**
Starting Position: straddle standing.
Procedure: Hold the hands behind the back, bend the trunk forward until parallel to the floor, and then left arms behind back as high as possible. Do not lock the knees.

FIGURE 14-57

FIGURE 14-58

3. **Arm Circles.**
Starting Position: moderate straddle standing, arms out to side.
Procedure: Circle arms (large circles—forward and backward) utilizing full range of motion; abdomen and buttocks held firm to minimize lumbar curve.

FIGURE 14-59

4. **Lateral Arm Pulls.**
Starting Position: moderate straddle standing.
Procedure: Move one arm shoulder high across midline of body; free arm reaches under and grasps extended arm right above elbow; pull arm to maximum position; repeat with other arm.

5. **Vertical Arm Pulls.**
Starting Position: moderate straddle standing.
Procedure: One arm reaches up the back to meet other arm reaching over the shoulder; grasp hands and hold in maximum stretch, alternate arms.

FIGURE 14-60

FIGURE 14-61

NECK

1. **Yes, No.**
Starting Position: moderate straddle standing, hands at sides.
Procedure: Stand tall in good posture; alternate rotating the head as far as possible to the right and then to the left (4 times), forward and backward (4 times); no circular rotations (that is, front, right, back, left in rapid sequence). *Caution should be taken not to hyperextend.*

FIGURE 14-62

2. **Neck Stretch.**
Starting Position: moderate straddle stand or cross-leg sit.
Procedure: Stand or sit tall in good posture; place left hand on top right side of head and gently pull head to the left; repeat with the right hand pulling head to the right; place both hands on back of head and gently pull chin to chest; move head up and backward so face is toward the ceiling. Keep back straight during entire exercise.

Selected Games, Dance, and Gymnastic Activities

Fortunately, there are numerous activities available that can be used to enhance the development of flexibility. Activities that involve stretching/bending, swinging/swaying, and twisting/turning movements provide excellent opportunities to achieve desired objectives. Most activities that do not contain these characteristics can be easily modified to be of benefit. For example, while children are waiting in line during a relay activity or a softball game, they can be doing static and dynamic stretching exercises. Table 14-8 presents a sample of game, dance, and gymnastic activities that may be used to enhance the development of flexibility.

MUSCULAR STRENGTH/ ENDURANCE ACTIVITIES

Muscular strength is demonstrated by the amount of force (intensity) that can be exerted by a muscle or group or muscles working against resistance. For the child, the resistance is often simply the movement of body parts against gravity. *Muscular endurance* is demonstrated by the length of time (duration) that a muscle(s) can persist in exertion. With slight modification (intensity and duration), most of the same exercises can be used to develop both muscular strength and endurance. The reader is reminded that although strength can be present without endurance, the reverse

is not true. To train for endurance, the resistance (intensity) is reduced so the duration of participation can be lengthened sufficiently to cause an overload (overtime) on the muscle(s) and/or organic system.

Review of Basic Principles & Teaching Hints

1. Muscular strength/endurance is developed through resistance exercises.
2. Isotonic exercise is dynamic resistance work that involves joint movement such as in performing curl-ups and exercises on resistive exercise machines.
3. Isometric exercise is static resistance work that involves no joint movement such as in performing a static push-up, flexed-arm hang, and pressing the legs or arms against an immovable object.
4. Frequency should be every other day or at least three days a week.
5. Isometric contractions should be held for five to eight seconds and repeated for three sets.
6. Simply lifting their own body weight offers enough isotonic resistance for strength building in children.
7. To increase muscular endurance, lighten the resistance and increase the repetitions.
8. Low-intensity activities, such as walking up steps and jumping jacks, should be done for at least one full minute to be effective. Beginners should start with fewer repetitions in one minute and work up to one per second (60 per minute).

Table 14-8

Sample of Enhancements for Flexibility

	Games	Dances	Gymnastics Activities
Levels I–II	Simon Says Do This Do That Shoe Twister Follow The Leader Over The Brook Islands Skin The Snake In and Out Popcorn Back To Back Chinese Hurdle Eyeglasses Fly Trap Here To There	Hickory Dickory Dock Hockey Pockey Turn the Glass Over Hansel and Gretel Cat's Meow Limbo (I–IV) Pease Porridge Hot Klapp Tanz Skip To My Lou Creative Dance (I–IV) (scarfs/streamers) Shoo Fly	(All Appropriate for I–IV) Row Your Boat Inch Worm Egg Roll Forward/Backward Roll Wring The Washrag The Bridge Blow Up The Balloon Animal Walks Leap Frog Stoop and Stretch Thread The Needle Straight Rope Pick The Grass Heel Slap Heel Click
Levels III–IV	Tag (I–IV) Hopscotch (I–IV)	Duchess Hustle Norwegian Mountain March Little Man in a Fix Poi-Poi Kool Kat Ten Pretty Girls The Bird Dance Ace of Diamonds Heads and Sides Waves of Tory Turnaround Cshebogar Virginia Reel The Boogie Beat	Toe Tuck Stick Jump Spanker Inverse Twister Twister Grapevine Rabbit Jump Back Scratcher Tuck Jump Twist Away Floor Touch Greet The Toe Corkscrew Rhythmic Gymnastics

9. Exercises of medium intensity such as sit-ups and push-ups should begin with six to eight repetitions and be increased until 25 are achieved. This may be repeated for three sets.

10. After 25 repetitions of an exercise is completed (in good form), the student may move on to the next progression.

11. All exercises should be done slowly (no faster than one per second).

12. To maintain flexibility, each exercised muscle and joint should be moved through a full range of motion.

13. Stress proper form and explain why it is important for efficiency and safety.

14. Along with the basic concepts of strength/endurance (Chapter 4), teach students the scientific and common names of the major muscle groups.

15. Teach proper breathing techniques—that is, the breath should not be held, but rather exhaled during exertion and inhaled during recovery.

16. Emphasize the importance of striving to perform as well or better than the student's last individual performance.

Recommended Activities

Upper Body

Chin-ups	Horizontal Ladder Movement	
Dips	Vertical Pole Climb	
Push-ups	Parachute Play	Paddleball
Gymnastics	Basketball	Handball
Rope Climbing	Swimming	Scooter Activities
Resistance Exercises	Rowing (Canoeing)	
Aerobic Dance	Wrestling	

Trunk (Abdomen)

Curl-ups	Wrestling	Aerobic Dance
Rope Climbing	Gymnastics	
Leg Lifts	Resistance Exercises	

Lower Body (Legs)

Running	Soccer
Jumping Rope	Basketball
Stair Climbing	Skiing
Hiking	Speedball
Cycling	Exercise Dance
	Aerobic Dance
	Folk Dance

Selected Activity Descriptions

LEGS

FIGURE 14-63

1. **Partial Squats**
   Starting Position: standing, arms at sides.
   Procedure: With torso leaning slightly forward and arms held out in front, sit on an imaginary stool (thighs parallel to the ground); hold position for a minimum of six seconds.

2. **Heel Walks**
   Starting Position: standing.
   Procedure: Walk on heels with legs straight throughout and toes pointed toward the ceiling; first attempt should be two sets of 10 yards each (see Figure 14-48).

3. **Running for Speed**
   Starting Position: standing.
   Procedure:
   a. Run short distances of up to 50 yards; relays;
   b. Alternate running for speed with quick stops;
   c. Additional challenges can be obtained from Chapter 10, Running.

4. **Puppy Run**
   Starting Position: on hands and feet, knees slightly bent, head up.
   Procedure: Run (scamper) about like a puppy, forward, backward, sideward.

5. **Bear Walk**
   Starting Position: weight primarily on feet but with hands touching floor in front.
   Procedure: Slowly travel forward by simultaneously moving the hand and foot on the same side; movements are slow, heavy, deliberate, nonsupporting arm and leg should be lifted high.

6. **Jumping**
   Starting Position: standing.
   Procedure:
   a. Jump repeatedly for height; arms at sides; arms extended to reach;
   b. Jump for distance;
   c. Jump into the air and click heels together (center, right, left);
   d. Additional challenges can be obtained from Chapter 10, Jumping.
   e. See Gymnastic or gymnastics later this chapter.

7. **Jump to Run**
   Starting Position: supine or prone position.
   Procedure: On signal, quickly get to feet and run to a designated area as fast as possible.

FIGURE 14-64

8. **Skier's Sit (and wall walk)**
   Starting Position: in a sitting position, Thighs parallel to the floor with entire back against the wall; arms held crossed in front of body at shoulder height. Pull chin in.

Procedure: Have students sit in the isometric position for six seconds. Then begin to scoot the body up the wall as the legs gradually straighten and the feet are walked back towards the wall. Firm contact with head and entire back is required.

FIGURE 14-65

9. **Get Up**
   Starting Position: children of equal size stand back-to-back with elbows hooked.
   Procedure: Slowly sit down while backs press against one another.

10. **Mountain Climber**
    Starting Position: front-leaning rest, head up.
    Procedure: Alternate drawing each leg up under the body; change speed from slow to fast.

FIGURE 14-66

11. **Jumping Jack**
    Starting Position: standing, arms at sides.
    Procedure: Simultaneously jump to a straddle position and repeat.

12. **Squat-Thrust**
    Starting Position: standing, arms at sides.
    Procedure: Child bends the knees and places hands on the floor in a squat position, thrusts the feet and legs backward, assuming a push-up position, and then returns to a squat position and stands erect.

FIGURE 14-67

One squat-thrust is counted each time the child resumes the standing position. A push-up may be added to the basic squat-thrust exercise.

13. **Partner Tug-of-War**
    Starting Position: (partners) holding on to opposite ends of an individual tug-o-rope, forward stride position.
    Procedure: On signal, both students begin pulling against one another; pulling continues until one student is pulled across the line separating the two students.

FIGURE 14-68

14. **Gymnastic Activities:**
    See Chapter 17 for descriptions.

Animal walks	Human spring	Leap frog
Walking chair	Knee slapper	Jumping swan
Rope stunts	Toe touch	Heel click
Inchworm	Kangaroo jump	Tuck jump
Rising sun	Bouncing ball	Rabbit jump
Knee jump	elevator	Heel slap
Turk stand	Jumping tubes	Foot push
Jacknife	Sitting balance	Angel stand
Split jump	Bent knee hop	Jump foot
Single squat	Vaulting	

See Chapter 11 (stretch/bend, turn/twist, sway/swing)

15. Dance Activities:
See Chapter 16 for descriptions.

Jump Jim Joe	Norwegian Mountain March
Cherkassiya	Rumunsko Kolo
Polka (any)	Teton Mountain Stomp
Hora	Tinikling
Limbo	Uno, Dos, Tres
Mayim! Mayim!	Zip Code 001 (variation No. 3)

TRUNK

FIGURE 14-69

1. Curl-Ups
Starting Position: hook lying, arms folded across chest or extended toward feet and outside of Ankles.

Procedure: Lift head, chin on chest, lift shoulders; hold this curled position for a minimum of 6 seconds (exhale). Do not hold feet except for assessment.

FIGURE 14-70

2. Crunchies
Starting Position: hook lying, arms folded across chest or extended toward feet.

Procedure: Lift head and shoulders from floor while simultaneously pressing the back against the floor and rolling pelvis backward; feet may come off the ground.

FIGURE 14-71

3. Reverse Curl-Ups
Starting Position: supine, arms held out to side.
Procedure: Bring legs to the chest and hold both knees tightly to chest; extend legs, repeat.

4. Back Press
Starting Position: hook lying, arms at sides.
Procedure: Inhale allowing abdomen to rise; exhale while pressing back flat against the floor. Continue pressing until all air is exhaled; repeat the procedure 4–6 times (see Figure 14-50; eliminate the initial pelvic tilt-arch).

5. Cocoon Hang
Starting Position: straight hang from a bar.
Procedure: Both legs are curled to chest and held for as long as possible; repeat as many times as possible.

FIGURE 14-72

FIGURE 14-73

6. Prancing Ponies
Starting Position: standing, arms at sides.
Procedure: Rhythmically lift knees to hip level in a prancing fashion; alternate slow to fast speeds; various arm positions can be used.

7. Swan Balance Variations
Starting Position: prone, arms at sides.
Procedure: Lift arms, head, hold a minimum of 6 seconds; with each repetition the arms move to a new position. (figure 14-174)

FIGURE 14-74
Swan Balance Variations

8. **Shoulder Girdle Developer**

Starting Position: Hook lying.

Procedure: Exercise has three parts

Part 1: Move arms 2–3 inches from body, and press palms strongly against floor for 10 seconds, relax for 3 seconds, 5 repetitions.

Part 2: Move upper arms to 90° angle from body, bend elbows 90° to assume a reverse "T" position. Press backs of hands strongly against floor for 10 seconds, relax for 3 seconds, 5 repetitions.

Part 3: Move arms directly overhead, arms fully extended, with upper arms hugging the head. Press backs of hands strongly against floor for 10 seconds, relax for 3 seconds, 5 repetitions.

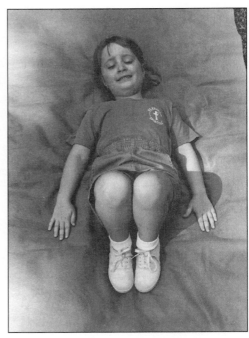

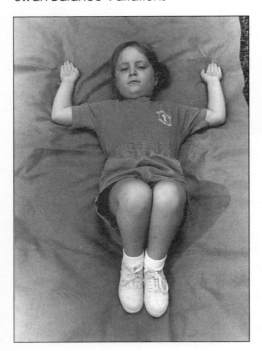
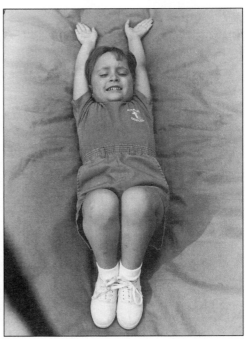

FIGURE 14-75

In all three positions, the shoulder blades (scapulae) should be squeezed together while the hands press against the floor. Although the hook lying position usually prevents arching of the back, additional attention may be needed (to keep the low back pressed to the floor) while arms are extended overhead.

9. **Prone Leg Lifts**

Starting Position: prone, arms bent, hands under face.

Procedure: Alternate lifting straight legs, attempting to free thigh from the floor. Stronger students will be able to lift both legs from the floor simultaneously.

FIGURE 14-76 a, b

10. **Mad Cat**

Starting Position: hands and knees, head up, back relaxed.

Procedure: Arch the back up by pulling the abdominals in, tightening the buttocks, lowering the head, and exhaling; hold until exhalation is completed then relax, letting the back sag while inhaling; repeat cycle rhythmically for 6 repetitions. (See Figure 14-51.)

10. **Gymnastic Activities:**

See Chapter 17 for descriptions.

Row your boat	Twist away	Stick twist
Long stretch	Camel walk	Who's behind
Egg sit	Gorilla walk	Straddle seat
Toe reach	Pick the grass	Toe touch
Inchworm	Blow up the balloon	Jumping swan
Stoop and stretch		
Top	Leap frog	Rabbit jump
Rocking horse	Tripod	Frog squat
	Toe push	Foot push

Rhythmic gymnastics   (wands, hoops, ribbons)

Coffee grinder	Split jump	Jackknife
Angel balance		
Vaulting	Egg roll	Body rolling (tumbling)

See Chapter 11 (stretch/bend, twist/turn, swing/sway).

11. **Dance Activities:**

See Chapter 16 for descriptions.

Tantoli	Limbo
Cherkassiya	
Mexican waltz	

ARM AND SHOULDER GIRDLE

1. **Birds and Butterflies**

Starting Position: standing, arms out to sides.

Procedure: Flap wings (arms) up and down in large, vigorous (birds) or floating (butterfly) type movements while moving, about quickly on tips of toes; encourage vigorous flaps for extended period of time. (See Figure 14-77.)

2. **Shoulder Shrugs**

Starting Position: standing, arms at sides.

Procedure: Alternate shrugging shoulders 10 times each side; shrug both shoulders simultaneously 10 times.

3. **Swimming**

Starting Position: moderate straddle stand.

Procedure: Bend trunk forward, head up: make crawl-stroke movements with the arms; stand erect and make back-crawl movements with the arms. Do not lock the knees.

4. **Sawing Wood**

Starting Position: slight stride stand, holding hands with partner.

Procedure: Arms make sawing movements back and forth; once movement is learned, encourage partners to offer mild resistance. (See Figure 14-78.)

FIGURE 14-77

FIGURE 14-78

5. **Flat Tire**

Starting Position: hands and feet.

Procedure: While students move about on hands and feet (as an automobile), an occasional "flat (left/front, right/rear) tire" will be called out by the teacher or a student. All "autos" will simulate the flat tire as it is called and then lift up as tire inflates. (See Figure 14-79.)

6. **Front Leaning Rest Variations**

Starting Position: front leaning rest.

Procedure:

a. Hold firm, straight position, head up;

b. Alternate lifting each hand (different heights for different abilities);

c. Alternate lifting each foot;

d. Alternate lifting one hand and one foot, and alternate slapping the chest with each hand in rhythm (marching tempo);

e. Move forward, backward, and sideways while maintaining the firm-straight position. (See Figures 14-80 and 14-81.)

FIGURE 14-79

FIGURE 14-80

FIGURE 14-81

FIGURE 14-82

7. **Let-Downs (and Push-ups)**

Starting Position: front-leaning rest.

Procedure: Let-Downs are reverse push-ups. Slowly lower the body until it touches the ground, then immediately assume the front-leaning rest position again; child can use any movement necessary to get back into the starting position, including placing the knees on the floor. The object is to keep the arm and shoulder girdle muscle groups in a contracted state for the longest time possible; rather than fighting gravity from the ground up, this exercise allows the child to resist gravity from the top down. Repeated push-ups can be done with knees on floor (easier) or in the straight leg position.

8. **Elevator Ride**

Starting Position: front-leaning rest.

Procedure: Teacher gives the "top floor" (starting position) a number and proceeds to call out the floors as the elevator moves down to ground level (lobby) and back up. If the elevator becomes stuck on a floor ("Oops, we're stuck on the second floor") the students must remain in that position until the teacher calls, "repair completed"; while "stuck" on a floor, students can also sound the emergency bell (yell).

FIGURE 14-83

9. **Wall Push-Ups**

Starting Position: standing 1 ½ to 2 feet from wall, hands on wall, shoulder height, elbows straight, feet slightly apart.

Procedure: Bend arms to bring chest as close as possible to the wall, then return to starting position; body and knees kept straight, feet pointed straight ahead.

10. **Mountain Climber:**

See Figure 14-66.

FIGURE 14-84

11. **Seal Crawl**

Starting Position: front-leaning rest, tops of feet on floor.

Procedure: Use the hands and arms to drag the stiff body forward; feet do not assist; strive for a distance of 15 feet. At first it is permissible to recline to prone position (and give seal grunts), if needed for intermittent rest.

FIGURE 14-85

12. **Elbow Crawl**

Starting Position: same as for seal crawl except weight is on elbows rather than hands.

Procedure: Use the elbows and arms to drag the body forward.

FIGURE 14-86

13. **Crab Variations**

Starting Position: crab.

Procedure: Alternate lifting each leg as high as possible; additional strength is required to lift an arm and leg in opposition.

FIGURE 14-87a, b

FIGURE 14-88

14. Ball Squeeze

Starting Position: moderate stride standing.

Procedure: Hold playground ball at chest height between palms of hands, elbows out; attempt to squeeze the air from the ball. For this exercise and the variations to follow, the ball should be squeezed for a minimum of 6 seconds with each repetition; exhale while squeezing.

FIGURE 14-89

Hold playground ball between knees and attempt to squeeze air from ball; hold for minimum of 6 seconds.

FIGURE 14-90

Hold ball between forearm and upper arm and attempt to squeeze air from ball; repeat with other arm.

FIGURE 14-91

15. Crab-Tug

Starting Position: crab position with one end of tug-o-rope looped around one foot; partners on either side of a line.

Procedure: Each student tries to pull opponent over the line.

FIGURE 14-92

Rope can also be held in hands.

FIGURE 14-93

16. Partner Arm Tugs

Starting Position: partners facing, moderate stride standing; both hands hold one end of a tug-o-rope (or a jump rope or deflated 10-speed bicycle tube).

Procedure: Partners alternate pulling and offering resistance to their partner's pulls; variations can include pulling with biceps only (upper arm held stationary), and pulling with a straight arm (downward, sideward, upward).

FIGURE 14-94

Partners can also position themselves back-to-back and pull over the shoulder and sideways.

A triceps pull can also be used. Partners bend forward approximately 45°. Partner A will flex right arm as partner B extends left arm; their opposite arms will work in opposition at the same time; rhythmical pulling in this manner will result in a pumping-arm action similar to that found in running. Children should be reminded to keep abdominal muscles tight and thereby avoid low back strain. These exercises can also be executed from a sitting position.

FIGURE 14-95

FIGURE 14-96

17. **Partner Pull-Ups**
   Starting Position: supine with partner in straddle-stand, feet placed approximately midway along trunk.
   Procedure: Partners assume double wrist grip; standing partner keeps trunk upright, tightens buttocks and abdominals, and flexes knees slightly to relieve pressure on back; supine partner pulls stiff body up; repeat 10 times. (See Figure 14-96.)

18. **Climbing Apparatus**
   See Chapter 10, Climbing, for ideas using stairs, boxes, ladders, ropes, frames, cargo nets, and poles.

19. **Medicine Ball Activities**
   Procedure:
   a. Lift the ball over the head with two hands while standing.
   b. Bend the body and slowly lower the medicine ball to the floor.
   c. Pick the medicine ball up from floor.
   d. Pass the medicine ball overhead, between legs, from the chest, underhand and over hand in circle group exercises.
   e. Carry the medicine ball in relay games.
   f. Play over and under relay games.
   g. Throw the medicine ball as far as possible, use progressively heavier balls.
   h. Play (self-catch) throwing the ball over head, catching it when it returns repeating as fast and as long as possible.
   i. Raise and lower the medicine ball using the arms from a supine position

20. **Gymnastic Activities**
   See Chapter 17 for descriptions.

Push and clap	Push-pull the wand	Inchworm
Gorilla walk	Partner pull-up	Leap frog
Crab walk	Rabbit jump	Elbow wrestling
Pull the donkey	Tripod	Hand wrestling
Coffee grinder	Seal slap	Frog stand, tip-up
Horizontal stand	Forearm balance	Handstand
Spanker	Rhythmic gymnastics (wands, ribbons)	Vaulting

Horizontal bar activities
Horizontal ladder activities

21. **Dance Activities**
   See Chapter 16 for descriptions.
   Kalvelis

Activities for Improving Posture

Good posture is defined as proper segmental alignment which allows individuals to perform a movement efficiently. Back pain, one of the most common medical problems of the average adult, can be minimized through appropriate strength and flexibility practices that are learned early in life. Postural problems due to improper use of muscles are usually not as prevalent or obvious in children as in older individuals. However, exercises are much more effective if presented as a preventive measure, or after early detection of a deviation. While several of the exercises used in the strength and flexibility program will enhance good posture, specific postural exercises should also be considered for inclusion in the fitness program. It is strongly suggested that specific exercises be utilized with common body misalignments only (not scoliosis) and with the advice and approval of the child's parents and physician.

REVIEW OF BASIC PRINCIPLES AND TEACHING HINTS

1. Adequate strength and flexibility are the foundation of proper body alignment (posture).

2. When all sets of muscles that surround a joint are equal in strength, that body part is in proper alignment. When attempting to correct a misaligned area, stretch the stronger of the muscles that control the body part and strengthen the weaker set of muscles.

3. The three most common deviations (and corrective procedures are):
   a. Forward Head—stretch muscles in the front of the neck and strengthen those in the back of the neck.
   b. Rounded Shoulders—stretch muscles across the upper chest and strengthen those across the upper back.
   c. Hollow Lower Back/Protruding Abdomen (lordosis)—stretch muscles in the lower back and hip flexors and strengthen the abdominal muscles and hamstrings. It is important that a neutral strength position be reached rather than one side (front or back) being stronger than the other.

4. Guidelines for avoiding back strain:
   a. When lifting, get close to the object, keep the back straight, bend at the knees, and let the muscles of the legs do most of the work.
   b. Do not turn with a load without changing position of the feet.
   c. Do not lift or carry a load that can be pushed or pulled efficiently.
   d. Do not work for long periods in a bent-over position.
   e. When lowering (squatting) to a sitting position, keep the back straight and hips tucked.

Selected exercises for correction and prevention of functional postural problems (descriptions found in Flexibility and Strength/Endurance sections).

HOLLOW BACK/PROTRUDING ABDOMEN (LORDOSIS)

Bent-knee curl-up (Fig. 14-69)
Reverse curl-up (Fig. 14-71)
Pelvic tilt (Fig. 14-50)
Psoas stretch (Fig. 14-52)
Low back stretch (Fig. 14-49)
Foot to head (Fig. 14-44)
Hula hoop movement (tilt pelvis backward and rotate around and around)
Supine tuck (Fig. 14-55)
Mad cat (Fig. 14-51)
Wall walk (Fig. 14-64)

ROUNDED SHOULDERS

Swan balance variations (Fig. 14-74)
Arm raises and circle motions (Fig. 14-58)
Vertical arm pulls (Fig. 14-60)
Raise elbows to shoulder level, clasp hands and pull evenly
Supine tuck (Fig. 14-55)
Shoulder girdle Developer (Fig. 14-75)
Skier's (wall) sit and Wall walk (Fig. 14-64)
Wall push-ups (also use corner; placing hands on each side and attempting to touch nose to corner) (Fig. 14-84)
Shoulder shrugs and rolls (emphasize the backward rolling motion)
Perform straight-arm hang on bar or rings (Fig. 14-72)

FORWARD HEAD

Walk with beanbag on head while keeping back straight and chin held in
Swan balance variations (Fig. 14-74)
In supine position (on back) push neck to floor and chin to chest
With back to wall and standing straight, press the back of head against the wall with chin held down
Tighten neck muscles while keeping chin in contact with the chest
Shoulder shrugs
Yes, No (Fig. 14-61)
Neck stretch (Fig. 14-62)
Mad cat (Fig. 14-51)
Shoulder girdle developer (Fig. 14-75)

REFERENCES

CORBIN, C. & LINDSEY, R. (1983). *Fitness for life*. Glenview, Ill: Scott, Foresman and Company.

SWEETGALL, R., & NEEVES, R. (1987). *Walking for little people*. Newark, DE: Creative Walking Inc.

The President's Council on Physical Education and Sports. (1986). *Health & fitness values of popular sports and other activities*. HHS. Office of Assistant Secretary for Health.

SHERRILL, C. (1986). *Adapted physical education and recreation*. Dubuque, IA: Wm. C. Brown.

TIMMERMANS, A. & MARTINS, M. (1987). Top ten potentially dangerous exercises. *Journal of Physical Education, Recreation, and Dance, 58* (6), 29–31.

15 *Games*

Probably the most recognized, yet many times misused, aspects of children's physical education are *games*. Because games are motivating and fun, they are considered one of the easiest forms of physical activity to teach. Although some forms of games are quite simple and require little teacher intervention (perhaps another reason for their popularity), games can be as diverse and complex as any physical activity. As previously noted in the general philosophy of the "developmental theme approach," games should serve as vehicles for enhancing and utilizing the fundamental movement abilities of children rather than as the primary objective of the lesson.

DEVELOPMENTAL VALUE

Games that are carefully selected can be a valuable part of the physical education program by contributing to the total development of children. Games offer a multitude of opportunities that may add significantly not only in support of motor–skill enhancement but also to cognitive and affective development.

Many game-type activities (discussed in the next section of this chapter) offer acceptable enhancement to the motor-skill foundation, and provide for the development and maintenance of physical fitness. Games have the potential to provide both of these assets along with a very effective element—fun!

The cognitive value of games is evident in several ways: (1) in many instances game complexity is not only related to skill but also to cognitive involvement (that is, understanding rules, responsibilities, options, and strategies); (2) when children are provided the

opportunity to modify and create their own games, cognitive stimulation occurs; and (3) games may be utilized to teach and reinforce specific academic concepts (as discussed in Chapter 2).

Although games offer children an opportunity to enhance their skills, fitness, and cognitive abilities, such activities may also present a tremendous benefit to social and emotional development. Many physical educators cite the primary importance of games as a medium to enhance the child's affective development (the authors of this text would also add the enhancement of skills and fitness). The physical education setting is an excellent environment where children may learn such values as sportsmanship, leadership, self-discipline, self-worth, honesty, cooperation, patience, and respect for others.

GAMES: STRUCTURE AND DIVERSITY

The structure and the diversity with which games may be presented are illustrated in Figure 15-1.

Conventional Games

Also referred to as *predesigned* or *structured* games, *conventional* games are activities that have been designed by others and are usually taught without modification. This form of game mandates the use of specific skills and is described in most elementary textbooks.

Typical of conventional games is a hierarchy that ranges from games of low organization (i.e., simple game activities such as tag and relays) to more complex, highly organized activities associated with sports

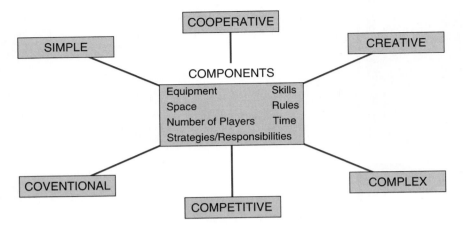

FIGURE 15-1

The structure and diversity of games.

and the Level III–IV program. Most conventional games, especially of the low-organized variety, are easy to teach and require little planning or background skill or knowledge. Because of their structured form, however, conventional games must be carefully selected with regard to the specific movement abilities that a theme emphasizes. Although many conventional games can be used in their intact form, instances will arise when the activity needs to be modified to increase its developmental value. The items featured in the center of Figure 15-1 present the components of a game that can be modified to meet specific needs. Morris (1976) popularized the idea that games can be changed in a multitude of ways to accommodate lesson objectives and needs of children. For a more recent discussion of this concept refer to Morris and Stiehl (1989). Frequent modifications in the intact game include changing the number and/or organization of players, equipment used, rules, scoring contingencies or, as presented in this text, altering the skill-utilization requirements to meet theme objectives.

Cooperative and Creative Games

Games may range on a continuum from simple to complex, cooperative to competitive, and also be conventional (predesigned) or created by individuals to fit specific needs and desires. In recent years, a strong movement has brought attention to what many educators describe as the most important (yet neglected) contributions of games—namely opportunities for achieving a goal through a cooperative spirit, and development of the child's creative and critical thinking abilities. Along with the focus upon these characteristics of the game has emerged a philosophy of game value as well as the creation of new games and an understanding of how to change existing activities to accommodate program objectives.

Evaluation and Selection

Although the majority of the games presented in this and other texts are predesigned, it is stressed that teachers, when appropriate, either create or modify game activities to meet the developmental needs of the children. With an understanding of game structure, teachers can learn to evaluate games by examining their various facets and, if needed, adapt new or modified activities. Davis and Isaacs (1992) support the use of a rating scale with which a game receives a high of "5" to a low of "1" for its contribution to each of the three developmental areas: psychomotor, affective, and cognitive. After the teacher has examined the game and determined a rating, the basis for modification is set. It is also noted that games that are rated fairly low still have developmental value if used prudently, provided that they are fun—an important aspect in the development of a positive attitude toward physical education.

The following are general points to remember when selecting games. Games should:

1. Be fun;
2. Provide maximum activity for all children; circle and relay games generally fail to qualify in this area;
3. Enhance the development of specifically determined motor skills and/or develop and maintain fitness; to do this, maximum activity for all is crucial;
4. Promote inclusion and not elimination. Such games as dodgeball and musical chairs are basically elimination activities and need to be modified to provide inclusion.

General Instructional Hints

The following general guidelines and hints may prove helpful in the selection and teaching of games.

1. Select a game progressive in nature and one that reflects the participants' abilities and the focus of the lesson plan.

2. Be sure participants have at least a basic understanding and utilization of skills needed in the game for an acceptable level of success.

3. When selecting games, progressively increase the number and complexity of rules and strategies.

4. Although the nature of some activities may be competitive, avoid excessive emphasis on winning and stress fair play and sportsmanship.

5. Provide equal opportunities regardless of skill, ability or sex.

6. Be thoroughly familiar with the activity and its basic needs (*i.e.*, number of students, equipment, space); don't hesitate to modify when necessary.

7. Demonstrate clearly and explain information thoroughly before active student participation. Make instructions as brief as possible.

8. Have equipment ready and mark boundry lines clearly.

9. Maximize participation.
   a. Select games that characteristically provide maximum play. Avoid elimination and most circle games, or modify to increase participation.
   b. Use lots of equipment; for example, a basketball for each participant during a dribbling drill is better than one for every three players.
   c. Maximize the use of space (and increase the number of groups who can play simultaneously). This may require modifications to the game, such as having two or three smaller courts (or circles) rather than one large area.
   d. Minimize waiting time in lines. For example, use more lines (if a relay-type game), modify game time (have two outs instead of three or 11 points instead of 15), and allow children to practice related skills in an adjoining space.

10. Use a method to select team members, trying to maintain equal competition and size.

11. If there are multiple teams, use distinguishing marks (*i.e.*, pennies, armbands, wristbands).

12. Enhance the activity.
    a. Actively teach and provide feedback as the game continues.
    b. When practical, rotate players so that all participants have an opportunity to play desired positions.
    c. Enforce rules consistently and fairly.
    d. If there isn't an understanding about the activity or new information needs to be presented, stop the game and get the attention of all participants.
    e. Use a whistle sparingly, but demand attention when it is used.
    f. Generally, do not start a new game if less than five minutes remains in the period.

13. Use the game to evaluate and enhance affective, as well as psychomotor, behavior.

14. Evaluate the game after it has been played.

15. Emphasize safety factors.
    a. While planning, keep in mind situations and conditions that are potentially hazardous.
    b. Check equipment and ground conditions (*e.g.*, broken glass) before the start of each day.
    c. Do not use walls as goals or boundary lines. Clearly marked lines should be 8 to 10 feet from a wall or any other hazard.
    d. Only sport shoes (rubber soled) should be worn on gym floors. If the floor is clean and free from splinters, children may play in bare feet, but never in socks alone.
    e. Traffic patterns for manipulative (*e.g.*, throwing) and locomotor (*e.g.*, running) movements should be established to avoid collisions.

GAME DESCRIPTIONS

Cooperative and Creative Games

COOPERATIVE GAMES

While some children love to challenge others because of their own competitive spirit, other youngsters prefer not to be placed in a competitive situation. Many physical educators believe that with our present game selections, too often competition has been emphasized at the expense of cooperation and other affective values. Perhaps the greatest criticism connected with children's sport programs has been the degree of competition and emotional stress generally associated with such programs. Although some degree of competition

FIGURE 15-2

Cooperative games emphasize a collective effort

stimulates interest and motivation, practices such as emphasizing winning and focusing on the score rarely if ever contribute to a healthy learning environment. Cooperative games emphasize the cooperation and sharing of people to achieve a common goal.

Terry Orlick, a leading authority on the subject and author of *The Cooperative Sports and Games Book*, describes the cooperative game concept thus:

> People play with one another rather than against one another; they play to overcome challenges, not to overcome the person; and they are freed by the very structure of the game to enjoy the play experience itself. (Orlick, 1982, p. 4)

Through cooperative experiences, individuals learn to be considerate of others, to be more aware of an individual's feelings, to practice sharing, and to be willing to perform with another's interests in mind.

To better understand the cooperative game philosophy and its value toward development of the individual, one should examine the primary aspects of cooperative activities. These aspects, the structural components, separate cooperative games from other game-type activities. The exciting aspects of cooperative games are that they provide freedom from competition (*cooperation*), freedom to *create*, freedom to *choose*, and freedom *from exclusion*.

The cooperative component serves to have individuals play with rather than against each other. The primary goal is to confront a challenge through cooperative action with others. The freedom to *create* is stressed in the fact that cooperative games should never be so rigid that they are resistant to creative input from the participants.

Orlick (1982) points out that cooperative games and their multiple variations have grown out of many people's creative thoughts, which is the basis for the cooperative game philosophy. Another vital aspect to the cooperative concept is the provision of *choice*. When children are given the freedom to choose, to offer suggestions, and to make decisions, motivation is enhanced immensely. The act of choice usually begins on a realistic, limited basis, then progresses to a level where children have almost total responsibility.

Regarding *freedom from exclusion*, one of the worst game choices that the teacher could make is an activity that removes individuals from the game (that is, exclusion, elimination-type games). Cooperative games eliminate these possibilities and reject the general concept of having winners and losers. Each game is designed so that all participants are involved as much as practically possible. Participants are making a contribution as a part of the activity and everybody has fun.

Whereas some predesigned cooperative game suggestions can be found in textbooks, the concept can be easily incorporated into traditional activities by changing various structural components (refer to Fig. 15-1). Basically the structural change should elicit the four freedoms previously described (cooperation, creativity, choice, nonexclusion). Orlick describes three general game categories: games with no losers, collective score game, and reversal activities.

The *no-loser* concept is promoted by having the goal of the game a challenge against a standard rather than against other individuals. *Collective score* games involve scoring contingencies where points are awarded when a number of teams cooperate to achieve a common goal. The *reversal* concept is manifested by de-emphasizing team membership. This may be accomplished by having team members systematically rotate from one team to another during the game. Orlick also suggests game structure change with traditional team sports to provide a semi-cooperative activity. In games such as basketball, hockey, and volleyball, for example, all participants would be required to handle the scoring object before a scoring attempt.

CREATIVE GAMES

As noted in Figure 15-1, games may range on a continuum from conventional (predesigned) to self-designed. Frequently teachers will use games in their intact form derived from a source. However, because of specific characteristics of the class (class size, skill level, equipment, objectives, and so forth), the teacher may be confronted with a need to modify the game or create a new activity to meet lesson objectives. As previously noted, the concept of changing games to meet lesson objectives has become an integral part of the educational games program. Whether modifying an existing game or creating a new one, the elements that are generally used in structural change are the basic game components, which may be initiated by the student as well as the teacher.

Creative games may be utilized in connection with any of the three phases of a lesson (fitness, skill development, and final activity). They may also stand on their own to develop basic skills (for example, activities to refine running, dodging, throwing, jumping) or be used to enhance a traditional game theme during the selection of a practice and final activity.

Creative games may be designed by: (1) the teacher, (2) the teacher/child, or (3) the child. The extent of change may vary from a simple component modification to a totally inventive activity. Although most game modifications are planned by the teacher to accommodate class needs and to facilitate skill development, occasions arise when modification of a predesigned activity does not seem adequate, or the teacher wishes to stimulate the creative and critical thinking abilities of the children. This end of the game continuum enters the cognitive/creativity barrier associated with *exploration* (teaching style) as presented in this text and Muska Mosston's (1981) *Going Beyond*.

Many teachers feel more comfortable using a guided approach that does not deter the number and quality of responses, but rather controls the general area of discovery. This is accomplished by first presenting the problem and then setting practical limitations related to boundaries, equipment, safety, and time.

Teacher/child and child-designed games, to be effective, require a greater understanding of class characteristics than those activities modified and invented by the teacher alone. When the teacher and children work cooperatively to design a game, the teacher presents the general problem and limitations. The teacher and child then work together to determine specifics of the structured components (that is, rules, equipment, boundaries). Activities of this type generally evolve slowly and require a different teaching style from most teacher-initiated activities. The teacher acting in a cooperative effort with the class serves as a facilitator who guides within general limitations, but does not impose strong ideas concerning alternatives and discoveries. It is no easy task to manage the creative processes involved with children, at the same time holding to a preplanned set of teacher-directed objectives (even though general).

Child-designed games—those activities that may be identified in the spectrum of learning associated with creativity—present a new dimension not only to the child but also the teacher. At this level of game creation, it is common for a number of groups to be playing several games at the same time, rather than the entire class responding to the teacher en masse. The teacher's primary role is to interact with groups, at the same time being sure not to interfere when not needed. This type of instruction requires an experienced and observant teacher, one who has an understanding of individual abilities in both the cognitive and motor–skill dimensions.

Graham (1977) has suggested the following guidelines for helping students create their own games:

1. Begin gradually. More structure will be needed at the beginning; however, as students become more adept, you should gradually lessen the imposed structure.
2. Limit your interference. If students are to learn to make significant decisions, they must be responsible for the consequences.
3. Always be aware of safety. Regardless of the level of decision-making given the child, a safe environment is the teacher's responsibility. An unsafe situation is one of the few times that the teacher must interfere. When possible, unless the situation calls for an immediate change, make the students aware of the potential hazard and allow them to decide on an alternative.
4. Allow students to enforce their own rules. If students are given the opportunity to make rules, they should enforce them as well. Keep the control in their hands and act only as a facilitator.
5. Remind students of the creative concept—the only rule is that the game can always be changed. Be flexible; if you are unhappy or can create another aspect, do so.
6. Teacher be patient! The creative process is often time-consuming. The process is as important as the product. Once the general idea of game components and how to manipulate them is mastered, the quality of responses will increase.

The following modifications are frequently made to simple games and team sports:

1. The kind of locomotion is changed.
2. The goal or restricted areas are made larger or smaller.
3. Boundaries are varied (generally to accommodate class size).
4. Scoring requirements are changed. For example, a number of players must handle the object before a scoring attempt, or only a specific type of shot (or kick) may be used to score.
5. The number of players is changed (usually increased).
6. The equipment is changed. For example: Beach-Ball Volleyball, more balls are going

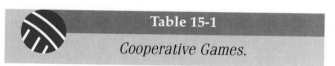

Table 15-1
Cooperative Games.

Descriptions are arranged alphabetically.

GAME	LEVEL
Fish Gobbler	I–III
Frozen Beanbag	
Modified Musical Chairs	I–IV
Caterpillar	
Hug Tag	
Big Turtle	
Runaway Train	
Balloon Bucket	II–IV
Parachute Golf	
Twister	
Circle of Friends	III–IV
Over and Over	
Juggle a Number	
Pass-A-Person	
Tug-of-Peace	
Handball/Paddleball	
Badminton (Goodminton)	
Blanket Volleyball	
Three-Sided Soccer	
Alaskan Baseball	
Cooperative Track and Field	
Airplanes	
Group Skip	

at once and two nets are placed in an X to accommodate four teams.

7. The rules are changed. For example, a maximum of five dribbles is allowed in basketball, or each volleyball player may strike the ball twice in a row.

One of the first organizations to develop written materials devoted to the New Games concept was the New Games Foundation,* which introduced *The New Games Book*, in 1976, and *More New Games*, in 1981. The philosophy behind this concept emphasizes the adaptation of predesigned games and the invention of new activities. A primary objective is challenge rather than competition. The focus is on challenges that are meaningful to all players, so that the participants remain the central element of the game. These games may also be considered as cooperative activities because of their attempt to temper the competitive spirit with a spirit of cooperation. Many new games are designed to create and communicate a feeling of trust.

The New Games material, along with Orlick's texts (see suggested readings) on cooperative activities, are highly recommended sources for the beginning (and experienced) teacher who wishes to establish a base for incorporating the creative and cooperative game philosophy into the curriculum. The following cooperative activities were derived from Orlick (1978: 1982) and Kirchner (1992).

AIRPLANES

Groups of five players begin behind a starting line. One player in each group lies face down with arms and legs extended sideways. Four carriers grasp the "airplane's" elbows and ankles and carry the plane around a cone and then back to the starting line. This is not a relay race; team members should carry their airplane back and forth at their own speed. This game should not be played on rough gravel or other dangerous surfaces, and for safety, the airplane must land feet first.

ALASKAN BASEBALL

The group is divided into two teams—preferably four or more on each side. The members of the batting team line up one behind the other. The fielding team scatters around the diamond, ready to receive the ball. The first batter moves out of the lineup and kicks a rubber ball (or bats a ball off a stationary tee or shoots a ball with a hockey stick). As soon as the player makes the hit, he or she begins to run, circling around the line of batters as many times as possible. Each time the batter passes the front of the line, one run is

scored. The first member of the fielding team who gets to the ball picks it up, and all the other fielders quickly line up behind this player. The ball is passed over their heads, one to another (or it can simply be thrown to each player on the field without lining up). When the last player receives the ball, he or she yells, "Stop!" At this time the batter's turn is up. The two teams can take turns at batting without changing positions on the field or court. A player from one team bats and runs, then a player from the other, without wasting time by having the entire team move from a special batting area to a special fielding area. If the game is played indoors or in a restricted space, a sponge ball, beach ball, or yarn ball is recommended.

BADMINTON (GOODMINTON)

Two players position themselves on each side of a rope or net and hit a balloon or small beach ball back and forth with a badminton (or paddleball) racket. The objective is to keep the "bird" in flight for as long as possible. Twenty serves make up a game, ten on each side of the court. The score is a running total of volleys, and the team score is the total number of volleys made in the 20 serves. A fault on either side ends a serve. If a large number of players wish to play on a limited number of courts, each doubles team plays for a small number of serves. The collective score for each team of four is added to the scores of all other teams to get a final group score. To add some challenge, the regulation service patterns could be followed, and two hits on one side of the net could be required before the ball is volleyed over. The first hit is a pass to the other player; the second hit is the volley over. The same player may not hit the ball twice in a row.

BALLOON BUCKET

Eight to ten Hula Hoops are spread out on the floor around the edges of the playing area. Partners bat balloons back and forth as they attempt to score. To score, one of the partners must pick up a hoop, get the balloon to pass through it, replace the hoop on the floor, and continue on with the partner to the next hoop while still batting the balloon back and forth. The object is for the entire group to score collectively as many hoops as possible in a certain time period. Players cannot run while holding the balloon or strike the balloon twice in succession.

BIG TURTLE

A group of about seven or eight children get on their hands and knees under a large "turtle shell" (mat, cardboard, mattress, or blanket) and try to make the "turtle" move in one direction. As the children improve, they might try to make the turtle go over the "mountains" (beams or rolled mats) or through an obstacle course.

---

*New Games Foundation, P.O. Box 7901, San Francisco, California 94120.

BLANKET VOLLEYBALL

Two teams of six or seven players are arranged on each side of a volleyball net or rope. Each team holds a blanket, keeping the net side open. One team starts with the ball on the blanket and tries to toss it over the net to the other team. As soon as the ball leaves the blanket, one player from the "sending team" crosses under the net and joins the other team. The receiving team tries to catch the ball in the blanket and return it to the other team. Each time the ball is returned, a player crosses under the net. Variations include having two or three players crossing under the net after each toss and using different types and sizes of balls.

CATERPILLAR

The students take partners. One player stands behind the other, bends forward, and grasps the ankles of the partner. On a signal, all partners move in a caterpillar-like fashion. When the teacher calls "fours," two partners join up and keep moving like a caterpillar. They continue to "eight" or "ten" and then start over. This may also be performed with children lying on their stomachs.

CIRCLE OF FRIENDS

About eight participants kneel down (or stand) and form a tight circle, shoulder to shoulder. Another person standing in the center of the circle stiffens the body and falls in any direction. Generally the person in the center keeps arms "glued" to the sides and is encouraged not to move the feet. This game helps develop trust, as the people forming the circle learn to work together to catch the center person in their hands and gently shove in another direction. Children take turns in the center. As proficiency increases, it is possible to back the circle up a bit (more room to fall).

COOPERATIVE TRACK AND FIELD

In cooperative running events the emphasis is placed on a collective fastest time, and no one is eliminated. Each runner tries to run the race as fast as possible, to get a "best time," but the individual times are added up or averaged. In using this collective-timing approach, intramurals become cooperative efforts in which one classroom of a school is sending out a runner to help another runner from another room. Both contribute something; both contribute their best. Collective runs can also be done without recording times. Each runner runs once around the track and hands off the baton to the next participant. Everyone gets one big run around the track (or, if two runners are paired up, each runs half the distance).

A similar collective approach can be followed in events involving walking, running for distances, jumping, throwing, and so on. The total score is simply an expression of all the human energies and skills that come together at that particular time.

FISH GOBBLER

You can play this game outdoors or indoors in a large space. The caller shouts "Ship," and all the children run toward the wall to which he or she points. On the shout, "Shore," they quickly change directions and run toward the opposite wall. On the signal "Fish Gobbler," they quickly drop to the floor on their stomachs and link arms, legs, or bodies together with one or more friends. The "Fish Gobbler" moves around the room with arms outstretched, looking for "fish" to "gobble," but the children are all "safe" as long as they are physically linked to someone else. Once the Fish Gobbler sees that everyone is safe, the signal "Rescue" is called. All the children jump to their feet, join hands, and yell "Yeah!" raising their joined hands in the air. Various calls could be added, such as "Sardines" (everyone sits on someone else's knee or knees), "Crabs" (they all back up to a partner, bend over, and reach under their own legs to hold hands), or "Fishnet" (the children use their imagination and decide how to make one).

FROZEN BEANBAG

The children begin by moving around the gym at their own pace, each balancing a beanbag on his or her head. The teacher can change the pace by asking the children to skip, hop, go backwards, and so on. If the beanbag falls off a child's head, he or she is frozen. Another child must then pick up the beanbag and place it back on the frozen player's head to free that child without losing his or her own beanbag. The object of the game is to help one's friends by keeping them unfrozen.

GROUP SKIP

Three to nine players stand beside a rope in a rope-jumping position. On a signal, players try to jump the rope together as the rope is turned. The teacher may wish to start the game with three or four players and then gradually increase the number.

HANDBALL AND PADDLEBALL

The basic idea is to keep the ball in play for as long as possible. This strategy is tied into the rules of the game. The game begins with 21 points; one point is deducted every time a ball is missed, a serve is broken, or the ball goes out of play. To maintain the challenge for players with higher skill levels, they may attempt to return the ball to a different wall from the one last hit.

HUG TAG

One person designated as "It" tries to tag the other players, who try to run away. Players are safe when they are hugging. Special rules should be set, such as "Partners may hug for a maximum of five seconds, fours for seven seconds, sixes for eight seconds," and so forth. Players should keep their own count.

JUGGLE A NUMBER

Five players begin in a circle formation. Each player is numbered in a random fashion rather than sequentially around the circle. Five balls are placed behind player 1. Player 1 throws a ball to player 2, 2 to 3, and so forth until the first ball is returned to player 1. This action is repeated two or three times, or until all the players know the rotation pattern. Members of each group decide how many balls they can keep moving; then player 1 starts by throwing the first ball to player 2, then a second ball, and so on until the selected number of balls are all moving from player to player. If a ball drops, any player may pick it up and try to get it back into the throwing sequence. Variations include using one hand or a balloon.

MODIFIED MUSICAL CHAIRS

This game is played like musical chairs, except no one is eliminated. It starts with the entire class and 15 to 20 chairs. When the music stops, players rush to sit down. Instead of eliminating the remaining players, they sit on the laps of seated players. There may be more than two per chair. The music is started again, one or more chairs are removed, and play continues until a "safe load" is questionable (usually five or six chairs).

OVER AND OVER (RELAY)

Players form two lines (one behind the other), about four and a half "kid-lengths" apart. The first person in each line has a ball, which is passed backward over his or her head to the next person in line. The lead person immediately turns around and shakes (or slaps) hands with the second person ("gimme five"), who must momentarily free one hand from the ball, balancing it with the other. The lead person then runs to the end of the second, adjoining line, where another ball is being passed along. The second person repeats this procedure, and so on over and over down the line. The common objective is to move both balls and both lines from one point to another as quickly as possible, perhaps from one end of the gym to the other.

For variation, two double lines are formed and partners use only their inside arms to pass the ball over their heads to the next set of partners, or partners lie on their backs side by side and use only their inside legs to pass a beach ball over their heads to the set of partners behind. The handshake is optional in this one. If the ball drops, it is picked up (with hands) and play continues from the last person to touch it.

PARACHUTE GOLF

With children holding the parachute at waist level, two different colored balls are placed on the chute. The object is for the group to drop the "red" ball through the hole, followed by the "blue" ball. As soon as the class has had a few successful games with two balls, add another "red" and "blue" ball, alternating a different color as each ball drops through the hole.

PASS-A-PERSON

Two groups (the class is divided) lie on their backs with heads touching and arms extending upward. One player starts from one end and is passed to the opposite end of line. The next player stands up and the action is repeated. As each player finishes, he or she joins the end of the line.

RUNAWAY TRAIN (LOOSE CABOOSE)

Groups of four or five participants form a "train" and chug around the play space. Players maintain contact by wrapping their arms around the waist of the person immediately in front of them. The front of each train attempts to link up to the back end (caboose) of any other train, while at the same time trying to avoid being linked up from behind by another train. If one train does hitch up with another, the two parts continue as one unit, trying to join up with other smaller pieces. Soon all the small trains will be linked into one large unit. The front engine can then try to catch and link up to the last car.

THREE-SIDED SOCCER

This game is played by three teams at the same time and with three goals. The three goals are set up on the field in the form of a triangle. The rules are similar to those of regulation soccer, except that the teams rotate from goal to goal at specified intervals while the goalies remain at the same goals throughout the game. Each team starts by defending one goal and is able to score on either of the other two goals. As the game progresses, the teams rotate so that they defend a different goal (and goalie).

For variation, several balls are put into play rather than just one, thus guaranteeing plenty of action for everybody. No official scoring system is necessary; the multiball, multigoal approach, along with team rotation, heightens the focus on play and diminishes concern about who wins.

TUG-OF-PEACE

Standing equal distance apart along the side of a rope, class members count off in two's and turn and face each other. On the signal pull, "ones" pull against "twos."

TWISTER

Five or six players are arranged in a circle. Each player joins each hand with a different person (not side by side). When all hands are joined, the group tries to untwist itself without letting go.

Simple Game Activities

The activities found in this section, simple games and relays, are frequently described as games of low organization, those activities on the simple end of the game complexity continuum. Games of low organization are usually so designated because they have simple rules, are easily organized, require little or no equipment, may be played in or out of doors, and can be varied in many ways (*e.g.*, to accommodate the number of players).

Simple group games should be fun and, most important, be utilized to develop fitness or motor skills. These activities provide the opportunity for individuals to develop and refine prerequisite skills needed in the performance of more complex activities. Although activities in this category are usually associated with Levels I–III, the use of simple group games at Level IV is also (aside from fitness and skill development) an excellent means for introducing individuals to each other, to classroom procedures, and to formations. They also offer the teacher an opportunity to evaluate individual ability and to provide feedback.

The list of simple games is almost endless. Regardless of type, the activity should be carefully evaluated for its value (psychomotor, cognitive, affective); this will of course depend on the objectives of the lesson. The teacher should keep in mind that almost any game can be modified to fit the characteristics of the class and the objectives of the lesson. Due to the size limitations of this text and the fact that simple game resources are abundant (refer to "Suggested Sources"), only a select number of activity descriptions are provided (Table 15-2).

BACK TO BACK
Area: Classroom; gymnasium
Equipment: None
Participants: Class
Formation: Scattered
Description: One child is chosen leader and gives instructions, such as "walk backward on knees" and "skip and run in place," that all must follow. When the leader calls "back to back" everyone must stand back to back with a partner. The last couple to get together, or anyone without a partner, gets one point (if there are an odd number of children). The children with the fewest points win.

BALL TOSS
Area: Playground; gymnasium
Equipment: A ball or beanbag for each group
Participants: Class; groups of six to eight
Formation: Circle with one player in center

Description: The center player throws the ball (using designated throwing skill) to each circle player, who returns the ball. Each player has a turn as center player. Two points are scored every time the center player makes a successful round in good form and with no fumbles. The group with the most points wins after a designated time.

BAT BALL
Area: Playground; gymnasium
Equipment: Rubber playground ball
Participants: Class; groups of 10 to 14
Formation: Baseball diamond

Description: One team fields the ball and the other team is at bat. The batter strikes the ball with a hand or fist. If the hit is successful, he or she runs to second base, tags it, and returns to home plate. A fielder tries to hit the runner below the waist. Players fielding the ball may take only two steps and can pass the ball to their teammates. A player is "out" if a fly ball is caught or if he or she is hit or misses the base. The game can be timed or played by innings. Two points are awarded for each complete run, and one point for a foul by a fielder.

BEACH-BALL NERFS
Area: Playground; gymnasium
Equipment: One beach ball per group
Participants: Class; groups of 10
Formation: Circle
Description: Players kneel in a circle. The ball is batted into the air, and the players try to keep it up by striking it with one hand. A player is a "Nerf" if he or she uses both hands or misses the ball in an attempt to strike it. After a designated time the team that has the fewest number of nerfs wins.

BEANBAGS
Area: Gymnasium; playground
Equipment: Beanbags; targets
Participants: Class (as individuals)
Formation: Scattered
Description: The wide surface and lack of rebound make the bean bag a valuable tool in helping young children learn how to throw and catch. Following are a few examples of how primary teachers can use the beanbag to develop hand-eye coordination:

1. Have the players toss the beanbag into the air and catch it with both hands, then with the left hand, and then with the right.
2. The players toss the beanbag into the air, change direction or perform a hand movement (clap hands or touch the floor), and then catch the beanbag.
3. The players place targets on the floor (hoops or milk cartons) and throw the beanbag into the target. The throwing skill or distance may be changed.
4. Have the children use a variety of locomotor skills (running, skipping, etc.) and throw and catch beanbags as they move about the instructional area.

Partner activities: To enhance throwing and catching skills, the players:

1. Throw the beanbag back and forth, changing the type of throw, distance, and position and angle of throw.
2. Throw and catch with two beanbags.
3. Throw and catch with one or both players on the move.

LEVELS I–III ACTIVITY DESCRIPTIONS

Table 15-2

Selected Simple Game Activities

NAME	SKILL(S)	NAME	SKILL(S)
Level I–III		Cross Over	Catch, throw
		Deck the Halls	Jump, hop
Box Ball	Ball rolling, locomotor	Fire Engine	Dodge, run, walk
Circle Ball	Catch, throw	Frozen Beanbag	Balance, body awareness, jump
Circle Kick Ball	Kick, trap	Guard the Toys	Directional, non-locomotor
Kick the Pin	Kick	Hit the Pins	Ball rolling
Moon Soccer	Kick	Human Tangles	Twist/Turn
Over the Brook	Balance, hop, jump, leap, spatial	Hurdle Race	Leap
		In & Out	Directional, stretch/bend, twist/turn
Level I and II		Indian Running	Directional, locomotor
		In the Creek	Balance, body awareness, hop, jump, leap, spatial
Beach-Ball Nerfs	Strike		
Bounce Ball	Bounce/dribble	Islands	Balance, directional, hop, jump, leap, spatial
Brownies & Fairies	Eye-hand, locomotor, spatial		
Caged Lion	Tag, locomotor	Mousetrap	Directional, dodge, locomotor
Charlie Over the Water	Body awareness, locomotor spatial	Newcomb	Catch, throw
Corners	Locomotor	O'Leary	Bounce, auditory
Forest Lookout	Run	One Step	Catch
Hoop-Hop	Balance, eye-foot, body awareness, hop, jump, leap, spatial	1,2,3, You're Set Free	Ball rolling
I Don't Want It (Poison Ball)	Throw	Parachute Play	Locomotor, nonlocomotor
Jet Pilot	Run, spatial	Pass & Duck	Catch
Kneeling Tag	Balance, eye-hand, run, walk	Put in Order	Tactile
Letter Race	Visual, locomotor	Rattlesnake	Spatial
Play Footsie	Jump, hop, walk	Ship Wreck	Directional, locomotor, nonlocomotor
Santa's Reindeer	Locomotor		
Scarecrows & Cranes	Locomotor	Shoe Twister	Twist/turn
Squirrels in the Trees	Direction, spatial, locomotor	Soccer Steal	Eye-foot
Throw & Go	Eye-hand	Sticky Popcorn	Hop, jump
Toss Jump-Pick	Jump	Weathervane	Jump
Traffic Cop	Eye-foot	Wild-Horse Round-up	Dodge, gallop, run
Walking Robot	Walk		
What to Play?	Locomotor, nonlocomotor		
Whistle Stop	Balance, locomotor, directional	**Level III**	
		Beanbags	Body awareness, catch
Level II		Blue & Gold	Dodge, eye-hand, locomotor
		Call A Guard	Throw, ball rolling, eye-hand
Ball Toss	Catch, throw	Chain Tag	Dodge, stretch/bend
Call a Guard	Ball rolling	Circle of Friends	Push/pull
		Goal Tag	Directional, dodge, stretch/bend, twist/turn
Level II and III		Hoop Activities	Catch
		Hot Ball	Directional, body awareness, catch, eye-foot, kick, trap
Back to Back	Balance, direction, dodge, stretch/bend, tactile		
Bat Ball	Catch, strike	My Ball	Eye-hand
Boundary Ball	Eye-foot, kick, trap	Overtake Ball	Catch
Bronco Tag	Eye-hand, locomotor	Par Three	Eye-hand
Canoes & Rapids	Locomotor, throw	Pull the Tail	Push/pull, dodge
Chinese Hurdle	Body awareness, hop, jump, leap	Scoot the Hoop	Eye-hand
Club Guard	Throw	Wall Ball	Bounce, dribble

Listings are arranged in approximate developmental
sequence, then in alphabetical order

The players pass and catch the beanbag with different parts of the body. They propel with the feet and catch with the hands or feet; they propel with the head and catch with the stomach or another part of the body.

BLUE AND GOLD

Area: Playground; gymnasium

Equipment: A cardboard disc painted blue on one side and gold on the other

Participants: Class

Formation: Two goal lines 40 feet apart; two center lines three feet apart

Description: The teams, called Blue and Gold, line up along their center lines. The leader throws the disc up in the air between the teams. The team bearing the name of the color that lands upward turns and runs (or other designated locomotor skill) to its goal. The members of the other team try to tag opponents before they cross the goal line. If tagged, a player must join the opposing team. The team with more players at the end of a specified time wins. Points can be given to a team rather than having players change teams when caught. Any two color combinations can be used.

BOUNCE BALL

Area: Gymnasium; playground

Equipment: Two volleyballs or playground balls

Participants: Class; two teams of eight to 15 players on each

Formation: A rectangular court 40 by 60 feet, divided into two halves by a center line

Description: Each team occupies one half the court and is given a volleyball. One or two players from each team should be assigned as ball chasers to retrieve balls behind their own end lines. The object of the game is to bounce or roll the ball over the opponent's end line. A ball thrown across the line on a fly does not count. Two scorers are needed, one at each end line. Players can move wherever they wish in their own areas but cannot cross the center line. After the starting signal, the balls are thrown or bounced back and forth.

BOUNDARY BALL

Area: Playground; gymnasium

Equipment: Two soccer balls

Participants: Class; 10 to 15 players per team

Formation: Three lines drawn 20 to 30 feet apart; two teams scattered on each side of center line

Description: Without touching the ball with their hands, players on each team kick a ball toward the opponent's goal line. Players may move freely on their half of the playing area and try to prevent the opponent's ball from crossing the goal line. Each time the ball crosses the opponent's goal line, one point is scored. Variations include kicking with the left foot, the inside of the foot, or the right foot and rolling the ball.

BOX BALL

Area: Playground; gymnasium

Equipment: One box and one ball per group

Participants: Class; groups of four to eight

Formation: File formation; three-foot alleys with distance of 10 feet from players to box

Description: Players line up and take turns rolling the ball down the alley into the box. One player is designated the retriever to return the rolled balls. Each player is allowed three turns, and one point is scored for each successful roll. The first group to get 10 points wins.

BRONCO TAG or LOOSE CABOOSE

Area: Playground; gymnasium

Equipment: None

Participants: Class

Formation: Several lines of three to six per line, formed by grasping hips

Description: The lines are arranged like the spokes of a wheel with "It" in the center. Each line is a "bronco." All the children in each line hold the hips of the child in front. "It" attempts to latch onto the "tail" of a bronco by grasping the hips of the last child in the line. If "It" latches onto a tail, the head of the line becomes "It." The first child in the line, or the head, should be encouraged to stay between "It" and the tail. He or she must also know where the tail is at all times.

BROWNIES AND FAIRIES

Area: Playground; gymnasium

Equipment: None

Participants: Class; two groups

Formation: Rectangular area with goal lines marked at each end

Description: The "Brownies" and "Fairies" each stand on their own goal line with their backs to the other team. On a silent signal from the teacher, one of the groups sneaks toward the other. For example, if the teacher signals to the Brownies, they will advance very quietly toward the Fairies, who are standing on their goal line. When the Brownies are within a reasonable distance for a good chase, the teacher calls, "The Brownies are coming." On this signal the Fairies turn and try to tag the Brownies, who run (or other designated locomotor skill) for safety behind their own goal line at the opposite end. And Brownie tagged becomes a Fairy. The game repeats, giving the Fairies a turn to sneak up on the Brownies.

CAGED LION

Area: Classroom; gymnasium

Equipment: None

Participants: Class

Formation: One player inside a 10-foot square and the other players around the outside of the square

Description: The "lion" will be within the square on hands and knees. The other players tease the lion, moving in and out of the cage. The lion will try to tag the other children. If the lion succeeds, they must take his or her place. If the lion isn't successful, after a reasonable amount of time a new lion is chosen.

CALL A GUARD

Area: Playground; gymnasium

Equipment: One playground ball and one Indian club per team

Participants: Class; two teams of 10 to 15

Formation: Two circles of equal size with an Indian club in the center of each circle

Description: The players of each team are numbered so that there is a player in each circle with a corresponding number. The teacher calls a number and those players go to the opponent's circle to compete for their own team. That player becomes a club guard and guards the club for his or her team, trying to keep the opponent from knocking it over by throwing or rolling the ball. The team that is first to knock the club over wins a point. The center players return to their circle, and another member is called. The team with more points after a designated time wins.

CANOES AND RAPIDS

Area: Playground; gymnasium

Equipment: Four to 10 playground balls

Participants: Class; groups of 10 to 15

Formation: Two parallel lines 40 feet apart to form the river, 60 feet in length.

Description: One group divides its players equally to form the river banks (parallel lines); the other group, the "canoes," run (or other designated locomotor skill) up and down the river trying to avoid the "rapids" (the rapidly thrown or rolled balls) moving back and forth across the river. If a canoe gets hit by a rapid, that player must go to the river bank. When all the canoes are hit (or in a designated time), the groups switch roles.

CHAIN TAG

Area: Gymnasium; playground

Equipment: None

Participants: Class

Formation: Two pairs of players with joined hands are "It"; remaining players are scattered

Description: Each "It" (two children) tries to tag (designated locomotor skill) the remaining players. "It" cannot come unjoined or else the tag is invalid. Tagged players join hands with the "It" and help capture other free players. The game is over when all players are captured. The winning team is the one with the longer chain.

CHARLIE OVER THE WATER

Area: Classroom; gymnasium; playground

Equipment: None

Participants: Class

Formation: One player is Charlie; all others stand in a single circle around Charlie

Description: Players race (designated skill) clockwise around the circle, chanting,

> Charlie over the water,
> Charlie over the sea,
> Charlie caught a blackbird,
> But he can't catch me!

As soon as they finish the verse, the players squat down. If "Charlie" can tag one of the players first, that player becomes the new Charlie, and the game is repeated. For variation, players can reverse direction or have a different safe position.

CHARLIE OVER THE WATER—BALL VERSION

Area: Playground; gymnasium

Equipment: One playground ball per group

Participants: Class

Formation: Circle with hands joined; one person in the center with ball

Description: "Charlie" is the player with the ball in the center of the circle. The circle players skip around the circle, chanting,

> Charlie over the water,
> Charlie over the sea,
> Charlie caught a bluebird,
> But he can't catch me!

on the word *me*, players drop their hands and scatter; at the same time Charlie tosses the ball in the air. He or she

catches it and calls "stop." All the players must freeze. Charlie rolls the ball in an attempt to hit one of the players. If he or she succeeds, the player hit becomes the new Charlie; but if Charlie misses, he or she will repeat the turn. After two misses Charlie picks someone to take his or her place.

CHINESE HURDLE

Area: Gymnasium; playground

Equipment: Ten sticks, candles, or pins

Participants: Class; six to 10 per line

Formation: Equal teams, single-file lines

Description: The sticks are laid out in a straight line about one foot apart. The first child in each line hurdles, hops, jumps, or leaps over the sticks one at a time. After clearing the last stick and remaining on one foot, the child will pick up that stick; turn and hurdle over the remaining nine sticks, picking up the last one; turn and hurdle over the remaining eight; and so on. This continues until all the sticks are picked up.

CIRCLE BALL

Area: Gymnasium; playground

Equipment: Basketball or utility ball

Participants: Class; 10 to 15 per circle

Formation: Circle with six to eight feet between each player

Description: The ball is passed from player to player around the circle. Once the ball is started, a second ball is passed in the same direction. A stopwatch could be used to time the speed, or the direction could be changed frequently to keep the children's interest.

CIRCLE KICKBALL

Area: Playground; gymnasium

Equipment: One playground ball per group

Participants: Class; groups of six to eight

Formation: Large circle

Description: The children see how many times they can kick the ball back and forth and all around inside the circle before it goes out. They use their feet and legs to stop it—not their hands. If the ball goes out, they begin counting over again. They should keep the ball low and not kick it too hard. The leader ensures that all the players have many turns. An option is to have the group with the most kicks declared the winner.

CLUB GUARD

Area: Playground; gymnasium

Equipment: Indian club; volleyball

Participants: Class; eight to 10 per group

Formation: Fifteen-foot circle with 18-inch circle drawn in middle for club; one guard with club; other players outside of a 15-foot circle

Description: The circle players throw the ball at the club and try to knock it down. The guard tries to block the throws with legs or other body parts. The guard must, however, stay out of the inner circle. If the guard steps into the inner circle, he or she loses his or her place to the player holding the ball or the player who just threw the ball. The circle players may pass the ball around rapidly to allow for a good shot at the club. The player who knocks the club over becomes the new guard. Note: A hoop makes a good inner circle.

CORNERS

Area: Gymnasium
Equipment: None
Participants: Class
Formation: Scattered

Description: The children will be scattered in various corners of the area. On a signal, the children will move from one corner to another, using the locomotor skills designated by the teacher or selected on their own.

CROSS OVER

Area: Playground; gymnasium
Equipment: One 10- to 18-inch utility ball per team
Participants: Class

Formation: Two parallel lines 20 feet apart (or to meet skill level) to designate starting and goal lines; players line up in file formation behind starting line.

Description: The first player in each line picks up the ball and runs to the goal line, turns to face the team and, with both feet behind the goal line, throws ball (using designated throw such as two-hand pass, overarm throw, or rolling) back to the second player on the team who has stepped up to the starting line. The second player repeats this action, and activity proceeds until every player has caught the ball and crossed to the goal line. If the throw is inadequate, the thrower must recover the ball and throw again from the goal line. If the player catching the ball fumbles, he or she must recover it and return behind the starting line before running. The team with all its members "crossed over" to the other side of the goal line wins first.

DECK THE HALLS

Area: Hallway; gymnasium
Equipment: Large cards and masking tape
Participants: Class
Formation: Single file

Description: The area is divided into sections by a strip of gym tape placed across the hall every 6 or 8 feet. These indicate "traffic lights," where the participants stop and change to the next position. There should be room for as many as 10 changes. A card is placed on the wall just inside each section indicating what kind of jump or hop is required. The card on the wall should illustrate the hop or jump with stick figures when possible.

FIRE ENGINE

Area: Gymnasium; playground
Equipment: None
Participants: Class
Formation: Two lines 40 feet apart and one in the center

Description: One child is chosen to be the "fire chief" and stands on the center line. All others stand on one of the end lines and are given a number between one and five, which represents the "alarm number." The fire chief begins to call out the numbers and after any of them, may yell, "Fire!" All the children with this number must run to the opposite line before being tagged. The first to cross the opposite line becomes the new fire chief. "General alarm" may be called, which signals that all must run.

FOREST LOOKOUT

Area: Playground; gymnasium
Equipment: None
Participants: Class; groups of eight to 10
Formation: Double circle facing in

Description: The inside circle represents the "trees." A "lookout" takes a place in the center and says, "Fire in the mountain, run, run, run!" and begins clapping. All on the outside circle behind the trees begin running clockwise. When they have gone around the circle once or twice, the lookout suddenly stops clapping and takes a place in front of a tree. The runners do the same. The one who cannot find a tree becomes a lookout, and the former trees are now runners.

GOAL TAG

Area: Gymnasium; playground
Equipment: Carpet squares or squares drawn on the floor
Participants: Class
Formation: Scattered; each child occupies one square

Description: One player is selected to be the tagger. When the tagger leaves his or her base, all others must leave their bases and stop in a new square. The tagger attempts to tag any player seeking a new base. No player may return to the base he or she has previously occupied until the player has stopped at three different squares. Two players may not share the same base. The person who is tagged becomes the new "It," and the game continues. Rapid play should be encouraged and the playing area restricted to a feasible size.

GUARD THE TOYS

Area: Classroom; gymnasium; playground
Equipment: Ten or more Indian clubs
Participants: Class
Formation: Seven- to 20-foot circle

Description: One child is the chaser; all others are runners. The chaser stands in a 20-foot circle along with ten or more Indian clubs (the toys). The players run in and out of the circle, trying to carry away the Indian clubs without being tagged by the chaser. The one caught becomes the new chaser, and a new game follows.

HIT THE PINS

Area: Gymnasium; playground
Equipment: Ten pins; 10 to 12 balls
Participants: Class, divided into two equal groups
Formation: Playing area is divided into half; a restraining line is drawn across the end line; the pins are set up in this area an equal distance apart.

Description: Each team has five balls. The players try to knock down the pins in their opponents' goal area and at the same time try to keep their own pins from being knocked down. The players must stay behind the restraining line and are allowed to handle only one ball at a time. The players may not stand in front of the pins and if a player accidently knocks over his or her own pin, it will count as a fallen pin. The group who knocks over the opponents' pins first wins and a new game starts.

HOOP ACTIVITIES

Area: Gymnasium; playground
Equipment: Hula-Hoops
Participants: Class (as individuals)
Formation: Scattered

Description: Hula hooping is normally performed with the hoop around the waist; however, other areas of the body, such as the arm, leg, wrist, and ankles, can also be used. The hoop can also be used as a jump rope. This is an effective substitute, particularly for primary children, who are instructed to:

1. Place the hoop on the floor and jump over it or across it.
2. Roll the hoop with a reverse spin.
3. Spin the hoop. While it is spinning, try to run around it or jump over it before it falls.
4. Place the hoop on the floor. Walk around the edge of the hoop or run and jump into the center and then out.

Partner Activities. The children can try the following:

1. The players play catch with one or two hoops.
2. One partner throws the hoop at a designated part of a partner, such as the arm or right leg. The distance can vary according to the level of skill.
3. One partner holds the hoop in a horizontal position while the other tries to run and jump over it or crawl under it.
4. One partner rolls the hoop while the other partner attempts to crawl through it.

HOOP HOP

Area: Gymnasium; playground; hard-top surface
Equipment: Hula-hoops or ropes
Participants: Class; four to six per line
Formation: Circles (objects) placed in a row (like an obstacle course); single file
Description: The child walks into the first hoop and jumps while counting "one" aloud. Then the child walks into the second hoop and jumps twice, saying, "one, two." Then the child walks into the third hoop, jumps three times, and so on. Various forms of jumping (or hopping) may be performed in each circle.

HOT BALL

Area: Classroom; gymnasium
Equipment: One to three balls per group
Participants: Class; eight to 10 per group
Formation: Circle
Description: Each group forms a circle around one or more balls. The children must keep the balls moving by using designated body parts. They pretend the balls are too hot to touch.

HURDLE RACE

Area: Gymnasium; playground
Equipment: Rope or broomstick for each team
Participants: Class, six to 10 per line
Formation: Single file
Description: The first and second children in each line, holding a rope between them approximately 6 inches off the floor, run down the line with their teammates between them. The teammates leap the rope as it moves to the end of the line. As soon as players number one and two reach the end of the line, number two will go to the front of the line and number three will be his or her partner. They will move the rope down the line. The game will continue in this manner until number one is again at the front of the line.

I DON'T WANT IT (POISON BALL)

Area: Playground; gymnasium
Equipment: Ten to 16 playground balls
Participants: Class; two groups of equal size
Formation: Two groups equally divided, with center line
Description: Each group begins the game with an equal number of balls. To start, players call, "I don't want it" and throw or roll the balls into opponents' area. The game continues as players throw or roll the ball back and forth across the center line. After a designated time (about two minutes), the team with fewer balls wins.

IN AND OUT

Area: Classroom; playground; gymnasium
Equipment: Two beach balls per group
Participants: Class; 10 to 15 per group
Formation: One group forms a circle around the other group
Description: The people on the outside of the circle throw a beach ball at those in the center. Two balls are in play. If the ball hits a player below the waist, that player switches places with the person who threw it. Thus everyone has a chance to be both inside and outside the circle, no one is really "out," and the beach ball doesn't hurt. Players may also be required to pass the ball once before throwing.

INDIAN RUNNING

Area: Classroom; gymnasium
Equipment: None
Participants: Class
Formation: Six players leave the room; others remain at their desks or seats
Description: The six students outside the room arrange themselves in any order, return and race (designated locomotor skill) around the class, and then re-exit. The remaining students try to name the six in order. The student who remembers correctly gets to choose five others to form the next team with him or her.

IN THE CREEK

Area: Gymnasium; playground
Equipment: None
Participants: Groups of six to eight
Formation: Two parallel lines two to three feet apart (the banks of the creek)
Description: The players line up facing the "creek." The leader gives one of two directions: "in the creek" or "on the bank." The players, following the command, jump to the other "bank" or in the creek. If the children are in the creek and that command is repeated, they must not move. An error is made when a child steps on a line, makes a wrong jump, or moves when he or she should remain still. All commands should be quick and clear.

ISLANDS

Area: Gymnasium; hard surface
Equipment: Balls, discs, or frisbees (islands)
Participants: Class
Formation: Relay or individual
Description: A number of "islands" (balls or discs) are drawn or placed on the floor. The object of the game is for the children to move (hop, leap, or jump) around the islands without error. The course layout will depend on the children's abilities. The islands may vary in size and arrangement. The first line to finish without error wins. An error is committed when the child touches or bumps into an island while traveling through them.

JET PILOT

Area: Gymnasium; playground

Equipment: None

Participants: Class

Formation: Two lines

Description: All players except one, who is the starter, are "jet pilots." The pilots stand behind the takeoff line. The starter, who stands in the middle, calls out, "Tower to pilots—take off!" The pilots then run (designated locomotor skill) to the turning line and back. As the pilots cross the finish line, they shout, "Checking in, " and the first pilot across is the new starter.

KICK THE PIN

Area: Gymnasium; playground

Equipment: Volleyball or rubber playground ball and Indian club or milk bottle for each group

Participants: Class; eight to ten per group

Formation: Circle

Description: Each circled group, with approximately six feet between players, tries to knock down the centered pin by kicking the ball. All kicking is done from the circle. Each group begins on a signal, and the first one to knock down the pin scores a point. The first group to reach ten points wins.

KNEELING TAG

Area: Gymnasium; playground

Equipment: None

Participants: Class

Formation: Free

Description: Two or more students are "It." They attempt to tag the other children, who can be safe by kneeling on one knee. The student tagged becomes "It." The teacher designates which knee is to be used and should change part way through the game. The game continues until about half of the players are "It"; then it is reorganized. Players kneeling on the wrong knee are not safe. The players should be encouraged to be daring.

LETTER RACE

Area: Classroom; gymnasium

Equipment: Two sets of the alphabet

Participants: Class, divided into two teams

Formation: Side-by-side line facing the center of the room

Description: The players stand a minimum of 4 feet from the side wall. One alphabet is scattered on the floor (face up) between the two teams. The other alphabet is placed on a table face, down, at the rear of the room. On the starting signal, the first player in each line runs (or other designated locomotor skill) to the table, picks up a letter, runs back to the head of the line, and passes the letter to the next player. The letter is passed quickly down the line until it reaches the last player, who then runs to the letters on the floor, finds the matching letter, runs around to the head of the line and behind it to the table, places both letters in a pile on his or her team's side of the table, takes another letter, runs to the head of the line, and passes the letter to the next player. This procedure is continued until all the letters have been picked up. The team with more letters is declared the winner. To increase familiarity with different kinds of lettering, the sets may be of different styles, for example, one printed and one scripted or one in capital letters and the other lower case.

MOON SOCCER

Area: Playground; gymnasium

Equipment: One slightly deflated soccer ball designated as green cheese

Participants: Class

Formation: Single circle designating the moon, with line drawn across the center

Description: One team of "moonies" fills in the area on each side of line. The leader ("man in the moon") rolls the "green cheese" across the circle. The object of the game is for each team of moonies to try to kick the ball (green cheese) out of the circle (moon) on the opponent's half of the playing area. The ball must go below waist level and out of the circle to score one point. If a player touches the ball, goes into the center while kicking, or kicks the ball above waist level, one point is awarded to the opposing team.

MOUSETRAP

Area: Playground; gymnasium

Equipment: None

Participants: Class

Formation: Large circle (the trap) of all but five players (the mice); circle players holding hands

Description: The teacher directs players to "open the trap" and raise and keep their hands clasped. Then the teacher says, "Run, little mice, run!" (or other designated locomotor skill) and the "mice" can move in and out of the circle. Players lower their hands when the teacher says, "Snap!" Any mice caught in the trap join the circle, and the game continues until all mice are caught. New mice can be chosen and the game repeated.

MY BALL

Area: Playground; gymnasium

Equipment: One club and one playground ball per team

Participants: Class; two teams of 10 to 15 each

Formation: Two circles of equal size

Description: The players of each team are numbered consecutively so there is a player in each circle with a corresponding number. Each numbered player goes to the center of the opponents' circle in turn and competes for his or her team against the circle of opponents. To begin, the number one players go to the opponent's circle. The circle players pass the ball from one to another while the center players try to touch it and say, "My ball." Whichever center player touches the ball first wins a point for that team. After the number one players have competed, they return to their own circle and the number two players go. This rotation continues until all players have had an opportunity to compete. The team with the most points wins.

NEWCOMB

Area: Volleyball court

Equipment: One to four volleyballs

Participants: Class; Teams of eight to 10 (two teams per game)

Formation: A team occupies each side of the court positioned in two or three lines

Description: The object of the game is to throw the ball underhand over the net in such a way that it will not be caught. The game starts with a member of one team throwing the ball into the opposite court. The ball is thrown back and forth until an error is committed. Each time a team commits an error, a point is scored for the opposite team. Errors include failure to catch the ball, not throwing the ball across the net, and throwing the ball so it falls out of bounds on the other side of the net. The first team reaching a score of 15 wins. There is no formal rotation, but the teacher can change the lines from front to back at times. The child nearest to a ball that touched the floor or went out of bounds starts the play with a throw. The ball may be passed from one player to another before it is thrown across the net. Numerous variations are possible, such as adding more balls and requiring that the ball bounce once before being caught. An official may be needed on each side.

O'LEARY
Area: Playground; gymnasium
Equipment: One ball per group or one ball per player
Participants: Class
Formation: Free
Description: This game can be played as an individual activity, or small groups may chant and bounce balls together. The chant is

One and *two* and *three* O'Leary
four and *five* and *six* O'Leary
seven and *eight* and *nine* O'Leary
ten O'Leary *postmen*

The player bounces the ball on each italicized word, gives one hard bounce on the word *postmen*, and catches the ball. Suggested stunts:

1. Bounce the ball on each italicized word then make a circle with arms and on *O'Leary* let the ball drop through the circle from above.
2. Bounce the ball then swing right or left leg over the ball on *O'Leary*.
3. Bounce, and then turn all the way around on *O'Leary*.

ONE STEP
Area: Gymnasium; playground
Equipment: Ball or beanbag for every two players
Participants: Class
Formation: Two parallel lines of players facing each other 3 feet apart
Description: The object of this game is to throw or toss the ball in the designated manner (underhand, overhand, with two hands, under one leg, around the back, etc.) so the partner can catch it *without moving his or her feet*. If the throw is successful, the thrower takes one step backward and gets ready to catch a throw from his or her partner. Catching may also be designated, such as with two hands, left hand, right to side, and so on. If an error occurs, partners move forward and start over. Challenges, such as who can throw to the greatest distance, are good motivation.

1-2-3 YOU'RE SET FREE
Area: Playground; gymnasium
Equipment: One ball and two Indian clubs or two milk cartons per group
Participants: Class; groups of six to eight
Formation: Circle
Description: Four clubs are arranged in a square about 3

feet apart in the middle of the circle. Two players are designated as pinsetters to set up the clubs as circle players attempt to roll the two balls at the pins and knock them over. When a player knocks over three out of four clubs, the pinsetter calls, "1-2-3, YOU'RE SET FREE!" and chooses two new pinsetters so the game will continue. After a designated time, the teacher can see how many out of each group were "set free."

OVERTAKE BALL
Area: Gymnasium; playground
Equipment: Two balls
Participants: Class; groups of 16 to 24
Formation: Double circle
Description: Half the class stands in an outer circle and the other half in an inner circle, both circles facing each other. Each circle counts off by two's. All number one players are one team, and number two players are the other team. On the signal "Go!" a player from the outer circle and a player from the inner circle start the balls. Each starter passes to his or her teammate on the other circle; inner player to outer player, outer to inner, and so on around the circle. Both balls go in the same direction around the circle. The balls must make two complete trips around the circle. The team finishing first, with the ball back in the hands of the first thrower, scores one point. If either team "overtakes" the other team with its ball, the overtaking team scores an additional point. The first team scoring five points wins.

OVER THE BROOK
Area: Playground; gymnasium
Equipment: None
Participants: Class
Formation: The brook is drawn with banks 2, 3, 4, 5 and 5 feet across at 10-foot intervals, children line up single file at the narrowest point
Description: Children must be able to cross the narrowest section a certain number of times before moving to the next width.

PARACHUTE PLAY
Area: Classroom; playground; gymnasium
Equipment: Parachute; eight to 10 beanbags; eight to 10 yarn balls
Participants: Class
Formation: Circle
Description: Play with a parachute is versatile and adaptable to many different fundamental skills. The following activities may be varied by changing the locomotor skills to be utilized or adding the musical or rhythmic accompaniment.

This is a group activity in which children must cooperate to achieve success. Therefore, it is important to develop specific starting and stopping signals. Action is started with "1, 2, 3, up." To stop activity, children return to a kneeling position, grasping the parachute loosely enough so that it sags in the center.

The grips may be done with one or two hands.
Overhand: palms facing the floor
Underhand: palms facing up
Mixed: one hand up; one hand down

1. Circular Movements: Circular movements, where the center hole in the parachute remains above the same spot, offer many opportunities for locomotor movements, either free or to the beat of a tom-tom. Rhythmic running, European style, is particularly appropriate. Holds can be one- or two-handed.

Many basic movements can be utilized while children move in a circular fashion, such as walking, running, hopping, skipping, galloping, sliding, taking draw steps or grapevine steps, and others. The parachute can be held at different levels.

2. Shaking the Rug and Making Waves: Shaking the Rug involves rapid movements, either light or heavy. Making Waves are large movements to send billows of cloth up and down like waves. Waves can be small, medium, or high. Children can take turns to see who can make the best waves.

3. Making a Dome: Begin with the parachute on the floor, children holding it with two hands and kneeling on one knee. To trap the air under the chute and make a dome shape, each child stands up quickly, thrusting arms above the head and returning to starting position. The activity can be varied by having all or some of the children change to the inside of the chute on the down movement, as in a cave. Domes can also be made while moving in a circle.

4. Chute Crawl: One half the class, either standing or kneeling, stretches the chute level with the floor. The remaining children crawl under the chute to the opposite side from their starting position.

5. Mushroom Activities: With the chute on the floor and students on one knee holding with two hands, they stand up quickly, thrusting arms overhead. Keeping the arms overhead, each walks forward three or four steps toward the center. The arms are held overhead until the chute is deflated.

6. Mushroom Release: All children release at the peak of inflation and either run out from under the chute or move to the center and sit down, with the chute descending on top of them.

7. Popcorn: A number of beanbags or fleece balls (six to 10) are placed on the chute. The players shake the chute to make the objects rise like popping corn.

Too few objects limit the fun. Too many on the chute makes them bunch up. Divide into teams and try to make them pop out over the opponents' heads.

8. Chute Ball: A small cage ball is placed in the parachute, and the players toss and catch it in the middle. They divide into two teams and try to roll the ball out over their opponents' heads. For the ultimate in cooperative effort, they try to roll the ball around the edge of the chute by using a steady wave-like motion.

PAR THREE
Area: Gymnasium
Equipment: Three basketballs; one goal; three bases per group
Participants: Class; groups of eight to 10
Formation: File

Description: Three bases are placed (or three spots marked) at random in front of a basketball goal; a ball is placed on each base. The object of the game, as in golf, is to score from each base in as few shots as possible. A running total is kept, and "par for the course" is three. Players start at the base of their choice, and three players start at the same time. Each shoots; if the player makes the shot, his or her score is one; if he or she misses, the player continues to shoot, counting one for each shot. As he or she makes a shot, the player gives the ball to the next player and moves on to another base. For example; if a player's score was four at the first base, his or her next shot from the next base would make five.

PASS AND DUCK
Area: Playground; gymnasium
Equipment: One playground ball per group
Participants: Groups of eight
Formation: See diagram

Description: The ball starts with player 1 who passes the ball to player 2 and then squats down. Player 2 passes over 1 to 3 and then squats down. The passing continues until all have "passed and ducked." Player 8 must pass to 1 and then duck. The game ends with player 1 standing and holding the caught ball high overhead. Various passes can be used, and various body positions can be assumed for the "duck" movement. This game should not be used in a relay until all the children are able to pass and catch accurately.

PLAY FOOTSIE
Area: Classroom; gymnasium; playground
Equipment: Paper footprints or circles
Participants: Class; groups of four to six
Formation: Single file

Description: Footprints are placed not more than 3 feet apart around the area. The player, may jump, hop, or walk their way through the course.

PULL THE TAIL
Area: Gymnasium; playground
Equipment: Two flags or ropes per student, 18 to 24 inches
Participants: Class
Formation: Three equal teams

Description: Two teams line up facing each other about 4 yards apart. The members of the third team are runners, who run between the lines, maneuvering to avoid having their tails pulled by the line players. Tail pullers may not cross over their designated lines. Each tail that remains unpulled counts one point for the runners. The line teams change with the runners until all have run. The team with the most points wins.

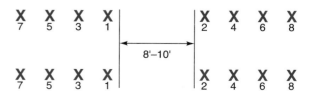

FIGURE 15-3

PUT IN ORDER

Area: Classroom; gymnasium; playground
Equipment: Blindfolds and various objects
Participants: Class
Formation: None

Description: Several objects are scattered on the floor. The children are blindfolded and told the type of object they must locate. They should begin with three types, locating them and placing them in order. For example, they should be told to find something round, then something hard, and then something smooth.

RATTLESNAKE

Area: Playground; gymnasium
Equipment: One blindfold for each hunter. One can or carton containing pebbles for each snake
Participants: Groups of 10 to 15
Formation: Single circle, facing center; hunter (blindfolded) and rattlesnake in center

Description: The blindfolded "hunter" attempts to catch the "snake," who must constantly rattle the carton of pebbles. If the hunter is successful, he or she joins the circle and the snake becomes the hunter. A new snake is chosen. Players in the circle can assist the hunter by hissing loudly when the hunter is moving towards the snake and softly when the hunter is moving away from the snake.

SANTA'S REINDEER

Area: Classroom; gymnasium; playground
Equipment: None
Participants: Class
Formation: Scattered

Description: When "Santa," who is standing in the center of the play area, claps once, the participants gallop (or other designated locomotor skill) around the area. Two claps and they form a circle and move to the left; three claps, they move to the right. On four claps they stop.

SCARECROWS AND CRANES

Area: Classroom; gymnasium
Equipment: None
Participants: Class
Formation: Circle

Description: Six to eight "cranes" scatter on the outside of the circle. The "scarecrow" assumes a characteristic pose inside the circle. The circle children raise their joined hands and let the cranes run through into the garden, where they pretend to eat. The scarecrow tries to tag one of the cranes, and the circle children help the cranes by raising their joined hands, allowing them to leave the circle but trying to hinder the scarecrow. If the scarecrow runs out of the circle, all the cranes immediately run into the garden and start to nibble the vegetables, while the circle children hinder the scarecrow's re-entry. When the scarecrow has caught one or two cranes (the teacher can decide), a new group of children is selected to be scarecrow and cranes. If after a reasonable period of time the scarecrow has failed to catch any cranes, a change should be made.

SCOOT THE HOOP

Area: Gymnasium; playground
Equipment: One scooter per person; one volleyball; two hoops (large box or basket)
Participants: Class; groups of 10 to 12
Formation: Hoops are at each end of playing area; players are scattered

Description: The hoops are the goals, and each team moves toward its goal. Players are moving about on scooters and may not advance the ball by carrying it, but rather by rolling from teammate to teammate. Once the ball is rolled in a position to score, the player attempts to bounce the ball into the hoop, scoring two points. At the designated time, the team with the most points wins.

SHIPWRECK

Area: Gymnasium; playground
Equipment: None
Participants: Class
Formation: Scattered

Description: This is a multidisciplinary game using marine terminology. The playing area is symbolic of a ship. The "captain" of the ship calls out commands, and the students perform certain tasks. The game is fast-moving, and students are required to listen and follow directions. The last player to accomplish the task can be given demerits and after three be sent to the brig, that is, do 15 jumping jacks or five push-ups. However, the excitability level and motivation of the students are usually so high no one necessarily counts demerits. The tasks commanded are as follows:

1. Name the parts of the ship—bow, port, starboard, and stern—all students run to these areas.
2. "Hit the deck"—students lie down flat.
3. "Roll call"—students form one long line and salute the captain.
4. "To the crow's nest"—students pretend they are climbing a ladder
5. "Sharks"—students get in a circle and hide their heads.
6. "Anchor's away"—students assume the bicycle exercise position, with legs in a V shape.
7. "Swab the deck"—students make a swaying motion with arms and body.
8. "Bring in the anchor"—students pretend they are pulling in an anchor.
9. "Abandon ship" (man the oars)—two people pretend to row.
10. "Man overboard"—one child is on all fours; another places a foot on the lower back and looks for the missing person by placing a hand over the brow to shade the sunshine.
11. "Mates in the galley"—groups of three sit and hold hands.
12. "Inspection"—students form a line of three or four.
13. "Man the pumps"—students drop to push-up position and do push-ups.
14. "Signal in the tower"—students move their arms in a flag-waving gesture.

SHOE TWISTER

Area: Classroom; gymnasium; playground
Equipment: Shoes
Participants: Class
Formation: Circle

Description: Players take off one shoe and place it in a pile. Everyone then retrieves someone else's shoe and holds it any way possible while the players all join hands again to form the circle. Each player must then locate and return the shoe he or she is holding without letting go of the joined hands.

SOCCER STEAL
Area: Playground; gymnasium
Equipment: Four balls per group; markers or lines
Participants: Class; groups of five
Formation: Small areas; players scattered
Description: Markers confine play to a specific area. The players move a ball with their feet, controlling it and staying within the boundary. Players may not touch the balls or other players with their hands. The player without a ball attempts to gain possession of any uncontrolled ball within the group. Play continues with no eliminations; if a player loses the ball, he or she then attempts to steal another. Note: Slightly deflated balls are easier to control.

SQUIRRELS IN THE TREES
Area: Gymnasium; playground
Equipment: None
Participants: Class; groups of three
Formation: Groups scattered
Description: Two players hold hands, forming a "tree" for the remaining participant to stand in. Two extra participants are named "squirrels" without a tree. When the signal is given, all the squirrels must find new trees. The extra squirrels also try to find a tree. Again there will be two left. Each time the signal is given, the squirrels will scramble for a tree. Emphasis is placed on finding a tree.

STICKY POPCORN
Area: Gymnasium; playground
Equipment: None
Participants: Class
Formation: Scattered
Description: The "popcorn" begins popping (children hopping or jumping) and looking for other pieces of popcorn. When one popcorn contacts another (hand contact), they stick together. This activity will continue until all the class is one popcorn ball. The children must be originally scattered.

THROW AND GO
Area: Gymnasium; playground
Equipment: One ball per team
Participants: Class; groups of three to six
Formation: File
Description: On the starting signal the first team member of each group throws the ball so that it goes straight ahead and as far as possible. The player then runs quickly to retrieve any ball other than his or her own and brings it back to the starting mark. The first runner to do so scores one point for the team.

TOSS—JUMP—PICK
Area: Gymnasium
Equipment: Beanbag for each child or team (if relay), line or lines
Participants: Class; five to six per group, or individual
Formation: Single file
Description: The player stands on the starting line and tosses the beanbag forward to a distance that can be jumped over. The player then jumps over the beanbag so that all parts of the feet are ahead of the bag. Then the player must pick up the bag and toss it forward again. This action is repeated until the player reaches the finish line. For variation, the players perform another skill while returning from the turning line to the finish (*e.g.*, balancing the beanbag on their head, running, and walking backward).

TRAFFIC COP
Area: Gymnasium; classroom
Equipment: A drum or suitable record
Participants: Entire class
Formation: Scattered or circle
Description: While a child plays walking beats on the drum (or a suitable record is played), the teacher or child leader directs the class with arms and hands, using different signals for walking forward, backward, sideward, in place, and turning. Although signaling is easier if the leader stands in front of the class, it may be done from the center of the room, with the children moving clockwise or counterclockwise. The arm signals should be large enough for all the class to see. The object is to maintain an accurate response to the pulse beats and to follow the direction signals. The leader must be ready to change signals before the class has moved as far as it can in any one direction.

WALKING ROBOT
Area: Gymnasium; classroom
Equipment: None
Participants: Class
Formation: Scattered
Description: After the children learn what a robot is, they are told to walk like a robot anywhere within the boundaries. They are told to move quietly so that they can hear the teacher's commands since the teacher is in charge of the robots. Some sample commands for some of the axial movements as they are walking could be these:
Stretch both arms straight up overhead.
Bend your right arm to touch your right hand to your right shoulder.
Shrug your shoulders.
Twist your feet so your toes point toward each other as you walk.
Swing your arms side to side in front of your body.
Turn around to your left.
Push hands against your hips.
The teacher's imagination is the only limit. All the body parts, directional terms, and axial movements that can be made as the children are walking should be used.
For variations, there could be changes in the kind of walking (*i.e.*, backward or sideward); in the speed, force, or direction of walking; or in the levels and ranges of walking.

WALL BALL (HANDBALL)
Area: Playground; gymnasium with smooth surfaced wall
Equipment: Playground ball
Participants: Class, divided into pairs
Formation: Two players facing the wall
Description: The first player bounces the ball against a wall. The second player is allowed one bounce before he must hit it. Shots are alternated until one player misses.

WEATHERVANE
Area: Playground; gymnasium
Equipment: None
Participants: Class
Formation: Scattered
Description: The players move through space in a designated or choice of locomotor movement. As they move, the leader calls out "north," "south," "east," or "west." When they hear the call, the players jump up and make a turn to the new direction and continue moving.

WHAT TO PLAY?
Area: Gymnasium; playground
Equipment: None
Participants: Class
Formation: Circle
Description: The children sing the following verse to the tune of "Mary Had a Little Lamb" (the leader's name could be used instead of Mary):

> Mary, show us what to play,
> What to play, what to play,
> Mary, show us what to play,
> Show us what to play.

When the class stops singing, the leader says, "Play this!" and then makes a pantomine action such as hopping, skipping, skating, shaking hands, or washing clothes. Everyone imitates this motion until the leader says, "Stop." Another player is chosen to be leader, and the game continues.

WHISTLE STOP
Area: Gymnasium; playground
Equipment: Whistle
Participants: Class
Formation: Scattered
Description: On the first whistle signal, the children run (or other designated locomotor skill) in all directions at varying speeds. On the second signal, the participants will freeze. The students need to move without contacting anyone, and must stop immediately on the given signal. Variations include: children listen for directional signals—such as go to the left, to the right, forward, reverse, circle right, circle left to the top, to the ground, or all around—and then move accordingly. When the whistle blows all action must stop as the students freeze. For another variation, the students could freeze like animals, cowboys, and so on.

WILD HORSE ROUNDUP
Area: Gymnasium; playground
Equipment: None
Participants: Class
Formation: Play area boundaries form the range; a 10-foot circle is drawn inside to be the corral
Description: Four to eight of the children are "cowboys" and "cowgirls," and all the others are "wild horses." One of the former is designated as the "foreman." When the foreman calls out "wild horses!" the horses must run (or other designated locomotor skill) from the "mountains" (the area immediately surrounding the range) into the "range," trying to avoid being tagged. The horses must stay within the confines; if caught, they go to the corral. The last child caught becomes the new foreman, who chooses three other players who have not served in the capacity previously as cowhands.

BALLOON BALL
Participants: Two teams of equal size
Equipment: Balloons
Description: Half the players on each team have balloons. When the teacher starts the game, they try to bat their balloons to a goal behind the other team. Those without balloons will try to take them away from the other team by batting toward the other goal. Balloons must be kept in the air at all times and may not be grabbed.

Table 15.3

Levels III–IV

NAME	SKILL(S)	NAME	SKILL(S)
Level III and IV		Grabbing Sticks	Dodge, run
		Star Wars	Run
		Whistle Ball	Catch, pass
Box Ball	Ball handling, run	Scooter Volley	Eye-hand, push/pull
Pirate's Gold	Dodge, run		
Balloon Ball	Eye-hand		*Level IV*
Busy Ball	Catch, throw		
Basket Baseball	Catch, run, throw, shoot	Borden Ball	Catch, throw
Baskets		California Kickball	Catch, kick, run, throw
Crab Soccer	Kick	Ricochet	Throw
Alaskan Baseball	Ball handling, kick, run, strike	Football Goal Catch	Catch, throw
End-zone Ball	Throw, catch	Dodge Alley	Dodge, run, throw
Long Base	Run, strike		

Listings are arranged in approximate developmental sequence; descriptions are in alphabetical order.
Additional group activities in the form of lead-ups may be found in the "Team Sports" section.

BASKET BASEBALL

Participants: Two teams of equal size

Equipment: Four bases; one basketball or soccer ball

Formation: A home base is placed at the free-throw line of the basketball court; the other three bases are placed as for a regular softball game; boundary lines are the same as for a regular softball game

Description: One team is at bat and stands along the first-base line. The fielding team is scattered throughout the playing field. One player is designated to be the catcher. The first batter throws the ball into the field and proceeds to run around the bases in order. The fielders attempt to catch or field the ball and relay it to the catcher, who attempts to make a basket. If a basket is made before the runner reaches home base, two points are scored. If the runner returns before a basket is made, two points are awarded to that team. Once everyone has run, the teams change sides. A new catcher should be designated each time the sides change. The distance between bases should be shortened if the fielding team always returns the ball to the catcher before the runner gets home. If the runner always beats the ball, the bases may be too close.

BORDEN BALL

Participants: Class, divided into two equal teams

Equipment: Football; two posts or traffic cones

Formation: Playing areas divided into two equal sections, with one team in each

Description: One goalie from each team stands in an eight-foot goal area in the center of each end line (the two posts or traffic cones are used as goal posts). Other players scatter in the area. The object is to throw the ball through the opponent's goal. The game is started with a jump ball between two opposing players. The ball may be thrown in any direction, but it may not be hit or kicked. A player may not hold the ball longer than three seconds or take more than three steps. On penalties, the ball is given to the nearest opponent. Members of the team that does not have possession of the ball may check the player with the ball, but they may not touch, hold, or push that player. One point is awarded for each goal. After a point is scored, at halftime, or at any official stopping of play, a jump ball starts play at the center. If the ball goes over the sidelines, a player on the opposing team throws it into the field of play.

BOX BALL

Participants: Class

Equipment: A sturdy box, two feet square and about 12 inches deep; four volleyballs (or similar balls)

Formation: Class is divided into four even teams, with six to ten players per team. Each team occupies one side of a hollow square at an equal distance from the center. Players face inward and number off consecutively from right to left.

Description: A box containing four balls is put in the center. The instructor calls a number, and the player from each team who has that number runs to the box, takes a ball, and runs to the head of the line, taking the place of the first player. In the meantime, the players in the line have moved to the left just enough to fill in the space left by the runner. On reaching the head of the line, the player passes the ball to the next person and so on down the line to the end player. The last player runs forward and returns the ball to the box. The first team to return the ball to the box scores a point.

The runner must not pass the ball down the line until in place at the head of the line. The ball must be caught and passed by each child. Runners stay at the head of the line, retaining their original number. Keeping the lines in consecutive number sequence is not important.

BUSY BALL

Participants: Two teams of 10 to 15

Equipment: An odd number of volleyballs, utility balls, soccer balls, or basketballs—at least nine; volleyball net.

Formation: Players scattered on each half of a volleyball court, the balls are divided equally between the two teams, the leader keeping the odd one

Description: The leader gives the signal to start, and members of both teams throw the balls over the net into the other team's court. The leader tosses the odd ball into one of the courts at the signal to start. The object is for a team to have the fewest balls on its side of the court when the whistle blows at the end of three minutes. The game may be repeated for a set number of playing periods. One variation is for players to hit balls over the net rather than throwing them.

CALIFORNIA KICKBALL

Participants: Nine per team

Equipment: Utility ball or volleyball; four bases

Formation: A playing area arranged as for a softball game; the length of bases and other rules may be modified according to space and other conditions

Description: The game is similar to softball, with the following modification: (1) A utility ball or old volleyball is used. (2) The ball is rolled and the "batter" kicks it. (3) The batter must run whether the ball goes fair or foul. (4) First base is the only base that the fielding team can touch to get a batter out; on all other bases the fielder must tag the runner or throw the ball and hit the runner for an out. (5) Any number on the batting team may get on a base and stay, running when they think it is safe to try for another base. (6) On any hit ball, if the fielding team throws the ball to the pitcher, any runner who is between bases must go back to the last base. (7) Any runner caught between bases on a caught fly ball is automatically out. (8) The teams are switched after everyone on the batting team has had a turn.

CRAB SOCCER

Participants: Class, divided into two teams

Equipment: Soccer or cage ball

Formation: Playing area approximately 40 by 60 foot, with two designated goal lines

Description: Teams line up on their goal lines and the ball is centered in the middle of the playing area. On a signal, members of each team (without touching the ball with their hands) try to kick the ball over the opposing team's goal line while moving in a crab walk (weight on hands and feet, with seat toward the floor). If the team is successful in kicking a goal, two points are awarded and the ball is centered for play to start again. The teacher will designate a time period, and the team with more points wins.

END-ZONE BALL

Area: Gymnasium; playground

Equipment: Volleyball or basketball

Participants: Class, divided into two teams

Formation: See illustration

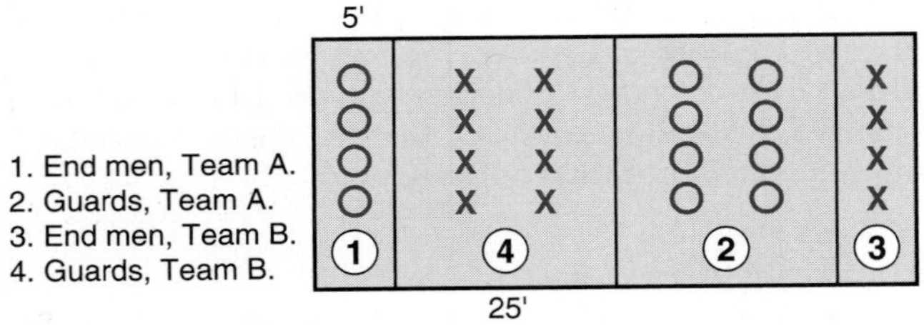

1. End men, Team A.
2. Guards, Team A.
3. End men, Team B.
4. Guards, Team B.

FIGURE 15-4

Description: One third of the players on each team are end men, and the others are guards. The object of the game is for the guards to throw the ball over the heads of the opposing guards to one of their own end men while the end men have both feet in their end area. A point is earned for each successful pass. The game may be played in three- to five-minute halves with one- to two-minute rest periods between halves. The game is started with a toss-up between two opponents who have come to the center; one player stands on each side of the center line, and both players attempt to bat the ball to their guards. Play is continuous. When an end man receives the ball, it is immediately thrown back to the guards. Guards may pass the ball to another guard or attempt to score with a throw to their end men. A ball that goes out of bounds is recovered by a nearby player, brought inside the boundary line at the point where it went out, and put into play. It is a foul for a guard to step across the center line or into the opponents' end area. The ball is given to the nearest opponent when a foul is committed. The team that scores more points within the playing time wins the game.

FOOTBALL GOAL CATCH
Participants: Class, divided into two teams
Equipment: Junior-size football
Formation: Playing area approximately 40 by 50 feet divided into halves; lines are drawn parallel to each end line about 6 feet away (this is the goal area); four players from each team are positioned in the goal area opposite their end of the field; the rest are field players scattered in their half of the field
Description: The ball is given to a goal-line player, who tries to throw it to a teammate at the opposite end of the playing field. Fielders then try to pass the ball to a goal-line player. If one catches it, the team receives one point. The opposing players try to intercept or knock down the pass and in turn try to throw it to one of their goal-line players. The team that has more points after a designated time wins. The field–and goal-line positions should be rotated frequently.

GRABBING STICKS
Participants: Two teams of 10 to 12 on opposite sides of a center line
Equipment: Eight to 10 lummi sticks
Formation: Playing area approximately 40 by 50 feet divided into halves

Description: Each team has a prison area and another area for its four sticks. Both teams attempt to cross over the center line, run through their opponents' territory, and secure a stick without being tagged. Only one stick may be stolen at a time. Once players cross the center line into opponents' territory, they may be tagged. Players successfully stealing a stick hold it high, and they may return to their team without danger of being tagged. A player tagged goes into the opponents' prison. Once there are prisoners, no stick may be stolen until all prisoners are free. If a player reaches a teammate held prisoner without being tagged, the two return to their team with hands joined to show their opponents that they may return without danger of being tagged. The team having more sticks at the end of the playing time wins. Boundaries should be well defined; any player running out of bounds to avoid being tagged becomes a prisoner.

LONG BASE
Participants: Class; of nine per team
Equipment: Softball, bat, and two bases
Formation: Softball diamond with 35 feet between bases; one team in the field, the other in a file formation behind a restraining line drawn 10 feet back and to the right of home plate
Description: Players are divided into two teams (each player numbered). Each team selects a pitcher and a catcher; other players are fielders or batters. When a ball is hit, the batter runs to first base and, if possible, returns home. The runner may stop on first base, and any number of runners may be on base at the same time. Runners may not steal home. Any hit is good; there are no fouls in this game. Batters are out when they strike out, are touched with the ball off base, steal home, throw the bat, or hit a fly ball that is caught. One point is awarded for each run to the base and back. Pitchers and catchers alternate, and pitchers can be moved closer as their skill indicates. The children should be kept away from the batters.

DODGE ALLEY
Participants: Class, divided into three teams
Equipment: Six 8 ½-inch playground balls
Formation: Parallel lines drawn about 25 feet apart and 40 feet long; team 1 lines up behind one of the lines, team 2 on the other; team 3 waits at the end of the lines
Description: Teams 1 and 2 are each given three balls. On a signal, players on team 3 run between the two lines to one end and back. Players on teams 2 and 3 repeatedly throw balls and try to hit players above the ankles or below the waist with a ball. Those who were not hit are counted, and the teams rotate: team 3 takes team 1's place; team 2 becomes the running team. After each team has run the line twice, scores are compared; the team with the most people who were not hit wins. Distances may be varied to fit the throwing ability of the groups, and more balls may be added.

SCOOTER VOLLEYBALL
Area: Gymnasium
Equipment: One beach ball (or volleyball) and one net per group; a scooter for each player

Participants: Class; groups of 10 to 12 (five to six on each side)

Formation: Scattered on each side of a four-foot-high net

Description: Play follows similar rules as regular volleyball.

PIRATES' GOLD

Participants: Two teams of 10 to 12

Equipment: A nickel

Formation: None

Description: One team is the "pirates" and the other the "coast guard." The pirates gather into a close huddle while the coast guard waits in the distance. A piece of gold (nickel) is given to one pirate although everyone pretends to possess it. On a signal, the pirates try to cross the "ocean" (designated area), and the coast guard must try to tag them. Upon being tagged, a pirate must stop. The coast guard then asks, "Do you have the gold?" The pirate must give up the gold if he or she has it. If the coast guard catches the pirate with the gold, they get one point. If the pirate with the gold gets to the safe base on the other side of the ocean, the pirates get a point. The two teams reverse roles, and the game begins again.

RICOCHET

Participants: Class

Equipment: One large utility ball and approximately 20 small balls

Formation: Two end lines approximately 3 feet from each wall; a line across the center of the playing area

Description: The class is divided in half and arranged along the end lines, and the teams are facing each other. Each team gets ten balls; the large utility ball is placed in the center of the playing area. On a signal, both teams begin to throw the small balls at the large utility ball, attempting to force it over the opponents' goal line. Players may retrieve the balls from their own half of the playing area; however, they must go back over their own end line before they attempt another throw. One point is awarded per goal.

STAR WARS

Participants: Class

Equipment: Four Indian clubs

Formation: A human square, about 10 yards on each side, is formed by four teams, each of which occupies one side, facing in

Description: The teams should be even in number, and the members of each team should count off consecutively from right to left. Hence, one person on each team has the same number as one person on each of the other three teams. The players are seated cross-legged. A number is called by the teacher and four players with the same number run to the right, all the way around the square, and through their own vacated space toward the center of the square. Near the center, in front of each team, stands an Indian club. The first child to put the Indian club down on the floor wins. The clubs should be at an equal distance in front of the teams and far enough away from each other to avoid collisions in the center. Scoring is accumulated by the words *Star Wars*. The player who puts the club down first gets two letters of the name, and the player who is second gets one letter. The first team to complete the name wins. Other words may also be used.

WHISTLE BALL

Participants: Entire class

Equipment: Ball for each group of six to eight players

Formation: Circle

Description: Eight or fewer children stand in a circle. One ball is passed rapidly back and forth in any order. The object is to be the player who stays in the game the longest. A player sits down if he or she makes any of the following errors:

1. The player has the ball when the whistle blows. (The teacher should blow a whistle at the end of a predetermined time period, which can be varied.)
2. The player makes a bad throw or fails to catch a good throw.
3. The player returns the ball directly to the person from whom it was received.

To keep this activity from being an elimination game, players should alternate sitting; hence, only one player is out until the next error is made.

RELAYS

Because of their versatility and popularity among children at all levels, relays may be a very useful (and developmentally appropriate) vehicle for enhancing fitness and motor skill development. They can be adapted to fit almost any fundamental objective and provide a means for practicing numerous sport skills (several of which can be found in the "Team Sports" section). Caution should be taken, however, for relays do have the potential for misuse. Because they are characteristically competitive, the teacher should attempt to de-emphasize this trait

when possible. Children should have an acceptable mastery of the skill before relays are introduced. Children (especially young learners) tend to forget the skill concepts learned when placed in a challenging position. Teachers should use relay activities primarily to develop skill levels and not as a contest of ability. Relays also offer the teacher an opportunity for individual observation and feedback. Because of the self-control and attention required in performing relays, teachers should carefully evaluate student readiness before selecting specific activities. Teachers should try not to place children in a position that brings out their worst and causes an uncomfortable situation for both parties.

GENERAL TEACHING CONSIDERATIONS

1. The class is divided into teams of four to eight players for maximum participation.
2. Ability should be equalized as much as possible. This may require changes during play.
3. Teams are arranged in formation. Organization and rules (with demonstrations during initial learning periods) are explained thoroughly. Team leaders are appointed when appropriate.
4. The relay is started with a definite signal (*e.g.*, whistle, verbal command, drum).
5. Student involvement in "creating" relays should be encouraged.
6. Basic safety rules should include
   a. The turning line put at a minimum of 8 feet from any wall or obstruction
   b. Traffic patterns clearly understood and followed by every player
   c. Adequate space between each team
7. Probably the easiest and most useful formation is the file: Players are lined up one behind the other, facing the starting line. Other formations are the shuttle (the team is divided in half; files are facing), line (side by side), and circle (players, are an equal distance apart, designated by marks).
8. Although competition may be inherent in most relays, the teacher should not place additional emphasis on winning through such actions as enthusiastically declaring the winner or providing a reward or punishment as a result of performance.

RELAY ACTIVITIES

The skills used in most relays are locomotor and stunt-type activities (which incorporate nonlocomotor movements). Teachers are reminded that relays are versatile and may be modified to accommodate lesson objectives.

BALLOON/FEATHER RELAY
Area: Classroom; playground; gymnasium
Equipment: Balloon or feather for each team
Participants: Six to 10 per line
Formation: Single file; equal teams
Description: Each player, in turn, blows a feather or balloon to the turning line and back to his or her team. If the

Table 15.4
Selected Relay Activities

NAME LEVEL	SKILL(S)
Level I–III	
Stunt Relay	Animal stunts
Level I–IV	
Locomotor Relay	Locomotor
Rescue Relay	Locomotor, stunt
Coffee-Can Stilt Relay	Locomotor
Balloon/Feather Relay	Locomotor, strike
Level II–IV	
Skipping Rope Relay	Rope jumping
Sack Relay	Balance, jump
Zigzag Relay	Locomotor
Over-and-Under Relay	Eye-hand, locomotor
Scooter Relay	Stunt, muscular endurance
Level III–IV	
Obstacle Relay	Locomotor, manipulative
Shuttle Relay	Locomotor
Hockey Relay	Strike, eye-hand
Two-Legged Relay	Hop
Three-Legged Relay	Stunt
Tire Relay	Roll
Wheelbarrow Relay	Stunt
Siamese Twins	Locomotor, stunt
Skin-the-Snake	Stunt

Descriptions are arranged in alphabetical order; listings in developmental sequence.

feather or balloon drops, the player must stop forward motion until the object is back in the air; hands may or may not be used. The first team to finish wins.

COFFEE-CAN STILT RELAY
Formation: Shuttle with four to eight per group
Equipment: Set of coffee-can stilts per group
Description: Each player takes a turn walking on the stilts to the turning line and back. The one-way distance should be 10 to 15 yards. Large cans (preferably #10), with the bottom taped to prevent slipping, should be used.

HOCKEY RELAY
Formation: File
Equipment: One hockey stick and ball (or puck) for each team
Description: A turning line is drawn about 20 to 50 feet in front of the starting line. The first player holds the stick in contact with the ball and guides it while running to the turning line and back. Play continues until every player has had a turn.

LOCOMOTOR RELAY

Formation: File

Description: A turning line is drawn 20 to 40 feet from the starting line (distance depends on ability). Each player performs a specified locomotor movement (*e.g.*, running, hopping, leaping, sliding, galloping, skipping, or skipping rope) to the turning line and back.

OBSTACLE RELAY

Formation: File

Equipment: Chairs, cones, or cartons

Description: Objects are placed 6 to 10 feet apart and directly in front of each team. The first player runs "in and out" around the objects and back around his or her team to the starting position. Play continues until every player has had a turn. This relay may include locomotor and manipulative skills, for example, running or dribbling (soccer, basketball, hockey).

OVER-AND-UNDER RELAY (AND SIDE TO SIDE)

Formation: File

Equipment: One ball for each team

Description: The first player in each file, on a signal, passes the ball, using both hands, over his or her head to the next player. This player then passes the ball between the legs to the third player, who passes it overhead to the fourth player, and so on until the last player receives the ball. The last player runs to the front of the file on the right. Each player in the file takes a step backward from the starting line. The relay continues until all players are in their original positions. The team wins that first has all players back at their starting positions. Another form of this relay has the players passing the ball behind, the left side, right side, left side, and so on.

RESCUE RELAY

Formation: File

Description: Each team stands in a line behind the starting line. The captains stand behind a second line drawn 20 feet in front of the starting line. On a signal the captains run to the first member of their team, grasp his or her hand, and run back with the player to their turning line. The players whom the captains brought over return to the starting line and bring the next player back. The relay is continued until the last child has been brought over the captain's line. For variation, changes can be made in the way players are brought back, such as holding both hands, locking elbows back to back, and piggyback.

SACK RELAY

Formation: Shuttle with six to eight per group

Equipment: One burlap sack per team

Description: Players place both feet in the sack and proceed (jump) to the turning line and back. This is an excellent activity for outdoors.

SCOOTER RELAY

Formation: File

Equipment: Twelve to 24 scooters

Description: Possible relay positions include sitting, using feet to propel; kneeling, using hands to propel; lying (on stomach).

SHUTTLE RELAY

Formation: Half of each team behind each of two restraining lines, spaced approximately 20 feet apart

Description: Players 1, 3, and 5 from half the team are placed on one side, and players 2, 4, and 6 on the other side. Player 1 runs across and tags player 2. Player 2 runs back and tags player 3, and so on, until all have had a turn.

SIAMESE TWINS

Formation: Partners in line, with six to eight per team

Equipment: One four-foot stick for each team

Description: The first pair stand back to back and straddle the stick, grasping it between their legs with both hands in front. Partner A faces the turning line about 20 to 30 feet away, and partner B faces the team. On a signal, the partners run to the turning line, partner A running forward and partner B running backward. Once they cross the line, they reverse positions and return to the starting line.

SKIN-THE-SNAKE RELAY

Formation: Line, with four to six per team

Description: The players extend their left hand back between their legs and grasp the right hand of the player behind. On a signal, each member of the team except the last player starts moving backward. The last player lies down on his or her back, still holding onto the player in front. The second rear player, after passing over the last player, lies down, still maintaining the grasp with both hands. This pattern continues until each player is lying down. As soon as all are lying on their backs, the one at the rear stands and moves forward, pulling the second player to his or her feet. Play continues until everyone is standing up.

SKIPPING-ROPE RELAY

Formation: Line, with three to four per team

Equipment: One skipping rope per team

Description: On a signal, the first player on each team skips to the turning line and back. Variations are numerous; see Chapter 8 for rope-jumping patterns.

STUNT RELAY

Formation: Line, with three to four per team

Description: On a signal, the first player on each team runs to the turning line and performs a stunt on the way back. Popular stunts are animal walks (*e.g.*, crab, lame puppy, seal, wicket, bear) and jumping activities (*e.g.*, kangaroo hop and rabbit jump).

THREE-LEGGED RELAY

Formation: Shuttle, with six to eight players per group

Equipment: Piece of rope or rubber band for each team

Description: After forming a double line, the first couple in each team bind their inside legs together and run to the turning line and back.

TIRE RELAY

Formation: Shuttle

Equipment: One tire per team

Description: Children line up in shuttle formation, with the players on each team divided into two groups and placed at opposite lines facing each other. On a signal, the first player rolls the tire to the turning line and gives it to the second player, who then rolls the tire back to the starting line, where it is given to the third player. This process continues until all players have exchanged places at opposite ends of the playing area.

TWO-LEGGED RELAY

Formation: Partners in a file

Description: Each team lines up in pairs. Partners grasp each other around the waist with their inside arms and raise their inside legs off the floor. On a signal, each pair hops to the turning line 20 to 30 feet away. Once behind the line, they change positions and hop on the other foot, returning to allow the next pair to go.

WHEELBARROW RELAY

Formation: Partners in a file

Description: Each team is divided into pairs of equal height and weight. On a signal, one partner places his or her hands on the floor and raises his or her legs to the other partner's hips. The standing partner holds the partner's feet close to his or her sides, and they walk to the turning line. When both have crossed the turning line, they exchange positions and return. The standing partner must not push the "wheel" partner but should walk steadily.

ZIGZAG RELAY

Formation: File, with players six to eight feet apart

Description: Player 1 runs in and out of his or her teammates in a zigzag pattern to the last player on the team, circles, and then repeats the movement back to the original position. Player 2 starts zigzagging backward around player 1 and continues the zigzag pattern up the line, back to the original position. The first team back in the original position wins the relay.

ACTIVITIES FOR INDIVIDUALS AND PARTNERS (LEVELS III AND IV)

With a diverse and functional foundation in movement skills, children should be ready for instruction and participation in advanced games (Levels III–IV) for individuals and partners. Such games are usually played by one to four individuals as a recreational activity; however, they also justify a place in the diverse developmental game curriculum. Such activities are strong in the areas of fitness, skill develop-

ment, and social interaction. The activities described in this section were selected on the basis of popularity and practicality in the school. Official golf, archery, bowling, and tennis have not been included; however, bowling- and tennis-related activities are presented.

Bowling Activities	Racquet Activities
Croquet	Paddleball
Deck Tennis	Paddle Tennis
Frisbee	Badminton
Hopscotch	Pickleball
Horshoes	Table Tennis
Shuffleboard	Hand Striking Activities
	Handball
	Sidewalk Tennis
	Volley Tennis

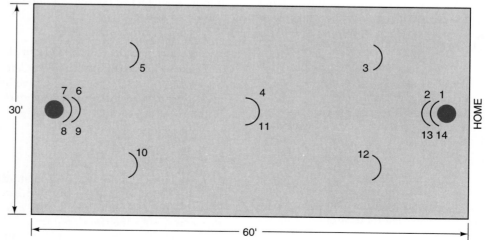

FIGURE 15-5

Croquet Area Layout

BOWLING (RELATED ACTIVITIES)

Equipment: Indian clubs, milk cartons, or plastic or regular pins as targets: eight-inch rubber playground ball; pins should be set up in a triangle with five pins in the back row, three in the next, two in the next, and one in the front; a space just as long as the pin should be left between the pins; it is best to mark the floor or an oilcloth or paper, where the pins are set; a foul line is marked 15 to 25 feet from the head pin

Players: Two to five

Skills: Stance. The stance is the position the bowler takes prior to the approach and delivery of the ball. A frequently used stance is one in which the bowler stands facing the pins, with the ball held in the right hand (slightly above the waist) and the weight of the ball supported by the left hand. The weight of the body is evenly distributed on both feet. The left foot may be placed slightly in front, or both feet may be even. The body may be in an upright, semi-crouched, or crouched position. The shoulders must be parallel to the foul line, and the toes should be pointed squarely toward the pins, regardless of the stance.

Approach. The approach is the series of movements performed to the foul line to deliver the ball. The number of steps taken depends on the point at which the bowler starts the approach. The steps (usually three to five) during the approach must be coordinated with the arm swing. As in the stance, the bowler must experiment with varying approaches to find one suitable.

Delivery. The delivery, or release, of the ball should be in a smooth motion, with the ball being rolled, not dropped. The release of the ball should coincide with the last step. The body at release should be slightly forward at the hips, with the knees bent and the body lowered a little. The shoulders must be parallel to the foul line at the time of release to ensure accuracy in the direction of the ball. A follow-through is made after each delivery. The arm continues forward after the release of the ball during the follow-through. The direction of the arm on the follow-through is toward the intended flight of the ball (at the pins) and ends up at shoulder level or as high as the face.

Each player rolls the ball at the pins in turn. If the player knocks all of them down on the first try, ten points are scored. If not, a second try at the remaining pins is allowed. The total number of pins knocked down on the two attempts is then recorded. The winner is the player who has the highest total after ten turns. One person is appointed pinsetter; after the first person has bowled, he or she becomes the pinsetter, and so on.

CROQUET

Area Layout: See Figure 15.5

Equipment: Croquet sets

The object of the game is for a player to hit the ball through each wicket around the course and be the first to reach home. Players decide on playing order and alternate turns. Each gets one hit in turn and an additional hit each time the ball goes through the wicket. If a player hits an opponent's ball, two bonus shots are awarded. One of the shots may be used to hit an opponent's ball out of the way. To do so, the hitter places both balls side by side and then puts a foot on his or her ball so that it remains in place as the mallet hits it.

DECK TENNIS

Court: An existing volleyball or badminton area; a minimum area of 25 by 25 feet, with a five-foot net across the middle and a line dividing each half (left and right)

Equipment: One deck tennis ring; can be made with two-inch tubing (seven-inch diameter)

Players: Two (singles) or four (doubles)

The object of the game is for a player to throw the ring across the net so the opponent will miss it. The game is started with a service by a player from behind the base line (from the right side of the court). The server must deliver the ring with a forehand delivery in an upward fashion to the opposite half of the court. The receiver must catch the ring with one hand and immediately return it. If the server or teammate makes a point, the server continues to serve from the left side of the court. The server continues to alternate serving from right to left court until his or her side makes an error or a foul. In doubles, the partner then has a term of service; in singles, the serve goes to the opponent. No point is scored if the serving side errs or fouls; the serve is won by the opponents. A game is won by the first team to get 15 points. If the score is tied at 14, one team must get two successive points to win. A time limit can be set, and the team with the most points at the end of it is the winner.

The fouls are:

1. Catching the ring with both hands
2. Changing the ring to the other hand before returning it
3. Holding the ring for more than three seconds
4. Failing to make the ring arc before it begins to descend into the opponent's court
5. Stepping over the base line when serving

FRISBEE

Frisbee activities are a enjoyable and beneficial form of sport and recreation. Frisbee may be played solo (frisbee golf), with a partner, or in groups. Unlike the throwing and catching skills involved in most recreational activities, the ability to throw and receive a frisbee may demand a considerable amount of guidance and practice.

Throwing and Receiving Skills: Backhand throw. The backhand throw is the most utilized throwing pattern. To secure the grip, the thumb is on top of the disc, the index finger along the rim, and the other fingers underneath. To throw with the right hand, the child stands in a sideways position with the right foot toward the target. The child then steps toward the target and throws the frisbee in a sideways motion across the body, snapping the wrist and trying to keep the disc flat upon release.

Underhand throw. The underhand pattern uses the same grip as in the backhand, with the child facing the target and holding the disc at the side of the body. The child steps forward with the leg opposite the throwing arm as the frisbee is brought forward. When the throwing arm is in front of the body, the frisbee is released. The trick is learning to release the disc so that it is parallel to the ground.

Key concepts for both techniques are (1) keeping the frisbee parallel to the ground at release and stepping toward the target and (2) follow-through.

Above and below waist catch. The thumb-down technique is used to catch the frisbee when it is received at waist level

FIGURE 15-6

Gripping the frisbee (backhand throw)

or above. The thumb points toward the ground. The frisbee should be tracked from the thrower's hand; this gives the catcher a clue to any tilt on the disc that will cause it to curve. The thumb-up technique is used when the frisbee is received below waist level. The thumb points up, and the fingers are spread.

Activities: After sufficient periods of variability in practice (*i.e.*, time, space, force) with a partner, the following activities are suggested:

1. A series of different-colored hoops are placed on the ground, each signifying point values. The children try to accumulate a number of points in a specific number of throws. If the frisbee lands in the middle, it is worth the whole value; on the hoop, one-half.

2. Working with a partner, the children try to complete as many catches and throws as possible in 30 seconds. A certain distance apart is set (based on ability), and the number of catches counted.

3. In groups of three, two of the children try to keep the frisbee away from the third person, who is in the middle.

4. For frisbee golf, one frisbee per player is needed. A golf course is laid out with hoops (lying on the ground) and marker flags designating the hole number. Holes should be placed to avoid the possibility of children being hit by the frisbee. Each throw counts as one point. Players continue to throw from where the frisbee stopped until they get it in the hoop. If the frisbee is touching the hoop, one additional point is added to the score. The lowest score represents the best performance. Distances between holes should vary, and hazards (*e.g.*, trees or tables) should be included to increase the difficulty.

AMERICAN HOPSCOTCH

Area: Marked surface; gymnasium; playground
Equipment: Lagger (buttons, beads, stones, or beanbags)
Participants: One to five
Formation: Line with first player facing area one
Description: The first player, holding a lagger, stands on one foot outside of area one. The player tosses the lagger into area one and then hops over this area, landing with the left foot in area two and the right foot in area three. The player then hops and lands on one foot in area four, then hops and lands with the left foot in area five and the right foot in area six. This pattern continues, the player hopping and landing with one foot in single spaces and both feet in adjacent areas. Two hops are permitted in area ten so that the player can turn around and get ready for the return. Upon landing in areas two and three, the player leans forward, picks up the lagger, and hops out.

The player now tosses the lagger into area two and repeats the pattern. The hopping pattern must then be modified to avoid area two. On the return, the player must land on one foot in area three, pick up the lagger, hop over to area two, then to area one, and hop out. This pattern is continued through area ten and back. A player is out if a line is stepped on, the lagger is tossed onto a line or into the wrong area, feet are changed on single hops, or a hand or other foot touches during any hopping or retrieving movement. When a child commits an error, that player goes to the back of the line.

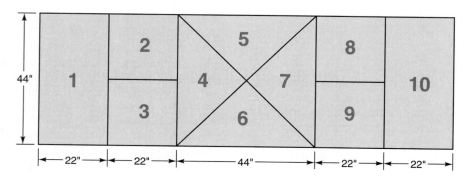

FIGURE 15-7

American hopscotch layout

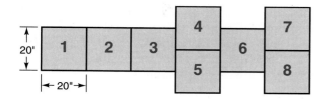

FIGURE 15-8

French hopscotch layout

FRENCH HOPSCOTCH

Area: Marked surface; gymnasium; playground

Equipment: Lagger (buttons, beads, stones, or beanbags)

Participants: Six to eight players

Formation: Line, with player one facing square one

Description: This game is similar to the American-style use of the lagger, with the player hopping on a single foot in single squares and landing with both feet in double areas. After landing in squares seven and eight, the player must jump up, turn around, land, and start in the opposite direction.

ITALIAN HOPSCOTCH

Area: Marked surface; gymnasium; playground

Equipment: Lagger (buttons, beads, or beanbags)

Participants: One to five players

Formation: Line, with player number one facing the first square

Description: The first player stands on one foot outside square one, holding a lagger. The player throws the lagger into square one and then hops into that area. Still standing on one foot, the player kicks the lagger into square two and then hops into that square. This pattern continues to square eight. When the player reaches square eight, he or she places both feet on the ground, picks up the lagger, and hops backward through all the squares to the starting position. A player is out if he or she steps on a line, throws the lagger on a line, places both feet in any square except eight, or changes feet. When an error is committed the player goes to the back of the line.

HORSESHOES

Equipment: Rubber or metal horseshoes (indoor sets of rubber stakes and shoes are available); four shoes and two stakes for each game; stakes are set 10 feet apart.

Players: Two to four

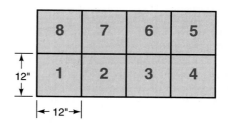

FIGURE 15-9

Italian hopscotch layout

In singles, the players alternate turns, each throwing both shoes each turn. In doubles, one player from each team is at each end. The play starts at one end, with players from opposing teams alternating turns. The object is to get the shoe over the stake or as near as possible while standing at the stake 30 feet away.

The following rules apply:

1. The horseshoe nearest the stake scores one point.
2. If both shoes of one player are nearer the stake, two points are scored.
3. A ringer (the horseshoe encircles the stake far enough to permit a stick or ruler to touch both ends of the shoes and still clear the stake) scores three points.
4. The game score for singles is 21, 50 for doubles.
5. When a player is throwing, the instep of the rear foot must not be farther forward than the stake. If it is, the position of the thrown shoe is disregarded.
6. Shoes that are hit and displaced by an opponent's shoe are scored where they finally rest; for example, displaced ringers are not counted as ringers.

SHUFFLEBOARD

Court: See the diagram; a smooth, flat surface such as a gymnasium floor is ideal

Equipment: Eight discs and two (singles) or four (doubles) cues.

Each player is given four discs (each player has a different color). Player 1 begins by pushing one of the discs with the cue from the right-hand side of the 10-off area, trying to get the disc into scoring position at the opposite end of the court. Player 2 then pushes one of the discs, trying either to get it into scoring position or to knock player 1's disc out of

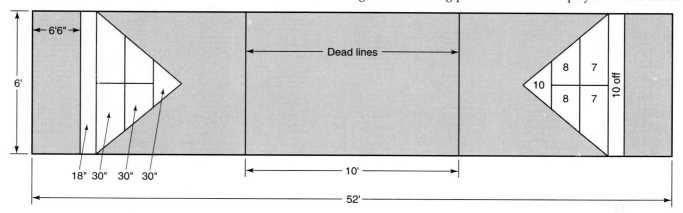

FIGURE 15-10

Shuffleboard court

scoring position. Both players shoot from the same 10-off area. The players take turns hitting their remaining discs until all eight have been played. Discs that land between the dead lines are taken off the playing surface. After the last disc is played, the players count their scores. If a disc lands in the 10-off zone, 10 points are deducted from the player's score. Discs that touch a line are not counted. Players start the second round at the opposite end of the court, and the process is repeated. Games may be played to 50, 75, or 100 points. For doubles, two opponents play from each end and remain there throughout the game; players from team 1 take turns, then team 2. Players should be taught to place the cue directly against the discs and then push forward gently.

RACQUET AND HAND STRIKING ACTIVITIES

RACQUET ACTIVITIES

Several basic skills are common in all racquet sports. With a sound Level II foundation, children should possess the fundamental skills needed for initial success in performance: eye-hand coordination and striking ability in various planes.

The following skills are fundamental to the racquet activities described in this section.

Grip. The implement is grasped as in shaking hands. The fingers and thumb are wrapped around the handle, forming a V along the handle. The handle is gripped by the fingers and not allowed to rest in the palm of the hand. This description generally characterizes the *forehand grip* and is used for strokes that are received on the right side of the body (if right-handed). A backhand grip is used for all strokes that are received on the left side of the body. From the forehand grip position the hand is moved one-quarter turn to the left so that the palm is directly over the handle as one looks down on the edge of the racquet. The thumb is placed along the back of the handle in a slightly diagonal direction.

Ready position and footwork. The ready position is assumed before attempting any stroke. This position is maintained, with the body in a semicrouched position, knees slightly bent and weight evenly distributed on both feet. The stance is toward the net, with the left foot slightly advanced. The racquet is held in front of the body. The stance allows quick changes of direction. After each shot the player returns to the "home position" on court, which is at the center and slightly back of midcourt. Movement should be made with short sliding steps.

Forehand stroke. There are three basic forehand stroke patterns: underhand, sidearm, and overhead. Each pattern resembles the movements used in throwing and striking (*e.g.*, volleyball). A step is taken toward the target (with the opposite foot), and for the sidearm and overhead motion, the elbow is bent before extension and there is a snap of the wrist at the point of contact.

Backhand stroke. The backhand stroke is used when hitting opposite the forehand side of the body. The player changes from the forehand grip to the backhand grip. The preparatory position and footwork for the stroke are the opposite of those for the forehand (sidearm) pattern; the striking side faces the target and a step is taken with the same foot. The backhand is a difficult stroke for the beginner, and many prefer to move to the racquet side to use the forehand. Practice and use of the backhand should be encouraged, especially with the more skilled players.

Performance Concepts.

1. Shake hands with racquet, rest butt against heel of hand, and hold firmly. For backhand, rotate racquet one-quarter turn to left and place thumb along back of handle.
2. Assume "ready position" (semicrouched: knees bent, body forward).
3. Keep eyes on the ball or bird.
4. Perform forehand strokes as throwing and striking patterns; take a step with the opposite foot.
5. For backhand stroke, turn striking side (shoulder) to net and take a step with the same side foot.
6. Bend elbow, swing, extend, and snap wrist at point of contact.
7. Transfer weight from back to front foot.
8. Follow through.
9. Use short sliding steps to get into position to hit.
10. Return to "home position" after hit.

FIGURE 15-11
Gripping the racquet

FIGURE 15-12
Backhand stroke

PADDLEBALL

Court: See Figure 15-13

Equipment: Paddles and ball (tennis, racquetball, or small sponge ball)

Players: Two (singles), three (cutthroat), or four (doubles)

Skills: Underhand, sidearm, and overhead strokes; the backhand stroke should also be introduced to advanced players

The rules are the same as for handball, except all serves and returned balls must hit the wall above the five-foot line.

PADDLE TENNIS

Court: An existing badminton area, with three-foot net dividing the court.

Equipment: Paddles and tennis or small sponge ball.

Players: Two (singles) or four (doubles)

Skills: Underhand, sidearm, and overhead strokes; the backhand stroke should also be introduced to advanced players

The server must stand behind the right base line to serve. The server must bounce the ball and then hit it over the net into the opponent's right forecourt. The receiver must hit the ball back after it has bounced once. After the receiver returns the serve, the ball may be hit "on the fly" or after one bounce. Each player serves until he or she loses by fault or fails to return a ball. The score may be 11, 15, or 21 points. For doubles, one player serves the full game. On each point, however, the server alternates, serving from right to left side and vice versa. Service changes after each game. After the receiver returns the service, the ball may be hit by either member of the team.

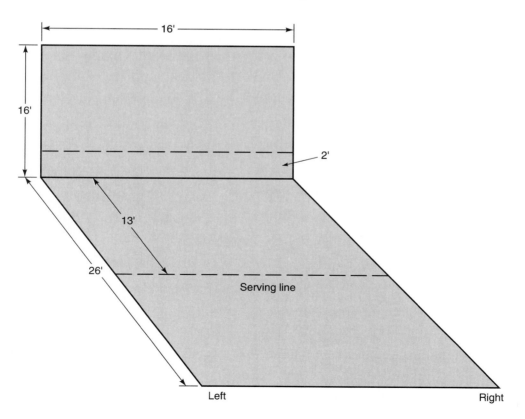

FIGURE 15-13
Paddleball Court

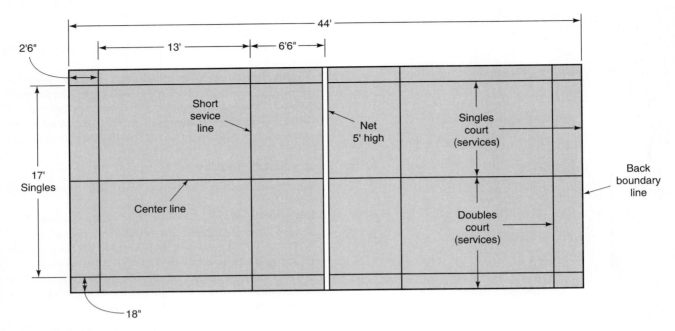

FIGURE 15-14

Badminton Court

The following rules apply:

1. The server has two chances to make a good serve.
2. The server must not step on or over the base line while serving the ball.
3. After each point, the service is made from alternate courts; the serve is from the right-hand court when the score is zero or an even number, and from the left-hand court when the score is an odd number.
4. The ball is served over if the ball hits the net and goes into the proper court.

BADMINTON

Court: An area approximately 20 by 40 feet with a 5-foot net (see diagram).

Equipment: Badminton racquets and shuttlecocks (birds) (long-handled badminton racquets may be difficult for the beginner to control; wooden, short-handled paddles may be substituted)

Players: Two (singles) or four (doubles)

Skills: Serve, clear, smash, and drop shot

Serve. The serve is much like the underhand serve in volleyball. As the racquet hits the bird, the top edge must be below the level of the wrist, and contact with the shuttle must be made below the waist. The bird is held by the base with the thumb and forefinger well out in front of the body the slightly above knee height. The wrist is cocked, and the racquet is held against the bird. The arm is swung back so that the racquet extends backward at hip height. It is then brought forward forcibly, the wrist flexing and the racquet whipping into the bird just as it is contacted. The bird is dropped as the forward swing begins. Body weight is shifted to the back foot with the start of the backswing and forward as the body leans into the hit; follow-through is high and toward the desired line of flight. Two types of serves (strategy) are used: short and long.

Clear. The clear is primarily a defensive shot used to hit the shuttle high and deep, forcing the opponent back near the base line. The clear may be made from the forehand or backhand side and with an underhand or overhead stroke. The underhand clear is executed in the same manner as the serve, except that the bird may be hit with the hand above the waist at the point of contact. The pattern for all overhead strokes is much like that for the overhand throw.

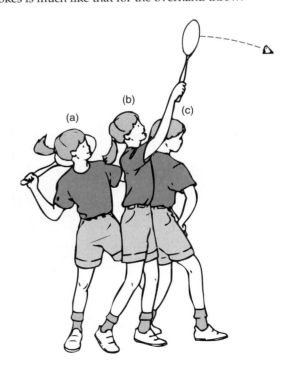

FIGURE 15-15

The Smash: (a) backswing, (b) upswing and contact, (c) follow-through

Smash. The smash is an offensive stroke. Its execution is similar to the overhead clear, except that the bird is contacted slightly ahead of the body, and the rotation of the body is greater. The bird is hit so that it travels at a sharp angle toward the net, the object being to barely clear the net with great force. See Figure 15-15.

Drop. The mechanics of the drop are the same as those for the smash except that the speed of the forward swing is checked just before the bird is contacted; there is little or no follow-through. The drop shot is used to catch the player off guard who is deep in the rear court.

The following basic concepts apply:

1. The clear is used for defense, the smash and drop for scoring.
2. The opponent is kept on the defensive by mixing shots and placement.
3. The use of long and short serves keeps the opponent off guard.

The game begins with an underhand serve from the right service court. The serve must be made with the bird no higher than the waist at the point of contact with the racquet. The bird must go diagonally into the opponent's right-hand court.

The same server continues to serve while making points. The service alternates after each point, from the right side when the server's score is zero or an even number, and from the left side when the server's score is an odd number. For doubles, one serve is allowed the side beginning the first inning, and two serves each subsequent inning. When the score is even, partners should be in the courts in which they started the game. The game may be played to 11 for singles and 15 for doubles. Two consecutive points are needed to break a tie.

Additional rules are as follows:

1. The bird must land in the proper court and may not pass through or under the net or hit a player before crossing the net.
2. A player may not touch the net with the body or racquet.
3. A player may not reach over the net to hit a bird.
4. A player can only hit the bird once during each play.
5. The bird may not be held or thrown: it must be hit with the racquet.
6. A serve that hits the net and goes into the proper court is good and must be played.

PICKLEBALL*

Pickleball, a relatively new game, may be described as a slowed-down version of tennis that incorporates rules similar to badminton. Easily adaptable to backyards, streets, driveways, and play areas, pickleball is quite challenging to the skilled individual and more adaptive to players of lower skill levels than such sports as badminton or volleyball.

Court: The official court is 20 by 44 feet; however, a badminton area may be used by lowering the net to three feet; if a badminton area is used, the short service line on each side may be used for a nonvolley zone (see diagram)

*Pickleball is the registered trademark of Pickle-ball, Inc., Room 530, 3131 Western Ave., Seattle, Wash. 98121.

Equipment: Wooden, short-handled paddles (official paddles have a squared-off head) and a plastic three-inch diameter perforated (whiffle-type) ball

Players: Two (singles) or four (doubles)

Skills: Forehand and backhand strokes (drives and volleys) and the serve

A side can score a point only when serving, and only one serve is permitted. The server, starting on the right side of the court, must serve the ball underhanded, contacting the ball below the waist. The ball must be hit in the air on the serve. For a serve to be good, it must be served diagonally to the receiver, clearing the seven-foot nonvolley zone. If the ball contacts the net on a serve, and still lands beyond the seven-foot nonvolley zone cross court, it is called a "let" and the serve is played over. The ball has to bounce once on each side of the net before it can be volleyed (hit in the air first without letting it bounce) in a rally. If a player sees that the ball is going to land in the nonvolley zone, the player can move into the zone before it bounces but must let it bounce before returning it.

In singles play, the server will always serve from the right side of the court with an even-numbered score, and the left side when the server has an odd-numbered score.

There are four ways to lose a point: (1) hitting the ball out of bounds (a ball landing on any line is considered good), (2) hitting the net, (3) stepping into the nonvolley

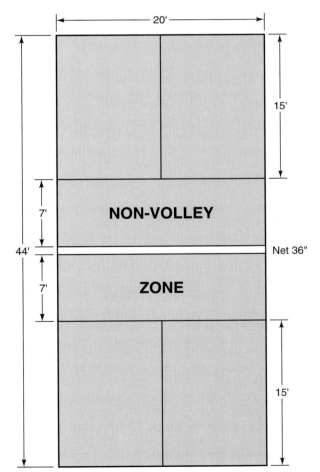

FIGURE 15-16
Pickleball Court

zone and volleying the opposition's ball, and (4) volleying the ball in a rally before it has bounced once on each side of the net.

In doubles play, the same basic rules apply except that two faults result in a loss of service. At the beginning of each game, the team serving first is allowed only one fault before turning the ball over to the opposition. Throughout the rest of the game, both team members will serve, alternating court sides until the receiving team has won two faults. When the serve is won by the receiving team, the player positioned on the right side of the court will always start serving first. In doubles, the serving team is usually back at the base line because of the double-bounce rule. The receiving team can play with one up at the edge of the seven-foot nonvolley zone and one back at the base line.

The serving team cannot charge the net until their opponents' return bounces first on their own side of the court. The receiver, after hitting a deep return, can advance to the edge of the seven-foot nonvolley zone with his or her teammate.

The game is played to 11 points; however a team must win by two points. A point can be scored only by the serving side.

The following basic concepts (strategy) apply:

1. A deep service is advantageous.
2. Low shots over the opponent's head (driving the player back) are also a good offensive action.
3. As in badminton, the smash and drop shot can be effective alternatives for scoring.

TABLE TENNIS

Table tennis, also known as ping-pong, is a popular recreational game and an excellent intramural (or recess) activity. Portable tables allow ease of organization, and a number of players can be accommodated in a relatively small area. Another asset is that table tennis can be played by individuals lacking the physical stamina required in many racquet-type activities (also those who are either temporarily or permanently handicapped).

Area: The table is nine feet long, five feet wide, and 30 inches above the floor; a six-inch-high net divides the playing surface

Equipment: Table tennis (ping-pong) paddles and ball

Players: Two (singles) or four (doubles)

Skills: Forehand and backhand strokes; the tennis grip is used to grasp the paddle; however as the player becomes experienced, modifications may be desirable. For right-handed players, the forehand stroke should be used when the ball approaches from the right, and the backhand when the ball approaches from the left. With the forehand stroke, the left shoulder should face the table, while with the backhand, the right shoulder is pointed toward the table

A game begins with the server making five consecutive serves. The receiver follows with five serves, each player alternating in this fashion for the duration of the game, unless the score becomes 20–20, in which case the receiver shall make one serve, followed by the original server with one serve, then the receiver, and so on, until a winner is declared. The winner of a match is the player who first scores 21 points, unless both players have 20 points, in which case the winner must gain a two-point lead. The

choice of ends and service at the start of the game shall be decided by a toss. Where the match consists of only one game or in the deciding game of a match, the players change ends at the score of ten. The player who started at one end of the table in one game shall start at the other end in the immediately subsequent game.

The service is delivered by dropping the ball (without spin) and striking it with the paddle outside the boundary of the court near the server's end. The ball shall be struck so that it first drops into the server's court and then into the receiver's side by passing directly over or around the net. The served ball shall be a let if it touches the net or its supports and lands in the receiver's court. A let shall also be declared when a serve is made before the receiver is ready, unless the receiver makes an effort to strike the ball. It is a let if either player, because of conditions not under his or her control, is prevented from making a serve or a return. A ball having been served or returned in play shall be struck by the player so that it only passes directly over or around the net and lands in the opponent's court.

In doubles, during the serve, the ball must pass from the server's right-half court to the receiver's right-half court. Each server serves for five points; at the end of each turn (of service), the one who was receiving becomes the server and the partner of the previous server becomes the receiver.

A point is lost:

1. For failure to make a good service, unless a let is declared;
2. If a good service or return is made by the opponent and not returned;
3. If the racket, or any part of the player or clothing, touches the net or its supports while the ball is in play;
4. When a player moves the table in any way while playing the ball;
5. If a player's free hand touches the table while the ball is in play;
6. If at any time a player hits the ball before it has bounced.

HAND STRIKING ACTIVITIES

HANDBALL (One-Wall)

Court: A court 20 feet wide by 20 feet long, with a 16-foot high wall; the service line should be 16 feet from the wall

Equipment: Tennis ball, small rubber ball, or family (soft) handball; gloves may be used, but they are not necessary unless a hard ball is used

Players: Two to four (singles, cutthroat, doubles)

Skills: Underhand, sidearm, and overhead stroke and the serve (which can be made with either of the three strokes)

The object of the game is for a player to hit the ball against the wall and have it rebound into the court area in order to cause the opponents to err in trying to return it to the wall. The server, while standing in back of the service line, drops the ball and hits it with the palm of the hand so that it hits the wall and rebounds into the court area behind the service line. The receiver tries to hit the ball so it will hit the wall and rebound anywhere in the court. The receiver may hit the ball on the fly or after the first bounce. Play continues with the server and opponent alternating hits until an error is made. The server receives a point if the receiving side is at fault. If the server commits the error, the serve goes

FIGURE 15-17

Handball Strokes: (a) overhand, (b) sidearm, (c) underhand

to the opponent. When three are playing (cutthroat), the server must play every other ball—two against one. After a "side out," the players rotate on the court counterclockwise for the serve. In doubles the ball must be hit alternately by a member from each team. The server has two trials to make a good serve. The serving team scores a point when an error is committed; 11 or 21 points constitute a game.

The following rules apply:

1. The serve must hit the wall first and then rebound beyond the service line or it is short; a second trial is allowed if the serve is short. The ball must rebound within the lines of the court. A line ball is good. The receiver may not stand in front of the service line when waiting for a serve.
2. The ball must be hit alternately by members of each team in doubles.
3. The ball may be hit with one hand only and may not touch any other part of the body.
4. The ball may be hit in the air or after the first bounce.
5. If a player intentionally interferes with an opponent, a foul is called. If the interference is unavoidable, the point is replayed.

SIDEWALK TENNIS

Court: Four squares of a sidewalk or as shown in diagram: a low net is optional

Equipment: Tennis ball or small rubber ball

Players: Two (singles) or four (doubles)

The server, standing behind the base line, bounces the ball and then strikes it with an underhand hit (palm of hand) over the net line. The ball must land in the opponent's court. After one bounce, the receiver must return (open palm) the ball over the net line. After the receiver has returned the first serve, players may return the ball while it is in the air or after the first bounce. For doubles, the same rules apply, with partners alternating on serves and returns. When a teammate loses a serve, it goes to an opponent. The server scores one point if the receiver fails to return the ball or commits one of the following fouls:

1. Hitting the ball with any part of the body other than the open palm;
2. When returning a serve, hitting the ball while it is in the air; if the server commits any of the following fouls, there is a change in servers:
   a. Stepping over the baseline when serving
   b. Serving the ball with a side or overhand serve.

Games may be played to 11, 15, or 21 points. If the score is tied, a player must make two consecutive points to win the game.

VOLLEY TENNIS

Court: Same as paddle tennis court.

Equipment: One volleyball

Players: Two (singles) or four (doubles) or six if court is enlarged.

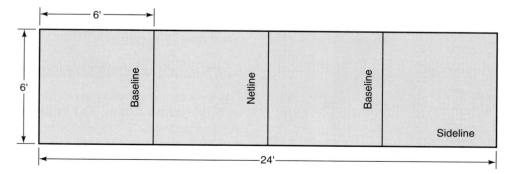

FIGURE 15-18

Sidewalk Tennis Court

The game begins with a serve from the right-hand base line to the court diagonally opposite. The ball must bounce once and be hit with the fist or open palm. The ball is returned anywhere in the court by the receiver. The ball may be hit while in the air or on the first bounce only after the serve is returned off the first bounce. The server continues to serve from alternate courts until an error or a foul is committed; then the serve goes to the opponent. When the opponent errs or commits a foul the server scores a point. The game may be played to 11, 15, or 21 points. If the score is tied, one side must make two consecutive points.

Fouls are:

1. Stepping over the base line when serving;
2. Allowing the ball to hit any part of the body but the hands;
3. Failing to hit the ball within the service court;
4. Failing to hit the ball within the boundary lines;
5. Catching or carrying the ball in hand;
6. Touching the net or reaching over it to hit a ball.

TEAM SPORTS AND LEAD-UP ACTIVITIES (LEVELS III AND IV)

Basketball	Volleyball	Track and Field
Soccer	Hockey (Field/Floor)	
Football Activities	Softball	

One of the major problems associated with childrens' physical education has been the implementation of traditional team sports before a diverse and proficient skill foundation has been established. With a Level II foundation, most children should be ready to enter, learn, and perform efficiently during initial periods of the sports-related phase of motor behavior. It is with fundamental skill proficiency, psychological readiness for team interaction, and a traditional spirit for sports that children enter Level III–IV with overwhelming enthusiasm.

The primary focus of the elementary sports program is concept and skill development; therefore playing of the official sport should be minimized. Participants should be given experiences that maximize specific skill development and individual participation.

This objective may be obtained through carefully selected practice and final activities. Final activities such as modified, creative, and lead-up games should be selected to progressively present elements of the sport with maximum benefit to participation and practice. It is with a Level IV proficiency that children have experienced the specifics of the sport and are ready for additional challenges in school and outside sport activities.

The format for each sport presented in this section includes the following:

Introduction
Instructional considerations
Developmental Skill Presentation Chart (Beg., Int., Adv.)
Skill description
Skill development activities
Game activities
Basic rules and regulations
Skill test suggestions

BASKETBALL

Since James Naismith created the game in 1891, it has become one of the most popular team sports. For involvement at post-Level II (usually above third grade), basketball is an excellent activity. The game includes most of the fundamental skills (*e.g.*, catching, throwing, running, and jumping), it can be vigorous, and it is easily adapted to most schools and playgrounds.

Because of the vast popularity of the sport, teachers will discover a wide variation in skill levels within each grade. Although most children will have acquired a Level II foundation in fundamental skills, many students may be well beyond this stage because of interest and participation in the community youth sport program. When practical, the teacher should address these differences in the planning and presentation of the unit (*e.g.*, through station work). Repetition in the form of practice, even for the more skilled students should be recognized as a contribution to skill refinement. Although playing the official game offers much to the skilled participant, the nature of the game in school provides limited activity—hence the emphasis on skill development and select final activities.

INSTRUCTIONAL CONSIDERATIONS

Equipment. Various types of balls, including soccer balls, playground balls, and volleyballs may be used in the intermediate grades for ball-handling practice and lead-up games.

Junior-size basketballs should be used at the elementary level. Baskets should be lowered to a height of 7 to 9 feet (regulation is 10 feet), depending on size and skill level.

Table 15-5

Basketball: Developmental Skills Presentation Chart

SKILLS	LEVEL		
	Beg.	*Inter.*	*Adv.*
Passing	(All to stationary target) Chest pass Bounce passes Baseball pass Underhand pass	To moving target	Overhead pass
Catching	Above the waist Below the waist	While moving	
Dribbling	Forward and backward Use of right and left hand	While weaving and pivoting	
Shooting	One-hand push Two-hand set Layup	Free throw	Jump shot Layup either hand
Additional Skills		Pivoting Feinting Guarding (defending)	Rebounding Jump ball
Rules	Traveling Out-of-bounds Scoring	Held ball Personal fouls	The game

Skill Presentation. The basic program should emphasize the refinement and development of skills and include activities that offer variability in practice. Each child should have an opportunity to practice all skills. This is not possible when a considerable portion of class time is devoted to playing regulation basketball on a full-length court. Children at the beginning Level III (frequently shown at the third or fourth grade level) should concentrate on refining the basic

FIGURE 15-19

Two-hand chest pass

skills used in basketball (*e.g.,* passing, catching, dribbling, and simple shooting). Students at the intermediate and advanced levels should practice using both hands, weaving, pivoting, shooting, and playing defense, as well as learning the rules needed to play regulation basketball.

SKILL DESCRIPTION

Passing. Passing is an offensive maneuver to transfer the ball from one player to another. The movement is performed from a stationary or dynamic position. Basic to all passing variations is the child's ability to throw with accuracy. Because of the size and weight of a basketball, in many instances power is a significant performance factor.

Two-Hand Chest Pass. The two-hand chest pass is one of the most useful and effective passes in basketball. It is generally used for transferring the ball short distances. To begin, the ball is held with the fingers spread around the sides of the ball; the thumbs should be close together. The ball is held at chest level and the elbows remain close to the sides of the body. The ball is projected by taking one step toward the intended receiver, extending the arms, snapping the wrists as if putting a reverse spin on the ball, and releasing the ball off the fingertips.

FIGURE 15-20
Two-hand bounce pass

FIGURE 15-21
Baseball pass

FIGURE 15-22
Underhand pass

Performance Concepts

1. Hold the ball with the fingers, thumbs behind ball.
2. Position elbows close to the sides of the body.
3. Step in the direction of the pass and shift the weight forward, extending arms.
4. Snap the wrists and fingers as the ball is released.
5. Follow through toward the target.

Bounce Pass. The bounce pass may be executed with either one or two hands. The two-hand bounce pass is performed like the two-hand chest pass except the ball is bounced on the floor before it reaches the receiver. The ball should strike the floor about three feet in front of the receiver so that it bounces up about waist high. For the one-hand bounce pass the ball is projected by bringing the ball with two hands to a position on the preferred side of the body while the push is made with one hand. The ball is bounced as described in the two-hand bounce pass.

Performance Concepts

1. Note the concepts for the two-hand chest pass.
2. Bounce the ball so it will reach the receiver at waist level.

Baseball Pass. This pass is most effective for long distances. The pass utilizes the overarm throwing pattern. Since a basketball is larger than the usual throw-

ing object and somewhat awkward for the child, the nonthrowing hand may be placed in front of the ball in the backswing to aid in stabilization. The throw is made by stepping with the foot opposite the throwing hand toward the intended receiver, projecting the ball with the throwing hand from behind the ear, extending the elbow, and snapping the wrist (as if waving good-bye). Body weight shifts from the back to the forward foot toward the receiver.

Performance Concepts

1. Throw the ball in an overarm pattern.
2. Keep the throwing hand behind the ball and follow through.

Underhand Pass. The underhand pass is most effective for short hand-offs. The pass utilizes the underhand throwing pattern. However, because of the large size of the ball, the left hand (if right-handed) is placed on top of the ball for stability during the backswing. During projection the right hand and arm follow through toward the target.

Performance Concepts

1. Keep the fingers of the throwing hand spread under the ball with the palm up.
2. Use this pass only to cover short distances.

Overhead Pass (two hands). The overhead pass is effective when a player wishes to pass the ball to a teammate above the reach of a shorter opponent. The pass begins with the feet in stride position and knees slightly bent. The ball is held above the head, with the hands on the sides of the ball. Projection is accomplished as the arms shift forward with a forceful wrist and finger snap.

Performance Concepts

1. Use a forceful arm action with wrist and finger snap.
2. Step toward the intended receiver whenever possible.

Catching. Catching a basketball is a fundamental skill. However, because of the size and weight of the object, specific performance elements should be

FIGURE 15-23
Overhead pass (two-hand)

FIGURE 15-24
Catching

understood by the receiver. Basically, there are two types of catching skills. The overhand position (fingers up) is used to receive the ball *above the waist*, and the underhand pattern (fingers down) is used for catching *below the waist*. With both styles the elbows are bent and held close to the sides of the body. The hands are extended toward the oncoming ball, with the fingers spread and slightly flexed. The ball is received on the finger tips, with the elbows bent to absorb the force.

Performance Concepts

1. Spread the fingers wide and curl them slightly.
2. Watch the ball until it is caught.
3. Move to meet the ball to shorten the distance.
4. Give with the hands on contact.
5. When applicable, draw the ball in toward the body and use the motion as the backswing for a pass.

Dribbling. Basically, dribbling is controlled bouncing of the ball in any direction and at varying speeds. The dribbler's feet should be placed in a narrow stride position and the body flexed at the knees with a slight forward trunk lean at the hips and waist. The ball is contacted with the fingers spread and propelled (pushed) to the floor by elbow extension and follow-through. The hand rides up with the

FIGURE 15-25
Dribbling

ball to the desired height before the next downward push. The height of the bounce is maintained at just above waist level. A low, controlled dribble should be used to protect the ball from the hands of a defensive player. When dribbling, a player must keep his or her eyes and head up rather than looking down at the ball. This will enable the dribbler to see the opponents better as well as possible opportunities for passing to an unguarded teammate.

Performance Concepts

1. Push the ball down and slightly forward with the fingers when dribbling forward.
2. Use the wrist and fingers to control bounce.
3. Keep the dribble low when guarded.
4. "Ride" the ball up; do not slap.

5. Do not look directly at the ball while dribbling; use peripheral vision.

Shooting.   Shooting is perhaps the most important and complex skill in basketball. Considerable practice is needed before a consistent level of proficiency can be achieved. To aid in skill acquisition, a junior-size basketball and lowering the height of the goal to 8 or 9 feet (regulation is 10 feet) is desirable. The following points should be stressed:

1. Watch the target and not the ball.
2. Before the shot starts, the wrist(s) should be cocked.
3. The arc of the shot should be approximately 45°.
4. Follow through with the shot.

FIGURE 15-26
One-hand shot

FIGURE 15-27
Two-hand set shot

One-Hand Push Shot. This type of shot is the most frequently used in the game. It can be attempted from a standing or moving position. To attempt this shot, the player should advance the same foot as the shooting hand. The knees are flexed and the trunk erect. The ball is held at shoulder level, with the shooting hand behind and slightly below the ball and the other hand (the guide hand) on the side and slightly to the front. As the ball is pushed, the shooting arm is extended upward and toward the basket—the wrist snapping just as the ball is released. Eyes should be on the target throughout the shot and the follow–through. The amount of knee bend and extension depends on the force needed to complete the distance.

Performance Concepts

1. Use the nonshooting hand to help get the ball in position for a shot.
2. Snap the wrist and release the ball off the finger tips.

Two-Hand Set Shot. This shot is similar to the chest pass, except the angle of release differs. The ball is released when the arms are fully extended toward a point just above the rim. This shot is usually attempted when the shooter is not closely guarded.

Performance Concepts

1. Snap the wrists.
2. Keep the fingers in contact with the ball as long as possible.

FIGURE 15-29

Underhand free throw

3. Use an equal amount of force with both hands.

Layup. A layup is a shot taken when the player is close to the basket, either as the result of a dribble or a pass. The shot may be executed from an angle, generally deflecting the ball off the backboard, or in front of the basket. The player should push off on the opposite foot of the shooting hand. The knee on the same side as the shooting hand is flexed and raised. The

FIGURE 15-28

Lay-up

FIGURE 15-30

Jump shot

ball is raised while the arms extend toward the basket. At the height of the upward leap, the ball rolls off the fingertips, laying it gently against the backboard for side shots and over the front edge of the rim for a front shot.

Performance Concepts

1. Reach high during the leap.
2. Lay the ball against the backboard for side shots and over the rim for front shots.
3. Use the nonshooting hand to guide the ball.

Free Throw. A variety of shooting styles may be used to complete free throws. The one-hand shot appears to be the most popular; however, the two-hand set shot and two-hand underhand shot are also used. Since the two-hand underhand shot has not been described (too easy to guard during play), it will be presented here.

To perform the underhand shot, the back is held straight, knees slightly bent and weight equally distributed on both feet. With the arms straight (pointing downward), the ball is held with the finger tips of both hands slightly under the ball. Simultaneously, the arms swing forward and upward as the knees straighten. The back should be held straight throughout the pattern and the ball released off the finger tips.

Jump Shot. The basic principles of the one-hand push shot also apply to the jump shot. The primary difference is exhibited in the jump. The player raises the ball with both hands, and with a two-footed jump, projects the ball by extending the shooting arm and snapping the wrist forward to impart a reverse spin on the ball. Ideally, the ball should be released at the height of the jump.

Additional Skills.   *Pivoting.* Pivoting is the technique of turning the body in different directions while on one foot. After the player declares a pivot foot, it must remain in the original spot. The pivot foot should be firmly planted, using the ball of the foot as a pivotal point. The free foot may be raised and moved as desired. While pivoting, the knees should be flexed, the ball held firmly with both hands, the elbows out to protect the ball, and the body crouched low.

Performance Concepts

1. Keep the feet spread for balance and the elbows out.
2. Keep the pivot foot firmly planted on the ground.
3. Face the basket whenever possible.

Feinting. Feinting is a deceptive movement in one direction when the original intent is to move in another direction. This may be accomplished by presenting faking movements with the eyes, head, foot, or whole body, such as faking a pass in a direction other than the direction used.

Guarding (defending). After the children have learned to control, move, and shoot the ball, they should be introduced to the basic skills of defending. Assuming a position between the opponent and the basket, the player bends at the knees and places the feet comfortably apart, with one foot slightly ahead of the other. The arms are outstretched to the side, with

FIGURE 15-31
Pivoting

FIGURE 15-32
Guarding (defending)

one arm up and one down. The body weight is slightly forward on the balls of the feet. The player's eyes are on the ball and the opponent. A sliding step is used to pursue the opponent while cutting off the opponent's path.

Performance Concepts

1. Stand with knees flexed and weight on the balls of the feet.
2. Position yourself between the basket and in front of the opponent.
3. Slide to move with the opponent.
4. Keep one hand up at all times.
5. Focus on the offensive player's midsection.

Rebounding. Rebounding is a positioning and timing of a jump to gain possession of the ball after an attempted shot. This is an advanced skill because of the timing involved between the jump and rebound of the ball off the backboard or rim. To begin, the player should assume a position between an opponent and the basket. The knees are flexed slightly and the jump taken from the toes. Usually the ball rebounds at the same angle at which it hit. After gaining possession, the player should land with feet spread and ready to dribble, pass, or shoot.

Jump Ball. The official game of basketball and many lead-up activities are started with a tossup of the ball between a player from each team. A jump ball may also be used if two opposing players both have possession or both cause a ball to go out of bounds. To jump for the ball, the two players stand side to side, each facing his or her basket. The knees are flexed and then extended, with thrust also being produced by the shoulders and toes. One arm is extended to tap or push the ball with the finger tips. If possible, the direction of the tapped ball should be toward a player on the same team. To achieve this, timing is critical and practice necessary.

Strategy Concepts. *Offensive*. Players should be aware of their teammates' positions, as well as their own. When dribbling, they should be alert for chances to cut toward the basket and move through empty spaces. The ball should be brought up court quickly, and passes in front of the basket should be avoided, unless a teammate is open. Short passes are generally more successful than long ones. Players should dribble only when a pass is risky or they have the best opportunity to advance the ball.

Defensive. Most guarding efforts should take place in a semicircle from the free-throw line toward the basket. Guards should position themselves between the basket and the player they are guarding. Players should be given specific guarding assignments. Guards should use a sliding motion to stay with dribblers.

SKILL DEVELOPMENT ACTIVITIES

Passing and Catching. *Circle Pass*. A circle is formed with a student in the middle. The center student has a ball in hand, and a student in the circle also has a ball. On the command, the student in the center passes his or her ball to any student standing in the circle except the one who already has a ball. As soon as the student in the center releases the ball, the student holding the other ball passes to the student in the center. This drill can be done quickly or slowly depending on the skill level of the students.

Circle-Pass Keep Away. The class is arranged in circles of six to seven, with a student in the center. The students making the circle pass the ball to each other, but they may not pass to the person on either side. The center student attempts to intercept the ball. If successful, he or she changes places with the last passer.

Circle-Pass Race. The class is divided into circles with even numbers of students. Each circle receives a ball. On a signal, the ball is passed twice around the circle. The circle finishing first wins.

Partner Passing. Partners scatter around the playing area and stand about 10 to 15 feet apart. Each student remains in a stationary position while passing. After a few minutes, one student remains stationary, and the other moves around him or her. After a few more minutes, both players move, pass, and catch.

Wall Passing. The class is arranged in lines around available wall surfaces. Players should stand approximately five feet from the wall and gradually move back as their skill increases. This drill can be used to practice all types of passing and catching skills. To increase complexity, lines or targets can be placed on the wall or timing contests added (for example, the number of hits in ten seconds).

Slide Circle Drill. In circles of four to six, students slide around a person in the center. The center person passes and receives to and from the sliding students. After the ball has gone around the circle twice, another student takes the center position.

Single-Line Pass. Students form two single facing lines about seven yards apart. The first student in line 1 passes to the first student in line 2, who passes the ball back to the second student in line 1. Each goes to the rear of the opposing line. The students should use all passes and keep moving.

Floor Catch. Students form two facing lines about 10 yards apart. The first student in line 1 bounces the ball hard to the floor. The first student in line 2 catches and returns the ball to line 1. Each goes to the rear of the opposing line.

Dribbling. *Kneeling and Standing Dribble*. Students kneel on one knee and begin dribbling with the same hand as the kneeling knee. This drill will eliminate unnecessary arm action. Movements include moving the ball backward and forward; moving the ball around the front of the opposite leg and change hands, moving the ball around the front of the opposite leg and changing hands, moving the ball under the leg to the other hand, bouncing the ball in rhythm, and playing follow the leader. These movements should also be performed while the students are standing.

File Dribble. In file formation, students dribble forward to and around an obstacle (*e.g.*, Indian club, cone, chair) and back to the line, where the next student repeats. For a variation each student should dribble down with one hand and back with the other.

Circle Dribble. The class is divided into circles, students spaced 4 feet apart. One student dribbles, weaving in and around other students in the circle. When the student returns to his or her position, he or she gives the ball to the player on the right.

Line Dribble. The class is divided into equal groups, and teams are divided into two parallel lines facing each other about 20 yards apart. The first player dribbles across, giving the ball to the first player in the opposite line, and taking his or her place. This player then dribbles to the second player in the line across, gives that player the ball, and replaces him or her in the line. Play continues until the last person in line receives the ball and dribbles back to the first person in line.

Shuttle Dribble. This variation begins at the head of a file. The first student dribbles across to another file, handing the ball to the student at the head. He or she then takes a place at the end of that file. The student receiving the ball then dribbles back to the first file. A number of shuttles can be arranged for dribbling crossways over a basketball court.

Figure-Eight Dribble. For figure-eight dribbling, four or more obstacles are set about 5 feet apart. The first student at the head of each file dribbles in and around each obstacle, changing hands so that the one opposite the obstacle is always used.

Shooting. *File Shooting.* The class is divided into groups, one group to each basket. Each group is in file formation at the foul line. The first student dribbles in to the basket for a layup or shoots (choice of style) from a designated mark, retrieves the ball, gives it to the next player in line, and goes to the rear of the line.

Set-Shot Shooting. Six to eight students form a semicircle near a basket. One student, the leader, is stationed under the basket with a ball. The leader passes the ball to the first player in the semicircle, who attempts a two-hand set shot (or one-hand push). The leader recovers each ball and passes it to each student in sequence. The distance from the basket may be adjusted according to the group's level of skill. Leaders should he changed regularly so that everyone has the opportunity to shoot and be a leader.

Layup Shooting. Two lines of students are arranged at a 45° angle to the basket. The first student in each line should be about 20 feet away from the basket. The first student in the shooting line dribbles toward the basket and attempts a layup and then goes to the end of the retrieving line. The first student in the retrieving line leaves the line at the same time as the shooting player to retrieve the ball and pass it to the next person in the shooting line. The retriever then goes to the end of the shooting line. The drill continues until everyone has had ample opportunity to practice; the drill is then repeated, the players shooting from the other side of the basket.

Pivoting. *Circle Pivot and Pass.* The class forms large circles. The student with the ball dribbles to the center of the circle, pivots, passes to another player in the circle, and takes his or her place. The students could perform front and reverse pivots when arriving in the center. A variation allows the center person to pivot and pass to all the students before changing places.

Pivot and Pass. In file formation, each student in turn dribbles forward to a designated line, stops, pivots, faces the file, and then passes back to the next player, who repeats the drill. The first student runs to a place at the end of the line.

Whistle Pivot. Students are scattered by pairs around the floor, one ball for each pair. On the first whistle, the front player of the pair dribbles in any direction and fashion on the court. On the second whistle, the student stops and pivots back and forth. On the third whistle, the student dribbles back and passes to a partner, who immediately dribbles forward, repeating the routine.

GAME ACTIVITIES

The following activities may be used to enhance the student's proficiency. Each activity stresses one or more of the skills practiced during the skill development phase of the lesson. Because large differences may be (and frequently are) present between and within groups, modification of the activities may be needed to meet each group's ability, as well as to accommodate equipment and facilities.

BATTLE

Players: Two equal teams

Two playing areas, with a neutral area between them, are designated. Half of each team is in a playing area. No one is permitted in the neutral area. The object is for a player to make a pass to a team member in the opposite area. Each good pass scores one point.

FIVE PASSES

Players: Four or five on a team

Two teams are arranged in a scattered formation on one side of the playing court or within a designated area. Play is started with a jump ball between any two opposing players. Basketball rules are adhered to with respect to traveling, fouling, and ball handling. Passes must be counted out loud by the passer. One point is awarded whenever a team completes five passes in a row. The ball cannot be passed back to the person from whom it was received, and no dribbling is allowed.

Table 15-6
Game Activities for Basketball

ACTIVITY	CATCHING	PASSING	DRIBBLING	SHOOTING	PIVOTING	GUARDING
Level *Beginning/Intermediate*						
Battle	X	X				
Odd and Even	X	X				
Five Passes	X	X				
Guard Ball	X	X				X
Keep Away	X	X	X		X	X
Circle Guard and Pass	X	X				X
Dribble 500			X	X		
Dribble, Pass shuttle Relay			X	X		
Twenty-One				X		
Pig (or Horse)				X		
Basketball Golf				X		
Pressure shooting				X		
Level *Intermediate/Advanced*						
Captain Basketball	X	X	X		X	X
In and out	X	X	X	X	X	X
Sideline Basketball	X	X	X	X	X	X
One Goal	X	X	X	X	X	X
Three-on-Three	X	X	X	X	X	X
Half-court Basketball	X	X	X	X	X	X

Whenever a series of passes is interrupted by an interception or a fumble, a new count is started by the team that gains possession of the ball. A free throw from one teammate to another is awarded to the team that did not commit the foul.

KEEP AWAY

Players: Eight to 10 on each team

Two teams are arranged in a scattered formation within a designated area. On a signal, the teacher gives the ball to one of the teams, which passes it among themselves, trying to keep it away from the other team. Players on the opposing team guard as in regular basketball. If teams are large and space is limited, players rotate every few minutes. For variation, players may be allowed only two dribbles.

DRIBBLE 500

Players: Six to eight per team

After dividing the class into relay teams, a circular track area is marked by pylons at each corner. At a signal, the first player from each team dribbles around the track, returns, and gives the ball to the next player, who repeats. A number of circles may be used. If space is a problem, each team can be timed.

ODD AND EVEN

Players: Eight to 12 per circle

Players are arranged in a circle and numbered by 1 and 2. Balls are started anywhere in the circle. The 1's throw in sequence to each other; 2's do the same. When the ball

returns to the person who started, he or she shouts, "Odds" ("Evens"), and all players on that team sit down. The first team to sit down wins. Balls can be started in opposite directions.

GUARD BALL

Players: Five on each of three teams

Two lines are drawn approximately 10 to 15 feet apart, with one team (1 and 2) behind each sideline, and the third (3) in the middle. On a signal, players on teams 1 and 2 try to pass the balls back and forth to each other. All passes must be below head height of the opposing player. Players on team 3 attempt to intercept the passes. If a pass is intercepted, player 3 returns the ball to the passer and stays in position while the game continues. The game continues for one minute, then the number of successful passes are counted. Teams are rotated after each game.

CIRCLE GUARD AND PASS

Players: Eight or 10 per team

The offensive team moves into formation around a large (30-foot) circle. One of the offensive players moves to the center. The defensive team is in position around a smaller (20-foot) circle inside the larger circle. On a signal, the offensive team tries to pass the ball to the center player. The players may pass the ball around the circle to each other before making an attempt to the center. The defensive team must bat the ball away but cannot catch it. After a stipulated time (one minute) offensive and defensive teams trade positions. Score can be kept, with two points awarded for each successful pass. More than one ball can be used, and different types of passes can be stipulated. Points can be awarded to the defensive team members each time they touch the ball.

TWENTY-ONE

Players: Six or seven players

Players of each group are arranged in a scattered formation around one basket. The object of the game is for any player to score 21 points by a combination of field shots and free throws. Player 1 shoots from the free-throw line while the other players stand wherever they wish in the playing area. Player 1 continues shooting from the free-throw line until he or she misses; each successful basket counts one point. When player 1 misses, any player who can get possession of the ball may try for a field goal; if successful, it counts two points. If the try for a field goal fails, any player who can get the ball may try for a field goal. Play is continued until a field goal is made. After a goal, the ball is given to player 2, who takes a turn at the free-throw line. Play continues until a player has 21 points.

PRESSURE SHOOTING

Players: Six to eight per team

One team is arranged in file formation behind the foul line of a basket. At a signal, each player in turn takes a shot, retrieves, and passes to the next player. Each completed basket counts one point. The team with the most points within a designated time limit wins.

IN AND OUT

Players: Six teams of five players each

Regular basketball rules apply, with the following modifications: (1) Two teams play, while the third team remains on the sidelines; (2) when a field goal or free throw is made, the third team takes the loser's place; and (3) each player is allowed only two dribbles. This game may be used to practice strategy, as well as skills. If goals are not being scored, a time limit may be used instead.

ONE GOAL

Players: Two to four on each team

The game is played by two teams according to the regular rules of basketball but with the following exceptions:

1. The game begins with a jump at the free-throw mark, with the centers facing the sidelines.
2. When a defensive player recovers the ball, either from the backboard or on an interception, the ball must be taken out beyond the foul-line circle before offensive play is started and an attempt at a goal can be made.
3. After a basket is made, the ball is taken in the same fashion away from the basket to the center of the floor, where the other team starts offensive play.
4. Regular free-throw shooting can be observed after a foul, or some use can be made of the rule whereby the offended team takes the ball out of bounds.
5. If an offensive player is tied up in a jump ball, he or she loses the ball to the other team. As many children as possible should be kept active; if only two goals are available, a rotation system should be used.

HALF-COURT BASKETBALL

Players: Five per team; however, four or six may be used

One half of a basketball court is utilized for each game; two games may be conducted at a time. The free–throw line is extended all the way across the court; both teams shoot at the same basket. The same rules are adhered to as in regular basketball, except that the team that gains possession of the ball must throw it to a team member behind the restraining line before it can be passed in for a shot at the basket.

DRIBBLE, PASS SHUTTLE RELAY

Players: Six to eight per team

Teams are divided into shuttle lines facing each other 30 yards apart. The first player dribbles to a designated 5-yard spot, stops, passes to the first player in the other line, and goes to the rear of the second line. The second player repeats.

PIG (or HORSE)

Players: Groups of four to six, each given a number for shooting order

The first player shoots from wherever he or she wishes with any type of shot. If successful, the next player must attempt the same style shot from the same place. If the shot is missed, the player receives the first letter of the name of the game, *P* (or *H*). The the next player may choose a style of shot and a place to shoot from. As long as the shot is made, the player who follows must attempt a shot of the same style and from the same place or receive a letter. When one player completes the name of the game, he or she is eliminated until the game starts over.

BASKETBALL GOLF

Players: Four to six per team

A team is assigned to each goal. Nine spots are designated on the floor in a semicircle near the basket. Each player shoots from spot 1 until a basket is made, and the number of shots required is counted. That player then shoots from spot 2, and so on. The player who completes the course with the fewest shots wins. Individuals may compete within a team or a team may compete against another team.

CAPTAIN BASKETBALL

Players: Six to eight on each team

Captain Basketball is played in much the same way as basketball. A team normally has three forwards, one captain, and four guards. The captain must keep one foot in his or her area (a line between the two foul restraining lines 4 feet out from the end line) under the basket. The game is started with a jump ball, after which the players advance the ball as in regulation basketball; however, the players may not cross the center line. The guards must bring the ball up to the center line and throw it to one of their forwards. The forwards maneuver and attempt to pass to the captain. A throw by one of the forwards to the captain scores two points; a free throw scores one point. Fouls are the same as in basketball, but in addition, stepping over the center line or a guard stepping into the captain's area is a foul.

SIDELINE BASKETBALL

Players: Ten to 12 per team

Five players from each team play in the court area, and the remaining players from both teams are placed alternately along the boundry lines. Equal spaces are left between line players. Basketball rules are adhered to, except that the ball may be passed to a sideline player. Sideline players cannot enter the court, dribble, or pass to another sideline player. The game is started with a jump ball in the center of the playing area. The team that gains possession is designated as the offensive team. If the defensive team intercepts the ball, it must pass to one of its sideline players before it becomes the offensive team. Stepping over the sideline gives the ball to opponents on their sideline. Players on the sidelines rotate with players on the floor.

THREE-ON-THREE

Players: Three to five teams of three players each

Playing on half of a court, an offensive team of three stands just forward of the center line, facing the basket. The center player has a basketball. Another team of three is on defense and waits for the offensive team in the area near the foul line. The remaining teams await their turns and stand beyond the end line. At a signal, using regular rules, the offensive team advances to score. After a score is made or the ball is recovered by the defense, the defensive team moves to the center of the floor and becomes the offensive unit. A waiting team comes out onto the floor and gets ready for defense. The old offensive team goes to the rear of the line of waiting players. Each team should keep its own score. Two games can be carried on at the same time, one in each half of the court.

The following are variations:

1. If the offensive team scores, it remains on the floor and the defensive team drops off in favor of the next team. If the defense recovers the ball, the offensive team rotates off the floor.
2. If a team commits a foul (by one of the players), that team rotates off the floor in favor of the next team.

3. A team wins when it scores three points. The contest becomes a regular scrimmage in which the offensive team becomes the defensive team upon recovering the ball. When a team scores three points, the other team is rotated off the floor.

4. The game can be played with four against four.

BASIC BASKETBALL RULES AND REGULATIONS

Court Area. The basketball court has recommended maximum and minimum dimensions (Figure 15-32), the small area being more appropriate for elementary school players.

Positions. A team has five players: two guards, one center, and two forwards. Although only five players are allowed to play at one time, substitutes are allowed to enter the game whenever the ball is not in play. During early learning stages (generally the fourth and fifth grade), a modified game may have six players on a team, three on offense and three on defense, with no crossing of the midcourt line. This arrangement helps children learn the specific responsibilities of a position without the confusion of dual roles (offense and defense).

The Game.

1. The game is started at the center circle with a jump ball. The referee tosses the ball in the air between two opposing players, who attempt to tap it to one of their teammates. The jump ball is also used (a) when the ball is "tied" by two opposing players (the jump is taken at the nearest key or center circle), (b) when the ball goes out of bounds and the referee is uncertain which team caused it to go out, and (c) to start the second half of the game.

2. After a successful basket, the ball is put into play at the end of the court by the defending team.

3. After a ball goes out of bounds, the ball is put into play from behind the line and immediately in front of the place where it went out. Any player from the team that did not cause it to go out may put it into play.

4. Two points are awarded for every field goal and one point for every successful free throw.

5. One or all substitutes may enter the game whenever the ball is not in play (out of bounds, before a jump ball, etc.).

6. The game is divided into four quarters, six minutes each.

Violations. The penalty for a violation is the award of the ball to the other team at a near out-of-bounds area. The following are violations:

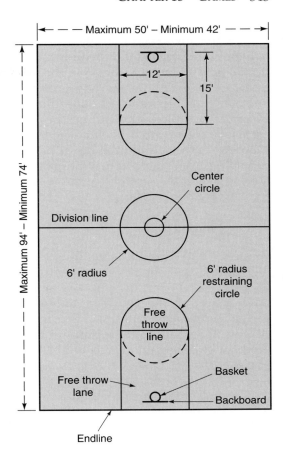

FIGURE 15-33
Basketball court

1. Traveling, that is, taking more than one step with the ball without passing, dribbling, or shooting

2. Stepping on or over a boundary line while having possession of the ball

3. Taking more than 10 seconds to cross the center line from the back to the front court (this rule does not apply in women's basketball); once in the forward court, the ball may not be returned to the back court by the team in control

4. Double dribbling, that is, taking a second series of dribbling without another player handling the ball; palming (not clearly batting) the ball; or dribbling the ball with both hands at once

5. Stepping on or over a restraining line during a jump ball or free throw

6. Kicking the ball

7. Remaining more than three seconds in the area under the offensive basket, bounded by the two sides of the free-throw lane, the free-throw line, and the end of the court

Fouls. A foul is charged against a player if he or she kicks, trips, pushes, holds, or charges another player. If a player commits unsportsmanlike conduct, a foul is also given. The penalty is one or two free throws to the nonoffending team from the free-throw line. One free throw is awarded if a player is fouled while participating in an activity other than shooting. If the free throw is successful, the defending team puts the ball into play from behind the end line. If the free throw is unsuccessful, the ball continues in play. Two free throws are given to a player who is fouled when shooting. If the second free throw is successful, the defending team puts the ball into play from behind the end line. If the second free throw is unsuccessful, the ball continues in play.

BASKETBALL SKILL TESTS

Passing.   *Check pass.* A target (6 feet wide by 4 feet high; 3 feet from the floor) is drawn on the wall. A restraining line 4 feet from the wall and parallel to it is also placed on the floor. The student must pass the ball against the wall repeatedly as many times as possible in 20 seconds. The ball must hit the target but need not be caught on the rebound. The total number of passes that hit the target is the score. The better of the two trials is recorded.

Baseball pass. Three concentric circles are drawn on a wall. The outer circle is 58 inches in diameter (and 3 feet from the floor), the second circle is 38 inches in diameter, and the inner circle is 18 inches in diameter. A restraining line is drawn on the floor parallel to the wall and 25 feet from it. The student uses a baseball pass to hit one of the circles on the wall. Ten passes are taken, and the point values for the inner, middle, and outer circles are three, two, and one, respectively. A maximum score of 30 is possible. Balls hitting a line are given the highest point value.

Dribbling.   Six chairs are set in a line with a distance of eight feet between them, and a line is drawn 10 feet from the first chair. The student starts from behind the line on a signal and dribbles the ball, going to the left of the first chair and to the right of the second, and continues to weave in and out down the line and back. A stopwatch is started on the signal and is stopped when the student crosses the finish line. Two trials are given, and the faster time is recorded.

Shooting.   *Layup.* A line is drawn at a 45⁻ angle and 30 feet away from the basket. Each student attempts 10 layup shots. The player must begin dribbling from the 30-foot line and attempt a shot when reaching the basket. Five points are awarded for each successful basket.

Free throws. The student stands at the free-throw line (the distance may be shortened according to the grade level being tested) and shoots 15 free throws, five at a time. Any method of shooting is permitted. One point is awarded for each basket made. A total of 15 points is possible.

Speed shooting. The student stands at the free-throw line, and on a signal, shoots for the basket. After

retrieving the ball, the student may shoot from anywhere. The object is to make as many goals as possible in one minute. Students must retrieve their own shots. Two trials are given, and the better of two is recorded.

SOCCER

Soccer is played with uniform rules in over 70 countries, making it one of the most popular team sports in the world. In recent years, the sport's popularity in the United States has shown a dramatic increase, especially at the youth sport level. Some of the factors underlining soccer's recognition are its vigorous nature (the main skills being running and kicking) and its appeal to both sexes. Also, it is relatively inexpensive, and it is not primarily dependent on physical size (*i.e.*, height and weight). Perhaps one of the most unique and intriguing facts about soccer is that the ball must be handled with body parts other than the hands (except by the goalie).

INSTRUCTIONAL CONSIDERATIONS

Equipment.   Balls should be smaller than those used in regular soccer; molded rubber or foam balls are appropriate. When balls are used indoors, they should be deflated so they may be more easily controlled. Cones, chairs, cartons, and jumping standards are acceptable substitutes for goals.

Safety.   Because of the vigorous nature of the game, the teacher must be aware of overfatigue; a method of rotation should be used to provide rest.

Since running and kicking are involved, rough play (*e.g.*, pushing, tripping, and kicking) must be controlled and the rules enforced.

Instruction should stress keeping the ball low and avoiding high kicking when near other players.

Children should be taught to protect their face if endangered by a ball that is kicked hard toward the face.

Skill Presentation.   Before an adequate level of skill can be expected, the child must possess a general rhythmic awareness and eye-foot coordination. If this foundation is not exhibited, general activities, such as ladder walking, hopscotch, and jumping with a focus on targets, should be provided. Beginning level activities should emphasize skill development with variations in practice before modified or regular soccer is introduced. The program should include basic kicking, dribbling, and passing the ball with either foot, as well as fundamental trapping; ball handling and control are of primary concern. With the intermediate level program, previously introduced skills are refined and more complex movements presented. To accommodate skill development and knowledge of the game, more advanced lead-up activities and rules and strategies are an essential part of the instructional program. It is with beginning and intermediate level competency that the child can play a variety of lead-

Table 15-7

Soccer: Developmental Skills Presentation Chart

SKILLS	LEVEL		
	Beg.	*Inter.*	*Adv.*
Kicking	Inside-of-foot kick	Outside of foot kick	Volley kick
	Instep kick	Punting	
Passing	With either foot		
Trapping	Sole-of-foot trap	Leg trap	Body trap
	Foot trap		
Dribbling	Inside of foot	Outside of foot kick	
Heading			Stationary and while moving
Tackling		Feet and shoulders	
Throw-in	From behind head		
Goalkeeping		Introduce	
Rules	Handing the ball	Free kick	The game
	Kick off	Penalty kick	
	Corner kick	Goalkeeping	
	Goal kick	Offsides	
	Throw-in rule		
	Charging		
	Position		

up games utilizing most of the skills needed in regular soccer. With the Level IV program, the teacher presents and refines the essentials (advanced skills and rules and strategies) needed for proficient performance; however, it is not recommended that the program consist entirely of an 11-player game. The instructional program should emphasize skill development with practice, which is best facilitated with modified games and activities.

SKILL DESCRIPTION

Kicking. *Inside-of-Foot Kick.* This type of kick is used to move a stationary ball a long distance, to pass to a teammate after trapping or dribbling, or to shoot for a goal. The ball is contacted with the inside edge of the foot. The kicking foot is turned outward, leg bent at the knee diagonally backward and outward. The leg is swung across in front of the body. The ball should be contacted slightly below center. The arms are used for balance, while the foot follows through toward the target. To increase force, a few running steps can be taken.

FIGURE 15-34

Kicking with inside of foot

Performance Concepts

1. Begin the kick with the ball alongside of the nonkicking foot.
2. Turn the kicking foot outward.
3. Bend the knee.
4. Swing the leg forward and across the body.
5. Keep the eyes on the ball and kick it at its midline, slightly below center.
6. Follow the foot through toward the target.

Instep Kick. The instep kick is the most common skill in soccer. It is used for passing and for shooting at the goal. Just before the ball is kicked, the nonkicking foot should be even with the ball and the head and trunk should be leaning forward, slightly bent. Eyes are focused on the ball and the arms extended sideways. As the kicking leg moves downward and forward, the knee moves forward and over the ball. The ankle extends downward to allow the top of the instep to contact the ball and then continues forward and upward with the kicking leg.

If the player wishes to make a low pass, the instep should contact the center of the ball; for a high loft pass over a defender's head, the instep must contact the ball just below the center.

Performance Concepts

1. Swing the leg straight back and forward.
2. Lean into the kick and use the top of the instep.
3. Contact the ball at its midline or slightly below center.
4. Follow the ball with the leg pointed at the target.

FIGURE 15-35

Instep kick

Outside-of-foot Kick. The outside foot kick is used primarily for short passes. The nonkicking foot steps more to the side than for the inside foot kick, with the backswing of the kicking foot taken across that leg. Contact with the ball is made with the outside of the foot along the sole line. This kick allows the player to pass while running without breaking stride. It is also useful for passing to the side and dodging to avoid a tackler.

Performance Concepts

1. Keep the ball within reach.
2. Swing the leg across and through.

Punting. The volley kick is perhaps the most difficult because it is performed when the ball is in flight. The player should stand with the nonkicking foot in front, the weight evenly distributed on both feet. As the ball approaches, the player's weight shifts to the support (non-kicking) foot and the kicking leg is lifted, with the knee slightly bent and the toes pointed down. Contact is made with the top of the instep and follow-through proceeds forward and upward. See Figure 15-36.

Trapping. *Sole-of-Foot Trap* (and Foot Trap). The sole-of-foot trap is best used with a slow-moving ball. In trapping a ball with the sole of the foot, the body is lined up with the flight of the ball and the weight is placed on the left foot. The knees are slightly bent and the sole of the right foot is placed on the ball, with the heel close to the ground behind the ball. Once the trap is made, the foot is removed and put into position for the next play.

Traps with the inside of the foot are made for low balls that are traveling faster than those for sole traps. The foot is rotated outward and the ball is contacted with the inside of the foot or the leg. If the ball

rolls too far away from the body, the sole of the foot can be used to stop it.

Performance Concepts

1. Keep eyes on the ball.
2. Get in line with the ball.
3. Place the sole down over the ball and trap between ground and foot; then release quickly.
4. For an inside-of-the-foot trap, rotate the foot outward.

FIGURE 15-36

Outside of foot kick

FIGURE 15-37
Punting

Leg Trap. The leg trap (upper or lower) is used to control balls dropping toward the receiver. As the ball rolls toward the player, the receiver assumes a position in line with the ball's flight. The trapping leg is raised to meet the ball with contact at midthigh or midcalf. The leg gives on impact, cushioning the ball as it drops in front of the player. The arms are spread to aid stability and avoid contact with the ball.

Performance Concepts

1. Keep eyes on the ball and get into its path.
2. Bend the knees
3. Keep weight on the nontrapping foot.
4. Contact with the midthigh or midcalf, not the knee.
5. Keep the arms spread at sides.
6. Drop the leg immediately upon contact.

Body Trap. A body trap is used when the ball is descending from a high level or when a player wants to prevent a high-rising ball from getting away. To perform the trap, the player brings his extended arms forward but does not touch the ball with the hands or arms. The arm position helps to create a pocket for the ball. However, the player's chest is held in a normal position up to the moment the ball makes contact. Upon contact, the player relaxes the chest muscles, thus creating a pocket for the ball, to stop it and drop it directly below.

Performance Concepts

1. Get in line with the ball.
2. "Give" with the body on chest traps.
3. Jump back slightly from the ball.

Dribbling.   *Inside-of-Foot Dribble.* Dribbling is a means of moving and keeping the ball under control. The ball is trapped gently with the inside edge of the foot. As the player runs, he or she should tap the ball with alternate feet. The ball should never be more

FIGURE 15-38
Sole-of-foot-trap

FIGURE 15-39
Lower leg trap

FIGURE 15-40
Body trap

than two feet ahead of the runner. As the children acquire more control of the ball, they should be taught to use both the inside and outside of the feet.

Performance Concepts

1. Keep the ball at a distance at which it can be controlled (2 feet or less).
2. Tap the ball lightly with the instep (or outside of foot).
3. Tap the ball with one foot, then the other, when running.

Heading.   Heading is volleying or redirecting the ball by hitting it with the head. The player gets in line with the ball, drops the head back, maintains a good stable stance, bends the knees, and bends the trunk backward at the hips. The ball contacts the forehead at the hairline. An upward and forward thrust of the body is made by extending the knees, and the body follows through in the new direction of the ball. This is a difficult skill because of the need to judge the speed and position or flight of the ball. During initial learning periods, a soft ball (e.g., beachball, foam soccer ball) should be used. See Figure 15-42.

Performance Concepts

1. Keep eyes on the ball.
2. Get the body in the path of the ball.
3. Bend the knees.
4. Control the direction by the angle of contact.

FIGURE 15-41
Dribbling

Tackling.   Tackling is a move by a player to gain possession of the ball from an opponent who is dribbling. The most common tackle is the front block, which involves contacting the ball with the inside of the foot just as the opponent touches it. The tackler reaches out with a leg and either brings the ball out to the side (hook motion) or kicks it between the opponent's legs and continues running to reach it. After a tackle, the forward momentum of the body must be checked to avoid body contact with the other player.

Performance Concepts

1. Keep eyes focused on the ball.
2. Reach for the ball with one foot.
3. Quickly clear the ball to a teammate or retrieve it.
4. Avoid contact with the opponent by stepping to the side.

Throw-in.   When balls go out of bounds over a sideline, they are put back into play by throw-ins. To make a throw-in, the ball is held over the head with both hands slightly to the rear of the ball, with the feet in a comfortable position. From either a running or standing start, a backward lean at the waist is assumed and the elbows are bent, with the ball behind the head. The body is brought forward with the arms extended, and the wrists are snapped to give added impetus to the throw.

FIGURE 15-42
Heading

Performance Concepts

1. Throw from overhead with bent elbows.
2. Release and follow through with the hands and arms.

Goalkeeping. Goalkeeping involves stopping shots by catching, blocking, and trapping the ball. The goalie may catch the ball and throw it out, punt it out, or block and trap and kick it out.

Players should get in the habit of catching low, rolling balls in much the same manner as a baseball outfielder does. The goalie gets down on one knee, with the body behind the ball to act as a backstop, and catches it with both hands, fingers pointing toward the ground.

FIGURE 15-43
Tackling

FIGURE 15-44
Throw-in

FIGURE 15-45

Eye contact is critical in goalkeeping

If it is necessary to dive for the ball, the goalie must throw the body behind it and cradle it with the hands. A goalie should always try to get the body behind the ball.

When catching a ball below the waist, the goalie should point the thumbs outward as the arms reach for the ball, with body and arms bent, and bring the ball into the abdomen. For balls above waist level, the thumbs should be turned inward, arms reaching to meet the ball and bending to guide it to the midsection.

Practice activities for goalies should offer a great deal of variety in level and angle of incoming balls, as well as changes in speed.

Strategy Concepts.

Offensive.

1. Have the ball under control before attempting a kick.
2. Pass ahead diagonally to a teammate.
3. Use short, controlled kicks.
4. Use the sidelines to dribble toward the goal.
5. Remember the responsibilities of the position and stay in that area.

Defensive.

1. Back blocker should be positioned behind forwards to pick up missed or intercepted balls.
2. If a back, be ready to tackle the ball as soon as the opponent receives it.
3. After gaining possession, pass the ball ahead to a teammate quickly.

SKILL DEVELOPMENT ACTIVITIES

Kicking, Passing, and Trapping. *Circle Kick and Trap.* Six to eight students form a circle with a leader in the middle. The student in the center rolls the ball to a player in the circle, who traps and kicks it back. Players use the left and right feet and different types of kicks.

Wall Kicking and Trapping. Students are in a line along a wall. Each player stands about 6 feet away from the wall, kicks the ball to the wall, and retrieves the rebound with a foot or shin trap. Variations include (1) having the student start several yards back, dribble to a line, kick the ball to the wall, and trap the rebound; and (2) placing a target on the wall for accuracy kicking. Partners can also use the wall for passing and trapping practice; one kicks and the other traps.

Partner Passing and Trapping. Partners stand about 10 to 15 feet apart. One player passes to the other, who traps the ball and returns the pass. For variations, one player remains stationary and the receiving player is on the move, or both players are on the move. Players may also move greater distances apart for distance kicking.

Line Kicking and Trapping. Players form two facing parallel lines and kick the ball back and forth. The lines should be 5 to 10 yards apart for inside and outside kicks and farther apart for instep kicks. Players trap the ball before kicking.

Goal Shooting. Partners have one ball and two traffic cones (or milk cartons). One partner kicks the ball through the cones, and the other partner traps the ball and repeats the kicking skill. Kicking should be performed at various distances and angles from the goal, with a variety of kicks and traps. For variation, each partner acts as the goalie (attempting not to let the ball pass).

Lead Passing and Shooting. Students form three lines about 20 yards from and facing the goal. The first player in line 1 passes to the first player in line 3, who passes the ball across and about 12 to 15 yards from the goal to the lead player in the line 2, who then shoots. Each player then goes to a different line. The order should be frequently varied.

Dribbling. *Individual Dribbling.* Each child has a ball and finds his or her own space. Children dribble anywhere within the playing area as long as they do not bump into other players.

File Dribbling. Students form two single lines 20 yards apart facing each other. Player 1 dribbles to the opposite line, gives the ball to player 2, and goes to the rear of the line. Player 2 repeats. Other skills such as dribble, pass, and trap may be added.

Shuttle Dribbling. The class is divided into groups of six to eight. Half of each group stands behind the second half 30 feet away. The first player dribbles the ball to the first person in the line directly across and stops it in front of that player. The receiver then dribbles the ball back to the other line. This process continues until all have completed dribbling.

Heading and Throw-in.   *Head and Shoot.* Two players, 7 yards apart, face each other with the goal at the side (two cones, chains or cartons). Player 1 throws the ball to player 2, who heads the ball, pivots, and shoots for the goal.

Pass, Head, and Shoot. Players form three lines about 15 yards from and facing the goal. Player 1 throws the ball in the air to player 2 (or 3), who heads the ball to player 3 (or 2), who shoots.

Throw-In and Head (Individual Practice). Each student has a ball and stands about 5 or 6 feet away from a wall. Each performs a throw-in and heads the rebound back to the wall. The student should attempt to head the ball to various spots on the wall.

Circle Heading. Students form small circles with a student leader in the middle. The person in the center throws the ball to a student in the circle, who heads it back.

Throw and Head (Partner). Partners face each other about 8 to 12 feet apart. One player, using the throw-in technique, passes the ball high in the air so that it descends just in front of the partner. That partner then attempts to head the ball forward and downward toward the first partner's feet. A partner may also be asked to head the ball to the center of a hoop.

Tackling.   *Take Away.* One player is given a ball and tries to keep it from his or her partner by dribbling, dodging, stopping, and pivoting. As soon as the defensive partner touches the ball, the players exchange positions and repeat the drill. A variation has partners beginning about 20 feet apart, facing each other. On a signal from the teacher, each approaches the other, the player with the ball trying to dribble past the opponent and the defensive player attempting to gain possession of the ball.

Shuttle Tackle. In basic shuttle relay formation (one line facing the other; leaders about 20 to 25 feet apart), one leader dribbles the ball toward the other line while the leader of that line moves out to tackle. The dribbler tries to reach the opposite line without being tackled. After about 30 seconds of play, the next two players should begin.

One on Two. Two players attempt to keep the ball away from a third player. If player 3 touches the ball, the opposing player who last touched it changes position with player 3. A variation includes adding a goal behind the tackler and requiring the two offensive players to try to score.

GAME ACTIVITIES

The following activities may be used to further enhance the student's skills. Each activity stresses one or more of the skills practiced during the skill development phase of the lesson. Because large differences may be (and frequently are) present between and within groups, modification of the activities may be needed to meet each group's ability, as well as accommodate equipment and facilities.

CIRCLE SOCCER

Players: Six to eight on each team

The class is divided into two teams, each team making up half of a circle. Each team tries to kick the soccer ball out of the circle through the half of the circle made up of opposing players. The ball must be kicked with the inside of the foot and below the shoulders of the opponents. A moving ball must be trapped and stopped before it may again be kicked. Team members must kick the ball from their place in the circle. If the ball becomes stationary, a player may go after it and dribble it back to his or her position in the circle. A point is made when the ball goes through the opponents' half of the circle. A ball kicked above the shoulders gives a point to the opponents. The first team to score a declared number of points wins.

KEEP AWAY

Players: Six to eight per team

Two teams are formed and confined to a designated area. Team 1 has possession of the ball and tries to retain possession by using soccer fundamentals. When team 2 gets possession, it attempts to keep the ball away from team 1.

Table 15-8

Game Activities for Soccer

SKILLS

ACTIVITY	KICKING	PASSING	TRAPPING	DRIBBLING	HEADING	TACKLING	GOALKEEPING
Level *Beginning/Intermediate*							
Circle Soccer	X		X				
Keep Away	X	X	X	X		X	
Soccer Touch Ball	X	X	X				
Soccer Dodgeball	X		X				
Boundary Ball	X		X				
Circle-Soccer Tag	X	X	X		X		
Line Soccer	X	X	X	X	X	X	
Soccer Goal Kick	X	X	X	X			
Level *Intermediate/Advanced*							
Three-Line Soccer	X	X	X	X	X	X	X
Seven-player Soccer (Mini-soccer)	X	X	X	X	X	X	X
Alley Soccer	X	X	X	X	X	X	X
Pin Soccer	X		X				
Punt Back	X		X				

SOCCER DODGEBALL

Players: Half of class on each team

Half the players form a large circle, and the other half scatters inside. The circle players attempt to hit the players inside by kicking the ball at them. Inside players cannot use their hands to stop the ball, except for a pass that may strike their faces. When a player is hit below the waist, he or she must join the circle. The winners are the last three players remaining inside the circle.

BOUNDARY BALL

Players: 10 to 15 players on each team

Players are scattered on their own side of a playing area divided into halves. Each team is given a ball, which is kicked toward the opponents' goal line. Players may move about freely in their own half of the field to prevent the opponents' ball from crossing the goal. However, they cannot touch the ball with their hands. One point is scored each time the ball crosses a goal line.

LINE SOCCER

Players: 10 to 15 players on each team

Equipment: Soccer ball, four markers, and four goal posts (cones or cartons)

Playing area and teams are arranged according to the diagram. Five players from each team line up inside the playing area. The other players line up outside the area. A kickoff by the center player starts the game and restarts it after each point. Once the game is started, inside players may move anywhere within the court; sideline players must stay behind the line but may shift sideward to the next player. Sideline players are allowed to trap and pass to court players, but only court players may score. If a ball goes over the sidelines or end lines, it is given to the nearest sideline opponent of the team that last touched it. The same procedure is followed for any other violation, such as players

touching the ball with their hands or sideline players entering the court area. One point is awarded for each goal. Sideline and field players, should rotate frequently.

SOCCER TOUCH BALL

Players: Eight to 10 per circle

Players are spaced around a circle about 10 yards in diameter, with one in the center. The object of the game is to keep the player in the center from touching the ball as it is passed back and forth. If the center player touches the ball with a foot, the person who kicked the ball goes to the center. Also, if there is an error (a missed ball), the person responsible changes places with the one in the center.

CIRCLE-SOCCER TAG

Players: 20 or fewer per circle

The class forms a large circle, with approximately 2 feet between players and with one player in the center. Circle players try to keep the center player ("It") from touching the ball. If the ball goes outside the circle, "It" is replaced by the person who missed the ball. If "It" touches the ball, he or she is replaced by the last person to kick the ball.

THREE-LINE SOCCER

Players: 15 to 20 on each team

This game is similar to Line Soccer. A center line bisects the field (approximately 100 feet by 50 feet). Each team is divided into three equal groups, who line up as forwards, guards, and goalies. Play begins with a kickoff, with both teams on their own side. The forwards stand at the center line for the kickoff and then move into the forward (other side) portion of the field. The guards are scattered in the back half of the field, and the goalies are on the goal lines. Thus, forwards compete against guards of the other team, while goalies guard the goal. Goalies may use their hands to defend their goal, but other players follow regular soccer rules. To

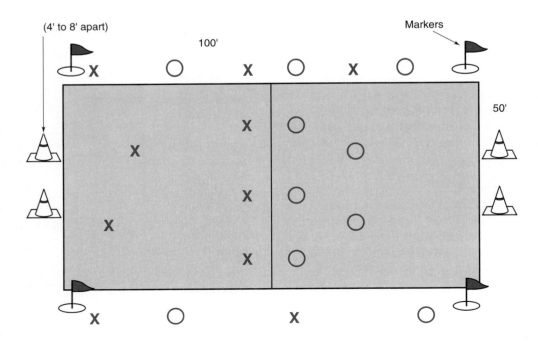

FIGURE 15-46
Line soccer layout

score, the ball is driven past the line of goalies below shoulder level. After each score, the team that did not score gets to kick off. Out-of-bounds balls are put into play with the regular soccer throw-in. Players rotate after each score, with forwards becoming guards, guards becoming goalies, and so on.

Rules should also be observed:

1. An illegal touch results in a free kick from the spot of the foul.
2. A personal foul by a player in his or her own front court results in a direct free kick for the opposing team. (A goal can be scored from this kick.)
3. A personal foul by a player in his or her own back court results in a penalty kick from 12 yards away, with only two goalkeepers defending.

SOCCER GOAL KICK

Players: Teams of eight to 10 each

Similar to One-Base Kickball, one team spreads in semicircular fashion in front of goal posts. The other team waits to the right of the goal posts for kicking turns. The kicker kicks the ball and runs to base, trying to get back to the goal posts before the fielding team can kick the ball between the goal post. The fielders should be encouraged to trap the ball and then kick for a goal, dribble closer before kicking, or pass to a teammate who is closer to the goal. A point is awarded to the kicking team if the player gets back to the goal before the ball crosses the goal line. The fielding team gets a point if the ball beats the kicker across the goal line. After a point is made, the kicker goes to the end of the line, the goalie becomes the kicker, and the next person in line becomes goalie.

SEVEN-PLAYER SOCCER (MINI-SOCCER)

Players: Seven per team

This game follows basic soccer rules. Since there are seven players on each team, this is an ideal game to accommodate an average-sized physical education class. The playing field is normally divided in half to allow two games to be played at the same time. To help facilitate the understanding of "position" play, forwards should remain in their opponents' half of the field and backs should remain in their own half of the field.

ALLEY SOCCER

Players: Two teams of 10 to 12 each

One player stands between the goal line and the restraining line of each lane and is the goal-line guard of that lane. One player stands in each lane on his or her team's side of the center line and is the forward-line player of that lane for the team. Forwards attempt to dribble the ball down the field and kick the ball over the opponents' goal line. The opposite forwards try to get the ball to go toward the other goal. The team with the ball is known as the attacking team; the team without the ball is the defending team. Play is started in the center alley at the center line, with the official giving the ball to one team. Forward-line players should pass the ball across alleys and down the field to the other forwards. After a goal, the ball is given to the nonscoring team at the center line. Players rotate one lane from left to right, starting at the left forward position. If there are more than 10 players on a team, the extra players become sideline guards. In that case the right forward moves into the right sideline guard position rather than moving directly to the right goal-line position. Sideline players put all balls in play

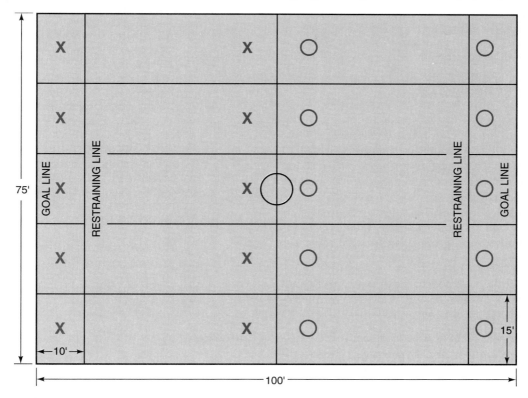

FIGURE 15-47
Alley soccer layout

on their side of the field. With the following fouls, a free kick is awarded from where the incident occurred.

1. Touching the ball with the hands
2. Stepping over alley lines
3. Pushing an opponent
4. Goal-line guards stepping over the restraining line to defend the goal
5. Forwards stepping over the restraining line to kick or retrieve the ball
6. Kicking the ball for a goal above shoulder height

PIN SOCCER

Players: Seven to 10 per team

Two teams stand about 20 yards apart facing each other. At least six pins are placed between the two lines of players. One ball is given to each team. Kicks are made from behind the team's line. Players should trap and concentrate on accuracy. Each pin knocked down scores a point for that team. Variations include the type of kick, distance away, and space between pins.

PUNT BACK

Players: Eight to 12 per team

Equipment: One soccer ball

Players on each team are in a scattered position on their own half of the field. The ball is placed in the middle of the field, and the captain of the kicking team kicks the ball to start the game. Once the game has started, opposing teams must stay at least 15 feet apart. Any member of the receiving team may trap the ball and must kick it toward the opponents' goal. If a player kicks the ball over the opponents' goal, the team receives one point. The team that did not score starts the ball from the center of the field. Any player who contacts another player while the latter is attempting to kick the ball commits a foul. A free kick is then awarded to the other team.

BASIC SOCCER RULES AND REGULATIONS

By the fifth grade many children are ready for participation in a modified game of soccer. Because different rules govern official soccer play for boys and girls, the rules presented in this section are essentially a compromise between the two.

Two modifications of the rules are noted: girls are allowed to fold their arms across their chests for protection when trapping chest-high balls; for girls, tackling is allowed only from the side.

The Playing Field.   A soccer field with minimum measurements of 240 feet by 120 feet is recommended for elementary school programs.

Positions.   Eleven players are on a team: forwards (one center, two insides, and two wings), three halfbacks, two fullbacks, and one goalkeeper. The duties of the various players are as follows:

Forwards: the offensive players. They advance the ball into position and attempt to score.

Halfbacks: both offensive and defensive players. They operate at midfield between the forwards and the defense.

Fullbacks: the last line of defense before the goalkeeper. They must stay in the back third of the field to defend against the forward players on the opposing team. They must be able to kick the ball for long distances to clear it to their forwards or halfbacks.

Goalkeeper: the last line of defense. The goalkeeper is the only player allowed to touch the ball with the hands, provided the ball is within the penalty area.

The Game.

1. *Kickoff.* The game is started with a kickoff in the center of the field by the center forward of one team. The ball may not be played again by this player until it has been kicked by another player of either team. No player may cross his or her restraining line until the kickoff is made by a center forward. A goal may not be scored on a direct kick at the kickoff.

2. *Scoring.* One point is awarded for each goal, that is, when any ball that is in play is kicked, headed, volleyed in any manner (except with hands or arms) across the goal line between the goal posts and under the crossbar. One point is also awarded for a successful penalty kick or direct free kick.

3. *Out of bounds.* Balls that cross the sideline are put in play by the opposing team with a throw-in from where it crossed the line. No opponent may be within 10 yards of the throw-in spot at the time of the throw.

   Balls that go over the end line, when caused by the offensive team, are put in play by a goal kick (from the point where it went out) by the defensive team. The ball should be kicked as far beyond the penalty area as possible.

   When the defensive team causes the ball to go out of bounds over the end line, it is placed in play by a corner kick (from the corner nearest the out-of-bounds spot) by the offensive team.

4. *Time.* Four six-minute quarters constitute a game. Two-minute rest periods are provided between quarters, and a 10-minute period between halves. If the period of time for the game is limited, shorter rest periods might be used.

Infractions.

1. *Penalty kick.* A penalty kick is awarded to the offensive team if a defensive player other than the goalie touches the ball in the penalty area. The kick is taken from a penalty mark (12 yards away) by any member of the offensive team.

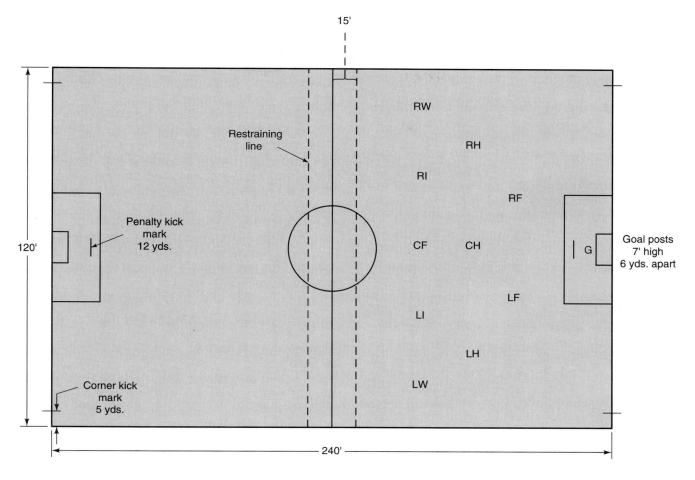

FIGURE 15-48

The Playing Field and Positions

2. *Free kicks (direct and indirect).* A goal may be scored directly by a direct free kick. The ball is kicked from where the infraction occurred. It is awarded when any opposing player commits an infraction outside the penalty area (inside, a penalty kick is awarded). The infractions are kicking an opponent, charging, tripping, handling the ball, and pushing. After such an infraction, the ball is placed where it occurred. Any player may take the kick as both teams stand in front and at least 10 yards away.

A goal cannot be scored directly with an indirect kick unless the ball is touched by another player (the goalie does not count as another player). An indirect kick is awarded when

a. A player kicks the ball a second consecutive time after a kickoff, free kick, goal kick, or corner kick
b. The ball is not kicked forward from a penalty kick
c. The goalie takes more than four steps carrying the ball (the goalie must bounce the ball before taking one or more steps)
d. Players exhibit unsportsmanlike conduct
e. A player is offsides
f. Obstruction other than holding is committed

3. *Corner and goal kicks.* A corner kick is awarded when the ball is kicked, headed, or legally forced over the end line by a defensive player. The ball is placed on the corner of the field—where the sideline meets the end line—on the side the ball went out. Usually a wing player kicks the ball into play. All other players may stand anywhere on the field, providing they are at least 10 yards away from the ball.

When the ball is kicked, headed, or legally forced over the end line by a player on the offensive team, a goal kick is awarded to the defensive team. The ball is placed in the goal area on the side nearest to where the ball crossed the line. Any defensive player may kick the ball; however, it must cross the penalty line to be in play. If it does not, the kick is taken over. The offensive team remains outside the penalty area until the ball has crossed the penalty line.

4. *Offside.* A player is offside when nearer the opponent's goal line than the ball at the moment the ball is played. The player is not offsides, however, if (1) the player is in his or her own half of the field; (2) there are two opponents nearer their goal than the play-

er is at the moment the ball is played; or (3) the player received a ball directly from a corner kick, a throw-in, or a goal kick.

SOCCER SKILL TESTS

Although there are numerous standardized tests to measure soccer skills, most have been designed for secondary- and college-level students. These tests, however, can be modified to meet the ability of elementary children. The following are examples of tests that can be administered without elaborate equipment and in a short period of time. Scores should be kept from year to year to develop appropriate norms for the school.

Kicking. *Distance.* Players are lined up in a file formation on a field marked with a number of parallel lines 6 feet apart. The first line is 20 or 30 feet from the kicking line. Student leaders mark the distance of the kick and retrieve the balls. The students who are taking the test kick the ball from behind a restraining line, either from a short running start or from a stationary position (place kick and punt). The best of the three scores is recorded.

Accuracy. Three circles 2 feet in diameter, labeled 1, 2, and 3, are drawn on an unobstructed wall. They are placed so that the circles are on different vertical and horizontal planes. The kicker has six trials to hit the targets (two per target) from a distance of 25 feet. A point is given for each successful hit on a target. The maximum number of points that may be earned from hitting any one target is two.

Kicking and Trapping. A line is drawn 5 to 10 feet from a wall. The ball is placed on the line. Each player attempts to kick the ball and hit the front wall as many times as possible within 30 seconds. All kicks must be taken from behind the five-foot line. If players lose control of the ball, they may retrieve it with their feet and continue kicking. The higher score of two trials is recorded.

Dribbling. Four objects (pins, cones, or chairs) are set 15 feet apart in a straight line, the first being 15 feet from a starting line. On a signal, a player dribbles the ball from the starting line, weaving around the objects to the end, and returns. A timer starts a stopwatch on the signal and stops the clock when the ball passes over the finish line. If the dribbler loses control of the ball or does not go around the objects in order, he or she must regain control or position and continue the course. The score, the time required to complete the dribble, is the better of two trials.

FOOTBALL ACTIVITIES

The American public in general and children specifically are engrossed in the mystique of competitive football. Although public opinion varies concerning the effects of this phenomenon on our youth, it still remains the most popular team sport in America, and football players' names have become household words. We do not support the sport of contact (tackle) football for children; however, through skill development and modified activities, the nature of the game can be learned.

Because the activities described in this section do not include tackling, it is strongly recommended that as with other team sports, teachers provide equal opportunities for boys and girls to participate. Because of the excitement and interest that football currently presents, teachers may wish to take advantage of the opportunity to enhance the child's movement repertoire; football activities provide a multitude of experiences in throwing, catching, kicking, and running. As with softball and basketball, skill levels may vary widely because of interest and participation outside of school.

INSTRUCTIONAL CONSIDERATIONS

Equipment and Safety. Junior-size footballs should be used.

Activities with the contact elements of football should be avoided; flag or the modified activities suggested should be substituted for touch (strips of cloth can be used if flags are not available).

Roughness and unsportsmanlike conduct must be controlled by supervision and the rules strictly enforced.

Although equal opportunity for the sexes is encouraged, some activities (*e.g.*, blocking) may not be suitable for general participation. Children do exhibit varying degrees of ability regardless of sex, and such issues deserve the teacher's consideration.

Skill Presentation. With a Level II proficiency, most children have acquired an acceptable throwing and catching ability that can be applied to basic football activities. The introduction of beginning level activities provides opportunities to refine throwing and catching skills with the oblong-shaped ball and emphasizes proper carrying technique. At intermediate levels, refinement should progress to increased accuracy between passer and receiver, and the ability to toss the ball laterally while moving rapidly should be evident. In addition, punting and blocking are prerequisities to many modified activities. It is with the skills described and knowledge of basic concepts that the child can effectively perform in modified football activities.

Positions should be rotated frequently so that different skills associated with various positions and strategies can be developed.

SKILL DESCRIPTION

Passing. Three passing techniques are frequently utilized in football activities: forward pass, lateral pass, and centering the ball. The forward passing

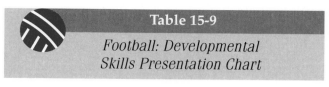

Table 15-9

Football: Developmental Skills Presentation Chart

SKILLS	LEVEL		
	Beg.	*Inter.*	*Adv.*
Passing	Forward pass Centering	Lateral pass	
Catching	Receiving the ball		
Additional Skills	Carrying the ball	Stance Blocking Punting	
Rules	Passing and receiving Scoring Kickoff	Line of scrimmage Safety Use of hands Downs	The game

motion utilizes the basic overhand throw, with a unique grip and release so that the ball spirals. The lateral pass is a sideward toss that is effective anywhere in the field. Centering the ball starts each play.

Forward Pass. In executing the forward pass, the grip is made by spreading the fingers across the top portion of the ball and on the laces. The thumb is pointed around the other side of the ball and toward the finger tips. The feet are in a forward-backward position, with the opposite foot pointing toward the target. The pass is executed by bringing the throwing

FIGURE 15-49

Forward pass

arm back past the ear with the elbow held high, weight on the back foot, the left shoulder pointing toward the throw. As the ball is brought forward, weight is transferred to the forward foot and the body rotated toward the target. The wrist is snapped as the ball is released to give added impetus to the throw. The wrist is also dropped to allow the ball to roll off the fingers and create a spiral action.

Performance Concepts

1. Point the opposite foot (left if right-handed) and the shoulder toward the target.
2. Grip the ball with the fingers across the laces.
3. Bring the ball back beyond the ear.
4. Snap the wrist just before the ball is released off the finger tips.
5. Follow through with the arm toward the target.

Lateral Pass. The lateral pass is a sideward toss of the ball. The ball is shifted from a one-arm carry to two hands. Once the ball is firmly held in both hands, it is shifted to the opposite side of the intended throw. The ball is then moved across the body and released about waist-high level.

Centering the Ball. Centering is used to start play from the line of scrimmage. The ball is passed from a player (center) on the line to a backfield player. The center takes a position with the feet well spread, toes pointed straight ahead, and knees bent. The center is close enough to the ball to reach it with a slight stretch. Body weight is well forward over the shoulders and arms. The right hand takes about the same grip as would be used for passing. The other hand is on the side near the back, acting as a guide. On a signal, the center extends the arms and hands backward through the legs.

Catching. The basic principles of catching (above and below the waist) apply to receiving a football, whether from a pass, punt, or center. The ball should be received with the fingers and brought close to the body to a carrying position. See Figure 15-52.

Performance Concepts

1. Keep eyes on the ball.
2. Reach out for the ball.
3. Catch the ball at the longest point from the body.
4. Wrap the fingers around the ball.
5. Relax the hands to cushion contact.
6. Bring the ball toward the body and tuck into the carrying position.

Additional Skills. *Carrying the Ball.* The ball should be carried with the arm on the outside and the end of the ball tucked into the notch formed by the elbow

FIGURE 15-50 (A), (B)
Lateral pass

FIGURE 15-51
Centering the ball

and arm. The hand is placed under and around the other end of the ball. See Figure 15-53.

Stance. The most utilized stance is the three-point stance (Fig. 15-53). The feet are positioned a shoulder-width apart (either parallel or with one foot slightly ahead of the other), knees bent, weight slightly forward and resting on the knuckles of one hand. The head is up and eyes focused straight ahead. Variations include a four-point stance (both arms forward and hands touching the ground) and a standing position with the body leaning forward and one foot slightly in front of the other.

Blocking. If blocking is utilized (alternative activities are encouraged), players in recreational football activities may block by simply placing their body in the way of an opponent. The blocker's feet must stay in contact with the ground and the hands may not be used. If blocking is permitted, contact from the rear should not be allowed.

Punting. Proficient punting is a skill that requires the precise timing and coordination of all movements from the instant the movement pattern begins. To begin the pattern, the football is held out in front of the right foot at shoulder height. The right hand is under the ball at the center; the left hand is on the front end and to the side of the ball. Generally, two forward steps precede the kick. The player steps forward onto the kicking leg, holding the ball in front of that leg with arms extended. The ball is dropped (not tossed up) before the support foot touches the ground, and the kicking leg is whipped forward with the toes pointed. The ball is contacted with the top and slightly outer side of the foot; follow-through is upward as the arms extend sideways for stability. See Figure 15-36 (soccer) for an illustration of punting form.

Performance Concepts

1. Drop the ball out in front; do not toss it up.
2. Take one or two preliminary steps.
3. Whip the kicking leg forward and use arm opposition.
4. Contact the ball with the top of the foot (not the toe).
5. Follow through toward the target and upward.

FIGURE 15-52
Catching an overhead ball

FIGURE 15-53
Carrying the ball

Strategy Concepts.

Offensive.

1. Be alert and ready to outguess the other team.
2. Look for open places to run and pass.
3. Carry the ball firmly and on the opposite side of the defensive player.

FIGURE 15-54
3-point stance

Defensive.

1. Be alert on all play; get a quick start.
2. Fake blockers.
3. Never leave your feet, or charge into another player.
4. Move in fast to block the ball.

SKILL DEVELOPMENT ACTIVITIES

Most of the skills described can be practiced with partner drills with a scattered formation in lots of space. For example, partners can pass and catch (utilizing the various techniques described), punt and catch, block, run and dodge, and create their own drills stressing variety. If enough balls are not avail-

FIGURE 15-55

Blocking

able, small groups can be formed. The following are specific activities generally involving groups and a combination of skills.

Keep Away (Pass and Catch).   Students form groups of four to six, and boundaries are designated. By passing and catching, one group attempts to keep the ball away from the other. When a player has the ball he or she is not permitted to take any steps.

Target Pass (Pass).   Students form groups of four to six in line formation. A tire suspended from a rope is swung back and forth while the students attempt to throw the ball through the tire.

Pass Defense (Pass, Receive, Center, Defend).   A line of pass receivers stands next to the center; a line of defenders stands opposite them. A passer waits in position to receive the ball from the center. As the ball is centered, the first receiver runs out to receive the pass. The first defender moves out and tries to intercept the ball. The students then rotate, including the center.

Punt Return (Punt, Receive, Center).   The students divide into groups of 9 to 12. Each group forms a triad of punter, center, and receiver (two lines of punters and receivers). The receiver is approximately 25 to 30 yards in front of the center. The center is positioned 5 to 7 feet from the punter. After the punter receives the ball from the center, it is punted to the receiver and returned to the center as quickly as possible. Students then rotate, including the center. A good variation includes placing cones in the field and having the punt returner zigzag through to the center.

GAME ACTIVITIES

The following activities can be used to further enhance the students' skills. Each activity stresses one or more of the skills practiced during the skill development phase of the lesson. Because large differences may be present (and frequently are) between and within groups, modification of the activities may be needed to meet each group's ability, as well as to accommodate equipment and facilities.

FIVE PASSES
Players: Six to ten per team

Players scatter on the field. One team tries to make five consecutive passes to five different players without losing control of the ball. This scores one point. The defensive team may go for the ball only and not make personal contact. No player may take more than three steps when in possession of the ball. More than three steps is traveling, and the ball is given to the other team. The ball is given to the opponents at the nearest out-of-bounds line for traveling, for minor contact fouls, after a point has been scored, and for causing the ball to go out of bounds. There is no penalty when the ball hits the ground. It remains in play, but this interrupts the five-pass sequence, which must begin anew. A jump ball is used when the ball is tied up or there is a pileup. The official should call out the pass sequence.

PUNT AND CATCH
Players: Eight or nine per team

A player from one team punts the ball over the center line into the opponent's area. The opponent closest to the ball tries to catch it; if successful, the player punts the ball back and the game continues. If an opponent misses a catch (it must be in the air), the kicking side is awarded one point. No score is awarded if the ball lands outside the playing area or it does not travel 5 yards.

Table 15-10				
Game Activities for Football				

			SKILLS		
ACTIVITY	PASSING	RECEIVING	CENTERING	PUNTING	BLOCKING
Level *Beginning/Intermediate*					
Five Passes	X	X			
One-Down Football	X	X	X		
Punt and Catch	X			X	
Ground Newcomb	X	X			
Fourth Down	X	X			
Punt Back		X		X	
Forward Pass	X	X	X		
25-Yard Football	X	X	X		

PUNT BACK

Players: Eight to 10 per team

The object of this game is to punt the ball over the opponents' goal line. One player begins the game by punting the ball from his or her own 25-yard line. Once the game is started, opposing players must stay at least 10 yards apart. If the ball is caught by a player on the opposite team, he or she calls "mark" and remains motionless for two seconds. The player then has two options: First, he or she may take five steps and then punt the ball or pass it to a teammate. If a player catches the ball, that player must kick it from the point of the catch. If the catcher moves his or her feet while catching the ball or fails to call "mark," he or she is allowed only three steps before kicking the ball. If the ball is not caught, the player who secures the ball must punt it from the point where it was stopped. A ball that goes over the sideline is punted back from the point where it went over the line. A ball that is caught in the air behind the goal line does not count as a point; it is put back into play by a punt from the goal line. One point is awarded for a successful punt over the goal line provided it is not caught. The ball is put into play again at the 25-yard line.

25-YARD FOOTBALL

Players: Two teams of four to six players

A playing area 20 by 25 yards is recommended. The object is for one team to cross the goal line 20 yards away in four downs or less. The ball is put into play on the offensive team's goal line and started with a hike from the center. In general, the rules are the same as for football. The team has four tries to make a goal by running with the ball, handing off, throwing a lateral, or passing from behind the line of scrimmage. When the offensive team fails to score in four downs or when the defending team intercepts a pass, the defending team puts the ball into play from its own goal line. When a goal is scored, the team scored against puts the ball into play from its own goal line. Each goal counts six points.

ONE-DOWN FOOTBALL

Players: Eight to 12 per team

Both teams line up on opposite sides of the center line. One team is designated to be the offense and is given one down to score a touchdown. Play begins with a hike from the center; then the ball may be run or passed any number of times in any direction from any position on the field. The defensive team attempts to tag the ball carrier below the waist with two hands. If a player is tagged before reaching the opponent's goal line, the ball is downed and the other team takes its down at this point. If a ball is intercepted, the game continues, the defensive team becoming the offensive team.

GROUND NEWCOMB

Players: Ten to 15 per team

A playing area 12 yards wide and 40 yards long has two parallel lines at the center, 10 yards apart, for a neutral zone. One team attempts to pass over the neutral zone and hit the ground with the ball. The second team repeats. Each time the ball hits the ground, one point is scored for the throwing team. If the ball is caught on the fly, one point is scored for the defending team. Fifteen points win a game.

FORWARD PASS

Players: Four to eight per team (two teams)

The object is to move the ball by completing forward passes and to score by completing a pass behind the opponent's goal line. One team starts the game at midfield by centering the ball to the passer. The passer is not allowed to run, and the defensive team may not rush the passer; but the ball must be passed within a slow count of five (one-thousand-one, one-thousand-two, etc.) or the opposing team is awarded the ball. The pass receiver may not run with the ball after it is caught. All completed forward passes give the offensive team another down with the ball put in play where the pass was completed. The opposing team takes possession of the ball on an incomplete or intercepted pass at the place of the last play. A touchdown is scored when one team completes a pass beyond the opponents' goal line. After each touchdown, the opponents' of the scoring team start play again at midfield by centering the ball.

FLICKERBALL (GAME ACTIVITIES)

Flickerball, an exciting alternative to traditional football, is played with a football and incorporates many features of basketball, football, speedball, and hockey. The object is to advance the ball by passing to a position from which a goal shot can be attempted. Any player on either team is allowed to handle the ball at anytime. The ball may be advanced toward the goal only by passing. The player in control of the ball is not allowed to advance toward the goal while in possession of the ball. However, the ball may be carried laterally or backward. No contact is allowed. The game is an extremely active sport (for all), with countless opportunities to run, pass, and receive the football. One of the novel features of flickerball is that an attempted goal results in losing the ball since the goals are situated out of bounds. Any shot, successful or unsuccessful, results in loss of the ball for the shooting team. Thus, the offensive team is forced to eliminate wild or haphazard shooting and work for better scoring opportunities. After a goal attempt, the defensive team puts the ball in play by throwing inward from behind its own end line. Another interesting feature is that a loose ball that remains on the playing field is a free ball and may be played by any player; this rule promotes fluidity of action. Running and physical stamina are important considerations in any team's success in flickerball.

Goal and Field. The goal is a board 4 feet by 5 feet, with a hole 2 feet by 3 feet. The goals are supported (similar to a basketball stand) so that the lower part of the opening is 6 feet (8 feet for secondary school children) above the ground.

The field is 53 yards long and 30 yards wide, with the goals set 15 feet behind the end line. The free-throw line is 10 yards in front of each end line.

The Game.

1. A team may have nine to 12 players.
2. A jump ball is used to start the game, at the half and in held-ball situations. A player other than the jumper must touch the ball before the jumper may again handle the ball. All players, except the jumpers, must be outside a 10-foot diameter circle until the ball is batted.
3. Players are not permitted to advance toward their goal while the ball is in their control; players may move only in a lateral or backward direction.
   a. If a player gains control of the ball while advancing toward the goal, a maximum of one and a half steps is allowed in which to stop the advance or to swerve to a lateral direction.
   b. If a player is called for traveling (illegally advancing with the ball), the ball is given to the nearest opponent.
4. No player may maintain possession of the ball for more than 10 seconds. As a penalty, the ball is awarded to the opposing team at that spot.
5. When the ball goes out of bounds, an opponent of the player who caused it to go out of bounds will be given possession at that point (out of bounds).
6. The ball may be thrown with any motion; however, no hand-offs are allowed.
7. The following rules apply to incomplete passes:
   a. If the offensive team attempts a forward pass that is incomplete through no interference on the part of a defensive player (*i.e.*, if the attempted pass is poorly aimed or the receiver muffs the ball), possession of the ball will be given immediately to a player on the defensive team. The ball is not dead until it touches the ground and is put into play at the spot when it touched the ground.
   b. If a forward pass is incomplete because of a defensive player, the ball remains a free ball and may be played by either team.
8. If the ball is kicked intentionally, opponents are given possession at the spot of infraction.
9. All balls will be dead as they cross the end line, whether the try for a goal is successful or not. In either case, possession of the ball is given to the defending team behind its own end line.
10. When a ball is out of bounds in the back court, the player must throw the ball in so that a player gains possession in the back court. The player may not throw the ball into the front court. Out-of-bounds rules apply when the ball is dead on the field after an incomplete pass.
11. When a team is given possession of the ball out of bounds, it will be given five seconds in which to put the ball in play. The penalty for violation is loss of ball at that point.
12. After a dead ball, a player must be allowed at least 3 feet in which to put the ball in play.
13. Whenever the ball becomes dead, the player to put the ball in play must hold the ball to the ground until the official whistles the ball alive. As soon as the official blows the whistle, the ball may be thrown into play. A pivot foot must be established by the player.
14. A player cannot pass the ball to himself or herself.
15. Although time is flexible, 10- or 15-minute halves are recommended. Time runs continuously.

Scoring.

1. A goal is scored by throwing the ball through the goal or striking the face of the board. A ball that passes through the hole in the board is worth three points; hitting the face is worth one point. After an attempt, the defensive team is given possession of the ball behind its own goal line.
2. An attempted shot that is blocked by a defensive player and remains on the field is a free ball and may be played by any player. An attempted shot that is blocked by a defensive player and rolls out of bounds over the end line will be given to the defensive team out of bounds.
3. A successful free-throw (penalty) shot counts three points if the ball goes through the goal and one point if it hits the goal.

Substitutions.   Any number of players may be substituted at one time; players out for a penalty may not re-enter until they are eligible.

Infractions.

1. No player is allowed to make personal contact with an opponent. For personal fouls (contact, kicking, pushing, tripping, etc.), the player committing the foul must leave the game for three minutes. The offended team will be given possession of the ball on the spot of the infraction. If the foul is committed against a player attempting a shot, all points resulting from the shot will be awarded, followed by a free-throw attempt. After the penalty shot, the defensive team takes possession of the ball at its own end line. Three personal fouls disqualify a player, a substitute may enter the game.
2. Any foul construed to be deliberate or any act of unsportsmanlike conduct will be handled as follows:
   a. A free throw is awarded and the fouled team is given possession of the ball out of bounds at a point parallel to the free-throw mark.
   b. The offending player leaves the game; a substitute may enter the game.

BASIC FOOTBALL RULES AND REGULATIONS

Playing Field.   Recommended playing areas are 60 by 30 and 80 by 40 yards. Lines are drawn or marked across the field at 20-yard intervals, and a line 10 yards behind each goal line designates the endzone.

Positions.   A team may have six to 10 players. If fewer than seven are playing, four are line players and two are backfield players. Two of the line players are ends and usually go out for passes. If eight or more play, no more than four backfield players are allowed.

The Game.   The objective of the game is to advance the ball to the endzone for a touchdown. The game consists of four four-minute quarters or two eight-minute periods.

Start. The game is started with a kickoff (punt or place kick) from the goal line of the team that is designated by lot or choice. If the ball is kicked out of bounds, it is brought back to the goal line and kicked again. If it goes out of bounds on the second kick, the other team starts play at its 20-yard line. The kickoff may not be recovered by the kicking team unless the other team touches and fumbles the ball.

Line of scrimmage. The ball is placed wherever a player is downed, and this is called the line of scrimmage. If a pass was attempted and was not caught or intercepted, it is returned to the line of scrimmage.

Downs. A team is allowed four downs, or attempts to move the ball either by running with it or passing it 20 yards or into the next zone. If players cannot move into the next zone in four downs, the ball is given to the other team at the line of scrimmage.

Huddle. This is the term applied when a team meets in a huddle or circle to plan the next play. After huddling, the teams line up; play is started when the ball is centered.

Offensive play. The offensive team must have at least three players on the scrimmage line when a play begins. The center must pass the ball backward through the legs. A backfield player who receives the ball can hand off or throw a lateral or forward pass from behind the line of scrimmage. Any player except the center may receive the forward pass. The offensive team can punt on any down, providing it announces its intentions. When this occurs, neither team may cross the scrimmage line until the punt receiver has caught the ball.

Defensive play. Defensive line players must remain 3 yards from the line of scrimmage on all plays. They are allowed to cross the line of scrimmage when the offensive team center snaps the ball on running and passing plays.

A defensive player must touch the ball carrier with two hands below the waist (touch football) or grab a flag and hold it up (flag football). No pushing, tackling, or roughing in any manner is allowed.

Blocking. A player may block only by putting the body in the way of an opponent. No hand or body contact is permitted.

Scoring. A touchdown scores six points. The point kicked after touchdown scores one point. After a touchdown, the team is given one play from a spot 3 yards from the goal to make an extra point by kicking ball over goal. A safety scores 2 points. A safety is called when the defending team causes the ball to go behind the goal line, either by catching an opponent chased over the goal line or by causing it to be fumbled. If a defensive player intercepts a ball behind the goal line and does not run it out or if an offensive player kicks the ball over the goal line, a touchback occurs; the ball is then taken to the 20-yard line and given to the team that was defending the goal.

Infractions.   Each of the following infractions results in a 5-yard penalty: offsides, delay of game, throwing a forward pass from in front of the scrimmage line, and failing to announce the intention to punt. A 10-yard penalty is given for illegal blocking, unsportsmanlike conduct, and illegal use of hands.

FOOTBALL SKILLS TESTS

Because most of the standardized tests designed to measure basic football skills are for secondary-level students, the teacher must modify activities to form a teacher-made test battery.

Passing.   *Accuracy.* A target is painted on the wall with three concentric circles measuring 2 feet, 4 feet, and 6 feet in diameter. A point value of three, two and one, respectively, is allotted to each circle. A restraining line is drawn 15 feet from the wall. The student is given five trials; the score is the total points earned. If the ball strikes a line, the highest value is given. A suspended tire, hung about shoulder height and 15 feet away, can also be used. Two points are scored for a "through" and one point for a hit; the score is the total after five throws.

Distance. Lines are placed on the field at 5-yard intervals from 10 to 15 yards. Stakes can be used as a substitute for gypsum lines. Each student must pass a regulation-size football from behind the restraining line. Where the ball lands is marked with a beanbag or small object. The highest score (yards) of three passes is recorded.

Pass receiving. The student runs down the field a designated distance (15 to 25 yards) and cuts to either right or left to receive a pass from a thrower who stands where the runner started. Each receiver has five tries and scores one point for each successful catch. Failure to catch a pass that was not within a reasonable catching distance does not count as a try.

Punting.   The same procedure as in passing for distance is used.

Ball-carrying run. Five pins or chairs are arranged in a straight line 10 feet apart, with the first pin 10 feet from a starting line. The student puts the ball in carrying position and on a signal runs to the right around the first pin; as the student moves to the left of the second pin, he or she changes the ball to the left arm and continues in and around each pin. Each time the student passes a pin, the ball is changed to the outside arm. When the student reaches the end pin, he or she turns and goes back to the starting line in the same manner. The stopwatch is started on the signal and stopped when the student crosses the starting line again. The player is given two trials, and the faster time is recorded.

VOLLEYBALL

Volleyball is one of the most adaptable and socially popular sporting activities played by children and adults in America. It can be a highly skillful professional sport or an informal recreational game for family members. Volleyball requires very little space and equipment, and it can be learned quickly. For years, volleyball has been a popular coeducational activity that can be played on a beach, ship, and playground as well as in the gymnasium.

The basic skills needed in volleyball are a sound movement foundation in eye-hand coordination and striking. With such a background, many children have the ability to participate in modified versions of the game at the beginning; however proficient play at the skilled level will demand a concentration on ball control in varied practice and team play.

INSTRUCTIONAL CONSIDERATIONS

Equipment.   Lightweight balls or beach balls should be used during the initial learning periods. Net height can vary from six feet (for fourth graders) to a maximum of 7 feet. Ropes with ribbons dangling from them may be substituted for nets.

Skill Presentation.   When possible, smaller courts with fewer players should be used to allow for maximum practice and participation.

The ball should be rolled under the net to the server; this saves valuable time. Walls should be used for practicing skills.

Basic to success in volleyball are eye-hand coordination and striking skills. Children at Level III, although generally having these competencies, should concentrate on the overhand volley and underhand serve. The use of a lightweight ball such as a beach ball can help those who lack sufficient arm and wrist strength. With variety in practice, most children will become skillful enough to participate in a number of lead-up games. Intermediate level skills necessitate the development of accuracy

and power in serving and volleying; the forearm volley is then introduced. It is at the advanced level that children are capable of playing a regular game of volleyball, utilizing the overhand serve, setup, spike, and block, and have the ability to recover balls hit into the net. Although regulation play should be provided, lead-up activities and variable practice should still be stressed because of the vast number of individual movement opportunities afforded.

SKILL DESCRIPTION

Volleying (Passing).   Proficiency with volleying (or passing) the ball is essential since most of the game involves this skill. It is used to pass the ball to teammates and to get the ball over the net. Balls that are contacted at chest level or above should be hit with the overhand volley. The underhand technique, called the forearm (or bump) volley, is used for balls that are hit below the chest.

Overhand. The overhand technique is a fundamental skill used to redirect a ball received at chest level or higher. The hands are held at eye level, with the fingers spread and thumbs and index fingers almost touching. This gives the appearance of a triangle or window to look through as the ball is hit. The wrists are hyperextended, elbows are flexed and out at shoulder height, and the knees are bent. As contact is made, the knees and arms extend forcibly upward and forward with a complete follow-through high in the air in the direction the ball is to travel. The ball is contacted by all the fingers and the thumbs simultaneously, as the wrists flex with a flicking motion. Emphasis should

Table 15-11

Volleyball: Developmental Skills Presentation Chart

SKILLS	LEVEL		
	Beg.	*Inter.*	*Adv.*
Volleying (passing)	Overhand	Forearm (bump)	
Serving	Underhand		Overhand
Setup, spike, block recovery from net			X
Rules	Simple	Basic game	Strategy and official rules

be on hitting the ball high, about 15 to 20 feet off the floor, and finishing with the whole body in a fully extended position.

Performance Concepts

1. Keep eyes on the ball.
2. Make a "window" with the hands.
3. Bend the knees.
4. Contact ball with the finger tips and with the wrists flexed.
5. Extend the body upward.
6. Strike ball with finger tips.
7. Arms/hand follow intended flight of ball.

Underhand. The forearm technique, also known as bumping, should be used when the ball must be hit (underhand) below the waist or when a player's back is toward the net. To execute the bump volley the player bends very low at the knees, the back remaining straight. The hands can be either clasped together to form fists or one hand can be placed in the palm of the other, with the thumbs folded. The ball is contacted with the forearms. In making contact with the ball, the player should make sure to get in line with the flight of the ball and extend the arms to meet the ball.

Performance Concepts

1. Get the body in line with the ball.
2. Grasp one hand securely in the other hand.
3. Keep the forearms together, extending arms/wrists.
4. Get in a low crouching position by bending at the knees.
5. Extend the knees/body upward
6. Contact ball with forearms.
7. Arms follow toward intended flight.

Serving. A player may serve the ball by either an underhand or overhand technique. The hand may be open or closed. Boys and girls in the intermediate grades are capable of developing a high level of skill in both serves. Students should begin with the underhand serve and, after sufficient skill has been developed, practice the overhand serve.

Underhand. The player stands with the left foot slightly ahead of the right (for a right-handed server) and knees bent. The ball is held in the left hand directly in front of and at the same level as the right hand as it hangs down at the side. The serving motion is like that of an underhand throw. Weight is on the rear foot, and the body is bent forward slightly. The right hand forms a fist, with the palm up. The right arm swings straight back and forth in a pendular motion. The ball is contacted slightly below center and hit off the hand. The right arm follows through above the shoulder in the direction of the target.

FIGURE 15-56
Overhead volley (pass)

FIGURE 15-57
Forearm volley (bump)

Performance Concepts

1. Keep eyes on the ball.
2. Turn the left shoulder toward the net (if right-handed).
3. Swing the arm backward and upward.
4. Hit the ball off the hand a little below center.
5. Follow through in the direction of the target.

Overhand. The overhand serve should be taught after a player has mastered the underhand technique. The merits of this technique are that it can be placed accurately and it has an element of deception caused by its "floating" action. A right-handed server stands in a slightly staggered stance, with the left foot forward. The knees are relaxed for comfort and ease, and the body is turned slightly. The ball is held with the left hand. The ball is tossed lightly 2 or 3 feet above the head so that it descends a foot or more in front of the shoulder of the striking hand. On the toss, body weight is transferred to the back foot. Contact is made in a motion resembling a baseball catcher's throw to second base. The arm is flexed and cocked, with the hand drawn back near the ear. The upper body rotates slightly to the right in a preparatory move. As the ball drops, body weight transfers to the front foot with a short step or a slide. The striking arm snaps forward from its cocked position. To assure a floater, little follow-through of the arm is made. Hand contact can be made in several ways—with an open hand, with a cupped hand (the knuckles make contact), or with a clenched fist. The wrist remains rigid as contact is made near the center of the ball.

Performance Concepts

1. Keep eyes on the ball.
2. If right-handed, turn left shoulder to net.
3. Shift weight to the back foot.
4. Toss the ball 2 or 3 feet above the head.
5. Step into the ball with the forward foot.
6. Strike ball with rigid wrist on heel of hand.
7. Follow through toward the target.

Setup.   A setup is usually the second hit in the series of three allowed. The ball is hit to a teammate so it is in position for a spike. The overhead technique is used; however, the set must be about 15 feet high and about 1 foot from the net in a position where a teammate can spike it over the net. Even before children can spike the ball, they should be taught to set the second ball high. A ball that is high and soft is much easier to redirect, no matter what kind of a hit is used.

Performance Concept

1. Hit the ball high and close to the net.

Spike.   The spike is the most effective series of movements used in volleyball. The spike is a ball that is sent smashing downward into the opponents' court. The spiker stands close to the net facing the direction from which the ball is coming. As the ball starts to come down, the spiker jumps high in the air

FIGURE 15-58
Underhand serve

FIGURE 15-59
Overhand serve

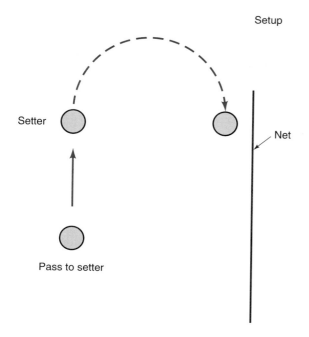

FIGURE 15-60
Setup

FIGURE 15-61
Spike

and swings the right arm upward. The hand is held open with the fingers spread and bent slightly into the shape of a ball. The ball is hit downward when it is still above the net. The body turns in the air, and the spiker lands facing the net. The ball must be set up high enough so that a hit can be downward on top of the ball. The net may be lowered for initial learning periods. Weight must be controlled so the body does not fall forward into the net.

Performance Concepts

1. Keep eyes on the ball.
2. Jump high enough into the air for the hand to make contact near the top of the ball as the ball starts downward.
3. Keep the upper body erect.
4. Time the jump to be at its height when the ball is slightly higher than the net.
5. Follow through with downward motion.

Block.   The block is a skill used to defend against the spike. One or two players attempt to block the path of the spiked ball in order to direct it back over the net or to reduce its speed and deflect it to a teammate. The block can be an individual effort or a multiple-player effort. Although a multiple-player block is the best defense against a skilled spiker, beginners should first focus on the individual, or one-player, block. The two-hand block is the best defense against an oncoming spiked ball. The blocker should face the net and jump up at the same time the spiker does. Both arms should swing upward to bring the hands to about six inches above the net, the palms facing the opponent.

The ball should rebound off the blocker's hands back over the net.

Performance Concepts

1. Keep eyes on the ball.
2. Jump with the player spiking.
3. Stretch out the hands, with thumbs close together.

Recovery.   When the ball hits the net it will rebound at different angles. Players should study this effect before attempting net recoveries. If there has been one or two hits, a player may hit the ball as it bounces off the net. The player faces the net, watches where the ball hits the net, quickly gets into position, bends the knees, and uses a two-hand dig to send the ball directly upward. In desperation a one-hand dig may be tried. This is a difficult skill because the timing is crucial.

Performance Concepts

1. Watch where the ball contacts the net and try to anticipate the angle of rebound.
2. Bend at the knees while getting under the ball.
3. Strike the ball upward.

Strategy Concepts.

Offensive.

1. Place the serve into open areas deep in the court and near the sidelines. Allow

FIGURE 15-62

Block

three hits before the ball is sent over the net. Follow the basic 1, 2, 3, attack in modified games as well as in official games, even though a spike cannot be executed:

    a. One is the initial pass made to a front-line player when the ball is received

    b. Two is the set to a front-line player

    c. Three is the spike or the volley over the net

2. Do not play (for forward-line players) with backs to the net.

3. Pass high.

Defensive.

1. Be in a position of readiness with eyes on the ball, weight evenly placed in a forward stride position.

2. Be ready to receive a pass (if a front-line player), for most serves are received by back-line players.

3. Always take a ball that goes above a front-line player's shoulders (for a player in back).

4. Always back up players (for back-line players) closest on the serve.

5. Call out, "Mine" when intending to take a ball and when there may be some doubt about who is going to take it.

SKILL DEVELOPMENT ACTIVITIES

Volleying (Passing). *Individual Volley.* Players are in scattered formation. Each student begins by throwing a ball into the air and catching it close to the forehead after one bounce. The teacher then gradually introduces the following variations.

1. Throw the ball up, perform an overhand volley on the returning ball, then catch it.

2. Throw, set, set, catch.

3. Throw, set, allow one bounce, set, catch.

4. Throw, kneel and set, stand and set, catch.

The class forms a line around the gym and approximately six feet from a wall. The students

1. Throw the ball against the wall, set, and catch.

2. Throw against the wall, set, set, and catch.

3. Throw against the wall, allow one bounce, set, and catch.

Circle Volley. The students form small circles of six to eight. One student throws the ball up and then volleys to anyone in the circle. The ball is volleyed until it falls to the floor or is caught, pushed, or thrown. A leader calls out the number of hits.

Wall Volleyball. The object of this game is to keep the ball bouncing against the wall above the line. Partners work with one another; one puts the ball in play with a serve against the wall. It must be returned by the next person, and play continues with alternate hits.

Shuttle Volley. The class is divided into three or four groups, each in a shuttle formation with about 6 feet between players. The first player throws the ball to the second player, who volleys it back to the third player, who has taken the first player's position. Each player goes to the end of the line after having volleyed the ball. The direction of the throw is reversed after everyone has had a turn. Variations include using the same formation with a net between lines, volleying with one or two hands, and bouncing the ball rather than making a direct throw.

Zigzag Volley. Students form groups of 10 that line up in two staggered lines so that each person faces an empty space. The lines are approximately 10 feet apart. The ball is started at one end. On a signal, the first student tosses the ball up and hits it to the first student in the opposite line. The ball zigzags back and forth between the two lines to the end and back to the first player, who catches it.

Basket Pass. Students form a semicircle around the foul circle of a basketball court. A leader is stationed under a basket. The leader throws a high lob pass to a student in the semicircle, who attempts to make a basket. The student cannot catch and throw the ball.

Serving. *Wall Serve.* Arranged around a wall, individual players repeatedly serve to a point on the wall 5 feet high from varying distances from the wall.

Partner Serve. Partners serve back and forth to one another from varying distances (15, 20, 25, 30 feet), depending on skill level. If there is not a ball for every two people, single-line formations on each side of the court may be used.

Single-Line Serve. Students form two facing lines, single file 10 yards apart. The first person in line 1 serves to the first player in line 2, and then goes to the rear of line 2. The first player in line 2 serves to the first player in line 1 and goes to the rear of line 1, and so on. The players should keep their heads down, eyes on the ball. They should work for proper fundamentals, interchanging types of serves and methods of hitting.

Base-Line Serve. The class is divided into two groups, with each evenly distributed along the base line. One student from each group is assigned to the retriever position. Any child on the base line may begin by serving the ball over the net. The ball is then served back by the child who retrieves it. No serving order need be kept. The retriever's job is to catch and pass the ball back to anyone on his or her team. For variation, more than one ball may be used.

Accuracy Serve. Each side of the playing court is divided into six equal squares with chalk. Students stand on each serving line. Before each serve, the instructor calls out the number of a square, and the player attempts to serve in that square. This activity may also be played as a game; each group is a team that receives a point for placing the ball in the proper square.

For variation, a rope is extended across the length of the court 3 feet above the net. Players stand on each serving line. The object is to serve the ball below the rope and over the net.

Setup, Spike and Block. Students form three lines on the same side of the net. Line 1 is the setting line, line 2 the passing line, and line 3 the spiking line. The first person in line 2 throws a high pass to the first person in line 1. The student executes a two-hand setup for the first person in line 3. Each student rotates clockwise to a different line. Keeping the setup pass high and close to the net is stressed. A fourth line may be set up across the net for retrieving. The retriever may become a blocker, or a couple of players may block as a unit.

Net Recovery. Working with partners, one player tosses the ball into the net, and the other tries to recover it. Two lines can be formed, and turns taken.

GAME ACTIVITIES

The following activities can be used to enhance the student's skills. Each activity stresses one or more of the skills practiced during the skill development phase of the lesson. Because large differences can be present (and frequently are) between and within groups, modification of the activities may be needed to meet each group's ability, as well as accommodate equipment and facilities.

TEN PASS
Players: Groups of six to eight
The class is divided into teams, each with a volleyball. A time limit is set. Each team maintains the ball in the air by using volleyball's passing fundamentals. A player cannot touch the ball twice in succession. For every 10 consecutive volleys, a point is scored. The team with more points wins.

BEACH-BALL VOLLEYBALL
Players: Six to nine per team
This game uses a beach ball and has the same rules as volleyball, with the following exceptions: two assists are permitted in serving; four passes are permitted.

KEEP IT UP
Players: Five to eight per circle
The object of the game is to see which team can make the most volleys in a specified time or which team can keep the ball in the air for the most consecutive volleys without error.

FOUR-SQUARE VOLLEYBALL
Players: Six to nine on each of four teams
Four separate teams are positioned on a court divided into four equal sections by two crossed nets. Players in courts 1 and 2 may serve only into courts 3 and 4; players in courts 3 and 4 may serve only into courts 1 and 2. After the serve, a team may hit the ball into any of the other three courts. When a fair serve is made and the ball touches the floor or fails to get out of the receiver's court within the allotted three hits,

Table 15-12
Game Activities for Volleyball

ACTIVITY	VOLLEYING	SERVING	SETUP	SPIKE	BLOCK
Level *Beginning/Intermediate*					
Ten Pass	X				
One-Bounce Volleyball	X	X			
Beach-Ball Volleyball	X	X			
Newcomb	X	X			
Keep It Up	X				
Level *Intermediate/Advanced*					
Keep Away	X				
Four-Square Volleyball	X	X			X
Progressive Volleyball	X	X	X	X	X
Mass Volleyball	X	X	X	X	X
Zone Volleyball	X	X	X	X	X

the serving team scores one point and continues serving as in regular volleyball. However, when a receiving team hits the ball into another court fairly, this team becomes the serving team the moment the ball leaves its court. If the new receiving team fails to pass the ball out of its court, the new serving team is awarded one point. All other volleyball rules apply.

ONE-BOUNCE VOLLEYBALL

Players: Six to 12 per team

The volleyball is put into play with a serve. The receiving team may let the ball bounce once before batting it back. The ball may bounce only once before being returned over the net. Any number of players may hit the ball one time before it is hit over the net. A score is made when the receiving team fails to return the ball within bounds. The receiving team gets the ball for service when the serving team misses. Team members rotate before each serve as in volleyball.

NEWCOMB

Players: Six to 12 per team

The game consists of throwing a volleyball back and forth over the net. The ball is thrown over the net from where it was caught. To start the game the ball is thrown from the end line. A score is made when a team fails to catch a thrown ball that lands in its playing area. If the ball is thrown out of bounds, the other team scores a point. The winner is the team that first scores 15 points.

VOLLEYBALL KEEP AWAY

Players: Any number on each team

Teams are arranged in a scattered formation within a designated area. By volleying the ball from one team member to another, the team with the ball tries to keep the ball away from the other team. Members of the other team try to intercept the ball. It can be intercepted only when it is dropping (on the downward arc). After the ball has been intercepted, the team in possession volleys the ball. The team volleying the ball more times wins. A time limit also can be used.

PROGRESSIVE VOLLEYBALL

Players: Six to 12 per team

Phase one: Newcomb is used to teach playing rules and rotation.

Phase two: Newcomb rules are used, with the following modifications: the regular volleyball service has an assist or a throwing serve; the ball is caught; one pass is made to a teammate; and the second pass is a high lob to a different teammate who must hit the ball over the net by using a regular volleyball hit.

Phase three: Newcomb rules are used, with the following modifications: the regular volleyball service is used; the ball is caught; a high lob pass is made to a teammate who sets it up for a third teammate, who hits the ball over the net.

Phase four: The ball must be hit by three different players on the same team before crossing the net: a pass, setup, and over the net.

Phase five: Regular volleyball is played.

ZONE VOLLEYBALL

Players: Six to eight per team

The game is played by the same rules as regular volleyball except that the players must remain in their respective zones during play. Areas within the zone are designated for positions.

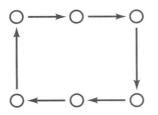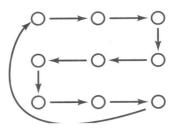

FIGURE 15-63
Rotation of Players

MASS VOLLEYBALL

Players: Six to 12 per team, arranged in rows of six

This game has the same rules as volleyball, but two balls and two servers are used. Play continues until both balls are dead. Each team alternates services. There should be an official for each ball.

BASIC VOLLEYBALL RULES AND REGULATIONS

Court Area. The court should be 30 feet wide and 60 feet long (a 25 by 50 foot court is also appropriate at the elementary level). Net height recommendations are 6 feet for fourth- and fifth-grade students and 7 feet for sixth-grade students.

Positions. The game of volleyball at the elementary level is played with six to nine players on each team (see Figure 15-63 for the rotation of players).

The Game. The object of the game is to serve the ball and volley it back and forth across the net until one team fails to return the ball. The team that wins the right to serve first decides whether it wishes to serve first or take a certain end of the court.

1. The serve is used to start the game and place the ball in play after each dead ball. The right back player puts the ball in play. The server has the responsibility to call out the score before each serve (the serving team's score is given first). The following are the rules for serving:
   a. The server must have both feet behind the end line until the ball is hit. (If students are unable to serve the ball from that distance, the service line may be moved up to 25 feet from the net.)
   b. The server may hit the ball with a hand or arm, but the underhand serve must be used.
   c. The ball must clear the net on the serve. If the ball hits the net and goes in the opponents' court, side out is called (the ball goes to the opponents). Fifth graders might be given two opportunities to serve if the first serve hits the net and goes in the opponents' court.

2. Players rotate after each side out, but only after the first server for each team completes a serve.

3. After the serve, the ball may hit the net as long as it goes into the opponents' court. Additional rules include the following:
   a. The ball may not be volleyed more than three times before being hit across the net.
   b. A player is not allowed to hit the ball twice in succession except after being one of two players to block a ball simultaneously.
   c. The ball may be hit with the hands or arms.
   d. No player is allowed to go into or over the net to play a ball.
   e. A player can play the ball from out of bounds.
   f. All balls hitting the boundary lines are good and should be played.

4. The game shall be eight minutes or less, depending on the score. The rules of scoring are as follows:
   a. Only the serving team can score.
   b. The team that reaches 15 points first wins, provided it is ahead by two points.
   c. If neither team scores 15 points in eight minutes, the team that is ahead at the end of eight minutes wins.

Violations. The penalties for the following violations listed are a side-out if committed by the serving team, and a point if committed by the receiving team. The violations are

1. Failing to make a legal serve
2. Hitting the ball twice in succession
3. Catching, pushing, or otherwise letting the ball rest on the hands before volleying it
4. Stepping over the end line before hitting the ball on the serve
5. Reaching over the net or touching the net when playing the ball near the net
6. Volleying the ball more than three times before hitting it over the net

VOLLEYBALL SKILLS TESTS

Volleying (Passing). A line is drawn on the wall 6 feet from the floor, representing the net. A restraining line is drawn on the floor 3 feet from the wall. The student stands behind the line and tosses the ball into the air, then volleys it against the wall. The student continues to volley the ball back and forth against the wall from behind the restraining line. If the ball does not hit above the net line, no score is counted. Whenever the ball hits the floor it may be started with another self-toss. One point is awarded for each hit above the line. At the end of 20 seconds the total number of hits is the score. Two trials are given, and the higher score is recorded.

Serving (for Accuracy). The receiving court is divided in half by a line drawn parallel to the net. The back half is divided into three equal parts. The server stands behind the serving line and attempts to serve into one of the three sections. A ball that lands in one of the two outside sections scores two points; one that lands in the center section scores one point. Ten serves are allowed, and the score is the total number of points; two trials are given.

HOCKEY

Field hockey, a game enjoyed by the early Greeks and Egyptians, has gained its greatest popularity in the United States among females at the secondary level. In recent years, however, with the increased emphasis in childrens' movements programs, hockey has become a popular team activity that is enjoyed equally by boys and girls.

Both field and floor hockey (use of a puck and generally played indoors) are excellent skill activities that are fast paced and easily adaptable to accommodate the conditions of the environment, as well as the abilities of the children.

INSTRUCTIONAL CONSIDERATIONS

Equipment. A plastic puck should be used indoors and a whiffle ball outdoors. Cones, cans, cartons, standards, and boxes may be substituted for net goals.

Safety. Hockey can be dangerous; proper stick handling and avoidance of violations should be stressed. Because fatigue could be a problem, players should be rotated and given ample rest periods.

Skill Presentation. Before an adequate level of skill proficiency can be expected, the child must possess an acceptable level of eye-hand coordination. General activities with the hockey stick should provide this foundation (Level II). With advanced control, the child can dribble simply, field a ball approaching from the front, and make short passes. Intermediate level skills require greater ball control with the ability to dodge and tackle an opponent. Greater playing proficiency can then be realized, with more sophisticated shooting abilities and knowledge of teamwork and the game.

SKILL DESCRIPTION

Grip and Carrying Position. A proper grip helps a player execute all the basic skills correctly. The position of the left hand, once placed, seldom changes on the stick (for a right-hander); the right hand may slide up or down the stick, depending on the particular skill being attempted.

Table 15-13		
Hockey: Developmental Skills Presentation Chart		

SKILLS	LEVEL		
	Beg.	*Inter.*	*Adv.*
Grip and carrying position	X		
Dribbling	Simple	Controlled	
Push pass	X		
Fielding	Front	Side Behind	
Driving	X	Scoop Flick Jab	
Face-off	X		
Tackling		X	
Dodging		X	
Roll-in		X	
Goalkeeping	X		
Rules	Simple	Positions Roll-in Offsides Fouls	The game

To attain proper grip, the right hand holds the stick in front of the body, parallel to the ground, with the flat side of the blade facing left and the toe of the stick facing up. The left hand grasps the butt end of the stick with a firm but comfortable "handshake" hold. The thumb and fingers wrap around the stick, and the butt end of the stick rests in or near the palm of the left hand. While maintaining this left-hand position, the player lowers the stick, so that it is perpendicular to the ground, and rotates the blade one-quarter turn clockwise, so that it faces forward. The right hand is now placed on the grip. A low position of the right hand improves control of the stick but restricts vision and ease of movement; a high position provides maximum vision and efficiency of movement while running but reduces the control of the blade end of the stick. Each player must choose a position for the right hand that is most comfortable and efficient for that player. The grip should be firm but not tight.

The player should carry the stick to the right of the body, with the blade close to the ground, while running. To ensure accuracy as well as safety, the stick must not be swung above waist height.

Performance Concepts

1. Grasp the stick with a firm "handshake."
2. Grasp the stick firmly but not tightly.
3. Do not allow the left hand (if right-handed) to rotate around the stick.

FIGURE 15-64

Proper grip and carry

Dribbling. The dribble is a controlled means of propelling the ball along the ground with the field hockey stick.

Simple Dribble. The simple dribble is an elementary form of moving the ball that demands less skill than controlled dribbling. In simple dribbling, the players push the ball 10 to 15 feet in front of them. The players move to the ball and give it another push, repeating the sequence. This type of dribble is used in open-field play, where there is little chance that an opponent will intercept the ball. It also is used to allow skilled players to run at maximum speed. The ball must be pushed with the flat side of the blade and kept in front of the body.

Controlled Dribble. For controlled dribbling, the ball should be dribbled slightly to the right of the feet by short taps with the flat side of the blade. The

FIGURE 15-65

Dribbling

movement should come from the shoulder rather than the wrists. The ball should be tapped 2 to 3 feet ahead, followed by a short running step, and then another tap. The flat side of the blade should always be toward the ball and close to the ground. The hands should be spread apart in order to rotate the blade quickly directly behind the ball.

Performance Concepts

1. For controlled dribbling, tap the ball rather than hit it.
2. Keep the ball to the right side.
3. Do not hold the arms too close to the body or use extensive wrist action.
4. Look upfield while dribbling.

Push Passing.   A push pass (quick hit) is a quick means of passing the ball over short distances that is usually executed directly from a dribble. The movement emphasizes accuracy rather than distance, as little if any backswing is required. The player spreads the feet with the toes pointed slightly forward. The ball is approached with the stick held low; then the left forearm and wrist pull back toward the body, keeping the ball in contact with the stick as long as possible. The ball is not hit but pushed or swept along the ground in the intended direction. The follow-through is low, with the arms extended away from the body as far as possible.

Fielding.   Being able to field the ball is a vital skill that all players should master. A player must be equally proficient in receiving balls from all directions and in receiving ground balls or aerial balls or slow balls or fast balls. Regardless of the angle of approach, the feet face the goal, and the blade of the stick is held away from the feet and close to the ground. Eyes focus on the ball during its approach. The weight of the body is held forward on the balls of the feet, enabling the player to move quickly should the need arise. The degree of trunk rotation in fielding depends on the ball's angle of approach. The ball is contacted when it is farthest from the body, while the stick is still perpendicular to the ground. Fielding a bouncing ball (the most difficult situation) requires that motions of the stick be timed with the varying movements of the ball.

Front Approach. The ball is contacted in front and very slightly to the right of the body. The flat portion of the blade faces forward, allowing the ball to rebound into an ideal position for the dribble.

Side Approach. If a player is fielding from the left, the ball is allowed to cross in front of the body. Contact is made in front and very slightly to the right of the body. The flat portion of the blade faces to the player's left, but at an angle that allows the ball to rebound into dribble position. When a player is fielding from the right, the ball is contacted near the right foot, thereby not allowing it to cross in front of the body. The blade of the stick is rotated clockwise so that the flat side faces the oncoming ball. The toe of the stick faces diagonally to the right behind the player, allowing the ball to rebound forward into dribbling position.

Approach from Behind. If the ball is approaching from behind, the player moves either to the right or left of the ball's pathway, thus fielding the ball from the right or left. By rotating the trunk to an extreme degree, the player can contact the ball behind or even with the body on the appropriate side.

FIGURE 15-66

Fielding (side approach)

Performance Concepts

1. Get in line with the ball.
2. Keep the stick close to the ground.
3. Contact the ball when it is farthest from the body.
4. Tilt the flat portion of the stick forward.
5. Relax the grip as the ball makes contact.

Driving.   Driving is a means of forcefully projecting the ball moderate to long distances and shooting at the goal. It differs from the push pass in that the hands are brought together more toward the end of the stick. As the player moves into position to strike the ball (the ball should be about 12 inches in front of the left foot), the right hand moves close to the left, and the left shoulder points in the direction of the drive, with the head over the ball. The arms swing back, keeping the stick below shoulder level, and the arms are brought forward and downward to contact the ball just off the left foot. The follow-through should be low and in the direction of the hit.

Performance Concepts

1. Hold the stick firmly, with the hands fairly close together.
2. Point the left shoulder in the direction of the target.

Scoop. The scoop shot is a stroke used to loft the ball slightly off the ground in order to dodge an opponent, to pass, or to shoot the ball into the corner of the goal. The player leans forward, with the right foot in front and the stick tilted back as it is placed under the ball. The player makes a strong lifting and shovel-like action with the right arm that is aided somewhat by the force of the legs in raising the body.

Flick. The flick is a combination of the scoop and push pass. The stroke utilizes the speed of the push pass and the lofting potential of the scoop. The flick may be used for a shot at the goal, or a pass, or as a clearing stroke. The ball is usually contacted farther out in front of the body than in the dribble. Initially the stick begins in contact with the ball. The left arm inclines the butt end of the stick laterally to the left prior to contact. The left elbow remains high and well away from the body. The follow-through is low, with the upper trunk and arms fully extended in the intended direction. Because of the flicking action of the wrists, the flat side of the blade faces either to the player's left or down toward the ground at the completion of the stroke.

Facing-off.   The face-off, or "bully," is used to start the game, after a goal is scored, and when the ball is prevented from further play by two opposing players. The face-off is taken between two opposing players, who stand on either side of the ball with their left sides facing their opponents' goal line. Both players start with the blades of their sticks on the ground and on their own side of the ball. Both players lift and touch their sticks over the ball and then touch the ground. They do this three times; then each tries to gain possession of the ball or pass to a teammate. See Figure 15-69

Tackling.   A tackle is a legal means of taking the ball away from an opponent. The defensive player should move in toward the opponent with eyes on

FIGURE 15-67
Driving

FIGURE 15-68
Scoop

FIGURE 15-69
Face-Off

the ball, body well forward, and weight evenly distributed over both feet. The blade of the stick should be held close to the ground. The tackle should be made when the ball is farthest from the opponent's stick. At that moment, the defensive player should place the face of the blade on the ball and perpendicular to the ground. As soon as the defensive player has possession of the ball, it should be immediately passed to another player or quickly dribbled away from the opponent.

FIGURE 15-70
Tackling

Performance Concepts

1. Keep eyes on the ball as the opponent approaches.
2. Time the tackle so it is unexpected.
3. Do not swing the stick forward.
4. Pass or dribble when possession is gained.

Jab. The jab is used only when a tackle is not possible. It is a one-handed poking shot that attempts to knock the ball away from an opponent.

Dodging. A dodge is an evasive movement that an offensive player uses to move the ball past an opponent. It is essentially a controlled pass to oneself. The dribbler pushes the ball to the right and then runs around the other side of the opponent to pick up the pass. The most important part of this movement is the timing. The ball must be pushed late enough to prevent the opponent from backing up to gain possession of the ball.

Performance Concepts

1. Do not slow down before attempting a dodge.
2. Keep the ball close enough to the body so the opponent cannot tackle.

Roll-in. A roll-in is a means of putting the ball back into play after it has been sent over the sideline. The roll-in is an underarm rolling action. The player must keep the feet and stick behind the sideline until the ball has been rolled into play.

Goalkeeping. The goalkeeper may intercept the ball with any part of the body or stick. Frequently the stick (or flat surface) and legs (a kick) are used to stop the ball. The player may not hold the ball or throw it toward the other end of the playing area (it may be cleared to the side by hand). The goalkeeper is positioned in front of the goal line and moves between the goal posts. When a ball is hit toward the goal, the goalkeeper should attempt to move in front of the ball and keep the feet together. This allows the body to block the ball should the stick miss it. After the block, the ball should be passed to a teammate immediately.

Performance Concepts

1. Align your body with the position of the ball.
2. Keep the stick close to the surface.
3. Clear the ball away quickly.

General Concepts

1. Do not raise the stick above the shoulder.
2. Do not touch an opponent with the stick or body.
3. Do not run in front of another player.

FIGURE 15-71
Goalkeeping

4. Use the flat side of the stick.
5. Move only in one's own territory.
6. Field the ball before hitting it; do not strike on the fly.
7. Move straight up and down the field.
8. Pass when a teammate is free to receive the ball rather than wait to draw an opponent.
9. Move away from a teammate with the ball to make a space into which the ball can be passed.
10. Move to meet an approaching pass and move away.
11. When receiving a pass from behind, look back over the shoulder and be in a running position with the feet going in the direction of the attacking goal.
12. To avoid obstruction, turn in a clockwise direction around the ball and never pull the ball around the body.
13. Keep a space between the line of forwards and the line of defense through which passes can be sent.

SKILL DEVELOPMENT ACTIVITIES

Dribbling. *Free Dribbling.* Students should practice dribbling the ball anywhere on the field, beginning with a walking speed, then increasing to a jog, and finally going to a run. Variations include dribbling forward, shift left, shift right, and stopping the ball.

Obstacle Dribbling. Students line up in groups of four to six, one player behind the other. The first player dribbles the object to the opposite end of the floor, weaving in and out of the markers (cones, chairs, cans, cartons) and back again.

Recommended dribbling activities for soccer can be modified for use with the stick. The remaining major hockey skills (passing, fielding, dodging, tackling) can also be enhanced by modifying the activities suggested for soccer.

GAME ACTIVITIES

The following activities can be used to enhance the student's skills. Each activity stresses one or more of the skills practiced during the skill development phase of the lesson. Because large differences may be present (and frequently are) between and within groups, modification of the activities may be needed to meet each group's ability, as well as accommodate equipment and facilities.

GOALKEEPER HOCKEY
Players: Two teams of equal size
Each team occupies two sides of a square. Team members are numbered consecutively from left to right. Two or three numbers are called by the instructor. These players enter the playing area and attempt to capture the ball that is placed in the center of the square and pass it through the opposing team. A point is scored when the ball goes through the opponents' side. Sideline players should concentrate on goalkeeping skills. When a score is made, the active players return to their positions, and new players are called.

LINE FIELD HOCKEY
Players: Six to eight per team
Players are numbered from one to the last player. The ball is placed in the middle of the field. On a signal, player 1 from each team runs out and tries to gain possession of the ball. Once in possession of the ball, a player may pass to any side player or try to shoot the ball over the opponents' goal line. No other player on that team may enter the field of play or score a goal. After each goal, players rotate and start the game again.

Table 15-14

Game Activities for Hockey

	SKILLS					
ACTIVITY	DRIBBLING	PASSING (DRIVE)	FIELDING	TACKLING	DODGING	GOALKEEPING
Level Beginning/Intermediate						
Star Wars	X					
Circle Keep-Away		X	X			
Mass Hockey	X	X	X	X	X	
Goalkeeper Hockey	X	X	X	X	X	X
Level Intermediate/Advanced						
Modified Hockey	X	X	X	X	X	
Line Field Hockey	X	X	X	X	X	
Sideline Hockey	X	X	X	X	X	
Zone Hockey	X	X	X	X	X	X

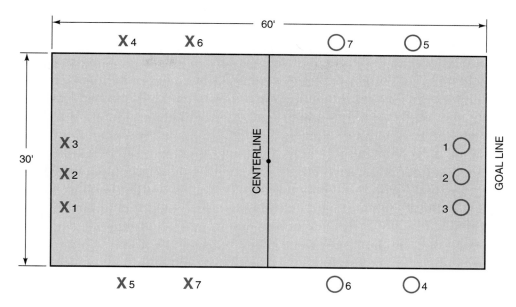

FIGURE 15-72
Line field hockey layout

CIRCLE KEEP-AWAY

Players: Eight to ten per group

Players are evenly spaced around a circle (20 to 25 feet), with one in the center. The object is to keep the player in the center from touching the ball. The ball is passed back and forth, with emphasis on accurate passing and fielding. If the player in the center touches the ball, the player who last passed takes the place of the center player.

SIDELINE HOCKEY

Players: Six to 12 players per team

Each team is divided into two groups. They are positioned as indicated in Figure 15-73 (eight players on each team). Half of each team is in the court; these are the active players; the others stand on the sidelines. No goalkeeper is used. A face-off at the center starts the game and puts the ball into play after each score. Each team attempts to score a goal with the aid of the sideline players. Sideline players help keep the ball in bounds and can

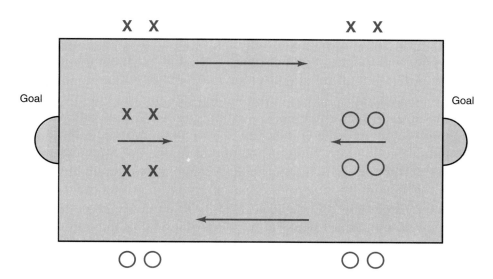

FIGURE 15-73
Sideline hockey setup

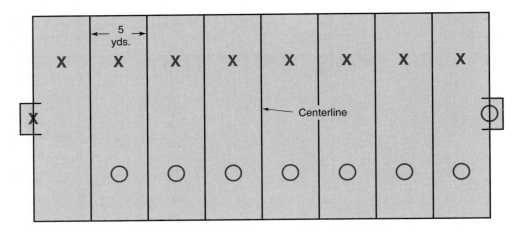

FIGURE 15-74

Zone field hockey layout

pass it into the court to the active players. Sideline players must pass only to an active player and not to each other. Any out-of-bounds play belongs to the team guarding that sideline and is put into play with a pass. An out-of-bounds ball over the end line that does not score a goal is put into play by the team defending the goal. The halves of the teams change places as soon as a goal is scored or after a specified time period. Minor infractions result in loss of the ball, and roughing fouls and illegal striking result in banishment to the sideline.

MODIFIED HOCKEY

Players: Seven to 11 per team

The teams may take any position on the field as long as they remain inside the boundaries. The object of the game is to hit the ball through the opponents' goal; however, no goalies are used. A face-off is used at the start and after each score.

STAR WARS HOCKEY

Players: Four teams of equal size

Each team is numbered consecutively and arranged to form one side of a square formation. Four balls are placed in the center. When a number is called, each player with that number goes to a ball and dribbles it back out of the square through the spot previously occupied, around the square counterclockwise, and back to the original spot. Circles 12 inches in diameter are drawn on the floor in the middle to provide a definite place to which the ball must be returned. If the game is played outdoors, hoops can mark the spot to which the balls must be returned.

MASS FIELD HOCKEY

Players: Half the class on each team

Any available field may be used. Markers are placed on the corners of the area, and a line is drawn across the middle. The game begins with each team lining up behind its own goal line (width of field). The ball is placed in the middle of the field. On a signal, each team tries to gain possession of the ball. A goal is scored when the ball crosses the opponents' goal line. A free hit is awarded for any foul or violation (see hockey rules) and is taken at the point where the foul occurred. If a ball passes over the sideline, a roll-in is taken by the nonoffending team.

ZONE FIELD HOCKEY

Players: Ten to 12 per team

The game starts with a face-off between two opposing players at the center of the field. All players must remain in their own five-yard zone. After each goal is scored, the player in the zone closest to the center line becomes the new goalie, and all other players move forward into the next zone.

BASIC FIELD HOCKEY RULES AND REGULATIONS

Playing Area.   The field is approximately 50 feet by 90 feet and set up as illustrated in Figure 15-75.

Positions.   The playing positions are the same as for soccer (11); however, this number can be modified, for example, seven players on a team using half the field (four teams at a time).

The Game.

1. *Scoring and time:* One point is awarded for each goal. Although the time can be flexible, three periods of eight minutes each with a three-minute rest between periods is suggested.

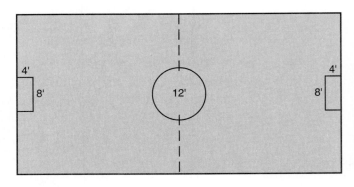

FIGURE 15-75

Elementary hockey field

2. *Face-off*: A face-off is taken at the center of the field at the start of the game, after each goal, and after halftime. After the third hit of the sticks, one of the two players must hit the ball and put it into play. During the face-off, all other players must stand on their own side of the face-off line until the ball is played.

3. *Play*: The clock starts when the ball is put into play and runs continuously until a goal is scored or a foul is called. Substitutions can be made only when the clock is stopped.

When a ball is forced over a sideline, a roll-in is awarded to the opposing team.

If a ball is sent over the endline by the attacking team, the defending team is awarded a free hit 15 yards from the endline opposite the spot where the ball crossed. If a ball is sent over the end line by the defending team, the attacking team is awarded a corner hit. The hit must be taken from a point on the end line within 5 yards from the corner of the field.

Goalkeepers may use their hands to clear the ball away from the goal but may not hold or throw the ball toward the other end of the playing area. If they do so, they are charged with a foul for holding the ball. The goalkeeper may be pulled from the goal area but cannot go beyond the center line. No other player may enter the restraining area without being charged with a foul.

Infractions.

1. Outside the penalty area (semicircles in front of goals), a free hit is awarded to the opposing team. All players must be five yards away from the player taking the hit. Fouls are as follows:
    a. Using any part of the stick except the flat surface of the blade
    b. "Sticking"—raising the stick above the waist
    c. Using any part of the body to propel the ball, although the hand may be used to stop the ball
    d. Hitting another player, hooking, slashing, or interfering with the opponents' half of the field (does not have possession of the ball and fewer than three opponents are between the player and the goal line)

2. Inside the penalty area, if a foul is committed by the attacking team, the defending team is awarded a free hit from anywhere inside the semicircle. If a foul is committed by the defending team, any player on the attacking team is given a free hit on a spot five yards in front of the center of the goal. All other players, except the goalie, must remain behind the 25-yard line until the penalty hit is taken.

BASIC FLOOR HOCKEY RULES AND REGULATIONS

Playing Area. Any area that is laid out for basketball—or any other smooth surface of comparable size—can be used. For elementary school children grade six and under, it is recommended that the playing area not exceed 50 by 75 feet. The goal should not exceed 60 inches in width and 54 inches in height. The nets are placed with the net frames directly against the wall or at the end of the court. The goal box is a restraining line five feet from the front of the goal and four feet from each side of the goal. (Note: When playing in gyms or other areas that do not have the proper lines, colored plastic tape can be used for lines, including the goal box.)

Positions. Each team has six players: one goalkeeper, who stops the puck with hands, feet, or stick; one center, who is the only player allowed to move full court and who leads the offensive play (the center's stick is stripped with black tape. In Canadian Poly

FIGURE 15-76
Floor hockey can be played indoors on a basketball court

Hockey, the center is often called the rover); two defense players, who cannot go past the center line into the offensive area and whose responsibility is to keep the puck out of their defensive half of the floor; and two forwards, who work with the center on offensive play and cannot go past the center line into their defensive area.

The Game.

1. The game has three periods of eight minutes each, with a five-minute rest between periods. Goals are changed after each period.
2. A coin is flipped for possession of the puck at the start of the game. Whichever team is behind at the end of the first and second periods is given possession of the puck at the start of the following period. In case of a tie game at the start of a period, a coin will again be flipped for possession.
3. When the game is played in gyms where the puck can go out of play in or under bleachers, for example, officials will carry extra pucks and will drop one into the play area so that play is continuous. There are no time-outs.
4. Free substitution is allowed. A player entering the game as a substitute should use the stick of the player being replaced. A change of goalies can take place only when the clock is stopped.

Scoring. A goal is scored when the puck touches or crosses the goal line or is above the goal line. On shots where the puck is deflected off a player or equipment into the goal, the goal counts. But a puck deliberately kicked or hit by hand into the goal does not count.

Goalkeeping. The goalkeeper may use either hands or stick to clear the puck away from the goal. At no time is the goalie exempt from a penalty for roughing, slashing, high sticking, or leaving his or her feet when going outside the goal box to play the puck. It is a misconduct when the goalie throws the puck out of play.

Infractions. When any player accumulates five fouls for roughing and/or misconduct, that player is out for the duration of the game. The following are classified as roughing fouls:

1. Slashing—when an opponent is hit with the stick and in the judgment of the official, the player slashing has no chance to hit the puck (playing through an opposing player).
2. Contact with an opposing player.
3. Contact with the goalie while in the goal box (crease).
4. Pushing.
5. Blocking with the body.
6. Tripping or hooking with the stick.

A player who is charged with a roughing or misconduct foul must sit out two minutes, and the team must play short-handed during this time. Fighting or deliberately fouling another player calls for automatic ejection from the game. Misconduct fouls include the following:

1. Deliberately stopping play by holding or placing the foot on the puck.
2. Except for the goalie, being in the goal box or playing the puck from the goal-box area (crease) with the sticks (a penalty should not be called if a player accidentally steps in the goal box while play is away from the goal, unless contact with the goalie is made).
3. Delaying the game.
4. Except for the goalie, catching or closing the hand on the puck (hitting the puck with the hand is allowed, but a puck played with the hand to a member of the same team will require a penalty—loss of possession. Play will resume at center circle.)
5. Deliberately hooking, grabbing, or kicking the stick out of an opponent's hand.
6. Swinging the stick above the waist during play.

HOCKEY SKILLS TESTS

Although there are numerous standardized tests for secondary-level students, few are usable with the elementary child. The following are examples of teacher-made tests that can be administered in a short period of time. A simple battery may be selected that subjectively and objectively evaluates the student's progress. If records are kept over a period of time, norms for the school may be helpful.

Driving. *Distance.* Players are lined up in a file formation on a field marked with a number of parallel lines 10 feet apart. The first line is 20 or 30 feet from the driving line. The ball is shot from behind a restraining line. The best score is recorded.

Accuracy. From a distance of 20 to 30 feet, the student attempts to pass the ball through two objects (cones, standards, cans) set three feet apart. Five attempts are given, each worth one point.

Dribbling Speed. Three cones are placed in a line eight feet apart. The first cone is placed 16 feet from a starting line. The student dribbles around the cones in a figure-eight fashion to finish at the original starting line. The score is recorded to the nearest tenth of a second. Two trials are given, and the faster trial is recorded.

Fielding. Three students designated as passers pass from different angles to a fielder. The ball must be stopped and controlled. Six passes, two from each angle, are taken, and one point is awarded for each successful field. The teacher will need to be at the location to judge whether the pass was a fair opportunity for the fielder.

SOFTBALL

Because of its similarity to America's favorite pastime (baseball), softball is one of the most familiar and popular team sports in the United States. Like basketball, most children are acquainted with the sport through participation in youth sports programs, television, and sandlot activities. Because of such familiarity, a wide range of skill proficiency is not uncommon. As with the other team sports described in this text, softball is a coeducational activity and every child should be given an opportunity to play all positions. Assigning only the more proficient players to key positions (catcher, pitcher, firstbase) is educationally unsound.

INSTRUCTIONAL CONSIDERATIONS

Equipment. Soft balls and gloves should be used when possible. A face mask is a must for the catcher; chest and shin protectors are also recommended. Batting tees and bats of varying sizes are needed. Care of equipment should be stressed; students should not bat rocks or throw down pieces of equipment.

Safety. The catcher should use protective equipment, especially a mask. All bats should be taped, and broken or cracked bats should not be used. No sliding should be permitted. Collisions in the field should be avoided by having players call for the ball. Not throwing the bat should be stressed; teammates should keep an appropriate distance away or if possible position themselves behind a protective fence (on the first-base side with a right-handed batter).

SKILL PRESENTATION

With a Level II movement foundation, children should have adequate ability in most of the skills (*i.e.,* throwing, catching, batting) used in softball activities. The beginning level program mainly stresses refinement of the basic skills and the introduction of pitching, fielding, fungo hitting, base running, and basic rules. With intermediate and advanced proficiency, the child has acquired the skills needed to play an official game that includes bunting, sidearm throwing, and the ability to play various positions.

Games with a pitcher should be avoided until some degree of pitching proficiency has been acquired. Batting skills should be stressed and an adequate amount of instruction and practice given. Tee Ball provides good opportunities for acquiring batting skills.

Because softball is basically not as active an activity as the teacher may desire, positions should be rotated often and lead-up activities selected that require fewer players and provide a more continuous flow of movement. When feasible, everyone on the batting team should bat before changing sides. The three-outs rule may also be modified to avoid the situation in which a fielding team does not get to bat.

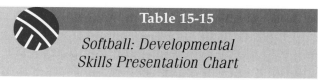

Table 15-15

Softball: Developmental Skills Presentation Chart

SKILLS	LEVEL		
	Beg.	*Inter.*	*Adv.*
Throwing	Grip Overarm Underhand Pitch	Sidearm Throw-in (from outfield)	
Catching and fielding	Fly balls Grounders		
Batting	Basic batting Fungo hitting		
Base running	To first base Around bases		
Additional skills		Positions Stealing Bases	Sacrifice Double play
Rules	Balls and strikes Safe and out Fair and foul ball Bunt rule	Pitching rule	The game Coaching at bases

To avoid the pitcher-batter duel during early learning periods, a member of the batting team can be chosen to pitch; a slow-pitcher or a no strike-out rule may also be considered. Children in the fifth and sixth grades should be allowed to act as umpire on a rotation basis. When possible this experience should be supervised by the teacher (or aide); guidance should be given to the group as well as to the individual to reinforce the learning of rules and regulations.

SKILL DESCRIPTION

Although the foundation for most of the skills used in softball is established earlier with a Level II proficiency, it is with the refinement and introduction of specific game skills that children can successfully perform at an optimum level.

Throwing. *Gripping the Ball.* Two basic grips are used in softball. If the hand is large enough, the ball can be held between the thumb and first two fingers, with the third and fourth fingers just resting against the side of the ball. Younger children with small hands may find it necessary to grip the ball with the thumb and all four fingers spread around the side and bottom of the ball. However, only the top surface of the fingers should touch the ball. A good check for the young thrower is being able to see daylight between the ball and the hand.

FIGURE 15-77
Gripping the ball

Overarm Throw. Basically a Level II skill, overarm throwing is the primary pattern for all players except the pitcher. The following summary characterizes the general movements associated with the overhand throwing pattern:

Feet are slightly apart with the forward foot opposite the throwing arm.

The trunk rotates to the throwing side and the weight shifts onto the rear foot.

There is a definite rotation through the hips, legs, spine and shoulders.

The weight shifts, and there is a step with the opposite foot.

Elbow extension occurs just before release as the body continues with a follow-through.

Underhand Toss. The underhand toss is used to make short, quick throws to players around the infield. To perform the toss, the player steps forward with the opposite foot while extending the arm backward. On the forward movement, the arm swings down and forward as the body weight shifts to the front foot. The ball is released at a light to medium force; follow-through is in the direction of the target.

Sidearm Throw. The sidearm throw is most effective when the ball needs to travel a short distance with speed, which is characteristic of infield play. The throw is similar to the overarm pattern, except the entire motion is kept near a horizontal plane. As the arm swings forward, the forearm drops and moves parallel to the ground. After release of the ball, the arm continues across the body.

FIGURE 15-78
Pitching (Underhand)

Pitching. The underhand throw is the only pattern allowed when pitching the ball. Although official rules require the pitcher to have both feet in contact with the pitcher's rubber, few elementary schools are so equipped. The pitcher can stand with both feet about even, facing the batter and holding the ball momentarily in front with both hands. The pitcher takes one hand from the ball, extends the other arm forward, and brings it back with a pendulum swing, positioning the ball well behind the body. A forward step toward the batter with the left foot (if a right-handed pitcher) begins the throwing sequence. The arm is brought forward with an underhand slingshot motion, and the weight is transferred to the leading foot. The ball is released when the hand is at a point just forward of a vertical line through the shoulder. Only one step is permitted. Fast-pitch softball techniques are not recommended for school programs.

Performance Concepts

1. Take a step forward with the foot opposite the throwing arm.
2. Extend the throwing arm back and up prior to the swing forward.
3. Keep the throwing arm close to the body.
4. Rotate the shoulders toward the left on the forward swing (for right-hander).
5. Release the ball at a point just below the hip.

Catching and Fielding. Catching in the game of softball requires a fundamental Level II proficiency (overhand and underhand catching); however, the complexity is increased because of the size of the ball and diversity of the conditions. Although gloves help to absorb some of the force, many children may not have one; therefore, a rubberized or softer ball should be used. Fielding involves catching or stopping the ball after it is propelled by the batter. If the ball is in flight, it is called a fly ball, a ball that rolls or bounces on the ground is called a grounder.

Fly Balls. When fielding fly balls, children should use basic underhand (balls approaching below waist) and overhand (balls approaching at higher level) catching principles. Players should keep their eyes on the ball from the time it leaves the bat, watch the pattern of its flight, and then move into position to catch it. Since a batted ball comes with great force, players must get in line with the ball. Beginners should be taught to catch high balls just above the chin by keeping their thumbs together. For low level balls, the little fingers should be together and the hands formed into a basket. The stride should be forward and backward, with knees flexed slightly and feet spread. This stance helps maintain balance and also allows a good position for the return throw. Fielders should give with their hands and provide sufficient squeeze to stop the ball's spin.

FIGURE 15-79
Fielding a fly ball

Performance Concepts

1. Keep eyes on the ball throughout its flight.
2. Get in line with the ball.
3. Catch a high ball with the thumbs together and palms out.
4. Catch low balls with the little fingers together.
5. On contact, squeeze and "give."

Grounders. To field a grounder, the player moves to meet the ball and get in line with it. With the left foot forward (if right-handed), the player bends at the ankles, knees, and hips and gets into a semicrouched position, keeping the upper part of the body almost erect. With the fingers pointing toward the ground, the hands are placed opposite the left foot. Eyes should be kept on the ball until it is firmly held. Once the ball is caught, the fielder begins to straighten up and takes a step in the direction of the throw. Another type of fielding that is used mainly by outfielders is the "sure stop." To keep the ball from going through the hands and allowing extra bases, the outfielder uses the body as a trap. The fielder turns toward the right and lowers one knee to the ground at the point where the ball is approaching. The hands catch the rolling ball, but if it is missed, the thigh and lower leg provide a good rebound surface.

FIGURE 15-80

Fielding a grounder ("sure stop")

Performance Concepts

1. Keep eyes on the ball until it is caught.
2. Move to meet the ball.
3. Get in line with the ball.
4. Bend at the ankles, knees, and waist, with fingers pointing down.
5. "Give" with the ball and bring it toward the body.

Batting.   There are three basic ways of striking a ball in softball. Basic batting is striking a pitched ball with near maximum or maximum force. Fungo batting is throwing the ball up with one hand, regrasping the bat, and striking the ball before it hits the ground. Bunting is a form of hitting a pitched ball; however, there are basic differences in grip, force, and follow-through.

Basic Batting. Important to batting performance is the grip. Children should get experience with the choke, long, and middle grips. Beginning batters can start with the choke grip. In any case, the grip should be light, since this relaxes the forearm muscles. In the long grip the hands are placed close to the bottom of the bat. For the medium grip, the hands are moved up about 1 or 2 inches. For the choke grip, the hands are about 3 to 4 inches away from the knob of the bat. In each grip, the bat is held with the hands together and the fingers and thumbs wrapped around the handle. For right-handed batters, the right hand grips the handle above the left hand. In the basic pattern, the batter stands facing home plate with feet shoulder width apart and pointing straight ahead toward the plate and parallel to it. The player reaches out with the bat and touches the far side of the plate. This helps a player judge how far from the plate to stand. The grip should be firm and the trademark of the bat should be facing

FIGURE 15-81

Mature batting form

the batter. The batter holds the bat away from the body with right elbow bent and out. The bat is held at shoulder height and points diagonally upward. The player's knees are bent and weight is on the back foot, but hips and shoulders remain level. The batter looks over the left shoulder at the pitcher and watches the ball as it approaches the plate. To initiate the forward swing, the player rolls the hips forward and takes a short step toward the pitcher. The bat is swung forward and level with the ground. The wrists are snapped as the bat contacts the ball and continues to roll over for the follow-through. Body weight is shifted to the forward foot. The bat is dropped on the first step toward first base.

Performance Concepts

1. Place left hand below right hand (right-handed batter).
2. Face home plate with the feet a shoulder's width apart.
3. Hold the bat back just over the right shoulder.
4. Keep the arms and elbows out and away from the body.
5. Keep eyes on the ball.
6. Start with the weight on the right foot.
7. Swing in a horizontal plane.
8. Shift the weight to the left foot.
9. Snap the wrists.
10. Roll the wrists over.
11. Follow through.
12. Drop the bat.

Fungo Batting. Fungo batting is useful for striking the ball during fielding practice and in many lead-up activities. The player starts with feet parallel, comfortably spread apart, and the weight evenly

FIGURE 15-82
Fungo batting

FIGURE 15-83
Bunting

distributed on both feet. The bat is suspended over the right shoulder while the ball is held in the left hand. Simultaneously the ball is tossed up, both hands grasp the bat, and the bat swings forward. Movement continues forward, the player transferring the weight to the front foot and twisting the body toward the left. The ball is hit approximately in front of the left foot; follow-through continues with a swing around the left shoulder.

Performance Concepts

1. Toss the ball up at approximately an arm's length way.
2. Swing horizontally.
3. Contact the ball with a firm grip on the bat.

Bunting. To bunt, the bat is positioned facing the path of the oncoming pitch, then allowed to "give" as the ball contacts the bat. As the ball moves toward the plate, the batter draws the rear foot forward and squares the body to the pitcher. Simultaneously, the batter slides the top hand up the bat, keeping the hand cupped and the fingers resting just behind the hitting surface. When the ball is hit, the bat should be angled in the direction of the intended bunt.

Performance Concepts

1. Move into the bunting stance as the ball is released by the pitcher.
2. "Give" with the bat on contact.

Base Running. As soon as a ball is hit, the batter should drop the bat and run as fast as possible to and "through" first base. The base runner should touch the foul line side of the bag. If the player decides to try to run to second base, he or she should begin to curve to the right a few feet before reaching first base,

touch the inside corner of the bag, and continue running to the next base. A runner waiting on base should assume a forward leaning position, with the left foot on the base and the right foot ready to push off as soon as the ball is hit.

Performance Concepts

1. Run after every hit.
2. Run "through" first base; do not slow down unless beginning the curve toward second base.

FIGURE 15-84
The baserunner's ready position

FIGURE 15-85
First-base stretch

ADDITIONAL SKILLS

Position. The general ready position for infielders is a semicrouch, with legs spread a shoulder's width apart, knees slightly bent, and hands on or in front of the knees. As the ball approaches, the weight shifts to the balls of the feet. Outfielders assume a similar posture, with the back slightly more erect.

Catcher. The catcher assumes a crouch, with the feet about a shoulder's width apart and the left foot slightly ahead of the right. The catcher should use a glove and wear a mask; also a body protector is desirable. The catcher is positioned just beyond the range of the swing of the bat. Although it is not recommended that anyone attempt to catch without at least a mask, the unprotected catcher should back up at least 8 to 9 feet from the plate and be extremely aware of a "loose" bat.

First-base stretch. When a ball is hit to the infield, the first-base player moves to the base, touching it with one foot. The player then judges the path of the ball, stepping toward it with one foot and stretching forward. The other foot remains in contact with the base.

Performance Concepts

1. Pitcher
   Fields balls hit to the mound area;
   Covers first base when the first-base player must field a hit ball;
   Backs up the third-base player on a hit to the outfield when base runners attempt to reach third;
   Backs up the catcher when a runner is on second;
   Covers home on a passed ball or a wild pitch.
2. Catcher
   Fields balls hit or bunted near the plate;
   Backs up the first-base player when no runner is on first.
3. First-base player
   Plays 10 feet to the right of the base when no one is on first;
   Fields all balls coming toward the first base area;
   Backs up the second-base player on throws from left and center fields when no one is on first.
4. Second-base player
   Plays between second and first base about 10 feet behind the base line and 12 feet from second base;
   Fields balls hit to the left of second base;
   Covers second base when hits are to the right side of the base;
   Covers second base on throws from the cather;
   Acts as a cutoff for throws from center fielders and right fielders to the infield.
5. Shortstop
   Plays about 10 feet behind the base line and halfway between third and second base;
   Fields balls between second and third base;
   Covers second base on balls hit to the first-base side of second base;
   Backs up the second-base player on balls thrown by the catcher;
   Relays throws from the left fielder to the infield.
6. Third-base player
   Plays about 8 feet to the left of third base and about 4 or 5 feet behind the base line;
   Fields balls hit to the left side of the field.
7. Left fielder
   Backs up the center fielder on balls hit to the center;
   Backs up the third-base player and shortstop.
8. Center fielder
   Backs up the left and right fielders on balls hit to those areas;
   Backs up the second-base player.
9. Right fielder
   Backs up the center fielder, second-base player, and first-base player on hit balls;
   Backs up plays at first base.

Sacrifice. The sacrifice bunt is a tactic performed when there are runners on first or first and second, with less than two outs. The batter bunts toward first or third in an effort to advance runners on base and get them into a scoring position. When there is a runner on second and on third with less than two outs, the batter should hit deep, giving the runner enough time to "tag up" and attempt to score.

Double Play. A double play is two consecutive put-outs occurring between the time the ball leaves the pitcher's hand and its return. The most frequent situation is a forced out and an out at first base. For example, there are runners on first and second; the hit ball is thrown to the third-base player, who tags the base before the runner (force) and throws the ball to the first-base player before the batter arrives. Similar situations can occur with runners on first (throw to second) or runners on first, second, and third (throw to home).

Stealing Bases. Stealing is advancing a base or bases without the batter's support (hitting). There are no lead-offs (the runner must stay in contact with the base until the ball leaves the pitcher's hand), so to be successful, the runner must leave the base with the pitch and run rapidly to the next base without being tagged out. This is an advanced skill and often causes confusion and dispute among children; therefore it is not recommended during game activities but can be introduced as a skill. Another consideration is sliding (frequently done with stealing), which many believe is not appropriate at the elementary level because of field conditions that result in torn clothes and injuries.

SKILL DEVELOPMENT ACTIVITIES

Throwing and Catching (Fielding). *Partner Activities.* Partners throw and catch, varying the distance, levels of throw (high, low, grounders), type of throw (overhand, sidearm, underhand), and speed.

Base Throwing. Three players are each assigned to a base. Two balls are thrown in sequence around the bases, with each player taking a turn. Both line throws and grounders should be used.

Fly Catching. One batter is at home plate, and the remaining players are in the field. The batter, using fungo batting, hits fly balls into the field. When a fielder catches a fly ball, he or she becomes the batter. Variations include placing all fielders in a large semicircle and requiring the batter to hit two balls to each player in turn; after the last player has received the second fly, places are rotated.

Pepper. Members of a group line up in a single line with about 9 feet between them; they are facing the leader. The leader stands 20 feet in front of the others. The first person in line throws the ball or pitches it to the leader, who tries to hit a ground ball to the next player in the line. This person then pitches it back to the batter, and the process is repeated. If a line player misses a ground ball, he or she goes to the end of the line, and everyone moves up one place. If the pitch is wild, the person who threw it must go to the end of the line. The object is to be batter as long as possible.

15. Students are divided into groups of six to eight, with one batter and the others scattered in the field. The batter hits balls into the field. Each time a player is in position to field a ball, the individual must yell, "Mine" and attempt the play. If the player catches a fly ball, five points are awarded. If the player catches a fly on the first bounce, three points are given; if a grounder, 1 point. The first person who reaches 15 points takes the place of the batter, who goes into the field.

Batting Accuracy. The class is divided into groups of six to eight. Each group forms a circle, with a batter in the middle. Each player pitches the ball to the batter, who hits it to the player on the pitcher's left. If the hit is missed, it must be replayed. The drill continues around the circle.

Five Swings. The class is divided into groups of 8 to 12. One half of the group fields; the other half bats. Each player is given five swings. After the last player has batted, the groups exchange places.

Number Fly Balls. The class is divided into groups of six to eight, each player getting a number. A designated thrower throws a fly ball, and a number is called out. The player with that number catches the fly ball.

Circle Fly Ball. The class is divided into groups of eight to ten. Five players (if the total is 10) make up a fielding team arranged inside a large circle. The throwing team is arranged on the outside of the circle. Each thrower takes a turn throwing a high fly ball into the circle. If the ball is missed and lands in the circle, one point is scored for the throwing team. After going around the circle, teams exchange places.

Overtake Base. The class is divided into groups of eight to ten and arranged around the bases, with player 1 at the pitcher's line, 2 on home plate, 3 on first base, 4 on second, and 5 on third. The remaining players form a line near home plate. On a signal, player 1 throws to 2, 2 throws to 3, and so on around the diamond to home plate. At the same time that player 1 throws the ball, player 6 takes off for first base and continues around the bases, attempting to reach home plate before the ball. Two rules apply: (1) The base runner must touch all bases, and (2) the players rotate after each run. Player 1 takes 2's position, 2 goes to 3, and 6 takes 1's place. Everyone shifts one place to the right, with the player on third—player 5—going to the back of the line.

Batting. *Tee Batting.* The class is divided into groups of four to five and placed at stations, each with a batting tee. There are a batter and a catcher, the others spreading out as fielders. Each batter is allowed five hits; then the group rotates. The catcher moves to bat, and a fielder moves to catcher.

Base Running. Students practice running to first base (through the base); then they concentrate on running around the bases.

Hunter and Hare. The class is divided into groups of four, one group in the field and the other at bat. On a signal, the first player from the batting team runs the bases. At the same time, the ball is thrown by the catcher to the first-base player, and so on around the bases. The object is for the batter to return home before the ball gets there.

GAME ACTIVITIES

The following activities can be used to enhance the student's skills. Each activity stresses one or more of the skills practiced during the skill development phase of the lesson. Because large differences may be present (and frequently are) between and within groups, modification of the activities may be needed to meet each group's ability, as well as accommodate equipment and facilities.

SCRUB

Players: Seven to 12 per game

The "scrub" is the first to bat. All other players are numbered; the catcher is 1, pitcher 2, first-base player 3, and fielders 4 and up. The batter hits a pitched ball and must run to first base and back (two bases are used). The batter is out if he or she is tagged at first or home, strikes out, slings the bat, or hits a fly ball that is caught. If the batter gets home, he or she bats again. The batter is allowed three times at bat; then he or she becomes the last fielder. If the batter is put out, every player moves up one position. If a player catches a fly ball, he or she exchanges positions with the batter. Two players may be up at the same time. In this situation, the first batter is permitted to stop on first base and be hit home by the other batter.

Table 15-16

Game Activities for Softball

ACTIVITY	THROWING	PITCHING	FIELDING	BATTING	BASE RUNNING
SKILLS					
Level *Beginning/Intermediate*					
Bat Ball	X		X		X
Throw It and Run	X		X		X
Six-Player Softball	X	X	X	X	X
Long Ball	X		X	X	X
Tee Ball	X		X	X	X
One Old Cat	X		X	X	X
21	X	X	X	X	X
Roll at the Bat	X		X	X	
Level *Intermediate/Advanced*					
Scrub	X	X	X	X	X
500	X		X	X	
Three-Team Softball	X	X	X	X	X
Slow-Pitch	X	X	X	X	X
Modified Slow-Pitch	X	X	X	X	X

THREE-TEAM SOFTBALL

Players: 12 to 15

The players are divided into three teams. The rules of softball apply, with the following exceptions:

1. One team is at bat, one team covers the infield (including the catcher), and the third team provides the outfielders and pitcher.
2. The team at bat must bat in a definite order. This means that because of the small number of batters on each side, instances can occur when the person due to bat is on base. The runner must be replaced by a player not on base and take a turn at bat.
3. After three outs, the teams rotate, with the outfield moving to the infield, the infield taking a turn at bat, and the batters going to the outfield.
4. An inning is over when all three teams have batted.
5. The pitcher should be limited to pitching one inning only. A player may repeat as pitcher only after all members of the team have had a chance to pitch.

BAT BALL

Players: 10 to 12 per team

Two teams play this game, using a home plate and first base and a volleyball as the ball. The batter strikes the ball with the hand or fist into the field and then runs to the base and back to home plate. The fielders, who are positioned on the field to cover it adequately, field the ball and attempt to hit the runner; fielders may not take more than two steps with the ball in their possessions, but they are permitted to pass to other teammates.

SIX-PLAYER SOFTBALL

Players: Six on each team

This game is similar to regular softball, but with the following modifications: (1) There are six complete innings; (2) there are four outs in each inning; (3) a batter is out after two strikes; (4) a foul ball counts half a strike; and (5) a base on balls is given after three balls rather than four. All players rotate one field position after each inning.

ONE OLD CAT

Players: Nine per team

The first player on the batting team hits the ball into the field and tries to run to first base and home (only two bases are used) in one complete trip. The runner may not stop on base. If the player makes a complete trip without being put out, one run is scored. Three outs retire a team.

21

Players: Nine to 10 per team

Softball rules are used, with the following exceptions: The batter gets three swings to hit the ball. When the batter hits the ball, he or she runs the bases until put out. A runner safe at first scores one point; safe at second, two points; safe at third, three points; and safe at home, four points. Teams exchange places after three outs. The first team to score 21 points wins.

ROLL AT THE BAT

Players: Four to nine per group

The first batter fungo-hits the ball anywhere into the field. If a player catches a fly ball, he or she rolls it back and tries to hit the bat, which has been placed on the ground.

The length of the bat must face each "roller." If the ball is not caught, it is thrown back to the batter. A fielder becomes the new batter when he or she (1) rolls a ball into the bat, (b) catches two fly balls, or (c) retrieves three grounders. All players start at zero when a new batter takes a turn.

500

Players: Four to nine players

One player is chosen to be the batter (fungo style), and the others scatter in the field. The object of the game is for each fielder to try to be the first to reach 500 points. Points are scored as follows: 100 for catching a ball on the fly, 75 for a ball caught on the first bounce, and 50 for fielding a grounder. The same number of points is deducted from a player's score if he or she commits an error. As soon as a player has reached 500 or more points, the player exchanges positions with the batter.

SLOW-PITCH SOFTBALL

Players: 10 per team

Slow-pitch involves slower pitching, and thus more hitting and more action on the bases and in the field. Outfielders are a very important part of the game since there are many long drives. Changes from the official game are as follows:

1. The pitch must be a slow-pitch. Any other pitch is illegal and is called a ball. The pitch must have an arc of 1 foot and it must not rise over 10 feet from the ground. Its legality depends on the umpire's call.
2. There are 10 players instead of nine; the extra, called the roving fielder, plays in the outfield. The extra player handles the line drives hit over the infielders.
3. The batter must take a full swing at the ball and is out if he or she chops at the ball or bunts.
4. If the batter is hit by a pitched ball, he or she is not entitled to first base. The pitch is merely called a ball. Otherwise, balls and strikes are called as in softball.
5. The runner must hold base until the pitch has reached or passed home plate; no stealing is permitted.

THROW IT AND RUN

Players: Nine to 12 per team (extra three in field)

The pitcher throws to the batter, and the batter throws the ball overhand to the field within the foul lines. The fielder throws the ball to the base where the runner is going. The ball is returned to the pitcher, and another batter throws. The team bats around once; then the teams change places. An inning is a division of the game during which each team has a turn at bat. When a batter completes the circle of bases without being put out, a run is scored. The team with more runs after an equal number of turns at bat wins.

LONG BALL

Players: Two teams of nine to 14 players

The object of the game is to hit the ball into the outfield between the fielders and run to as many bases as possible without being put out. The batter hits the ball fungo style (there is no pitcher). Once the ball is batted, the rules of softball are in effect except that points are awarded in the following manner: one point for a single, two points for a double, three points for a triple, four points for a home run, and four points for each run scored. Three outs retire the side. Teams can play for a certain number of innings or until one team gets a set number of points.

TEE BALL

Players: Nine per team

This game is similar to softball, with the following modifications:

1. The batter is allowed one hit off the tee.
2. Since there is no pitcher, no one is permitted to steal a base. A runner must stay on the base until the ball is hit by a teammate.

MODIFIED SLOW PITCH

Players: Nine to 12 per team

The hitting team provides its own pitcher, who must remain on the mound during any play and may in no way interfere with any fielders. The pitcher does bat in order. Batters receive a maximum of two pitches. If they accept the first pitch and swing, they must hit a fair ball or they are out. Hitters can elect to let the first pitch pass; but they must then hit a fair ball on the second pitch or they are out. (Foul balls are out; a swing and miss is out.) No bunting is allowed; hitters must take a full swing at the ball or they are called out. There is no stealing or sliding.

SOFTBALL RULES AND REGULATIONS

Although general softball rules are suggested, it is recommended that base runners remain on base until the ball is hit and no stealing be permitted. The level of pitching speed should be monitored by the teacher to control fast pitching.

Playing Field. The official softball field has 60-foot base lines and a pitching distance of 46 feet. Although distances may be flexible, it is recommended that play in the intermediate grades should be with base lines no longer than 45 feet and a pitching distance of 35 feet or less.

Positions. Softball is played with nine players (the same as baseball): Figure 15-85 designates playing positions.

The Game. The game is played for seven innings. Each team gets to bat in its half of the inning, and when both teams make three outs the inning is over. One team is at bat while the other team is in the field. Games of fewer than seven innings can also be played.

Batting Order. Players are permitted to hit in any order; however it is wise to have players bat according to their positions. Once an order is established, it cannot be changed, even if players change their positions.

Getting on Base. A batter gets on base when:

1. A base hit is made;
2. A fielder commits an error;
3. Four balls are thrown by the pitcher.

Advancing on Base. The runner may advance to a base when:

1. A player gets a hit;
2. The player behind walks;
3. The ball is overthrown to a base player; only one base is allowed if the ball is thrown into foul territory; two bases if in the infield;
4. A fly is caught.

Batter Out. The batter is out when he or she:

1. Has three strikes;
2. Is thrown out at first;
3. Is tagged before reaching first base;
4. Hits the third strike and the ball is caught by the catcher;
5. Hits a fair or foul ball that is caught on the fly;
6. Bunts a foul on the third strike;
7. Throws the bat more than 10 feet;
8. Steps on home plate when batting;
9. Interferes with the catcher when he or she is catching a fly or putting out a runner coming home;
10. Fouls any ball to the catcher that rises above the batter's head and is caught.

Runner Out. The runner is out when:

1. A defensive player reaches first base with the ball before the runner touches the base;
2. The runner is tagged with the ball before reaching a base;
3. The player leaves a base before a batter hits the ball;
4. The player leaves a base before a fly ball is caught and is not able to get back before the fielder tags the player or the base;
5. A player is on base behind the runner and the fielder touches the player or the base to which the player is advancing;
6. A batted ball hits the player going from one base to another;
7. The player intentionally interferes with a fielder who is playing the ball;
8. The player runs out of the base line to avoid being tagged;
9. The player slides into a base (For safety purposes, students should not be permitted to slide).

Pitching. The pitcher must face the batter with both feet on the pitching rubber, with the ball held in front with both hands. The pitcher is allowed one step toward the batter and must deliver the ball while taking that step. The ball must be pitched underhand. The player cannot fake a pitch or make any motion toward the plate without delivering the ball. It is illegal to roll or bounce the ball to the batter. No quick return is allowed before the batter is ready. To be called a strike, a pitch must be over the plate and

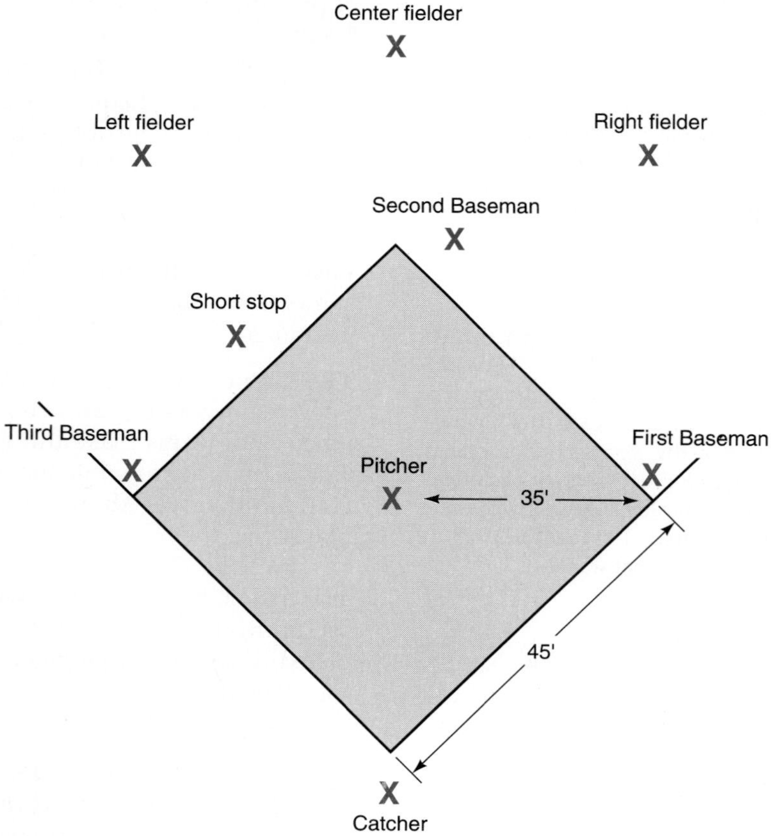

FIGURE 15-86
The playing field

between the knees and shoulders of the batter. A ball is a pitch that does not go through this area.

Scoring. A run is scored when the base runner goes around the bases (first, second, third, and home) before the batting team has three outs. If the third out is a forced out, no run is scored even if the runner crossed home plate before the out was actually made.

The situation needing the most clarification occurs when a runner is on base with one out and the batter hits a fly ball that is caught, making the second out. The runner is forced to return to the base previously occupied before the ball reaches that base or it is an out. If the player makes the third out as the result of failure to return to the base in time, no run is scored.

SOFTBALL SKILLS TESTS

Throwing. *Distance*. From a standing or running start from between two restraining lines 6 feet apart and parallel to each other, the student throws a softball as far as possible. Three throws are allowed, and the distance (to the nearest foot) of the best throw is recorded.

Accuracy. A target is drawn on the wall, or a hoop or tire is hung from the ceiling. The thrower stands 40 to 50 feet away and attempts to throw the ball within the target. The score is the number of successful throws out of 10.

Pitching. A target 17 inches wide and 36 inches high is drawn on the wall 16 inches from the floor. A line is drawn 35 feet from the wall in front of the target. The pitcher, using a legal underhand pitch and keeping one foot on the pitching line before the ball is released, is given 15 consecutive trials. One point is scored for every ball that hits the target.

Fielding. The student takes a position behind a line marked on the field. The teacher throws three grounders and three flies; the score is the number of balls caught. All throws must be consistently difficult and provide a fair opportunity for success.

Batting. Each student is allowed five hits (slow pitches by the teacher); three strikes are considered to be a hit. A grounder in the infield is worth one point: a fly ball in the outfield, two points; and a home run (a point past the designated marker), four points. The same point system may be used to evaluate the student's fungo-batting ability. Bunting ability can be evaluated by the number of successful bunts out of five pitches.

Base Running. On a signal, the batter swings the bat at an imaginary pitched ball, puts the bat down, and circles the bases, which are set at the distance the class is used to having in the game. A timer starts the stopwatch when the signal to hit is given. The bat must not be thrown or carried more than 12 feet. Each base must be touched in order. The watch is stopped when the runner touches home plate. Two trials are given, and the better trial is recorded as the score.

TRACK AND FIELD

Track-and-field events provide special excitement for the child because of their self-testing nature and association with Olympic athletes. Boys and girls love to race, jump, throw objects, and test their physical abilities. Since these skills are involved in track-and-field events, children are easily motivated to learn and perform during the unit. It is also encouraging and beneficial from a physical fitness perspective, especially with the recent interest in long-distance and cross-country running.

INSTRUCTIONAL CONSIDERATIONS

Equipment and Safety. Warm-up activities should precede jumping and sprints. Light jogging and flexibility (bending and stretching) are recommended.

If possible, children should wear proper running shoes (not heels or flip-flops) and run on surfaces free from stones and large holes. Spiked running shoes should not be permitted.

Recommendations for running and jumping facilities are in the latter part of this section.

Two wooden paddles or blocks of wood clapped together make an adequate starting signal if a starter's gun is not available.

All facilities and equipment should be checked before class, especially for broken glass and other hazardous objects.

Figure 15.87 presents an example of a track–and-field outdoor activity setup. The cross-country and long distance courses should incorporate larger areas around the school or, if needed and possible, adjacent facilities such as parks or recreational areas.

SKILL PRESENTATION

There are two basic types of events in track and field: running events, which include sprints, hurdles, and endurance runs; and field events, including the high jump, long jump, triple jump, and shot put. These skills should be taught to all students, regardless of their sex or ability. Once the children have been exposed to these skills, they should be allowed to select and concentrate on those events best suited to their interest and potential capabilities.

Since optimal performance is based primarily on proficiency in the fundamental skills of jumping, running, and throwing, the teacher should assess movement pattern proficiency and strive toward the mature level.

Opportunity for individual practice is critical; therefore, station work with small groups is highly recommended. Good form should always be emphasized. Children should be made aware of times and distances during the unit (stimulates motivation and presents goals).

Table 15-17

Track and Field: Developmental Skills Presentation Chart

SKILLS		LEVEL	
	Beg.	*Inter.*	*Adv.*
Running	Starts (standing and sprinting) Sprints (40 to 60 yards) Distance running Cross-country	(50 to 80 yards) Relays Hurdling	(50 to 100 yards)
Jumping	Standing long jump Running long jump High jump (scissors)	Straddle	Triple jump Fosbury Flop
Throwing	Softball		Shot put

If school norms are established that utilize consistently accurate layouts (*i.e.*, distance), scores recorded during the unit or culminating activity may be used for evaluation. Other considerations may be form and progress.

The amount of activity, particularly with distance running, should be increased gradually. In some cases (especially with overweight children), the progress may be from a fast walk to a slow jog before a run.

Some type of culminating activity (*e.g.*, track-and–field meet), is suggested to provide a goal for the students.

SKILL DESCRIPTION

Running.   Running-related activities appropriate at the elementary level include sprints, distance running, relays, hurdles, and cross-country.

Starting Stance. Common to all running events mentioned is a starting stance. For races of a relatively short distance (40 to 60 yards), the sprint start is used, and distances beyond that are generally begun in a standing position.

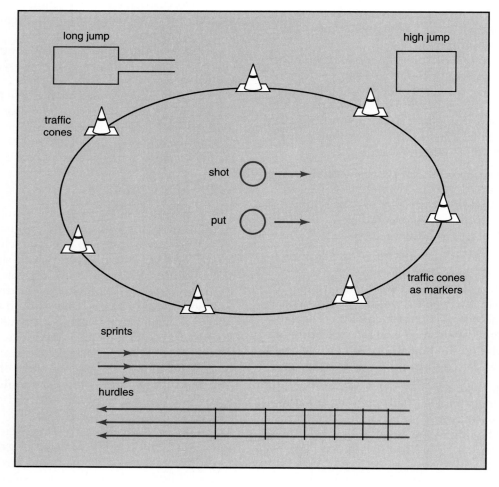

FIGURE 15-87
An outdoor activity setup

FIGURE 15-88
Standing start

FIGURE 15-89
Sprint start

In the *standing start* (Fig. 15.88), one foot is close to the starting line and the other is slightly to the rear (a half-stride position). The head is up, the trunk is bent forward, the knees are slightly flexed, and the weight is on the front foot. The opposite arm to the lead foot is held forward with the elbow flexed; the other arm is down and slightly back.

A quick start is one of the most critical aspects of success in short distances. For the *sprint start*, the body position is assumed according to the commands of the starter. The commands are "On your mark, set, go." When the starter calls out "On your mark," the runners get down in a crouched position with one knee touching the ground and their heads hanging down. Their hands are placed behind the starting line with the thumb and forefinger of each hand forming a base on which to lean. On the command "set," the runners raise their hips to a level even with or slightly above the shoulders. The weight of the body is mostly on the support formed by the thumbs and forefingers. After a two-second pause, the command "go" is given. The runners drive quickly and powerfully out of the crouched position, with the front foot pushing hard off the ground and the rear foot making the first stride over the starting line.

Sprints. The most common sprinting distances are 50, 60, 75, and 100 yards. With a sprint start, on the word "go" or the sound of the whistle, the race is started by a push-off from the toes to overbalance the body weight forward. The runner keeps the body low and uses short, hard, driving steps and a powerful swing of both arms to regain balance and pick up speed. Shifting into full stride, the runner's knees should be lifted high and brought down forcefully, the toes pointed straight forward and the arms bent at the elbow and moved back and forth forcefully, with contact continued with the ball or front of the foot.

Distance Running. Generally, distances of 440 yards, 600 yard, 880 yards, and one mile are considered appropriate for elementary school children; however with a good fitness program and background, distances of two and three miles are also recommended. With a standing start, the body is more erect than with a sprint; weight is taken on the heel, and then rocked forward. The elbows are bent slightly, and the arm action is less vigorous than in sprinting.

Performance Concepts

1. Run in a comfortable manner.
2. Establish a pace and don't sprint until the finish line is within a short distance.

Cross-Country. Rapidly becoming one of the most popular long-distance running events in the nation, cross-country takes the individual off the track onto an open course. Participation may be on a competitive level or for personal improvement. Frequently used distances are one mile to one and a half miles across a grassy area (open field or golf course) with some variations of grade levels. Markers (cones, flags, trees) can be used to indicate the path of the course.

As with all long-distance events, it is important that students learn the concept of pace. One technique is to place cones at similar intervals and challenge students to run from cone to cone at a designated pace (*i.e.*, time). A student or the instructor can call out the time at each cone, and runners can adjust their pace. Another method is to break down long-distance times into smaller segments to enable runners to get a feel for how fast they must run the shorter distance to equal a certain time over a longer distance.

Relays. A relay is a team event in which a runner runs a specified distance and passes a baton to a teammate. Generally, four runners make up a relay team. When each runner covers the same distance, the race is referred to by the total distance, for example, 4 by 220 yards, 4 by 440 yards, 4 by 880 yards. If the dis-

FIGURE 15-90

The baton exchange

tances for runners vary, the race is called a medley relay. In these events all the runners run in the same direction; some people refer to them as pursuit relays. In straight relay racing there is a 10- to 20-yard passing zone in which the baton must be exchanged. In baton passing, the runner holds the baton in the left hand and puts it in the right hand of the runner ahead. The runner should carry the baton like a candle when passing. The receiver reaches back with the right hand, with fingers pointed down and thumb to the inside, and begins to move ahead when the advancing runner is three to five yards back. The receiver grasps the baton and immediately shifts it to the left hand while moving. The exchange to the next runner should be made on the move, with the front runner timing the start and increase of speed to the pace of the runner coming in.

Another kind of relay is the shuttle relay. These are run in straight lines, with half of each team at opposite ends of the distance to be run. In shuttle relays the runners touch each other's hands or pass a baton. All runners tag each other with their right hands, passing by their right shoulders.

Performance Concepts

1. Start to run just before the runner approaches with the baton.
2. Make the exchange of the baton within the zone.
3. Form a V with the right hand to receive the baton.

Hurdling. Hurdling involves sprinting between hurdles and leaping over them. The takeoff begins about three to five feet in front of the hurdle, with the lead leg kicking straight up in front of the body. At the same time the leg is kicked up, the arms are thrust forward to give more lift to the body. The lead leg stretches forward as far as possible. As the lead leg

FIGURE 15-91

Hurdling

crosses the hurdle, the trailing leg is bent, with the knee pointing directly to the side. The toe of the trailing leg must be raised high enough to clear the hurdle. The lead leg is brought down and touches the gound as close to the hurdle as possible. As the lead leg starts down, the trailing leg comes around and takes the first step toward the next hurdle. The faster the foot touches the ground, the quicker the move toward the next hurdle. Body lean is important. An odd number of steps should be taken between hurdles.

Hurdles can be formed from electric conduit pipes or wands supported on blocks or cones. Height should begin at about 12 inches and increase to 18 inches. Hurdles should be placed about 25 feet apart.

Performance Concepts

1. Start the takeoff between three and five feet from the hurdle.
2. Bring the knee of the lead leg up quickly toward the hurdle.
3. Use arms to add lift over the hurdle.
4. Lean forward into the hurdle to acquire good balance.
5. Bring the lead leg down quickly.
6. Snap the trailing leg through quickly into the next running stride.
7. Always lean forward when doing the hurdle, never backward.

Jumping. Jumping events appropriate at the elementary school level include standing long jump, running long jump, high jump, and triple jump.

Standing Long Jump. The jumper stands with toes just behind the takeoff line, feet comfortably spread, knees bent, and trunk well forward. The arms are brought forward in a preliminary swing, then back and forward and upward vigorously. As soon as the feet leave the ground, the legs extend and the arms remain forward. The landing is with feet parallel and trunk and arms extended in a forward direction.

FIGURE 15-92

Standing long jump form

Running Long Jump. In the running long jump a preliminary run is taken toward the takeoff board before the jump. The run is fast, and the last stride is shortened to enable the jumper to adjust the center of gravity and to step flat-footed on the takeoff board. A hard and flat-footed step on the takeoff board should be made to gain drive and spring for the forward lift. The jump is made by pushing off vigorously and extending one or both legs. When the top of the jump is reached, the jumper is in a sitting, running, or lay-out position in the air. Upon landing, the arms are snapped back to ensure forward motion. The runner should then reach forward.

High Jump (Scissors Style). If right-footed, the jumper approaches the bar from the left at a slight angle. The jumper takes a few steps, plants the right, or take-off foot, and then swings the left foot high into the air. The left leg continues over the bar, followed by the right in a scissors action. Simultaneously, the arms swing forward and upward, assisting the upward lift of the body. The right foot should land first, followed by the left, completing the jump.

High Jump (Straddle Style). The approach for this style of high jump is slower than for the scissors tech-

nique. The takeoff is begun about an arm's length from the bar by kicking the outside leg high and toward the bar. The push-off is made from the foot nearest the bar (inside foot) when the center of gravity is directly over the take-off foot. The swing of the outside leg should turn the body so that the abdomen and chest face the bar at the height of the jump. The takeoff leg is rolled over the bar. The landing is made on the lead leg and both hands.

Regardless of which jumping technique is taught, it is essential that a safe landing surface be provided. Children will not learn to jump correctly if they are afraid to land in the pit. Although foam rubber is recommended, shavings or an improvised rubber tube pit provide a satisfactory landing surface.

High Jump (Fosbury Flop). The Fosbury flop is the newest style used in high jumping. The approach is similar to the straddle, although more speed is required and the angle of approach and takeoff is usually less. If jumping from the right side, the jumper uses the left foot as the takeoff foot. As the push-off is being made, the body begins to rotate to the right (if approaching from the right side) so that the back of the jumper is toward the bar. As the jumper reaches the top of the jump, the upper body (with the back facing the bar) is thrust down, thus

FIGURE 15-93

Scissors-style high jump

FIGURE 15-94

Straddle-style high jump

FIGURE 15-95

Fosbury flop

providing the momentum to carry the lower body over the bar. The jumper lands on his or her back.

Triple Jump. Also referred to by the primary skills involved, "hop, step, and jump," the triple jump is an Olympic event that has gained immense popularity among older children. The runner starts 30 to 40 yards back to gain maximum speed at the takeoff mark. The first stage is a hop on the right foot from the takeoff board; the left leg drives forward and the jumper lands on the right foot. The jumper continues forward with a thrust of the left leg, lands on the heel of the left foot, and rocks forward toward the toe. The runner continues the forward movement by pushing off from the left foot and landing on both feet.

Throwing.   *Softball Throw (for Distance).* Although not a standard track-and-field event, a softball throw for distance is frequently included in an elementary school unit. An overhand throwing pattern is used. A running approach is taken from behind the restraining line.

Shotput. Shotputs weighing four to eight pounds are appropriate for most intermediate-level children. The shot should always be pushed rather than thrown. The shot is held in the right hand at the base of the three middle fingers and balanced on the sides by the thumb and little finger. The elbow is bent and away from the body. The shot is rested against the neck and collarbone and is nestled into the side of the chin. The thrower stands with the side to the intended target and the feet spread about a shoulder's width apart with the weight on the rear foot. The front leg is swung across the body and then forward. A short hop is taken with the rear foot, and as the front foot hits the ground, the

body rotates forward. The "putting" arm pushes the shot forward with the body until the body weight is over the front foot. The elbow is straightened and the wrist and fingers extend to propel the shot forward and upward. The front leg and arm swing around, and all the body weight is taken on the front foot.

Performance Concepts

1. Rest the shot in the hand at the base of the fingers; balance with the thumb.
2. Tuck the shot into the neck.
3. Bend the elbow away from the body.
4. Swing the front leg across the body and then forward.
5. Hop on the rear foot.
6. As the forefoot hits the ground, twist the body.
7. Push the shot forward and upward.
8. Follow around with the foreleg and arm. Take weight on the forefoot.

SKILL DEVELOPMENT ACTIVITIES

Proficiency in track-and-field skills necessitates a sound physical foundation and a great deal of individual practice. If proper attention has been given to the health-related fitness components (*i.e.,* flexibility, muscular endurance, cardio-respiratory function), skill-related tasks such as those described can be challenging, with a greater potential for success. Warm-up activities, including light jogging and flexibility exercises, should be engaged in before practice.

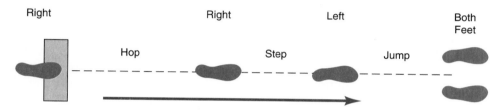

FIGURE 15-96
Triple jump

FIGURE 15-97
Shotput

Running.   *Conditioning Running.* A distance of one to one and a half miles is established. Each child runs as far as possible and then walks the remainder. With practice, children should gradually increase the running distance. Cones or sticks designating distance (tenths of a mile) should be set up along the course to provide goals and perspective.

   Fartlek (Change-of-Pace) Running. The children should be taught the difference between jogging and running. A jog is about half speed and a run is full speed. To start, students jog around an area designated with markers (an oval area is suggested). A blow of the whistle means that everyone should run; a second blow means a jog, and so on. A double blow of the whistle means to slow down gradually to a fast walk. If hills are available, they can also be added for variety and conditioning.

Interval Training. Interval training consists of running at a set speed for a designated distance and then decreasing to a more comfortable rate for a given distance (usually the same distance as that covered with speed). This type of training can be done on an oval track (*e.g.*, one lap at speed, one at a jog) or straight lane (the runner jogs back to the starting line).

Starting Drill. The class forms lines, six to eight in each line. Half the team stands behind each of two starting lines 25 feet apart. The teacher uses the following commands: "Take your marks, set, go," or blows a whistle. On the whistle, runners on each team behind opposite lines make fast starts (sprint and standing) and run until they pass each other, passing on the right. At the passing point each player slows to a walk and goes to the rear of the line.

Baton Passing. The class is divided into groups of four to six runners and placed in a single line approximately four to five feet apart. The runner in the back line walks and passes with the left hand to the runner in front, who takes the baton in the right hand and immediately brings it forward into the left hand in preparation for the next pass. When the baton reaches the front of the line, everyone turns around and the drill is repeated. After the runners have the feel of passing the baton while walking, they should do it during a slow jog and then a run. The distance between runners will have to be increased.

Jumping and Throwing. Jumping and throwing events are primarily task specific and allow little variation. Tasks are usually individually practiced, with as many stations as possible.

Conducting Track-and-Field Events. After learning the skills of a game, a culminating activity in the form of the game is usually conducted. Track-and-field skills are not so directly applicable in a game situation; consequently, a meet is frequently planned to offer children the fun and opportunity of trying their newly acquired skills. The event may be within a class, among grades, or for the whole school.

The organization of a meet requires that certain details must be cared for before the day of the meet. For intraclass competition, such planning may be included in the lesson plan; however, the plans for an intramural activity need to be more detailed and should to be made far enough in advance of the chosen day to allow individuals and teams sufficient time to prepare for participation.

Facilities. Facilities can be constructed on most outdoor play areas (see Figure 15-86). A high-jump pit should be 12 feet long and 10 feet wide. Foam pieces or a commercial landing mat should fill the pit. If a steel rod is not available, a bamboo pole or rope is adequate.

Events. The number of events can vary, depending on student population and time. Events can be conducted one at a time or two to three during the same period. Although some teachers may elect to drop those events already featured during tests of physical fitness (*e.g.*, standing long jump, 50-yard dash, softball throw, mile run), other teachers may have enough time (and desire) to provide these activities as well as popular events such as a sack race, tug of war, obstacle course and Frisbee throw (distance and/or accuracy).

Officials. Fellow teachers, parents and, if need be, dependable students should be assigned the following responsibilities:

1. Starters for track events
2. Finish judges (one for each place or time needed) and recorder
3. Field judges (with one or two helpers), spotter, recorder, and so on
4. Announcer (the meet director may wish to do this) and head recorder

Eligibility and Awards. Considerations for eligibility and participation include the following: (1) number of events each participant may enter (*e.g.*, each child could enter two track events and two field events) and (2) classification of participants (*i.e.*, age, grade, and sex). Another consideration is number of places and point awards if team standings are kept. For team points, a first place can be five points, a second four points, and so on. In case of a tie, the team with the most first place awards wins. The giving of awards and places has become somewhat of a controversial issue. Although some teachers support giving distinguishing awards (generally ribbons or certificates) to first, second, and third place, others feel more comfortable with participation awards (the same) for all. Whatever the method, serious thought should be given to the decision.

NONTRADITIONAL TEAM SPORTS (LEVELS III AND IV)

Korfball	Netball
Modified Speedball	Pillo Polo
Modified Team Handball	

Just as an increasing number of sports programs are adopting the creative and cooperative game philosophy, many teachers are also incorporating the use of nontraditional team sports (examples of traditional activities are basketball, football, and soccer) into the Levels III–IV curriculum. Aside from being novel, nontraditional sports provide skill development and creative alternatives that enrich the physical education curriculum. Games of this nature can serve as separate units or supplement other activity areas such as lead-up games.

One of the primary reasons for the recent popularity of these lesser known team activities lies in their developmental value and adaptability to the school or recreational setting. Another important asset is that most of the activities presented can be initiated with little formal instruction, thereby maximizing participation. In addition, these activities can be adapted to programs with limited facilities and small budgets by the use of innovative or homemade equipment. In general, regardless of skill level, most students will have some degree of success in nontraditional team sports. For the beginner, success during initial learning periods promotes enjoyment and incentive for further participation and skill development. The more advanced players, on the other hand, can be challenged to the point of refining their motor skills and problem–solving abilities. Thus, the activities described in this section have the potential to enhance a sports program's diversity as well as the students' game skills.

KORFBALL

Korfball is a favorite pastime in many European countries and is rapidly gaining popularity in physical education classes in this country. The game closely resembles netball and basketball, but it is unique in that teams of eight players (if played indoors) are made up of four boys and four girls. If the game is played outdoors, a team is made up of six boys and six girls. The object of the game is to advance the ball by passing and cutting and, ultimately, to shoot the ball through the basket and outscore the opponents. The strategy is similar to traditional girls' basketball, in which the defense is on one side of the playing area and the offense on the other side.

The baskets are located a distance from the end lines so that an offensive player can score from anywhere around the basket. Each time two goals are scored, the players change ends of the floor, or divisions, as they are commonly called in Korfball.

GOAL AND FIELD

The goal is a basket (resembling a wicker basket) attached to a two- to three-inch thick post 11 ½ feet above the ground. A height of 8 to 9 ½ feet may be more appropriate for the elementary school levels. The posts can be permanently fixed into the ground or attached to a sufficiently heavy baseplate. The bas-

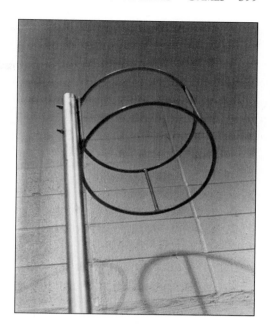

FIGURE 15-98

Improvised goal

kets are 15 to 17 inches in diameter, must face the center of the playing area, and do not have a backboard.

The dimensions of the court or field should be at least 132 feet by 66 feet and no more than 164 feet by 82 feet. The ratio of length to width should be 2:1. The court is divided into equal halves, or divisions, as they are properly termed.

The Game.

1. Teams of eight to 12 players each are matched up wherever possible so that males are guarding males and females are guarding females.
2. To start the game, one player standing near the center of the court throws the ball (a soccer ball or a volleyball) to a teammate on the offensive, or attack, division of the floor.
3. The ball may only be advanced by passing. *Dribbling or running with the ball is not permitted.*
4. Students who do not have possession of the ball should be encouraged to be cutting and moving to free themselves from their guards.
5. Shots at the basket may be taken only by an offensive player who is in an unguarded position.
6. The defensive players' objective is to stay between the person they are guarding and the basket and to intercept a pass whenever possible.
7. Defense players may not hit the ball out of the hands of an offensive player.
8. If a player should fall down with the ball, the individual simply stands back up and retains possession.

9. After every two goals the players change to the other division. After half-time the teams change baskets, and again the players change divisions.

10. When two opponents seize the ball simultaneously, the referee stops play and throws the ball up. The same applies when play must be restarted without one side being entitled to the ball. For this purpose the referee chooses two players from the division concerned, who must be of the same sex.

Scoring.

1. A team scores a goal when the ball has fallen completely through the basket of the opposing team.

2. All baskets, including the foul shots, count one point.

3. A goal stands even when the referee has previously blown a whistle for an infringement committed by a defender, provided the ball had left the hands of the shooting attacker at the moment the whistle was sounded.

4. Only offensive players may score.

Infractions.

1. The following violations result in a free throw for the offended team:
   a. Running with the ball
   b. Hitting the ball out of another player's hands
   c. Touching the ball with a leg or foot
   d. Pushing or shoving other players
   e. Taking hold of a post and using it to change direction or for any other purpose
   f. Attempting a score from the defensive division of the floor
   g. Disregarding the eight and a half foot free space while an opponent is either attempting a free throw or dribbling in the ball.

2. A free throw is awarded for any of the preceeding violations, for intentionally causing danger, or for unnecessarily delaying the game. The free throw is taken from the spot where the infringement occurred.

3. A penalty throw is awarded when an infringement results in the loss of a scoring opportunity or for other infringements that improperly hinder the attack. The penalty throw is a free throw taken at a distance of 13 feet in front of the basket. When taking the penalty throw, players may not touch the ground between the post and the penalty mark with any part of the body before the ball has left their hands. The other players have to observe a distance of eight and a half feet and refrain from any action that disturbs the thrower. The ball is in play following the missed free throw or penalty throw.

Adapted from *How We Do It Game Book* (3rd ed.). American Alliance for Health, Physical Education, Recreation, and Dance. 1900 Association Drive, Reston, VA.: AAHPERD Publications.

MODIFIED SPEEDBALL

In the early 1900s two fall sports were commonly played by students in the various elementary schools, secondary schools, and colleges in the United States: touch football and soccer. Soccer was not popular then because of the restrictions regulating the use of hands, and touch football very often was dominated by a few players. The need therefore arose for another active game that would involve all players and could be played outdoors. It was because of this need that the game of speedball was developed. Speedball is a combination of soccer, touch football, and basketball. If the ball is on the ground, it is kicked as in soccer; but under certain circumstances, passing and catching (similar to that in basketball) is also a part of the game. Different point values are awarded, depending on the method of scoring (*i.e.*, kicking, passing, or drop kicking). Much of the strategy in speedball is similar to that used in soccer, especially when playing a ground ball. The attempt should be made whenever possible to convert ground balls to aerial balls so that control of the ball can be more secure.

FIELD AND GOAL

The playing field (Figure 15.99) should be rectangular and approximately 100 yards long and 60 yards wide, although the size may vary. The longer boundary lines are called the sidelines, and the shorter lines extend the entire length of the field. There is a line drawn five yards from the front of each goal post that extends from sideline to sideline, marking off the penalty area. There is also a line drawn opposite the center and 12 yards from the goal line: this line is the penalty kick mark. The goal posts are on the goal line an equal distance from the sidelines.

The Game.

1. Each team has 11 players, one of whom is the goalkeeper. Any number of players, however, can participate in the game.

2. Speedball has four equal periods of eight minutes. Points are scored by a field goal, a touchdown, a penalty kick, or a drop kick.

3. The game starts with a kickoff similar to that used in soccer, with each team spread out on the half of the field it is defending.

4. The ball may be advanced toward the opponents' goal by kicking or dribbling, as in soccer, and by passing or catching, as in basketball. Another method of advancing the ball is air-dribbling (*i.e.*, tossed or tapped into the air and caught by the same player).

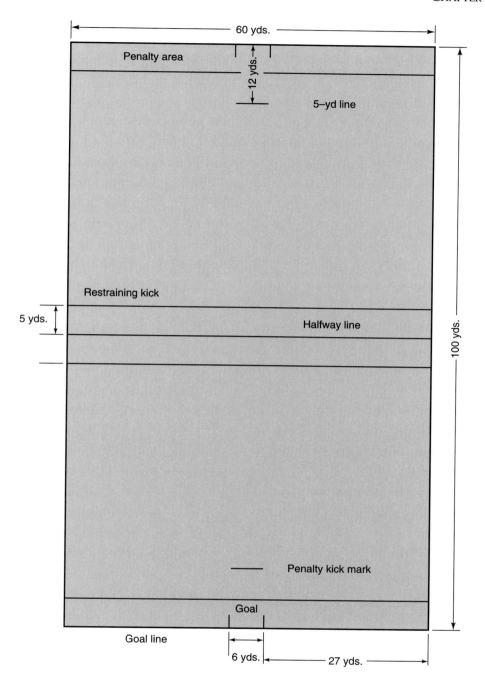

FIGURE 15-99

Playing field.

5. If the ball is rolling, bouncing, or stationary on the ground, it is considered a ground ball and may be advanced by kicking, dribbling as in soccer, volleying, blocking, or heading.

6. If the ball is raised into the air from a direct kick or by using one of the conversion techniques (two-foot lift, single-foot lift, lift to partner, etc.), it becomes an aerial ball and may be advanced by throwing, air-dribbling, volleying, blocking, heading, or kicking. However, running with the ball is not permitted.

7. A player holding an aerial ball has five seconds to pass, punt, air-dribble, or advance the ball with the feet.

8. It is illegal to charge, block, trip, kick, or push an opponent.

9. If a foul occurs outside of the penalty area, a free kick is awarded to the offended team.

10. If a player is fouled while holding the ball, a free throw is given to the offended team.

11. In both the free kick and the free throw the opponents must remain at least five yards

from the player with the ball until the ball is passed or kicked.

12. If a foul occurs within a team's penalty area, a penalty kick is given to the offended team.

13. When a ball passes wholly over the sideline, a player of the opposite team (that which played it out) shall use a throw-in to return the ball to play. The player throwing the ball must stand behind the sideline (where the ball went out of bounds) and throw the ball into the field with any kind of one-hand or two-hand throw.

Scoring.

1. *Field goal—three points.* A field goal is scored when a ground ball is kicked or legally given impetus with the body so that it passes over the goal line between the goal posts and under the crossbar. A field goal may be scored from any spot within the field by any player. In addition, a field goal is scored when a ball has been legally drop kicked and passes under the crossbar or falls to the ground and rolls or bounces across the goal line under the crossbar and between the goalposts.

2. *Touchdown—two points.* A touchdown is scored by the completion of a forward pass, the ball being thrown by an attacking player who is outside the penalty area in the field of play, and caught by a teammate who is in back of the goal line extending from sideline to sideline. A pass received by a player standing behind the goal line between the goal posts does not score, and the ball is awarded to the defense.

3. *Penalty kick—one point.* A penalty kick is attempted following a contact foul by the defense in its own penalty area or following a foul by the defense behind its own goal line during an attempted forward pass for a touchdown. The kick must be a drop kick and may be taken by any member of the attacking team.

4. *Drop kick—four points.* A drop kick is a play in which the person with the ball drops it to the ground and kicks it as it bounces on the ground. A drop kick is scored if the ball goes over the crossbar and between the uprights of the goal posts or their imaginary extensions, provided the kicker is outside the penalty area and in the field of play.

Substitutions.   Free substitution is allowed.

Infractions.   Individual fouls include the following: blocking (personal contact that impedes the progress of an opponent), charging, charging the goalkeeper, dangerous kicking, pushing, hacking, holding, tripping, touching a ground ball that has not been properly converted by one of the conversion techniques, traveling with the ball, holding the ball for more than

five seconds, unnecessary roughness, delaying the game, air-dribbling the ball more than once, drop kicking for a goal, or attempting a forward pass for a touchdown while within the penalty area. The penalty for these fouls is either a free kick, a free throw, or a penalty kick. It is up to the discretion of the official concerning the severity of and the subsequent penalty for each infraction.

Adapted from *National Association for Girls and Women's Sport Guide, Flag Football—Speedball.* (June 1978-June 1980). American Alliance for Health, Physical Education, Recreation, and Dance, Reston, VA.: AAHPERD Publications. Adapted from GUSTAFSON, JOHN, (1980). *Team Sports.* Winston-Salem, N.C.: Hunter Publishing Co.

MODIFIED TEAM HANDBALL

Modified team handball combines the skills of basketball with the strategy of soccer. The object of this game is to throw the ball (a six-inch playground ball or volleyball) between two markers set 12 feet apart or approximately the width of the three-second lane on a basketball court. The scoring area can be wider or narrower, depending on the skill level of the students. A semicircular restraining line in front of each goal identifies the area from which scoring is prohibited. To advance the ball, an offensive player must either throw it or dribble (basketball style). There is, however, a limited number of steps permitted.

The game is very good for Levels III and IV and can be played indoors on a basketball court or outdoors on a football field. Team play and positioning are basically the same as in soccer when outdoors, and as basketball indoors. Games may be limited in length by a specified time or a certain number of scores.

GOAL AND FIELD

The goals are two markers (*e.g.,* cones, tin cans, tape on a wall) set approximately 12 feet apart. The playing area can be either a basketball court if indoors or a football field. A semicircle, with a 30-foot diameter indoors and a 50-foot diameter outdoors (Fig. 15-100), is drawn in front of each goal. It is referred to as the restraining line.

The Game.

1. Five to eight players per team are needed when playing indoors and 11 players per team are preferable for outdoors.

2. The game is started by a jump ball in the center of the court.

3. The ball may be advanced only by throwing or dribbling (basketball style).

4. The person in possession of the ball is allowed to complete a sequence of three steps, a dribble, and three more steps, or

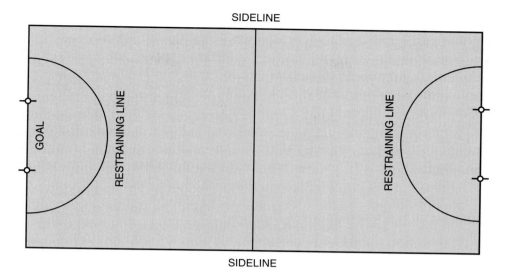

SIDELINE

GOAL

RESTRAINING LINE

RESTRAINING LINE

SIDELINE

FIGURE 15-100

Semicircle in front of each goal

any portion of that sequence. At any time during this sequence the player may pass the ball or attempt to score.

5. If a player stops at any point in this sequence, five seconds are allowed for the player to pass or attempt to score or to go on to the next stage in the sequence. Failure to do this results in a throw-in from the sideline nearest the infraction by a member of the opposing team.

6. All throws at the goal must come from outside the restraining line.

7. When a shot is attempted, the goalie can stop the ball from passing through the two goal markers by catching or deflecting it.

8. If the ball is deflected by the goalie and goes out of bounds, the ball is awarded to the shooting team at the sideline where the ball went out.

9. After a score, a throw-in is taken by the opposing team from the middle of the sideline.

Infractions.

1. Fouls and violations are the same as in basketball, and the penalty is a throw-in from the nearest sideline by the team fouled.

2. Offensive fouls result in a penalty throw from outside the restraining line by the team fouled. The goalie is the only player during the penalty shot who is allowed inside the goal area, and everyone else must remain outside the restraining line.

3. As soon as the penalty shot is taken, play resumes.

Adapted from BENNET, JOHN O. (May 1978). Modified team handball. *Journal of Health, Physical Education, and Recreation*, 57.

NETBALL

The game of netball originated from the Olympic game of team handball. It is played on a regulation basketball court with two portable floor hockey net goals and a six-inch rubber playground ball. The game follows basketball rules up to the point of scoring. Instead of shooting a basket, the offensive player attempts to throw the ball into the hockey net for a goal. The defending goalie is given special privileges to prevent the ball from going into the goal. The strategy used is very similar to traditional girls' basketball; the offense is on one side and the defense on the other, with no crossing the midcourt line. Thus, netball, a unique combination of team handball and basketball, provides an opportunity for developing a number of problem-solving skills. It can also serve as an enjoyable lead-up game to basketball, promoting ball-handling skills and a better understanding of the strategy and rules.

Netball can be modified to accommodate class size and skill level. One of the best features of the game is that the beginner can experience early success in scoring. The game can be played by any number of players, but seven or nine per team is preferred. Scoring and the length of each game may vary, depending on the time and the number of students in the class. Ideally, ten minutes or five goals are allowed for each game; however basketball time limits are quite satisfactory. Rules regarding substitutions, the number of personal fouls allowed before a player must retire, the size of the goalie box, and the distance of the free-throw line to the goal can and should be adjusted to the level of the players.

GOAL AND FIELD

The goal is a portable floor hockey net goal. If a floor hockey net is not available, two strips of tape (each approximately four feet in length) placed perpendicular to the ground and six feet apart on the wall at each end can serve as goals.

The playing area is a regulation basketball court or any space of similar size. The goalie is protected in a goalie's box, which is 12 feet by eight feet and surrounds the front of the hockey goal.

The Game.

1. Netball is played by two teams of seven or nine players; if seven are used, three offensive and four defensive players (one goalie) constitute a team. The object of the game is to score by throwing the ball into the opponents' goal.
2. The game starts with a jump ball at center court, just as in basketball.
3. After the jump, basic basketball rules prevail. No double dribble, no traveling, and so on.
4. No one can step into the goalie's box except the goalie. The goalie may step out of the box, but when doing so, the goalie must dribble just as the other players.
5. If an offensive player steps into the opposing team's goalie box with the ball, the opposing team is awarded a free shot from a free-throw line 15 feet away, with only the goalie protecting. The ball is dead after the shot and given to the goalie to return.
6. If a player from the same team steps into the goalie's box to help defend the net, a free shot is given to the opposing team.
7. A player is allowed two personal fouls and must retire on the third, although this rule is quite flexible.

Scoring.

1. A goal is scored when an offensive player throws the ball into the hockey net that is being defended by the opponents.
2. The entire ball must pass over the goal line.

Infractions.

1. If a personal foul (those dictated by basketball rules) occurs, the offensive player is awarded a free shot from the free-throw line, with only the goalie defending.
2. Any other violation, such as double dribbling, traveling, and so on, results in loss of the ball.

Adapted from GABBARD, CARL. (May 1978). Netball. *Journal of Physical Education and Recreation*, 57.

PILLO POLO

The game and strategy of Pillo Polo are very similar to hockey, except that in Pillo Polo there are no red or blue lines and the goalie is allowed to pick up the ball and throw it downfield. This rule makes goaltending exciting and a more satisfying position. Each player has a Pillo Polo stick (31-inch-long plastic stick with soft, flexible foam padding on the hitting end), and the object is to hit the seven-inch foam ball into the opponents' net. There is a very low fear factor involved, and the game itself was designed with safety in mind. Therefore, no masks, elbow pads, or shin guards are required. The game can be played on almost any surface, indoors or out.

GOAL AND FIELD

Pillo Polo has its own regulation goals which are 1½-inch nylon mesh net around aluminum tubing (43 inches by 41 inches by 20 inches). Floor hockey nets, cones, or any homemade goals can also serve as goals. The goals are placed along the center of each end line.

The playing field depends on the space available. The ideal size is 100 feet by 50 feet. The length should be twice the width, with a line or other marker to show the center line.

The Game.

1. A team has five or six players. The positions are *center*, two *wings*, two *defense players*, and a *goalie*; one wing is dropped if there are five players per team. The class is divided into as many teams as necessary, a team is rotated each time a goal is scored.
2. It is recommended that only three offensive players be allowed to cross the center line, which means that two defensive players and the goalie must stay behind the line. This rule can eliminates congestion.
3. When there are only two teams, three ten-minute periods are recommended.
4. Play begins with a face-off in the center.
5. Each team attempts to advance the ball toward its respective goal by hitting it with the padded end of the stick.
6. The ball should not be caught or held in the hand except by the goalie. The ball can, however, be knocked down by hand.
7. The ball should not be kicked.
8. A player cannot pass the ball to any teammate across the center line. The ball must precede the player across the center line. This rule prevents "hanging around the goal." If this occurs, off-sides or "center line" is called and the opponents take possession of the ball at the center line.

9. If the ball goes out of bounds the last team to have contact loses possession.
10. The opposing team starts play where the ball went out. However, to have a more active game with fewer interruptions, side-lines and end lines can be eliminated.
11. A goal is scored when the entire ball crosses the front plane of the goal.

Scoring.

1. If the goal is made by deflection off any player, or propelled by a stick, the goal is good.
2. If the offensive player deliberately kicks or throws the ball into the net, the goal is not allowed.
3. If a defensive player shoots, kicks, or throws the ball into the opponents' net, the goal is awarded to the offensive team.

Infractions.

One free shot with only the goalie on defense is given for the following violations:

cross-checking	holding	hooking
kneeing	throwing the	tripping
hacking with the	stick	rough play
stick	charging	elbowing
high sticking	falling on	
	the ball	

One regular penalty dictates a *single* free shot by a player on the goal from a distance, starting the approach, no less than 20 feet in front of the goal, with the goalie defending. No rebounds are allowed. If any infraction is severe, a major penalty can be given or the attending player can be banned from the game. Play resumes after the ball is touched by the goalie.

Adapted from *Pillo Polo Official Rules.* U.S. Games, Inc., Melbourne, Fla 32935.

REFERENCES

DAVIS, R. G., & ISSACS, L. D. (1992). *Elementary physical education: Growing through movement* (3rd ed.). Winston-Salem, NC: Hunter.

GRAHAM, G. (1977). Games for elementary school children. *Journal of Physical Education and Recreation.* September 1977, 17–35.

KIRCHNER, G. (1992). *Physical Education for elementary school children* (8th ed.). Dubuque, Iowa: Wm. C. Brown.

MORRIS, D. G. S. (1976). *How to change the games children play.* Minneapolis: Burgess.

MORRIS, D. G. S., & STIEHL, J. (1989). *Changing Kid's Games.* Champaign, Ill: Human Kinetics.

MOSSTON, M. (1981). *Teaching physical education.* Columbus, OH: Chas. E. Merrill.

ORLICK, T. (1982). *The second cooperative sports and games book.* New York: Pantheon.

SUGGESTED GENERAL READINGS

Games Teaching. *Journal of Physical Education and Recreation.* Special feature on games for elementary school children. September 1977, 17–35. (Authors include Graham, Morris, Barret, Riley, Orlick)

LOGSDON, B. J., BARRETT, K. R., AMMONS, M., *et al.* (1984). *Physical education for children: A focus on the teaching process,* (2nd ed.). Philadelphia: Lea & Febiger.

MAULDON, E., & REDFERN, H. B. (1981). *Games teaching* (2nd ed.). London: Macdonald & Evans.

SUGGESTED READINGS AND SOURCES

Cooperative and Creative Games

DECKER, J., & STERNE, M. (1990). The new way to play: cooperation in physical education. *Strategies*, May, 13–16.

MORRIS, D. G. S., & STIEHL, J. (1989). *Changing Kid's Games*. Champaign, Ill: Human Kinetics.

New Games Foundation. (1981). *More new games*. Garden City, NY: Doubleday.

New Games Foundation. (1976). *The new games book*. Garden City, NY: Doubleday.

ORLICK, T. (1978). *The cooperative sports & games book*. New York: Pantheon.

ORLICK, T. (1982). *The second cooperative sports & games book*. New York: Pantheon.

Simple Game Activities

ARNOLD, A. (1972). *The World Book of children's games*. New York: World Publishing.

FARINA, A. (1981). *Developmental games and rhythms for children*. Springfield, IL: Charles C. Thomas.

HEATON, A. (1981). *Double fun: 100 out and indoor games*. Provo, Utah: Brigham Young University Press.

Individual And Partner Activities

BLOSS, M. V. (1971). *Badminton*. Dubuque, IA: Wm. C. Brown.

CHALTON, J. (1977). *Croquet: A complete guide to history, strategy, rules, and records*. New York: Turtle Press.

DOLAN, E. F. (1974). *Complete beginner's guide to bowling*. Garden City, NY: Doubleday.

TIPS, C. (1979). *Frisbee: Sports and games*. Millbrae, CA: Celestial Arts.

VARNER, M., & HARRISON, J. R. (1968). *Table Tennis*. Dubuque, IA: Wm. C. Brown.

VERNER, B. (1977). *Raquetball*. Palo Alto, CA: Mayfield.

YURIC, T. (1972). *Handball*. Philadelphia: W.B. Saunders.

Team Sports

GENERAL TEXTS

BLAKE, W. O., & VOLP, A. M. (1964). *Lead-up games to team sports*. Englewood Cliffs, NJ: Prentice Hall.

BLAKENMORE, C., HAWKES, N., & BURTON, E. (1991). *Drill to skill*. Dubuque, IA: Wm. C. Brown.

DAUER, V. P., & PANGRAZI, R. P. (1992). *Dynamic physical education for elementary school children (10th ed.)*. Minneapolis, MN: Burgess.

HUMPHREY, J. H., & HUMPHREY, J. N. (1980). *Sports skills for boys and girls*. Springfield, IL: Charles C. Thomas.

KIRCHNER, G. (1992). *Physical education for elementary school children (8th ed.)*. Dubuque, IA: Wm. C. Brown.

MARTENS, R., CHRISTINA. R. W., HARVEY, J. S., JR. & SHARKEY, B. J. (1981). *Coaching young athletes*. Champaign, IL: Human Kinetics.

PHILIPP, J. A., & WILDERSON, J. D. (1990). *Teaching team sports*. Champaign, IL: Human Kinetics.

SEATON, D. C. (1984). *Physical education handbook*. Englewood Cliffs, NJ: Prentice Hall.

SEIDEL, B. L., BILES, F. R., GIGLEY, G. E., & NEUMAN, B. J. (1980). *Sports skills*. Dubuque, IA: Wm. C. Brown.

Specific Sport

BASKETBALL

EBERT, F., & CHEATUM, B. A. (1977). *Basketball*. Philadelphia: W.B. Saunders.

FERRELL, J. (Ed.). (1979). *Youth basketball association leader's manual*. Colorado Springs, CO: National Board of YMCA's.

SOCCER

BEIM, G. (1978). *Principles of modern soccer*. Boston: Houghton Mifflin.

CHYZOWYCH, W. (1978). *The official soccer book*. Chicago: Rand McNally.

FERRELL, J. (Ed.). (1980). *YMCA youth soccer coaches manual*. Colorado Springs, CO: National Board of YMCA's.

HAIGHT, A. L. (1979). *The soccer coaching guide*. San Diego, CA: Barnes.

OLSON, J. R. (1983). Basic team concepts for beginner level soccer players. *JOPERD*, Nov./Dec.

FOOTBALL

FERRELL, J., & FERRELL, M. A. (1980). *Coaching flag football*. Colorado Springs, CO: National Board of the YMCA's.

FRIEND, J. (1980). *Coaching youth league football*. North Palm Beach, FL: Athletic Institute.

LITTLE, M., DOWELL, L., & JEETER, J. (1977). *Recreational football: Flag and touch*. Minneapolis, MN: Burgess.

VOLLEYBALL

COX, R. H. (1980). *Teaching volleyball*. Minneapolis, MN: Burgess.

SCATES, A. E. (1976). *Winning volleyball fundamentals, tactics and strategy (2nd ed.)*. Boston: Allyn & Bacon.

HOCKEY

KELLY, J., & SCHMIDT, M. (1974). *Hockey: Bantam to Pro*. Boston: Allyn & Bacon.

MEAGHER, J. W. (1972). *Coaching hockey: Fundamentals, team play, and techniques*. Englewood Cliffs, NJ: Prentice Hall.

SOFTBALL

BROWN, P. (1978). *Coaching youth softball*. North Palm Beach, FL: Athletic Institute.

WALSH, L. (1978). *Contemporary softball*. Chicago: Contemporary Books.

TRACK AND FIELD

Athletic Institute. (1986). *Track and field for elementary school children and junior high school girls*. Chicago.

COLFER, G. (1977). *Handbook for coaching cross country and running events*. West Nyack, NY: Parker.

FOREMAN, K. E., & HUSTED, V. (1977). *Track and field for girls and women (3rd ed.)*. Dubuque, IA: Wm. C. Brown.

Recommended Films

VOLLEYBALL

Volleyball. (16 min.) The Athletic Institute

Volleyball for Intermediate Grades. (26 min.) Thomas Howe Assoc.

BASKETBALL

Basketball for Intermediate Grades. (28 min.) Thomas Howe Assoc.

Basketball. (13 min.) The Athletic Institute.

FIELD/FLOOR HOCKEY

Floor Hockey. (13 min.) The Athletic Institute

Field Hockey—Dribbling, The Drive, Goalkeeping, Shooting (series). Champions on Film.

FOOTBALL

Football—Kicking, Centering, Passing, Quarterback Play (series). Champions on Film.

Touch/Flag Football: How to Play. (12 min.) The Athletic Institute.

SOCCER

Soccer—Basic Goal Keeping, Dribbling, Kicking, Trapping (series). Champions on Film.

Soccer. (14 min.) The Athletic Institute.

SOFTBALL

Softball: How to Play. (11 min.) The Athletic Institute.

Softball—Batting, Fielding Techniques, Throwing and Catching (series). Champions on Film.

TRACK AND FIELD

Track and Field. The Athletic Institute.

Track and Field for Intermediate Grades. Thomas Howe Assoc.

Addresses

Champions on Films, Box 1941, 745 State Circle, Ann Arbor, MI 48106

The Athletic Institute, 200 Castlewood Drive, North Palm Beach, FL 33408

Thomas Howe Associates, 1226 Homer Street, Vancouver, BC VGB 2Y5

University of Wisconsin—Madison, Bureau of Audio Visual Instruction, 1327 University Ave., Madison, WI 53706

16

Rhythms and Dance

The dance and rhythmic activities discussed in this chapter will serve as excellent enhancement activities for children in the process of building their movement foundation. The child's urge for self-expression through movement can be well served by the teacher's presentation of appropriate dance activities in a manner that frees the child to express thoughts and feelings through movement. Unfortunately the teaching of dance is often avoided by physical education teachers due to an erroneous notion that dance can only be taught by those who have a great deal of dance experience. This is an unfortunate notion that, hopefully, we can dispel.

All human movement is manipulated and controlled by the environment of the situation. In dance, the movement is manipulated by the rhythm of the music (or words, as in the case of rhymes), emotion, or an idea. Dance then is merely a sequence of fundamental skills in which rhythm is the manipulator. All movement has rhythm; the difference found in dance is that rhythm is a *controlling* element rather than one of many elements as in movements used in games/sports and gymnastics. Through dance, the child is given the opportunity to use the entire body in a very individualistic manner that is satisfying to both the child and the teacher.

The many forms of dance suitable for the elementary school program include creative, aerobic, folk and square. This chapter offers methodology related to the teaching of each of these dance forms.

The objectives of the elementary dance program include the following:

Psychomotor: motor control, balance, agility, coordination, flexibility, muscular strength and endurance, and cardiorespiratory endurance (if danced vigorously over an extended period of time).

Cognitive: sequencing, synchronization of movement to accompaniment, knowledge about different cultures, creativity, concentration, laterality.

Affective: cooperative effort with others, personal expression of movement, joy of success.

Additional information associated with the teaching of fundamental rhythmic activities may be found in the Rhythmic Awarenesses section of Chapter 13.

PROGRESSIONS

The progressions found in dance closely parallel the progressive psychomotor, cognitive, and affective developmental characteristics of children. In other words, the egocentric child will find pleasure in using the developing fundamental movement skills in simple combinations that allow freedom of expression and are not encumbered by the encroachment of a partner. With increased development, children in Levels III–IV can concentrate on the refinement of fundamental skills; therefore, dances become more structured, creative challenges more complex, and synchronization with a partner more feasible. Rhythm and dance activities for Levels I and II serve as enhancements for the development of fundamental skills and movement awarenesses. Total lessons will be built around the performance of creative and structured dances for Levels III and IV.

The following progressions for Levels I–IV are offered as flexible guidelines for the teacher:

Opportunities for creative expression are numerous in dance.

Level I

Rhythm knowledge to be learned by students at this level include underlying beat, tempo, and simple accents. If the school supports a good school music curriculum, the physical educator and the music educator could coordinate many of their lessons.

Rhythmical movement using fundamental locomotor and nonlocomotor skills to move expressively with an accompaniment (for example, percussion, records, singing, rhymes). Locomotor movement receives the strongest focus.

Creative dance in which feelings and/or thoughts are expressed with accompaniment (percussion, records, story plays, and other imaginative instrumentation) are centered around the use of fundamental skills, as in rhythmical movement.

Finger plays in which manipulating the hands and fingers to accompanying songs reinforce the child's rhythmic awareness and finger dexterity. These skills are continued at this level from preschool experiences.

Structured dance in which students learn simple choreographed dances with accompaniment (singing nursery rhymes, chants).

Level II

Rhythm knowledge to be learned includes accents, even and uneven rhythms, measures, and simple rhythmic patterns.

Rhythmical movement focuses on locomotor and nonlocomotor skills and simple sequences of both. Variability of space, time, force, and relationship is stressed. Simple exercises and jump-rope routines are presented as are simple ball, hoop, and streamer routines.

Creative dance for this level continues to focus on the child's interpretation of stimuli provided by the teacher. The creation of short movement sequences is also introduced. Longer sessions of creative dance are possible.

Structured dances are longer and sometimes involve more movements in the sequence. Suggested formations for Levels I and II are scattered, single, and double circles. Specific dance steps include the slide, Schottische, and step hop.

Level III

Rhythm knowledge to be learned includes rhythmic patterns, phrasing, note values.

Rhythmical movement will focus on quality of movement as movement combinations are continued and variations are increased.

Creative dance for this level focuses on more specific problem solving and increased variability of improvisation. Children should also be challenged more frequently with abstract stimuli. They enjoy performing in small groups.

Structured dance includes the additions of small groups, double lines, quadrilles, and squares. Simple dance positions such as the promenade and open position are introduced as are simple figures (honor, elbow, and two-hand turn; reel, do-si-do, grand right and left, allemande, and promenade). Dance steps include the two-step, grapevine, bleking, and polka.

Level IV

Rhythm knowledge to be learned includes syncopated rhythm and more complex rhythmic patterns. The use of musical phrasing for cues will become more prominent.

Rhythmical movement will continue to focus on quality of movement and combinations of step patterns. Synchronization with partner and group becomes more important. Accuracy is emphasized.

Creative dance for this level can rely more on abstract stimuli and children enjoy small group improvisation. Children at this level are capable of providing their own stimuli for creative challenges.

Structured dances includes the addition of more square dances. Folk dances are more complex due to faster rhythm. Increased difficulty is also due to sequences demanding more movement such as frequent changing of partners. Dance steps include the sweep step, waltz, mazurka, buzz step and balance.

CREATIVE DANCE

Generally, creative dance lessons for Levels I and II should contain activities that allow for individualization and require the use of fundamental skills (hop, skip, slide, for example) with simple variability introduced through the use of space, time, force, and relationship variables. Creative dance and dance challenges (that is, movement dramatization of the rhyme or story play) offer excellent opportunities for the child to use large movements involving the total body without being encumbered by correctness or incorrectness of performance. Children need opportunities where they feel *free* to move creatively. Naturally, the main objective for using a dance-enhancement activity is to provide opportunities for the development of a sense of rhythm as it is expressed through movement. The child moves from an inner stimuli (rhythmic awareness) to an external stimuli (record, drum, song, rhyme). The only control asked of the child is that an attempt be made for the movement to suggest harmony between body and stimuli. Any other encumbrance (controls) would inhibit the creative expression being elicited.

Creative dance provides children with the following advantages:

1. Gradual progression from moving to an internal beat to responding to an external beat.
2. The lack of rigid structure (as found in aerobic and folk dance) encourages the development of an attitude of freedom (physically, mentally, emotionally).
3. Children can use a familiar movement vocabulary (fundamental skills) rather than having to learn new moves. New challenges can be experienced as these familiar fundamental skills are sequenced in many different ways.
4. Promotes creativity expression and a sense of success.
5. The possibility for individualization makes it more efficient for classes with diversified skill levels.
6. Offers a natural outlet for the many feelings that are naturally felt by children. They will feel encouraged to develop and expand their power of creative thinking abilities.

Scarfs and appropriate music encourage full extensions.

Teaching Styles

Creative dance can only be productive when the teacher creates an atmosphere of openness, acceptance and freedom for the children. The children must feel that their movement ideas and performance are acceptable answers for the challenges set forth by the teacher. Demonstrations (motor or verbal) have no place in a creative dance lesson. The child is encouraged towards individual movement expression using the fundamental movement skills already existing in his/her movement schema. Creative dance can be performed in solo or group.

It is important for the teacher to be familiar with the stimuli that will be used for a particular lesson. *Poems* must be read with voice inflection and appropriate pauses so the children will be helped to *feel* the movement suggested by the poem. *Music* should be chosen carefully and the children must first listen (without movement or only hand movements) prior to being encouraged to respond with full body movement. *Color, nature, and sensory* stimuli require some verbal discussion using a variety of verbal descriptors prior to movement. It is best if the classroom teacher attends to this phase of learning. Stories (fantasy or everyday life) and word pictures sometimes create a problem in that the children may simply want to pantomime (with restricted everyday gestures or singular moves). Through the use of guided discovery and problem-solving questions the teacher can encourage large (even outlandish) movements that serve to free the child and elicit more creativity.

Class Organization

The most efficient formation for creative dance is a scattered arrangement in which each child occupies enough "self space" to feel free to move with abandonment. Level I and II students will most often perform in solo whereas Level III and IV children will profit from both solo and group experiences. The teacher must remember that structure (beyond what is necessary for efficient class management) is to be avoided.

The child needs to sense freedom to move about in the space available. A good understanding of the "self space" principle described in Chapter 13 will permit the children this freedom without becoming a class management problem. Creativity can even be a part of the minimal structure the teacher may deem necessary. For example, rather than identifying the play space with boundary lines the teacher may use imaginary peanut butter or glue for the out-of-bounds area. Other techniques include asking the whole class to make a shape like a big chocolate chip cookie (circle), a doughnut (double circle), a piece of uncooked spaghetti (line), a two-sticked popsicle (double lines), eyeglasses (side by side circles), or a giant box (square).

Some teachers have found it helpful to use a double circle formation with outside circle facing out and inner circle facing in. This enables the children to move without being restricted by others watching.

Stimuli for Creative Dance

Poems, being rhythmical in structure, offer a good beginning stimulus for creative dance. Begin with poems that contain a moving character or familiar object (for example, nursery rhymes) and progress to poems that express ideas and emotions. The teacher may choose to have the children act out (emphasizing big movements) the poem as it is read, or the poem can be read to the class beforehand, discussed, and then the children can describe the poem through movement. Help from the classroom teacher can be very supportive.

Music (tapes and records) provides an excellent stimulus and many fine records are available commercially. Choose music that has meaning to the children and make sure the rhythm pattern is simple (marches, light classical, and folk music are good choices). Some of today's contemporary music contains too many different sounds for children to clearly hear the underlying beat. Themes from some contemporary movies and TV programs may also provide an appropriate creative stimulus.

Percussion instruments (drums, tambourines, finger spoons, sticks) are a favorite of children. The teacher should begin by providing the percussion and gradually allowing students opportunities to manipulate the instruments.

Color is an exciting stimulus for creative dance in which the students demonstrate through movement the feeling that each color elicits for them. The teacher should remember that these responses may not follow a norm (that is, to some, red may signal danger or anger, and to others happiness or excitement).

Stories provide very appropriate outlets for dramatization. As with poems, children should be encouraged to use exaggerated movements to express the emotions of the story rather than simply pantomime the actions suggested by the story. Children at Levels I and II should be allowed to interpret the story line by line. Older children, however, can usually perform in phrases.

Everyday life and "real people" offer opportunities for the teacher to observe the perceptions children have about a police officer, teacher, sanitation worker, physician, doughnut maker, and others.

Nature offers both simple and complex challenges as a child responds to stimuli ranging from animals to more abstract things (sunbeams, moonlight, lightning).

Sensory information provides abstract stimuli for Level III and IV students who are able, for example, to demonstrate an individual perception of what the sound of a drippy faucet might look like.

Word pictures are perhaps the most elementary of abstract stimuli. Children must know the meaning of the words that are used. For example, a child could demonstrate individual perceptions of such words as short, tall, snappy, gooey, straight, crooked, happy, sad, young, and old. Level IV students could respond to situational pictures such as a family reunion, fans of the winning (losing) team, death of a pet, failing a test.

Teaching Hints

1. Remember not to evaluate "good" and "bad" movement; rather, encourage exploration.
2. Reinforce expressions of freedom, variety, honesty.
3. Allow for considerable exploration prior to problem-solving challenges.
4. Show enthusiasm for efforts in a way children can understand (children think a teacher is really "with it" when the teacher is able to get excited about what happens in the class; in other words, it's okay for the teacher occasionally to seem hyper with excitement over the children's performance).
5. Begin with individuals, then partners, and finally small groups for those who are ready.
6. Allow for time to practice (repetition) and refine movements.
7. If time permits, allow time for those who want to share their creative dance with the class.
8. After a required presentation by individuals or groups, be prepared to offer an evaluation. Begin with the positives and move on to areas for improvement (for example, "Mark, you certainly moved well at the medium level. Can you think of a nifty and smooth way to also move at the low and high levels?").
9. Remember that the *process* is often more important than the *product*. Thus provide ample time for rhythmical exploration through movement.
10. If the term "dance" seems to affect the children negatively, call it something else (rhythmic play, musical moves).
11. Begin with rather well-known stimuli (nursery rhymes, animals, holidays, birthdays, sports).
12. Use simple props (streamers, lummi sticks, drums, etc.) to help children expand feelings and thoughts beyond themselves.
13. Use variability of space, time, force, and relationships during the dance activity to help challenge and stimulate excitement in the students.
14. Observe the children carefully and use their movement as a stimulus to become more creative in planning future lessons.

STRUCTURED DANCE

Structured dance (*e.g.*, singing dances, folk dances, aerobic dances) are available for all levels of students. The teacher should carefully select the dance most appropriate for the motor, cognitive, and emotional needs of the children at each level. Structured dances are comprised of specific patterns and sequences and are often handed down as part of different cultures. Physical educators should, whenever possible, teach folk dances in conjunction with the social studies and music curricula.

Teaching Styles

Structured dance is easier to teach for most teachers because it has definite steps, formations and rhythms that must be adhered to for the student (and teacher) to experience success. The command style of teaching is best suited for the teaching of folk, square and aerobic dance. Demonstration, cues, transitions and repetitive practice are of utmost importance. Structured dance is a group activity and students are expected to perform in synchrony with the other dancers.

Class Organization

Generally, children should learn each dance within two lessons, and if this is not achieved the teacher should seriously question the appropriateness of the dance that the students are being taught. Remember, learning in small doses with frequent successes is an important key to motivation. Children will feel joyful and proud to be able to perform simple dances well and with flair, whereas inappropriately difficult dances will elicit feelings of frustration and trigger avoidance behaviors to dance in general.

Unlike the freedom of creative dance, structured dance generally requires a strict adherence to specific formations and synchronization with a partner or a small to large group.

The following terms, to be taught as the dances require, are appropriate for children at all levels.

Positions

Open—Girl usually on right of boy; inside hands are joined. (Figure 16-1).

FIGURE 16-1
Open position.

Two-hand closed—Partners face and join both hands. (Figure 16-2).

FIGURE 16-2
Two-hand closed position

Skating or promenade—Partners are side by side facing same direction; girl is on boy's right, right hands held above left hands. (Figure 16-3).

FIGURE 16-3
Skating or promenade position.

Schottische Position.   The girl is on the boy's right, the boy's right arm around the girl's waist, their right hands clasped; the girl's left hand is on the boy's right shoulder (Figure 16-4).

FIGURE 16-4
Schottische position

Shoulder Waist Position.   Partners face each other, the boy's hand on the girl's waist, the girl's hands on the boy's shoulders (Figure 16-5).

FIGURE 16-5
Shoulder-waist position

Banjo Position.   This is also called the right shoulder or side position. Partners face a little to one side of each other; the boys' right side is adjacent to the girls' right side (Figure 16-6).

FIGURE 16-6
Banjo position

Basic Position.   The arms are down but not stiff; hands are clasped at about waist level (Figure 16-7).

FIGURE 16-7
Basic position

Swings—While running or walking, partners hook elbows or hold hands, single or both hands, to turn one another twice around quickly.

FIGURE 16-8
Swings

Buzz—Using single hand or elbow hook; one foot is planted while the other foot pushes the couple into a pivoting turn. Movement in turns and swings is usually clockwise.

FIGURE 16-9
Buzz

Shoulder Position. The children's arms are up and outstretched to their sides, their hands resting lightly on their neighbors' shoulders (Figure 16-10).

FIGURE 16-10
Shoulder position

V-Position. All children face the same direction, their arms held down but not stiff, their hands clasped at about hip level (Figure 16-11).

FIGURE 16-11
V-position

Varsouvienne Position. The girl is on the boy's right side, right hands clasped at the girl's right (at shoulder level, but not resting on the shoulder); left hands are clasped to the left of the girl's left shoulder (Figure 16-12).

Formations.

Scattered—Individuals, couples, or small groups positioned at random in the area.
Single circle—All stand facing the same direction (center out, clockwise counterclockwise). (Figure 16-13).

Counterclockwise (CCW) Circle Formation. This is the direction most often used in structured dances (Figure 16-13).

FIGURE 16-12
Varsouvienne position

FIGURE 16-13
Counterclockwise circle formation

FIGURE 16-14
Double circle formation

Double Circle. In a circle of couples, partners can face each other (boys' backs to the center), or all face counterclockwise (CCW) or clockwise (CW). Both partners can also face in or out. The circles can move in the same direction or in opposition (Figure 16-14). Couples can also face one another (one couple facing CCW and the next, CW). The circle can also have more than a couple, for example, trios (Figure 16-15), as found in the Troika.

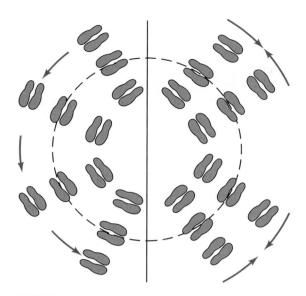

FIGURE 16-15
Triple circle formation

Free Formation. Dancers are alone, in partners, in trios, or in larger groups scattered freely around the area.

Line Formation. Students form a file, one behind the other, facing CCW and CW.

Single Circle, Broken. A circle of dancers is broken at one end. The dancer at one end (usually the right end) is the leader. Movement can follow that used in a circle, serpentine, or line.

Single Circle, Closed. The circle has no break; dancers can face CCW or CW, to center, or away from center.

Trios. Students form a group of three dancers; if possible, the center dancer should be of opposite gender to the two side persons. All can move in the same direction, or trios can move towards one another (Figure 16-15).

FORMATIONS

Contra or Longways. Children form lines of couples, with partners facing one another (Figure 16-16).

FIGURE 16-16
Contra or longways formation

Grand Right and Left. Partners begin by taking right hands and proceeding past one another. They continue moving around the square or circle, alternating right and left hands (Figure 16-17).

FIGURE 16-17
Grand right and left

STEPS IN TEACHING STRUCTURED DANCE

Step 1: Setting the Stage

Children are naturally curious, so a brief statement about any interesting cultural information concerning the dance will oftentimes pique their interest. Naturally, the name of the dance should be repeated several times during this phase. The teacher's innate enthusiasm for the dance will also stimulate the children's interest. If the dance is to be among those performed at an upcoming open house, this is the time to make the fact known as this information will also motivate rapid learning.

Step 2: Demonstration

The children's first view of the dance should be as close to the desired finished product as possible, and this includes dancing to the music at correct tempo. If the dance involves a partner, it is best for the teacher to have one of the more alert students be a part of the demonstration. However, if this is not possible, simply demonstrating (with music) the steps that will be used will suffice. The teacher should dance for about one minute, calling attention to the step pattern and how it fits to the music. Simple cues can be called out as the step pattern is performed.

See Table 16-1 for additional information.

Step 3: Listening to the Music

Listening to the music for about one minute acquaints the children with the tempo. Clapping out the rhythm is helpful, as is clapping the step pattern while the teacher continues to demonstrate and give verbal cues. Children should be encouraged to chant these verbal cues as they clap the music and/or perform the step pattern in their own personal space.

Step 4: Learning and Practicing the Steps

Regardless of the formation called for in the dance, the children should be in scattered- or multiple-line formation to complete the initial learning of the steps. The teacher must make sure everyone can see. Depending on the complexity of the step, the teacher may choose to face the class or face away. It is often easier on the children perceptually if they are behind the teacher's back. However, if the step does not involve a turn, it is permissible for the teacher to face the class. In this case the teacher must teach in opposition (that is, call "step right, close left" but actually demonstrate moving to the left and closing right), thereby providing a mirror image for the child to imitate (Fig. 16-18). Cues must be very clear, concise, and timely. It is a good idea also to have students verbalize the cues as this will enhance their memorization of the step patterns. When the class can call the cues as it practices, the teacher is free to move about and give individual help. Liberal use of praise and corrective feedback during this stage is very important.

Step 5: Music

As soon as most of the class is familiar with the step pattern, begin using the music. The music should be used as soon as the step pattern (for example, schottische) can be executed rather than waiting until part or all of the dance (for example, Buggy Schottische) can be executed. As new steps or phases of the dance are being taught, the music should be removed. Music not only keeps the children interested but it also facilitates learning the dance (that is, the music stimulates the appropriate rhythm). Students should continue giving the verbal cues, but now they can state them quietly to themselves as they learn to coordinate their movements with the music. As early in the learning process as is appropriate, the children should be encouraged to depend on the phrasing of the music for their cues. The teacher should continue to move freely about the class giving individual help unless the teacher's image is needed by most of the class, in which case it is best to remain dancing at the front of the class. As soon as several children are successfully performing the steps to the music, they can come to the front of the class and lead with their backs to the class. Leadership opportunities such as this should be rotated among all of the students.

Step 6: Formations

When most of the students are reasonably comfortable with both the steps and the music, the class should assume the required formation of the dance. If this formation is a circle, the teacher becomes a part of the circle (Fig. 16-19) while talking to the class. The teacher should switch positions in the circle several times so that all of the children have the opportunity to view the teacher's movement. Generally it is a good idea to have a trial run without the music and at a slightly reduced pace so students become familiar with the circular movement. It is important to remind the children not to watch others directly across from them in the circle as they may become confused when right and left moves are made. If an image is needed it is best to watch the dancers to either side rather than across the circle. The best place for the teacher to be to help an unsure dancer is to either side of that dancer, or, if necessary, directly in front of the performer.

Have a definite procedure for the selection of partners if boy/girl partners are necessary. For example, have the boys form an inner circle and the girls an

FIGURE 16-18
Teaching in opposition.

FIGURE 16-19
Teaching in circle formation.

outer circle. Each circle moves in opposite directions, and when the music stops the circles face each other with partners being directly across. Whenever possible it is best for children to form partners without reference to sex, in which case the two circles would be mixed.

During this phase, extra practice may be needed on the transitions from one step to the next. Also, the ending of the dance should be practiced several times. A strong ending makes the dancers feel good even if parts of the dance are still rough.

Step 7: Dance the Entire Dance

The first time the dance is attempted in its entirety may require playing the music at a slightly reduced tempo (a variable-speed record player is really a must!) so students will experience early success. However, if in the previous periods the music has been at full operational speed and the class has been successful, then reducing the tempo is not necessary. During this phase the teacher should be free to observe the dancers and make

note of the students having difficulty with rhythm, step pattern, or motivation. Sometimes the teacher can correct this by becoming a part of the dance and offering additional instruction to each student. If several students demonstrate a lack of readiness for this phase, it is best to arrange them into a separate group for additional practice with the teacher. This practice can be scheduled for the end of the class period or the beginning of class the next day. The students who know the dance can be performing at the same time in their separate groups.

It is important to remember that a class should complete steps 1 through 7 within two class periods. At all times, the teacher should strive enthusiastically to promote learning the dance. Positive reinforcement is often the most effective teaching tool.

Step 8: Refinement

Once the students can perform the steps of the dance in rhythm to the music, they should perform the dance often so it can become a permanent part of their dance schema. Each time they perform the dance the teacher should be alert for ways in which to refine their movement (that is, body carriage, styling of moves, and so forth). It is during this stage of relaxed performance that the children will demonstrate their gracefulness (or lack of it). Often this phase is omitted, which robs the children of an integral part of the total dance experience—relaxed, graceful expressive movement.

Teaching Hints

1. Approach each dance with enthusiasm.
2. Do not hesitate to withdraw a dance that turns out to be too difficult (*i.e.*, cannot be learned in two class meetings).
3. Place students who have rhythmical difficulties between students who do not.

Table 16-1
Teaching Dance

Procedure	Teacher	Students
1. Set the stage	Enthusiastic verbalization	Active listening
2. Demonstrate	Perform the steps with music	Active watching
3. Study the music	Clap rhythm and chant cues	Clap rhythm and chant cues
4. Practice	Continue to perform steps and call cues	Perform steps and chant some cues
5. Practice with the music	Continue to call cues, give individual help and perform steps	Call cues and dance in rhythm to the music
6. Implement the formation	Teach the appropriate formation	Call cues, dance in rhythm and in formation
7. Dance	Positive group feedback and individual help	Enjoy and continue to learn
8. Refinement	Give individual help; where needed introduce subtle styling	Dance in the spirit intended for the dance and refine the movements

Table 16-2

Progressions for Structured Dance. Dances are organized by predominant step pattern and listed in progressive order (Levels II–IV).

Walk or Run	Level
Come Let Us Be Joyful	II
Dance of Greeting	II
Bingo	II
Greensleeves	II
Jump, Jim Joe	II
Grand March	III–IV
Gustaf's Skoal	III

Polka	Level
Klumpakojis	III
Mayim! Mayim!	III
The Bird Dance	III
Ace of Diamonds	IV
Norwegian Mountain March	IV
Teton Mountain Stomp	IV
Cshebogar	IV
All American Promenade	IV
Put Your Little Foot	IV
Turkey in the Oven	IV
Wearin' O' the Green	IV
Brown-Eyed Mary	IV

Step-Hop	Level
Crested Hen	II
Schottische	II
Hora	III
Hopp Mor Anika	III
Tantoli	IV
Milanovo Kolo	IV
Rumunsko Kolo	IV
Cherkassiya	IV
Susan's Gavotte	IV
Turkey in the Oven	IV
Buggy Schottische	IV
Korobushka	IV

Two-Step	Level
Badger Gavotte	II
Teton Mountain Stomp	IV
Grand March	III–IV
Susan's Gavotte	IV
Cotton-Eyed Joe	IV
Miserlou	IV
Irish Washerwoman	IV

Sweep Step	Level
Put Your Little Foot	IV

Schottische	Level
Bleking	II
Danish Schottische	II
Rumunsko Kolo	IV
Korobushka	IV
Buggy Schottische	IV

Heel-Toe	Level
Patty-Cake Polka	IV
Tantoli	IV
Cotton-Eyed Joe	IV

Polka	Level
Kalvelis	III
Klumpakojis	III
Hopp Mor Anika	III
Tantoli	IV
Ace of Diamonds	IV
Cotton-Eyed Joe	IV
Lott Ist Tod	IV

Waltz	Level
Norwegian Mountain March	IV
Little Man in a Fix	IV
Susan's Gavotte	IV
Rye Waltz	IV

Grapevine	Level
Alunelul	IV
Milanovo Kolo	IV
Hora	III
Mayim! Mayim!	III
Cherkassiya	IV
Miserlou	IV

Bleking	Level
Bleking	II
Uno, Dos, Tres	III

Buzz Step	Level
Cshebogar	IV
Teton Mountain Stomp	IV

Balance	Level
All-American Promenade	IV
Korobushka	IV

Promenade	Level
Carousel	II
Glowworm	II
Irish Washerwoman	IV

Grand Right and Left	Level
Bingo	II
Irish Washerwoman	IV
O'Susanna	IV
Turkey in the Oven	IV

Do-Si-Do	Level
Wearin' O' The Green	IV

Allemande	Level
Wearin' O' The Green	IV

4. If at all possible, secure a variable-speed record player.

5. Prior to performing a previously taught dance, have the students listen to the music and call cues or dance in place.

6. Keep directions short and clear.

7. Use the music as early in the learning process as possible.

8. Maintain the same cues and sequence of cues for each individual dance.

9. Occasionally use vigorous dances that are well known by the children for fitness activities.

10. Use the questioning technique to test students' knowledge of terms, dance names, and cultural information.

11. Whenever possible coordinate the use of dance enhancement activities with related information being learned in other classes, like social studies, art, and English.

12. Teach in phrases and repeat previous phrases when progress is shown.

13. Because of the nature of dance and the hesitancy of some students to dance, handle evaluation very carefully. Participation and variability of movement are the focus when evaluating the students' performance of creative dance. Students of structured dance should be required to know the origin of the dance and to perform the dance without major mistakes. Therefore, give the students ample opportunity for high-quality repetitive practice once the dance has been learned.

14. Be alert for ways to turn dances into social "mixers." This enhances the complexity of the dance and encourages acceptance by the students.

Table 16-2 organizes the dances in progressive order from simple to complex within the more common step patterns found in structured dance.

Dance Glossary

ACCENT—Stress that is placed on a beat to make it stronger or louder than another. Usually the accent is on the first beat of the measure. However, if the rhythm is syncopated, the accent will fall on the off beat. Some music utilizes more than one accent per measure.

ALLEMANDE LEFT—Square dance pattern in which "corners" take left hands and turn each other once around and then return home.

ARCH—Square pattern in which two persons in the center (or at the end) of a line grasp both hands and make an arch for the other dancers to pass under.

BACK TO BACK—(Back to back, face to face) pattern in which couples move either facing or back to back, inside hands joined. It is most often used in conjunction with the two-step, polka, or waltz. Couples alternate moving in the same direction while facing and while back to back.

BALANCE—Used in folk, square, and social dancing. A step is made with one foot; as weight is transferred to the ball of that foot, the other foot closes to the first foot, with weight remaining on the first foot. Alternating steps are taken (*i.e.*, balance L, balance R).

BLEKING STEP—Quick change of the feet in an uneven rhythm. The dancer stays in place and hops on one foot while the opposite leg extends forward and the heel of that foot is placed on the floor. The extended foot is brought back in place as the opposite foot is extended and the heel placed on the floor. The count is hop ("*ah*"), heel ("*one*"), hop ("*ah*"), heel ("*two*").

BUZZ STEP—Found in many square and folk dances and some social dances. Partners are positioned in a waist swing, although the hand or elbow swing may also be used. (This step can also be done alone.) Couples turn clockwise on the ball of the right foot as the left foot pushes off. If counterclockwise movement is called for, the left foot becomes the pivot foot (see Figure 16-9).

CAST-OFF—A method for progressing couples along a line, for example, from head couple to foot couple in a reel. Partners separate, with the boys going down one side and the girls the other, usually meeting to form an arch.

CCW—Symbol for counterclockwise movement around a circle or as dancers turn individually. The terminology is derived from the movement of hands on a clock. Movement is to the right. This is also referred to as "line of direction" (see Figure 16-13).

CHA-CHA-CHA—Social dance-step from Cuba. A step forward is followed by a rock back onto the opposite foot and then three quick stamps in place. Cues would be *right* (forward), *left* (in place). R, L, R.

CONTRA DANCE FORMATION—Refers to *Longway set* (see Figure 16-16).

CORNER—Square dance term to denote that the girl is on the boy's left. The girl's corner is the boy on the right.

COUNTING—Use of *ah* or *and* in the cues to indicate half of the beat value (*and*) or one-quarter of the beat value (*ah*). See *Polka* and *Bleking*.

CW—Symbol for clockwise movement. Movement is to the left. This is also referred to as "reverse line of direction."

DO-SI-DO—Square dance term in which the boy and girl move toward each other and pass each other right shoulder to right shoulder, back to back, and left shoulder to left shoulder as they move backward into position.

DRAW STEP—Step to the side followed by the other foot being dragged up to it. The cue is usually *step-together-step*.

ELBOW SWING—Dancers hook right or left elbows and turn around once (see Figure 16-8).

FACE TO FACE—See *Back to Back*.

GRAND RIGHT AND LEFT—Square and folk dance pattern in which partners take right hands as they move past each other and on to the next person, alternating left and right hands until the partner is met. The boys move counterclockwise while the girls move clockwise (see Figure 16-17).

GRAPEVINE—Dancers step left to side, cross right behind, step left to side, cross right in front. Weight is on the balls of the feet, knees are bent, and there is free hip movement either right or left. The crossing step may begin front or back and may move to the right or left.

HEAD COUPLE—Refers to the first and third couples in a set of four couples, or the first two couples in a longways set.

HOME POSITION—Original positions of the dancers at the beginning of the dance.

HUNGARIAN BREAK STEP—Dancers hop on left foot while touching right toe in front of left, hop again on left while right toe touches out to right side, and draw right foot to left (clicking heels together); hold for the fourth count. The cue is *cross, side, click, hold*, each move receiving one count.

LEFT-FACE TURN—Individual dancers turn one full turn to the left (CCW).

LINE OF DIRECTION—Refers to counterclockwise movement of the dancers around the circle.

LONGWAY SET—Double line of couples: boys in one line, girls in opposite line. Partners may face each other or stand side by side facing the head of the lines. This is also known as *Contra dance formation* (see Figure 16-16).

PIVOT—Turning clockwise or counterclockwise on the balls of one or both feet.

POLKA—two counts hop left (*ah*), step forward right (*one*), close left to right (*and*), and step right (*two*). Dancers continue alternating the lead hop.

PROMENADE—Square dance term describing counterclockwise movement of couples (in promenade position, boys on inside) around the set (see Figure 16-3).

REEL—Figure in longway dances in which the head couple begins by turning each other around one full turn in the middle of the set. The boy will now be facing the girl's line and the girl will be facing the boy's line. The boy will go on to swing the second girl in line and so on down the line. The girl does the same with the boys. In between each swing the head couple meets for a swing in the middle of the set.

REVERSE LINE OF DIRECTION—Refers to clockwise movement around the circle.

RIGHT-HAND LADY—Square dance term describing the girl of the *couple* to the right.

ROCK—Dance step in which the weight is shifted from forward to backward (or vice versa).

SCHOTTISCHE—Four-count, even time, dance step: Step right, step left, step right, hop right. Continue alternating the lead foot.

SIDE COUPLES—Refers to second and fourth couples in a four-couple set.

STEP-CLOSE—Dancers step to the side, bringing the other foot up to the first foot and transferring the weight.

STEP-DRAW—Dancers step to the side, lightly dragging the other foot to the first foot and transferring the weight.

STEP-HOP—Dancers step and hop on the same foot.

STEP-POINT—Dancers step, pointing the free foot.

STEP-SWING—Dancers step, swinging the other foot lightly in the direction specified.

SWEEP STEP—Right foot sweeps across left foot and diagonally backward, then forward to step and carry weight.

Table 16-3
Levels I–IV—Rhythms.

NAME	SKILL(S)	NAME	SKILL(S)
RHYTHMIC GAMES		JUMP-ROPE RHYMES	
Level I–II		*Level II-IV*	
Crazy Clock	Rhythmic	All in Together	Jump, eye-foot, rhythmic
Levels	Rhythmic	Apple, Apple	"
Orchestra Leader	Directional, rhythmic	Ask Mother	"
Level II (Beginning)		Be Nimble, Be Quick	"
Lummi Sticks	Eye-hand, rhythmic	Birthday	"
Morse Code	Eye-hand	Bobby, Bobby	"
Names in a Rhythm	Eye-hand, rhythmic	Bubble Gum	"
Rhythmic Echo	Eye-hand, rhythmic	Bulldog	"
Level II (Intermediate)		Charlie McCarthy	"
Line or Circle Clap	Rhythmic	Chickety Chop	"
Reverse Ranks	Rhythmic, directional	Cinderella	"
Threes and Sevens	Rhythmic, directional	Down in the Valley	"
FINGER PLAYS		Hippity Hop	"
Level I and II		Hokey Pokey	"
Follow the Beats	Rhythmic	I Love Coffee	"
SINGING RHYTHMS		Ice-Cream Soda	"
Level I		Lady, Lady	"
Head, Shoulders, Knees, and Toes	Body awareness	Mabel, Mabel	"
Keep It Moving	Rhythmic, body awareness	Mama, Mama	"
Muffin Man	Spatial, skip	One, Two, Buckle My Shoe	"
This Is the Circle, That Is My Head	Body awareness	Peanuts, Popcorn	"
		Teddie Bear, Teddie Bear	"
		Tick tock	"
		Vote, Vote	"

SYNCOPATION—Temporary displacement of the natural accent in music, such as shifting the accent from the first and third beat to the second and fourth beat.

THREE STEP TURN—Dancer makes a complete turn, using three steps. If the turn is clockwise, the steps are right, left, right. If the turn is counterclockwise, the steps are left, right, left. Either turn will position the dancer facing the original direction when completed.

TWO-STEP—Two counts, uneven time, step R, close L, step R, pause. Continue by alternating lead foot.

WALTZ—An even step pattern, simply a walk, with a specific floor pattern. Step forward right, step to side left, close right to left, and take weight on right.

WRING THE DISHRAG—Partner clasp hands (right over left) raise arms and turn back to back under arch performed by their raised arms.

RHYTHM/DANCE DESCRIPTIONS

Explanation of Activity Descriptions for Levels I–II

The rhythmical activities and dances have been arranged to give the teacher the greatest ease in teaching unfamiliar activities. The reader will note that in some cases (*i.e.,* singing, and rhythms) the exact count of measures is not given for each step pattern. The verses of the rhyme that are matched with the step patterns serve the same purpose as do the measure counts for the more complex dances. When rhymes are used, the students should chant the rhyme rhythmically prior to learning the dance. Some of the singing rhythms are simple enough (they simply mimic the rhymes) so that cues are not given because the rhyme actually cues each movement. They are almost like pantomimes. The teacher will recognize that many of the variations and teaching hints are applicable to more than one dance and have not been redundantly included.

Table 16-4

Levels I–II—Dances.

DANCE	ORIGIN	SKILL(S)	FORMATION	RECORD
		Level I-II		
A Hunting We Will Go	England	Slide, skip, visual, rhythmic	Line (P)	FK 1191; RCA 45-5064, 22759
Baa, Baa, Black Sheep	England	Rhythmic, skip, slide, walk	Circle (P)	FK 1191, CR VII R700A 701
Bluebird	USA	Walk, spatial	Circle	FK 1180
Chimes of Dunkirk	France	Auditory, directional, slide, skip, spatial	Circle (P)	FK 1187; WFD 1624
Hickory Dickory Dock	England	Rhythmic, run, swing/sway	Circle	CR Series 7, No. 702
Hokey Pokey	USA	Auditory, body awareness, kick, rhythmic, balance, spatial, stretch/bend	Circle	Capitol 2427, 6026
I See You	USA	Rhythmic, skip	Line (P)	FK 1197; RCA 20-432
Marching	England	Eye-foot, directional, rhythmic	Scattered at first	Any marching record
Muffin Man	England	Skip	Circle	FK 1188; RCA 45-5065
Oats, Peas, Beans, and Barley	England	Rhythmic, skip, walk	Circle	FK 1182; RCA 45-5067
Sing a Song Of Sixpence	England	Rhythmic, walk	Circle	FK 1180; RCA 22706
Turn the Glasses Over	USA	Directional, spatial twist/turn	Circle	WOF 2B (M112)

Level II

Ach-Ja	Germany	Rhythmic, slide, walk, grapevine	Circle (P)	CR-VII
Badger Gavotte	USA	Two-step	Circle (P)	FK 1094; 1416
Bingo	USA	Auditory, rhythmic, walk, grand right and left	Circle	FK 1189; RCA 45-6711
Bleking	Sweden	Hop, jump, Bleking, Schottische	Circle (P)	FK 1188
Bow Belinda	USA	Hop, skip	Line (P)	FK 1189
Carousel	Sweden	Slide, skip, promenade	Circle (P)	FK 1183; WFD 1625
Come Let Us Be Joyful	Germany	Walk	Trios/Circle	WFD 1622; WOF 4-A (M102)
Crested Hen	Denmark	Step-hop, rhythmic, spatial	Sets of 3	FK 1194; 1159; RCA 45-6176, 21619
Dance of Greeting	Denmark	Eye-hand, rhythmic, run	Circle	FK 1187, FK 1187; WFD RCA 1625
Danish Schottische	Denmark	Rhythmic, Schottische, step-hop	Circle (P)	WFD 1622; WOF 4-A (M102)
Glowworm	USA	Rhythmic, walk, promenade	Circle (P)	McGregor 310-B; Windsor 4613-B
Greensleeves	England	Directional, rhythmic, spatial walk	Circle (P)	WFD 1624; V-45-6175
How Do You Do, My Partner?	USA	Rhythmic, skip	Circle (P)	FK 1190; Pioneer 3012
Jolly Is the Miller	USA	Rhythmic, skip, visual, walk	Circle (P)	FK 1192; RCA 45-5067
Jump, Jim Joe	USA	Jump, run, slide	Circle (P)	FK 1180; Bowmar-III
Kinderpolka	Germany	Slide, spatial	Circle	FK 1181; WFD RCA 1625; RCA 45-6179
Klapptanz	Sweden	Auditory, rhythmic, twist/turn	Circle (P)	WOF 7-A (M114)
Lummi Sticks	USA	Eye-hand, rhythmic, spatial		FK 1167; Twinson "Koo-EE"
Limbo	Caribbean	Balance, rhythmic, stretch/bend	Line	Hoc 1608B
Maypole Dance	USA	Skip	Circle	FK 1178; EA-20
Round and Round the Village	England	Directional, rhythmic, skip	Circle	FK 1191; WFD 1625
Seven Jumps	Denmark	Balance, jump, kick, rhythmic, skip, spatial	Circle	FK 1163; WFD 1623
Shoo, Fly	USA	Rhythmic, skip, swing/sway, visual, walk	Circle (P)	FK 1102; 1185; Decca 1822
The Wheat	Czechoslovakia	Rhythmic, skip, walk	Sets of 3	RCA 1625
Schottische	Scotland	Walk, step-hop	Circle	Victor 4131; WOF 4A (M102)
Skip to My Lou	USA	Rhythmic, skip, spatial, swing/sway, walk	Circle (P)	FK 1192-A; RCA 45-5066

CR = Childhood Rhythms	KIM = Kimbo	WFD = World of Folk Dance
DWP = Dances Without Partners	MH = Melody House	W = White, Rhythms Productions
EA = Educational Activities	(P) = Denotes partners required	WOF = World of Fun
FK = Folkraft	R = Russell	
HOC = Hoctor	RCA = RCA Victor	

Listings and descriptions are arranged by approximate developmental level and in alphabetical order within each level.

ACH-JA

Level: II
Records: Ruth Evans, Childhood Rhythms, Series VII

Formation: Double circle, partners facing CCW, inside hands joined
Skills: Grapevine, stomp, slide

VERSE

1. *When my father and my mother take the children to the fair,*
2. *Ach, ja; ach ja!*
3. *Oh, they have but little money but it's little they care,*
4. *Ach ja; ach, ja!*
5. *Tra la la, tra la la, tra la la la la la la,*
6. *Tra la la, tra la la, tra la la la la la la,*
7. *Ach ja; ach ja!*

CUES

1. Walk 2, . . . 8
2. Face and bow
3. Backs and bow
4. Repeat of cues 1-3
5. Slide 2, . . . 4
6. Slide 2, . . . 4
7. Face and bow
8. New partner . . . and bow

MEASURES	MOVEMENTS
1–2	1. In partners, walk eight steps CCW.
3	2. Drop hands, face each other, and bow.
4	3. Turn back to back and bow.
5–8	4. Repeat patterns 1-3.
9–10	5. Join both hands and slide four CCW.
11–12	6. Slide four CW.
13	7. Drop hands, face partners, and bow.
14	8. Boys walk CCW to the next girl. New partners bow. Repeat the dance with new partners.

VARIATIONS AND TEACHING HINTS:

1. This dance offers a progression to "bow to your corner" (3).
2. CW and CCW are taught as the direction of movement in the circle and not as right and left since this is not the movement within a single circle.
3. Once the dance is learned, a turn by the girl under the boy's right arm at the fourth slide adds a challenge.

A HUNTING WE WILL GO

Levels: I and II
Records: Folkcraft 1191; RCA 45-5064, 22759

Formation: Two parallel lines with boys and girls facing each other
Skills: Skip, slide, rhythmic

VERSE

1. *Oh, a hunting we will go, A-hunting we will go,*
2. *We'll catch a fox and put him in a box,*
   And then we'll let him go.

(CHORUS)

3. *Tra, la, la, la, la, la, la,*
   Tra, la, la, la, la, la,
   Tra, la, la, la, la, la,
4. *la, la, la, la,*
   Tra, la, la, la, la, la,

CUES

1. Skip down . . . 8
2. Skip back . . . 8
3. Skip L . . . 8
4. Arch

MOVEMENTS

1. Head couple joins inside hands and skips down between the lines to the foot of the set.
2. Head couple turns around, changes hands, and skips back to the head of the set. All other players clap hands while the head couple skips down and back.
3. Head couple skips around the left side of the set, followed by other couples.
4. When the head couple reaches the foot of the line it forms an arch under which all other couples pass.
5. Head couple remains while the second couple becomes the head couple. (Repeat the dance with a new head couple.)

VARIATIONS AND TEACHING HINTS

1. Level I students should walk through the floor pattern.
2. Students should skip to the beat of the verse.
3. If music is not available, this dance can still be performed while students sing the verses and chorus.

BAA, BAA, BLACK SHEEP

Levels: I and II
Records: Folkcraft 1191; Childhood Rhythms, Series 7, No. 701; Russell 700A; Victor E-83

VERSE

1. *Baa baa, black sheep,*
   Have you any wool?
2. *Yes sir, yes sir.*
   Three bags full.

5. Skip . . . 16

Formation: Circle; girls on the boys' right, facing the center with hands joined
Skills: Walk, skip, slide, rhythmic

MOVEMENTS

1. Stamp three times. Shake fingers.
2. Nod head twice. Hold three fingers up.

3. *One for my master,*
   One for my dame,
4. *And one for the little boy*
   Who lives in the lane.
   Lines 1-2
   Lines 3-4
   Lines 5-6

CUES

First option:

1. Stamp 2, 3; shake 2, 3;
2. Nod, 2; fingers
3. Right and bow/curtsy; left and bow/curtsy
4. Turn and bow/curtsy
5. Skip . . . 16

Second option:

1. Slide R . . . 8
2. Slide L . . . 8
3. Walk in, 3, 4 walk out, 3, 4
4. Walk in, 3, 4 walk out, 3, 4

3. Turn right and bow or curtsy. Turn left and bow or curtsy.
4. Turn around. Face center and bow or curtsy.
5. Chorus: Join inside hands and take sixteen steps (walk or skip) CCW.
   Alternate movements:
6. Slide eight steps right (CW) with hands joined.
7. Slide eight steps left (CCW).
8. Take four steps in and four steps out of circle, joined hands raised. Repeat four in, four out (chorus same as before).

VARIATIONS AND TEACHING HINTS

1. Students should try to dramatize the bow and curtsy. This will serve to require more vigorous movements (*e.g.*, stretch of arms, backs, and legs).

BINGO

Level: II
Records: RCA Victor 45-6177 or 41-6172; Folkcraft 1189

Formation: With partners, a double circle facing CCW
Skills: Walk, promenade, grand right and left

VERSE	MEASURES	MOVEMENTS
There was an old farmer	1–2	Promenade while singing the song.
Who had an old dog,	3–4	
And Bingo was his name.	5–10	
Bingo, Bingo, Bingo,	11–12	
Bingo was his name.	13–14	Take partner by right hand as all say B. A grand right and left follows as each person takes the next person by the left hand and says I, the next by the right hand (N), the next by the left hand (G), and the next by the right hand (O).
B-I-N-G-O,		
Bingo was his name.		
	15–16	Persons meeting on O swing once around and prepare to promenade again with a new partner.

BLEKING

Level: II
Record: Folkcraft 1188

Formation: Single circle; partners facing, both hands joined
Skills: Bleking, Schottische

CUES	MEASURES	MOVEMENTS
1. Right, pause, left, pause	1	1. Both beginning right, thrust right arm and right leg forward, heel placed on floor; pause. Thrust left arm and left leg forward; pause.
2. Right, left, right		
3. Left, pause, right, pause, left, right, left	2	2. Beginning right, perform one Bleking step (right, left, right).
4. Right, pause, left, pause, right, left, right Left, pause, right, pause, left, right, left	3–4	3. Repeat patterns 1 and 2, beginning left.
5. Step-hop... 16	5–8	4. Repeat patterns 1–3.
	9–16	5. In Schottische position, beginning right, do 16 step-hops.
		6. Repeat the dance.

VARIATIONS AND TEACHING HINTS

This music can also be used for a simple Schottische.

BOW BELINDA

Level: II
Records: Burns, Evans, Wheeler, *Folk Dances,* Series I;
Folkcraft 1189

Formation: Two lines, partners facing; boys in one line, girls in the other; six to eight couples per set
Skills: Hop, skip, bow, do-si-do.

VERSE

Bow, bow, O Belinda,
Bow, bow, O Belinda
Bow, bow, O Belinda
Won't you be my darling?
Right hands round, O Belinda, etc.
Left hands round, O Belinda, etc.
Both hands round, O Belinda, etc.
Back to back, O Belinda, etc.
Skip, skip, O Belinda, etc.

MOVEMENTS

1. Partners walk toward each other, bow, and walk backward to place. Repeat.
2. Partners turn each other with right hand.
3. Partners turn each other with left hand.
4. Partners turn each other with both hands.
5. Partners walk back to back, passing right shoulders, and walk backward to place.
6. Partners join hands and skip around set, following the head couple. The head couple may lead its own line down the outside of the set, meet at the foot, and make an arch, each following couple meeting and skipping under the arch. The dance is then repeated with a new head couple.

HICKORY, DICKORY, DOCK

Levels: I and II
Records: Childhood Rhythms, series 7, No. 702; Square Dance Association, Album 12, No. 8

Formation: Double circle; inside hand on partner's shoulder; both facing CCW; one child is the "mouse" and the other is the "clock"
Skills: Rhythmic, sway, stamp, run

VERSE

Hickory, dickory, dock!
The mouse ran up the clock.
The clock struck one.
The mouse ran down.
Hickory, dickory, dock.

MOVEMENTS

1. Sway toward center of circle.
2. Sway toward outside of circle. Stamp one foot, then the other foot.
3. Mouse runs CW around partner, then stamps feet as above.
4. Clock claps hands on word "one."
5. Mouse runs CCW.
6. Repeat swaying and stamping movements.

HOW DO YOU DO MY PARTNER?

Level: II
Records: Folkcraft 1190; RCA Victor 21-685; Pioneer 3012

Formation: Double circle, girls outside
Skills: Skip, turn

VERSE

How d'ye do my partner
How d'ye do today?
Will you skip in a circle?
I will show you the way.
Tra, la, la, la, la, la,
Tra, la, la, la, la, la,
Tra, la, la, la, la, la,
Tra, la, la, la, la, la,
(Repeat song.)
And I thank you, Good day.

MEASURES

1–2
3–4
5–6
7–8
1–8
1–6
7–8

MOVEMENTS

1. Boys bow to their partners.
2. Girls curtsy to their partners.
3. Boys offer hands to their partners.
4. Join inside hands and turn CCW.
5. With joined hands skip around the circle.
6. Repeat the directions for measures 1-6.
7. Stop, release hands, and face partners: boys bow and girls curtsy. Change partners by moving one step to right. Repeat the singing game.

I SEE YOU

Levels: I and II
Records: Folkcraft 1197; Victor 20432

Formation: Two double lines facing each other; one line of boys, the other of girls
Skills: Rhythmic, skip

VERSE

I see you, I see you
Tra, la, la, la, la, la,
I see you, I see you
Tra, la, la, la, la, la,
I see you and you see me.
I take you and you take me.

MOVEMENTS

1. Active dancers are the back two lines. On the first "I see you," they look over their partners' left shoulders peek-a-boo style. On the second "I see you," they look over their partners' right shoulders.
2. To double tempo, partners make three quick peek-a-boo movements: left, right, left.
3. Dancers repeat line 1 but peek-a-boo to the right first.
4. Dancers repeat line 2 but peek-a-boo to the right first.
5. They clap on the first note; active players skip to the center, passing to the left of their partners and joining hands in the center with a two-hand swing.
6. They clap again; active players face partners, skip around them once, and finish in the front as their partners become the new active players.
7. They repeat from line 1.

JOLLY IS THE MILLER

Level: II
Records: Folkcraft 1192; RCA 45-5067; Victor 45-5067; Old Timer 8089; American Play Party 1185

Formation: Partners form a double circle (side by side), facing CCW with the girls on the inside; one child is chosen as the "miller," who stands in the center
Skills: Walk, skip, visual

VERSE

Jolly is the miller who lives by the mill,
The wheel turns around of its own free will,
One hand in the hopper and the other in the sack,
The girl steps forward and the boy steps back.

MOVEMENTS

1. Couples join inside hands and walk (or skip) CCW, singing the song.
2. During the second line, children in the inner circle extend their left arms sideward to form a mill wheel.
3. On the last word of the song ("back"), partners drop hands; children in the inner circle step forward, while those in the outer circle step backward. The extra dancer tries to secure a partner during this exchange. The child without a partner goes to the center.

JUMP, JIM JOE

Level: II
Records: Folkcraft 1180; Bowman Album 3

Formation: Two circles, boys outside and girls inside; partners facing
Skills: Jump, run, slide

VERSE

Jump, jump and jump, Jim Joe,
Take a little twirl and away we go,
Slide, slide, and stamp just so—and
Take another partner and jump, Jim Joe.

MOVEMENTS

1. Take two slow and then three fast jumps in place.
2. Run around partners CW in a small circle and return to position.
3. With hands on hips, move to left with two slide steps (step left, close right; step left, close right), followed by three stamps. Each person then has a new partner.
4. Join hands with the new partner and run around each other back to place, finishing the turn with three light jumps on the words "jump, Jim Joe."

KLAPPTANZ

Level: II
Record: Klapptan Tampet, World of Fun 7-A (M114)

Formation: Double circle, boys on inside with backs to the middle
Skills: Auditory, twist, turn, rhythmic

VERSE

Now with your hands go clap, clap, clap.
Now with your feet go stamp, stamp, stamp.
Shake—shake—shake.
Shake—shake—shake.

MOVEMENTS

1. Bend at hips and clap hands three times after words "Now with your hands."
2. Place hands on hips and stamp feet three times—left-right-left or right-left-right—after words "Now with your feet."
3. Shake right finger at partner three times; free hand can be on hip or on elbow of right hand.
4. Shake left finger; same as above.
5. Slap partner's right hand in the middle and spin around to the left back to position; stamp feet three times.
6. Repeat movements 1 through 5.
7. Skip around circle with partner, holding inside hands.
8. Repeat entire dance.

VARIATIONS AND TEACHING HINTS

Once the children learn the dance and the movements, the dance could become a progressive dance, that is, one in which the children change partners at movement 5 or 7; each person would move to the right one person to a new partner.

MUFFIN MAN

Levels: I and II
Records: Folkcraft 1188; RCA Victor 45-5065

Formation: Circle, facing center; "Muffin Man" in the center
Skills: Skip

VERSE

Oh, have you seen the muffin man, the muffin man, the muffin man,
Oh, have you seen the muffin man, who lives across the way.
Oh, yes, we've seen the muffin man the muffin man, the muffin man,
Oh, yes, we've seen the muffin man the muffin man, who lives across the way.

MOVEMENTS

1. Join hands and circle to the left, using a walk or a slow skip.
2. Stand facing center and clap hands while singing.
3. The child in the center chooses a partner from the circle and brings him or her back to the center (in the skaters' position). This child becomes the new muffin man while the old partner returns to the circle.

OATS, PEAS, BEANS, AND BARLEY

Levels: I and II
Records: Folkcraft 1182; RCA Victor Pioneer 3012; Folk Dancer MH 1110-A

Formation: Circle, facing center with hands joined; a child is chosen to be the "farmer," who stands in the center
Skills: Skip, rhythmic, walk

VERSE

1. Oats, peas, beans, and barley grow,
Oats, peas, beans, and barley grow,
Do you or I or anyone know
How oats, peas, beans, and barley grow?
2. First the farmer sows his seed,
Then he stands and takes his ease.
Stamps his foot and claps his hand.
And turns around to view the land.
3. Waiting for a partner,
Waiting for a partner,
Open the ring and choose one in.
While we all gladly dance
4. Tra, la, la, la, la, la,
Tra, la, la, la, la, la,
Tra, la, la, la, la, la,
Tra, la, la, la, la, la,

MOVEMENTS

1. Farmer in center stands while children in the circle walk left, taking small steps. Circle players stop, point to the farmer, shrug, turn right, and stamp their feet.
2. Children in the circle stop, face the center, and dramatize the words of the song.
3. Children in the circle skip left as the farmer skips around inside the circle and picks a new partner. The farmer and new partner skip around inside the circle.
4. The two farmers continue to skip inside the circle while the others join hands and circle left. The "old farmer" joins the circle, and the "new farmer" repeats the pattern.

ORCHESTRA LEADER

Levels: I and II

Formation: Semicircle; leader in front
Skills: Directional rhythmic

VERSE

Though there are no verses, the following commands are said:
Get ready
And
TWO COUNT
Say "one"
Say "two"
THREE COUNT
Say "one"
Say "two"
Say "three"
FOUR COUNT
Say "one"
Say "two"
Say "three"
Say "four"

MOVEMENTS

Begin each rhythm with the following:
Arms wide and to the side (Get ready)
Arms straight up and overhead (and)
Arms straight down to the thighs (one)
Arms back to overhead position (two)
Arms drop strongly down to the thighs (one)
Arms open out to the sides (two)
Arms return overhead (three)
Arms drop to the thighs (one)
Arms cross in front of the body (two)
Arms open out to the side (three)
Arms return overhead (four)

VARIATIONS AND TEACHING CUES

Movements should be sharp and strong.

OVER THE HILLS

Levels: I and II

Formation: Scattered
Skills: Rhythmic

VERSE

Over the hills and far away
We skip and run and laugh and play.
Smell the flowers and fish the streams.
Lie in the sunshine and dream sweet dreams.

MOVEMENTS

1. Make a pounding motion with hands.
2. Clap hands.
3. Sniff a flower; cast a line.
4. Sleep, cheek on hand.

ROUND AND ROUND THE VILLAGE

Level: II
Records: Folkcraft 1191; Pioneer 3001-B; World of Folk Dance 1625

Formation: Circle, facing the center with hands joined; one or more players on the outside
Skills: Directional, skip, rhythmic

VERSE

Go round and round the village,
Go round and round the village,
Go round and round the village,
As we have done before.
Go in and out the windows,
Go in and out the windows,
Go in and out the windows,
As we have done before.
Now go and choose a partner,
Now go and choose a partner,
Now go and choose a partner,
As we have done before.
Now follow me to London,
Now follow me to London,
Now follow me to London,
As we have done before.
Shake hands before you leave me,
Shake hands before you leave me,
Shake hands before you leave me,
As we have done before.

MOVEMENTS

1. Children join hands as "It" skips to the right around the outside.
2. "It" skips in and out under the raised arms ("windows").
3. "It" skips around the inside of the circle, stops, and bows or curtsies in front of a partner "It" has chosen.
4. "It" skips around inside the circle, followed by the new partner. Circle players skip in the opposite direction.
5. The circle players remain in place, clap their hands, and sing while the inside players shake hands and bow or curtsy. The chosen players then go to the outside of the circle while the other players return to the circle.

SHOO, FLY

Level: II
Records: Folkcraft 1102, 1185; Decca 1822

VERSE

Shoo, fly, don't bother me;
Shoo, fly, don't bother me.
Shoo, fly, don't bother me,
For I belong to somebody.
(Repeat all of above)
I feel, I feel,
I feel like a morning star;
I feel, I feel,
I feel like a morning star.

Formation: Circle, with partners facing center and hands joined; girls on the right side of boys
Skills: Skip, swing, sway, visual, walk
Description: The dance is in two parts and finishes with a change of partners.

MEASURES	MOVEMENTS
1–2	**1.** Partners walk forward four steps toward the center of the circle, arms swinging back and forth.
3–4	**2.** They walk four steps backward, arms swinging back and forth.
5–8	**3.** They repeat all of the above.
9–16	**4.** Each boy turns to the girl on his right, takes hold of both of her hands, and skips around in a small circle, finishing so that this girl will be on his left when the dance is re-formed. His new partner is on his right.
	5. The dance is repeated with new partners.

SKIP TO MY LOU

Level: II
Records: Victor 45-5066; Bowman Singing Games, Album 3, No. 1522-A; Folkcraft 1192-A; Folk Dancers MH111-A; Pioneer 3003-A

VERSE

Flies in the buttermilk, two by two,
Flies in the buttermilk, two by two,
Flies in the buttermilk, two by two,
Skip to my Lou my darlin'
Little red wagon painted blue. . . .
Purty as a red bird, purtier too. . . .
She is gone and I'll go too
Get me another'n as purty as you. . . .

Formation: Circle of partners
Skills: Skip, spatial, swing, sway, walk

MOVEMENTS

1. One couple chooses another player, and all three skip around in the center of the circle, while those forming the circle go the opposite way.
2. On the word "skip," the chosen player in the center skips under the arch formed by the arms of the couple in the center.
3. The original couple joins the circle while the odd dancer chooses another couple. He or she takes the new girl or boy for his or her partner.
4. They form the next arch, and the dance continues for as long as desired.

CUES

1. Walk 2, 3, 4
2. Slide 2, 3, cross-touch
3. Walk 2, 3, 4
   Slide 2, 3, cross-touch
4. Two-step . . . 8

VARIATIONS AND TEACHING HINTS

While in scattered formation (prior to assuming double circle formation) have students practice the 3 sliding steps with the toe touch and two step. Using the music at this time will facilitate smooth movement in the circle formation.

BLUEBIRD

Levels: I and II
Record: Folkcraft 1180

VERSE

Bluebird, bluebird, in and out my windows,
Bluebird, bluebird, in and out my windows,
Oh! Johnny, I am tired.

CHORUS

Take a little boy and tap him on the shoulders,
Take a little boy and tap him on the shoulders,
Oh! Johnny, I am tired.

Formation: Circle; students facing center with hands joined and held high to form arches; a chosen "bluebird" stands in the center
Skills: Walk, spatial

MOVEMENTS

1. Bluebird walks around the circle, weaving in and out under the arches.
2. Bluebird stops behind a boy.
3. Bluebird places his or her hands on the shoulders of a child and taps lightly through the chorus.
4. The dance is repeated, with the boy becoming the leader and the girl following behind with her hands on his shoulders. The game continues until all are chosen. "Jenny" is substituted for "Johnny" when girls are chosen.

CAROUSEL

Level: II
Records: World of Folk Dance 1625; Victor 45-6179; Folkcraft 1183
Formation: Double circle, all facing toward center; boys—horses inside circle, hands joined; girls—riders outside, hands on partner's shoulder
Skills: Slide, stamp, gallop, promenade

MEASURES		MOVEMENTS
1–3	**1.**	All take 14 slow slides to the left. Stamp three times (Left, Right, Left). Take 16 fast gallop slides left (CW) and 12 gallop slides right (CCW). Partners change places with four walking steps.
5–8	**2.**	Promenade CW with eight walking steps.
9–12	**3.**	Pass right shoulders, back to back; then step back to place.
13–16	**4.**	Turn to the right, face new partner, and do-si-do with eight running steps.

CUES

1. Promenade . . . 7 and turn
2. Promenade . . . 8
3. Shoulder, back, and home
4. New partner and do-si-do

CHIMES OF DUNKIRK

Levels: I and II
Records: Folkcraft 1187; Columbia A-3016; Victor 45-6176, 17327; World of Folkdance 1624
Formation: Circle, with girls and boys alternating; partners face each other with hands on own hips
Skills: Auditory, directional, slide, skip, spatial

MEASURES		MOVEMENTS
1–2	**1.**	All stamp lightly left, right, left.
3–4	**2.**	Clap hands overhead while swaying back and forth.
5–8	**3.**	Join hands with partner and make one complete turn in place CW.
9–16	**4.**	All join hands in a single circle, facing the center, and slide left 16 times.

CUES

1. L, R, L
2. Clap and sway
3. Turn 2, 3, 4
4. Slide . . . 16

COME LET US BE JOYFUL

Level: II
Records: Victor 415-6177; World of Folk Dance 1622; Folkcraft 1195; World of Fun 4-A (M102)
Formation: A large circle, with groups of three arranged like wheel spokes. Figure 16-5
Skills: Walk

MEASURES		MOVEMENTS
1–2	**1.**	Starting with left foot, walk forward three steps. Girls curtsy; boys bow.
3–4	**2.**	Starting with right foot, walk backward three steps. Girls curtsy; boys bow.
5–8	**3.**	Repeat steps 1 and 2.

9–10	**4.**	Middle child hooks right elbows with child on the left and skips four steps.
11–12	**5.**	Middle child hooks left elbows with child on the right and skips four steps.
13–16	**6.**	Repeat patterns 4 and 5.
17–20	**7.**	Repeat patterns 1 and 2.
21–22	**8.**	Threesomes walk forward eight steps, meshing through threesome facing them, passing left shoulders, and advancing to a new partner. Repeat the dance.

CUES

1. Walk forward and bow/curtsy
2. Walk backward and bow/curtsy
3. Forward . . . bow; backward . . . bow
4. Hook R, 2, 3, 4
5. Hook L, 2, 3, 4
6. Hook R, 2, 3, 4
   Hook L, 2, 3, 4
7. Walk forward and bow/curtsy; walk backward and bow/curtsy
8. Walk and pass through . . . 8

CRAZY CLOCK

Levels: I and II
Formation: Scattered
Skills: Rhythmic
Description: The children clasp their hands and swing their arms in imitation of the pendulum of a grandfather clock, the tempo of the swinging having been set beforehand. At any time during the swinging, the teacher or a child leader calls a number from one to 12, and the children strike that hour. Striking the hour must be done in exactly the same rhythm as the swing but with some kind of audible movement—a series of stamps, walks in place, claps in any direction, slaps of the thighs, or any combination of movement sounds. The swinging pendulum is then resumed without pause in the same rhythm. Some of the hour signals may be in numerical sequence, but it is more fun if they are not. The timing of the swing should always be moderate to slow in speed. As the tendency in this game is to shorten the intervals and speed up the timing, an accompaniment is indicated for the pendulum swing. This may be provided by a piano or drum or by the children themselves saying "tick-tock" as they swing.

CRESTED HEN

Level: II
Records: Folkcraft 1194, 1159; RCA 45-6176, 51619
Formation: Scattered about the room in sets of three each set forming its own circle
Skills: Step-hop, spatial

MEASURES		MOVEMENTS
		Use the step-hop throughout, all sets performing simultaneously.
1–8	**1.**	Beginning left, take eight step-hops, moving CW and leaning back while circling.
9–12	**2.**	Repeat the step-hops CCW.
	3.	Girls release their hands, putting them on their hips. Boys do not ever release their hands. Girl at left of boy does eight step-hops to move in front of him and under the arch made by the raised hands of the two dancers on the right.
13–16	**4.**	Repeat the same action, with the person on the right passing through the arch. Repeat the dance.

CUES

1. Left hop, 2 . . . 8
2. Right hop, 2 . . . 8
3. Turn, 2 . . . 8
4. Turn, 2 . . . 8

VARIATIONS AND TEACHING HINTS

Boy (or center dancer) turns under own arms as outside dancer passes under the arch.

DANCE OF GREETING

Level: II
Records: Victor 17158; Folkcraft 1187; Russell 726; World of Folk Dance 1625
Formation: Circle, facing center with hands on hips
Skills: Run, eye-hand, bow

MEASURES	MOVEMENTS
1–2	1. Clap hands twice; turn to partner and bow. Clap hands twice; turn to neighbor and bow.
3–4	2. Stamp right, stamp left; turn in place with four running steps.
1–4	3. Repeat measures 1 and 2.
5–8	4. All join hands and take 16 running steps to the right (CCW). Repeat to the left. Repeat the dance.

CUES

1. Clap, 2, and bow
   Clap, 2, and bow
2. Stamp R, L; turn 2, 3, 4
3. Clap, 2, and bow
   Clap, 2, and bow
   R, L; turn 2, 3, 4
4. Run R . . . 16
   Run L . . . 16

DANISH SCHOTTISCHE

Level: II
Record: World of Fun 4-A (M102); RCA 1622
Formation: Double circle, facing CCW; boys in outside "skaters' position" (promenade)
Skills: Schottische, step-hop.

MEASURES	MOVEMENTS
1–2	1. Schottische right and left.
3–4	2. Step-hop right, left, right, left.
5–8	3. Repeat patterns 1-2. On the last step-hop partners turn to face each other. They hold left hands.
9	4. Schottische step to the left (back to your partner).
10	5. Schottische step to the right (back to partner).
11	6. Sweep right hand in a big circular motion over partner's head; place right hands on partner's back.
12	7. Partners look at each other and turn CW with four step-hops. Repeat from the beginning.

CUES

1. Step R, L, R; hop
   Step L, R, L; hop

2. Step-hop R, L, R, L
3. Step R, L, R; hop
   Step L, R, L, R
   Step-hop R, L, R, L
4. Step L, R, L; hop
5. Step R, L, R; hop
6. Sweep
7. Turn, 2 . . . 4

FOLLOW THE BEATS

Levels: I and II
Area: Gymnasium, playground, classroom
Records: Percussion or strong rhythmic music
Formation: Children in small groups with one leader
Skills: Rhythmic
Description: The child leader performs a series of movements to the beat of the music. The group imitates the leader, changing when he or she changes and keeping the same accurate time. The leader should not change too rapidly and should include both locomotor and nonlocomotor movements.

GLOWWORM

Level: II
Records: MacGregor 310-B; Windsor 4613-B
Formation: Double circle, facing CCW; boys on inside with inside hands joined
Skills: Walk, rhythmic, promenade

MEASURES	MOVEMENTS
1–4	1. Promenade CCW with eight walking steps.
5–8	2. Promenade CW with eight walking steps.
9–12	3. Pass right shoulders, back to back; then step back to place.
13–16	4. Turn to the right, face new partner, and do-si-do with eight running steps.

CUES

1. Promenade . . . 7 and turn
2. Promenade . . . 8
3. Shoulder, back, and home
4. New partner and do-si-do

GREENSLEVEES

Level: II
Records: Victor 45-6175; World of Folk Dance 1624; *Honor Your Partner*, Album #13
Formation: Double circle, boys on inside with inside hands joined; two couples form a set, facing CCW
Skills: Directional, spatial, rhythmic, walk

MEASURES	MOVEMENTS
1–8	1. Walk CCW 16 steps.
9–12	2. Both members of couple 1 turn individually to face the couple behind them.
13–16	3. Both couples join right hands to form star position for eight steps (CW).
	4. Couples reverse and form left-hand star.
	5. Couple 1 goes back to place and faces CCW.
17–20	6. Couples 2 arches, and couple 1 backs under four steps.
	7. Couple 2 moves forward four steps.
	8. Couple 1 repeats same movements.
21–24	9. Repeat patterns 6-8.

CUES

1. Walk . . . 16
2. Turn
3. Star, 2, 3 . . . 8
4. Star L, 2, 3 . . . 8
5. Go home
6. Arch, back, 3, 4
7. Forward, 2, 3, 4
8. Arch, back, 3, 4
9. Forward, 2, 3, 4

HEADS AND SHOULDERS KNEES AND TOES

Level: I
Formation: Scattered
Skills: Body awareness

VERSE

Head shoulders, knees and toes, knees and toes
Head, shoulders, knees and toes, knees and toes
And eyes and ears and mouth and nose,
Head, shoulders, knees and toes, knees and toes.
(Repeat, eliminating vocals for each body part, one at a time.)

MOVEMENTS

Children touch body parts as called for in the song.

HOKEY POKEY

Levels: I and II
Record: Capitol 2427, 6026
Formation: Circle
Skills: Rhythmic, balance, spatial

VERSE

You put your right foot in,
You pull your right foot out,
You put your right foot in,
And you shake it all about.
You do the hokey pokey
And you turn yourself around.
That's what it's all about.
Repeat using left foot
  right hand
  left hand
  head
  back side, and so on*

MOVEMENTS

1. Act out the words.
2. Hold hands over the head, palms out, and do a type of hula while turning around.

JUMP-ROPE RHYMES

Level: II
Equipment: Jump ropes
Formation: Scattered

MAMA, MAMA

Mama, Mama, I am sick,
Send for the doctor, quick, quick, quick.
Mama, Mama, turn around,
Mama, Mama, touch the ground.

---
*Use any body part

Mama, Mama, are you through?
Mama, Mama, spell your name.
(Child performs actions indicated in the verse.)

BIRTHDAY

(Children jump while saying the following, but each child jumps out on the month of his or her birthday.)
All together, girls.
Never mind the weather, boys,
Till January, February, March. . . .

HIPPITY HOP

Hippity hop to the barber shop,
How many times before I stop?
One, two, three, etc.

BULLDOG

Bulldog, poodle, bow wow wow,
How many doggies have we now?
One, two, three, etc.

ALL IN TOGETHER

All in together, this fine weather,
January, February, March, etc.
(Jumper runs in on the month of birthday.)
All out together, this fine weather,
January, February, March, etc.
(Jumper runs out on month of birthday).

ASK MOTHER

I asked my Mother for 15 cents
To see the elephant jump the fence.
He jumped so high he reached the sky;
And never came back 'till the Fourth of July.

VOTE, VOTE

Vote, vote for dear old (name of jumper)
Calling (jumper calls another jumper in) at the door.
(Name of new jumper) is the one who has the jolly fun,
And we won't vote for (old jumper) any more.
(Old jumper runs out, leaving new jumper to continue).

BUBBLE GUM

Bubble gum, bubble gum,
Chew and blow,
Bubble gum, bubble gum,
Scrape your toe.
Bubble gum, bubble gum,
Tastes so sweet
Get that bubble gum off your feet (run out).

DOWN IN THE VALLEY

Down in the valley
Where the green grass grows
Sat little Mary as sweet as a rose.
Along came Johnny
And kissed her on the nose.
How many kisses did she get?
One, two, three, four, five, six, (and so on until a miss is made).

PEANUTS, POPCORN

Peanuts, popcorn, soda pop,
How many jumps before you stop.
Close your eyes and you will see
How many jumps that this will be!

CHICKETY CHOP

Chickety, chickety, chickety, chop,
How many times before I stop?
One, two, three, four, etc.

KEEP IT MOVING

Level: I
Formation: Circle or scattered
Skills: Body awareness

VERSE

Keep it moving, keep it moving.
I've got a hand so
keep it moving, keep it moving,
I've got a hand, so keep it moving.

MOVEMENTS

The teacher inserts various body parts and movements into the song. Once the children have learned the chant they should lead the movements.

KINDERPOLKA

Level: II
Records: World of Folk Dance 1625; Victor 45-6179; Folkcraft 1181; Pioneer 3004-B
Formation: Circle, with arms extended sideways and hands joined; partners side by side.
Skills: Slide, spatial

MEASURES		MOVEMENTS
1–2	**1.**	Take two slides toward center; stamp lightly three times.
3–4	**2.**	Take two slides away from center; stamp lightly three times.
5–8	**3.**	Repeat patterns 1 and 2.
9–10	**4.**	Slap knees once, clap hands once, and slap partners' hands three times.
11–12	**5.**	Repeat pattern 4.
13–14	**6.**	Hop, placing right heel forward; place right elbow in left hand, and shake finger three times. Repeat with left foot, shaking left finger three times.
15–16	**7.**	Turn in place with four running steps and stamp lightly three times.

CUES

1. Slide in, 2, stamp, 2, 3
2. Slide out, 2, stamp, 2, 3
3. Slide in, 2, stamp, 2, 3
Slide out, 2, stamp, 2, 3

4. Knees, hands, partner, 2, 3
5. Knees, hands, partner, 2, 3
6. Hop and shake R, 2, 3
Hop and shake L, 2, 3
7. Turn, 2, 3, 4; stamp, 2, 3

LEVELS

Levels: I and II
Area: Gymnasium, playground, classroom
Equipment: Moderate accompaniment
Formation: Scattered or lines
Description: Children walk forward for eight beats, each child on his or her own path. On the second group of eight beats everyone makes a change of level downward and comes back again to a standing position, ready to repeat the walk without pause. It is a good idea at first to assign a specific action for the level change, such as touching the floor with both elbows or touching the seat, the chin, one shoulder, the top of the head, or the upper back. The object is to lower the body and regain a standing position again on exactly the eight beats—no more, no less. Later, children may make their own level changes, and the number of beats for the two phrases may be decreased or increased. This is a good game to play in two opposing groups, one walking and the other starting with the level change. If the phrase is long enough, the lowering process may start with an extension upward.

LIMBO

Level: II
Record: Hoctor Dance Records 1608B
Equipment: Limbo pole (bamboo)
Formation: Double line
Skills: Balance
Description: A limbo pole can be set up on adjustable high-jump standards, or a stretch rope may be used. Children go under two at a time. The bar is set at the shoulder height of the smallest child in the class. Each time the class goes under, the pole is lowered two inches.

VERSE

Wiggle the ankle.
Wiggle the knee
Under the bar
Like a willow tree.

MOVEMENTS

Keep knees flexed, pelvic girdle tilted back, hips and shoulders dropped, and head back. Knees turn out and ankles roll in as knees come closer to the floor. Go forward with the rhyme.

LINE OR CIRCLE CLAP

Level: II
Area: Gymnasium, playground, classroom
Participants: Entire class, divided into groups of eight to 10
Formation: Line, closed, or open circle
Description: Children may sit or stand in one of the formations. The teacher sets the tempo for a pattern by clapping or using an instrument. The pattern may be two quarter notes and one half note or quick-quick-slow. The series is passed along, each child clapping one pattern in turn, beginning at either end of the line or open circle or any place in the closed circle. The intervals between notes and between patterns set by the leader must be maintained precisely until every child has had a turn. The tempo may be made faster in later trials. Other short series of notes may be assigned, such as a measure of four, three, or two quarter notes. The most difficult

interval to maintain precisely is that in which each child claps only one note, immediately followed by the child next to him after the appropriate interval. The game is made more difficult by substituting stamping, jumping, or any other audible movement for clapping or by tossing a beanbag or ball in succession in the exact timing of the sequence.

LUMMI STICKS

Level: II
Records: Twinson Koo-EE
Formation: Scattered
Equipment: Lummi sticks; 12-inch wands
Skills: Eye-hand, rhythmic
Description: Children sit Indian fashion facing each other about 18 to 20 inches apart. The sticks are grasped by the thumb and fingers (not the fist) around the bottom third of the stick. Routines are based on sets of six movements; each movement is completed in one count. There are many possibilities for routines. THe following basic one-count movements are presented here as suggestions. The teacher should adjust the movements to fit the skill level of the children. The children will enjoy creating their own routines.

Vertical tap: Tap both upright sticks to the floor.
Partner tap: Tap partner's stick right to right or left to left.
End tap: Tilt sticks forward or sideward and tap ends to floor.
Cross-tap: Cross hands and tap upper ends of stick to floor.
Side tap: Tap upper ends to side.
Flip: Toss one stick in the air, giving it a half turn. Catch the other end.
Tap together: Hold sticks parallel and tap together.
Toss right (or left): Toss right-hand stick to partner's right hand, at the same time receiving partner's right-hand stick.
Pass: Lay stick on the floor and pick up partner's stick.
Toss right and left: Toss quickly right to right and left to left, all in the time of one count.

Lummi routines are traditionally performed to a rhythm chant (see end of chapter for record resource). They also can be effectively performed to any 3/4 or 4/4 music deemed appropriate by the teacher.

MARCHING

Levels: I and II
Area: Gymnasium, classroom
Record: Any good march record
Formation: Scattered at first (see following patterns)
Skills: Eye-foot, directional, rhythmic
Description: The following progression should be followed when teaching marching before the formations are attempted.

1. Clap hands to the rhythm of the march music or drum.
2. Step in place, stepping first on the left foot, in time to the music.
3. Maintain good posture, head up, eyes straight ahead, rib cage up.
4. March forward in time to the music.
5. Maintain an even space in relation to the person in front.
6. Keep in step and learn the quick step-close-step to return to step.

Patterns: Levels I and II (See diagrams, page 435)

1. In a circle formation march single file, by twos, and then by threes.
2. In a square formation march single file, by twos, and then by threes. Make square turns at corners; those on the outside pivot around inside marcher.
3. See Grand March (Levels III and IV).

MAYPOLE DANCE

Level: II
Records: Victor 20990; Educational Activities-20, Folkcraft 1178, R4132
Equipment: Maypole and streamers
Formation: Circle, facing CW around a Maypole
Skills: Skip

MEASURES	MOVEMENTS
8	1. Holding streamer in inside hand, skip 16 times around circle CCW.
8	2. Face center; take four skips in toward pole, four skips backward to place, and eight skips circling in place.
8	3. Take 16 skips CW.
8	4. Face center; take four skips in toward pole, four skips backward to place, and eight skips circling in place.
16	5. Facing alternate directions, as for grand right and left, skip around circle, passing streamer over and under, "braiding" streamers around the pole.

CUES

1. Skip R . . . 16
2. Skip in, 2, 3, 4;
   skip out, 2, 3, 4;
   skip circle, 2, 3 . . . 8
3. Skip L . . . 16
4. Skip in, 2, 3, 4;
   skip out, 2, 3, 4;
   skip circle, 2, 3, . . . 8
5. Streamers around pole . . . 16

VARIATIONS AND TEACHING HINTS

Students should keep the streamers "gently" taut.

REVERSE RANKS

Level: II
Area: Gymnasium, playground
Formation: Scattered
Skills: Walk, directional, rhythmic
Description: Children walk forward to moderate timing. At the signal "four," "three," "six," and so on, the children walk that number of steps backward in the same rhythm without accompaniment; they then go forward again, with a strong accent on the first forward step. Because it is impossible to change direction immediately on the signal, the first number of the signaled count has to be another forward step, which shifts the direction from forward to backward and occurs directly after the signal. Signals may be given at irregular intervals; the same number may be given twice in succession if practice is needed. A run may be used, with the reverse taken in place or backward. This game can be played without accompaniment, the class maintaining a unison beat. A speedup in tempo should be avoided.

RHYTHMIC ECHO

Level: II
Area: Gymnasium, playground,
Equipment: Rhythm drum for the teacher
Formation: Divided into teams; sitting by rows
Skills: Eye-hand, rhythmic
Description: Each row represents a team. The teacher stands in front of each row in turn and claps out a rhythm pattern, such as *dum da da dum da da dum dum dum*. The chil-

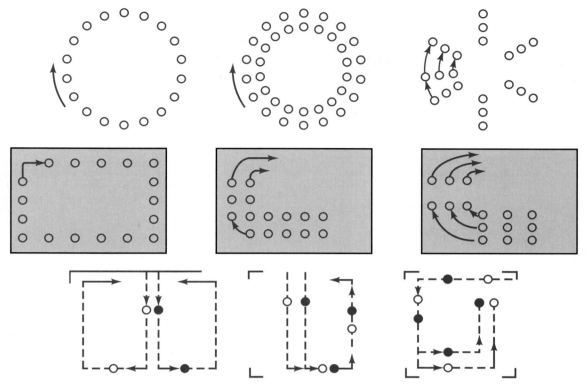

Formations for marching.

dren in the row must clap the rhythm exactly as it was given. If they succeed, their row is given a point and the teacher goes on to the next row with a different rhythm. If they fail, the teacher gives the same rhythm to the next row. After the children develop a memory for the sound patterns, they will enjoy working out movement patterns to fit the rhythm. For example, *dum da da dum da da dum dum dum* might be interpreted as step, hop, hop, step, hop, hop, leap, leap, leap. The children will be quick to offer many suggestions.

NAMES IN A RHYTHM

Level: II
Area: Gymnasium, playground, classroom
Formation: Scattered in pairs or small groups
Skills: Rhythmic, eye-hand

Description: Children say and clap their names out loud. Each name is prefaced by the statement "My name is. . . ." Attention should be paid to the long and short sounds unique to each child's name. The children should make a locomotor pattern of walks, hops, jumps, and so on to match the pattern of their name. Several children may put their names together to form a movement sequence, or they may create a song or chant around the rhythm of each name. They could try different sentences, such as "I live on . . ." and "I am . . . years old."

RADIO OR MORSE CODE SIGNALS

Level: II
Area: Gymnasium, playground, classroom
Formation: Children in two or more groups
Skills: Eye-hand

Description: This game is an extension of the echo game. The class divides into two or more groups, and each group takes the name of a city or a radio station. The accompaniment, which is the "home station," follows a pattern (coded message). It may be repeated several times before a starting

signal is given. The pattern is then picked up and clapped or stepped by each "station" in turn without pause in a predetermined order. Accurate reception throughout without blurring the pattern or accelerating the tempo indicates that no "static" is present. Any station may make a pattern and initiate the message. The patterns must be of one or more 4/4 measures, preferably ending on a quarter or half note. Otherwise it is difficult for the next group to come in promptly at the beginning of the following measure. This game may also be played with individuals instead of groups.

SCHOTTISCHE

Level: II
Records: Victor 26-0017, 4131 any moderate Schottische
Formation: Double circle, facing CCW with inside hands joined; boys on inside, or Schottische position (see Figure 16-20).
Skills: Walk, step-hop, Schottische

MEASURES		MOVEMENTS
1–2	**1.**	Beginning with the outside feet, walk three steps and hop.
3–4	**2.**	Beginning with the inside foot, walk three steps and hop.
5–8	**3.**	Beginning with the outside feet take four step-hops.

CUES

1. Walk, 2, 3, hop
2. Walk, 2, 3, hop
3. Step-hop, step-hop;
   step-hop, step-hop

VARIATIONS AND TEACHING HINTS

A number of different movement patterns can be used while the four step-hops are taken.

1. Children drop hands, turn away from each other on the four step-hops, and rejoin hands again in original position.
2. Children turn in two-hand position CW.
3. Children join both hands and execute the dishrag turn, moving CCW. Boys dip left shoulder, girls right as they turn under the joined hands, back to back, face to face. The hands are held above the head throughout the maneuver.
4. The boy kneels and girl takes the step-hops around him CCW.
5. Older students may consent to using the Schottische position.

SEVEN JUMPS

Level: II
Records: Victor 17777; Folkcraft 1163; World of Folkcraft 1623
Formation: Circle, facing in
Skills: Balance, jump, kick, skip, spatial

MEASURES	MOVEMENTS
1–16	1. Skip (slide or gallop) 16 in circle ccw.
17	2. Raise one foot off the floor, knee held high.
	3. Replace foot.
18	4. Repeat the locomotor skill; this time, raise and lower the other leg. On each repetition add an additional movement at the end.
	5. Measures 17 and 18 will be repeated for each additional movement; the last time through, the dance ends with seven movements: a. Raise one leg and lower it. b. Raise the other leg and lower it. c. Go down on one knee. d. Go down on both knees. e. Put one elbow to the floor. f. Put the other elbow to the floor. g. Touch the head to the floor.

SING A SONG OF SIXPENCE

Levels: I and II
Records: Folkcraft 1180; RCA Victor 22706
Formation: Circle facing center; six to eight children crouched in the center as "blackbirds"
Skills: Rhythmic, walk

VERSE

Sing a song of sixpence, a pocket full of rye.
Four and twenty blackbirds, baked in a pie,
When the pie was opened the birds began to sing.
Wasn't that a dainty dish to set before the king?
The king was in his counting house, counting out his money,
The queen was in the pantry, eating bread and honey,
The maid was in the garden, hanging out the clothes.
And down came a blackbird and snipped off her nose!

MOVEMENTS

1. Players walk around in a circle.
2. Circle players walk with shortened steps toward the center of the circle, with arms outstretched forward.
3. Players walk backward with arms up. The blackbirds in the center fly around.
4. Circle players kneel as if presenting a dish (blackbirds continue to fly around).
5. Pantomime action of words; counting out money, eating, and hanging up clothes.
6. Each blackbird snips off the nose of a circle player, who then becomes a blackbird for the next game.

THE WHEAT

Level: II
Records: Victor 45-6182; RCA Victor 1625
Formation: Sets of three, facing CCW around a circle
Skills: Walk, skip

MEASURES	MOVEMENTS
1–4	1. All walk forward 16 bouncy steps.
5–8	2. The middle child hooks right elbow with child on the right. Together, they skip eight steps in a circle in place.
8–12	3. The middle child hooks left elbow with child on the left. Together, they skip six steps in circle in place.
12–16	4. During the last two skips, the middle child moves forward one set to new partners.

CUES

1. Walk, 2, 3 . . . 16
2. Swing R . . . 8
3. Swing L . . . 8
4. New partner

THIS IS THE CIRCLE THAT IS MY HEAD

Level: I
Formation: Scattered or in a line
Skills: Body awareness

VERSE

This is the circle that is my head.
This is my mouth with which words are said.
These are my eyes with which I see.
This is my nose that's a part of me.
This is the hair that grows on my head.
This is my hat all pretty and red.
This is the feather so bright and gay.
Now I'm all ready for school, today.

MOVEMENTS

1. Raise arms above head to make a circle.
2. Point to mouth.
3. Point to eyes.
4. Point to nose.
5. Point to hair.
6. Put hands on head and make a pointed hat.
7. Use pointing finger to make a feather.

THREES AND SEVENS

Level: II
Formation: Scattered or in lines
Skills: Rhythmic, directional
Description: A common sequence in folk dance involves movement to two, threes, and seven to a 16-beat phrase. There is a pause after each three and seven. When counted out it sounds like this: one, two, three, pause, five, six, seven, pause; one, two, three, four, five, six, seven, pause. Children can then move to this pattern. They walk forward three steps, clap, and repeat; then they walk seven steps forward and clap. An inaudible body movement can be substituted for the clap. The children can experiment by moving in different directions—forward, backward, and sideward. An accompaniment can be added, and the children can invent their own sequences.

Table 16-5

Levels III–IV—Dances.

Dance	Origin	Skill (s)	Formation	Record
		Level III		
The Bird Dance	Europe	Walk, skip, elbow swing, star	Circle or scattered	Avia Disk AD-831-A
Grand March	USA	Rhythmic, skip, spatial, walk, two-step	Line	Any march or square dance record
Gustaf's Skoal	Sweden	Walk, skip, turn	Square	WOF 7-B (M102), WII
Hora	Israel	Grapevine, swing, hop, kick	Circle	WFD 1623; RCA-EPA-4140; FK-1110, 1106, 1118
Hopp Mor Anika	Sweden	Step-hop, skip, polka	Circle (P)	WFD 1624; RCA 4142
Kalvelis	Lithuania	Polka	Circle (P)	WOF 7-B (M101)
Klumpakojis	Lithuania	Polka	Double circle (P)	FK 1416; WFD 1624
Mayim! Mayim!	Israel	Walk, hop, grapevine	Circle	WOF 6-B (M119); FK 1108
Uno, Dos, Tres	USA	Bleking	Line	DWP EA 32
		Level IV (Beginning)		
Ace of Diamonds	Denmark	Back to back, Bleking, polka, elbow swing	Circle (P)	WFD 1622; WOF 4-A (M102)
Norwegian Mountain March	Norway	Waltz, run, turn	Sets of three	WFD 1622; FK 1177
Oh, Susanna	USA	Slide, skip, grand right and left	Circle (P)	WFD 1623; FK 1186; RCA-EPA 4140
Patty-Cake Polka	USA	Heel-toe, slide, skip	Circle (P)	FK 1260; WOF 1-B (M107); WFD 1625
Tantoli	Sweden	Heel-toe, polka, step-hop	Circle (P)	WFD 1621
		Level IV (Intermediate)		
All-American Promenade	USA	Walk, balance	Circle (P)	FK 1061
Alunelul	Romania	Grapevine, stomp	Circle	FK 1549; FD-MH-1120
Cherkassiya	Israel	Grapevine, step-hop	Circle	RCA EPA 4140; WFD 1623
Cotton-Eyed Joe	USA	Heel-toe polka, two-step, chug	Free or line (P)	WOF 2-A (M118); WFD 1621 FK 1255
Cshebogar	Hungary	Walk, skip, slide, Hungarian turn, buzz	Circle (P)	WFD 1624; WOF 6-A (M101)
Little Man in a Fix	Denmark	Waltz, run, turn, draw step	Sets of two couples	WOF 4-B (M121)
Lott 1st Tod	Sweden	Slide, face-to-face and back-to-back polka	Circle (P)	WFD 1622
Milanovo Kolo	Yugoslavia	Step-hop, grapevine	Circle	WFD 1620
Put Your Little Foot		Sweep step, point, walk	Circle (P)	FK 1165; WOF 1-B (M107)

Dance	Origin	Skill(s)	Formation	Record
Romunsko Kolo	Yugoslavia	Schottische, rock, step-hop	Circle	FK 1402; W-Vol. 3
Susan's Gavotte	USA	Walk, slide, step swing, two-step	Circle (P)	"Lili Marlene," WOF 1-A (M113) FK 1096
Teton Mountain Stomp	USA	Walk, two-step	Circle (P)	FK 1482
Tinikling	Philippine Islands	Tinikling steps	Sets of three	WFD 1619
Turkey in the Oven	USA	Grand right and left	Circle	EA 20
Wearin' O' the Green	USA	Allemande, do-si-do, promenade	Square, circle	EA 20

Level IV (Advanced)

Dance	Origin	Skill(s)	Formation	Record
Brown-Eyed Mary	USA	Walk, skip, promenade, turn	Circle (P)	WOF-3-A (M117); any lively polka
Buggy Schottische	USA	Schottische	Sets of four	WFD 1620
Irish Washerwoman	Ireland	Grand right and left, allemande left, promenade	Square (P)	RCA EPA 4140; WFD 1623
Kool Kat	USA	Walk, skip, turn	Varsouviene (P)	MH-39
Korobushka	Russia	Schottische, balance, 3-step turn	Free (P)	WOF 3-B (M108); FK 1170
Miserlou	Greece	Step-point, grapevine pivot, walk	Line, circle	WFD 1620; W-Vol. 5 FK-1060
Rye Waltz	USA	Slide, waltz, walk, skip	Circle (P)	FK 1103

CR = Childhood Rhythms
DWP = Dances Without Partners
EA = Educational Activities
FK = Folkraft
HOC = Hoctor
Kim = Kimbo
MH = Melody House
(P) = Denotes partners required
R = Russell

RCA = RCA Victor
WFD = World of Folk Dance
W = White Rhythms Productions
WOF = World of Fun

Listings and descriptions are arranged by approximate developmental level and in alphabetical order within each level.

The reference to beginning, intermediate, and advanced in Levels III and IV dances is an attempt to indicate difficulty *within* these two levels. The teacher is encouraged to make these decisions for the specific learners' experience in dance. Some of the dances in Levels III and IV will take considerable practice to achieve the fluidity of movement desired. However, students must feel that they are progressing at the end of each class setting.

Explanation of Activity Descriptions for Levels III–IV

A comprehensive listing of dances for Levels III–IV can be found in Table 16-5.

The reader will note that detailed cues are given for each dance and in most descriptions the measure count is also provided. The measure indicators provide a valuable learning tool for the teacher as steps and music must articulate for the successful performance of the dance. The cues are for the students' benefit and they should be encouraged to chant the cues along with the teacher. The brevity of the cues is to aid the verbalization of the rhythm as well as to assist with the memory of the step sequence.

ACE OF DIAMONDS

Levels: IV (Beginning)
Records: FK 1176; WOF 4A (102); World of Folk Dance 1622
Formation: Double circle, partners facing each other.
Skills: Walk, elbow swing, bleking, skip, polka

MEASURES	MOVEMENTS
1	1. Clap hands once; stamp left foot. Hook right elbows and swing around once with six skipping steps.
2–4	2. Clap hands once, stamp right foot. Hook left elbows and swing around once with six skipping steps. Face partners, hands on hips.
9–12	3. Hop on left foot, extending right leg forward so right heel is on the floor (pause). Repeat with a right-foot hop, extending left leg, heel to the floor (pause). Repeat for four hops with no pause in between.
13–16	4. Repeat all of the hopping sequence.
17–24	5. Join partners' hands and move CCW with 16 skips.

CUES

1. Clap, stamp left, 2 . . . 6
2. Clap, stamp right, 2 . . . 6
3. Right pause, left pause, and right and left and right and left; right pause, left pause, and right and left and right and left
4. R pause, L pause, and R and L and R and L R pause, L pause, and R and L and R and L
5. Skip 16

VARIATIONS

1. The skips can be replaced by polkas.
2. For the 16 skips (eight polkas) at the end, students can assume the skaters' position or shoulder-waist position.
3. There are *many* versions of "Ace of Diamonds".
4. This dance can be used as a mixer by allowing the inside partner to move forward one position on the last four skips (two polkas).

ALL-AMERICAN PROMENADE

Level: IV (Intermediate)
Records: Folkcraft 1061
Formation: Double circle facing line of direction (CCW)
Skills: Walk, balance, left and right face turns

MEASURES	MOVEMENTS
1–2	1. Facing CCW, inside hands joined and beginning with the outside foot, walk four steps forward (CCW); on fourth step turn toward partner to face reverse line of direction (CW) and join inside hands. Walk four steps backward (CCW).
3–4	2. Repeat 1 and 2 in reverse line of direction (CW). Begin with four steps forward (CW) and continue through pattern.
5	3. Inside hands joined and free hand on waist, balance apart (1, 2) and together with partner (3, 4). Face line of direction during balance.
6	4. Girl does a left-face turn (four steps), crossing in front of boy. Boy uses four steps to move to his right, crossing behind girl. Release hands during turn; rejoin inside hands at end of turn.
7	5. Join inside hands: balance with partner together (1, 2) and apart (3, 4).
8	6. Raise joined hands. Girl does right face turn under arms, moving back four steps to new partner. Boy moves forward four steps to new partner.

CUES

1. Forward, 2, 3, turn
   Back, 2, 3, *turn*
2. Forward, 2, 3, turn
   Back, 2, 3, *turn*
3. Apart, 2, together, 4
4. Cross, turn, 3, 4
5. Together, 2, apart, 4
6. Turn to new partner

VARIATIONS AND TEACHING HINTS

1. In step 6, various patterns from simple to complex can be used to move to a new partner. This offers an excellent opportunity to allow the students to demonstrate some creativity.
2. Children should show a good change of level on the balance step by rising to the balls of their feet.
3. This dance will fit to almost any march-like tune.

ALUNELUL

Levels: IV (Intermediate)
Records: Folkcraft 1549; Folk Dancer MH-1120
Formation: Single circle, facing center; hands on shoulders; arms straight
Skills: Grapevine, stomp

MEASURES	MOVEMENTS
1–2	1. Take five steps plus two stomps: Sidestep right, cross left behind, sidestep right, cross left behind, sidestep right, stomp twice with left foot.
3–4	2. Beginning with the left foot, repeat the action, moving left.
5–8	3. Repeat patterns 1 and 2.
9–10	4. Take three steps plus one stomp: Sidestep right, cross left behind, sidestep right. Sidestep left, cross right behind, sidestep left, stomp with the right foot.
11–12	5. Repeat pattern 4.
13–14	6. In place, step right, stomp left, step left, stomp right, step right, stomp left, stomp left.
15–16	7. Beginning left, repeat pattern 6.

CUES

1. 5 + 2 R, cross L, R, cross L, R, stomp L, stomp L
2. 5 + 2 L, cross R, L, cross R, L, stomp R, stomp R
3. 5 + 2 moving R
   5 + 2 moving L
4. 3 + 1 R, cross L, R, stomp L, L, cross R, L, stomp R
5. 3 + 1
   3 + 1
6. In place R, stomp L, L, stomp R, R, stomp L, stomp L
7. In place L, stomp R, R, stomp L, L, stomp R, stomp R

VARIATIONS AND TEACHING HINTS

1. Alunelul is pronounced "ah-loo-NAY-loo." This dance is called "Little Hazelnut," and the stomping action depicts the breaking of the hazelnuts.
2. Stomps should be made close to the supporting foot.
3. The dance should be taught in scattered formation—then in a circle, children just holding hands. Hands on the shoulders requires more skill and should be presented only after the children can dance confidently.

THE BIRD DANCE

Level: III
Records: Avia Disk AD-831-A
Formation: Circle or scattered, with or without partners
Skills: Walk, skip, elbow swing

MEASURES	MOVEMENTS
1	1. If in couples, face partners. Snap fingers four times.
2	2. Flap arms (hands in armpits) four times.
3	3. Do wiggle the hips (knees bent, body low) four times.
4	4. Clap hands four times.
5–16	5. Repeat 1–4 three more times
17–20	6. With a partner take 16 walks or skips in.
	7. Repeat 1–6.

BROWN-EYED MARY

Level: IV (Advanced)
Records: World of Fun 3-A (M117); any lively polka
Formation: Circle, couples facing CCW, promenade position
Skills: Promenade, turns

VERSE

If perchance, we should meet on the wide, wide prairie,
In my arms would I embrace my darling brown-eyed Mary.

Turn your partner halfway 'round.
Turn your opposite lady.
Turn your partner all th' way 'round
And take the forward lady.

MEASURES		MOVEMENTS
1–8	**1.**	Couples promenade CCW until next pattern is called.
9–12	**2.**	Partners face, join right hands, and do a half turn. (The boy is now on the outside of circle, facing CW; the girl is on the inside, facing CCW.)
13–16	**3.**	They drop hands. The boy gives his left hand to the girl who was behind him in the promenade; they make one turn.
17–20	**4.**	Moving CCW, the boy gives his right hand to his partner, and they make one full turn.
21–28	**5.**	Continuing CCW, the boy moves on to a new partner and promenades.

CUES

1. Promenade
2. Partner turn
3. Corner turn
4. Partner turn
5. New partner

VARIATIONS AND TEACHING HINTS

The corner girl position should be taught carefully. Wrist bands on the girls' left wrists may help cue which girl is the corner girl.

BUGGY SCHOTTISCHE

Level: IV (Advanced)
Records: World of Folk Dance 1620
Formation: Two couples per each set, all facing same direction, one couple behind the other; partners hold outside hands with other couple (Figure 16-20A).
Skills: Schottische, "buggy figures"

MEASURES		MOVEMENTS
		All in the set perform the steps simultaneously.
1–2	**1.**	Beginning with outside feet, do two Schottische steps.
3–4	**2.**	Step-hop four forward.
5–6	**3.**	Repeat pattern 1.
7–8	**4.**	While doing the four step-hops (front couple), drop own hands (keep hand contact with back couple) and "cast off" (Figure 16-20b), moving behind back couple and rejoining hands.
9–10	**5.**	Repeat pattern (with new lead couple). Continue the dance, executing different patterns during the four step-hops, causing a change of lead couples each time.

CUES

1. Step, 2, 3, hop
  Step, 2, 3, hop
2. Step-hop, 2, 3, 4
3. Step, 2, 3, hop
  Step, 2, 3, hop
4. Front break, 2, 3, 4
5. Step, 2, 3, hop
  Step, 2, 3, hop

FIGURE 16-20A
Buggy Schottische, starting position

VARIATIONS AND TEACHING HINTS

1. The following variations will be appropriate:
  Back break: the back couple drops their own hands and moves forward, turning under the outside arms of the front couple and rejoining hands as the new front couple (Figure 16-20B).
  Back arch: without dropping hands, front couple backs under the arch made by the back couple. Back couple turns under their own arms as front couple passes by. This twisting turn is referred to as "wringing the dishrag."
  Front arch: without dropping hands, back couple moves forward under the front arch, with front couple wringing the dishrag.
2. Only on break variations are any of the hands unclasped.
3. To keep everyone in step, it is best to do patterns 1 and 2 in between each of the variations.
4. One person in each "buggy" should call the commands for the variations.

CHERKASSIYA

Level: IV (Intermediate)
Records: World of Folk Dance 1623; RCA EPA 4140
Formation: Single circle, closed or broken; no hands joined throughout
Skills: Grapevine, step-hop

FIGURE 16-20B
Buggy Schottische, break

MEASURES		MOVEMENTS
1–8	1.	Chorus: moving to the left (CCW), the grapevine, crossing right foot in front of left with a stamp; steps to side with left. Step right and cross behind left; step to side left. Repeat pattern three more times.
9–16	2.	All step to side right; the left leg extends and then quickly crosses behind the right, taking the weight and bending both knees slightly. This is almost a running step (two steps for each measure). Repeat seven more times.
17–24	3.	Repeat chorus (pattern 1).
25–32	4.	Continue holding hands; all face right (CCW); beginning right, take eight step-hops and extend free leg in back on each; this should resemble a horse trotting.
8	5.	Repeat chorus (pattern 1).
	6.	Circle, moving to right, feet held together, weight on heels; move toes to the right, then both heels to the right with weight on toes; maintain contact with the floor. Repeat seven more times.
8	7.	Repeat chorus (pattern 1).
	8.	Beginning right, kick feet forward, alternating for 16 kicks.
8	9.	Repeat chorus (pattern 1).
	10.	Kick feet backward, alternating 16 times.
8	11.	Repeat chorus (pattern 1).
8	12.	Still holding hands, turn to right (CW). In a semicrouched position shuffle 16 steps. Repeat the dance.

CUES

1. Chorus: Cross R, L, back R, L, (repeat three more times)
2. Right, cross L, 2 . . . 8
3. Chorus
4. Step-hop, 2 . . . 8
5. Chorus
6. Toes, heels, toes, heels, 3 . . . 8
7. Chorus
8. Kick R, L, 3 . . . 16
9. Chorus
10. Back R, L, 3 . . . 16
11. Chorus
12. Shuffle . . . 16

VARIATIONS AND TEACHING HINTS

1. The chorus (pattern 1) and each verse should be taught separately and put together after two verses are learned: chorus, verse, chorus, verse, chorus. Gradually more verses are added. It is best not to teach this entire dance in one day because the students should be really familiar with two or three verses and the rhythm before more verses are added. Though the dance seems complex, it is not and can be enjoyed by beginners.
2. The dance movements should suggest the movements of horse and rider.
3. Hands can also be placed on shoulders or joined behind the back of the adjacent dancer, gripping hands of the next dancer.
4. This can also be danced in facing lines, after the steps are learned.
5. In the chorus; dancers always move to the left (CCW).
6. The chorus and each step pattern require eight measures of music. There are six different step patterns (2, 4, 6, 8, 10, 12).
7. In patterns 8 and 10, dancers face the center.

COTTON-EYED JOE—TEXAS STYLE

Level: IV (Intermediate)
Records: World of Fun 2-A (M 118); Folkraft 1255; World of Folk Dance 1621
Formation: Line; partner not necessary
Skills: Polka

MEASURES		MOVEMENTS
1–2	1.	Begin with two kicks of the right foot. The first small kick is across the left foot and pulling backward. The second kick is forward.
3–4	2.	Beginning with the right foot, take three running steps backward.
5–6	3.	Beginning with the left foot, kick twice, as in step 1.
7–8	4.	Beginning with the left foot, take three running steps backward.
9–16	5.	Repeat steps 1–4.
17–24	6.	Beginning with the right foot, take eight polka steps forward.

CUES

1. Right kick, 2
2. Back, 2, 3
3. Left kick, 2
4. Back, 2, 3
5. Same as 1–4
6. Polka 2, 3, 4, 5, 6, 7, 8

VARIATIONS AND TEACHING HINTS

The polka step can be replaced by the two-step, with the second step being a cross behind (country western style).

CSHEBOGAR

Level: IV (Intermediate)
Records: World of Folk Dance 1624; Folkraft 1196; World of Fun 6-A(M-101)
Formation: Single circle, partners facing center, hands joined; girls on boys' right
Skills: Slides, step-draw, skip, buzz

MEASURES		MOVEMENTS
1–4	1.	Slide eight steps to the left (CW).
5–8	2.	Repeat to the right (CCW).
9–12	3.	While raising arms high, walk three steps to center and stamp on fourth. While lowering arms, walk three steps backward and stamp on fourth.
13–16	4.	Face partners, right hands joined; beginning left, walk eight steps (CW) to turn.
17–20	5.	Face partners, both hands joined, arms extended out to side. Take four draw steps (step, close) toward the center of the circle, not putting weight on the last step. Move arms up and down slowly (like a moth).
21–24	6.	Take four draw steps back to periphery of circle.
25–26	7.	In a single circle, hands joined, all facing center, and beginning right, cautiously take four small steps toward center (bent over like a moth creeping up on the fire, arms moving slowly up and down).
27–28	8.	Beginning right, run backward with eight running steps, hands fluttering above heads.
29–32	9.	Turn partners as in step 4. Finish in a circle, all facing center.

CUES

1. Slide left . . . 8
2. Slide right . . . 8
3. Center, 2, 3, stamp; back, 2, 3, stamp
4. Right turn, 2, 3 . . . 8
5. In, 2, 3 . . . 8
6. Out, 2, 3 . . . 8
7. In, 2, 3, 4
8. Out fast, 3, 4, 5, 6, 7, 8
9. Right turn, 2, 3 . . . 8

VARIATIONS AND TEACHING HINTS

1. On turns, the walk can be replaced with skips; the Hungarian turn (right arms around waists, left arms raised high) can replace the right-hand turn.
2. Movement in and out of the circle can be regular walks, draw steps, or skips.
3. The dance is meant to simulate the movement of moths being attracted to a flame and then escaping, only to try again.

GRAND MARCH

Levels: III and IV
Records: World of Fun 5-B (M116); any lively polka, two-step, or march
Formation: Girls on left side of room, boys on right side, all facing the foot of the hall; first couple is the lead couple
Skills: Walk, grand march figures

MEASURES

The size of the group will determine the length of music needed.

MOVEMENTS

1. March toward the foot of hall and turn toward the opposite line; upon meeting, march up the hall couple by couple.
2. As the couples get to the head of the hall, the odd-numbered couples go right and the even-numbered couples go left, meeting at the foot of the hall.
3. Form foursomes and march up the hall four abreast.
4. At the head of the hall the foursomes break, one couple casting off to the left and the other to the right.
5. At the foot of hall, the lead couple forms an arch.
6. Each couple goes under the arch and then becomes part of the "arch tunnel" by forming its own arch.
7. At leader's discretion, the couples coming out of the tunnel of arches cast off right and left.
8. As lead couples get to the foot of the hall, they crisscross with the oncoming couple so that they lead their sides into a circle formation. Each couple will crisscross; the lines will be moving alongside each other but going in opposite directions.
9. Dancers end up in a large single circle.

CUES

1. March around and meet at the foot of the hall; come up the center in twos
2. Break by twos, R and L
3. Come up the center in fours
4. Break by twos, R and L
5. Arch and tunnel
6. Arch and tunnel
7. Cast off in twos, R and L
8. Crisscross and make a grand circle.

VARIATIONS AND TEACHING HINTS

1. Many geometric "traffic" variations can be created.
2. A "traffic director" is needed at all times.
3. By using more vigorous locomotor patterns such as slides and skips, the grand march can be used as a vigorous aerobic warmup.
4. Depending on the level of the children, the grand march can be simple or complex. Even adults enjoy the Grand March. (See diagram pp. 680)

GUSTAF'S SKOAL

Level: III
Records: W. White, *Rhythms Productions*, Vol II; World of Fun 7B (M 102)
Formation: Set of four couples, as in square dancing; girl on left of boy, inside hands joined, outside hands on hips
Skills: Walk, skip, turn

MEASURES	MOVEMENTS
1–2	1. Head couples forward three steps, bow, and move three steps back to place and bow to each other.
3–4	2. Side couples walk forward three steps, bow, and move back three steps to place and bow.
5–8	3. Dancers repeat steps 1 and 2.
9–12	4. Side couples raise inside joined hands to form an arch. Head couples skip to the center; meet; drop partners' hands; and taking inside hand of facing dancer, skip through the nearest arch. After passing under the arch they drop hands, peek around at their partners, and skip back home toward their original partners (eight counts).
13–16	5. All clap on first count of measure 13 (just before reaching partners). All join both hands, lean away from each other, and skip once around (CW).
17–20	6. All repeat step with head couples forming an arch.
21–24	7. This is the same as step 5.

CUES

1. Head couples forward 2, 3, bow; back 2, 3, bow
2. Sides 2, 3, bow; back 2, 3, bow
3. Forward, 2, 3, bow; back 2, 3, bow; forward 2, 3, bow; back, 2, 3, bow
4. Sides arch, 2, 3, split 5, 6 . . . 8
5. Clap, skip, 3, 4, 5 . . . 8
6. Heads arch, 2, 3, split 5, 6 . . . 8
7. Clap, skip, 3, 4, 5 . . . 8

VARIATIONS AND TEACHING HINTS

1. The first part of the dance is slow, stately, and quiet; it should represent royalty.
2. The second part is faster and lighter and represents the fun and frolic of the peasant class; it can also be noisy.

HOPP MOR ANIKA

Level: III
Records: Victor 21618; RCA 4142 World of Folk Dance 1624
Formation: Double circle; partners facing with inside hands joined
Skills: Bow, skip, stamp, polka

MEASURES	MOVEMENTS
1–8	**1.** Bow to partners and face CCW. Beginning right, walk 16 steps CCW, arms swinging forward and backward.
9–16	**2.** Beginning right, skip in the same direction, stop, and face partners.
17–20	**3.** Stamp the right foot and clap right hands with partner. Stamp the left foot and clap left hands with partner. Stamp right and clap both hands with partner. Stamp left and clap own hands.
21–24	**4.** Repeat pattern 3.
25–32	**5.** Join inside hands and polka 16 steps to the right.
	6. Repeat the dance, boys moving ahead (CCW) one partner on "Introduction."

CUES

1. Walk, 2, 3, . . . 16
2. Skip, 2, 3 . . . 15, face
3. Stamp R, clap R, stamp L, clap L, stamp R, clap both, stamp L, clap own
4. Repeat cue 3
5. Polka, 2, 3 . . . 16
6. New partners

VARIATIONS AND TEACHING HINTS

1. The Polka of step 5 can be changed to 16 two-steps. Once students learn the dance, the two-step can be replaced with the polka.
2. After the first time through the dance, the bow is eliminated and the time is used for the boys to move ahead (CCW) to their new partners. During this time the girls can perform a two-step in place.

HORA (Hava Nagila)

Level: III
Records: World of Folk Dance 1623; any recording of *Hava Nagila*; Folkraft 1106, 1110, 1118, 1122
Formation: Circle; hands on shoulders
Skills: Step-hop, grapevine, kick

MEASURES	MOVEMENTS
1–3	**1.** Moving CCW, step side right, cross left behind right, step right, kick left diagonally to right, step left, and kick right.
	2. Repeat this pattern throughout the dance. The tempo builds from slow to fast.

CUES

1. Step, cross, step, kick, step, kick
2. Step, cross, step, kick, step, kick

VARIATIONS AND TEACHING HINTS

1. The word *Hora* means tempo or movement. *Hava Nagila* means "Come, let us be gay," and the dance should be danced with building enthusiasm.
2. As the tempo becomes faster, the steps should be performed with more vigor (i.e., each step becomes a tiny hop that builds to a larger hop).
3. Dancers should extend their arms (holding their own weight) and lean slightly back, keeping their heads up.
4. Toward the end of the dance, the hop prior to the kick can be made more vigorous by hopping on two feet (jump) on the first hop. The cue would be "jump," "kick."

5. The dance may be danced either to the right (CCW) or to the left (CW). Steps are reversed to the left.
6. Large groups should form concentric circles. Alternating circles can dance clockwise (begin right) and CCW (begin left).
7. Dancing with hands joined requires less skill than hands on shoulders.

IRISH WASHERWOMAN

Level: IV (Advanced)
Records: WFD 1623 or any good reel
Formation: Square sets of four couples, girls on right, all facing center
Skills: Balance, allemande left, grand right and left

CALL

1. All four gents to the right of the ring and when you get there you balance and swing.
2. Now allemande left with your corner, all and grand right and left around the hall.
3. Now promenade first girl.

MOVEMENTS

1. Boys step behind partners' place, "balance," and swing once in with next girl on the right. The new partner finishes on the boy's right.
2. Facing the corner, allemande left, followed by grand right and left; continue until boys meet their original partners.
3. Finish with a promenade.

VARIATION (SIMPLE)

1. All join hands and skip to the middle.
2. Let your foot pat-a-pat in time to the fiddle.
3. And when you get back listen well to my call.
4. Swing your corner girl and promenade the hall.

MOVEMENTS

1. Take four steps to the center.
2. Stamp two slow and three fast in place.
3. Return to place with four backward steps.
4. Swing the corner girl and promenade CCW.

VARIATIONS AND TEACHING HINTS

1. Many variations can be used. For example, the girls can begin the dance by executing the same action as the boys. "All ladies to the right. . . ."
2. An interesting introduction is the following: "All into the center and give a big shout, back to your places and circle about."

KALVELIS

Level: III
Records: Folkcraft 1051A; World of Fun 7-B (M101) White III
Formation: Single circle; partners, girls on the right
Skills: Polka

MEASURES	MOVEMENTS
1–4	**1.** Join hands and circle right (CCW) with eight polka steps.
5–8	**2.** Circle left (CW) with eight polka steps.
	3. Chorus: Face partners.

9–10	Hammering—Hammer hands, beginning with the left hand on top (left, right, left, right) (four counts). (Figure 16-21).
11–12	Turn—Link right elbows and turn halfway around with two polka steps, starting with the left foot.
13–14	Hammering—Repeat as above, beginning with the right hand on top (right, left, right, left) (four counts).
15–16	Turn—Link left elbows and turn halfway around with two polka steps, starting with the right foot.
17–24	Repeat the entire chorus (measures 9–16).

4. Beginning with the right foot, girls move to center with three light polka steps and stamp three times lightly and quickly (left, right, left).

5. Turn quickly, and with three light polka steps, move back to periphery of circle and stamp three times (left, right, left).

6. Boys repeat pattern 4 and 5, using heavier polka steps.

7. Repeat chorus, as in step 3.

8. Face partners, join right hands, and do a grand right and left around the circle, using 16 polka steps. Having ended with a new partner, repeat the chorus.

9. Repeat chorus, as in step 3.

CUES

1. Circle right, 2, 3, 4 . . . 8
2. Circle left, 2, 3, 4 . . . 8
3. Hammer left, right, left, right
   Turn right, 2
   Hammer right, left, right, left
   Turn left, 2
   Hammer left, right, left, right
   Turn right, 2
   Hammer right, left, right, left
   Turn left, 2
4. Girls in (pause), stamp 2, 3
5. Girls out (pause), stamp 2, 3
6. Boys in (pause), stamp 2, 3
   Boys out (pause), stamp 2, 3
7. Chorus: Hammer left . . . etc.
8. Grand right and left . . . 16

VARIATIONS AND TEACHING HINTS

1. *Kalvelis* means "little smith." The actions of the chorus imitate the blacksmith at the forge.
2. In patterns 4 and 5 girls can swish skirts.
3. In pattern 6 boys may fold their arms on their chests.

FIGURE 16-21
Kalvelis—"Hammering"

KLUMPAKOJIS

Level: III
Records: Folkraft 1416; World of Folk Dance 1624
Formation: Double circle; inside hands joined at shoulder height; outside hand on hips
Skills: Walk, polka

MEASURES	MOVEMENTS
1–4	1. Beginning with outside feet, take eight brisk steps CCW, turning toward partner to face CW direction on last step.
5–8	2. Beginning with inside feet, join inside hands at shoulder height, outside hands on hips; take eight brisk steps moving CW.
9–16	3. Face partner and join right hands, head high, elbows bent, left hand on hip; take eight steps, turning CW. Clap on eighth count, join left hands, and again turn around, this time moving CCW for eight steps; clap on eighth count.
17–20	4. Wait two counts (1 and 2 and); then stamp three.
21–24	5. Wait two counts, and then clap hands three times.
25–28	6. Hold right elbow in left hand and shake right forefinger at partner (as though scolding) for three counts; pause (one count). Shake left forefinger at partner for three counts; pause. Clap right hand of partner and turn alone CCW in place one full turn. Face partner and quickly stamp feet three times.
29–36	7. Repeat steps 4, 5, and 6.
	8. In varsouvienne position, beginning left, take 16 polka steps forward (CCW). On the last two polka steps, boys move forward to new partners.

CUES

1. Walk, 2, 3 . . . 7 and turn
2. Walk, 2, 3 . . . 7 and turn
3. Turn 2, 3 . . . 7 and clap
   Turn 2, 3 . . . 7 and clap
4. Wait 2, and stamp 2, 3
5. Wait 2, and clap 2, 3
6. Shake R, 2, 3; shake L, 2, 3
   Turn (or swing or duck) 2, 3
   Stamp 2, 3
   Shake R, 2, 3; shake L, 2, 3
   Turn (or swing or duck) 2, 3
   Stamp 2, 3
7. Repeat 4, 5, and 6
8. Polka 2, 3 . . . 16

VARIATIONS AND TEACHING HINTS

1. This is one of the "finger-polka" (shaking finger at partner) folk dances, and there are many clever variations.
2. The walking steps of patterns 1–3 can be taken as scuff steps (scuffing the heel just prior to the firm step).
3. In pattern 5 the partners can pretend to try and slap one another as they turn. The first time the outside dancer swings the right arm as if to hit the partner, who ducks (squats) while the outside partner completes a pivot turn to be left. The next time the inside partner swings while the other ducks (squats).
4. This dance is sometimes refered to as "wooden shoes." The term *Klumpakojis* actually translates as "wooden footed" or "clumsy footed."

KOOL KAT

Level: IV (Advanced)
Records: Melody House, No. 39
Formation: Scattered or circle, facing CCW; varsouvienne
Skills: Walk, skip, turn

MEASURES	MOVEMENTS
1	**1.** Begin right, step right, cross left behind, step right, and kick left.
2	**2.** Step left, cross right behind, step left, and kick right.
3–4	**3.** Step forward right, lifting left knee up; step forward left, lifting right knee up. Repeat for two more steps, finishing with weight on the left foot. (This is to simulate a skipping motion.)
5–8	**4.** Repeat patterns 1-3.
9	**5.** Touch right heel forward and back to place; touch left heel forward and back to place.
10	**6.** With weight on toes and feet together, move heels apart and then click them together, stomp right foot in place; stomp left foot in place.
11–14	**7.** Step forward right, lifting left knee up; step forward left, lifting right knee up. Repeat for two more steps, finishing with weight on the left foot.
15–20	**8.** Repeat patterns 5-7. For "Salty-Dog Rag" steps,
21	**9.** Face partners, drop right hands, and repeat step 1: Step right, cross left behind, step right, and kick left. If dance is being performed in a circle, partners will finish with the boys facing out and the girls facing in.
22	**10.** Dropping left hands, take three steps to turn across front of partner (partners now have exchanged places) and kick right. Finish in a right-hand star with partner.
23–24	**11.** Beginning right, walk four steps while turning the star (CW).
25–26	**12.** Repeat patterns 9 and 10.
27–28	**13.** In the star formation the boy walks around the girl while the girl takes four small steps back to original position; each step equals two counts.

CUES

1. R, cross L, R, kick
2. L, cross R, L, kick
3. Forward R, and L, and R, and L
4. R, cross L, R, kick
L, cross R, L, kick
Forward, and L, R, and L, and
5. Right heel, back, left heel, back
6. Apart, together, R, L
7. Forward, and L, and R, and L, and
8. Right-heel, back, left-heel, back, apart, together, R, L, forward, and L, and R, and L, and
9. Face, R, L, R, kick
10. Turn, 2, 3, kick
11. Star, and 2, and 3, and 4, and
12. Repeat patterns 9 and 10
13. Walk, and 2, and 3, and 4, and

VARIATIONS AND TEACHING HINTS

1. This is a variation of the "Salty-Dog Rag." If patterns 5–7 are omitted, the dance becomes the Salty-Dog Rag.
2. Patterns 1–3, 5–7, and 9–11 should be learned as separate segments and performed without hesitation prior to moving to the next segment.

3. The music is rather fast; therefore, a variable speed record player is desirable.
4. Students can be encouraged to add their own creative additions once the dance is learned (e.g., the girl can turn under the boy's right arm in pattern 13).

KOROBUSHKA

Level: IV (Advanced)
Records: Folkraft 1170; World of Fun 3-B (M108)
Formation: Double circle; boy's back to center, partners' facing, both hands joined
Skills: Step-hop, Schottische, balance

MEASURES	MOVEMENTS
1	**1.** All do a Schottische (step, step, step, hop) away from the center of the circle. Boys begin with left foot and move forward. Girls begin with right foot and move backward. On the hop the free leg swings in front of the hopping foot.
2	**2.** All Schottische into center (boys begin right; girls begin left).
3	**3.** All Schottische away from center as in step 1.
4	**4.** Each dancer does the Hungarian break step. Boys hop left and touch right toe across left foot, hop left and touch right toe to right side, hop left and click right heel to left heel, and pause. Girls do the same, beginning the hop on the right foot.
5	**5.** Both hands on own hips, partners do a sideways Schottische step to their own right sides (moving apart from each other).
6	**6.** Beginning left, partners do a sideways Schottische step to return to each other.
7	**7.** Holding right hands, both balance forward with a step-hop right and back with a step-hop left.
8	**8.** Holding right hands, beginning left, partners take four step-hops to turn clockwise, finishing with the girls' backs to the center.
9	**9.** Steps 5-8 are repeated. Now boys will once again have their backs to the center.

CUES

1. Out, 2, 3, hop
2. In, 2, 3
3. Out, 2, 3
4. Point, side, click
5. Right, together, right, hop
6. Left, together, left, hop
7. Forward, hop; back, hop
8. Change, 2, 3, 4
9. Repeat patterns 5–8

VARIATIONS AND TEACHING HINTS

1. This dance is alleged to have originated in the United States by a group of Russian immigrants shortly after World War I.
2. To use as a mixer, boys do the last four step-hops to move CCW to a new partner.
3. Any number of couples can be used in a longways set—not as a mixer.
4. Step-hops of pattern 8 can be replaced with four walking steps.

FIGURE 16-22A
Little man In a fix

FIGURE 16-22B
Little man in a fix, arch

LITTLE MAN IN A FIX

Level: IV (Intermediate)
Records: World of Fun 4-B (M121)
Formation: Free formation; sets of two couples hooked together at boys' left elbows; couples face opposite direction (Figure 16-22a).
Skills: Running step, waltz

MEASURES	MOVEMENTS
1–8	**1.** Beginning left, take 24 running steps forward (eight running waltz). Lightly accent the first step of each waltz. The set will turn CCW. Girls lean slightly forward.
9–16	**2.** Boys release elbows and join hands (left); release waist of girl and join her hand (boy goes right, girl goes left). Girls take 12 running steps under the arch formed by the boys' uplifted arms (CCW through the arch) (Figure 16-22b). Girls face partners and join right hands across (boys' left hands are still joined). Now the set runs CCW 12 steps.
17–20	**3.** Boys drop hands; couples do four open waltz steps, beginning with outside foot.
21–24	**4.** Couples do four closed turning waltzes.
	5. Repeat steps 3 and 4.
	6. Repeat the dance with a new couple.

CUES

1. Forward turn . . . 8
2. Ladies under . . . 12
  Cross hands turn . . . 12
3. Waltz, 2, 3, 4
4. Turn 2, 3, 4
5. Waltz 2, 3, 4, turn, 2, 3, 4

VARIATIONS AND TEACHING HINTS

1. If there is an odd number of couples, the "odd couple" can "cut in" during the closed waltz pattern on another set. The odd couple becomes the "Little Man in a Fix."
2. All the maneuvers with the arches should be walked through carefully.
3. The waltz step of pattern 4 can also be a straightforward waltz in an open position or a turning waltz in the two-hand position.

LOTT IST TOD

Level: IV (Intermediate)
Records: World of Folk Dance 1622
Formation: Circle; partners, boys' backs to center
Skills: Slide; face-to-face and back-to-back polka

MEASURES	MOVEMENTS
1–2	**1.** Take four step-draws (slow slides) CCW.
3–4	**2.** Take eight quick slides in opposite direction (CW).
5–6	**3.** Repeat step 1.
7–8	**4.** Repeat step 2.
	5. Do 16 polkas, turning and traveling CCW. Repeat the dance.

CUES

1. 1 and, 2 and, 3 and, 4 and
2. Fast, 2, 3 . . . 8
3. 1 and, 2 and, 3 and, 4 and
4. Fast, 2, 3, . . . 8
5. Polka, 2, 3 . . . 16

VARIATIONS AND TEACHING HINTS

1. There are many variations of this popular folk dance. Humor is incorporated as the boys try to drag the resisting girls to the center of the circle and the girls, with the boys following, quickly scamper back to the edge.
2. Skipping can replace the polkas.

MAYIM! MAYIM!

Level: III
Records: Folkcraft 1108; World of Fun 6-B (M119)
Formation: Single circle, facing center; hands joined and held down
Skills: Grapevine ("Circassia" steps), walk, hop

MEASURES	MOVEMENTS
1–4	**1.** Take four "circassia" (grapevine) steps, beginning with the right foot crossing over the left; step left, cross right behind left, and step left. Accent the first count on the right foot. This is one circassia step. Repeat three more times. Accent each fourth step.

5–6	**2.** Walk to center in eight steps while raising joined hands high. Walk backward to place in eight steps, lowering hands (16 counts).
7–8	**3.** Repeat step 2.
9	**4.** Moving clockwise and beginning with the right foot, take three running steps; on the fourth count, face center, weight remains on right foot.
10	**5.** Hop right, touch left across right, hop right, and touch left to left side. Repeat
11	**6.** Repeat step 5.
12	**7.** Repeat step 5, beginning with the right foot touching in front. (Arm movements are optional.) Hop left, touch right across right, and clap hands directly in front (fully extended arms); hop left, touch right to right side, and swing arms out to sides at shoulder height; hop left, touch right across left, and clap hands—arms extended in front; hop left, touch right to right side, and swing arms out at shoulder height. The hops and touches occur on the same count.
13	**8.** Repeat pattern 7

CUES

1. Cross R, left, back R, left
   (repeat three more times)
2. Walk, 2, 3 . . . 8
   Back, 2, 3 . . . 8
3. Walk, 2, 3 . . . 8
   Back, 2, 3 . . . 8
4. Go left, 2, 3, 4
5. Touch L, side, front, side
6. Touch L, side, front, side
7. Touch R, side, front, side
8. Touch R, side, front, side

VARIATIONS AND TEACHING HINTS

1. This dance originated in a kibbutz on the shores of Galilee. Mayim means water. The Jewish people dance to celebrate the finding of water in an arid land, and the movements should imitate the motion of waves as they break on the shore.
2. Words to the chorus:
   Ma-yim, Ma-yim, Ma-yim, Ma-yim, V-ma-yim bi-sa-son

MILANOVO KOLO

Level: IV (Intermediate)
Records: World of Folk Dances 1620
Formation: Single circle, facing center, with hands joined; no partners; circle can be broken, with leader at one end
Skills: Step-hop, grapevine

MEASURES	MOVEMENTS
1–2	1. Facing slightly to the right, begin on the right foot with a step-hop; then step-hop left. Face center and step with the right foot forward; step behind the right foot; take three quick steps, right, left, right, in place.
3–4	2. Repeat pattern to the left. Step-hop left, step-hop right, step left, cross right, and step left, right, left, quickly.
5–6	3. Raise joined hands straight forward to shoulder level. Moving to center, beginning right, step-together-step, pause, step-together-step (left), pause.
7–8	4. Move back with right step-together-step, pause; then left step-together-step, pause.
	5. Repeat from the beginning.

CUES

1. Right hop, left hop, right, cross left, R, L, R
2. Left hop, right hop, left, cross right, L, R, L
3. Forward, R together, step, pause, L together, step, pause
4. Back, R together, step, pause, L together, step, pause

VARIATIONS AND TEACHING HINTS

1. During the first part of the dance, note that joined hands are held straight down, close to the body, and the body is very erect.
2. Sounds such as *Hey! Hup! Hi!* can accompany the dance.

MISERLOU

Level: IV (Advanced)
Records: Folkcraft 1060; World of Folk Dance 1620; White V
Formation: Broken circle; hands joined, elbows bent, little fingers linked; lead dancer on right
Skills: Two-step, grapevine, pivot

MEASURES	MOVEMENTS
1	1. Begin right, step in place (count 1) pause (count 2), touch left toe forward (count 3), and pause (count 4).
2	2. Arc left leg (keeping the toe close to the floor) to the left to be placed behind the right foot. This is a sweeping motion (count 1). Continue the grapevine movement by placing the right foot to right side (count 2), and cross left in front of right (count 3). Pivot CCW (with an arc movement of the right leg; the sweep is slightly higher than the previous sweep of the left leg) a half turn to the left to face CW (count 4).
3	3. Moving CW and beginning right (count 1), close left (count 2), step right (count 3), and pause (count 4). Weight should be slightly on the ball of the right foot, left leg lifted slightly in the back. There will be a slight rocking motion as the next step is taken.
4	4. Beginning left, step back (count 1), right side (count 2), cross left over right (count 3), and pause (count 4).

CUES

1. Step R, hold, point L, arc
2. Cross back, side, cross front, hold
3. Right, close, right, hold
4. Back, side, cross, hold

VARIATIONS AND TEACHING HINTS

1. This is a modified version of the Greek dance Kritikos. It originated in Pittsburgh in 1945 and is now danced all over the world.
2. The lead dancer at the right end of the broken circle leads the dancers in serpentine fashion.
3. Several broken circles can create an interesting kaleidoscopic effect.
4. The dance should be danced with grace and serenity.
5. Pattern 2 can be simplified by stepping in place left, right, left, after the toe touch.

FIGURE 16-23A

Norwegian mountain march, starting position

NORWEGIAN MOUNTAIN MARCH

Level: IV (Beginning)
Records: World of Folk Dance 1622; Folkcraft 1177
Formation: Circle in sets of three, all facing CCW; triangles, with center slightly in front of outside dancers; hands are joined, and front dancer extends arms backwards (Figure 16-23a).
Skills: Waltz, run, turn

MEASURES	MOVEMENTS
1–8	**1.** Beginning with the right foot, all take eight running waltz steps (24 steps). The first of every three steps should be accented.
9–10	**2.** The center dancer moves backward with six running steps under the arch formed by the two dancers in the back of the triangle (Figure 16-23b).
11–12	**3.** The dancer on the left takes six steps to cross in front of and under the arch formed by the center and right-side dancer.
13–14	**4.** The dancer on the right takes six steps to turn under the raised right arm of the center dancer.
15–16	**5.** The center dancer takes six steps to turn under his or her right arm, and all assume original position.
	6. Repeat the dance.

CUES

1. Waltz run, 2, 3 . . . 8
2. Center back, 2, 3 . . . 6
3. Left under, 2, 3 . . . 6
4. Right turn, 2, 3 . . . 6
5. Center turn, 2, 3 . . . 6

VARIATIONS AND TEACHING HINTS

1. If boys and girls make up the triangles, the center dancer should be a boy.
2. Handkerchiefs may join each dancer in the triangle; three handkerchiefs will be needed (See Figure 16-23a).
3. The dance represents a guide leading climbers up and down the mountain. Therefore, the center (guide) at times looks over his or her shoulder to check on the climbers. Keeping the "chain" untangled is the challenge.

FIGURE 16-23B

Norwegian mountain march, arch

OH SUSANNA

Level: IV (Beginning)
Records: World of Folkdance 1623; Folkcraft 1186; RCA EPA 4140
Formation: Grand circle; partners facing center. hands joined, girl to the boy's right side
Skills: Grand right and left, slide, skip

MEASURES	MOVEMENTS
1–4	**1.** Girls walk forward four and back four, as boys clap the time.
5–8	**2.** Boys walk four forward and four back while girls clap.
9–16	**3.** Partners face each other, remaining in a single circle; all perform a grand right and left by grasping their partners' right hand, passing on to the next person and grasping left hands, and so on. They continue until the music reaches the "Oh, Susanna" chorus.
17–32	**4.** At the chorus, all assume the skating position with new partners and walk CCW for two full choruses.
	5. The dance is repeated from the beginning, each time with new partners.

CUES

1. Girls forward, 2, 3, 4 and back, 2, 3, 4
2. Boys forward, 2, 3, 4 and back, 2, 3, 4
3. Partners, grand right and left
4. New partners walk, 2, 3, 4, 5, 6 . . .

VARIATIONS AND TEACHING HINTS

1. Skipping can take the place of walking.
2. The chorus can be sung while the dancers are moving.
3. Partners can turn under one another's arms while walking through the chorus.

PATTY-CAKE POLKA

Level: IV
Records: Folkcraft 1260; World of Folk Dance 1625; World of Fun 1-B (M107)
Formation: Circle; partners facing with both hands joined; boys' backs to center
Skills: Heel-toe, slide, skip, elbow swing

MEASURES	MOVEMENTS
1–2	**1.** Moving CCW, heel-toe twice (boys left, girls right).
3–4	Slide four to the boy's left, still moving CCW. Finish with the boy's right and left girl's foot free.
5–8	**2.** Repeat the pattern to the boy's right, moving CW.
9–12	**3.** Facing partners, clap right hands three times; clap left hands three times; clap both hands three times; slap own thighs three times.
13–14	**4.** Partners perform right elbow swing with four walking steps.
15–16	**5.** Walk four steps left to a new partner. Repeat the entire dance with a new partner.

CUES

1. Heel-toe, heel-toe, slide, 2, 3, 4
2. Heel-toe, heel-toe, slide, 2, 3, 4
3. Clap right, 2, 3
   Clap left, 2, 3
   Clap both, 2, 3
   Clap thighs, 2, 3
4. Swing, 2, 3, 4
5. And on to a new partner

VARIATIONS AND TEACHING HINTS

1. A skip or polka can replace the walk in the elbow swing.
2. Various clapping patterns can be used to keep the students motivated.

PUT YOUR LITTLE FOOT

Level: IV (Intermediate)
Records: Folkcraft 1165; World of Fun 1-8 (M107)
Formation: Couples in varsovienne position, scattered or in double circle, boys on the inside
Skills: Sweep step, point, walk, turn

MEASURES	MOVEMENTS
1	**1.** Facing CCW and with weight on the right foot, draw the left foot across the right instep with a sweeping motion. Step diagonally forward on the left foot, and close with the right foot.
2	**2.** Repeat step 1.
3–4	**3.** Sweep the left foot as previously; then take three steps (left, right, left) and point the right toe. The boy takes the three steps in place while the girl steps side left, cross right, side left, point right, to cross over in front of the boy to his left side. Dancers are still facing CCW.
5–8	**4.** Repeat steps 1, 2, and 3, sweeping with the right foot.
9–16	**5.** For the chorus, do four of the sweep-three-steps-point pattern, beginning left.

CUES

1. Sweep L, step L, close R
2. Sweep L, step L, close R
3. Sweep L, step L, cross R, step L, point R
4. Sweep R, step R, close L,
   Sweep R, step R, close L,
   Sweep R, step R, cross L, step R, point L

CHORUS:

5. Sweep L, step L, cross R, step L, point R
   Sweep R, step R, cross R, step R, point L,
   Sweep L, step L, cross R, step L, point R,
   Sweep R, step R, cross L, step R, point L

VARIATIONS AND TEACHING HINTS

1. There are many variations of this popular American version of the European varsovienne.
2. During the third pattern, the dancers may choose to pivot during the three steps to turn and face the opposite (CW) direction. The arms change vertical positions but are never released.

RUMUNSKO KOLO

Level: IV (Intermediate)
Records: Folkcraft 1402
Formation: Broken circle; leader at right end; joined hands held down
Skills: Step-hop, Schottische, rock, stamp

MEASURES	MOVEMENTS
1–2	**1.** Beginning right and facing the line of direction (CCW), take two step-hops forward.
3	**2.** Step right, step with the left foot behind the right, making a half turn left to face reverse direction.
4	**3.** Step-hop right backward.
5–6	**4.** Moving backward, step-hop left and step-hop right.
7–8	**5.** Beginning left, take one Schottische step, turning on hop to face center (1/4 turn).
9–10	**6.** Facing center and beginning right, cross the right foot over the left (count 1) as the left foot is displaced backward; rock back onto the left foot (count 2); step right and swing the left foot forward to repeat the entire pattern.
11–12	**7.** Repeat pattern 6, beginning left.
13–14	**8.** Repeat pattern 6, beginning right.
15–16	**9.** Stamp three times, all with the left foot; pause.
17–18	**10.** Beginning left, repeat patterns 6–9.

CUES

1. Step-hop R, step-hop L
2. Step, cross turn
3. Back-hop R
4. Back-hop L, step-hop R
5. Schottische L, R, L, hop, turn
6. Cross R, L, R, hop
7. Cross L, R, L, hop
8. Cross R, L, R, hop
9. Stamp L, L, L, hold
10. Cross L, R, L, hop
    Cross R, L, R, hop
    Cross L, R, L, hop
    Stamp R, R, R, hold

VARIATIONS AND TEACHING HINTS

1. Beginning dancers should listen to the first four measures to become familiar with the rhythm; calling the cues as they listen will also help them learn the dance.
2. On each step-hop the free foot should swing forward.

RYE WALTZ

Level: IV (Advanced)
Records: Folkcraft 1103
Formation: Double circle; boys' backs to center; open dance position
Skills: Slide and waltz

MEASURES	MOVEMENTS
1–4	**1.** Moving CCW, touch opposite toes (boys left, girls right) to side; then draw the same foot to cross behind the other foot (toes touching the floor). Repeat; then with three slides, move CCW.
5–8	**2.** Repeat, beginning with the other foot (boys right, girls left).
9–16	**3.** Dance four waltz steps.

CUES

1. Out, in, out, in slide, 2, 3
2. Out, in, out, in slide, 2, 3
3. Waltz

VARIATIONS AND TEACHING HINTS

Beginning students may want to replace the open position with the two-hand facing position.

SUSAN'S GAVOTTE

Level: IV (Intermediate)
Records: Any recording of "Lili Marlene"; Folkraft 1096; World of Fun 1A (M113)
Formation: Double circle of couples, facing CCW
Skills: Slide, kick, two-step

MEASURES	MOVEMENTS
1	**1.** Beginning with outside foot, walk forward four steps (CCW).
2	**2.** Face partners, join both hands, and slide four steps in the same direction (CCW).
3–4	**3.** Turn to face clockwise and repeat the four walks and four slides.
5–6	**4.** Face partners with both hands joined. Boys step left in place and swing their right foot across the left; then they step right in place and swing the left foot across the right (step left, swing right, step right, swing left). Girls simultaneously perform the same movements in opposition (step right, swing left, step left, swing right)
7–8	**5.** In the closed dance position, facing CCW, take three steps forward (beginning on the boys' left), turn toward partner, and point toe (boy right, girl left) in the reverse direction (CW).
9–10	**6.** Moving clockwise and beginning on the boys' right, repeat step 5.
11–13	**7.** In the open position, with inside hands joined and outside hands on waist, and traveling CCW beginning with the outside feet, do a two-step apart (back to back) and together (face to face). Repeat this action two more times.
14	**8.** Releasing hands, take four walking steps in individual circles (boys left, girls right) and circle by turning away from each other (boys begin left, girls begin right). The boy moves CW to the girl behind him, who becomes his new partner; girls finish their circles by coming back to their places.

CUES

1. Walk, 2, 3, 4
2. Slide, 2, 3, 4
3. Turn-walk, 2, 3, 4
4. Step, swing, step, swing
5. Walk, 2, 3, point
6. Walk, 2, 3, point
7. Step-together-step, face-together-step, apart-together-step, face-together-step, apart-together-step, face-together-step
8. Turn, 2, 3, 4 to a partner

VARIATIONS AND TEACHING HINTS

This is a popular variation of the dance Lili Marlene. It was composed by Susan Gentry of Oklahoma.

TANTOLI

Level: IV (Beginning)
Records: World of Folk Dance 1621
Formation: Partners in circle all facing CCW; open dance position
Skills: Step-hop, heel-toe, polka

MEASURES	MOVEMENTS
1–2	**1.** Beginning with outside foot, point toe forward (body leans back) and point toe backward (body leans forward); Schottische, beginning with the outside foot.
3–4	**2.** Repeat, beginning with the inside foot.
5–8	**3.** Repeat the entire pattern.
9–16	**4.** Take eight Schottisches, beginning with the outside foot (right, left, right, hop, repeated eight times, alternating lead foot).

CUES

1. Point, back, step, close, step, hop
2. Point, back, step, close, step, hop
3. Repeat cues 1 and 2
4. Schottische, 2 . . . 8

VARIATIONS AND TEACHING HINTS

1. Each of the Scandinavian countries has its own version of the Tantoli; this is one of the simpler versions.
2. During the Schottisches at the end, the girls can turn under the boys' right arm on the step-hops.

TETON MOUNTAIN STOMP

Level: IV (Intermediate)
Records: Folkcraft 1482; Western Jubilee 725; Windsor 7615
Formation: Single circle of couples, boys facing CCW, girls facing CW; two-hand position or closed position
Skills: Walk, stamp, two-step, buzz step

MEASURES	MOVEMENTS
1–2	**1.** In the two-hand or closed position, move sideways toward the center (the boy moving left, the girl right) with a step, close, step, stamp.
3–4	**2.** Move away from the center with the same steps (the boy moving right, the girl left).
5–6	**3.** Take one step toward the center and stamp the other foot; take one step away from center and stamp the other foot.

7–8	**4.** In the banjo position, walk four steps in the line of direction (CCW); the girl moves backward.
9–10	**5.** On the fourth step reverse the position (left sides adjacent); now the girl is walking four forward as the boy walks four back; the boy is still inside the circle.
11–12	**6.** Walk four steps forward to meet new partner (boy makes half turn to right). Pass right shoulders.
13–16	**7.** In the two-hand or closed position, with new partners, turn CW with four two-steps or eight buzz steps.

CUES

1. In, close, step, stamp
2. Out, close, step, stamp
3. In, stamp, out, stamp
4. Walk, 2, 3 turn (CCW)
5. Walk, 2, 3, turn (CCW)
6. Break, 2, 3, 4
7. Turn, 2, 3, 4, 5, 6, 7, 8

VARIATIONS AND TEACHING HINTS

1. The two-hand position is better for young children.
2. Buzz steps (eight) at the end will make the dance easier.

TINIKLING

Level: IV (Beginning)
Records: World of Folk dance 1619; any tune of moderate speed in 4/4 time
Equipment: Two bamboo poles (9 to 10 feet by 1 ½ inches) for every four to six children; two wooden blocks (30 inches by 2 inches)
Formation: Group of four (two pole beaters, two dancers)
Skills: Hopping, jumping
Description: Tinikling comes to us from the Philippine Islands. It is a very energetic folk dance in which the dancers depict the movements of the long-legged, long-necked tinikling bird "high-stepping" through the rice paddies. The dancers maneuver their feet in various patterns through the poles that are being manipulated in a rhythmic pattern by two students.

Although the "pole people" give the appearance of trying to trap the feet of the "birds," this aspect is not to be stressed with the students.

The original dance is lengthy and rather complicated. The following patterns (simple to complex) can be learned quickly by students who have developed rhythmic awareness. Additional patterns can be found in *Games Dance Gymnastics Activities* (Gabbard, Le Blanc, Lowy) 1989.

Two dancers dance with each set of poles if the poles are at least nine feet long.

Pole Movements: To start, the poles are apart and resting on the wooden blocks. The poles are manipulated by sliding them together and tapping them in the center of the blocks. The poles should never be more than one or two inches above the blocks. On the count of one the poles are clapped together. If music is in 3/4 meter, the rhythm cues should be together, apart, apart or close, tap, tap, with the first beat being accented; if the music is in 4/4 meter, the rhythm cues should be together, together, apart, apart or close, close, tap, tap. Those holding the poles should hold them lightly between thumb and fingers. If a dancer hits or steps on a pole the pole should be allowed to drop so the dancer will not be injured. Separation of poles will depend on the size of the dancers; 15 inches should be the maximum.

The original dance is performed to 3/4 meter music. However, this original music is sometimes hard to find. Actually any 3/4 music will give the appropriate rhythm, but the music may not seem appropriate to the movements being performed. In recent years several albums have been released with 4/4 music. Elementary children enjoy Tinikling to a good vigorous march, which stimulates them to make their hops and jumps precise and energetic.

Dancer Movements: Dancers stand with the poles to their right side, weight on both feet. Only one foot at a time will be on the floor during this dance (with the exception of the straddle step).

BASIC STEP—3/4 METER

1. Step slightly forward with the outside foot (left) (count 1 as poles are brought together).
2. Step with the right foot between the poles (count 2 as the poles are separated and tapped on the supporting blocks once).
3. Step with the left foot between the poles (count 3 as the separated poles are tapped again on the blocks. Hold the right foot up (remember the "high-stepping" birds).
4. Step with the right foot outside the poles to the right (count 4 as the poles are brought together).
5. Step with the left foot between the poles (count 5).
6. Step with the right foot between the poles (count 6).
7. Continue with left foot out, right in, left in, right out, and so on, from one side of the poles back to the other.

BASIC STEP—4/4 METER

1. Beginning left, step slightly forward with a step-hop (in even rhythm: count 1, 2, as poles are tapped against each other twice).
2. Step with the right foot between the poles (count 3).
3. Step with the left foot between the poles (count 4).
4. Step-hop with the right foot outside and to the right side of the poles (count 5, 6).
5. Step with the left foot between the poles (count 7).
6. Step with the right foot between the poles (count 8).
7. Continue with an even rhythm, moving from side to side of the poles.

VARIATIONS AND TEACHING HINTS

For all steps keep poles on the right side of the dancers for starting position.

STRADDLE STEP—3/4 METER

Begin with both feet inside the poles.
Jump to straddle the poles (count 1).
Jump twice on both feet inside the poles (count 2, 3).

CROSSOVER STEP—3/4 METER

Step with the right foot, outside (count 1).
Cross-step left, inside (2).
Step right, inside (3).
Cross-step left, outside (4).
Step right, inside (5).
Step left, inside (6).
Cross-step right, outside (1).
Continue to cross-step to get in or out.

STRADDLE STEP—4/4 METER

Begin with both feet inside the poles.
Make two straddle jumps outside (1, 2).
Jump twice inside (3, 4).

CROSSOVER STEP—4/4 METER

Step-hop right (1).
Cross-step left, inside (2).
Step right, inside (3).
Cross-step-hop left, outside (4).
Step right, inside (5).
Step left, inside (6).
Cross-step-hop right, outside (1).

POLE ROCK STEP—3/4 METER

Facing the poles, rock back on the left foot, outside the poles (1).
Step right, inside (2).
Step left, inside (3).
Step right foot forward, outside (4).
Step left foot backward, inside (5).
Step right, inside (6).
Step left foot backward, outside (1).

SIDE JUMP—3/4 METER

Jump lightly in place (1).
Jump inside the poles (2).
Jump inside (3).

POLE ROCK STEP—4/4 METER

Rock back on the left foot, outside (1).
Hop left, outside (2).
Step right, inside (3).
Step left, inside (4).
Step right, outside (5).
Hop right, outside (6).
Step left, inside (7).
Step right, inside (8).
Step-hop left, outside (1).

SIDE JUMP—4/4 METER

Jump twice outside (1, 2).
Jump twice inside (3, 4).
Jump twice to the other side (1, 2).

COMBO I—3/4 METER

Do a basic step (count 1–12).
Straddle jump (count 13–24).

COMBO I—4/4 METER

Step left, outside (1).
Hop left, outside (2).
Step right, inside (3).
Step left, inside (4).
Straddle jump, outside (5).

Straddle jump, outside (6).
Jump with both feet, inside (7).
Jump with both feet, inside (8).
Step right, outside (1).

TOUCHDOWN

1. The class is divided into four lines.
2. All dancers begin simultaneously.
3. They continue to dance the basic step as they progress to the end of the next line.
4. The goal is to have everyone active, with no waiting time.

VARIATIONS AND TEACHING HINTS

1. Dancers may assume various body positions in relation to one another (front to front, back to back, front to back) and make various movements with their arms and hands (holding hands or clapping). Dancers can also work in mirror fashion or on opposite sides of the poles.
2. Once the dancers become proficient, it is fun to increase the speed of the music.
3. Depending on the choice of music, the dancers may dance delicately (as the original dance is performed) or vigorously.
4. Various arm movements can be added creatively.
5. Progressions (cues for feet should be quietly verbalized during patterns 1–3; cues for poles should be quietly verbalized during patterns 4–5) are as follows:
   a. Listen to music and clap hands to beat.
   b. Standing in place, move feet to the beat.
   c. Practice steps with lines on the floor for poles.
   d. Practice steps over stationary poles.
   e. Practice moving hands in pole movements but without poles (clap, apart, apart or clap, clap, apart, apart).
6. The 4/4 pattern is easier for the beginner and should be presented first.
7. Pole tappers should chant their cues quietly. Cues for feet are as follows:

3/4 METER	4/4 METER
out, in, in	out, out, in, in

Cues for poles:

3/4 METER	4/4 METER
together, apart, apart	together, together, apart, apart

The "out" and "in" cues should never be used by the pole tappers because the cues are diametrically opposed to the movement of the dancers' feet!

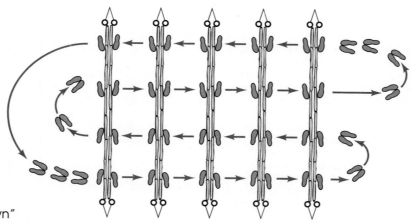

FIGURE 16-24
Tinikling, "Touchdown"

TURKEY IN THE OVEN

Level: IV (Intermediate)
Records Holiday Dances. Educational Activities No. 20; or any recording of "Turkey in the Straw"
Formation: Circle of partners, hands joined
Skills: Grand right and left

VERSE

We have some turkeys in the oven.
We have some turkeys in the oven.
We have some turkeys in the oven.
And they are tender too.

MOVEMENTS

1. Those without partners stand in the center of the circle; they are the "turkeys."
   Beginning with the right foot, walk three steps into the center and three steps back, singing the verse.
2. Repeat step 1.
3. Face partner and do the grand right and left. Turkeys scatter and join the grand right and left. Girls must move in the same direction as the girls already in the circle (CW), and the boys should move CCW.
4. When the whistle blows, take a new partner (the person whose hand is held) and promenade. Those left over become the new turkeys.
5. Join hands and repeat the dance (on the long musical chord).

CUES

1. In, 2, 3, stamp
   Out, 2, 3, stamp
2. In, 2, 3, stamp
   Out, 2, 3, stamp
3. Grand right and left
4. Promenade partner

VARIATIONS AND TEACHING HINTS

1. The children should walk through the procedure for pattern 3.
2. The students should be quizzed verbally on the appropriate movements for the grand right and left (e.g., boys move CCW; girls move CW).
3. Right, cross L, R, turn
4. Back, 2, 3, touch

UNO DOS TRES

Level: III
Records: Any recording of Linda Mujer; Dancing Without Partners EA 32
Formation: Line, double lines facing, or circle
Skills: Bleking

MEASURES	MOVEMENTS
1–4	1. Stepping in place, step left, right, left, pause; right, left, right, pause; left, right left, pause; right, left, right, pause.
5–6	2. Beginning and moving left, step left, close right, step left, close right, step left, close right, step left, pause. Step right, close left, step right, close left, step right, close left, step right, pause.
7–8	3. To perform Bleking, jump lightly in place and extend the right leg forward (heel on the floor). Jump lightly in place and extend the left leg forward (heel on the floor). Repeat with the right foot forward; pause.
9	4. Repeat pattern 3, beginning with the left leg forward.

11–12	5. Repeat steps 3 and 4. Note: There are 12 jump steps, with a pause after each third one (steps 3–5).
13	6. Beginning left, walk four steps forward, finishing with feet together.
14	7. In place, step left, right, left, hold.
15	8. Beginning right, walk four steps backward, ending with feet together.
16	9. In place, step right, left, right, hold.

CUES

1. L, R, L, hold
   R, L, R, hold
   L, R, L, hold
   R, L, R, hold
2. L, close, L, close, L close, L, hold
   Right, close, R, close, R close, R, hold.
3. Right, left, right, hold
4. L, R, L, L hold
5. Repeat cues 3 and 4
6. Walk L, 2, 3, 4
7. Step L, R, L, hold
8. Back, 2, 3, 4
9. Step R, L, R, hold

VARIATIONS AND TEACHING HINTS

1. A turning jump can be executed on the pauses in step
2. This will make the dance more vigorous.

WEARIN' O' THE GREEN

Level: IV (Intermediate)
Records: Honor Your Partner, Educational Activities No. 20
Formation: Circle of partners or square of four couples
Skills: Allemande, do-si-do, promenade

VERSE

Swing your corner
Swing your partner
Face your corner and Allemande
Swing your own
Do-si-do your partner
Do-si-do your partner
Swing corner girl around
Take some corner girl and promenade
Join hands, circle right
Now circle left
Allemande left your corner
All into the center and say "hello"

MOVEMENTS

1. Honor your partner, circle left, circle right, and promenade.
2. Swing the corner using left elbows.
3. Swing partner, using right elbows.
4. Allemande left the corner, using left elbows.
5. Swing partner, using right elbows.
6. Do-si-do the corner, passing right shoulders, backs, left shoulders.
7. Do-si-do partner, passing right shoulders, backs, left shoulders.
8. Swing the corner, using left elbows.
9. Promenade the corner, the girls on the outside.
10. Repeat steps 1–8.
11. Chorus: Circle right (CCW), hands joined, eight steps.
    Circle left (CW), hands joined, eight steps.
    Allemande left the corner, with eight steps.
    Walk into the center, four steps in, four steps out.

CUES

These references are for the teacher only since the calls are on the record.

1. Honor partner
2. Swing corner
3. Swing partner
4. Allemande left
5. Swing partner
6. Do-si-do corner
7. Do-si-do partner
8. Swing corner
9. Promenade corner

10. Repeat 1–8
11. Chorus: Circle R . . . 8
    Circle L . . . 8
    Allemande L . . . 8
    In . . . 4 "hello"
    Out . . . 4

VARIATIONS AND TEACHING HINTS

1. This is a simple folk dance but fast moving.
2. Students should be quizzed verbally about the appropriate hands and elbows with which to swing their partners (right) and corners (left).

RECORD SOURCES

CASEY, B. (1976). *The complete book of square dancing.* New York: Doubleday.

DAUER, V. P., & Pangrazi, R. P. (1992) *Dynamic physical education for elementary school children.* Minneapolis, MN: Burgess.

GILBERT, C. (1974). *International folk dance at a glance.* Minneapolis, MN: Burgess.

HALL, J. T. (1963). *Dance! Complete guide to social, folk, and square dancing.* Belmont, CA: Wadsworth.

HARRIS, J. A., Pitman, A. M., & WALLER, MARY (1994). *Dance a while* (9th Ed.). New York: Macmillan.

HEATON, A. (1965). *Recreational dancing.* Provo, Utah: Brigham Young University Press.

HERMAN, M. (1953). *Folk dance syllabus 1.* New York: Folk Dance House.

KIRCHNER, G. (1992). *Physical education for elementary school children.* Dubuque, IA: Wm. C. Brown.

KRAUS, R. (1969). *Folk dancing.* New York: Macmillan.

KULBITSKY, O., & Kaltman, F. L. (1959). *Teacher's dance handbook number one: Kindergarten to sixth year.* Newark, NJ: Bluebird Publishing.

MYNATT, C. V., & KAIMAN, B. D. (1968). *Folk dancing for students and teachers.* Dubuque, IA: Wm. C. Brown.

WEIKERT, P. (1989). *Teaching Movement and Dance.* Ypsilanti, Mi. The High Scope Press.

SUGGESTED SOURCES AND READINGS

Bowmar Records
622 Rodier Drive
Glendale, CA 91201

Educational Activities, Inc.
P.O. Box 392
Freeport, NY 11520

Educational Recordings of America, Inc.
P.O. Box 210
Ansomia, CN 06401

Educational Record Center
3233 Burnt Mill Dr.
Suite 100
Wilmington, N.C. 28403-2655

Folkraft Records
% Gail Shifrin
Florham Park, NJ 07932

Kimbo
Box 477
Long Branch, NJ 07740

Melody House Publ.
819 NW 92nd St.
Oklahoma City, OK 73114

Merrbach Record Service
P.O. Box 7308
323 W. 14th St.
Houston, TX 77008

Rhythm Productions Records
Dept. J., Box 34485
Los Angeles, CA. 90034

World Tone Music
230 7th Ave
New York, NY 10011

17

Gymnastics

Gymnastic activities are fun and inherently challenging across all skill levels. Such activities provide children with enjoyable opportunities to self-test emerging abilities, while allowing for immediate feedback. Gymnastics also provide children with opportunities to create movements that defy gravity and enhance the development of several health- and skill-related fitness components (flexibility, muscular endurance, balance, coordination, among others). These activities offer an excellent vehicle for developing an understanding of the laws of motion and fostering cooperation among students.

As children learn to transfer and support their weight on various body parts, unique and satisfying movements occur. Children learn to trust in their abilities and determine individually just how far to go, and how difficult a task to attempt. The child is generally the best judge of when to progress to a more difficult challenge. Consequently, it is the teacher's task to establish an environment that is safe, challenging, and provides for maximum participation.

Bearing in mind the fact that no two children in a class will perform the same stunt at the same time with an equal degree of proficiency, the teacher can use various teaching styles and types of class organization to create a learning environment that is safe and challenging for all children.

It must be noted that the gymnastics activities presented in this chapter are to be used as an extension of the schema developing movement activities suggested in the fundamental skill and movement awareness chapters (10–13). The specific skills are taught to enhance the development of specific body management capabilities for the child and not as "tricks" to be mastered for show as in Olympic gymnastics programs. The emphasis here must be on increasing the children's body awareness to the extent that they can control their bodies against the force of gravity both on the floor and on equipment. The term "educational gymnastics" is often used to describe this type of approach so as not to be confused with Olympic gymnastics where children are learning a set of predetermined skills to be used in competition. Skills such as the handstand, handspring and cartwheel, which are normally associated with Olympic gymnastics are, however, included here for children who are developmentally ready for these challenges. The following section outlines specific considerations for planning these self-testing educational gymnastics activities.

Establish Rules

For the teacher to establish a safe environment where youngsters can learn gymnastic skills, children must have certain responsibilities, and it is imperative that they are aware of what those responsibilities entail. Rules for conduct need to be established and posted where everyone can see them. They should include:

1. *Proper attire:* No loose or bulky clothes, jewelry, belts, or clothing that could catch on equipment or individuals.
2. *Proper conduct in the gymnasium:* No horseplay, unsupervised activity, or gum chewing.
3. *Proper use of spotters:* Children as spotters should only try to break a fall and should not be expected or be encouraged to carry or lift another student through a stunt.
4. *Movement in the area:* children should not walk across mats but should go around them to return, in order to prevent collisions.

Other rules may be added according to need; however, the list should be kept simple so that children can easily remember the rules. Table 17-1 presents an example of a gymnastics rules poster.

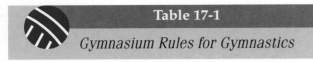

Table 17-1

Gymnasium Rules for Gymnastics

1. Move only when the teacher is in the gym.
2. Wear clothes that are not loose and bulky but enable you to move freely; NO JEANS!
3. Take off belts and jewelry; spit out gum.
4. Always have a partner to help break a fall.
5. Do not bug each other while you are working.
6. Only go one at a time on equipment unless otherwise directed.

Develop Strength and Flexibility

The fitness activity before gymnastic skills are presented should include general flexibility exercises that move all parts of the body, including the head and neck, through a complete range of motion, and strength exercises specific to the activities (see Chapter 14 Physical Fitness Activities, for exercise suggestions).

FOLLOW PROPER PROGRESSIONS

The teacher is responsible for presenting activities that are commensurate with the child's abilities and that follow an accepted progression. The activities listed in this chapter are grouped according to suggested levels and categories of skills; however, most classes are not homogeneous in abilities. Consequently, the teacher must assume responsibility for determining which activities are appropriate for the students' varying skill levels and which also enhance the theme being developed.

As previously noted in the description of this curricular model, Level I–II activities should be used primarily as enhancements to skill themes, whereas Level III–IV activities are themes (skills) to be introduced in the skill-development portion of the lesson.

The focus of the primary gymnastics program (Level I–II) is on developing movement awareness and the self-confidence necessary for performance. Variations in movement patterns are highly encouraged as children move to discover the multitude of possible patterns within each skill theme being explored. The enhancement activities are presented as logical extensions of the skills being perfected. Within each skill theme, a variety of enhancements should be used. For diversity, the activities can be divided into the following categories:

Animal movements	Partner balances
Individual stunts	Pyramids
Partner stunts	Small-equipment activities
Individual balance stunts	Large-equipment activities
Tumbling and inverted balance	

Activities within each category should be chosen to enhance each theme.

At Level III–IV, the same categories exist as the skills become more complex and attention to detail more rigorous. During these phases, students are encouraged to refine movements mechanically, aesthetically, and to combine various skills into sequences and routines.

At both the foundation and utilization levels, the child's readiness for specifically prescribed movements is determined by individual levels of strength, flexibility, vestibular awareness, and experience. Students should be required to demonstrate proficiency at less difficult skills before being permitted to attempt the more demanding and complex activities. Checklists and task sheets are extremely effective for keeping track of individual levels of proficiency in order to determine appropriate activities for each child (refer to Chapter 8, Evaluation, and Chapter 6, Organization and Instruction, for more detailed information on formulating task sheets).

The following general progression is recommended:

1. Perform alone on the floor
2. Work with a partner on the floor
3. Use small manipulative equipment with skills
4. Perform skills on large equipment

The incorporation of small manipulative equipment such as beanbags, hoops, and wands into the theme or unit increases task complexity and serves to increase interest during the repetitive practice necessary to refine the skills. For example, when practicing the forward roll, the progression of activities might be:

1. Forward roll in tuck position, from one foot, a straddle or a pike position;
2. Forward roll to a one foot, straight leg or straddle landing;
3. Forward roll with a partner, holding hands, starting back to back, or in a circle;
4. Forward roll over a beanbag, wand, or hoop;
5. Forward roll and catch a ball tossed by a partner;
6. Roll a hoop and forward roll next to it, stopping it at the completion of the roll;
7. Forward roll across a padded vaulting box;
8. Forward roll across a bench;
9. Forward roll across a padded vaulting box through a hoop held by a partner.

There are many more options to this forward-roll progression. A thorough examination of time, space, force, and relationship variations will turn up a multitude of possibilities. The important concept to remember is that within each activity described or outlined in this chapter, there are many possibilities for variability. The following pieces of small manipulative equipment may be successfully used with gymnastics activities:

Balls—playground (small size), yarn, nerf
Hoops
Wands
Beanbags

Indian clubs
Ropes—jump ropes and stretch ropes
Cones
Parachute

Develop an Atmosphere of Trust and Responsibility

The teacher's attitude about gymnastics is perhaps one of the most important factors in establishing a safe environment for learning. Students should always be encouraged for their efforts and not be expected to compete with classmates, but rather, with themselves. The teacher needs to remember that obstacle courses and relay races utilizing newly learned skills may not be conducive to initial skill acquisition and may be extremely unsafe. An atmosphere of trust and responsibility must be established.

TEACHING STYLE

The teaching style chosen for any particular lesson must by necessity establish a safe and controlled environment while at the same time enable children to work at their own pace. The greatest success will be achieved by using a variety of teaching styles and frequently more than one within a particular lesson.

The command style and demonstrations should be used for making specific skill points on complex stunts and also for establishing a controlled atmosphere. Frequently gymnastics lessons need to be highly structured so that children perform only when they are signaled to do so and do only what they are told to do. Structuring lessons for control helps to show children how to take turns, and directs their performance toward a specific goal.

As children demonstrate more responsible behavior (that is, taking turns, proper spotting, and directed practice habits), the guided discovery, problem solving, and exploration teaching styles should become more prevalent. Guided discovery is very useful in developing quality performance as well as teaching the laws of motion. Through guided-discovery techniques the child develops the much desired concept and movement schema associated with control in

varying positions, at the same time allowing the teacher more control of the outcome (that is, specific objectives are predetermined).

The problem-solving style offers the greatest reward in terms of individualizing and self-pacing as the child chooses his or her own movement solutions to such problems as: "How many ways can you balance on one body part?" and "Show me how to move across the floor touching three different body parts as you go." As children move, they develop ideas, with and from each other, and they self-perpetuate activity. The movements that emerge will greatly resemble the patterns described in this section, except that the children will have the satisfaction of discovery and will have learned about the uniqueness of their own movements. This approach to gymnastics is often referred to as *educational gymnastics*, and it plays an important role in the total gymnastics program. The themes most applicable to educational gymnastics (goals of good body awareness off and on equipment) are jumping and landing, rolling (Chapter 10); bending/stretching, swinging/swaying (Chapter 11); body, spatial, and vestibular awareness (Chapter 13).

A second way of using the problem-solving style is to expand on the specific skills described in this chapter by introducing movement variability as proficiency develops. For example, the child who has refined the basic handstand would be encouraged to try different ways of getting into the position, different ways of getting out of the position, and various body shapes while in the balanced position—thus expanding on the basic pattern. In this way children put movements together to first form sequences and eventually form routines linking the various categories of stunts together. It is the ultimate goal of the gymnastics program to produce quality movement sequences at each level. To this end, the problem-solving approach may be quite effective.

For a more detailed discussion of teaching styles, refer to Chapter 6, Organization and Instruction.

CLASS ORGANIZATION

The organization of the class into formations for the most effective teaching will be determined primarily by the equipment available and the activity. Individual mats or large carpet squares can be utilized effectively for a variety of activities, especially those that are nonlocomotive. A scattered formation (Fig. 17-1) can be utilized with each child working on an individual mat. Proper spacing should be encouraged along with reminders about self-space. Strip-tumbling-type mats may be linked together to form one long mat or separated into individual sections and used for activities that require locomotion or soft padding.

FIGURE 17-1

Scattered on individual mats

FIGURE 17-2

Mats in rows and children doing return activities beside them

If the mats are separated, the children may need to share in groups; therefore, some type of traffic pattern and return activity for the floor space between the mats should be planned to maximize activity. For example, a forward roll may be done on the mat and a seal walk done between the mats as a return activity. Figure 17-3 illustrates a useful formation. The demonstration mat can be used by children for practice after the teacher demonstrates.

The mats can also be linked together with velcro strips and utilized as one long piece with the children working individually across the width of the mat as illustrated in Figure 17-4.

Those activities which demand movement from one end of a mat to the other should be well organized. Children can be lined up on one side of a large activity mat, for example, and a "wave plan" used to allow turns (Fig. 17-5), or they can be lined up in groups at one side and move across in turn ("line plan"), waiting at the opposite side for return activities (Fig. 17-6).

Wave plan: Each child begins movement as the child to the left completes one movement of a series across the mat.

Line plan: Each row completes a turn across the mat at one time, then the next row takes a turn.

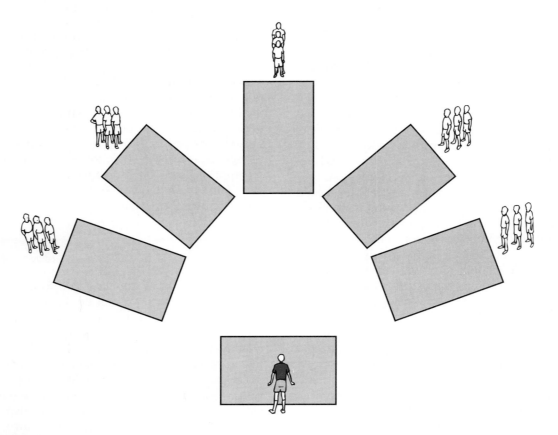

FIGURE 17-3

Mats in semicircle with demonstration mat in the middle.

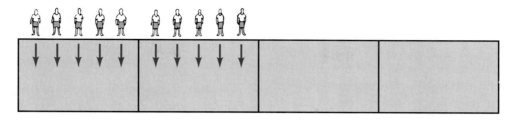

FIGURE 17-4

Mats hooked together with the children working widthwise across them provides more activity.

FIGURE 17-5

Wave plan

Generally, a station or group organization works best for utilizing available mats and equipment. In a group, children can be rotated among stations on a signal from the teacher, or individually they can progress according to their accomplishment of certain tasks. The teacher will find the use of station cards or posters that outline suggested problems or activities very helpful. Task sheets are very appropriate and desirable as a technique for facilitating station work (see Chapter 6, Organization and Instruction, for details concerning organization and class formations). When using stations, remember that the teacher should be safety conscious and not allow potentially dangerous activities (stations) to be unsupervised.

FIGURE 17-6

Line plan

SMALL EQUIPMENT

In order to incorporate small manipulative equipment into gymnastic activities, one should examine the basics of movement variability. A progression of complexity can then be established. The following list reveals the possibilities of movements in relationship to equipment and the suggested progression for incorporation with the activities:

1. Equipment stationary (for example, use prescribed movement to move over, around, through, and under the equipment);
2. Equipment carried or balanced on the body (use prescribed movement while carrying or balancing equipment in hands, under arms, on head, on shoulders, on knees, between legs, knees, ankles);
3. Equipment moving (roll ball and roll self next to it, or roll hoop and frog-hop through it);
4. Equipment manipulated before or after start (that is, throwing, catching, rolling, striking, kicking before or after stunt);
5. Equipment manipulated during stunt (throwing, catching, rolling, striking, kicking as stunt is performed). Not all skills will be adaptable to this variation.

LARGE EQUIPMENT

Most schools do not have sufficient numbers of apparatus (for example, horse, large beam) to allow the teacher effectively to involve all the students in the same activity at the same time. For example, it would not be a good idea to require 30 children to wait in line to cross one of two balance beams. Therefore, the teacher must be creative in organizing apparatus activities and using an appropriate teaching style. The teacher can use a variety of equipment and mats in one lesson to maximize activity or first have children use the floor and imitate the activity to be done on the apparatus (lines on the floor serve well as practice balance beams). The teacher should endeavor to set up creative arrangements of apparatus and mats to stimulate and challenge the children's capabilities. An example of one gymnasium organization (stations) is provided in Fig. 17-7. Whether the children rotate on a signal or at their own pace will be determined by the teaching style employed. If they rotate as a group, there must be enough stations so that there are no more than three or four students at each station.

Whatever the equipment used, the teacher must be sure that sufficient ground padding is provided (in relationship to the height of the apparatus and type of skill being practiced), and that the equipment is well spaced in the gymnasium or play area. The space required for performers and those waiting will be a

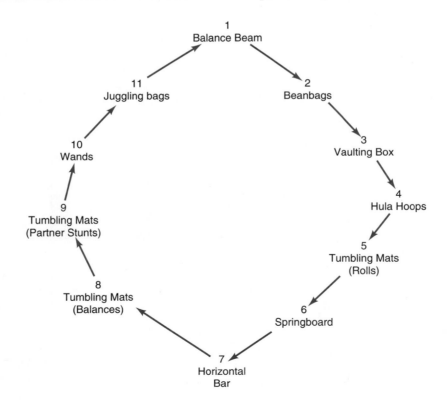

FIGURE 17-7

Gymnastic station plan

key consideration when choosing the teaching style and class organization.

For Levels III–IV, specific skills are recommended for the various pieces of equipment. Large-equipment activities for Levels I–II are incorporated into the skill themes under the additional movement variations sections. Movement variations with large equipment should be reviewed with Level III–IV children before they progress to the skills outlined in this chapter.

PROGRESSION

The most important concept to adhere to in the teaching of gymnastic activities is *proper progression*. The following general progression outline is provided to assist the teacher in choosing activities wisely.

1. Animal Walks and Movements (for example, bunny hop, measuring worm, bouncing ball, rocker). These simple movements should stress placing part of the body weight on the hands; the more weight, the more difficult the stunt. A further importance of these stunts is in their development of flexibility and abdominal strength, necessary for more advanced activities.
2. Individual and Partner Stunts (for example, coffee grinder, double walk, Chinese get-up). These serve to increase flexibility and strength, and they demand coordination of movements between two children.
3. Individual Balance Stunts (for example, balance stand, thread the needle, turk stand, rooster hop, crane stand). These stunts enable children to practice balancing in a variety of positions; the more complicated the position and the narrower the base of support, the more difficult the stunt.

The previously described categories of stunts should be worked on simultaneously, choosing the simplest stunts in each category and gradually progressing to the more difficult. Follow the same procedure for the next three categories.

4. Tumbling and Inverted Balance (forward roll, headstand, handstand). Each of these stunts may be performed in a variety of positions, each of which changes the difficulty of the stunt. For example, a forward roll from a tuck position is less difficult to perform than a forward roll from a pike position. Generally, the more force received in the transfer of weight the more difficult the stunt (that is, the farther from the ground at the start of the movement).
5. Partner Balances and Combatives (for example, angel balance, sitting balance, rooster fight, hand wrestling). These stunts demand considerable strength on the part of both performers, and they should not be attempted without due consideration.

Partners should be paired according to similar height and weight for maximum safety.

6. Pyramid Building demands careful adjustments based on the positions required and the varying amounts of strength possessed by the children. Most pyramids should be reserved for Level II through Level IV, and then only when children have demonstrated proficiency at partner balancing.
7. Large Apparatus. Once proficiency on the floor is established, certain stunts may be attempted on apparatus. The following pieces of apparatus provide gradually increasing difficulty, and the child should progress only as proficiency is established on each piece. Many activities successfully performed on the floor can be tried on equipment, and specific skills for each piece can be taught. For Levels I–II, review the following skill themes for specific large-equipment activities.

Jumping and Landing	(Chapter 10)
Rolling	(Chapter 10)
Climbing	(Chapter 10)
Swinging and Swaying	(Chapter 11)
Vestibular Awareness	(Chapter 13)

The following pieces of large equipment are recommended for elementary school use:

Low padded box (two ft.).
Low bench
Incline board (wide)
Low balance board (on the ground)
Ladder on the ground
Incline board (narrow)
Incline ladder
High horizontal ladder (three ft. to five ft. from the floor)
High balance beam (one ft. to three ft. from the floor)
Low horizontal bar
Climbing rope (single)
Double ropes
Rings
Vaulting horse or box (adjustable height)
Mini-Trampoline
Trampoline (more appropriate with small individualized programs using a qualified adult supervisor. Several states prohibit its use in public schools).

RHYTHMIC GYMNASTICS

The current rise in popularity of rhythmic gymnastics in the United States warrants its inclusion in this chapter for intermediate Level II (and higher level) students. The key concept in rhythmic gymnastics is the rhythmical performance of specifically prescribed movement skills incorporating specialized small equipment. Children will derive great pleasure from practicing and finally mastering these unique skills because they are novel, challenging and offer a great deal of task complexity. The specific skills performed with a ball, hoop, wand or ribbon are described in detail in the activities chapter of this text. As proficiency with single skills is developed, children should be encouraged to put the skills together into routines.

Teachers will find that the inclusion of rhythmic gymnastics into their programs expands the possibilities for challenging skill development. Some basic suggestions to enhance success include:

1. Use music in ¾ time.
2. Always practice with music.
3. Use a variety of music to encourage creativity and interest.
4. Space children so that there is no danger of a tossed and missed implement striking another child.
5. Stress reaching for and giving with arms and knees simultaneously as objects are caught.
6. Stress full extension of the body when objects are projected from the body (Levels III and IV).
7. Practice all skills on both sides of the body.
8. Allow children to create their own skills and routines.
9. Allow children the opportunity to perform their routines for others.

TEACHING HINTS

1. Use task sheets extensively to determine student readiness and progress.
2. Maximize activity by increasing the number of stations and using small manipulative equipment with large equipment.
3. Establish a responsible atmosphere, with a supportive attitude and specific safety rules.
4. Children should be encouraged to sequence skills and formulate routines utilizing their knowledge of space, time and force variables.
5. Stress transferring body weight smoothly using a variety of body parts (that is, not just hands to feet and feet to hands).
6. Lessons should flow smoothly from skill-development to enhancement activities, and frequently these parts may be indistinguishable. Large apparatus work may encompass both these parts of the lesson.
7. Combine locomotor-type stunts with balance and agility stunts at each level to maintain interest and offer the most diverse program possible.
8. Encourage responsible behavior by having children work in pairs. Spotting habits should be stressed and children should be taught where to stand in order to break or prevent a child's fall on the floor or on large equipment.

9. Use small equipment to increase the complexity of specific skills and maintain interest.
10. Gymnastics, being a developmental activity, will enhance the development of strength and flexibility.

GYMNASTIC ACTIVITIES

SEAL WALK

The seal walk is started in a lying position, stomach down, with the legs held straight. The arms are held as straight as possible and used to move the body, with the legs dragging.

ROW YOUR BOAT

Partners sit facing each other with legs spread and soles of feet touching. One person leans forward and the other leans backward pulling gently on each other; then they reverse. This could be tried with legs crossed. (See Figure 17-8).

FIGURE 17-8

SEAT CIRCLE

Sit on the floor with knees bent and hands placed behind the seat. Push with the hands and lift the feet off the floor and spin in a circle. Do this both ways; then try to hold a beanbag between the knees or toes, and spin without dropping it.

LONG STRETCH

Stand with feet together behind a line. With a piece of chalk in one hand, squat down and place free hand on the floor. Walk forward on hands as far as possible and mark distance with the chalk. Return to squat position and stand. (Equipment: chalk.)

EGG SIT

Sit in a tuck position and grasp right toes with right hand and left toes with left hand. Then rock back on seat and straighten legs without letting go of the toes. Balance in this "V-sit" position without grasping the toes.

Table 17-2

Listings and descriptions are arranged in approximate developmental order and category of movement. See Chapter 10 for rolling skills.

Levels I & II

NAME		LEVEL	NAME		LEVEL
Seal Walk	Animal movement	I & II	Free Standing		
Giraffe Walk			Single Squat		
Frog Jump			Spanker		
Bear Walk			Row Your Boat	Partner stunt	I & II
Duck Walk			Walking Chair		
Camel Walk			Inverse Twister		
Lame-Puppy Walk			Partner Pull-up		
Inchworm			Stand-up		
Gorilla Walk			Push 'em into Balance		
Elephant Walk			Wring the Dishrag		
Crocodile Crawl			Twist Away		
Animal Walk			Who's Behind?		
Crab Walk	Animal movement	II	Churn the Butter		
Rabbit Jump			Bouncing Ball		
	Individual stunt	I & II	Leapfrog		
Seat Circle			Rocking Horse		
Long Stretch			Wheelbarrow		
Egg Sit			Double Walk		
Rag Doll			Coffee Grinder	Partner stunt	II
Clown Trick			Toe Push		
Ankle Walk			Rooster Fight		
Blow up the Balloon			Greet the Toe	Individual balance stunt	II
Jack-in-the-Box			Tightrope Walker		
Missile Man			Tummy Balance		
Corkscrew		II	Double-Knee Balance		
Crazy Walk			Crane Dive		
Rising Sun			Balance Stand-Front Scale		
Crane Twist			Leg Roll	Tumbling and inverted balance	I & II
Knee Slapper			Side Roll	(See chapter 10)	
Toe Touch			Egg Roll		
Top			Forward Roll		
Jumping Swan			Forward Rolling Using a Springboard		
Tuck Jump			Rolling with a Tumbling Table		
Heel Slap			Human Ball		II Beg.
Heel Click			Step Jump Roll		
Turk Stand			Reach Over Roll		
Upspring			Back Shoulder Roll		
Thread the Needle			Tripod		
Seal Slap			Mule Kick		
Split Jump			Frog Stand Tip-up		
Jackknife			Headstand		
Bent-Knee Hop			Backward Roll	(See chapter 10)	
Jump Foot			Crossing Arms		

Levels I–III

NAME		LEVEL	NAME		LEVEL
Backward Rolling with a Table	(See chapter 10)		Rope Stunts:	Small-equipment skills	I & II
Dive Roll		II Int.	Lazy Rope		
Handstand			Snake Rope		
Cartwheel			Circle Rope		
Forearm Balance—Tiger Stand			Straight Rope		
People Pyramids	Partner balance stunts	II Int.	V-Rope		
Sitting Balance			Rope Rings		
Horizontal Balance			Wands:		II
Angel Balance			Floor Touch		
Thigh Balance			Thread the Needle		

Back Scratcher			Horizontal Bar (Swing and Sway):	(See chapter 11)	I & II
Twist Under			One-Foot Touch		
Stick Twist			Swing Back		
Rope Jumping	(See chapter 10)	I & II	Swing Back and Catch		II
Two-Foot step			Drop to Basket		
Alternate-Foot step			Front Support Variations		II & III
Swing Step		II Beg.	Skin the Cat		
One-Foot Hop			Basket		
Rocker Step			Pull-Over Progression		
Stride Step			Balance Beam (Vestibular Awareness): (See		I & II
Cross-Leg Step			Locomotor Movements	chapter 13)	
Side Shuffle Step		II Int.	Manipulative Movements		
Juggling:	(See chapter 13)	II Int.	Tires (Vestibular Awareness) (See chapter 13)		
Rope Climbing:	Large-equipment skills	I & II	Balance Board (Vestibular Awareness): (See chapter 13)		
Lying to sitting			Individual Variations		I & III
Lying to standing position (See chapter 10)			Manipulative Movements		II
Hanging			Trampoline (Vestibular Awareness) :(See chapter 13)		
Climbing			Jumping Variations (turns)		I & II
Swinging			Jumping Rope		II
Vaulting (jumping):	(See chapter 10)	I & II	Manipulative Movements		II
Squat			Horizontal Ladder on Ground (Vestibular Awareness):		
Flank			Locomotor Variations (See chapter 13)		I & II
Straddle		II Beg.	Manipulative Movements		II
Head		II Int.	Hoops, Wands, or Ropes (See chapter 13)		I & II
			Bean Bags	(See chapter 13)	

RAG DOLL

Stand with feet together and arms at sides. Count 1, bend head forward to touch chin to chest; count 2, rotate head sideward to position above right shoulder; count 3, rotate head backward to look at ceiling; count 4, rotate head sideward to position above left shoulder.

GIRAFFE WALK

Extend the arms straight up next to the ears and hook thumbs over the head. Bend the hands at the wrist to make the giraffe's head. Without bending the knees, walk on tiptoes. Bend slowly forward to take a drink of water.

WALKING CHAIR

Positioned one behind the other (two or three children may engage), holding onto the hips of the one in front, all sit back so the legs touch the thighs of the one behind. In unison, all move in the desired direction (initially forward). (See Figure 17-9.)

CLOWN TRICK

Lie on back on the floor; place a beanbag on the forehead. Get up to a standing position and return to a lying position without touching or dropping the beanbag.

ROPE STUNTS

All involve various arrangements and designated forms of jumping or hopping (or both).

LAZY ROPE

Figure 17-10

SNAKE ROPE

Figure 17-11

CIRCLE ROPE

(This is also a game.) One person stands outside the circle, the other inside. As the outside person jumps in, the inside person jumps out.

STRAIGHT ROPE

(This is also a game.) One partner stands on each side of a straight rope (or a line) holding one ankle and stretching the free hand with palm open toward the opponent. They hop on one foot and try to push each other off balance.

FIGURE 17-9

FIGURE 17-10
Lazy rope

FIGURE 17-11
Snake rope

FIGURE 17-12
Straight rope

V-ROPE

Jump (or hop) over the "V" at various widths (Figure 17-13). As a game, divide the "V" into sections and assign a point value to reach (Figure 17-14).

FIGURE 17-13
V-rope

ROPE RINGS

Figure 17-15

FROG JUMP

Squat down with hands on the floor (leaning over) and arms between the knees. Jump forward by pushing equally with the hands and feet. The landing should be on both feet and then the hands.

FIGURE 17-14
V-rope game

FIGURE 17-15
Rope rings

FIGURE 17-16
Camel walk

FIGURE 17-17
Lame-puppy walk

FIGURE 17-18
Blow up the balloon

BEAR WALK

Bending over to the "all fours" position, move in the desired direction trying to keep the legs and arms stiff and the head up.

DUCK WALK

Squatting down with knees turned out wide and hands under the armpits, move in the desired direction by swinging each foot wide to the side while flapping the wings.

ANKLE WALK

While grasping the ankles and keeping the head up, walk slowly in various directions.

CAMEL WALK

With one foot placed in front of the other and the body bent over at the waist, lock hands behind back (the camel's hump) and walk slowly, raising the head and chest with each step. (See Figure 17-16.)

LAME-PUPPY WALK

Start the lame-puppy position by placing both hands and one foot on the floor. Then walk on "all threes," optionally changing direction and hand position (close, wide, one hand in front of the other). (See Figure 17-17.)

INCHWORM

Beginning in a push-up position (without moving the arms), take short steps with the feet until the feet come as close to the hands as possible. Then, without moving the feet, take small steps with the hands until the body returns to the push-up position. The sequence of these movements may be reversed (*i.e.*, hand movements first).

GORILLA WALK

Bend the knees and the trunk forward. While moving in the desired direction (forward, backward, or sideward), periodically touch or drag the fingers across the floor.

ELEPHANT WALK

Begin by bending forward at the waist and clasping the hands together to simulate an elephant trunk. While moving, swing the trunk side to side like a pendulum. The trunk may also be used to imitate an elephant drinking water, eating, or washing.

CROCODILE CRAWL

Move along the ground on the stomach by advancing the same arm and leg: then do so with the opposite arm and leg, and finally on the back with hands bent and placed alongside the body.

BLOW UP THE BALLOON

Stand with feet a shoulder width apart: then squat and place hands on the floor in front of the feet. Keeping the hands flat on the floor, straighten the legs slowly by raising the hips upward and tightening the abdominals. To let the air out of the balloon, slowly return to the original position. (See Figure 17-18.)

JACK-IN-THE-BOX

Squat with all fours on the floor (leaning over), using the fingers for balance. When the signal is given (drum, whistle), jump up and extend the arms and legs. Variation: Use different sounds, but only one is the signal to jump. (Equipment: drum, sticks, or whistle for signal.)

MISSILE MAN

Cross the arms over the chest and move down into a squat position. On a signal (Blast off!), jump up into the air and then land with the feet in various positions (*e.g.*, one leg extended in front, or to the side, other foot extended, or on two feet).

FIGURE 17-19
Inverse twister

INVERSE TWISTER

Partners stand back to back, bend over, reach with right hands between the legs, and hold hands. Maintaining the hand grip, one partner leans to the right and lifts the left leg over partner's back. The movement is reversed to return to the original position. They may hold left hands also. (See Figure 17-19.)

PARTNER PULL-UP

Partners sit facing each other with legs in front and toes touching. They grasp hands, bend knees if necessary, and then pull together until standing. Then they try to return to a sitting position. This can also be done in groups.

STAND-UP

Partners sit on the ground back to back with knees bent and elbows locked. Partners push against each other and try to stand up without letting go of each other. If they are successful, add one more person. Try four, five, six, even more. See how many can get up successfully.

FIGURE 17-20
Stand-up

PUSH 'EM INTO BALANCE

Partners begin standing, with palms of hands together. They take one step or several, depending on the challenge needed, and lean on each other for balance. On a signal, they try to push each other back into balance without moving their feet. Be sure their feet are secure on the floor to avoid slipping. When executed properly, this looks like a standing push-up done on a mirror.

WRING THE DISHRAG

Partners face each other, holding hands. They raise one arm on the same side (right arm for one and left for the other) and turn back to back. They continue around by repeating with the other arm and return to the original position. This may also be done by grasping a wand. (See Figure 17-21.)

FIGURE 17-21
Wring the dishrag

FLOOR TOUCH

Partners sit cross-legged facing each other and grasp a wand with the palms facing down and arms extended. The wand is parallel to the floor. On a signal, they try to touch the wand to the floor on the right side. Then they change sides and grips on the wand. (Equipment: one wand per pair.)

TWIST AWAY

Partners face each other with feet comfortably apart and grasp a wand with palms down. They try to twist to the right, forcing the other person to lose the grip. The contest begins again when one partner has released the grip. They may use different grips and body positions.

BACK SCRATCHER

Grasp the wand with an underhand grip and arms crossed in front. Bring the wand over and behind head: then pass the wand over and behind head and down the body from the shoulders to heels without letting go. (See Figure 17-22.)

FIGURE 17-22

TWIST UNDER

Hold the wand upright with either right or left hand: twist under the arm without letting go or lifting the wand off the floor. Do not touch knee to the floor while performing this stunt.

STICK TWIST

Place the wand behind head and drape arms over it from behind. Very slowly, rotate the body to the right or left and touch the opposite knee with the end of the wand.

CORKSCREW

Stand with feet a shoulder width apart: place left arm behind back. Place right arm across body and behind left knee and touch the toes of the right foot by bending the knees and balancing on the toes. Use the left arm. (See Figure 17-23.)

FIGURE 17-23

CRAZY WALK

Try to walk forward by bringing one foot behind and around the other. Do this going backward, bringing the foot in front each time.

RISING SUN

Start by lying on the back with arms over the head to represent the sun. Slowly rise to a standing position by bending the knees, placing feet on the floor, and then raising the arms, head, shoulders, and trunk, pushing to a standing position.

CRANE TWIST

Stand on a line two feet from the wall and facing it. Then place forehead carefully on the wall and try to turn completely around without taking head from the wall. Try to turn both ways.

WHO'S BEHIND?

Choose a partner: one stands behind the other. On a signal from the teacher, the persons standing behind change places quietly. The person in front tries to determine "Who's behind?" by bending straight backward and looking behind.

GREET THE TOE

Stand on one leg and try to raise the toes of the opposite foot to touch the forehead, using the arms to grasp the foot. (See Figure 17-24.)

CHURN THE BUTTER

Partners of similar size stand back to back and lock elbows. One partner bends forward at the hips; the other partner gently springs from the floor, leans back, and lifts up his or her feet. They repeat by changing roles.

FIGURE 17-24

KNEE SLAPPER

Jump upward, drawing the knees toward the chest. As the knees move upward, slap the legs with the hands near the knees. Variations: Slap one knee at a time; slap double time on both knees; cross-slap each knee; perform an "ankle slapper."

TOE TOUCH

While jumping upward, extend the legs forward and upward with the feet apart. At the height of the jump, touch the toes while trying to maintain a vertical back position. The landing should be on both feet. (Equipment: minitramp—optional.)

BOUNCING BALL

Starting in a bent-knee position (squat), begin with a jump that is high and then lower each jump to simulate a bouncing ball that loses height with each bounce. Variations: Partners pretend to bounce (or dribble) each other. Bounce to music, or bounce next to a real bouncing ball.

TOP

With hands at the side, squat down and jump into space, trying a half, quarter, or full turn. The landing should be as the start, with hands at the side. This may also be executed with the arms in various starting positions (e.g., folded, straight out, or extended to the side).

LEAPFROG

The formation should be two single-file lines with four to six feet between people. The leapfrog has two units: the base and the frog. The "base" bends forward into a stationary creeping, knees-and-hands position. The head should be tucked down. The "frog" runs, places the hands on the base's back, and pushes off with the legs straddled and extended to the sides. The landing is on two feet with knees slightly bent. The activity may be performed alone or as a relay.

TIGHTROPE WALKER

Using a line drawn on the floor, with one foot in front of the other, walk (forward or backward), placing the toe and then heel on the line. Initially, the arms should be extended sideward; however, variability in arm position can be practiced. (Equipment: floor tape or chalk.)

CRAB WALK

Beginning in the sitting position, lift the seat off the floor, transferring body weight support to the hands and feet. The back should be held fairly straight. The direction of movement may be either forward, backward, or sideward. (See Figure 17-25.)

FIGURE 17-25
Crab walk

JUMPING SWAN

While jumping upward, pull the arms high overhead and arch the body. The hips are moved forward, and the head and shoulders pulled back hard with the legs extended to the rear. The landing should be on both feet with the body vertical. (See Figure 17-26.)

TUCK JUMP

Jump upward, drawing the knees to the chest while grasping the shins (tuck). The back should remain as vertical as possible, and the landing should be on both feet.

FIGURE 17-26
Jumping swan

RABBIT JUMP

Start in a squatting position, back straight, body weight over the toes. Jump forward, bringing the seat high; land on the hands and then both feet. Variations: Jump backward; click heels together; kick feet out as a donkey.

FIGURE 17-27
Rabbit jump

HEEL SLAP

Starting in a relaxed, standing position, jump up, kicking the legs back behind the body, bending them at the knees. Slap the hands to the soles of the feet. Before landing, straighten the legs but allow a slight bend to cushion the shock. Variation: Jump up and touch hands to toes, extended in front of the body.

FIGURE 17-28
Heel slap

HEEL CLICK

Stand with feet comfortably apart and ready to jump. Jump into the air and click feet together while in flight. Upon landing, bend the knees slightly to cushion the shock. (See Figure 17-29.)

FIGURE 17-29
Heel click

TUMMY BALANCE

Lie on stomach, keeping arms and legs straight. Raise arms, legs, head, and chest off the floor and balance on tummy.

ROCKING HORSE

Partners sit on each other's toes, facing and grasping forearms. One partner leans back and raises the other off the floor. The partner being raised straightens the legs, sits back, and raises the other partner off the floor. A rhythmic rocking should be the goal. (See Figure 17-30.)

FIGURE 17-30

DOUBLE-KNEE BALANCE

On knees, grasp right foot with right hand and hold it off the floor. Then repeat with the left foot and hand. Try raising both feet off the floor at the same time, maintaining balance on the knees.

CRANE DIVE

Take a front-scale position and slowly lean forward as far as possible without losing balance. Change the position of the arms; then attempt to pick up an object on the floor.

PEOPLE PYRAMIDS

Children should be encouraged to design their own balance structures, first working in pairs, then threes, fours, fives, and so on. A few safety precautions need to be observed:

1. Place weight over a firmly supported base, never in the small of the back or at a joint.
2. Form pyramids carefully by climbing to high positions; do not jump onto another person.
3. One child is responsible for signaling to "squash" or dismantle the pyramid. To squash a pyramid, all children should extend arms forward and legs back at the same time. Use this technique only with hands and knees pyramids.
4. Always use mats.

Pyramids can be formed by using a variety of balance stunts and shapes as the focus. (See Figures. 17-68 to 17-70.)

TURK STAND

With arms folded across the chest, sit cross-legged on the floor. Stand without using the hands or changing the position of the feet.

TRIPOD

In a squatting position, place hands flat on the mat; place crown of head at hairline about one foot in front of hands so the three points form a triangular base; lift body weight, resting knees on bent elbows. Maintain this position. (See Figure 17-31.)

UPSPRING

Kneel with toes pointed and ankles extended; swing the arms backward and then forward, creating lift, while simultaneously pushing the feet. The result should be an upswing to the standing position.

FIGURE 17-31
Tripod

MULE KICK

Place both hands on the mat; bend knees, and kick one leg at a time into the air. Return to the floor, and stand.

BALANCE STAND—FRONT SCALE

Stand on either foot, bend forward at the waist to form a right angle, and extend free leg behind and arms out to the side.

WHEELBARROW

One person grasps the legs of another at the knees and walks as if guiding a wheelbarrow. The front "wheel" walks on hands and keeps back straight.

DOUBLE WALK

Partners face and grasp upper arms. One person steps diagonally across the insteps of the other, who walks forward. The person on top shifts weight as the other walks.

THREAD THE NEEDLE OR GRAPEVINE

Standing, grasp hands or hold wand in front of body. Bend forward and step over hands or wand one foot at a time and finish with hands still clasped behind. Reverse, and return to original position. This can also be done while lying on the back, with the knees bent, by passing the feet up and under the hands or wand without touching them and then returning to the original position. (See Figure 17-32.)

FIGURE 17-32

COFFEE GRINDER

Place one hand on the floor; extend the other arm up and the legs out. Keeping arms straight, walk around the stationary hand, using it as a pivot point.

TOE PUSH

Partners sit facing, raise legs in a V position, and clasp hands under knees. On a signal, they try to force each other off balance by pushing against the other's feet with the toes.

FIGURE 17-33
Toe push

PUSH WAR

Partners stand opposite each other across the center line and place hands on the other's shoulders. On a signal, they attempt to push the opponent back over the end line. (Equipment: three lines drawn 20 to 30 feet apart.)

ROOSTER FIGHT

Partners stand on one leg opposite each other with arms folded across the chest. On a signal, they attempt to push the other off balance; they do not hit. When one partner touches the floor with the free leg, the other partner is declared the winner.

SEAL SLAP

Start in a front-lying position with hands directly under the shoulders and toes on the mat. Push off from the hands and toes, and at the same time, clap hands in the air. Then return to the starting position (Figure 17-34).

FIGURE 17-34
Seal slap

FROG STAND TIP-UP

Squat down, place hands on floor about a shoulder width apart, and bend elbows out away from the midline of the body. Place inside of knees on elbows and raise feet from floor to balance. (See Figure 17-35.)

FIGURE 17-37

FIGURE 17-35

SITTING BALANCE

The base (bottom person) lies on the mat with legs raised and knees slightly bent. The top sits on the base's feet and extends arms back, grasping the base's hands. The base straightens legs and releases the top's hands; the top extends arms to sides to help maintain balance. (See Figure 17-36.)

HORIZONTAL STAND

The base lies on the back with knees bent. The top stands with feet just behind the base's head and hands on the base's knees. The base grasps the ankles of the top. As the top springs up and shifts weight to hands, the base raises arms perpendicular to the floor. (See Figure 17-37.)

ANGEL BALANCE

The base lies on the back with legs raised, knees slightly bent, and feet placed diagonally alongside the top's pelvic bones. The base takes the top's hands and slowly raises the top into a balanced position. Hands are let go, and the top balances with arms out to side. On a signal, the base bends the knees and lowers the top to the floor, whereupon the top returns to a standing position. (See Figure 17-38.)

FOREARM BALANCE—TIGER STAND

In a kneeling position with forearms on the mat, palms down, index fingers and thumbs touching, head between them, extend right leg and swing it up overhead. At the same time, spring off the left leg and bring both legs into a straight balanced position. (See Figure 17-39.)

THIGH BALANCE

The base stands directly behind the top in a semi-squat position with the back straight and the feet about a shoulder width apart. The top places one foot

FIGURE 17-36

FIGURE 17-38
Angel balance

FIGURE 17-39

on the thigh of the base, and the base grasps the leg at the knee. Then the top places the other foot on the other leg while the base grasps the other knee. The top should lean forward and straighten up to form a balanced position. To return to the ground, the top jumps down, and the base lets go of the legs. Partners should be of equal weight, or the base can be heavier.

HEADSTAND

Take a tripod position and extend the legs over the head, keeping the legs straight and toes pointed. Maintain balance. To come down, bend the knees and let the body weight come down into a squat. A partner may stand beside and hold an arm across and behind the other person so the legs can be stopped from flying over too far. The partner should not lift the legs.

HANDSTAND

Extend arms straight up beside the ears: place one leg in front of the other. Step on the front leg, and kick the back leg up, placing the hands on the floor and maintaining the head between the arms' position.

FIGURE 17-40
Headstand

FIGURE 17-41A
Hand stand (beginning)

Bring the second leg to the first, point toes, and tighten abdomen and buttocks to maintain a straight body position. Bend one leg at a time, and step back to the original position. A partner may assist by standing beside the performer and extending an arm behind the legs to prevent overbalancing. The spotter should never lift the legs. (See Figures 17-41A and 17-41B.)

FIGURE 17-41B
Hand stand

SPLIT JUMP

Jump upward, spreading the arms overhead and the feet as wide as possible. Land with the feet together.

JACKKNIFE

This is similar to Toe Touch except that while the legs are extended forward and upward during the upward movement, the feet are together (not apart) to touch the toes. (See Figure 17-42.)

FIGURE 17-42

BENT-KNEE HOP

Squat and take a tuck position (arms and hands wrapped around knees). Proceed to hop (two feet) on the balls of the feet.

JUMP FOOT

Stand with the outside foot against the wall, about 12 inches from the floor and in front of the inside leg. Spring from the inside foot, and jump over the leg.

FREE STANDING

Lie on the back on the mat with arms folded across the chest. Come to a standing position without unfolding the arms or using the elbows.

SINGLE SQUAT

Stand on the mat and raise the arms to the side for balance. Raise one leg in front, keeping the knee straight. Squat, keeping the weight well over the supporting leg. Return to a standing position without losing balance.

SPANKER

Take position as for the Crab Walk. Raise both feet in the air, and slap seat with right hand, then left hand. Advanced: Hop, extend right leg, and spank with left hand: hop, extend left leg, and spank with right hand. (See Figure 17-43.)

FIGURE 17-43

CARTWHEEL (TO THE RIGHT SIDE)

Stand sideways with right side leading. Raise both arms straight overhead, a shoulder distance apart: raise the right leg and step onto it, placing the right hand on the floor as the left leg is kicked overhead. The left hand is then placed on the floor as both legs come overhead and are split in the air. Land on the left foot, followed by the right foot, facing the original position. There should be an even 4-count rhythm to this movement (*i.e.*, right hand, count 1; left hand, count 2; left foot, count 3; right foot, count 4).

DOUBLE LAME DOG

Move across the floor on one hand and one foot. Use all the combinations possible (four total). Do this only a short distance (10 feet) as this is very strenuous.

TURTLE

Take a push-up position on the floor with the arms and legs spread wide apart. Move in small increments in various directions. Maintain body plane about the same distance from the floor throughout.

WALRUS WALK AND SLAP

Take a front-leaning rest position with toes pointed and fingers pointed out. Move forward by pushing off both hands at the same time (jumping). Try to clap hands on each step.

INDIVIDUAL DROPS

Knee drop: Kneeling on a mat with the body erect, lift the feet off the floor and fall forward, maintaining a straight body position. Break the fall with the hands and arms.

Front drop: Stand on one leg with the other extended straight back and arms extended up over the head. Slowly lean forward, reaching the arms toward the floor until overbalanced; then break the fall with the hands and arms. Keep both legs straight and lift the back leg as the weight is taken on the hands. The head is held erect throughout the stunt.

Dead fall: Stand on both feet and fall forward slowly, keeping the knees straight. Take the weight on the hands and arms and end in a push-up position. The feet should not move.

FRONT TO BACK

Start in a push-up position: bend the elbows and push the body upward. Turn over and land in a back-leaning rest position.

WALK AND JUMP THROUGH

Take a push-up position on the floor. Using small steps, walk the feet through the hands until the body is fully extended in a back-leaning rest position. The hands stay on the floor throughout. Return to the original position by reversing the procedure. Try this stunt by pushing off both feet simultaneously and shooting them between the arms in one continuous motion (jump through). The hips must be raised sufficiently to permit the feet to pass between the hands. It may be easier to swing the legs to one side, lifting one hand to allow the legs to pass under them at first. (See Figure 17-45.)

BOUNCER

From a push-up position, bounce up and down, leaving both hands and feet at the same time. Try clapping while airborne or moving in different directions.

Table 17-3

Listings and descriptions are arranged in approximate developmental order and by category of movement.

Levels III & IV

NAME		LEVEL	NAME	LEVEL
Double Lame Dog	Animal movement	III & IV	Straight Hang	
Turtle			L-Hang	IV
Walrus Walk and Slap			Inverted Hang	
Donkey Kick			Double Hanging Ropes:	III & IV
Knee Drop	Individual stunts	III & IV	Straight-Arm Hang	
Front Drop			Tuck Hang	
Front to Back (Rolling the Log)			L-Hang	
Dead Fall		IV	Skin the Cat	IV
Walk and Jump Through			Inverted Hang	
Bouncer			Climbing	
Pretzel			Balance Beam:	
Single-Leg Circle			Locomotor Movements	III & IV
Backbend Down and Up			Turning	
Balance Jump	Individual balance stunts	III & IV	Manipulative Movements	
Fish Hawk Dive			Individual Balance Stunts	
V-Up			Animal Movements	
Front Seat Support			Tumbling Skills (on beam)	IV
Elbow Balance			Forward Roll	
Judo Roll	Tumbling and inverted balance	III & IV	Backward Roll	
Forward Roll Variations			Cartwheel	
Backward Roll Variations			Vaulting:	III & IV
Backward Extension Roll			Squat	
Headstand Variations			Flank	
Handstand Variations			Wolf	
Neck Spring			Straddle	
Cartwheel Variations			Head	
Round-off			Handspring	IV
Headspring			Trampoline:	III & IV
Handspring			Seat Drop	
Wheelbarrow Variations	Partner stunts	III & IV	Hands and Knees Drop	
Dromedary Walk			Knee Drop	
Centipede			Front Drop	
Eskimo or Double Roll		IV	Combine with Turns	IV
Circle High Jump			Horizontal Bar:	III & IV
Triple Roll (Monkey Roll)			Monkey Hang	
Double Bear	Partner balance	III & IV	Pull-ups	
Front sit			Skin the Cat	
Back Layout			Scramble Over	
Stand on Partner's Knees			Pull-over	
Chest Stand			Knee Swing	
Handstand Hip Support		IV	Penny Drop	
Knee and Shoulder Stand			Horizontal Ladder:	III & IV
People Pyramids (advanced)			Chinning	
Rope Jumping: (Combine primary individual rope skills into routines)		III	Swing and Drop	
			Single-Rung Travel	
			Double-Rung Travel	
Double Dutch Long Rope		III & IV	Side-Rail Travel	
Juggling			Rung Travel Sideways	
Single Hanging Rope:	Large-equipment skills		Rings:	III & IV
Lying to Standing			Tuck Hang	
Climbing			L-Hang	
Swing and Jump			Inverted Hang	
			Skin the Cat	
			Basket	

FIGURE 17-44A

DONKEY KICK

In a squatting position place the hands on the floor in front of the feet. Support the weight on the hands momentarily as the legs are kicked up and out together. Two kicks can be attempted before returning the feet to the floor. (See Figures 17-44A and 17-44B.)

PRETZEL

From a front-lying position, raise the head and trunk and try to bring the feet up to touch the back of the head. Another child may measure the distance to go by a hand span. If only a hand span away, try to reach the back of the head with one foot at a time.

SINGLE LEG CIRCLE

From a squatting position with the hands on the floor in front of the feet, extend one leg out to the side (right). Bring the right leg forward and under the right hand; continue around and under the left hand and left foot, returning to the original position. Do several leg circles in succession. Repeat with the left leg (Fig. 17-46.)

FIGURE 17-44B
Donkey kick

BACK BEND AND UP

Stand erect with feet about a shoulder width apart. Stretch arms straight up over the head, and lift chin and drop head back; bend back at the waist, leading with the hands and complete with hands and feet on the floor and back arched. To return to the original position, rock back gently onto the arms keeping chin up and head back, push arms off the floor shifting weight to the feet and stand up. It is good technique to keep the arms over the head and the head back throughout the entire movement.

BALANCE JUMP

Stand in a front scale position with arms out to the side and one leg extended back. Keeping the upper body parallel to the ground, quickly change weight to the other leg.

FIGURE 17-45
Walk and jump through

FIGURE 17-46
Single leg circle

FISH HAWK DIVE

Fold an 8 ½-by-11-inch piece of paper in half and place it on the floor in front of the body. Kneel on one leg; extend the arms out to the side and hold one leg back. Lean forward carefully, pick up the piece of paper with the teeth, and return to the original position. If this is too difficult at first, have a partner hold the piece of paper. When the stunt is completed successfully, fold the paper in half again and try for a lower target. (See Figure 17-47.)

V-UP

From a straight-lying position on the back with arms overhead and legs straight, simultaneously bring the legs and arms up to make a V-shape while balanced on the seat. Try to hold the position for five seconds. This stunt may be difficult at first so start with the knees slightly bent; the arms may also be placed in back of the body in the V-position for more balance.

FRONT SEAT SUPPORT

From a sitting position with legs extended straight out in front, place the hands pointing forward and flat on the floor between the hips and knees. Push down on arms and lift the seat off the floor; then try to lift the heels off also. Hold this position for three to five seconds.

FIGURE 17-47
Fish hawk dive

ELBOW BALANCE

From a front-lying position, bend the elbows and point the hands toward the feet on the floor. Support the body on the forehead and toes, working the arms underneath the body for support; eventually take all the weight on two hands, with the elbows providing the leverage under the body. Try this for three seconds at first. This stunt is difficult to perform so children need to be able to find their center of gravity to balance in this position. The elbow support divides the upper and lower body into equal weights. (See Figure 17-48.)

FIGURE 17-48
Elbow balance

JUDO ROLL (SAFETY ROLL)

This roll is used to prevent injury from a fall by enabling the child better to absorb the impact of a fall. The roll is executed on the shoulder and upper part of the back by bringing one arm down across the body and throwing that shoulder toward the mat and curling the body to roll on the side.

FORWARD ROLL VARIATIONS

Try a variety of leg positions to start the roll and a variety to finish the roll (*i.e.*, bent knees, straight legs, straddle, from one foot, and to and from various balance positions). Perform several rolls in succession. Tape a line on the mat to help in rolling in a straight line.

FIGURE 17-49
Backward roll variations

Combine the forward roll with other stunts, either rolling from another stunt like a bear walk or headstand or rolling into another stunt like a cartwheel or a jackknife. Combining skills adds greatly to the interest and increases the joy of practicing.

BACKWARD ROLL VARIATIONS

Emphasize the push-off with the hands while continuing to work on this roll. Vary the beginning and ending leg positions.

Tuck position: Start in the squat and end in the same position, or change the landing. Some possibilities include landing on straight legs, straddled legs, one foot, two feet and jumping up, and so on.

Pike position: Start with legs straight; bend over at the waist and reach hands toward the floor behind; as you lose your balance back over your heels, catch yourself on your hands and then quickly move hands back over the head as your seat touches the floor. Complete the roll as previously described, landing in one of a variety of positions. (See Figure 17-49.)

STRADDLE POSITION

Start with the legs straight and spread wide apart. Bend over at the waist and reach hands back between the legs, catching the weight on the hands as you drop back. Again quickly move the hands over the head to push, as in other backward rolls, and land on the feet.

Perform several rolls in succession. Combine the roll with other stunts. Try these combinations:

Crab walk, Backward roll
Jump through, Backward roll
Leg dip, Backward roll
Backward roll to a front scale
Backward roll to a headstand
Backward roll to a forward roll

HEADSTAND VARIATIONS

Review the basic headstand, positioning spotter(s) to grasp at the hips to prevent overbalancing. Arrive at the balanced position in a variety of ways. Lift both legs simultaneously, keeping knees straight; lift one leg at a time, knees straight; or start by lying flat on the stomach, pike at the waist, and then lift both legs up. Balance with the legs in various positions: stride, straddle, one knee bent, or changing while maintaining balance. Return to feet by stepping down, bending knees, and pushing the waist with the arms to snap back to a stand or by tucking the head and rolling forward. (See Figure 17-50.)

HANDSTAND VARIATIONS

The handstand may be varied similarly to the headstand, and spotters should position themselves to give support at the hips. Children should turn to step down as balance is lost when performing without spotters. A handstand may be begun by kicking up, jumping up, straddling, or piking up into position. Various leg positions can be attempted while balanced; the return to the feet can be accomplished by stepping, piking, or straddling down and by rolling out forward.

To roll out forward, first overbalance slightly, leading with the shoulders; then tuck the chin into the chest, bend the elbows and roll forward.

Once a free balance is accomplished, try walking on the hands. Walk in a forward direction, bending knees slightly to lead with the feet. (See Figure 17-51.)

BACKWARD EXTENSION ROLL

Before attempting this roll students must be able to execute a good backward roll, using the hands correctly. Begin the stunt from a stand, back to the mat; bend knees and roll back immediately as for a backward roll. When the hips are almost above the head, extend the arms and legs forcefully and simultaneously upward, pushing against the mat with hands,

FIGURE 17-50
Headstand variations

FIGURE 17-51
Handstand variations

head, and neck. Pull the head under and up to finish in a handstand position, holding momentarily. Practice these only for short periods as they are very fatiguing. (See Figure 17-52.)

NECKSPRING

Roll backward in a tuck position, keeping the feet over the head. When the knees are over the head and the shoulders and hands are bearing the weight, begin the forward motion by opening hips and driving the feet up toward the ceiling while pushing with the hands as the shoulders come off the mat. Extend the body and come to a standing position with a snapping action of the arms, neck, and legs. (See Figure 17-53.)

FIGURE 17-52
Backward extension roll

CARTWHEEL VARIATIONS

Variations for the cartwheel should include a light run with a skip for a takeoff, one arm (inside and outside), and a cartwheel to a handstand. Before attempting any of these variations the child should be able to cartwheel to each side. The one-arm inside cartwheel is done by placing the first hand down on the mat and immediately kicking the first leg over the head. The second arm is held at the side while the cartwheel is completed by stepping onto the second leg and coming to an upright position. The one-arm outside cartwheel is slightly more difficult and is done by starting in a sideways position with the arms extended overhead (Figure 17-54). As the step is taken to initiate the movement, the inside arm is drawn in across the body as the outside arm is placed on the floor. The legs extend over the head in the same way as they do for other cartwheels. To cartwheel to a handstand, the hands are placed on the mat one at a time, taking the weight as the legs are brought up and over the head one at a time and finishing together in a handstand position. The spotter should stand behind the performer and place the hands at the hips to prevent overbalancing. (See Figure 17-54.)

FIGURE 17-53
Neckspring

ROUND-OFF (RIGHT SIDE)

The round-off is started with a light run and a skip for takeoff; the hands are placed on the floor with the right hand in the same position as for a cartwheel, fingers to the side. The left hand is placed diagonally in front of the right hand with fingers facing the starting position. The feet are brought together over the head, and a quarter turn is made to land facing the starting point. The round-off is frequently the first movement that begins a backward tumbling sequence and can be followed by a backward roll or other backward tumbling stunt.

FIGURE 17-55
Double wheelbarrow

FIGURE 17-54
Cartwheel variations

HEADSPRING

Place the forehead and hands on the mat as for a headstand. Bend at the hips and gradually overbalance; as the weight shifts outside the base, thrust the feet forward over the head and toward the floor, pushing with the hands to arrive at a standing position with the knees slightly bent. The headspring is sometimes taught with a rolled-up mat for the head to provide elevation for the stunt.

Two spotters should stand on either side of the performer. The spotters each place one hand under the performer's hips and one under the shoulder, elevating the shoulders as the stunt is completed.

HANDSPRING

Begin with a light run and a skip takeoff. Place both hands on the mat and drive the first leg up and over the head, bringing the second leg to it over the head. Continue snapping both legs downward to the mat while pushing with arms and shoulders (shoulder shrug). Land in an upright position with legs slightly bent and arms over the head. Two spotters should stand on either side of the performer and place one hand on the middle of the back and one hand on the shoulder to help lift the performer to an upright position.

WHEELBARROW VARIATIONS

Wheelbarrow lifting: The pusher lifts the partner's legs as high as possible without changing the grip on the legs. The pusher lifts until the bottom child's body is at about a 45° angle with the floor.

The camel lift: The bottom child pikes at the waist to lift the seat as high in the air as possible. The "camels" can raise or lower their seat as they are being pushed.

Dumping the wheelbarrow: The bottom child is walked over to a mat where he or she ducks the head under (chin to chest). The seat is raised by piking at the waist, and a forward roll is made onto the mat.

Double wheelbarrow: Three children are needed. One child assumes a hands-and-knees position; the second child places the hands about 2 feet in front of the first child and then places the legs and body on top of the first child. The third child takes a position at the first child's legs and lifts them as in the regular wheelbarrow. The double wheelbarrow moves forward, synchronizing arm and leg movements. (See Figure 17-55.)

Two-way wheelbarrow: One child holds two wheelbarrows facing in opposite directions. The first wheelbarrow is secured in the forward position, and the second is added by placing the ankles over the already established hand position of the holder. The front moves forward as the back moves backward. (See Figure 17-56.)

FIGURE 17-56
Two-way wheelbarrow

DROMEDARY WALK

One child assumes a hands-and-knees position on the mat; the other child sits on the bottom child's back, facing the opposite direction. The top child wraps the legs around the bottom child's chest and leans forward to grasp the ankles of the bottom child. Once in this position the bottom child raises up off the knees, taking the weight of the top child and walking forward with the help of the top child.

CENTIPEDE

The centipede is started like the double wheelbarrow, with one child on hands and knees (the stronger, larger child is in the first position). The second child places the hands about 2 feet in front, and the third child is added at the front in the same position as the second child. The second and third children should spread their legs apart and place their ankles together. The walk is done with the bottom child raising off the knees and walking on hands and feet while the other two children walk on their hands only. (See Figure 17-57.)

FIGURE 17-58
Eskimo or double roll

CIRCLE HIGH JUMP

Three children of somewhat equal height stand in a circle holding hands. One child jumps forward over the opposite pair of joined hands. Jumping backward is not recommended. The children may take a short run together before the jumper explodes upward over the arms on a signal. (See Figure 17-59.)

TRIPLE ROLL

Three children assume a hands-and-knees position on a mat facing in the same direction. The middle child lowers to the mat and rolls to the right; the child on the right dives over the roller, lands in the middle position, and starts immediately rolling to the left. The child on the left must then dive over the roller to the middle and roll to the right again, starting the sequence all over.

FIGURE 17-57
Centipede

ESKIMO OR DOUBLE ROLL

One child lies on the mat in a hook position with the feet pointing in the direction of the roll. The second child stands with the feet on either side of the first child's head. The first child grasps the second's ankles with the thumbs on the inside and then raises his or her own feet so the other child can grasp them in a similar fashion. The child on top pushes off with the feet, diving forward and tucking the head under to roll forward as the bottom child is pulled to a sitting and then standing position, becoming the top child. The stunt may then be performed again. As the top child propels forward, it is important for the bottom child to keep the knees bent and place the feet on the floor. (See Figure 17-58.)

FIGURE 17-59
Circle high jump

FIGURE 17-60
Double bear

FIGURE 17-61
Front sit

DOUBLE BEAR

The bottom child takes a hands-and-knees position on the mat. The top child balances on the back in a hands-and-knees position with the hands over the shoulders and the knees over the hips. Both children raise their heads and look forward to finish the stunt. (See Figure 17-60.)

FRONT SIT

The bottom partner takes a back lying position and extends the legs upward. The top partner straddles the base so that they are looking at each other. The top partner then steps back and sits on the base's feet, extending his or her own legs forward as the base grasps the ankles and raises the partner up with the legs. The top partner should extend the arms outward to help balance. (See Figure. 17-61.)

BACK LAYOUT

The bottom partner takes the same position as for the front sit. The top partner places the small of the back on the base's feet and extends the arms out to the side as he or she lies back to balance. The base grasps the top partner's wrists and slowly extends the legs up to complete the stunt. (See Figure 17-62.)

STAND ON PARTNER'S KNEES

The bottom partner assumes a hook-lying position with hands placed beside the ears, palms up. The top partner stands with balls of feet on the hands of the bottom partner and leans forward to place hands on partner's knees. The bottom partner extends the arms up to complete the balanced position. (See Figure 17-63.) This may also be done with the top partner facing the opposite way, placing the hands on the partner's hands and the feet on the partner's knees. (See Figure 17-64.)

FIGURE 17-62
Back Layout

FIGURE 17-63
Stand on partner's knees

FIGURE 17-64
Stand on partner's knees

HANDSTAND HIP SUPPORT

The bottom partner takes a hook-sitting position with feet flat on the floor. The top partner approaches the stunt from behind the bottom partner, reaching over the head of the base to place the hands on the knees. The base partner then places the hands on the hips of the top as the top kicks up into a handstand position. The base maintains contact with the top's hips throughout the balance. Two spotters should be positioned on either side of the partner balancing on the hands. This stunt should be attempted only by students able to perform a handstand on the floor. (See Figure 17-65.)

CHEST STAND

The bottom partner takes a firm hands-and-knees position. The top child hooks forearms and hands under the base's chest and waist. Leaning across the base's back the top child kicks the legs up to an inverted position to balance. Spotters should be positioned on the far side of the performers to prevent overbalancing. (See Figure 17-66.)

KNEE AND SHOULDER STAND

The bottom child assumes a hook-lying position with hands up ready to support the top partner. The top child stands in front of the base's knees, placing the hands on the knees and leaning forward to rest shoulders on the bottom child's hands. The legs are kicked up to the inverted position, with spotters on either side of the performers to prevent overbalancing. The top partner should keep the arms straight and the head up. (See Figure 17-67.)

FIGURE 17-65
Handstand hip support

FIGURE 17-66
Chest stand

top children mount and assume their position; and on the third signal, a finished balance position is assumed by extending arms and legs. The fourth signal is given to break down the pyramid and return the children to the edge of the mat. Forming pyramids under a parachute is challenging and also exciting material for gym shows. (See Figures 17-68 to 17-70.)

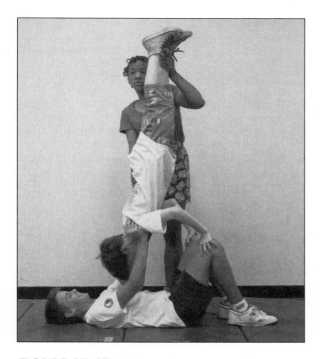

FIGURE 17-67
Knee and shoulder stand

PEOPLE PYRAMIDS (ADVANCED)

Children who have mastered the partner balances are ready for and may enjoy the following group balances (people pyramids). The illustrations show groups of five children, but the numbers can be adjusted either higher or lower depending on the purpose of the project. Pyramid building may also be used as a creative activity, with the children deciding on specific support and balance positions and building their own unique statues. Signals can be used for increasing orderliness or for demonstrations. Children begin by standing at attention on the edge of the mat. On the first signal, the base children assume their position on the mat; on the second signal, the

FIGURE 17-69
People pyramids

FIGURE 17-70
People Pyramids

FIGURE 17-68
People Pyramids

ROPE JUMPING

Review the primary rope-jumping skills for Levels I–II and combine several of the skills into rope-jumping routines. Music and chants should be used to establish a cadence.

DOUBLE DUTCH LONG ROPE

Two ropes are held by two turners, one in each hand. The ropes are turned toward each other so that one is up when the other is on the floor. A single-beat jump is required to keep up the timing of the ropes passing under the feet. The child should watch the front-door rope and enter the ropes at an angle, jumping over the back-door rope as he or she begins to jump. Turning the ropes for Double Dutch is quite tiring, and the turners should be rotated frequently. Double Irish is a variation of Double Dutch, except the ropes are turned away from each other; the jumper enters at an angle following the front-door rope and jumps the back-door rope. A single-beat jump is required for this skill also.

JUGGLING

Review the progression for juggling at Levels I–II. When the students are able to maintain three objects for five consecutive rotations, they may try juggling scarves and small balls. One final skill that can be tried with balls is juggling to a wall.

Juggling to the wall: The following progression is described for children whose right hand is dominant. Left-handed students should start with the left hand where the right hand is indicated. Students should practice this skill with a partner. A retrieving partner should be about 5 feet behind the juggler. Students should have 10 successes at each step before progressing to the next step.

1. Practice throwing the ball (handball, racquetball, or tennis ball) to the wall and catching it to determine the rebound effect of the ball chosen on the wall being used. Small juggling balls are also available and are a suitable size for children.
2. Toss with the right hand and catch with the left hand. A target on the wall should be about shoulder height. Repeat by tossing with the left and catching with the right.
3. Place two balls in the right hand. Toss one ball and catch in the left hand. Toss back with the left hand and time the toss of the second ball with the right hand to be able to receive the left toss as it rebounds back from the wall. Verbalize the sequence as follows: toss right, catch left, toss left, toss right, catch right, catch left.
4. Using three balls, place two in the right hand and one in the left. Throw and catch the three balls and stop (one rotation). The sequence is as follows: toss right, toss left, catch left, toss right, catch right, catch left. The balls can be numbered: the two balls in the right hand are numbers 1 and 3: the ball in the left hand is number 2. Toss balls in number order. Repeat this sequence, starting with two balls in the left hand. An auditory clue that can help the timing of the tosses is to release the second ball as the sound of the first ball hitting the wall is heard.
5. Progressively add on rotations, two to three to four until wall juggling becomes continuous.

SINGLE HANGING ROPE

Review the following skills for Levels I–II: lying to standing, climbing, swinging, and hanging.

L-hang: Reach up and grasp the rope in two hands as high as possible without jumping. Raise both legs off the floor and hold straight out from the body to form an L position with the body and legs. This requires good abdominal strength and should be held for about three seconds. (See Figure 17-71.)

FIGURE 17-71
L-hang

Inverted hang: Grasp the rope in front of the face and kick both legs up and over the head until they balance against the rope over the head. Hold the inverted position for three seconds. The rope may start to swing as the legs are kicked over the head, so a spotter should steady the rope and also place a hand under the shoulder of the child who is upside down.

DOUBLE HANGING ROPES

Straight-arm hang: Jump up and grasp the ropes as high as possible, bending the arms and keeping the body straight. Stay in the pull-up position for three seconds and then return to the feet. Keep the ropes from swinging by not jumping too vigorously.

Tuck hang: Begin as for the straight-arm hang and then bring the knees up to the tuck position and hold for three seconds.

L-hang: Begin as for the straight-arm hang and then raise both legs together to the L position and hold.

Skin the cat: Grasp the ropes at eye level and kick the legs up and between the arms, letting them drop back toward the ground over the head. Before the legs touch the ground, draw them back up using the abdominal muscles, and return to the original standing position. The legs may be allowed to touch the ground while the child is in the inverted position, so that to return to the starting position the child will have to spring off the feet to begin the return motion. The ropes may start swinging as the child starts the stunt with the leg kick, so a spotter can help steady the ropes, being careful not to impede the movement of the performer. (See Figure 17-72.)

FIGURE 17-72
Skin the cat

Inverted hang: Grasp the ropes at eye level and kick the legs up and over the head until they are straight up overhead. A spotter is needed to steady the ropes and protect the performer by placing one hand under the performer's shoulder. The inverted position should be held for three seconds: the legs may be placed against the ropes for balance. (See Figure 17-73.)

Climbing: Climbing the double ropes is difficult because the legs are not used to push. As a lead-up to climbing, the children should first practice pulling up from a lying position between the two ropes, using just the arms. The body is pulled up by alternating hands, pulling first with one hand and then the other. The child should pull first to the sitting position, then

FIGURE 17-73
Inverted hang

to a standing position. Once this is accomplished, the child may continue pulling with the arms and raise the feet off the floor.

BALANCE BEAM

For all movements along the beam the head should be held erect and the eyes should be focused on the beam. A straight body alignment is important to maintain balance and may be achieved by squeezing the muscles of the shoulders and buttocks together.

Locomotor movements: The locomotor movements used on the beam are walking, running, skipping, hopping, jumping, leaping, and galloping. (Rolling will be described later in this section.) Each of the locomotors may be done forward or backward and in some cases sideways. The arms should be held out to the side to aid in balance, and spotters can be positioned on either side of the beam to give a hand for balance when needed.

Turning: Turns should be done on the ball of the foot, starting first with a half turn on two feet to get the feel of rising up onto the toes and turning. The focus should be redirected to the beam as the turn is completed. Then the children should try turning in a squatting position or on one foot. The children should be encouraged to make up their own ways of turning and to vary the body parts used for support. For example, turns may be done on the knees or the seat.

Manipulative movements: Manipulative movements on the beam may include throwing, catching, and bouncing. When manipulating an object while on the beam, a straight body position is important and the eyes should still focus on the beam more than on the object. Some other manipulative skills that may be tried include juggling and using the Hula-Hoop.

Individual balance stunts: Any of the individual balance stunts that are performed on the floor may be attempted on the balance beam. The child must, however, be proficient at the skill on the floor before attempting it on the beam (Consult descriptions for these stunts for Levels I–II and III–IV.) Again, it is necessary to focus on the beam and maintain a tight body for better balance.

Animal movements: Animal movements are challenging and fun to attempt on the beam. (Consult descriptions for these in both Levels I–II and III–IV.)

TUMBLING SKILLS ON BEAM

Forward roll: Start in a squat and place hands on top of the beam with the thumbs together and the fingers around the sides of the beam. Lift the hips and tuck the head under between the arms. Roll forward, taking the weight on the upper back and squeezing the elbows together. The hands may be shifted to an undergrip, with the fingers sliding under the beam to grasp it. Finish the roll in a one-leg squat, releasing the beam as the foot touches the beam. The roll may also be completed in a sitting position as shown in Figure 17-74.

FIGURE 17-74
Forward roll

Backward roll: Start in a back-lying position: reach over the head and grasp the beam with the thumbs together and fingers alongside the beam. Squeeze the elbows together and bring the knees up to roll backward. Push with the hands and land on one foot or the knee. Spotters should be positioned for both rolls to support the hips as the roll is performed. (See Figure 17-75.)

Cartwheel: The cartwheel on the beam is executed just like the cartwheel on the floor. The body must stay very straight. This may be practiced on a line on the floor until the child develops confidence and a good straight cartwheel. A spotter can stand behind the performer to prevent overbalancing but should not stand in front. (See Figure 17-76.)

VAULTING

Review vaulting skills from Levels I–II (squat, flank, straddle, and head).

Wolf: Use a running approach and a two-foot takeoff on a springboard. Place hands on the vaulting box, bring one knee up between the hands, and extend the other leg to the side. Push off with the hands and bring feet together on the landing, flexing the knees slightly.

Handspring: Review the head vault before attempting this vault. Use a two-feet take off, extend the arms over the head and onto the horse; keep the body straight as the legs go over the horse through the handstand position. The weight rolls from the hands to the fingers; push off to land on the feet with the knees slightly bent. This stunt demands a lot of power off the springboard to complete and should only be attempted by the highly skilled child. Two spotters should be on either side of the performer on the far side of the horse, grasping wrists and supporting shoulders.

FIGURE 17-76
Cartwheel

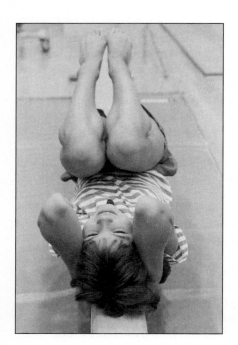

FIGURE 17-75
Backward roll

TRAMPOLINE

During practice on the trampoline, class members should be positioned around the trampoline to act as guards by gently pushing performers who lose control back on the trampoline. The minimum number of spotters is six, one on each end and two on each side. First the bounce and break (stop) should be taught. When bouncing, the child's feet are a shoulder width apart on the bed and are brought together in the air. The arms circle from a low position in front of the body to above shoulder level. The focus is about five or six feet in front of the performer at the edge of the bed. A mark can be placed on the bed as a ready reference. The break is done by bending the knees and stopping the action of the trampoline. The child must be proficient at this on command before being permitted to practice the other skills.

Seat drop: From the vertical position in the air, lift the feet up and land on the seat with the legs extended forward. The hands are pointed forward and positioned at the hips. Hands and feet hit the bed simultaneously, rebounding the performer to a standing position.

Hands and knees drop (four points): From the vertical position in the air, raise the hips, keeping the trunk parallel to the bed, and drop on the knees; lower legs and hands simultaneously. The head is held in line with the trunk.

Knee drop: From the vertical position in the air, bend the knees, keeping the head, back, and shoulders in line. The knees and lower legs only land on the bed, causing the rebound to the feet. Children must be sure to keep the back straight and not bend at the hips.

Front drop: Try this first from the hands and knees position. As the body rebounds off the bed from the hands and knees, extend the arms forward and the legs back. The weight is taken on the forearms and thighs. The waist should land where the feet were. From the standing position, when the body is in the air, lift the hips to a horizontal position and drop onto the bed, with the waist landing where the feet were. Once several of their skills have been mastered the child should be encouraged to put them together in combinations with turns.

HORIZONTAL BAR

The bar may be grasped in an undergrip as for chin-ups or in an overgrip as for pull-ups. There should be at least a two-inch mat underneath for the low bar and a four-inch mat for the high bar. (Review the pull-over, skin the cat, and knee swing for Levels I–II.)

Monkey hang: Stand under the bar and parallel with it. Reach up and grasp the bar with the hands facing each other and about 12 inches apart. Bring one leg up and place the heel on top of the bar; then bring the other leg up and place the heel on top of the other foot. Hang like a monkey.

Pull-ups: A high bar should be used and grasped in an overgrip, that is, with the hands over the bar and the fingers wrapped over the bar and the thumbs underneath. The body is pulled up by using the arms until the chin comes over the top of the bar; then the arms are used to let the body down to the straight hang position. The procedure is repeated as many times as possible. This is quite difficult for children, and so a spotter may grasp the legs to help support the weight of the child as the pull-up is done.

Scramble over: Start in a front support position, with the arms straight and palms down. Lift one leg up and over the bar to a rest position next to the hand. Release that hand, shift the weight to the thigh, and re-grasp the bar on the outside of the leg. Swing the other leg over and bring both legs together as they come down on the opposite side of the bar.

Penny drop: The low bar should be used for the penny drop. Grasp the bar with an overgrip and swing the legs up and between the hands as for the skin the cat. Hook the knees over the bar and release the hands. Keeping the knees bent and the head erect, swing back and forth. When the body is parallel to the floor on the forward swing, release the knees from the bar and bring the feet down to the ground. A spotter may assist by standing in front of the bar and supporting at the hips as the performer releases from the bar. (See Figure 17-77.)

HORIZONTAL LADDER

The horizontal ladder activities described here require a great deal of muscular strength and endurance and so should be added on gradually. That is, children should be encouraged to travel only one-quarter of the distance to start; then they gradually

FIGURE 17-77
Penny drop

work up to the full distance as strength and endurance improve. The children should keep track of the number of rungs they have passed, adding one each day to increase the challenge. Some safety procedures should be observed. Children should be required to travel in the same direction and wait their turn at least five feet from the ladder. Two parts of the body should be in contact with the apparatus for maximum safety.

Chinning: An over- or undergrip may be used. Pull up until the chin is over the bar and then return to the straight hang position before dropping to the ground or repeating the chin move.

Swing and drop: Swing forward and back by alternately raising the legs forward, using the abdominals, and pushing them back as the body swings with a pendular motion. Stop swinging before dropping off. Look down to spot the landing place and release both hands simultaneously, landing gently on the balls of the feet and bending the knees.

Single-rung travel: Stand on the top rung of the vertical ladder and reach the first and second rungs by grasping with the overgrip, one hand on each rung. Start the traveling by simultaneously shifting the body forward and releasing the back hand. The back hand reaches forward and regrasps the third bar. Continue the movement by letting go with the new back hand and alternately regrasping. It is best to maintain some momentum by keeping the movements sequential, that is, not stopping between each rung.

Double-rung travel: Start with both hands on one rung; swing legs forward and backward as in the swing and drop. When the legs are forward, release both hands and regrasp the next rung with both hands.

Side-rail travel: Grasp one side rail with both hands facing each other. Travel along the rail by using the hand-over-hand method.

Rung travel sideways: Hang with hands on separate rungs, hands facing each other and the body facing one side rail. Shift the right hand to the same rung as the left hand. Let go with the left hand and regrasp the next rung with the palms facing the head. Travel with the body swinging from side to side, and always lead with the same hand, either right or left.

RINGS

The rings can be used in much the same way as the double hanging ropes. The tuck hang, L-hang, inverted hang, and skin the cat are all executed in the same way as for the ropes, except the hand grip is below the rings with the palms facing each other. For safety purposes a spotter should be positioned at the shoulders for the inverted hang and skin the cat.

Basket: Grasp the rings with the palms facing each other; kick one leg up over the head and bring the other leg to the inverted position. When the body is inverted, bend the knees and place one foot in each ring. Arch the back and raise the head and hold this position. Carefully remove one foot at a time from the rings and return to the straight hang position. (See Figure 17-78.)

FIGURE 17-78
Basket

SUGGESTED SOURCES

Activities

COOPER, P. S. & TRINKA, M. (1994). \(3rd Ed.). New York: Macmillan

DAUER, V., & PANGRAZI, R. (1992). *Dynamic physical education for elementary school children* (10th ed.). New York: Macmillan.

KIRCHNER, G. (1992). *Physical education for elementary school children* (8th ed.). Dubuque, IA: Wm. C. Brown.

LOKEN, N., & WILLOUGHBY, R. (1977). *Complete book of gymnastics* (3rd ed.). Englewood Cliffs, NJ: Prentice Hall.

O'QUINN, G. (1990). *Teaching Developmental Gymnastics: Building physical skills for children.* Austin, TX: University of Texas Press.

RYER, O. E. & BROWN, J. R. (1980). *A manual for tumbling and apparatus stunts* (7th ed.). Dubuque, IA: Wm. C. Brown.

SKOLNIK, P. L. (1974). *Jump rope.* New York: W. P. Workman.

SZYPULA, G. (1968). *Tumbling and balancing for all.* (2nd ed.). Dubuque, IA: Wm. C. Brown.

Readings

BOUCHER, A. (Sept., 1978). Educational gymnastics is for everyone. *Journal of Physical Education and Recreation.* 48–50.

PARENT, S. (Ed.). (Sept., 1978). Educational gymnastics. *Journal of Physical Education and Recreation.* 31–50.

SANDER, A. & GRIFFIN, M. (January, 1991). *Skill, Fitness and Critical Thinking Through Gymnastics. Strategies,* 10–13.

18

Intramural Activities and Special Events

Intramurals are supplemental activities that allow opportunity for participation outside the basic instructional program. With time during the instructional program being devoted primarily to fitness and specific skill development, intramurals provide extra practice and fun for interested children. Children need more activity than the 20- to 45-minutes the instructional program provides. Just as there are intellectually gifted individuals, there are athletically endowed children who desire extra stimulation and refinement of skills. Because several of the activities are inherently competitive, participation should always be on a voluntary basis with primary emphasis on involvement, not winning. A strong intramural program can make a significant contribution toward skill refinement, fitness, school spirit and involvement.

Time of Day

Basically, the time options are before school, noon and after the school day. An hour (or less) before or after school can be an effective time, especially if children arrive and stay late due to bus schedules or working parents. Generally around lunch time is the most popular period because it provides an opportunity for more student participation.

Personnel

The success of any program depends largely upon personnel and supervision. While the physical education teacher may have primary responsibility, an effective program must have support (active and passive) from the administration and staff. Support per-

sonnel may include teachers, parents, adult volunteers and students. Regardless of the type of personnel, ideally a system should be developed that places individuals into designated time slots (and responsibilities) rather than a pool of volunteers (which in some cases can also also be efficient). Help can be solicited from administrative personnel, the parent-teacher organization, or a contact with the local adult volunteer program. Students can also be effective

FIGURE 18-1

Intramurals provide an opportunity to self test motor skills workers and should be given responsibility for planning and operating their program. Examples of responsibilities include set-up and storing of equipment, recordkeeping and scorekeeping. See suggestions for an Intramural Council later in this chapter.

Organizing for Play

One of the key elements for success with intramural programs is the procedure used to group children for play. The process should stress equality in competition and provide maximum participation. The following methods warrant consideration.

Grade and Homeroom. This method is currently the most popular. Teams or individuals are selected within their homeroom to compete against others in the same grade. The selection process (within homeroom) can be based upon teachers choice, students choice (vote), or skill (as determined by the physical education teacher and/or assessment).

Skill. If the intramural director is planning a specific tournament and wishes to select teams from a pool of designated participants, skill level can be a desirable consideration. Participants can be identified as A or B players and placed into appropriate groups. The teacher's assessment of skill levels is crucial for the success of this method. The physical education teacher may use results from skill tests administered at completion of instructional units. Intramural activities are generally offered after the completion of instructional units.

Classification. There are various factors other then skill level that the teacher can use in the classification process; age, weight, height, and date of birth. Many times the nature of the activity dictates the method needed, such as wrestling, when weight should be a primary consideration. Many teachers find it desirable to use an index that considers a combination of factors such as 10 (constant) X age + weight. The merit of such a method would be in the "general" selection from a large group of individuals (*e.g.*, 50 fifth and sixth graders registered for a noon volleyball tournament) for placement into leagues and teams. In this case, cutoff scores could be used to classify individuals for league and/or team play.

While none of the methods described offer absolute equality, the teacher should strive to gather the most accurate information available and implement the method that best fits the circumstances. Age and weight factors, for example can be misleading, due to the differences between a child who is 10 years and one month and one who is 10 years and 10 months.

Tournament Planning

While most tournament planning will be conducted for intramural activities, teachers may also wish to provide tournaments at the completion of instructional units (generally at Level IV). If conducted properly, tournaments provide great motivational value as well as giving children an opportunity to utilize and refine newly acquired skills. Some teachers (during the instructional period) use tournament time to evaluate student performance. The technique has several built-in problems:

1. Prevents the teacher from being able to continue teaching through feedback.
2. Puts unnecessary stress on students not ready for intense competition.
3. May take focus of instructional program away from the development of physical fitness and motor skills.

There are numerous ways individuals or teams can challenge. The type of tournament selected depends upon the activity, space available, time and number of participants. An *Olympic meet plan* is the only tournament that is feasible for multi-event activities (*e.g.*, gymnastics, track, superstars). *Elimination* and *round-robin tournaments* can be used for a variety of individual and team sports, while *ladder-type tournaments* are very useful for individual activities that can be played with minimal supervision during any suitable period of the day. Careful consideration should be given to the strengths and weaknesses of each type of tournament on the basis of time, space, and number of participants.

Elimination Tournaments

If time and number of participants are major considerations, an elimination tournament is desirable. It is the easiest to organize and a winner can be determined in a very short period. If used in the instructional program (after a unit), the teacher should be aware that the elimination feature does not provide much activity for immediate losers; thus alternatives (depending on the situation) should be considered.

Table 18-1

Number of Games To Be Played

Teams	Byes needed	Games to be played
3	1	2
4	0	3
5	3	4
6	2	5
7	1	6
8	0	7
9	7	8
10	6	9

SINGLE ELIMINATION

In the elimination tournament of this type, the number of games required to find the winner is always one less than the number of teams (N-1 = number of games to be scheduled). When there are an even number of teams no byes (no play) are required. With an odd number of teams (or an even number not equaling a power of 2), byes are required in the first round. The following chart provides information for byes and number of games to be played for up to 10 teams.

Two examples; tournaments for an even number and odd number of teams are presented in Figure 18-2.

Additional planning considerations.

1. Byes should be placed near the top and bottom of the first round
2. If they can be identified, the strongest teams should be given byes (seeded) so they do not meet in the first round.
3. When teams are generally of equal strength, consider drawing team names at random and placing the first round in order of drawing.

ELIMINATION WITH CONSOLATION (AND DOUBLE ELIMINATION)

While the single elimination tournaments described are efficient, there are two inherent problems that teachers should consider; a team eliminated in the first round is out for the remainder of the tournament, and the second best team can be defeated in the first round (by the best team). An alternative and addition to the elimination method is a consolation bracket. This addition enhances participation and the possible problem of early elimination of a strong team; each team plays at least twice. Another feature to the consolation-type tournament is that it can be considered double elimination. The losers in the first round move into the consolation contenders bracket. The winners of both brackets meet in the final game. Should the loser's bracket champ win, the teams are rematched until one has lost twice. This method is generally used with eight teams or less. Figure 18-3 illustrates the use of a single elimination with consolation and a double elimination bracket.

Tournament with even number of teams

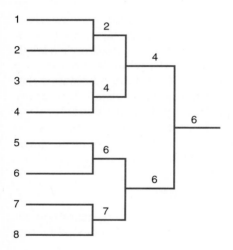

Tournament with odd number of teams

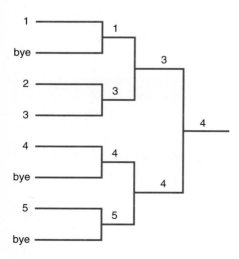

FIGURE 18-2

Single elimination tournaments

FIGURE 18-3

Single elimination with consolation (or double elimination)

CONSOLATION BRACKET   WINNER'S BRACKET

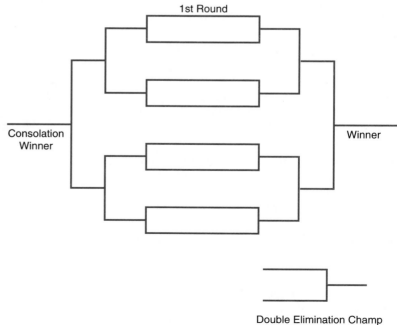

Double Elimination Champ

ROUND ROBIN

If time is not a major factor, a round robin is one of the best tournaments. With this method, every team or individual plays every other team or individual once; no one is eliminated and participation is maximized. Final standings are determined on a point basis or percentage of games won.

Planning Considerations:

1. To determine the number of games to be played, the following formula is used (N = number of teams): $N(N-1) \div 2$

   Example with $\dfrac{6(6-1)}{2} = \dfrac{6 \times 5}{2} = \dfrac{30}{2} = 15 \text{ games}$
   6 teams

2. Number the teams and arrange in two columns (down the first/up the second) to the first round.

3. Hold the number one team constant and rotate all other teams one place in a counterclockwise direction, until all games have been scheduled. There will always be one less round than the number of teams or individuals in the tournament.

Example (six teams):

Round 1	Round 2	Round 3	Round 4	Round 5
1 vs. 6	1 vs. 5	1 vs. 4	1 vs. 3	1 vs. 2
2 vs. 5	6 vs. 4	5 vs. 3	4 vs. 2	3 vs. 6
3 vs. 4	2 vs. 3	6 vs. 2	5 vs. 6	4 vs. 5

4. If planning for an uneven number of teams, a bye is given to one team each round. The bye becomes the constant and there is always the same number of rounds as there are number of teams.

Example (five teams):

Round 1	Round 2	Round 3	Round 4	Round 5
Bye 5	Bye 4	Bye 3	Bye 2	Bye 1
1 vs. 4	5 vs. 3	4 vs. 2	3 vs. 1	2 vs. 5
2 vs. 3	1 vs. 2	5 vs. 1	4 vs. 5	3 vs. 4

5. Determination of standings. Two methods may be used; a point system or percentage of games won. With the point system, a team is given two points for each win, one point for a tie, and no points for a loss (team with most points wins). Percentage standings are found by dividing the number of games won by the number of games played.

LADDER

Ladder tournaments are an efficient means of conducting continuous play with minimal supervision. This type of tournament is especially suited to individual sport activities such as tetherball, free-throws, handball, paddleball, ping-pong and horseshoes. The object is to climb (through challenge) to the top of the ladder and remain there until the end of the tournament.

Planning Considerations:

1. Construct a ladder board. This can be a portable blackboard, plastic cover with grease pencil, or board with name tags (*e.g.*, key tags) arranged one above the other (Fig. 18-4). Additional slots should be available for newcomers if play is over a long period of time (and rules permit).

2. If known, place the better players near the bottom of the ladder to start and/or draw names for placement.

3. Set a date for the beginning and the completion of the tournament. Also include times at which play can be conducted (*e.g.*, before school, noon, after school, or a combination).

4. It is essential that players understand the rules! Post a set of rules next to the ladder and, if possible, provide verbal classification. Time and personnel permitting, provide an individual knowledgeable about the rules to supervise.

Suggested rules:

   a. A player may challenge others one or two rungs above his placement.

   b. The winner changes places on the ladder with the person that was defeated (if the winner was the challenger).

   c. Challenges must be met within a specified period (depending upon how frequently the opportunity for play arises; usually two or three days).

   d. Set rules for specifics of the tournament (*e.g.*, rules for game, score).

```
         CHALLENGE LADDER
            PADDLEBALL

  1.   Bill        11.   Frieda
  2.   Sally       12.   Stan
  3.   Karl        13.   Mike
  4.   Cindy       14.   Steven
  5.   Max         15.   James
  6.   Ashley
  7.   David
  8.   Pete
  9.   Ellen
 10.   Sam
```

FIGURE 18-4

Ladder tournament format

PYRAMID

A pyramid tournament is a variation of the ladder concept with more diversity. With this system, an individual or team may challenge any opponent one level above their level. However, they must win a match at their level before challenging a higher level opponent.

Procedure

1. Construct a pyramid and place 16 or more circles (representing number of players) in rows.
2. Establish rules similar to the ladder tournament.
3. All players (or teams) begin by challenging each other for bottom row positions. Losers challenge each other for open positions as they become available (bottom row). First round pairings may be done through a random drawing of names.
4. Once on the bottom row, a player may challenge any other player on that row (only); winners move up.
5. If a player defeats an opponent from a higher row, they exchange positions.
6. Newcomers, if allowed to enter (a short team tournament may require all to register at the beginning), begin play by challenging a player on the bottom row.

OLYMPIC PLAN

An olympic plan is appropriate for events that include a number of separate activities, such as superstar, track and field, and gymnastic contests. Individuals or teams (cumulative score) are awarded points for placement in each activity, with the total points determining final standings. If there are at least 10 entries, for example, first place (in each activity) is awarded 10 points, second place nine points,. . . , and 10th place one point. After all events have been completed, the entry with the greatest total is the winner. If there is a tie score, the entry with the most first place awards wins (if that is also a tie, the most second place awards, etc.).

Additional Considerations

1. Boys and girls should receive equal opportunity to participate, just as disabled individuals should be allowed to engage in activity within their range of abilities.
2. Publicity is very important. A bulletin board with pertinent information should be maintained and updated on a regular basis. Also important is location; place the board where students can gather without blocking passageways. Tables or packet holders are helpful in securing loose materials.
3. For students who desire to participate in sponsored activities before or after regular school hours, parental permission (forms, including activity information) should be obtained. While generally already available, a physician's release should be required and filed.
4. *An Intramural Council.* As previously noted, for an intramural program to be a success, a cooperative effort is required. An avenue that may help to maximize this effort is an intramural council. The primary duties of the council are to plan (decision making), distribute the work effort and disseminate information. Figure 18-5 presents an illustrative example of a Council and primary responsibilities.
5. *Sport and Special Interest Clubs.* Two other excellent activities that complement both the instructional and intramural programs are sports and special interest clubs. These activities can be an extension of the instructional program (*e.g.,* gymnastics, tennis, handball, running), or of a special interest such as backpacking, twirling, skating, and cycling. Club success requires effective leadership and membership support. General guidelines can be established through the Intramural Council, with

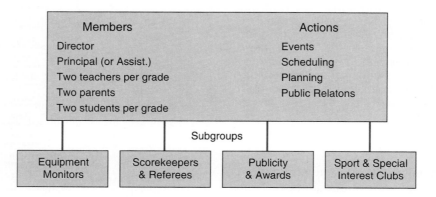

FIGURE 18-5
Intramural Council

leadership comprised of interested teachers, students, parents, and outside talent. Such activities as field trips, programs and extramural events are just a few of the possibilities that clubs can organize and enjoy. The recent popularity of rope jumping, jogging, and unicycling, has launched a number of clubs into outside-of-school exposure.

6. *Awards.* An award system can be established to recognize individuals, teams, and homerooms, for skill, sportsmanship and leadership. The creation of such an award system should foster the development of these desirable qualities and offer suitable recognition while not placing excessive emphasis on winning. To facilitate skill performance ratings, a point system similar to the Olympic Plan may be used. For each activity, a number of points are awarded per placement (*e.g.,* 10 for first, nine for second, etc.). The number of points for each activity can be different; this should be determined in advance by the Intramural Council and posted. Such factors as number of participants, task difficulty and skill level should be considered.

Due to the subjective nature of ratings for leadership and sportsmanship (compared to objectively rated skill performance), careful consideration should be given to the award criteria. Such criteria may be established and monitored through a subcommittee that strongly represents students. Special service award categories can include managers, scorekeepers, referees, as well as recognition for special helpers.

The type of award (*e.g.,* trophy, ribbon, certificate) should also be given thorough consideration. Trophies are nice, but generally expensive. An aggregate (score) trophy that is won each year by a homeroom is quite popular. Plaques with an individual's or homeroom's name inscribed are an inexpensive, yet very appreciated form of recognition. It is desirable to present intramural awards at the yearly award assembly, along with other achievement presentations.

SPECIAL EVENTS

Teachers should be looking for opportunities to show colleagues and the public highlights of the physical education program. It is through such events that the teacher and program gain recognition for its significant role in the school curriculum. Potential support for future endeavors can be realized through these events. Special events such as school programs and public demonstrations provide excellent opportunities for exhibiting selected aspects of the program, and allow students to display motor skill proficiency. Just as with the intramural program, special events involve extensive planning and preparation.

SCHOOL PROGRAMS AND PUBLIC DEMONSTRATIONS

These special events can be conducted after school hours, during the school day, or on a Saturday. They are frequently held in conjunction with Parent/Teacher meetings, or as a special event at a community center or shopping mall.

Such programs differ somewhat from demonstrations given to the general public. Since parents are usually in the audience, school programs highlight the year's activities and involve more children than public demonstrations. Public demonstrations might involve a specific aspect of the program or involve members of sport clubs such as Gymnastics Club, Jump-Rope Team, or Folk Dance Club. Another popular demonstration (that can also be a part of the school program) is an event which shows children performing various fitness activities (aerobic dance, rope-jumping, calisthenic routines). The following guidelines should be considered when developing and implementing the school program:

1. Involve as many children as feasible.
2. Enlist the aid of parents and classroom teachers for supervising and helping with the program.
3. Exhibit activities that represent the most important aspects of the curriculum—that is, health-related fitness and motor-skill development. Samples of Level III-IV game, dance, and gymnastics curriculum are also appropriate.
4. Keep the program time under one hour.
5. Allow some time to practice, but do not spend a lot of time working for a polished performance. It is important that a complete run-through be done prior to the event.
6. Provide the audience with a printed handout, summarizing the program and objectives of the school curriculum, and thanking the parents for continued support.
7. When possible, use colorful backgrounds, clothing, and props (*e.g.,* parachutes, streamers, musical accompaniment, hoops, scarfs). Careful deliberation should be conducted before requiring specific outfits, especially if all the children will be participating. For some parents such a request may present a financial or time burden and cause a less than favorable view of the program.
8. Send an early memo home (at least one week in advance) announcing the program. A permission form may also be needed if the program is conducted in the evening. This also lets the teacher know how many children will participate.
9. Invite school administrators, public officials, and local media representatives who may have an interest in (or influence on) the school program.

NATIONAL PHYSICAL EDUCATION AND SPORT WEEK

One week each spring is National Physical Education and Sport Week. During this time educational institutions are asked to focus on sports and physical fitness in hope the benefits of physical education will be acknowledged by the public. This is an opportune time to present a school program, give a public demonstration, and invite the public to visit during school hours. Popular events during this week include a focus on developing health-related fitness, fundamental motor-skill development, and sport-skill exhibition. It is recommended that a schedule of the week's activities be sent home with students and specific days be organized to depict selected events. Since it may be difficult for parents to visit more than once, each day should include a demonstration of health-related fitness and motor skill activities.

PHYSICAL EDUCATION NEWSLETTER

Communicating with parents is vital to gaining and maintaining program support. The physical education profession, in comparison to elementary education in general, needs a lot of improvement in this area. Frequently, elementary school teachers send home a child's papers for the week depicting student progress and describing future activities. Physical education teachers could also benefit from regular communication with parents in the form of a newsletter that might have student progress reports attached (see task evaluation sheet descriptions in Chapter 8). Physical education newsletters are usually sent home on a biweekly or monthly basis. Suggested items for inclusion are:

1. The motor skills that will be covered over the next two to four weeks.
2. Activity suggestions for practicing motor skills and fitness conditioning at home.
3. Special upcoming events and future activities that will require the aid of parent volunteers (e.g., fitness testing, field days, demonstrations), with the accompanying (tear-off) volunteer form.
4. A call for materials that can be used to make equipment (e.g., milk jugs, coffee cans, sash cord, old scarfs, records, tires).
5. A section that recognizes improvement and exceptional achievement and parent participation.
6. Notice of upcoming television and community programs that are related to physical education.
7. Invitations for parents with special skills to visit and discuss their expertise (e.g., triathletes, runners, softball players, judo participants, volleyball players, dancers).

Extramurals

In recent years there has been much discussion related to children in competition and organized contests between schools. As a result of this debate, many school systems have encouraged and developed diverse intramural programs. While some degree of competitive spirit appears to be innate and a healthy avenue for motivation and enjoyment, excessive emphasis upon winning (such as frequently found at the high school, college and professional levels) is not appropriate for the young, maturing child. At the pre-high school level, emphasis should be on skill development, participation and social interaction, all of which a good intramural program provides.

Occasionally, with the proper guidance, extramural events stemming from the intramural program can be conducted on a limited basis. Descriptions of popular formats follow.

Play Days.   Play days are among the most popular and cooperatively-spirited (rather than school-identifying and competitive) formats available. A play day involves children from two or more schools participating cooperatively on the same teams. One example is a volleyball play day involving three schools. Players can be selected from a random drawing (in this case three from each school to fill nine-person teams) or pre-assigned by teachers to equalize skill level. In this case, identified A, B, and C players would be assigned (to equalize skill level) to different teams.

Field Days.   A field day usually involves one school inviting two or more neighboring schools to participate in selected activities. One example would be a track and field day involving three schools on a Friday afternoon or Saturday. Students participate in selected activities without keeping an aggregate school score, thus the emphasis is on fun and social interaction.

Sports Days.   Sports days are similar to play days except that the teams keep their school identity. Schools enter teams in an elimination or round-robin tournament, with one school eventually declared the winner.

BILL OF RIGHTS FOR YOUNG ATHLETES

The following "Bill of Rights for Young Athletes" (Thomas, 1977), originally written for parents and coaches involved with youth sport programs (outside the school), communicates a strong and encouraging philosophy, "Child first, winning second". These "rights" are directly applicable to the physical education and intramural setting, where "fitness", "skill development" and "fun" are primary objectives.

Right to participate in sports
Right to participate at a level commensurate with each child's maturity and ability
Right to have qualified adult leadership

Right to play as a child and not an adult

Right to share in the leadership and decision making of their sport participation

Right to participate in safe and healthy environments

Right to proper preparation for participation in sports

Right to an equal opportunity to strive for success

Right to be treated with dignity

Right to have fun in sports.

REFERENCES

THOMAS, J. (Ed.). (1977). *Youth sports guide.* Reston, VA: AAHPERD Publications.

SUGGESTED READINGS

BLACKWELL, D. (1981). Elementary superstars. *Journal of Physical Education, Recreation, and Dance.* 52 (7), 28.

FEIGLEY, D. (1987). Intramural and recreational sport program award. *Journal of Physical Education, Recreation, and Dance, 58* (2), 50.

HYATT, R. W. (1977). *Intramural sports organization and administration.* St. Louis: C.V. Mosby.

MANJONE, J. A., & BOWEN, R. T. (1978). *Co-rec intramural sports handbook.* New York: Leisure Press.

ROKOSZ, F. M. (1982). *Administrative procedures for conducting recreational sports tournaments: From archery to wrestling.* Springfield: Charles C. Thomas.

SMALL, F., MAGILL, R., & ASH, M. (Eds.). (1988). *Children in Sport* (3rd. ed.). Champaign, IL: Human Kinetics.

STEIN, ERIC (Ed.). (1983). *Starting intramural programs. Journal of Physical Education, Recreation, and Dance.* February, 19–31.

A Appendix

Educational Record Center
3233 Burnt Mill Drive
Suite 100
Wilmington, NC 28403–2655

RECORD NAME	RECORD NUMBER	
Aerobic Express	2KB	9092
Aerobic Fitness	2KB	6035
Aerobic Dances for Kids	2EA	93
Aerobics for Kids	2KB	7052
Break in to Exercise	2MH	68
Feel in Good	2FS	7450
Fit Kids	2CY	909
Funfit—Workout for Kids	2CB	161
Jump Aerobics	2KB	2095
Jump to the Beat	2KB	8097
Kids in Motion	2YT	38
Mousercise	2DY	6251
Primary Fitness	2MH	63
Rope Activities	2MH	64
Rope Jumping	2KB	1132
Slashdance	2DY	6252

Kimbo Educational Records
P.O. Box 246
Deal, NJ 07723

RECORD NAME	RECORD NUMBER	CASSETTE NUMBER
A Fitness Experience	KEA 1110	KEA 1110C
A Thriller for Kids	KIM 7065	KIM7065C
Aerobic Express for Kids, The	KIM 9092	KIM 9095C
Aerobics For Kids	KIM 7043	KIM 7043C

	RECORD NUMBER	CASSETTE NUMBER
Aerobics USA	KIM 8065	KIM 8065C
Chicken Fat	KIM 290	—
Circle Jumpnastics	KIM 6005	KIM 6005C
Disco for Kids	KIM 7035	KIM 7035C
Elementary Aerobics Dance	KEA 1126	KEA 1126C
Fit Kids	CY 909	—
Fitness Can Be Fun	KIM 3010–20	KIM 3010–20C
Five Minutes for Fitness	KIM 235	—
Get a Good Start	KIM 7054	KIM 7054C
Good Morning Ex. for Kids	KIM 9098	KIM 9098C
Have Fun, Keep Fit	KEA 1120	KEA 1120C
J.S.'s Aerobics Club for Kids	KIM 1230	KIM 1230C
Jump Aerobics	KIM 2095	KIM 2095C
Jump to the Beat	KIM 8097	KIM 8097C
Jumpnastics	KIM 6000	KIM 6000C
Musical Fitness	KIM JJ 2	KIM JJ 2C
Rhythmic Rope Jumping	KIM 4001	KIM 4001C
Rope Jumping	KIM 1132	KIM 1132C
Walk, Jog, Run	KEA 1143	KEA 1143C

Melody House
819 N.W. 92nd Street
Oklahoma City, OK 73114

RECORD NAME	RECORD NUMBER	CASSETTE NUMBER
Exercise to Disco	MH–70	MHC–70C
Fit as a Fiddle	MH–67	MHC–67
Hokey Pokey, The	MH–33	MHC–33
Pre-School Fitness	MH–61	MHC–61
Primary Fitness	MH–63	MHC–63
Rhythmic Aerobics	MH–76	MHC–76
Rope Activities	MH–64	—
Swing to Fitness	MH–66	MHC–66
What Can I Be?	MH–60	MHC–60

ADDITIONAL RESOURCES

Educational Record Center
3233 Burnt Mill Dr., Suite 100
Wilmington, NC 28403–2655

Educational Record Sales
157 Chambers St.
Monroe, CT 06468

Educational Recordings of America, Inc.
P.O. Box 210
Ansomia, CT 06401

Folk Dancer Record Service
P.O. Box 201
Flushing, NY 11520

Hoctor Dance Record, Inc.
159 Franklin Turnpike
P.O. Box 38
Waldwick, NJ 07463

B

Appendix

Jump Aerobics	2KB	2095
Jump to the Beat	2KB	8097
Rope Activities	2MH	64
Rope Jumping	2KB	1132

KIMBRO

RECORD NAME	RECORD NUMBER	CASSETTE NUMBER
Circle Jumpnastics	KIM 6005	KIM 6005C
Jump Aerobics	KIM 2095	KIM 2095C
Jump to the Beat	KIM 8097	KIM 8097C
Jumpnastics	KIM 6000	KIM 6000C
Rhythmic Rope Jumping	KIM 4001	KIM 4001C
Rope Jumping	KIM 1132	KIM 1132C

MELODY HOUSE

RECORD NAME	RECORD NUMBER	CASSETTE NUMBER
Rope Activities	MH–64	—

"Rope Skipping for Fun and Fitness"
By Bob Melson & Vicki Worrell
Woodlawn Publishers, Inc.
P.O. Box 2334
Wichita, KS 67201
(VHS tape available)

"Skip It For Fun"
By Richard Cendali
P.O. Box 3307
Boulder, CO 80307
303/530–7179

"So You Want To Jump Rope"
By Dan Blackwell
Jefferson Elementary School
Riverton, WY 82501

"A Developmental Jump Rope Task Card Program"
By Cliff Carnes & Mark Sutherland
The Education Company
3949 Linus Way
Carmichael, CA 95608

"Aerobic Rope Skipping"
By Paul Smith
Educational Activities, Inc.
Freeport, NY 11520
(Record Available)

"Jump For The Health Of It"
(1) Basic Tricks
(2) Intermediate Single & Double Dutch Skills
American Heart Association
7320 Greenville Avenue
Dallas, TX 75231
800/527–6941
(VHS tapes and wall charts available)

Index

AAHPERD Physical Best (test), 48
Abdomen, protruding (lordosis), 296
Academic concepts, 6
Academic reinforcement, 28
Accents, 244, 418
Accommodation, 10
Accuracy serve, 369
Ace of Diamonds, 437
Ach-Ja, 421–23
Active participation, 28
"Activity" approach, traditional, 3
Adams position, 46
Adaptation, 9, 10
Adipose tissue, 41
Adventure activities, 30
Aerobic activity
    dance, 267–68, 269
    duration of, 39
    jumping, 276
Aerobic fitness. *See* Cardiorespiratory fitness
Affective behavior, 6, 8, 28–30
    attitudes, 30
    self-concept, 29–30
    socialization, 28–29
Affective objectives, 76
Agility, 42, 51
A Hunting We Will Go, 423
Aides, teacher, 3
Ailments, common, 260
Airplanes (game), 302
Alaskan Baseball, 302
All-American Promenade, 437–38
Allemande left, 418
Alley Soccer, 353–54
"All in Together," 431
Alternate-foot step (rope jumping), 150
Alunelul, 438
American Academy of Pediatrics, 2, 39, 55
American Alliance for Health, Physical
    Education, Recreation, and Dance, 2, 39,
    50
American Hopscotch, 324
Anaerobic activities, 39, 40
Angel balance, 473
Angels in the Snow (movement activity), 232

Animal walks and movements, 461
Ankle walk, 467
Arch, 418
Arching, 261
Area layout, 79
Arink, E.A., 88
Arm, strength/endurance activities for,
    291–96
Arm circles, 284
Arm pulls, lateral, 284
Arm tugs, partner, 294–95
Arnheim, D., *31*, 121
Arousal, 35
Ashworth, S., *98*
"Ask Mother," 431
Assessment, 1, 43–54. *See also* Evaluation;
    Observation; Testing
    conditioning/practice for, 51–52
    considerations for, 44–46
    criterion- and norm-referenced tests, 46–51
    of exceptional child, 54
    recording/reporting results of, 52
    remedial intervention, 52–54
    time of year for, 51
Assimilation, 10
Atrophy, 40
Attention, selective, 34–35
Attitudes, 30, 107–8
Auditory awareness, 26, 255–57
Auditory communication, 97
Auditory constancy, 255
Auditory discrimination, 255
Auditory figure-ground, 255
Auditory impairment, 135
Auditory rhythmic activities, 247
Awareness. *See* Movement awareness

Baa, Baa, Black Sheep, 423
Back balance, 169
Back bend and up, 477
Back bend (arching), 261
Back door entry (jumping rope), 149
Back layout, 483
Back press, 289
Back rocker, 167, 169

Back scratcher (gymnastic activity), 468
Back shoulder roll, 169
Back to Back (game), 305, 418
Backward diagonal roll, 171
Backward extension roll, 479–80
Backward roll, 170, 488
    variations on, 479
Badminton (Goodminton), 302, 328–29
Balance, 23–24, 42, 419
    inverted, 461
Balance beam, 235–36, 487–88
Balance board, 236
Balance jump, 477
Balances, partner, 461
Balance stand, 472
Balance (vestibular awareness), 23–24, 61,
    233–38
Ball-carrying run, 364
Ballistic ballet bar stretches, 262
Balloon Ball (game), 316
Balloon Bucket (game), 302
Balloon/Feather Relay, 320
Ball rolling, 197–99
Ball squeeze, 294
Ball Toss (game), 305
Banjo position, 413
Baranowski, T., 37, 57
Baseball
    challenger programs, 132
    creative games of, 302
    simple games of, 317
Baseball pass, 334–35, 344
Base-line serve, 369
Base running in softball, 385, 391
Basic Motor Ability Test-Revised, 121
Basket, 192
Basketball, 332–44
    game activities, 340–42
    instructional considerations, 332–33
    rules and regulations, 343–44
    skill description, 333–38
    skill development activities, 339–40
    skill tests, 344
Basketball Golf (game), 342
Basket Baseball (game), 317

Basket pass, 368
Bat Ball (game), 305, 388
Baton exchange, 394
Baton passing, 398
Batting, 218–19
   in softball, 384–85, 387, 391
Battle (game), 340
Baumgartner, T., 49
Beach-Ball Nerfs, 305
Beach-Ball Volleyball, 369
Beanbag activities, 233, 237, 305–7
Bear walk, 287, 467
Beats, pulse, 244
Bee, D., 37, 57
Behavior, total, 103–4
Behavioral objectives, 77
Behavioral verbs, 77
Behavior games, 116–17
Bending, 186–88
Bent-knee curl-up, 48, 49
Bent-knee hop, 474
Bent leg (low level) stretches, 262
Bicycle, inverted, 261
Big Turtle (game), 302
Bilateral movements, 13
"Bill of Rights for Young Athletes," 498–99
Bingo, 424
Binocular vision, 24
Bird Dance, The, 438
Birds and butterflies (exercise), 291
"Birthday," 430
Blanket Volleyball (game), 303
Bledsoe, C.J., 28, *31*
Bleking, 424
Bleking step, 419
Blocking
   in football, 358, 360
   in volleyball, 367, 368, 369
Block plan, 76
Blow up the balloon (gymnastic activity), 466, 467
Blue and Gold (game), 307
Bluebird, 428
Body awareness (image, schema), 22, 223–28
Body composition, 41, 49–51
Body fat, 41
Body mass, 39
Body Mass Index, 44, 51
Body rolling, 166–77
Body trap, 347, 348
Body weight/height, 15–17, 44
Bones, 15
Borden Ball, 317
Bounce Ball, 307
Bounce off, 153
Bounce pass, 334
Bouncer (gymnastic activity), 477
Bouncing ball (gymnastic activity), 469
Bouncing/dribbling, 214–17
Boundary Ball (game), 307, 352
Bow Belinda, 424
Bowling (related activities), 323
Box Ball (game), 307, 317
Boxes, 182
Brain, 14, 15
Braley, W.T., 122
Break, fitness, 57
Bredekamp, S., *1*, 7
Bronco Tag, 307
Brookfield, S.D., *98*
Brown-Eyed Mary, 438–39
Brownies and Fairies (game), 307

Bruininks-Oseretsky Test of Motor
   Proficiency, 121
"Bubble Gum," 431
Buggy Schottische, 439
"Building the Foundation" curriculum,
   61–62, 66–70, 80
"Bulldog," 431
Bunny hop, 166, 172
Bunting, 385
Busy Ball, 317
Butterfly (stretch), 280
Buzz, 413
Buzz step, 419

Caged Lion (game), 307
Calf and arch stretch, 281
Calf stretch, 281
California Kickball, 317
Calipers, skinfold, 49–51
Calisthenics, 266–67
Call a Guard (game), 307
Calories, 42
Camel lift, 481
Camel walk, 466, 467
Canoes and Rapids (game), 308
Captain Basketball, 342
Cardiac muscle, 17
Cardiorespiratory fitness
   activities for, 268–77
     aerobic jumping, 276
     basic concepts and principles, 268–71
     jogging, 139, 273–74
     jumping rope, 275–76
     vigorous games and dances, 276, 277
     walking, 271–73
   assessment of, 47–48
   endurance, 39–40
Cardiovascular problems, 37, 135
Cargo nets, 182
Carousel, 428
Carrying the ball, 357–58, 359
Cartwheel, 474, 488
   variations on, 480, 481
Cast-off, 419
Catcher in softball, position of, 386
Catching, 204–7, 213
   in basketball, 335, 339
   in football, 357
   in softball, 383–84, 387
Caterpillar (game), 303
CCW (counterclockwise movement), 419
Cell body, 15
Centering the ball, 357, 358
Centipede (gymnastic activity), 482
Cephalocaudal development, 13
Cerebellum, 15
Cerebral cortex, 14, 15
Cerebral palsy, 135
Cha-cha-cha, 419
Chain Tag, 308
Challenge (obstacle) courses, 266, 267
Challenger baseball programs, 132
Challenges, appropriate, 81
Change-of-pace running, 274, 397
Chants, 250
Charlie over the Water (game), 308
Check pass, 344
Cherkassiya, 439–40
Chest stand, 484
"Chickety Chop," 431
Child, physical educated, 6–7
Child-designed games, 300–301

Child development. *See* Development, child
Children, physical fitness levels of, 2
Chimes of Dunkirk, 428
Chinese Hurdle (game), 308
Chin-up, 49
Choice in cooperative games, 300
Christopher, J.R., 28
Churn the butter (gymnastic activity), 469
Circle Ball, 308
Circle clap, 432
Circle dribble, 340
Circle Guard and Pass (game), 341
Circle heading, 351
Circle high jump, 482
Circle Keep-Away, 377
Circle kick and trap, 350
Circle Kickball, 308
Circle of Friends (game), 303
Circle pass, 339
Circle-pass keep away, 339
Circle-pass race, 339
Circle pivot and pass, 340
Circle rope, 464
Circle Soccer, 351
Circle-Soccer Tag, 352
Circle volley (game), 368
Circuits, 264–66
Class instruction, 14, 94. *See also* Teaching
Class management, 101–18. *See also*
   Discipline
   behavior expectations in the gymnasium,
     106–7
   communication skills and, 108–9
   consequences, 107, 113–14
   control theory and reality therapy, 102–4, 105
   defined, 101
   managerial skills and, 109–12
   positive attitude development and, 107–8
   positive learning environment and, 105–6
   restitution, 113
   teacher-parent conferences, 115–16
   teacher-student conferences, 114–15
Climatic conditions, 260
Climbing, 177–83, 487
Climbing apparatus, 295
Clown trick (gymnastic activity), 464
Club Guard (game), 308
Cocoon hang, 289
Coercion, 105, 106
Coffee-Can Stilt Relay, 320
Coffee grinder (gymnastic activity), 472
Cognitive behavior, 5–6, 8, 27–28
   evaluation of, 124–25
Cognitive objectives, 76
Coincident timing, 219
Collective score games, 300
Color as stimulus for dance, 411
Combatives, 461
Come Let Us Be Joyful, 428
Command style of teaching, 88, 90, 412, 457
Communication
   class management and, 108–9
   with disabled student, 135
   intersensory, 21
   modes of, 97–98
   nonverbal, 90
   self-concept and, 30
Competition, introduction of, 29–30
Comprehensive approach to fitness devel-
   opment, 57
Concentration, motor-skill acquisition and,
   34–35
Concepts, problem solving style and, 93

Concrete operations stage, 10–11
Conditioning for fitness assessment, 51–52
Conditioning running, 397
Conferences
    teacher-parent, 115–16
    teacher-student, 114–15
Consequences of misbehavior, 107, 113–14
Constancy
    auditory, 255
    perceptual, 24
Content placement, 65–67
Contingency plans, 73, 75
Continued jog method, 274
Contra dance formation, 419
Controlled dribble, 372–73
Control theory, 102–3, 105
Conventional games, 297–98
Cooperative games, 298, 299–300, 301
Cooperative learning, 89
Coordination, 42
    eye-hand, eye-foot, 28–44
Corbin, C., 38, 58, 261, 296
Corkscrew (gymnastic activity), 469
Corners (game), 309
Corner (square dance term), 419
Coronary heart disease (CHD), 37
Cotton-Eyed Joe—Texas Style, 440
Council on Physical Education for Children
    (COPEC), 1
Counting, 419
Couples, side, 420
Crab position, 279
Crab Soccer, 317
Crab-tug, 294
Crab variations, 293
Crab walk, 470
Crane dive (gymnastic activity), 471
Crane twist, 469
Crazy Clock, 428, 429
Crazy walk, 469
Creative dance, 247–48, 409–11
Creative games, 298, 300–305
Creativity, 90, 246
Crested Hen, 428, 429
Criterion-referenced fitness tests, 46–51
Critical thinking skills, 90
Crocodile crawl, 467
Croquet, 323
Cross-country running, 393
Cross-lateral pattern, 178
Cross-leg sit, 278
Cross-leg step, 150
Cross over (game), 309
Crouse, S., 58
Crunchies, 289
Cshebogar, 440–41
Culminating activity, 74–75, 76
Curling, 186–88
Curl-ups, 48, 49, 289
Curricular approach to motor skill develop-
    ment, 3
Curricular content, 55–57
Curriculum, 1, 59–64
    "Building the Foundation," 61–62, 66–70, 80
    categories of, 59
    generic levels of skill proficiency and, 59–60
    "Utilization of the Foundation," 62–64, 70
CW (clockwise movement), 419

Daily planning. See Planning
Dance(s), 3, 63, 147. See also Enhancement
    activities

activity descriptions, 421–53
    Levels I–II, 421–35
    Levels III–IV, 435–53
    aerobic, 267–68, 269
    creative, 247–48, 409–11
    for flexibility, 285
    glossary, 418–20
    hop in, 160
    progressions in, 408–9
    structured. See Structured dance
    vigorous, 276, 277
Dance activities, 288, 291, 295
Dance of Greeting, 428, 429
"Dangles," 111–12
Danish Schottische, 428, 429
Davis, R.G., 298, 405
Dayton Sensory Motor Awareness Survey
    for 4- and 5-Year-Olds, 120
Dead fall (gymnastic activity), 474
Decision making in teaching, 85–86
Deck tennis, 323
Deck the Halls (game), 309
Deep knee bends, 262
Defensive strategy
    in basketball, 339
    in football, 359
    in soccer, 350
    in volleyball, 368
Demonstration, 88
    public, 497
Dendrites, 15
Denver Developmental Screening Test, 121
DeOreo, K., 21, 23
Depth perception, 24, 251
Development, child, 8–31
    affective behavior, 6, 8, 28–30
    cognitive behavior and, 8, 27–28
        evaluation of, 124–25
    development, defined, 8
    psychomotor. See Psychomotor development
    total. See Total child development
Developmentally appropriate activities, 29
Developmental skill theme approach, 3
Developmental value of games, 297
Dewey, J., 27
Diagonal roll, 170
Diaphysis, 15
Diet, 42–43
Dietz, W.H., 37, 58
Differences, individual, 14
Differentiation, 13
Direction, line of, 420
Directional awareness, 22–23, 228, 231–33
Directional awareness task sheet, 126
Directionality, 23, 231
Direct services, 132
Disabled children, 4, 131–36. See also
    Handicapped children
    accommodation in regular physical edu-
        cation, 134
    defined, 131
    Individual Education Program (IEP), 4,
        132–33
    instructional strategies, 134–35
    least restrictive environment for, 133–34
    legislation related to, 131–32
    mainstreaming of, 4
    physical fitness assessment of, 54
    special services for, 132
    specific disabilities, 135–36

Discipline. See also Class management
    behavior games, 116–17
    defined, 101
    eye contact and, 117
    punishment, 116
    strategies for, 112, 117–18
    time-out, 114
Discovery, guided, 91–92, 94, 457
Discrimination
    auditory, 26, 255
    figure-ground, 24, 26, 251, 255
    form, 24, 251
    gender, 4
    tactile, 26–27
Distance, jumping for, 143
Distance perception, 24
Distance running, 393
Dive roll, 168
Dodge Alley (game), 318
Dodging, 184–86
    in hockey, 375
Dog roll, 174
Donkey kick (gymnastic activity), 474
Do-si-do, 419
Double bear (gymnastic activity), 483
Double dutch long rope, 486
Double elimination tournaments, 494
Double hanging ropes, 486–87
Double-knee balance, 471
Double lame dog (gymnastic activity), 474
Double play, 386–87
Double roll, 482
Double walk, 472
Double wheelbarrow, 481
"Down in the Valley," 431
Draw step, 419
Dribble, Pass Shuttle Relay, 342
Dribble 500 (game), 341
Dribbling
    in basketball, 335–36, 339–40, 344
    foot, 207, 209, 210
    hand, 214–17
    in hockey, 372–73, 376, 380
    in soccer, 347–48, 350–51, 356
Driving in hockey, 374, 380
Dromedary walk, 482
Duck walk, 467
Dumping the wheelbarrow, 481
Dunn, S., 98
Duple meter, 245
Dynamic balance, 23, 24, 42, 234

Eckert, H.D., 178, 183
Educational gymnastics, 457
Education Amendments Act of 1972 (Title
    IX), 4
Education of the Handicapped Act of 1975
    (P.L. 94–142), 4, 131, 132
Egg roll, 177
Egg sit (gymnastic activity), 462
Egocentric localization, 22, 228
Egocentric stage, 28
Elbow balance, 478
Elbow crawl, 293
Elbow swing, 419
Elephant walk, 467
Elevator ride, 292
Elimination tournaments, 493–96
Emotional disabilities, 136
Encouragement, 30
Endurance
    cardiorespiratory, 39–40
    muscular, 40, 42, 48–49

Endurance activities. *See* Muscular strength/endurance activities
End-Zone Ball, 317–18
Enhancement
  of bending and stretching, 188
  of climbing, 183
  of dodging, 185
  of galloping, 162
  of hopping, 161
  of jumping and landing, 157
  of leaping, 158
  of pushing and pulling, 196
  of rolling, 177
  of running, 142
  of skipping, 165
  of sliding, 164
  of swinging and swaying, 194
  of twisting and turning, 190
Enhancement activities, 74, 76, 81
  auditory awareness, 257
  ball rolling, 199
  body awareness, 227
  bouncing/dribbling, 217
  catching, 207
  daily planning for, 82–83
  directional awareness, 233
  eye-hand, eye-foot coordination, 243
  for flexibility, 286
  kicking, 211
  for Levels I–II, 82
  for Levels III–IV, 82–83
  rhythmic awareness, 249–50
  spatial awareness, 230
  striking, 222
  tactile awareness, 255
  throwing, 204
  trapping, 214
  vestibular awareness (balance), 239
  visual awareness, 253
Environment
  least restrictive, 133–34
  positive learning, 105–6
Epilepsy, 135
Epiphyses, 15
Equipment. *See also specific names of activities*
  for entire theme, 73
  for jumping role, 148
Eskimo roll, 482
Espenschade, A.S., 178, *183*
Evaluation, 119–30. *See also* Observation
  through observation, 119–20
  procedures, 74
  of program, 129
  of students, 120–26
  of teachers, 126–29
Exceptional children, fitness assessment of, 54
Exclusion, freedom from, 300
Exercise(s)
  anaerobic, 39
  intensity of, 39
  isometric, 40, 285
  isotonic, 40, 285
  misconceptions associated with, 37–38
  potentially harmful, 260–63
  precautions for, 260–63
  resistance, 40
  stretching, 280–85
Expectations
  of behavior in gymnasium, 106–7
  reasonable, 30
Experience, 9, 14

Exploration teaching style, 94, 300
External feedback, 35
Extramurals, 498–99
Eye contact when disciplining student, 117
Eye-hand, eye-foot coordination, 24, 238–44
  activities for, 61

Face to face, 418
Facing-off, 374, 375
Falls, H.B., 39, *58*
Fartlek (change-of-pace) training, 274, 397
Fat, body, 41
Feedback, 111
  motor-skill acquisition and, 35
Feedback checklist, 128
Feedback phase of daily lesson, 83–84
Feinting in basketball, 338
Field days, 498
Fielding
  in hockey, 373–74, 380
  in softball, 383–84, 387, 391
Fifth grade curriculum, 70, 71
Fifth graders, characteristic behaviors of, 12
Figure-eight dribble, 340
Figure-ground discrimination (perception), 24, 251
  auditory, 26, 255
File dribble, 340, 350
File shooting, 340
Fine-motor manipulative skills, 242
Finger plays, 247, 409
Fire Engine (game), 309
First-base stretch, 386
First grade curriculum, 66, 67, 68
First graders, characteristic behaviors of, 11
Fish Gobbler (game), 303
Fish hawk dive (gymnastic activity), 478
Fitness. *See* Health-related fitness; Physical fitness
Fitnessgram, 48
Fitness objectives, 77
Fitness-oriented recess, 57
Fitness Phase, specific, 56
Fitness stations, 54, 95, 264–66
Fitts, P., 35, *36*
Fit Youth Today (FYT) program, 48, 50
500 (game), 389
Five Passes (game), 340–41, 360
Flank vault, 155
Flat tire, 292
Flexed-arm-hang, 49
Flexibility, 40–41
  assessment of, 48
  gymnastics safety and, 456
  posture and, 42
Flexibility activities, 276–85
  basic principles and teaching hints, 276
  descriptions of, 279–85
  enhancements for, 286
  recommended, 277
  selected games, dance, and gymnastic activities, 285
  starting positions for, 277–79
Flick, 374
Flickerball, 361–62
"Flip-flops," 111–12
Floor body, building a, 226–27
Floor catch, 339
Floor touch, 468
Fly balls, 383
Follow the Beats, 429–30
Food groups, basic, 42–43

Football activities, 356–64
  flickerball, 361–62
  game activities, 360–61
  instructional considerations, 356
  rules and regulations, 363
  skill description, 356–59
  skill development activities, 359–60
  skill tests, 363–64
Football Goal Catch, 318
Foot dribbling, 207, 209, 210
Foot-to-head stretch, 280
Foot trap, 346, 347
Force, variability in practice in, 34
Forearm balance—tiger stand, 473
Forest Lookout (game), 309
Formal operations period, 11
Formations, 96–97
Form discrimination (perception), 24, 251
Forward head, exercises for correction and prevention of, 296
Forward motion rolling, 174
Forward pass, 357
Forward Pass (game), 361
Forward roll, 166–67, 170
  variations on, 478–79
Forward rolling progression using spring board, 172–74
Forward shoulders (rounded shoulders), 45
Fosbury flop, 395–96
Four-Square Volleyball, 369
Fourth grade curriculum, 70
Fourth graders, characteristic behaviors of, 12
Fragmentation, 112
Frames, 182
Francis, R., 54
Frantz, R.N., 28, *31*
Freedom from exclusion, 300
Free dribbling, 376
Free standing, 474
Free throw, 337, 338, 344
French Hopscotch, 325
Frisbee, 323–24
Frog jump (gymnastic activity), 465
Frog stand tip-up, 473
Front door entry (jumping rope), 149
Front drop, 474, 489
Front leaning rest, 278
  variations, 292
Front seat support, 478
Front sit (gymnastic activity), 483
Front to back (gymnastic activity), 474
Frozen Beanbag (game), 303
Full twist, 174
Fundamental Movement Pattern Assessment Instrument, 121
Fundamental-movement phase, 18–19
Fundamental skill, 18
Fundamental skill task sheet, 123
Fungo batting, 384–85

Gabbard, C., 28, *31*, 32, *36*, *58*, 85, 87, *98*, 450
Gallahue, D.L., 29, *31*, 121, 140, 143, *183*
Galloping, 161–62
Games, 3, 63, 297–406. *See also* Enhancement activities
  behavior, 116–17
  conventional, 297–98
  cooperative, 298, 299–300, 301
  creative, 298, 300–305
  developmental value of, 297
  for flexibility, 285

for individuals and partners (Levels III–IV), 322–32
  hand striking activities, 330–32
  racquet activities, 326–30
observation of body awareness in, 223–24
relay activities, 320–22
simple, 305–20
structure and diversity of, 297–99
team sports and lead-up activities (Levels III–IV), 332–405
  basketball, 332–44
  football activities, 356–64
  hockey, 371–80
  korfball, 399–400
  modified speedball, 400–402
  modified team handball, 402–3
  netball, 403–4
  Pillo Polo, 404–5
  soccer, 344–56
  softball, 381–91
  track and field, 391–98
  volleyball, 364–71
vigorous, 276, 277
Gender discrimination, 4
Gesell, A., *31*
Giraffe walk (gymnastic activity), 464
Glasser, W., 101, 103, 115, *118*
Glowworm, 430
Goalkeeper Hockey (game), 376
Goalkeeping
  in hockey, 375, 376
  in soccer, 349–50
Goal of physical education, 64
Goal shooting in soccer, 350
Goal Tag (game), 309
Go-For-Health Project, 57
Golf, creative game of, 304
Goodminton, 302
Goodman, 302
Gorilla walk, 467
Gortmaker, S.L., 37, *58*
Gossen, D.C., 113, *118*
Grabbing Sticks (game), 318
Graham, G., 301, *405*
Grand March, 441
Grand right and left, 419
Grapevine (gymnastic activity), 419, 472
Greensleeves, 430
Greet the toe (gymnastic activity), 469
Grip in hockey, 371–72
Gripping the ball, 381
Gross-motor manipulative skills, 240, 242
Gross to fine (mass to specific) motor control, 13
Grounders, 383, 384
Ground Newcomb (game), 361
Group instruction, 94
Group organization, 134
Group Skip (game), 303
Growth, 9, 14–17
Growth phase, 20
Guard Ball (game), 341
Guarding (defending) in basketball, 338–39
Guard the Toys (game), 309
Guided discovery, 91–92, 94, 457
Gustaf's Skoal, 441
Gymnasium, behavior expectations in the, 106–7
Gymnastic activities, 3, 63, 147, 288, 291, 295, 462–90
  for flexibility, 285
  vaulting, 153–56

Gymnastics, 455–91. *See also* Enhancement activities
  class organization for, 457–59
  educational, 457
  large equipment, 460–61
  progression in, 456–57, 461
  rhythmic, 461–62
  safety in, 455–57
  small equipment, 460
  teaching hints, 462
  teaching style for, 457

Half-Court Basketball (game), 342
Half-squats, 262
Hamstring stretch, 280
Handball, 315, 330–31
  cooperative, 303
  modified team, 402–3
Handedness, 22–23
Handicapped children. *See* Disabled children
Hands and knees drop, 489
Hands and knees position, 279
Handspring, 481, 488
Handstand, 474
  variations on, 479, 480
Handstand and hip support, 484
Hand striking activities, 330–32
"Hand-under-hand" technique, 179
Haskell, E., 55, *58*
Head, forward, 296
Head and shoot, 351
Head couple, 419
Heading in soccer, 348, 349, 351
Heads and Shoulders Knees and Toes, 430
Headspring, 481
Headstand, 474
  variations on, 479
Head vault, 155–56
Health, evaluation of, 120
Health-related benefits of selected physical activities, 264
Health-related fitness, 2, 39–41. *See also* Physical fitness
  assessment of
    body composition, 49–51
    cardiorespiratory, 47–48
    flexibility, 48
    muscular strength/endurance, 48–49
  cardiorespiratory endurance and, 39–40
  daily planning for, 80
  flexibility and, 39, 40–41
  misconceptions about, 37–38
  muscular strength/endurance, 39, 40
Heart (pulse) rates
  measuring, 270–71
  target, 270
Heart Smart Program, 57
Heart Treasure Chest, 57
Heel click, 471
Heels, sitting on, 278
Heel slap, 470
Heel walk, 281, 287
Height
  assessment of, 44
  jumping for, 143
Heredity, 9
Hickory, Dickory, Dock, 424
High jump
  circle, 482
  Fosbury flop, 395–96
  scissors style, 395
  straddle style, 395
"Hippity Hop," 431

Hit the Pins (game), 309
Hockey, 371–80
  game activities, 376–78
  instructional considerations, 371
  rules and regulations, 378–80
  skill description, 371–76
  skill development activities, 376
  skill tests, 380
Hockey Relay, 320
Hoffmann, 96
Hokey Pokey, 430
Hollow back/protruding abdomen (lordosis), 296
Home position, 419
Hook lying, 278
Hook sit, 278
Hoop Activities, 309–10
Hoop Hop (game), 310
Hoops, 237
Hopping, 159–61
Hopp Mor Anika, 441–42
Hopscotch, 324–25
Hora (Hava Nagila), 442
Horizontal bar, 489
Horizontal ladder, 489–90
Horizontal stand, 473
Horse (game), 342
Horseshoes, 325
Hot Ball (game), 310
How Do You Do My Partner?, 425
Huddle (review and feedback) phase of daily lesson, 83–84
Hug tag, 304
Human ball, 177
Human Kinetics Publishers, 50
Human sticks, 226
Hunchback (kyphosis), 42, 45
Hungarian break step, 419
Hurdle activities, 308
Hurdle Race (game), 310
Hurdler's stretch, 262
Hurdling, 394
Hyperextension, neck, 262
Hypertrophy, 17, 40

I Don't Want It (Poison Ball), 310
Imitative activities, 246
Impairments, sensory, 135
In and out (game), 310, 341–42
Inchworm (gymnastic activity), 467
Indian running, 274
Indian Running (game), 310
Individual differences, 14
Individual dribbling, 350
Individual Education Program (IEP), 4, 132–33
Individual instruction, 94
Individual organization, 134
Individuals with Disabilities Education Act (IDEA) of 1990 (P.L. 101–476), 131
Individual volley, 368
Indy 500, 272
Inside-of-foot dribble, 347–48
Inside-of-foot kick, 345
Instep kick, 345
Instruction(s), 14, 94. *See also* Teaching
  evaluating teachers', 126–28
  strategies for disabled children, 134–35
  tape-recording of, 127
Instructional objectives, 73, 77
Integration, 13
Interaction checklist, 127–28

Interest, motor-skill acquisition and, 35
Internal feedback, 35
Interpretative activities, 246
Intersensory communication, 21
Intersensory integration, 27
Interval training, 398
Intervention, remedial, 52–54
In the Creek (game), 310
Intramural activities, 492–97
Intrasensory functioning, 21
Intuitive stage, 10
Inverse twister, 467–68
Inverted balance, 461
Inverted bicycle, 261
Inverted hang, 486, 487
Irish Washerwoman, 442
Isaacs, L.D., 298, *405*
I See You, 425
Islands (game), 310
Isometric exercise, 40, 285
Isotonic exercise, 40, 285
Italian Hopscotch, 325

Jab, 375
Jack-in-the-box (gymnastic activity), 467
Jack knife, 173, 474
Jet Pilot (game), 311
Jogging, 139, 273–74
Jog-walk-jog method, 274
Johnson, B., 121, *130*
Joint movement variable resistance, 40
Joint suppleness, 40–41
Jolly Is the Miller, 425
Judo roll (safety roll), 478
Juggle a Number (game), 304
Juggling, 241, 486
Jump, Jim Joe, 425
Jump ball, 339
Jump foot, 474
Jumping, 287
  aerobic, 276
  and landing, 143–47, 157
  in track and field, 394–96, 398
Jumping jack, 288
Jumping rope, 26, 148–53, 275–76
Jumping swan (gymnastic activity), 470
Jump Rope for Heart program, 275, 276
Jump-rope rhymes, 421, 430–31
Jump shot, 337, 338
Jump to run, 287

Kalvelis, 442–43
Kangaroo hop, 153
Karpovich, 38
Keep Away (game), 341, 351
Keep It Moving, 431
Keep It Up (game), 369
Kerr, R., 33, *36*
Kickball, simple game activities of, 308, 317
Kicking, 207–12, 217
  in soccer, 345–46, 350, 356
  visual-motor coordination and, 25
Kick roll up, 175
Kick the Pin (game), 311
Kindergarten children, characteristic behaviors of, 11
Kindergarten curriculum, 66, 67, 68
Kinderpolka, 431–32
Kinesthetic perception, 21–24
Kirchner, G., 302, *405*
Klapptanz, 425–26
Klesius, 96

Klumpakojis, 443
Knee and shoulder stand, 484–85
Knee bends, deep, 262
Knee drop, 474, 489
Kneeling and standing dribble, 339–40
Kneeling Tag (game), 311
Knee slapper (gymnastic activity), 172, 173, 469
Kolbe, L., 37, 57
Kool Kat, 444
Korfball, 399–400
Korobushka, 444–45
Kounin, J., 111, 112
Kyphosis (roundback), 42, 45

Ladder(s), 183, 236
  horizontal, 489–90
Ladder-type tournaments, 493, 495
Lame-puppy walk, 466, 467
Landing, 172
  jumping and, 143–47, 157
Large-group play, 29
Laterality, 22–23, 231
Lateral pass, 357, 358
Lateral straddle stretch, 262, 280
Lawrence, G., 108
Layout
  area, 79
  back, 483
Layup, 337–38
  in basketball, 344
Layup shooting, 340
Lazy rope (gymnastic activity), 465
Lead passing and shooting, 350
Leapfrog, 470
Leaping, 156–59, 176
Learning, 9
  cooperative, 89
  whole and part, 35
Learning centers (stations), 95
Learning disabilities, 136
Learning environment, positive, 105–6
Least restrictive environment, 133–34
Le Blanc, 450
Left-face turn, 420
Leg, foot, back stretch, 281
Legislation related to disabled children, 131–32
Leg lifts
  double, 261
  prone, 291
Legs, strength/endurance activities for, 287–89
Leg trap, 347
Let-downs, 292
Letter Race (game), 311
L-hang, 487
Lifespan motor development, 13
Limbo, 432
Limits, problem solving style and, 93
Lindsey, R., 261, *296*
Line clap, 432
Line dribble, 340
Line Field Hockey, 377
Line kicking and trapping, 350
Line of direction, 420
Line plan, 458, 459
Line Soccer, 352
Little Man in a Fix, 445
Localization
  egocentric, 22, 228
  objective, 22, 228

sound, 26, 255
Locomotion, 9
Locomotor Relay, 321
Locomotor skills, 19, 61, 62, 137–83, 242
  body rolling, 166–77
  climbing, 177–83, 487
  galloping, 161–62
  hopping, 159–61
  jumping and landing, 143–47, 157
  jumping rope, 26, 148–53, 275–76
  leaping, 156–59, 176
  pulse beats and, 244
  running, 139–43
  skipping, 161, 164–66
  sliding, 163–64
  vaulting, 153–56, 488
  walking, 137–39, 271–73
Log roll, 166
Long Ball (game), 389
Long Base (game), 318
Long sit, 278
Long stretch (gymnastic activity), 462
Longway set, 420
Look behind (activity), 166
Loose Caboose (game), 304, 307
Lordosis (swayback), 42, 45
  exercises to correct and prevent, 296
Lott Ist Tod, 445
Low back stretch, 282
Low-back syndrome, 40
Lowy, 450
Lummi sticks, 432

McClenaghan, B.A., 121, 140, 143, *183*
McGraw, M.B., *31*
Mad cat, 282, 291
Mainstreaming, 4, 133
Making Waves (parachute play), 313
"Mama, Mama," 430
Managerial skills, 109–12
  evaluation of, 128–29
Manipulative skills, 19, 61–62, 197–222
  ball rolling, 197–99
  bouncing/dribbling, 214–17
  catching, 204–7, 213
  fine-motor, 242
  gross-motor, 240, 242
  kicking, 207–12, 217
  striking, 217–22
  throwing, 199–204
  trapping, 212–14
Marching, 432–33
Marking-time pattern, 178
Martins, M., 260, *296*
Mass, body, 39
Mass Field Hockey, 378
Mass to specific (gross to fine) motor control, 13
Mass Volleyball, 370
Mats, 457–58, 459
Maturation, 9, 14
Mayim! Mayim!, 445–46
Maypole dance, 433
Mazurka, 160
Measures, 244–45
Media calf skinfold, 50–51
Medicine ball activities, 295
Medley relay, 394
Memory, tactile, 26, 27
Mental retardation, 135–36
Meter, 245
Midbrain, 14

Milanovo Kolo, 446
Mini-Soccer (game), 353
Mirror activities, 227
Miserlou, 446–47
Missile man (gymnastic activity), 467
Modified Hockey, 378
Modified method of content placement, 65, 66, 67
Modified Slow Pitch (game), 389
Monkey hang, 489
Monocular vision, 24
Montessori, 27
Montoye, H., 55, *58*
Moon Soccer, 311
Moral education, 6
Morris, D.G.S., 298
Mosston, M., 85, 91, 92, 93, *98*, *99*, 300
Motivation, 27, 28
  as internal, 103
  motor-skill acquisition and, 35
Motor behavior, 13
Motor control, mass to specific (gross to fine), 13
Motor development, 13. *See also* Perceptual-motor development; Psychomotor development
Motor program
  auditory awareness combined with, 256
  body awareness combined with, 224
  directional awareness combined with, 232
  eye-hand, eye-foot coordination combined with, 240–42
  rhythmic awareness combined with, 247–48
  spatial awareness combined with, 229
  visual awareness combined with, 252
Motor-skill acquisition, 32–36
  feedback and, 35
  interest and, 35
  motivation and, 35
  overlearning and, 35–36
  retention and, 35–36
  schema theory of, 32–34
  selective attention and, 34–35
  whole and part learning and, 35
Motor-skill days, 56–57
Motor skill development, 17–20
  curricular approach to, 3
  evaluation of, 120–24
Mountain climber, 288, 293
Mousetrap (game), 311
Movement, cognitive stimulation and, 5–6
Movement awareness, 20, 61–62, 223–53
  auditory awareness, 26, 255–57
  body awareness, 22, 223–28
  directional awareness, 22–23, 228, 231–33
  eye-hand, eye-foot coordination, 238–44
  rhythmic awareness, 26, 244–50
  spatial awareness, 22, 24, 228–31
  tactile awareness, 26–27, 253–55
  vestibular awareness (balance), 23–24, 61, 233–38
  visual awareness, 24–25, 250–53
Movement awareness task sheet, 123
Movement-pattern variability, 33
Movement schema, 32
Movement skills
  fundamental, 61, 62
  proficiency levels, 59–60
Movement stories, 279
Movement variability. *See* Variability, movement
Moving object, perception of, 25

Muffin Man, 426
Mule kick, 472
Multisensory approach, 28
Muscular development, 17
Muscular strength/endurance, 40
  assessment of, 48–49
  posture and, 42
Muscular strength/endurance activities, 285–95
  basic principles and teaching hints, 285–86
  descriptions of, 287–95
  recommended, 287
Musculoskeletal conditions, 135
Mushroom activities (parachute play), 313
Music, 416
  calisthenics to, 267
  as stimulus for dance, 411
Musical Chairs, Modified, 304
My Ball (game), 311
Myelination, 14
"My Job—Your Job" technique, 109

Names, learning children's, 106
Names in a Rhythm, 434
National Association for Sport and Physical Education (NASPE), 6–7
National Association for the Education of Young Children, 1
National Children and Youth Fitness Study, 2, 55
Nature as stimulus for dance, 411
Neck hyperextension, 262
Neckspring, 480
Neck stretch, 285
Needs, basic, 102, 103, 106
  satisfaction of, 107–8
Neeves, R., 272, *296*
Nelson, J., 121, *130*
Nerfs, Beach-Ball (game), 305
Nerve fiber, 15
Nervous system, 14–15
Netball, 403–4
Net recovery, 367, 369
Neurological disorders, 135
Newcomb (game), 311–12, 370
New Games concept, 302
New Games Foundation, 302
Newsletter, physical education, 498
No-loser concept, 300
Nonlocomotor skills, 61, 62, 184–96
  dodging, 184–86
  pulse beats and, 244
  pushing and pulling, 194–96
  stretching and bending, 186–88
  swinging and swaying, 190–94
  twisting and turning, 188–90
Nonverbal communication, 90
Norm-referenced fitness tests, 46–51
Norwegian Mountain March, 447
Nursery rhymes, 250
Nutrients, essential, 42
Nutrition, 42–43

Oats, Peas, Beans, and Barley, 426
Obesity, 37, 41
Objective evaluation, 121–24
Objective localization, 22, 228
Objectives
  of daily lesson plan, 79
  instructional, 73, 77
  writing of, 76–77

Objective sport skill task sheet, 124
Object permanence, 10
Observation
  of auditory awareness, 255–56
  of ball rolling, 197–98
  of bending and stretching, 186–87
  of body awareness, 223–24
  of bouncing/dribbling, 215–16
  of catching, 205–6
  of climbing, 180–81
  of directional awareness, 231
  of dodging, 184
  of eye-hand, eye-foot coordination, 238–40
  of galloping, 161
  of hopping, 159
  of jumping, 145–46
  of kicking, 208–10
  of leaping, 156–57
  of pushing and pulling, 195
  of rhythmic awareness, 246
  of rolling, 170–71
  of rope jumping, 151
  of running, 140–41
  of skipping, 164
  of sliding, 163
  of spatial awareness, 228–29
  of striking, 219–20
  of swinging and swaying, 191
  of tactile awareness, 253
  of throwing, 202–3
  of trapping, 212–13
  of twisting and turning, 188–89
  of unusual characteristics or behavior, 260
  of vestibular awareness (balance), 234
  of visual awareness, 251
  of walking, 137–38
Obstacle courses, 266, 267
Obstacle dribbling, 376
Obstacle Relay, 321
Odd and Even (game), 341
Offensive strategy
  in basketball, 339
  in football, 359
  in soccer, 350
  in volleyball, 367–68
O'Hara, N., 37, 57
Oh Susanna, 447–48
O'Leary (game), 312
Olympic meet plan, 493, 496
One-Bounce Volleyball, 370
One-Down Football, 361
One-foot hop (rope jumping), 150
One Goal (game), 342
One-hand push shot, 336, 337
One Old Cat (game), 388
One on two, 351
One Step (game), 312
"One third time" program, 6
1-2-3 You're Set Free (game), 312
Ontogenetic activities, 14
Ontogenetic behaviors, 13
Open position, 412
O'Quinn, G., Jr., 153, 166, 172, *183*
Orchestra Leader, 426
Orenstein, D., 55, *58*
Organizational patterns, 89, 94–97. *See also specific names of activities*
  formations, 96–97
  station arrangements, 95
Organizational procedures, 73
Orlick, T., 300, 302

Ossification, 15
Outcomes of Quality Physical Education Programs, 6–7
Outside-of-foot kick, 346
Over and Over (relay), 304
Over-and-under Relay (and Side to Side), 321
Overarm throw, 200–201, 382
Overdwelling, 112
Overhand serve, 366
Overhand volleying, 364–65
Overhead pass (two hands), 335
Overlearning, motor-skill acquisition and, 35–36
Overload principle, 40
Overtake Ball (game), 312
Over the Brook (game), 312
Over the Hills, 427
Overweight, 41

Paddleball, 327
  cooperative, 303
Paddle tennis, 327–28
Parachute Golf, 304
Parachute Play (game), 312–13
Parallel play, 28
Parcel, G.S., 37, 57
Parent-teacher conferences, 115–16
Parent volunteers, 3
Par Three (game), 313
Partial squats, 287
Part learning, motor-skill acquisition and, 35
Partner balances, 461
Partnering for disabled child, 135
Partner passing, 339
Partner passing and trapping, 350
Partner pull-up (gymnastic activity), 468
Partner serve, 369
Partnership teaching style, 88–89
Pass, head, and shoot, 351
Pass and Duck (game), 313
Pass-a-Person (game), 304
Passing, 333–35
  in basketball, 339, 344
  in football, 356–57, 363
  in soccer, 350
  in volleyball, 364–65, 368, 371
Pate, R., 49
Patterns, 245
Patty-Cake Polka, 448
"Peanuts, Popcorn," 431
Peer relations, 28–29
Pelvic tilt, 282
Penman, K.A., 28
Penny drop (gymnastic activity), 489
People pyramid, 471, 485
Perception
  cognitive development and, 27
  depth, 24, 251
  figure-ground, 24, 251
    auditory, 26, 255
  form, 24, 251
  kinesthetic, 21–24
  of moving object, 25
  of reality, 103
  temporal auditory, 255
Perceptual constancy, 24
Perceptual-motor concepts, 6
Perceptual-motor development, 20–27
  auditory awareness, 26, 255–57
  evaluation of, 120
  intersensory integration, 27

kinesthetic perception, 21–24
tactile awareness, 26–27, 253–55
temporal awareness, 26
visual awareness, 24–25, 250–53
Percussion instruments, as stimulus for dance, 411
Performance, quality, 101–2, 107
Personnel, 492–93
Phylogenetic skills, 13, 14
Physical disabilities, 135
Physical Education and Sport Week, 498
Physical education for children, 1–7
  developmentally appropriate, 1–3
  goal of, 64
  other trends in, 3–4
  values and purposes of, 4–7
Physical Education Resolution, 2–3
Physical fitness, 2–3, 37–58
  assessment of. *See* Assessment
  defining, 38
  health concerns and, 37–38
  health-related, 2, 39–41
    cardiorespiratory endurance and, 39–40
    flexibility and, 39, 40–41
    misconceptions about, 37–38
    muscular strength/endurance, 39, 40
  models of, 55–57
  nutrition and, 42–43
  posture and, 42
  skill-related, 41–42
Physical fitness program, 259–96
  basic instructional guidelines, 259–60
  cardiorespiratory fitness activities, 268–77
    aerobic jumping, 276
    basic concepts and principles, 268–71
    jogging, 139, 273–74
    jumping rope, 275–76
    vigorous games and dances, 276, 277
    walking, 271–73
  exercise precautions, 260–63
  fitness values of selected activities, 263–64
  flexibility activities, 276–85
    basic principles and teaching hints, 276
    descriptions of, 279–85
    enhancements for, 286
    recommended, 277
    selected games, dance, and gymnastic activities, 285
    starting positions for, 277–79
  general activity formats, 264–68
    aerobic dance, 267–68, 269
    calisthenics, 266–67
    fitness stations (circuits), 264–66
  muscular strength/endurance activities, 285–95
    basic principles and teaching hints, 285–86
    descriptions of, 287–95
    recommended, 287
  posture-improving activities, 295–96
Physical growth and development, 14–17
  muscular development, 17
  nervous system, 14–15
  skeletal development and body weight, 15–17
Physically educated child, 6–7
Physical needs, 102
Piaget, J., 5, 9–12, 27
Pickleball, 329–30
Pig (or Horse) (game), 342
Pike position, 479
Pike roll down, 176

Pillo Polo, 404–5
Ping-pong, 330
Pin Soccer, 354
Pirates' Gold (game), 319
Pitching in softball, 382, 383, 391
Pivot, 420
Pivot and pass, 340
Pivoting in basketball, 338, 340
Placekick, 207, 208–9, 210
Placheck (planned activity check), 128
Planning, 64–70
  contingency plans, 73, 75
  daily, 77–84
    content of, 79
    enhancement phase of, 82–83
    evaluation section, 84
    health-related fitness phase of, 80
    huddle (review and feedback) phase of, 83–84
    skill-development phase of, 80–82
  theme development, 70–75
  unit, 75–77
  yearly, 64–70
    "Building the Foundation" curriculum, 66–70
    content placement, 65–67
    primary considerations in, 64–65
    procedures for, 65
    "Utilization of the Foundation" curriculum, 70
Plato, 27
Play
  cognitive development and, 27
  finger plays, 247, 409
  large-group, 29
  parallel, 28
  Piaget's theories and, 12
  small-group, 29
  socialization and, 28
  speed, 274
Play days, 498
Play Footsie (game), 313
Plough, 261
Poems, 247, 411
Poison Ball (game), 310
Poles, 183
Polka, 160, 420
Popcorn (parachute play), 313
Position in softball, 386
Posner, M., 35, 36
Postural balance, 23, 42
Postural skills, 18–19
Posture, 42, 276
  assessment of, 44–46, 47
Posture-improving activities, 295–96
Power, 42
  measurement of, 51
Practice, 14
  for fitness assessment, 51–52
  variability in, 33–34
Practice opportunities, 129
Practice opportunities checklist, 129
Prancing ponies, 289
Preconceptual stage, 10
Predesigned games, 297–98
Preferences, problem solving style and, 93
Preoperational period, 10
Preschool children, characteristic behaviors of, 11
Preschool-kindergarten curriculum, 66, 67, 68
President's Challenge, The, 48

President's Council on Physical Education and Sports, 263
Pressure Shooting (game), 341
Pretzel (gymnastic activity), 477
Problem solving teaching style, 92–94, 457
    disabled student and, 135
Program evaluation, 129
Programs, school, 497. *See also* Physical fitness program
Progressive Volleyball, 370
Progress reports, student, 125
Promenade, 420
Promenade position, 412
Prone position, 277
Propulsive skills, 19
Protruding abdomen, 296
Proximodistal development, 13
Psoas stretch, 282
Psychological needs, 102, 106
Psychomotor development, 5, 8, 13–27
    general trends and terminology, 13–14
    motor skills development, 17–20
    perceptual-motor development, 20–27
    physical growth and development, 14–17
Public demonstrations, 497
Public Law 94–142 (Federal Education for All Handicapped Children Act of 1975), 4, 131, 132
Pulling, 194–96
Pullover, 193–94
Pull the Tail (game), 313
Pull-up/chin-up, 49
Pull-ups, 295, 489
Pulse beats, 244
Pulse (heart rate), measuring, 270–71
Punishment, 113, 116
Punt, punting, 209–10
    in football, 358, 363–64
    in soccer, 346, 347
Punt and Catch (game), 360
Punt Back (game), 354, 361
Puppy run, 287
Purser, D.J., 28, *31*
Push 'em into balance (gymnastic activity), 468
Pushing, 194–96
Push off, 153
    high, 154
Push passing in hockey, 373
Push-ups, 292
    wall, 293
Push war (gymnastic activity), 472
Put in Order (game), 314
Put Your Little Foot, 448
Pyramid, people, 471, 485
Pyramid building, 461
Pyramid tournaments, 496

Quadriceps stretch, 262, 280
Quadruple meter, 245
Qualities, 245
Quality performance, 101–2, 107
Quality Schools Movement, 101–2
Quantity, problem solving style and, 93
Questionnaires, student, 127

Rabbit jump, 470
Racquet activities, 326–30
Radio Or Morse Code Signals, 434
Rag doll (gymnastic activity), 464
Rarick, L., 54
Rattlesnake (game), 314

Reach and look, 169
Reach-over roll, 168
Reaction time, 41
Readiness, 14
Reality, perception of, 103
Reality therapy, 103–4, 106
    evaluative questions, 114
Reasonable expectations, 30
Rebounding, 339
    in rope jumping, 149
Receptive skills, 19
Recess, fitness-oriented, 57
Reciprocal teaching style, 88–90
Recovery in volleyball, 367, 369
Recreational pursuits, 263
Reel, 420
References
    in daily lesson plan, 79
    in theme packet, 75
Refinement phase, 20
Reflexive behavior, 18
Regression of motor behavior, 20
Reinforcement
    academic, 28
    in problem solving process, 93
Related services, 132
Relationships, problem solving style and, 93
Relativism, 11
Relay activities, 304, 320–22
Relays, 319–20
    running, 393–94
Remedial intervention, 52–54
Reminders, safety, 73, 75
Rescue Relay, 321
Resistance exercises, 40
Responsibility, atmosphere of, 457
Restitution, 113
Retardation, mental, 135–36
Retention, 28
    motor-skill acquisition and, 35–36
Reversal concept, 300
Reverse curl-ups, 289
Reverse line of direction, 420
Reverse Ranks, 433–34
Reversibility, 11
Review periods, 36
Review phase of daily lesson, 83–84
Rhymes, 247, 250
    jump-rope, 430–31
Rhythmic activities, European, 232
Rhythmical movement, 409
Rhythmic awareness, 26, 244–50
Rhythmic Echo, 434
Rhythmic gymnastics, 461–62
Rhythmic running, European, 274
Rhythm knowledge, 409
Rhythms, 63. *See also* Enhancement activities
    activity descriptions, 420–21, 430–35
    progressions in, 408–9
Ricochet (game), 319
Right-hand lady, 420
Rings, 490
Rising sun (gymnastic activity), 469
Rock, 420
Rocker board, 236
Rocker step (rope jumping), 150
Rocking horse (gymnastic activity), 471
Roll at the Bat (game), 388–89
Roll back, 176
Rolling, body, 166–77
Rooster fight (gymnastic activity), 472
Rope activities, 486

Rope climbing, 179–80
Rope jumping, 486
Rope rings, 466
Ropes, 183, 237
Rope skipping, 148–53, 275–76
Rope stunts (gymnastic activity), 464
Ross, J., 49
Round and Round the Village, 427
Roundback (kyphosis), 42, 45
Rounded shoulders (forward shoulders), 45
    exercises to correct and prevent, 296
Round-off, 480
Round-robin tournaments, 493, 495
Row your boat (gymnastic activity), 462
Rudimentary phase, 18
Rules, posting of, 107
Rumunsko Kolo, 448–49
Run, puppy, 287
Runaway Train (Loose Caboose) (game), 304
Running, 139–43
    European rhythmic, 274
    Indian, 274
    for speed, 287
    in track and field, 392–94, 397–98
Running long jump, 395
Running speed, measurement of, 51
Rye Waltz, 449
Sack Relay, 321
Sacrifice, 386
Safety in gymnastics, 455–57
Safety reminders, 73, 75
Safety roll (judo roll), 478
Santa's Reindeer (game), 314
Sawing wood, 291
Sayings, 250
Scanning, 120
Scarecrows and Cranes (game), 314
Schema, 10
Schema enhancement, 74
Schema theory of motor-skill acquisition, 32–34
Schmidt, R.A., 32, 33, *36*
School programs, 497
Schottische, 160, 420, 434
Schottische position, 412
Scissors-style high jump, 395
Scoliosis, 42, 45–46
Scoop, 374
Scooter Relay, 321
Scooter Volleyball, 319
Scoot the Hoop (game), 314
Scramble over (gymnastic activity), 489
Scrub (game), 388
Seal crawl, 293
Seal slap (gymnastic activity), 472
Seal walk (gymnastic activity), 462
Seat circle (gymnastic activity), 462
Seat drop, 489
Seat kicker, 173
Seat lifter, 167
Second grade curriculum, 66, 68
Second graders, characteristic behaviors of, 12
Selective attention, 34–35
Self-concept, 29–30
    academic success and, 27–28
    reciprocal teaching style and, 89
Self-discipline, 108
Self-esteem, messages that block or enhance, 109, 110
Self-evaluation by student, 115, 116
"Self space" principle, 410
Sensorimotor period, 10

Sensory impairments, 135
Sensory information as stimulus for dance, 411
Separate-fitness-days programs, 56–57
Sequencing of tasks, 29–30
Serving in volleyball, 365–66, 369, 371
Set-shot shooting, 340
Setup in volleyball, 366, 367, 369
Seven Jumps, 434
Seven-Player Soccer (Mini-Soccer), 353
Shaking the Rug (parachute play), 313
Shapes, recognition of, 251
Shapiro, D.C., 33
Shea, C., 28, *31*
Sherrill, C., *296*
Shipwreck (game), 314
Shoe Twister (game), 314–15
Shoo, Fly, 427
Shooting in basketball, 336–38, 340, 344
Shotput, 396, 397
Shoulder balance, 169
Shoulder girdle, strength/endurance activities for, 291–96
Shoulder girdle developer, 290–91
Shoulder position (dance), 414
Shoulders, rounded (forward shoulders), 45
    exercises to correct and prevent, 296
Shoulder shrugs, 291
Shoulder stretch, 284
Shoulder-waist position, 413
Shuffleboard, 325–26
Shuttle dribble, 340, 350–51
Shuttle Relay, 321, 394
Shuttle tackle, 351
Shuttle volley, 368
Siamese Twins (relay), 321
Sidearm throw, 382
Side couples, 420
Side leaning rest, 279
Sideline Basketball, 342
Sideline Hockey, 377–78
Side roll, 168
Side-shuffle step (rope jumping), 151
Sidewalk Tennis, 331
Sideward rolling variations, 177
Siedentop, D., 116, 128
Signals for starting and stopping class, 106
"Simon Says," 223
Simons-Morton, B.G., 37, 57
Simple dribble, 372
Sinclair, W.A., *31*, 121
Sing a Song of Sixpence, 435
Singing rhythms, 247
Single hanging rope, 486
Single leg circle, 477
Single-line pass, 339
Single-line serve, 369
Single squat, 474
Sit-and-reach position, 48, 49
Sit back, 169
Sit back to shoulder roll (diagonal roll), 170
Sitting balance, 473
Sitting on heels, 278
Sit-up, 48, 49, 261
Six-Player Softball, 388
Sixth grade curriculum, 72
Sixth graders, characteristic behaviors of, 12
Sixth sense, 21
Skating position, 412
Skeletal development, 15–17
Skeletal muscle, 17
Skier's sit (wall walk), 287–88

Skill(s). *See also* Locomotor skills; Manipulative skills; Nonlocomotor skills
    acquisition of, early training and, 14
    fundamental, 18
    phylogenetic, 13, 14
    postural, 18–19
    sport, 19, 20
    stability, 19
Skill development
    daily planning for, 80–82
    in unit plan, 76
Skill-development check sheet, 124, 125
Skill development/movement variability activities, 74
Skill-related activities, 263
Skill-related benefits of selected physical activities, 165
Skill-related fitness, 41–42
    assessment of, 51
Skills/movement variability, problem solving style and, 93
Skinfold calipers, 49–51
Skin the cat, 192, 487
Skin-the-Snake Relay, 321
Skipping, 161, 164–66
Skipping-Rope Relay, 321
Skip to My Lou, 427–28
Slide circle drill, 339
Sliding, 163–64
Slow-Pitch Softball (game), 389
Small-group play, 29
Smooth muscle, 17
Snake rope (gymnastic activity), 465
Sobol, A.N., 37, *58*
Soccer, 344–56
    game activities, 351–54
    instructional considerations, 344–45
    rules and regulations, 354–56
    simple games of, 311, 317
    skill description, 345–50
    skill development activities, 350–51
    skill tests, 356
    three-sided, 304
Soccer Dodgeball, 352
Soccer Goal Kick, 353
Soccer Steal, 315
Soccer Touch Ball, 352
Social development, evaluation of, 124
Social Development Checklist, 125
Socialization, 28–29
Socrates, 27
Softball, 381–91
    game activities, 388–89
    instructional considerations, 381
    rules and regulations, 389–91
    skill description, 381–85
    skill development activities, 387
    skill presentation, 381
    skill tests, 391
Softball throw, 51, 396
Sole-of-foot trap, 346, 347
Solid (block) method of content placement, 65
Sound localization, 26, 255
Space walk, 227
Spanker (gymnastic activity), 474
Sparks, R., 49
Spatial awareness, 22, 24, 228–31
Spatial dimension, variability in practice in, 33–34

Special events, 497–98
Specialist, physical education, 3
Special-needs children. *See* Disabled children
Specificity, principle of, 40
Speed, 42
    running for, 287
Speedball, modified, 400–402
Speed play, 274
Speed shooting, 344
Spike, 366–67, 369
Spine, lateral curvature of (scoliosis), 42, 45–46
Split jump, 474
Sports days, 498
Sport skills, 19, 20
    evaluation of, 120–24
Spotting, 170–71
Spring board, forward rolling progression using, 172–74
Sprints, 393
Sprint start, 393
Squat, 172
    partial, 287
    single, 474
Squat-thrust, 288
Squat vault, 155
Squirrels in the Trees (game), 315
Stability skills, 19
Stairs, 182
Stance, 358, 359
Standing, 278
Standing long jump, 143, 144–45, 394, 395
Standing start, 393
Standing toe touch, 262
Stand on partner's knees, 483
Stand-up, 468
Starting drill, 398
Starting stance, 392–93
Star Wars (game), 319
Star Wars Hockey, 378
Static balance, 23, 24, 42, 234
Stations, fitness, 54, 95, 264–66
Stature by age percentiles, boys' and girls', 16
Stealing bases, 387
Step-close, 420
Step-draw, 420
Step-hop, 160, 420
Step jump, 175
Step-jump roll, 168
Step-point, 420
Step-swing, 420
Stevens, Ted, 3
Stick twist (gymnastic activity), 469
Sticky Popcorn (game), 315
Stiehl, J., 298
Stories
    movement, 279
    as stimulus for dance, 411
Straddle, 175, 176
Straddle bounce, 173
Straddle position, 479
Straddle roll back, 176
Straddle roll down, 176
Straddle sit, 278
Straddle stand, 278
Straddle-style high jump, 395
Straddle vault, 155
Straight rope (gymnastic activity), 464, 465
Straw Walk, 272
Strength, muscular, 40. *See also* Muscular strength/endurance activities

assessment of, 48–49
gymnastics safety and, 456
posture and, 42
Stretching, 186–88
Stretching exercises, 280–85
Stride step (rope jumping), 150
Striking, 217–22
Structured dance, 409, 412–18
    class organization for, 412
    formations in, 414–15, 416–17
    positions in, 412–14
    steps in teaching, 415–19
    teaching styles, 412
Structured games, 297–98
Student questionnaires, 127
Students, evaluation of, 120–26
    cognitive development, 124–25
    fundamental motor skills/sport skills, 120–24
    health, 120
    perceptual motor skill, 120
    reporting progress, 125–26
    social development, 124
Stunt Relay, 321
Stunts, 461
Styles, teaching. See Teaching
Subjective evaluation, 124
Subscapular skinfold test, 51
Sun Flower Project, 57
Supine position, 277
Supine tuck, 282
Suppleness, joint, 40–41
Support group for teachers, 129
Susan's Gavotte, 449
Swan balance variations, 289
Swayback (lordosis), 42, 45
Swaying, 190–94
Sweep step, 420
Sweetgall, Robert, 272, 296
Swimming, 291
Swinging, 180, 190–94
Swings, 413
Swing step (rope jumping), 150
Symbols, recognition of, 251
Syncopation, 420

Table tennis, 330
Tackling
    in hockey, 374–75
    in soccer, 348, 349, 351
Tactile awareness, 26–27, 253–55
Tag, games of, 304, 307, 308, 309, 311
Take away, 351
Tantoli, 449–50
Tape-recording of instructions, 127
Task(s)
    modification for disabled child, 134–35
    open vs. closed, 33
    sequencing of, 29–30
Task materials, 97–98, 99
Task sheets, 123–24, 126, 459
T-Ball, 220
Teacher(s)
    evaluation of, 126–29
    ineffective behaviors of, 111–12
    physical education for children and, 3–4
    positive behaviors of, 112
    roles of, 80, 82, 83–84, 94
    self-concept and, 30
    voice of, 90–91
Teacher aides, 3

Teacher/child-designed games, 300–301
Teacher-parent conferences, 115–16
Teacher-student conferences, 114–15
Teaching, 85–99
    communication modes, 97–98
    decision making in, 85–86
    organizational patterns, 89, 94–97
    strategies for, 87–88
    styles of, 87, 88–94
        command, 88, 90, 412, 457
        communication and, 90–91
        for dance, 410, 412
        exploration, 94
        guided discovery, 91–92, 94, 457
        for gymnastics, 457
        problem solving, 92–94, 135, 457
        reciprocal, 88–90
Team handball, modified, 402–3
Team sports and lead-up activities (Levels III–IV), 332–405
    basketball, 332–44
    football activities, 356–64
    hockey, 371–80
    korfball, 399–400
    modified speedball, 400–402
    modified team handball, 402–3
    netball, 403–4
    Pillo Polo, 404–5
    soccer, 344–56
    softball, 381–91
    track and field, 391–98
    volleyball, 364–71
Tee Ball (game), 389
Temporal auditory perception, 26, 255
Temporal awareness, 26
Tennis activities, 323, 330, 331–32
Ten Pass (game), 369
Testing, 1. See also Assessment
Test of Gross Motor Development, 121
Teton Mountain Stomp, 450
Theme development, 70–75
Thigh balance, 473–74
Thinking skills, critical, 90
Third grade curriculum, 69, 70
Third graders, characteristic behaviors of, 12
This Is the Circle That Is My Head, 435
Thomas, J., 498, 499
Thread the needle (gymnastic activity), 472
Three-Legged Relay, 321
Three-Line Soccer, 352–53
Three-on-Three (game), 342–43
Threes and Sevens, 435
Three-Sided Soccer, 304
Three step turn, 420
Three-Team Softball, 388
Throw and Go (game), 315
Throw and head (partner), 351
Throw-in and head (individual practice), 351
Throwing, 199–204
    free throw, 337, 338, 344
    in softball, 51, 381–82, 387, 391
    in track and field, 396, 398
Throw-in in soccer, 348–49, 351
Throw It and Run (game), 389
Tightrope walker, 470
Time, emphasizing importance of, 111
Time dimension, variability in practice in, 34
Time-out, 114
Timing, coincident, 219
Timmermans, A., 260, 296
Tinikling, 450–52

Tip over (activity), 167, 172, 173, 174, 176
Tire Relay, 321
Tires, 236
Title IX (Education Amendments Act of 1972), 4
Toe push, 472
Toe touch, 154, 169, 469
    standing, 262
Toe touch (gymnastic activity), 469
Toole, T., 88
Toss-Jump-Pick (game), 315
Total behavior, 103–4
Total child development, 4–5, 8–12
    characteristic behaviors and, 11–12
    Piaget's theory of, 9–12
    stages of, 9
    terminology, 8–9
Touch, sense of, 26–27
Tournaments, intramural, 493–96
Track and field, 391–98
    cooperative, 303
    instructional considerations, 391
    skill description, 392–96
    skill development activities, 396–98
    skill presentation, 391–92
Traditional "activity" approach, 3
Traffic Cop (game), 315
Training
    early, effects on skill acquisition, 14
    Fartlek, 274, 397
    frequency of, 39
    interval, 398
Trampoline, 236, 489
Transitions, 109
    jerky, 111
Trapping, 212–14
    in soccer, 346–47, 350, 356
Trees (stretch), 282
Triceps pull, 295
Triceps skinfold test, 50, 51
Triple jump, 396, 397
Triple meter, 245
Triple roll, 482
Tripod (gymnastic activity), 471
Trunk, strength/endurance activities for, 289–91
Trunk rotation, 203
Trust, atmosphere of, 457
Tuck hang, 487
Tuck jump, 470
Tuck position, 479
Tuck roll back, 176
Tuck roll down, 175
Tug-of-Peace, 304
Tug-of-war, partner, 288
Tumbling, 461
    backward roll, 170, 479, 488
    on balance beam, 488
Tumbling table log roll, 174
Tummy balance, 471
Turkey in the Oven, 452
Turk stand (gymnastic activity), 471
Turning, 188–90
Turtle (gymnastic activity), 474
25-Yard Football, 361
Twenty-One (game), 341, 388
Twist away (gymnastic activity), 468
Twist board activities, 233
Twister, 305
    inverse, 467–68
Twisting, 188–90
Twist under (gymnastic activity), 469

Two-foot step (rope jumping), 150
Two-hand bounce pass, 334
Two-hand chest pass, 333–34
Two-hand closed position, 412
Two-hand set shot, 336, 337
Two-Legged Relay, 322
Two-step, 420
Two-way wheelbarrow, 481

Ulrich, D., 121
Underhand free throw, 337
Underhand pass, 334–35
Underhand serve, 365, 366
Underhand throw, 200, 201–2
Underhand toss, 382
Underhand volley, 365
Unilateral movements, 13
Unit planning, 75–77
Uno Dos Tres, 452–53
Upspring, 471
"Utilization of the Foundation" curriculum,
    62–64, 70

Vanves experiments, 6
Variability
    of bending and stretching, 187
    in climbing, 181–82
    of dodging, 184–86
    in galloping, 162
    in hopping, 159–60
    in jumping, 146–47
    in leaping, 157–58
    in practice, 33–34
    of pushing and pulling, 195–96
    in rolling, 171–77
    in rope jumping, 151–53
    in running, 141
    in skipping, 164–66
    in sliding, 163–64
    of swinging and swaying, 191–94
    of twisting and turning, 189
    in walking, 138–39
Variability, movement, 80
    in auditory awareness, 256–57
    in ball rolling, 198–99
    in body awareness, 224–28
    in bouncing/dribbling, 216–17
    in catching, 206–7
    in directional awareness, 231–33
    in eye-hand, eye-foot coordination, 240–42
    in kicking, 210–11
    in rhythmic awareness, 246–49
    in spatial awareness, 229–31
    in tactile awareness, 254
    in throwing, 203
    in trapping, 213
    in vestibular awareness (balance), 234–37
    in visual awareness, 251–52
Varsouvienne position, 414
Vaulting, 153–56, 488
Verbal communication, 97
Verbs, behavioral, 77
Vertical jump and reach, 143, 144
Vestibular awareness (balance), 23–24, 61,
    233–38
Visual awareness, 24–25, 250–53
Visual communication, 97, 98
Visual impairment, 135
Visual modality, 21–22
Visual-motor coordination, 24, 238–44
    activities for, 61
Voice of teacher, 90–91

Volleyball, 364–71
    creative game of, 303
    game activities, 369–70
    instructional considerations, 364
    rules and regulations, 370–71
    simple games of, 319
    skill description, 364–68
    skill development activities, 368–69
    skill tests, 371
Volleyball Keep Away, 370
Volleying (passing) in volleyball, 364–65,
    368, 371
Volley Tennis, 331–32
Volunteers, parent, 3
"Vote, Vote," 431
V-position, 414
V-rope (gymnastic activity), 465, 466
V-up (gymnastic activity), 478

Walk
    bear, 287
    heel, 281, 287
    space, 227
    wall, 287–88
Walk and jump through (gymnastic activi-
    ty), 475–77
Walking, 137–39, 271–73
Walking chair (gymnastic activity), 464
Walking for Little Children (Sweetgall), 272
Walking Robot (game), 315
Walk the Ball, 272
Wall ball. *See* Handball
Wall kicking and trapping, 350
Wall passing, 339
Wall push-ups, 293
Wall serve, 369
Wall volleyball, 368
Wall walk, 287–88
Walrus walk and slap (gymnastic activity),
    474
Waltz, 420
Wands, 237, 279
Washing machine twist, 282
Wave plan, 458, 459
Weathervane (game), 316
Wehler, C.A., 37, *58*
Weight
    by age percentiles, boys' and girls', 16
    assessment of, 44
    body, 15–17
    losing, 42
Weight control, 41, 42
What to Play? (game), 316
Wheat, The, 435
Wheelbarrow, 472
    variations on, 481
Wheelbarrow Relay, 322
Whistle Ball (game), 319
Whistle pivot, 340
Whistle Stop (game), 316
Whole learning, motor-skill acquisition and,
    35
Who's behind (gymnastic activity), 469
Wickstrom, R.L., 140, 143, *183*, 199, 218, 219,
    222
Wild Horse Roundup (game), 316
Williams, H.G., 21, 23, 25
Wilson, R., *98*
Winnick, J., *54*
"With-itness," 112
Wolf (vault), 488
Wood, G., 28

Word pictures as stimulus for dance, 411
Wrestler's bridge, 261
Wring the dishrag (gymnastic activity), 420,
    468
Written communication, 97

Yearly planning. *See* Planning

"Zero score" dilemma, 49
Zigzag Relay, 322
Zigzag volley, 368
Zone Field Hockey, 378
Zone Volleyball, 370